COME TOGETHER

TITLE

COME TOGETHER

SUBTITLE

The Rise of Cooperative Art and Design

AUTHOR

FRANCESCO SPAMPINATO

PUBLISHER

Princeton Architectural Press

CITY

New York, NY

For my grandfather, Francesco

TABLE OF CONTENTS

COME TOGETHER

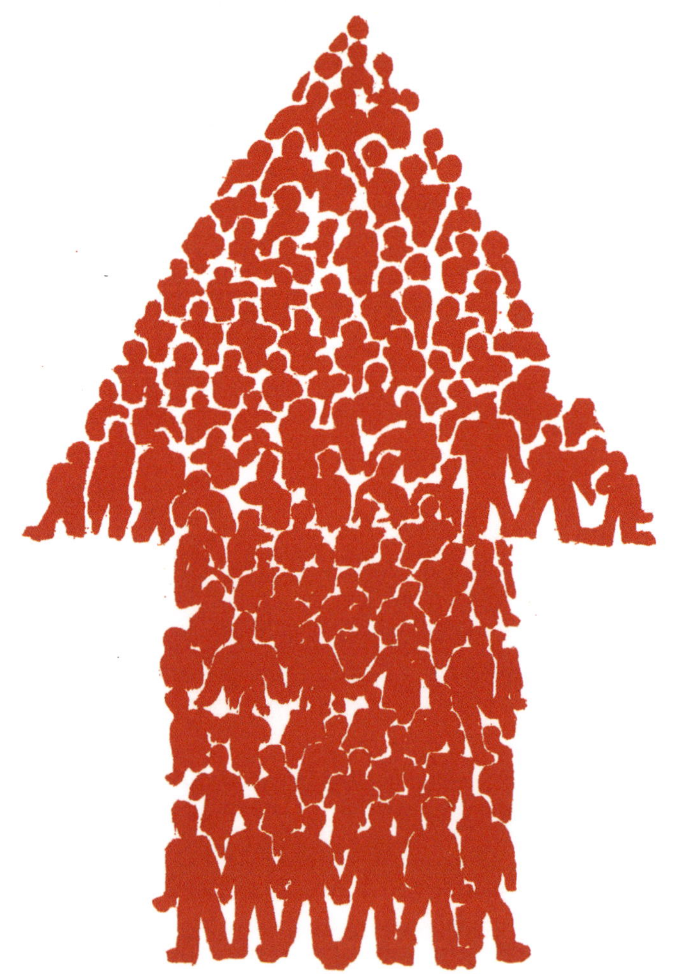

Fig. 1 – **Atelier Populaire, "Spirits are high for a protracted struggle," poster, Paris, June 1968**

INTRODUCTION

The Author Is Almost Dead

The role of the author is undergoing a massive transformation process. If, contrary to what Roland Barthes once famously wrote, the author is not dead, the idea of a sole creator working alone has certainly lost credibility and appeal.[1] In its place new forms of cultural production are emerging: open, collective, horizontal, and participatory. Come Together: The Rise of Cooperative Art and Design presents some of the most representative art groups of the past few years and explores the mechanisms that lie behind the collective production of visual culture today.

The forty groups and duos featured in this book were invited to answer a series of questions about the motivations, logistics, and objectives that drive artists to give up their egos and embrace anonymous and shared operations. What emerges is a common desire to transform viewers into producers, making them aware of their potential as agents of change. Borrowing strategies and symbols from mass media, the global market, and the entertainment industry, these collectives unravel and overthrow social, political, and cultural power structures.

The notion of art produced by groups is as old as human history, but the origins of today's collective art date to the last century's avant-garde movements such as Dadaism, futurism, Constructivism, Bauhaus, and situationism. Since the sixties, however, things have gotten more complicated. Over the decades, we've witnessed the rise of intellectual critiques of representation, ranging from postmodernism to relational aesthetics to the current postdigital generation. Concurrent with those trends in the art world, we have a series of social movements: 1968, the struggles against AIDS of the eighties, the antiglobalization movement of the late nineties, and the more recent Occupy! movement. Both of these spheres have turned out to be fruitful for collective operations.

The most representative collectives of the second half of the last century belong to the world of the visual arts (Art & Language, General Idea, Group Material), architecture (Archigram, Ant Farm), or graphic design (Atelier Populaire). [**Fig. 1**] But we find references to contemporary collectivism even in theater troupes (Bread and Puppet Theater), music bands (Destroy All Monsters, Laibach), pranksters (Provos, The Church of the SubGenius), and media activists (Raindance Corporation, Critical Art Ensemble), as well as in the arena of feminism (Guerrilla Girls), queer activism (Gran Fury), those struggling against the confines of cultural institutions (Art Workers Coalition), or those speaking to the issues of specific ethnic groups (Asco) or communities (WockenKlausur).

The Aesthetics of Conversation

The groups featured in this book are usually associated with the world of visual arts and design, but they are also involved in a variety of multidisciplinary activities. These can include everything from performance and publishing, to the organization of interventions and community projects that range from activism to curating to the creation of temporary spaces—actual or virtual—in which to experiment with new forms of cultural production.

Like those before them, these collectives are often born from preexisting communities, such as nonprofit organizations and squats, or other situations with common interests: theater, publishing, music, fashion, media. We will use the term "art," in a broader sense, to refer to these various creative fields, as insisting on their separation has become increasingly outmoded.

While the collectives showcased are vastly different on the surface, they share several common characteristics, including how they use images. Rather than simply creating imagery to be contemplated by the viewer, collective art often uses imagery as a direct communication tool. Many, in fact, appropriate familiar signs and symbols from pop culture and mass media in an attempt to unravel the mechanisms of representation that lie at their root.

In general, a work of art from a contemporary collective is an invitation to engage in a conversation with the public. As Umberto Eco notes in Opera Aperta, "Every reception of a work of art is both an interpretation and a performance of it, because in every reception the work takes on a fresh perspective for itself."[2] Following a similar approach, theorists have variously called the activities of these groups "context art" (Peter Weibel), "new genre public art" (Suzanne Lacy), "connective aesthetics" (Suzi Gablik), "relational aesthetics" (Nicolas Bourriaud), "social aesthetics" (Lars Bang Larsen), "dialogical art" (Grant Kester), and "participatory art" (Claire Bishop).[3]

The Group as Content

Another obvious common element in these collectives is the very fact that they work collectively, which is not only their modus operandi, but also often their message. On the model of past groups such as General Idea (1967–1994) and Art Club 2000 (1992–1993), these new collectives often produce self-portraits in parallel to their projects. These portraits work as promotional materials, but serve equally as well as a declaration of intent and a tool to interpret the group's activities.

The content of the activities of hobbypopMUSEUM, divided between Düsseldorf and London, is almost always subordinate to the form: the group. In the photos and videos that document their performances, we see them naked, covered with mud after a thermal treatment, or ranged around a white sofa, women sitting and men standing upright, wearing preppy clothing, with serious looks and heavily made-up faces. The images remind us of those of General Idea, who often portrayed themselves in ironic contexts, donning long poodle ears or posed under blankets with the wide-eyed innocence of babies ready to be fed. [Fig.2]

Many self-portraits of today's groups reflect on the tendency of youth to conform to the norms of their culture. Throughout their work, Berlin-based Discoteca Flaming Star and Reykjavík-based The Icelandic Love Corporation refer to music subcultures such as glam, folk, and metal. Not that they are interested in exploring content and lifestyles associated with them. They just borrow formal traits (costumes, symbols) and ritual aspects. Their performances, where music often has a crucial role, develop a direct and personal language with the public, within confined spaces and timelines, much like at an actual band's performance.

Communities and Participation

Other groups are less interested in the common traits of their communities than they are in how the disparate elements within them interact and grow. The concept of community is ever ripe for discussion and debate. A community is a social unit whose members share common values based on anything from religion to location to lifestyle, but what remains continually interesting to many art collectives is exploring how communities are formed and how they interact with each other. Being communities themselves, this exploration comes naturally to the collectives. They have only to expand their practices to the public, fostering participation in activities and projects inside and outside the art world. The Canadian group Instant Coffee's installations, for example, are made of chairs, tables, and pillows. "It does not have to be good to be meaningful," we read on a wall: on the one hand, it illustrates a problem; on the other, it provides the means to solve it.

The fashion-forward Parisian collective Andrea Crews is also divided between representation and participation. It produces images, events, and clothing, sold online or in trendy boutiques, that reflect on the values imposed by fashion. At the same time, in its workshops it teaches the general public how to make its own fashion. Similarly, Chicago-based Temporary Services—which plays a crucial role in the understanding and documentation of collectively produced art—is known for publications on "creative anonymous public phenomena," "self-reliance" libraries, and metacommercial installations: nonprofit banquets and markets.

Exhibitions, debates, and publications have been developed around the concept of participation in relation to the visual arts, design, and architecture. A common concern in these works is embodied in a warning from architect and writer Markus Miessen: "Participation is often stipulated and promoted as a false nostalgic desire."[4] The main target of this concern is relational aesthetics, a theory formulated by French curator Nicolas Bourriaud in the nineties, to explain the interactive installations and performances of artists like Rirkrit Tiravanija, Olafur Eliasson, Carsten Höller, and Philippe Parreno, among others. Relational aesthetics has often been accused of developing relationships that are utopian, for their own sake, or protected by the art world. It is precisely in response to Bourriaud that American theorist Claire Bishop opens the way to an understanding of a new kind of participatory art, with social purposes, when she writes that "if relational art produces human relations, then the next logical question to ask is what 'types' of relations are being produced, for whom, and why?"[5]

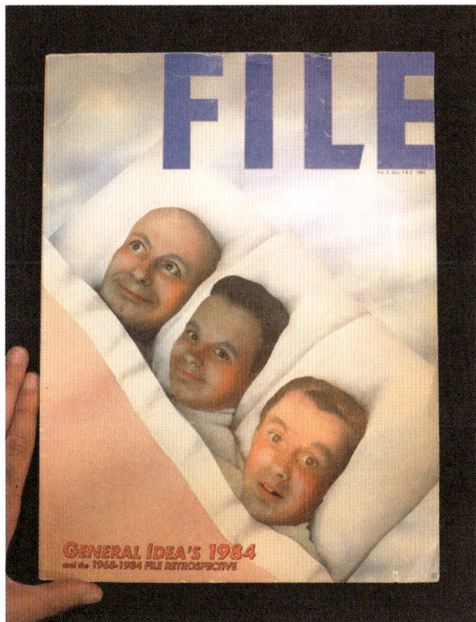

Fig. 2 – **General Idea, Baby Makes 3, on the cover of its FILE magazine, vol. 6, no. 1 and 2, 1984**

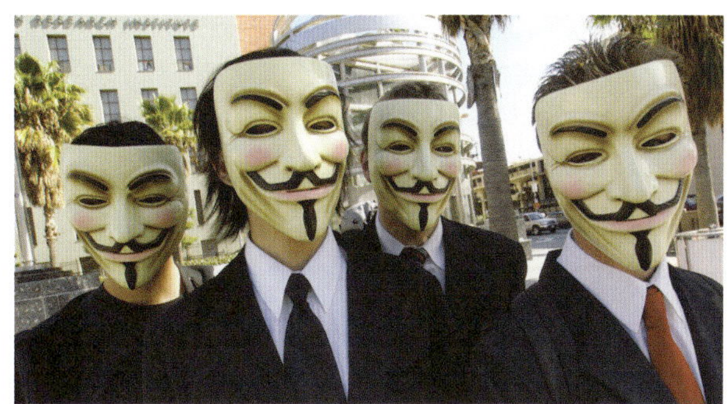

Fig. 3 – **Anonymous with Guy Fawkes masks at the Scientology area in Los Angeles, 2008**

Redesigning the City

The "hypothesis of constructions of situations," as suggested by Guy Debord, is at the heart of how many of these groups define their surroundings.[6] For the purpose of engaging as wide an audience as possible, they assign new values to the street and the city through the construction of emotionally powerful temporary spaces. As a consequence of situationism, the concept of the T.A.Z. (Temporary Autonomous Zone), drawn up by anarchist writer Hakim Bey, is also relevant. A T.A.Z. is "a guerrilla operation which liberates an area (of land, of time, of imagination) and then dissolves itself to re-form elsewhere/elsewhen, before the State can crush it."[7]

Through these models, the New York–based group Improv Everywhere helped give birth to the phenomenon of the flash mob—an open and highly participatory event organized online that comes to life in the real world. Flash mobs gather suddenly in public places and perform unusual acts—swimming competitions in fountains, "psychogeographical" visits to parks, musicals in supermarkets—and then they disperse. The idea is to provoke passersby and suggest new uses of the public sphere.

These operations are inherently festive; even when they offer up social critiques, they aim to make one smile. Many such events hope to raise ecological awareness. Tokyo Picnic Club, for example, organizes picnics in streets and parks, offering a physical and metaphorical break in the metropolitan rhythms. So does the Swedish R A K E T A with video projections that transform streets and monotonous facades into woods, or the Berlin-based Club Real, maker of cardboard trees and carrier of an imagery linked to outdoor excursions and campsites. The American-based SIMPARCH, instead, takes us directly to the countryside with mobile living units and wooden recreational structures intended for skateboarding or meditation.

Creative Dissent

Others have an interventionist approach to the public sphere. Rather than "art," in their case I will talk about "artivism." Artivists run operations of protest and dissent, against wars or globalization, or in favor of human, civil, or environmental causes that go beyond the boundaries of what art has traditionally dealt with. They are the proof, as Michael Hardt and Antonio Negri write in Empire, that "The creative forces of the multitude that sustain the Empire are able to build themselves as a counter-Empire."[8]

Several art collectives collect signatures for causes, organize sit-ins and hunger strikes, and guide public events. Many are aligned with the antiglobalization and Occupy! movements, or belong to the network of protesters know as Anonymous. [**Fig.3**] Many art collectives also employ the tried-and-true tactics of these groups, such as anonymity, engaging the carnivalesque spirit, the use of technology, and the production of propaganda. In Great Britain AAS, Reactor, and Space Hijackers use a guerrilla-themed vocabulary (fires, terrorist-like symbols, placards, tanks), but in a festive and peaceful way. They organize public demonstrations or occupy squares or disused buildings, with their faces masked or wearing police uniforms.

Fallen Fruit is a Los Angeles–based collective that organizes happenings and workshops built around the idea of fruit as a universal language. If you encounter the members, they'll invite you to take part in "condo jams"—off-the-cuff community events based around collecting fruit and making jam—or they will give you a map of the fruit trees of your neighborhood, asking you to "Take only what you need. Say 'hi' to strangers. Share your food. Take a friend. Go by foot." Thanks to Fallen Fruit, LA's Del Aire Park became the first public park in California dedicated to the cultivation and distribution of free fruit.

Détourned Economics and Media

Among those collectives moved by a political agenda, many develop a complex relationship with economics, imitating its language to overturn its symbols. Dutch sociologist Olav Velthuis, who has written extensively on the connections between art and economy, defines "imaginary economics" as those cultural operations that borrow techniques and strategies from the world of commerce "not as an instrument of exploitation and alienation, but of liberation and democratization."[9] Artists thus approach the signing of contracts, the registration of companies, and the management of enterprises out of intellectual purpose rather than economic necessity.

SUPERFLEX is a Danish collective that invites us to imagine alternative products and services that could nonetheless realistically enter the market: open-source beers, "biogas" units to make remote human settlements self-sufficient, and "free shops" where all the store's items are free of charge. With similar purposes, Italians Eva and Franco Mattes, a.k.a. 0100101110101101.ORG, spread through the Internet and an information kiosk the alarming false news that Karlsplatz in Vienna was bought by Nike and will be renamed Nikeplatz. The Spanish PSJM transforms names of philosophers and artists into trademarks with high commercial appeal: not even Marx remains immune from the trends of the market.

These activities are affected by the climate of anti-globalization and are echoed in the theories expressed by Naomi Klein in No Logo, as well as in the plagiarist practice of "culture jamming" that Canadian magazine Adbusters trumpets.[10] These new forms of situationist "détournement"—literally "diversion"—are also known as "tactical media," since their overt intention is to reverse the power of the media.

When it is not enough to attack the brands, however, one needs to focus on their distributional and promotional channels: mass media. The Yes Men, for example, raise awareness by posing as representatives of American companies and organizations, as when Yes Man Andy Bichlbaum, in the guise of a Dow Chemical executive, went on the BBC to assume responsibility for an ecological disaster that had cost hundreds of lives in India twenty years before.

Hallucinations and Fun

Often, the discourse on art collectives begins in underground subcultures. Paper Rad and Dearraindrop, (respectively via Providence and Virginia Beach) both emerged from New York City's downtown art scene of the early 2000s. Their work mainly consists of the appropriation of mass media icons and symbols of childhood and youth. In their varied media projects, we find the familiar faces of cartoons and video games, regurgitated in works that take the form of hallucinations reminiscent of the extramusical productions of Ann Arbor art-punk collective Destroy All Monsters (formed 1974).

Their practice is linked to the coeval open-source culture, from Linux to Creative Commons, a true intellectual revolution that extols the abolition of copyright and legitimate forms of digital banditry. [Fig.4] Technology, however, plays only a small part in their production, which is mainly handmade, lo-fi, and childlike—although many parents would certainly not be happy to show these pictures to their children. The works of the American group Friends With You, on the other hand, seem designed for children: smiling harmless creatures that first come to life on the screen, and then on paper and gadgets, or as mascots of amusement parks and parades, all characterized by a buoyantly good mood.

The festive aspect is also at the center of the hypnotic installations of Assume Vivid Astro Focus, active between New York, São Paulo, and Paris, that create a graphic hallucinogenic universe, hearkening to both Brazilian Tropicália and West Coast psychedelia. Taking images from mass culture and colorfully distorting them into fluorescents and acid tones, its performances are halfway between the Rio Carnaval and a rave party, animated by half-naked drag queens and masked characters on the edge of glamour.

Abstracting Spectacle

An important aspect of Assume Vivid Astro Focus's activities is its queer dimension, allowing its installations to function as temporary spaces for the liberation of sexual identity. A recurrent concern in collective art is the way in which mass media represent behavioral models. The worlds of art, fashion, music, and the underground, in response, have always provided countermodels and haveve given space to identities excluded or misrepresented by mass media.

The New York City–based members of DIS often perform in their multimedia operations, organized on their website into the categories of "discover," "distaste," "dystopia," "disco," and "discussion." They produce fake promotional campaigns, surreal sitcoms, and dysfunctional design inventions that make us think about how much our lives look like the images stored in a digital archive of stock photography. Similarly, the installations of London-based

Fig. 4 – **Creative Commons logo**

Fig. 5 – **George Maciunas in collaboration with other artists from Fluxus, Fluxkit, 1964–1965**

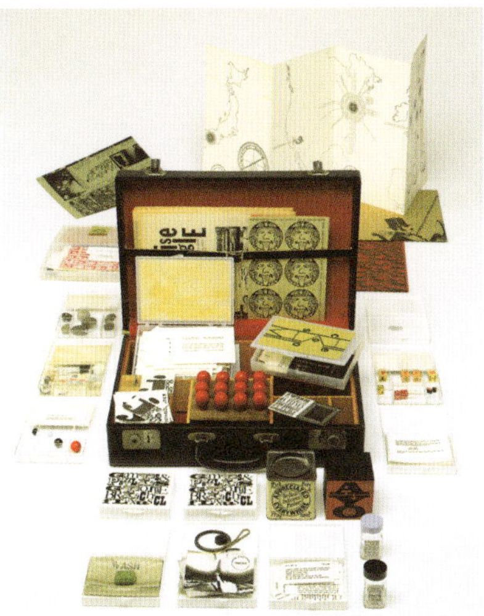

Lucky PDF resemble television studios in which they make parodies of talk shows and other genres of televisual entertainment, unraveling how mass media produce stereotypes we tend to identify with.

Like DIS and Lucky PDF, DAS INSTITUT, a New York–based German duo, incorporates elements taken from mass culture in its work, borrowing from the worlds of fashion, the Internet, and marketing, but mixing them in a highly abstract structure. Designs for fingernails, tanning beds, and graphic statistics are remixed in patterns that evoke modernism or biology; sometimes painted, sometimes digital, the images come to life on fabrics or industrial sheets of acetate. Like other groups, DAS INSTITUT presents itself as a company, proudly registered as a LLP (limited liability partnership).

Magic Games

Rather than the creation of products, many collectives are interested in what sociologist Maurizio Lazzarato calls immaterial labor, basically the idea that our current production model creates a sort of "cultural collateral." Lazzarato defines this "cultural content" as arising out of "a series of activities that are not normally recognized as 'work,' in other words, the kinds of activities involved in defining and fixing cultural and artistic standards, fashions, tastes, consumer norms, and more strategically, public opinion."[11]

We live in an era in which not only has the production of consumer goods been expanded into branding operations, but also "work" itself has often been removed from labor—"work" might mean sitting in front of a computer, answering a phone, or analyzing data. And as the work is dematerialized, so also is the worker: like a magician, he disappears. Mechanisms of disappearance are central to the activities of the Californian Center of Tactical Magic, which creates imagery linked to magic and mysterious energies that it uses as metaphors to address social and political issues: Houdini meets the Black Panthers.

Magical elements are also present in the productions of Åbäke, a London studio responsible for independent, transdisciplinary, and participatory metadesign projects, including an espionage agency and culinary events in exhibition spaces. This is a magazine, active between Milan and Perth, Australia, also uses magic to ask ironic questions about how design controls the transmission of culture. Its publications evoke certain games created by artist members of Fluxus, one of the most provocative postwar avant-gardes: the cover might be a sculpture to be cut out and assembled; hidden inside there could be encrypted messages, puzzles, directions to a place, or questionnaires about the meaning of life and art to fill in and return to sender. [**Fig.5**]

Fictional Politics

French philosopher Jacques Ranciere argues that "politics and art, like forms of knowledge, construct 'fictions,' that is to say material rearrangements of signs and images, relationships between what is seen and what is said, between what is done and what can be done."[12] Many collectives use this fictive power of art to reflect upon the actual fictions that lie behind politics and the mass media.

The Israeli collective Public Movement, for example, organizes public events that investigate democratic mechanisms. Their choreographed performances, sometimes featuring audience participation, simulate the processes of government action. It is no coincidence, then, that the group often collaborates with local state institutions. The idea is to involve the public in a form of collective learning about how governments produce consensus.

Those collectives from postsocialist countries act similarly. Zagreb-based curatorial collective What How and for Whom/WHW, whose name alone is illustrative of the group's intentions, has selected a number of these collectives for its exhibitions. These include Russian Chto Delat and Argentine Etcétera..., both using socialist icons in graphics, installations, and theatrical performances. The former organizes choirs and musicals of propagandistic nature, assigning utopian and often positive values to the theatricalization of life under socialism. The latter is the author of installations, public interventions, and cabarets built around the concept of "errorism" and aimed to provoke immobile viewers to become aware of their social status and act.

Contextual Practices

As for the groups just mentioned, the content of many collectives is context-specific. They cope with local issues, be they political, economic, or artistic, as Ruangrupa does through the organization of exhibitions, workshops, film festivals, and musical events in Jakarta. Its attention is focused on local creative resources in order to encourage the formation of an art scene in Indonesia.

The Propeller Group, divided between Saigon and Los Angeles, produces objects, videos, drawings, and installations in which religious symbols and political ideologies are presented as a PR firm might use them, to showcase how the commercial world has decayed their intrinsic value. In their hands, communism becomes the subject of a television advertising campaign and "Vietnam" the topic of a branding campaign that includes a world tour entrusted to a team of street artists.

Slanguage is also interested in the way in which local phenomena become universal. The composition of the very word Slanguage reflects a process of community integration that the members of the group, Californians of Latino origin, must know well. Like The Propeller Group, Slanguage is interested in anonymous creative street phenomena. Murals and folk culture are frequently the object or the final product of workshops, installations, and performances that involve the general public in which language is both the framework for and subject of the final product.

Structuring Language

As we have seen, the critique of representation (of mass media, economics, politics) goes hand in hand with an investigation of language: not the letters or characters that make up words, but how the articulation of words reflects certain territorial areas or structures of power. The group Slavs and Tatars explores political, religious, and cultural phenomena from the loosely defined geographical region of Eurasia. Its publications, installations, and lectures on Iranian or Polish events and personalities offer opportunities to reflect on dynamics behind the understanding of the Middle East and Eastern Europe.

Symbols and language are also the focus of New York studio Project Projects, whose pedagogically inspired activities often take the form of lectures or questionnaires. Its name itself is, after all, a linguistic play on the concept of "project." In the installations of Paris-based Société Réaliste, we find symbols of mathematic and bureaucratic origin. Its attention is focused on linguistic infrastructure—legalese and bureaucratic constructs that help sustain and define states. The project in which Société Réaliste proposes to replace the alphabet with a new code based on Esperanto is representative of the group's difficulties in identifying with its culture.

Esperanto is an artificial language, created in 1870 by a Russian ophthalmologist, aimed to connect people from different countries. Micronations—a phenomenon with which art collectives share much in common—have made abundant use of Esperanto. Micronations are self-declared, independent, and bureaucratic entities that claim sovereignty over some physical territory. Not surprisingly, one of the main projects of the Dutch duo Metahaven was the rebranding of the Principality of Sealand, the micronation par excellence. Their graphic operations, which also take the form of installations and publications, are all associated with liberated spaces both real (Sealand) and virtual (WikiLeaks). [**Fig.6**] In these projects, Metahaven reflects on how the language of design articulates the structures of power—economic, political, and media—that regulate the communities of the global village.

Everyone Is an Artist!

In this text I have tried to highlight the commonalities and differences of these groups. From time to time in the preceding paragraphs, I associated names of duos and collectives with thematic contents and particular modes of operation. Many of these names, however, may be interchangeable; it is not my intention to label them in this book. The activities of each, in fact, are much more complex and articulated, as clearly emerges from the following pages. If you wish to know more about any of them, explore the websites or publications suggested that precede each of this book's interviews.

My interest in the phenomenon of art collectives was born out of intellectual reasons: mostly art historical but also generational. As a scholar, writer, artist, and educator, I have often been at the center of the collective mechanisms that are more and more recurrent in the world of visual arts and design today, as well as more generally in our society.

Fig. 6 – **The Principality of Sealand shot from a helicopter, November 13, 1999**

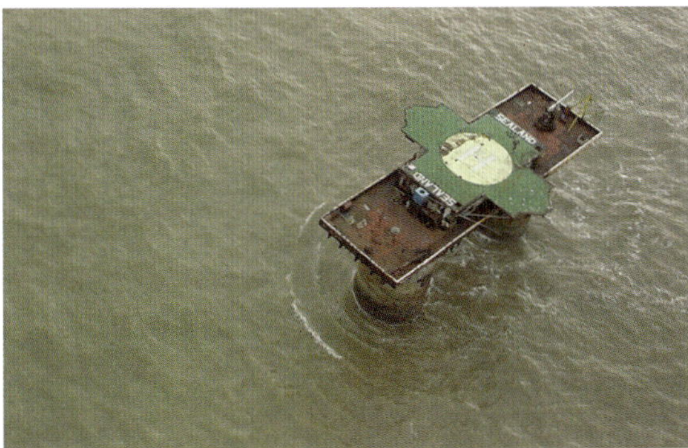

Collective art and design has always peaked at times when the political, economic, and social structures of power have lost their balance. It stands to reason that the continuing rise of collectivism in art and design is symptomatic of the shaky geopolitical structure of the past few decades. However, it is also the result of a sort of democratization of art enabled by the mass diffusion of technology that allows anyone to become a producer. As Ellen Lupton writes, in a key text on understanding graphic design today, "There exist opportunities to seize control—intellectually and economically—of the means of production, and to share that control with the reading public, empowering them to become producers as well as consumers of meaning."[13]

Indeed, this phenomenon is symptomatic not only of a redefinition of the role of the professional artist in our society, but also a shift in understanding the potential for a widespread and expanded use of art. Freed from the search for contemplation in the visual arts and for functionality in design, today we find art whenever an image, an event, or an object causes us to reflect on the role that images, events, and objects play in our lives and pushes us to ask: who produces them and for what purposes?

Whether it's a publication, a performance, or an installation, we read these collective productions primarily as critical simulations of realities that look familiar but are not necessarily natural. These simulations are implemented by often anonymous figures, with transdisciplinary or extradisciplinary training, who experiment with democratic and participatory dynamics that many states and human communities should learn from.

NOTES

1 Roland Barthes, "The Death of the Author," Aspen (1967). Later appeared in Roland Barthes, Image-Music-Text (New York: Hill & Wang, 1978).

2 Umberto Eco, Opera Aperta (Milan: Bompiani, 1967).

3 Peter Weibel, Kontextkunst—Kunst der 90er Jahre, (Cologne: Du Mont Verlag, 1994);
Suzanne Lacy, ed., Mapping the Terrain: New Genre Public Art (Seattle: Bay Press, 1995);
Suzi Gablik, "Connective Aesthetics: Art After Individualism" in Suzanne Lacy, ed., Mapping the Terrain: New Genre Public Art (Seattle: Bay Press, 1995);
Nicolas Bourriaud, Esthétique Relationnelle (Dijon, France: Les Presses du Réel, 1998. Translated as Relational Aesthetics in 2002);
Lars Bang Larsen, Social Aesthetics: 11 Examples to Begin With, in the Light of Parallel History, Afterall no. 1 (Fall/Winter 2000). Reprinted in Claire Bishop, ed., Participation (Cambridge, MA: Whitechapel & MIT Press, 2006);
Grant H. Kester, Conversation Pieces (Berkeley: University of California Press, 2004);
Claire Bishop, Artificial Hells: Participatory Art and the Politics of Spectatorship (London/New York: Verso, 2012).

4 Markus Miessen, The Nightmare of Participation (Berlin: Sternberg Press, 2010), pp. 41–42.

5 Claire Bishop, "Antagonism and Relational Aesthetics", October, no. 110 (Fall 2004): pp. 51–79

6 Guy Debord, "Rapport sur la Construction des Situations et sur les Conditions de l'Organisation et l'Action de la Tendente Situationniste Internationale" (Internationale Lettriste, July 1957. Translated as "Toward a Situationist International" in Tom McDonough, ed., Guy Debord and the Situationist International: Texts and Documents (Cambridge, MA: MIT Press, 2002) and reprinted in Claire Bishop, ed., Participation (Cambridge, MA: Whitechapel & MIT Press, 2006).

7 Hakim Bey, T.A.Z.: The Temporary Autonomous Zone, Ontological Anarchy, Poetic Terrorism (New York: Autonomedia, 1991).

8 Michael Hardt and Antonio Negri, Empire, (Cambridge, MA: Harvard University Press, 2001).

9 Olav Velthuis, Imaginary Economics: Contemporary Artists and the World of Big Money (Rotterdam: NAi Publishers, 2005).

10 Naomi Klein, No Logo (New York: Picador, 2000).

11 Maurizio Lazzarato, Lavoro Immateriale. Forme di Vita e Produzione di Soggettività (Verona: Ombre Corte, 1997).

12 Jacques Ranciere, Le Partage du sensibile: Esthétique et politique, La Fabrique-éditions, 2000). English translation by Gabriel Rockhill, The Politics of Aesthetics (London/New York: Continuum, 2004).

13 Ellen Lupton, The Designer as Producer in Steven Heller (ed.), The Education of a Graphic Designer (New York: Allworth Press, 1998), pp. 159–162.

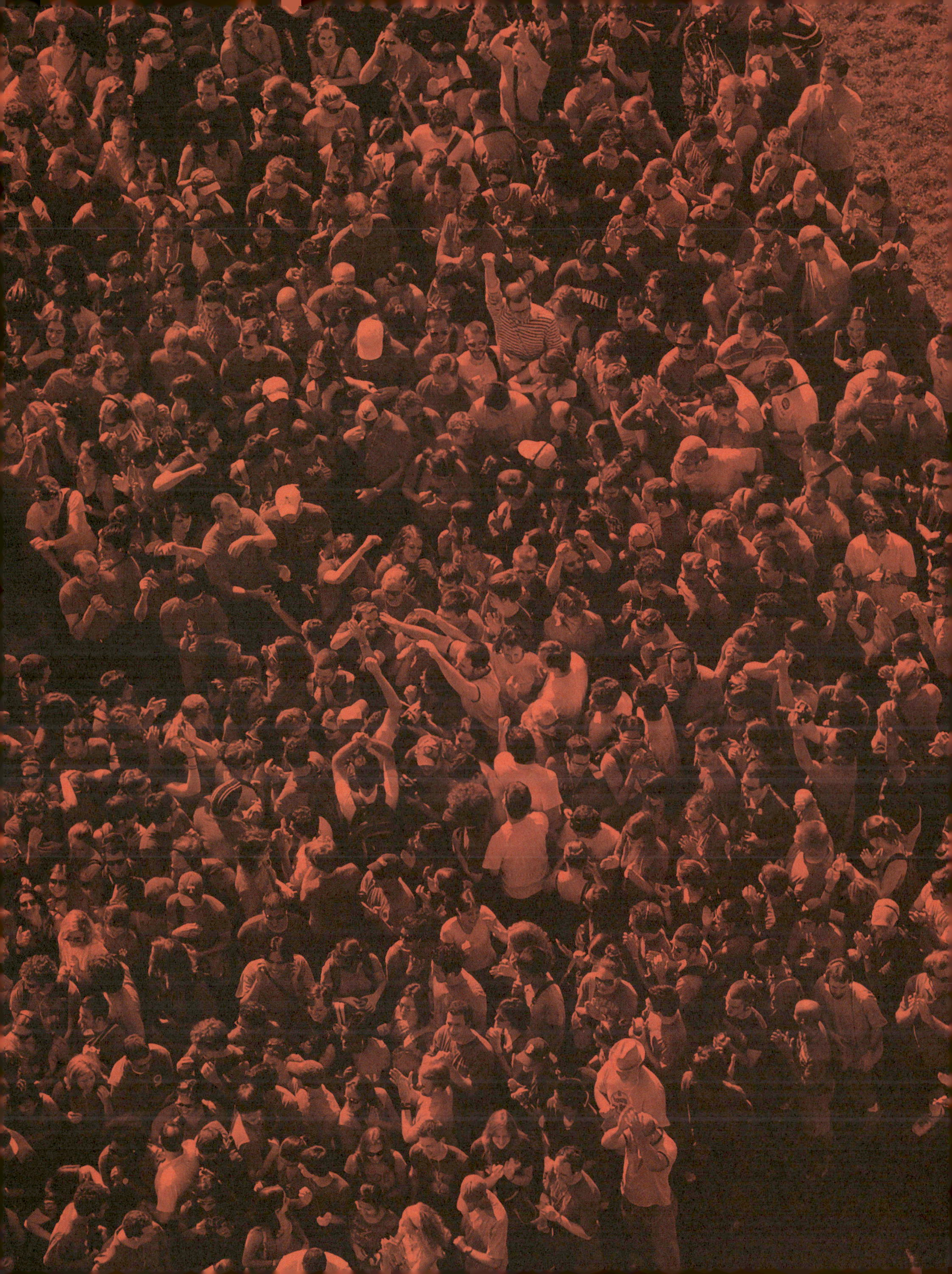

ACTIVE SINCE	CITY	WEBSITE
2001	London, UK	aasgroup.net

AAS

MEMBERS	ACTIVITIES	RECOMMENDED PUBLICATION
Ana Benlloch, Alex Marzeta, Vanessa Page, and Stuart Tait	Curating, Internet Art, Merchandising, Music, Painting / Sculpture / Installation, Public Performance, Publishing, Urban Interventions	Stuart Tait, Becoming Multiple: Collaboration in Contemporary Art Practice, (Thesis), Birmingham Institute of Art and Design, Birmingham City University, Birmingham, 2010

With a passion for science fiction and secret societies, AAS's practice reflects mainly on the issue and idea of technocracy. A parallel concern is how groups form, grow, and work: a subject AAS member Stuart Tait explores in his seminars through the use of rhizomatic graphics.

Why work collaboratively?

Although there are a variety of reasons for working with other artists, for example sharing the workload or studio rent, collaborative practice or collective working is also one of the strategies that artists have used, as Craig Saper notes in his book Networked Art, "to promote their work outside the entrenched gallery system." Most accounts of collaboration are based on the assumption that social groups are made up from people who have something in common, tending to treat groups as having a fixed identity, as being a "body." AAS tends to be more fluid than that, with additional members joining the group on a project-by-project basis. We believe that through assemblage with other people and collectives, new capacities to act become actualized.

How do you determine membership? Does physical location matter in this regard?

Core membership of the group is relatively stable at the moment, but at various points in AAS's history the group stated that there were no members and that AAS was an imaginary art group. This was not done in order to be awkward or deceptive, but to attempt to explore the notion that the nature of collectivity depended on imagination and belief in the life of the collective. Rather than thinking in terms of "members," we are each a "part" or component of AAS. So membership is determined as a kind of emergent property of a "becoming AAS" that each person goes through. Some people consider themselves to be AAS while not engaged in projects, while others simply slip away.

If considered separately, how do your individual artistic practices contribute to or detract from your work as a group?

While standard discussions of collaboration tend to be built upon a series of identities—individuals, groups, projects, and the world, which are all dealt with as discrete unities—our collaboration tends to be more molecular than that. There is very little focus on distinguishing between individual practice and group practice. In this sense AAS designates a kind of practice, an adjective that describes a particular territory. Work we carry out individually and with other groups only serves to increase our capacity to act.

How are decisions made?

Major decisions are made by consensus. We all have to agree on a direction for it to work, everyone has to be fully behind an idea so that we're motivated and want to make it happen.

We use the idea of AAS to help us think about what's right for the group, to get outside of our individual concerns, while still being able to bring our different perspectives to things. This generally happens through discussion; we try to all agree on what will be

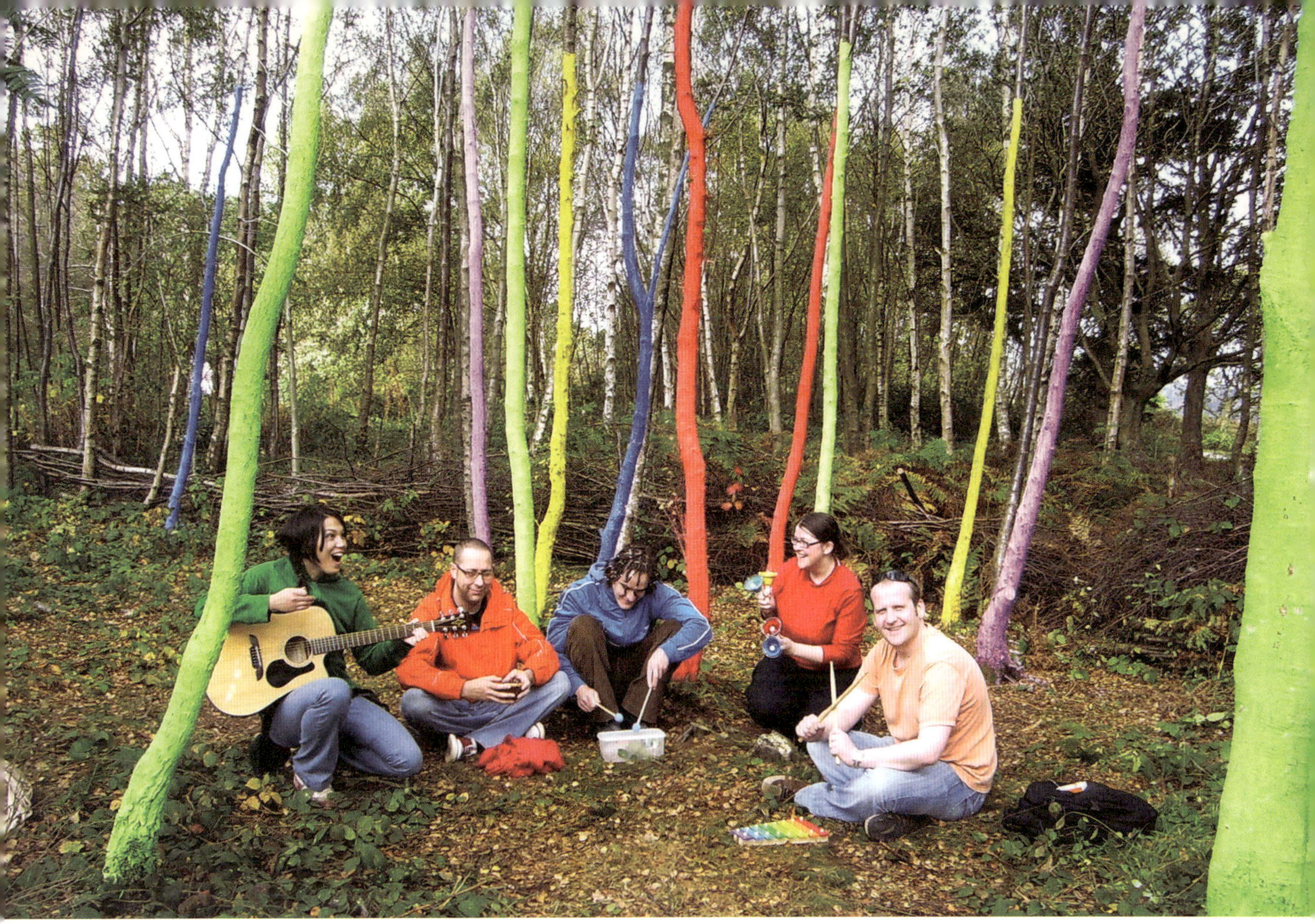

1

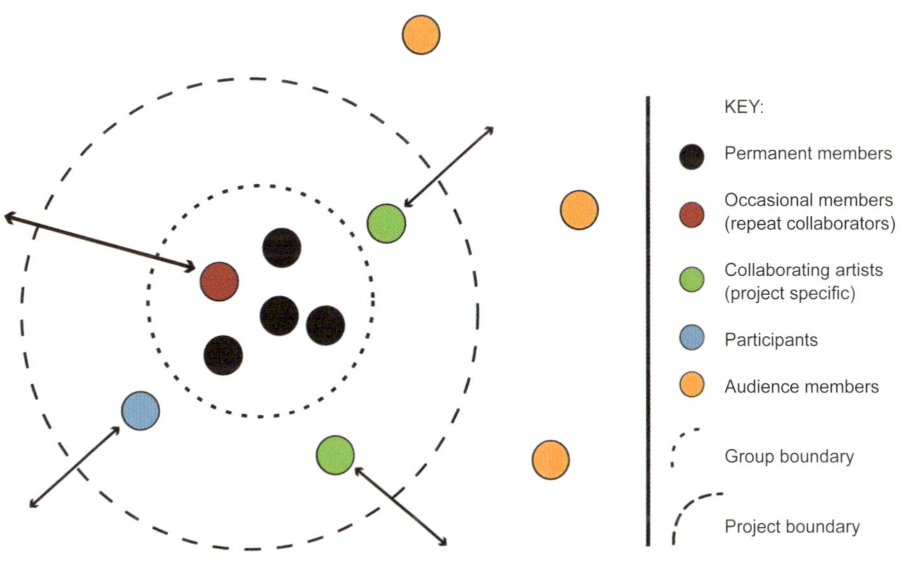

1 – The Family (Song Writing), performance, 2009

2 – Group structure graphics, 2008

most effective and achieve our previously defined aims. Occasionally, due to time constraints we just have to trust each other to make the right decisions, but we still have the group aims in mind.

Once a project has been agreed upon, we often devise a set of protocols to provide a structure and to act as guidance for anyone else joining in.

Does each of you have a clearly defined role? If so, what are some of each member's distinct responsibilities?

There are no clearly defined job roles in AAS and work tends to get distributed due to availability and capacity to perform a particular job. If someone has certain skills (e.g., web design), he or she may be more efficient at doing a job, but if he or she is too busy, someone else will step in.

How important is each group member's individuality, both in terms of your artistic production and in terms of your relationship with the media? Does anonymity come into play?

AAS does not ever really have a "relationship" with the media, but any publicity for projects is always presented simply as AAS and never lists the names of the artists involved. From the point of view of practice, a group member's individuality is important, because the collective, as an assemblage, is a form of multiplicity in which each part has a qualitative effect on the whole. When a new member joins, or a new coparticipant engages with the project, then all other parts of the work make adjustments to their positions and roles. In this way, each individual's impact on the work is particular and not simply as a homogenous unit.

What is the relationship between your working methods and your art's "content"? In this sense, does technology tend to play more of a supporting role, or does it lead you in new directions?

Our work is often coparticipatory with people who are not "members" of the group and is focused on the production of group states of mind. The development of a kind of group mentality is then transmitted to our coparticipants for further development together in a form of molecular collaboration. Technology plays a supporting role in the initial development of works in the form of Skype meetings and the use of a collaborative wiki. It has also played a supporting role in some projects in the form of project-specific social hubs/portals where coparticipants can interact with each other.

How does your collaboration relate to its cultural, institutional, and commercial contexts? In other words, how would you respond to those who call this a trend?

Although we generally respond to our cultural context, this is only one aspect among many and is not our primary aim. Whenever we manage to have a period of institutional support, commissions, and funding, we do respond to this specific relationship, often involving staff in our practice and accessing areas not normally used for art projects. We do struggle to capitalize on such support, however. We are still unclear about whether this is due to something in our practice or whether this is other collaborative groups' experience too. Our collaboration does not specifically consider its commercial context, although the practice has naturally developed in a direction where elements are available to purchase.

The idea that collaboration is a trend is nonsense. Art practice has been largely collaborative since people started painting in caves and dancing together.

Who is your audience?

There are various levels of audience for AAS projects: a pre-project audience that is first exposed to the narrative of the work before it materializes; a number of coparticipants who engage with and affect the work directly from "inside"; and a series of secondary audiences that experience the work at a distance via the Internet, lectures, and documentation.

Does your engagement with one another translate into an engagement with the public? How so?

The type of engagement we have with each other as a group often ends up carrying over into relations with coparticipants. For instance, in the 2009 project, The Family, we devised a procedure for roles within the expanded group to be randomly swapped at mealtimes to break people's habitual ways of behaving and interacting. This has been less the case in recent projects, which have been more about performing to an audience in a more conventional performer-audience relationship. In short, we have no fixed modes of engagement with each other and audiences.

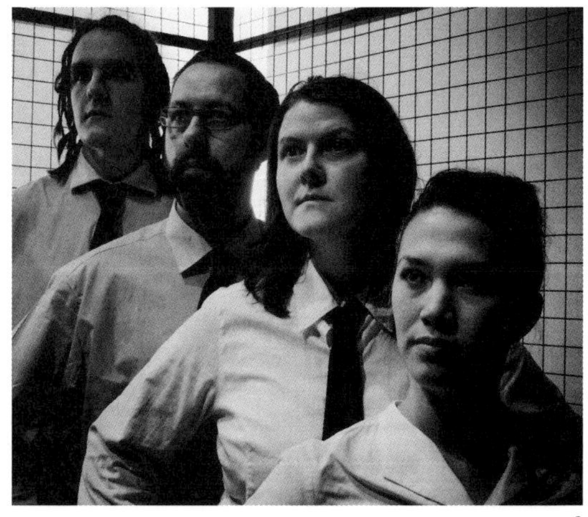

3

3 – **Group photo, 2010**

4 – **Drone Dose, performance, 2013**

5 – **Receivers' Temple, installation, 2012**

6 – **Phase IV logo, 2011**

7 – **House Lights Up, performance, 2003**

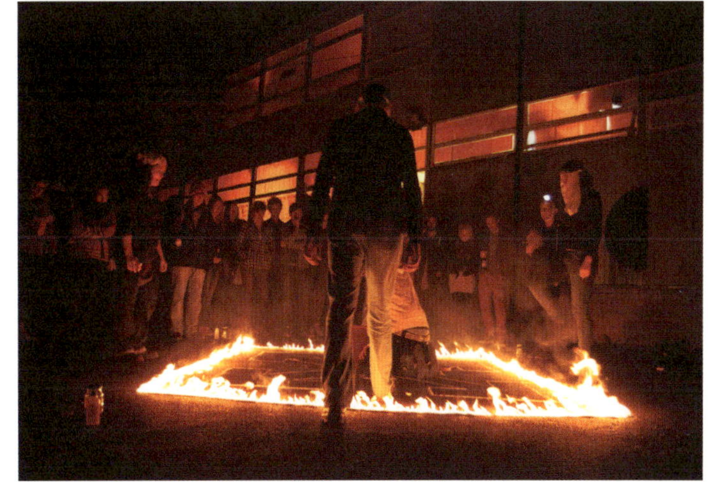

4

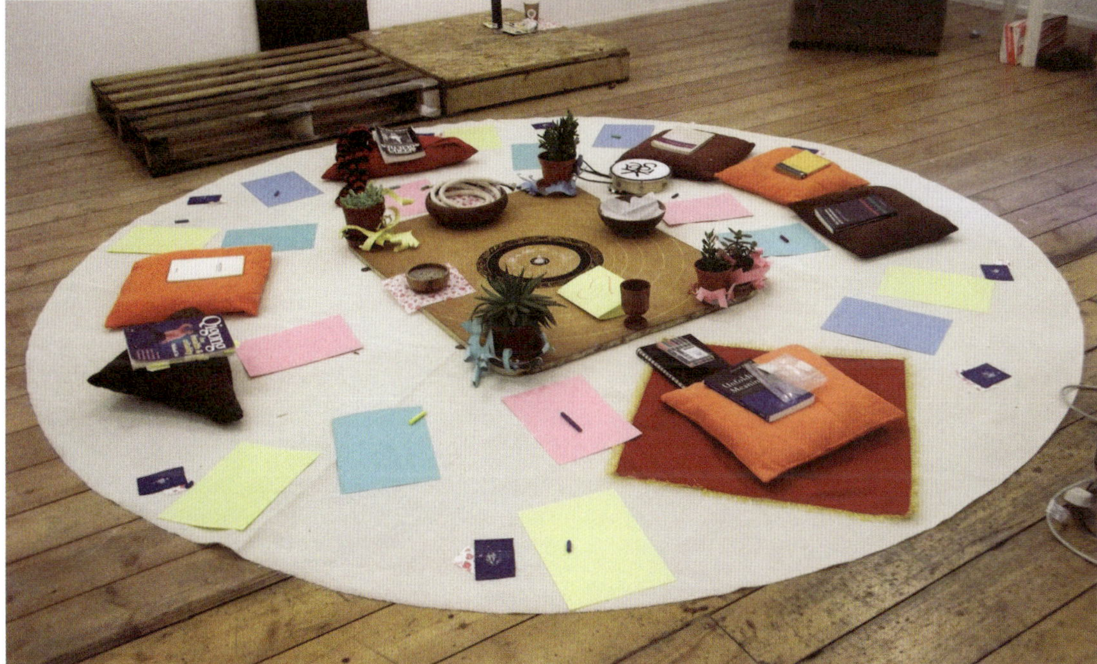

5

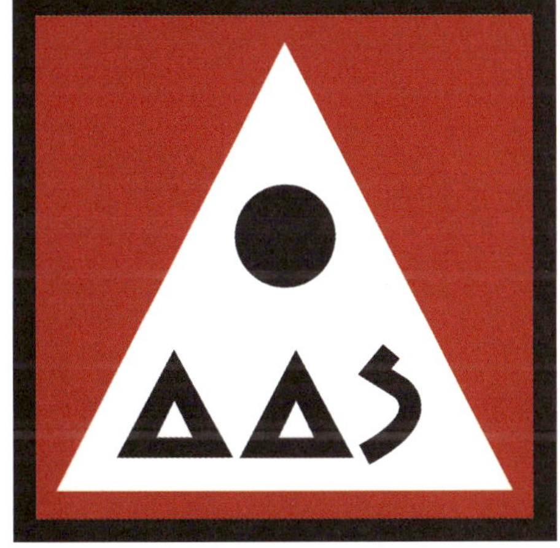

6

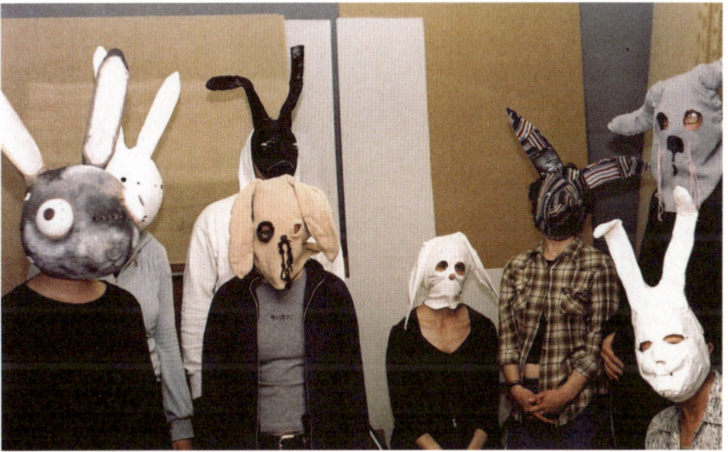

7

ACTIVE SINCE	CITY	WEBSITE
2000	London, UK	abake.fr

Åbäke

MEMBERS	ACTIVITIES	RECOMMENDED PUBLICATION
Patrick Lacey, Benjamin Reichen, Kajsa Ståhl, and Maki Suzuki	Community Projects, Curating, Merchandising, Installation, Public Performance, Publishing, Urban Interventions	the one you are reading

On one hand, Åbäke—the Swedish word for a large and cumbersome object—works as a traditional design studio; on the other, it is responsible for self-initiated projects that deconstruct the conventions and processes of design. These include the digital platform for architecture Sexymachinery, the interactive culinary events of Trattoria, the publishing project Dent-De-Leone, the propaganda for the imaginary Victoria & Alferd Museum, and the spy agency Åffice Suzuki.

NOTE: The following may contain an alteration of reality for entertainment purposes or simply because of a lack of distance to self-assessment. It may also be difficult to read, as it has been written by up to eight hands, and our wish was to keep the voice differences as well as the inevitable contradictions, which simply show we are not absolutely certain of what is being stated.

Why work collaboratively?

It is difficult to imagine working without other people but thirteen years after choosing a name to work under or behind, we can find several reasons. We met at the Royal College of Art, London, where there were precedents of collectives graduating from the course and it is perhaps what appealed to us even if the implications of working as a group were unknown to us. Let's say what follows are assumptions about then. First of all, it might have been the promise of autonomy or some relative form of authorship, in direct opposition to working for someone. There was perhaps the arrogance associated with studenthood that we could not imagine working for a boss on top of having to deal with the hierarchy imposed by a commissioner or a client. How many people do we want between the work and ourselves? We always spoke of why we became a group as a solving of two flaws we identified with the "job": money and ego. Money was to be shared equally whatever the so-called amount of effort by individuals, even from our teaching or other obvious individual endeavors. In the beginning, it was very easy, given that all projects were handled by the four of us. Very quickly, we established that two people would be working on each project in different combinations between the four. Today, we even do projects individually but the money still goes into the same account and the work is credited as Åbäke's. Back to the RCA years there was a natural atmosphere of working with each other, and we can safely say that "collaboration" was ultimately a positive word and attitude, perhaps naively. Everybody worked with everybody and the first sign of a darker side to collaboration appeared when a prize was taunting the students. What was informal became more organized in order to gain the money that would have launched a collective (in fact, this prize was for any project but for some reason everybody decided to enter as a collective). This, in retrospect, was both exciting and pathetic, groups forming, members defecting, name sessions and other paraphernalia meetings happening. I don't think we had uniform or logo meetings, but almost. Each creation of a group came with alienation of other people. Come to think of it, there was also the slightly absurd idea to collaborate with people who had the same age, culture, education, and even skills. Our business card, which we only really use in Japan, shows what has become of the group after more than a decade of working. We still want to work collaboratively but not necessarily within the four of us. In 2008 we participated in a group show at the Somerset house in a project we called

1 – Limbtypography: On Purpose, performance, cocurated with Nav Haq, Arnolfini, Bristol, 2008

2 – We Connect invitation, Studio Camuffo, Venice, 2004

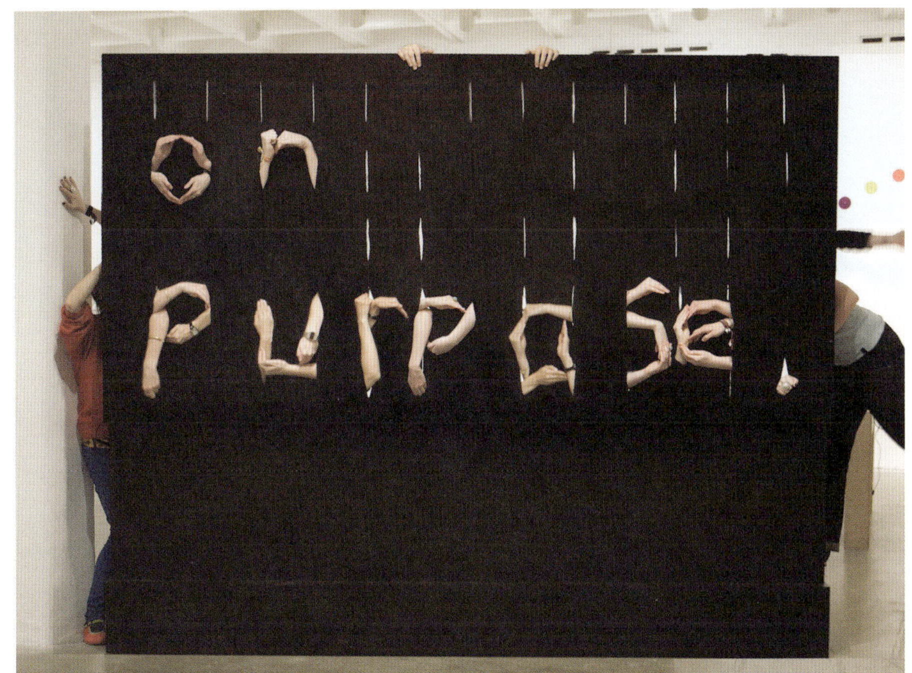

1

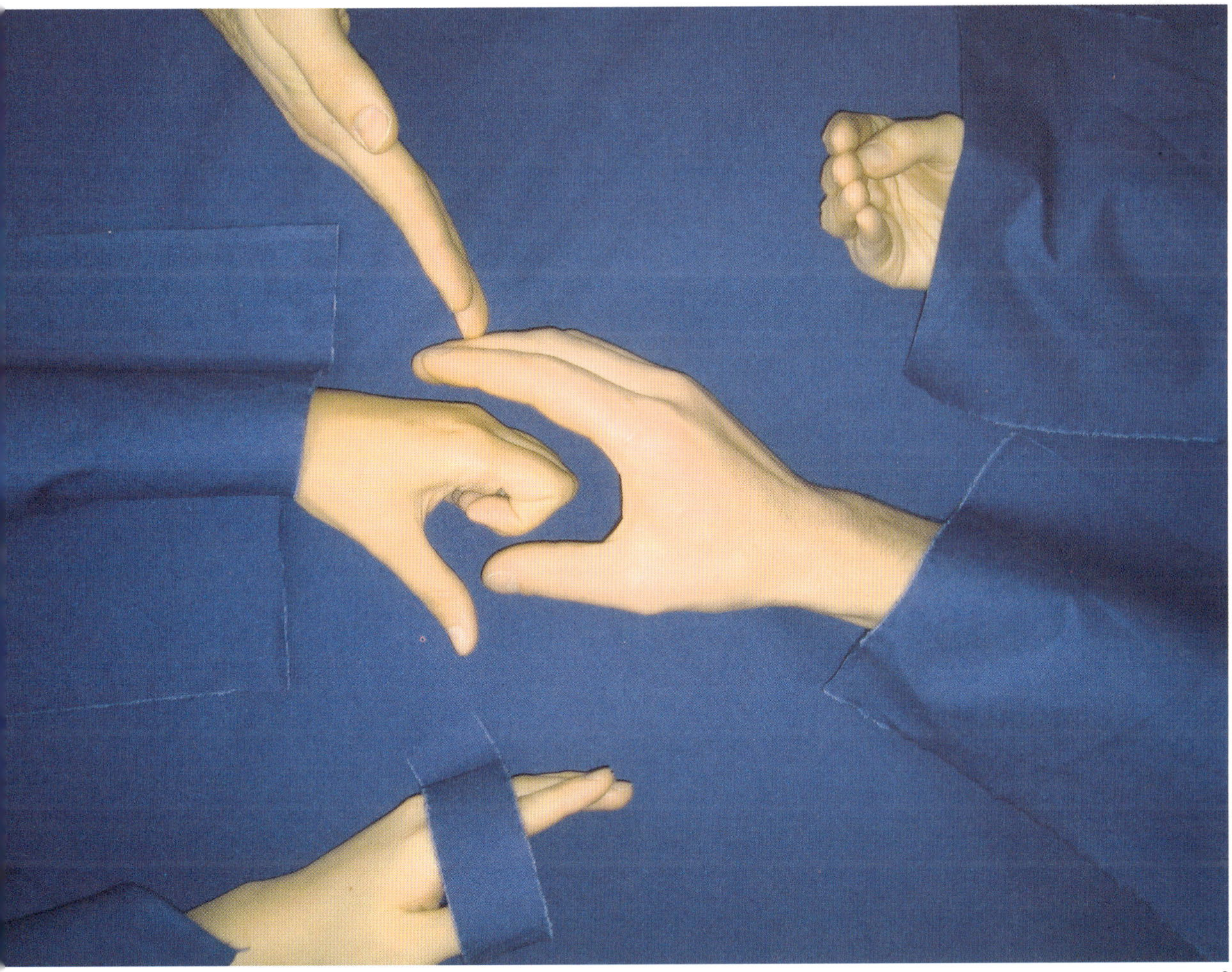

2

An Inventory of Aliases for which our studio was moved to the gallery and every day the installation changed to accommodate the thirteen or so different collaborative projects we had developed over the years with other people, such as designers, architects, band managers, teachers, artists, musicians, or others.

As mentioned before, the very idea of "collaboration" is vague, and half of us being French, we cannot completely forget that the word has a very dark connotation, as this is how we described the period of Germany occupying France during the Second World War. To this we would like to add what Arrabal said of his work with Jodorowski: "We never collaborated, there was a 'connivance'—a trust—between us."

More recently, the will to share or work with others is more related to being able to wander in other fields. Less a passport but rather a mean to dance even as a graphic designer. Our long-term project Trattoria started with the hope we would learn to cook by practicing in public, before being "ready." We are not interested in becoming the best in our field.

How do you determine membership? Does physical location matter in this regard?

We recently identified the internship in our practice as a place of education, with the existence of a strict contract about what we can ask, what should not happen, how the students are treated, etc. At some point the idea of creating a diploma—basically a testimonial, a proof-object—came up. We had to create a membership. The ones who belong and the ones who don't.

We decided to drop the idea.

As a group of four we had very early on agreed that expansion did not make sense and that there would be no legacy of Åbäke as a separate entity to the four of us. This is not the X-Men or Genesis (even if we can appreciate some Phil Collins tunes, of course). The physical location does matter in the work. Long-distance projects have mostly proven deceiving, and we favor direct contact and exchange despite having agreed to participate in this very book without having met with the editor. However, our collective has recently survived relocation in other countries, mainly for residencies, of up to six months. The trust seems to stretch even if some members do not see each other for half a year.

If considered separately, how do your individual artistic practices contribute to or detract from your work as a group?

I very much like Thom Yorke's solo album as well as being a fan of Morrissey. I equally appreciate the Smiths or Radiohead. The solo albums in general are, however, a mistake, more often than not. KISS created a hybrid of individuality within the band's system in 1978 by having an album each.

Apart from the self-flattering choice of analogy—we do not compare ourselves to the Smiths—our group does not separate what could be seen as an individual practice from the group's work. It may be artificial, as there are clear preferences and difference of approaches between the four of us, such as aversion to education for some, need of including it in the practice for others. We have so far not seen the need to separate the practices. We are obviously growing, although we do not absorb new people in the group but create connective points, which are more important in the action and the project created than its status.

As a matter of fact, speaking in such metacontext is preferred by myself but rejected or ignored by others.

At this point it is important to speak of the very context of this book. Why do we speak? How biased are our statements? What are the motivations of answering the questions? As students in our BA, some of us went to see practitioners with the embarrassing question: "When will I be famous?" implying they were, implying it has a form of value.

A better question would have been: "Why do stand-up comedians rarely collaborate?"

How are decisions made?

We have heard of the better situation of an uneven number of members in order to make decisions. We don't really believe in this—well, we're four; we don't have a choice—and neither do we believe in proposing three or more options for a client to decide on. We always present one proposal and even if we have had to admit several painful times that the idea was not so good, we are open to changing based on discussions. In this matter we have seen similarities between design commissions and participating in exhibitions.

Most of our projects are contextually driven in a wide sense. It can be the history of the place but equally the curator's favorite fruit. They are integrated to tell a story, however short or long.

Seriously Forks is a talk about talks. This work came up after a disastrous conference about our projects. The subjects were very badly spoken of by us and the lack of enthusiasm that plagued the two excruciating hours led us to understand it is more interesting to do than to represent, which as graphic designers is a bummer. The talk then almost wrote itself and resembles a talk, albeit one that only speaks of itself, never really starting before the end.

Does each of you have a clearly defined role? If so, what are some of each member's distinct responsibilities?

Four members, all straight, one girl, three guys who people thought were gay in college, mostly with long hair, one daughter each, using English as the language of work, two French, one Welsh, one Swedish. A few years back a friend had defined each one of us in relation to the Spice Girls.

3 – Trattoria, pop-up dinner moments with Alex Rich and Martino Gamper, 2004–ongoing

4 – All the Knives catalog for an exhibition curated by Åbäke at Z33, Hasselt, Belgium, 2012–2013

5 – Happy 93rd Birthday Ellen, event, from Åbäke's residency at Serpentine Gallery Skills Exchange, London, 2010

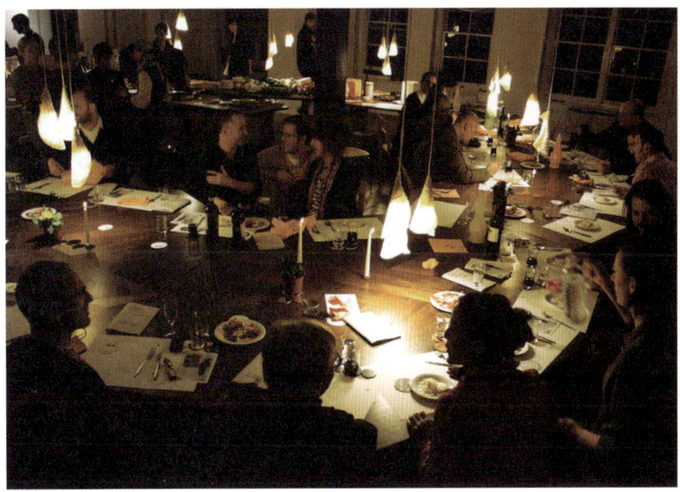

3

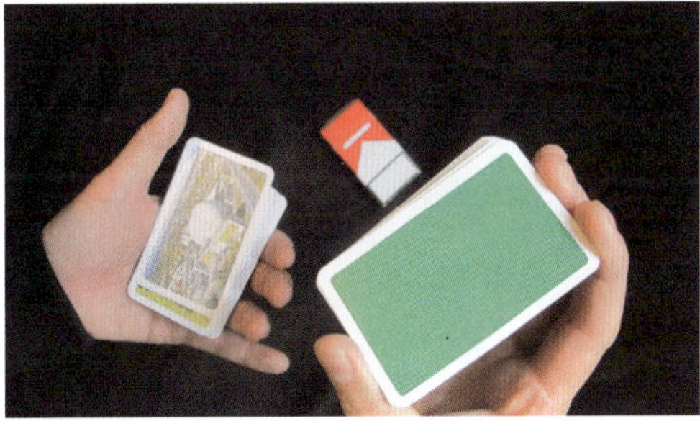

4

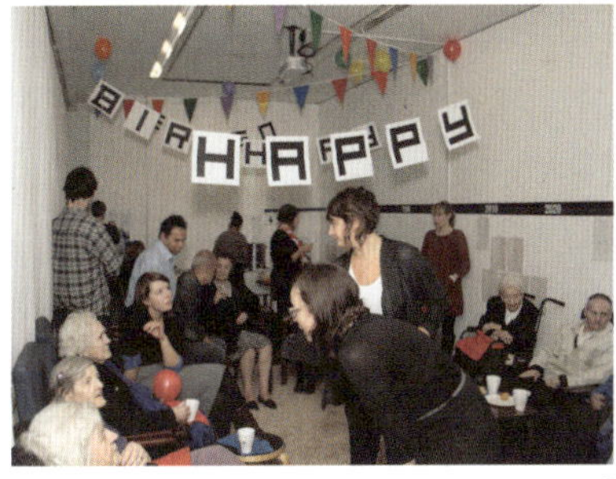

5

Like them, we cannot sing very well and like them, he continued, some people like to work with one rather than the other. One is the heart, one the brain, one the mysterious one, and the other is ginger. We were therefore pigeon-holed in a place between The Wizard of Oz and a band strategically groomed for those who like a sporty girl, a posh girl, a baby girl, a scary girl, and ginger. I don't want to be the ginger, said one of us, I am not even ginger.

We have had two email addresses, both used by the four of us. New clients or collaborators often ask how difficult it is to have only one address. They sometimes never meet the three others and possibly don't need or want to.

How important is each group member's individuality, both in terms of your artistic production and in terms of your relationship with the media? Does anonymity come into play?

Very important but not to the media. It is rather about letting each person go and do something personal within the group practice. We are not anonymous but we don't feel it important to distinguish who in the collective did what when there is already a signature. The problem comes more often from the outside: an artist asking for a text to be signed in one's name or a journalist mentioning a name of a person rather than the collective.

What is the relationship between your working methods and your art's "content"? In this sense, does technology tend to play more of a supporting role, or does it lead you in new directions?

The content and the methods are connected in a narrative sense, rather than a functionally logical way. Technology or media are supportive but equally exciting whenever there is something new we can learn.

How does your collaboration relate to its cultural, institutional, and commercial contexts? In other words, how would you respond to those who call this a trend?

It might be a trend but then a painful one. It is more difficult to work in a group, so why inflict this on oneself for a passing fad?

Who is your audience?

A very important parameter to any project, despite the almost impossible task to define it. For the present example, both you, the editor of the book, and the readers, then perhaps ourselves.

Does your engagement with one another translate into an engagement with the public? How so?

With is certainly possible, for is not preferred. We sometimes do not care about the audience or the buyers. as we refuse to engage in a service relationship. We love them, however.

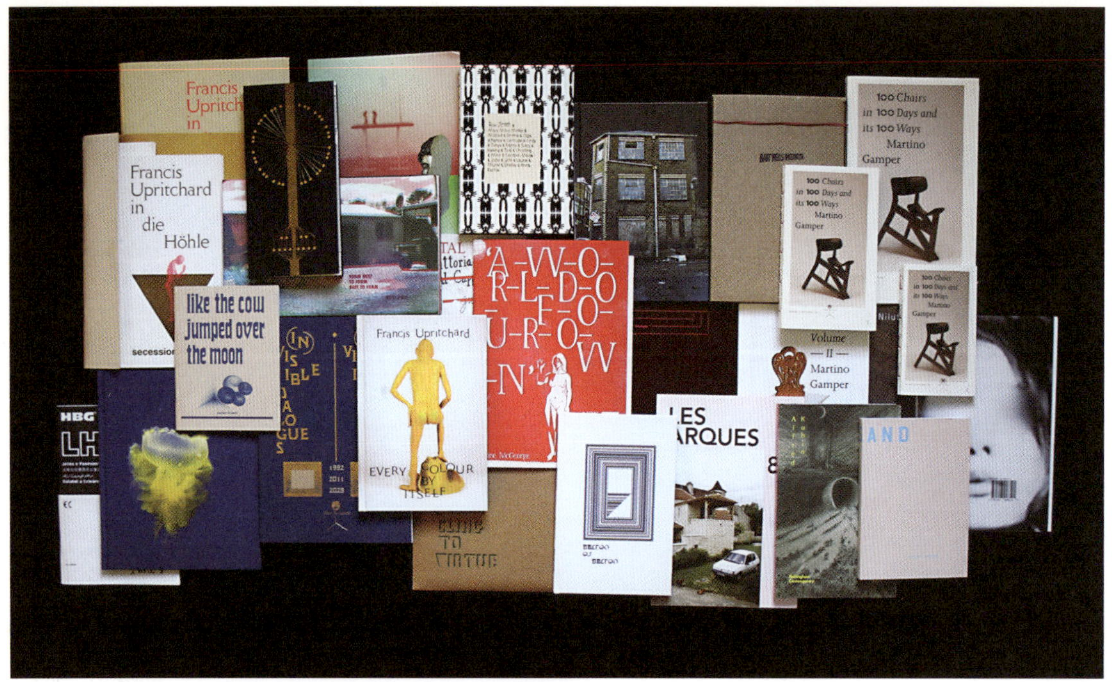

6

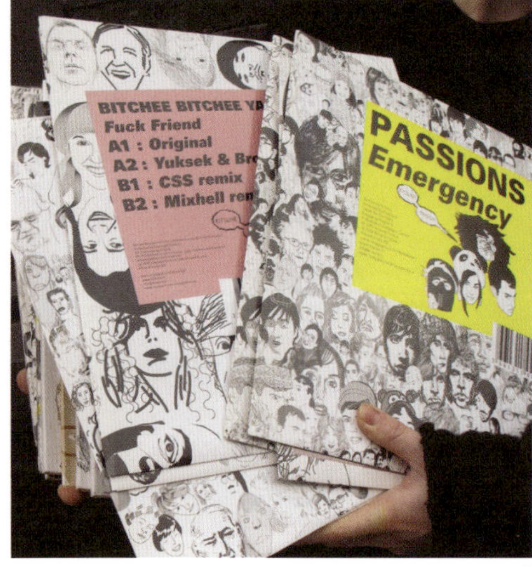

7

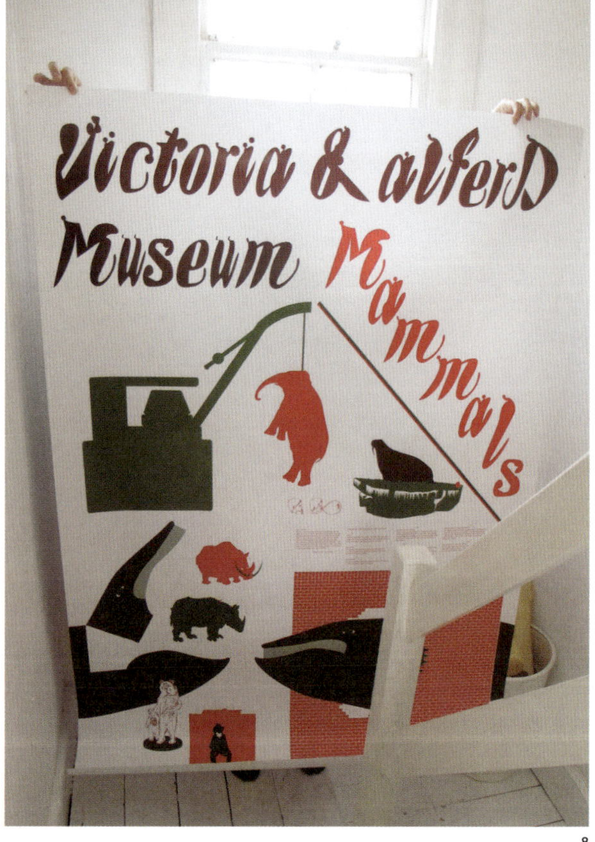

8

6 – Dent-De-Leone books, Åbäke's Maki Suzuki and Kajsa Ståhl's own publishing house run together with Martino Gamper. All books designed by Åbäke, 2004–2013

7 – Kitsuné Maison records, 2002–2013

8 – Victoria & Alferd Museum: Mammals, poster, Museum Show Part 1, Arnolfini, Bristol, 2011

opposite
9 – When is a yes a no?, poster insert for Graphic no. 20, 2011

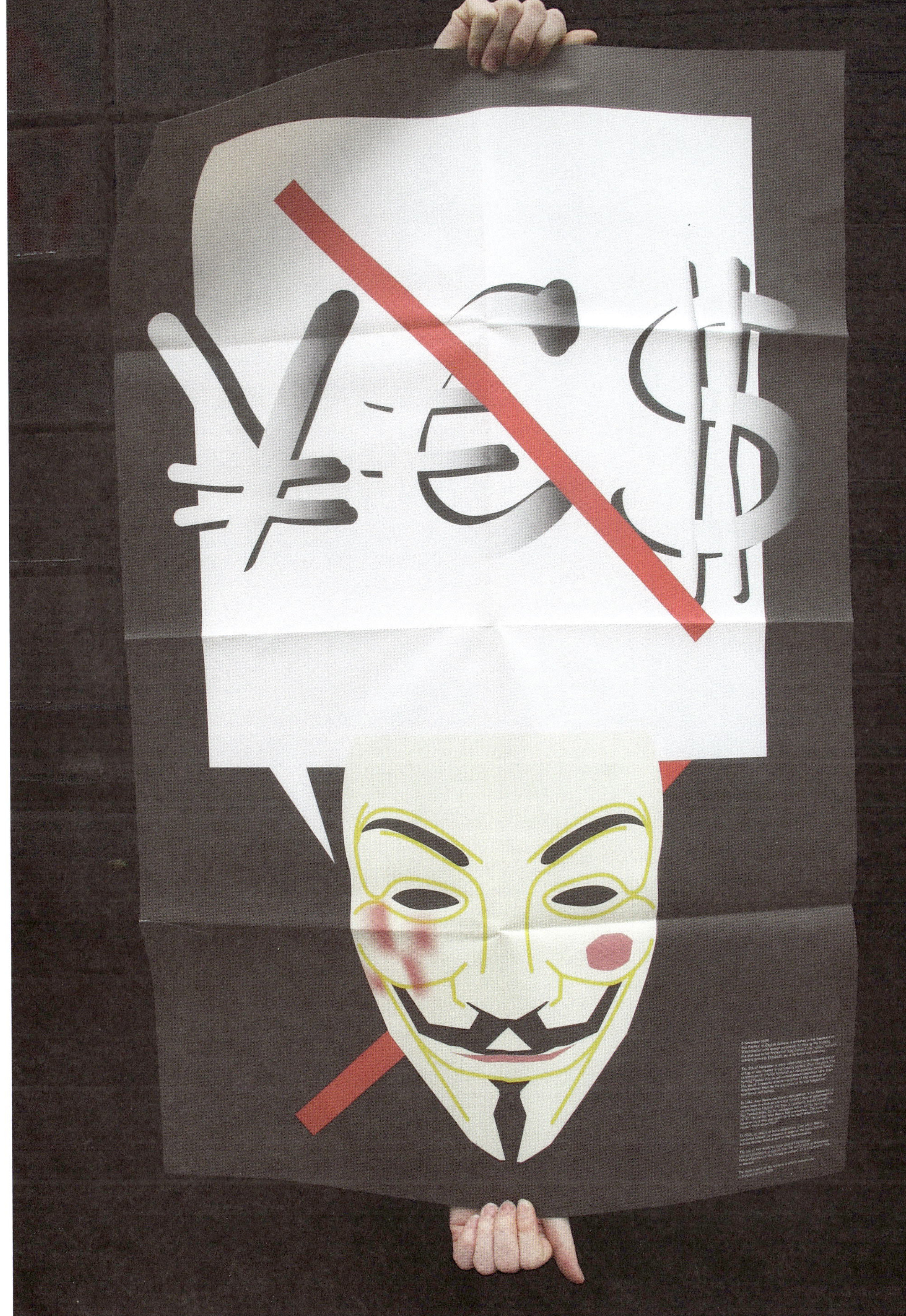

ACTIVE SINCE	CITY	WEBSITE
2002	Paris, France	andreacrews.com

Andrea Crews

MEMBERS	ACTIVITIES	RECOMMENDED PUBLICATION
from 1 to 100,000	Clothing, Community Projects, Merchandising, Public Performance, Urban Interventions	Lauren Bastide, Florence Parot, Lorent Idir, I AM ANDREA CREWS, Édition B-42, Paris, 2012

Led by Maroussia Rebecq, the Parisian collective, brand, and creative agency is known for creating clothing and projects that reflect on the meaning of fashion in our society. Working under the motto Fashion, Art, Activism, Andrea Crews's workshops and performances are characterized by a neo-hippie atmosphere in which used clothing becomes a tool for the reimagination of fashion and crafts from outside the traditional gilded realm of high fashion.

Why work collaboratively?

Collaboration makes the work and inspiration arises through movement; it creates an everyday "remise en question" and makes every idea stronger. We all feel we have a lot of energy to share. Also, working with people keeps us engaged by our own ideas; it's always challenging! It boosts up le savoir-faire!

How do you determine membership? Does physical location matter in this regard?

It's organic: friends of friends, time to time, practice to practice, we have a lot of worldwide connection and friends. It can be designers, musicians, performers, writers, muses—some people might call them "influencers."

The world is small and big is the family!

But let's say we are mostly a band of Parisian girls, all quite fashionable ☺, and we can recognize one another with simply a glance, and we love being together! (And boys are very welcome with their sexy and strong bodies).

If considered separately, how do your individual artistic practices contribute to or detract from your work as a group?

We give all our personal work to our community, and the community gives it back to us.

To make Andrea Crews an aesthetic and energetic empire is the main personal project of most of us. As an individual artist, Maroussia Rebecq wanted to build a system, a living system (the idea of the total work of art of the avant-gardes comes to mind). Andrea Crews now is a creative workshop, an interactive space, a clothing brand, and an innovating company. It's a very unique energy and it takes a lot of time—it is the main activity—it is the life itself of Maroussia.

How are decisions made?

Maroussia is the leader of Andrea Crews in a participative system, which seems paradoxical, but everybody always does their best for the others, and inspiration and good sense fill in the rest! It's very intuitive and it can be messy. But we learn every day, we meet every week, we make reports every month, and we structure the multiple creative projects as a business development.

Does each of you have a clearly defined role? If so, what are some of each member's distinct responsibilities?

Let's say in our everyday life, Maroussia has the vision, Anji the reason, and Nina the tools.

Maroussia is the founder, the eldest, and she takes care of the girls ☺, "her" girls; they are the smartest and the sexiest, and they take care of her in return. She brings the wisdom and the energy; they bring the freshness and the motivation. Most of the time, to produce our projects we mix up our skills to make an innovative and experimental cocktail.

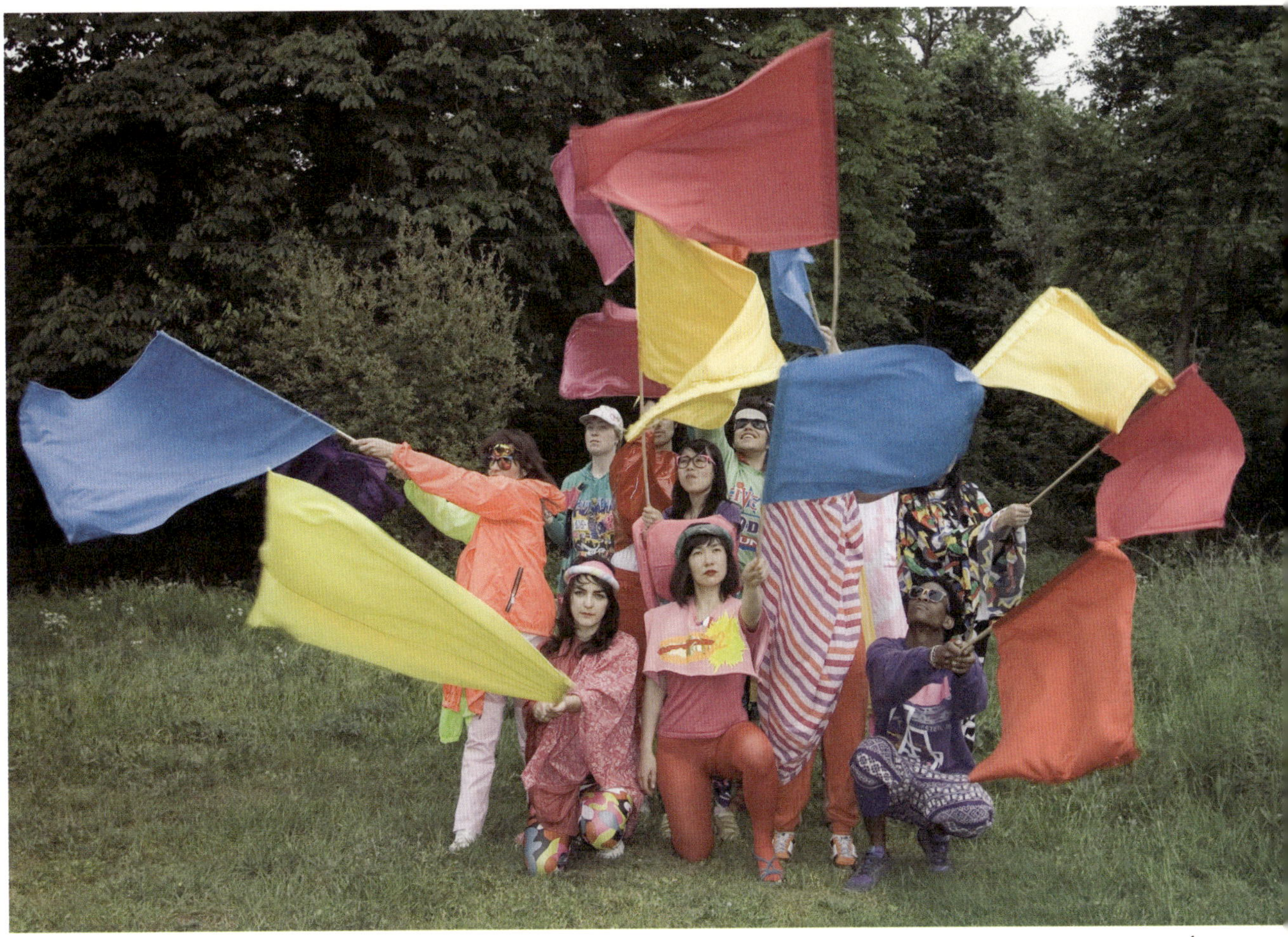

1

1 – Color Explosion, performance, Paris, 2009

2 – Sunset Empire, Gallerie LHK, 2010

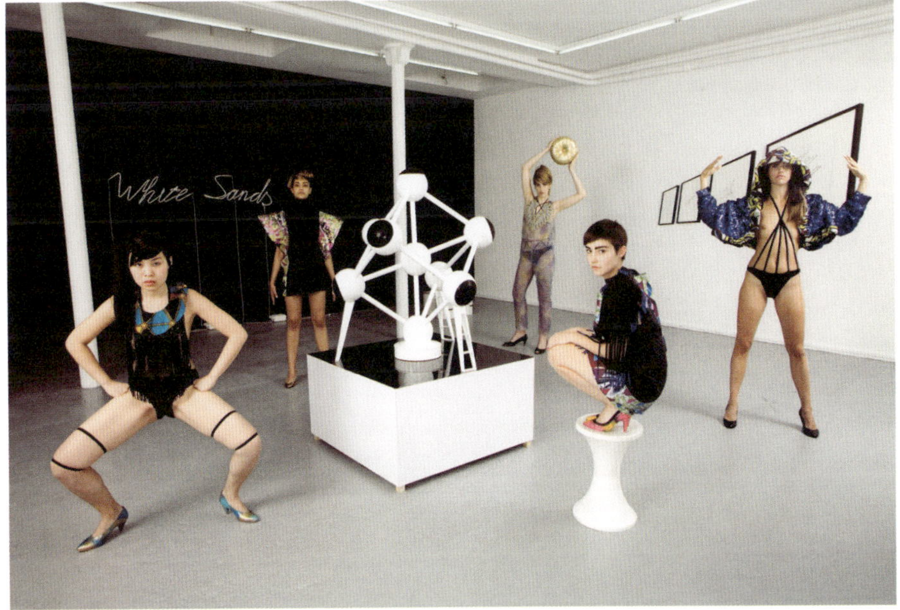

2

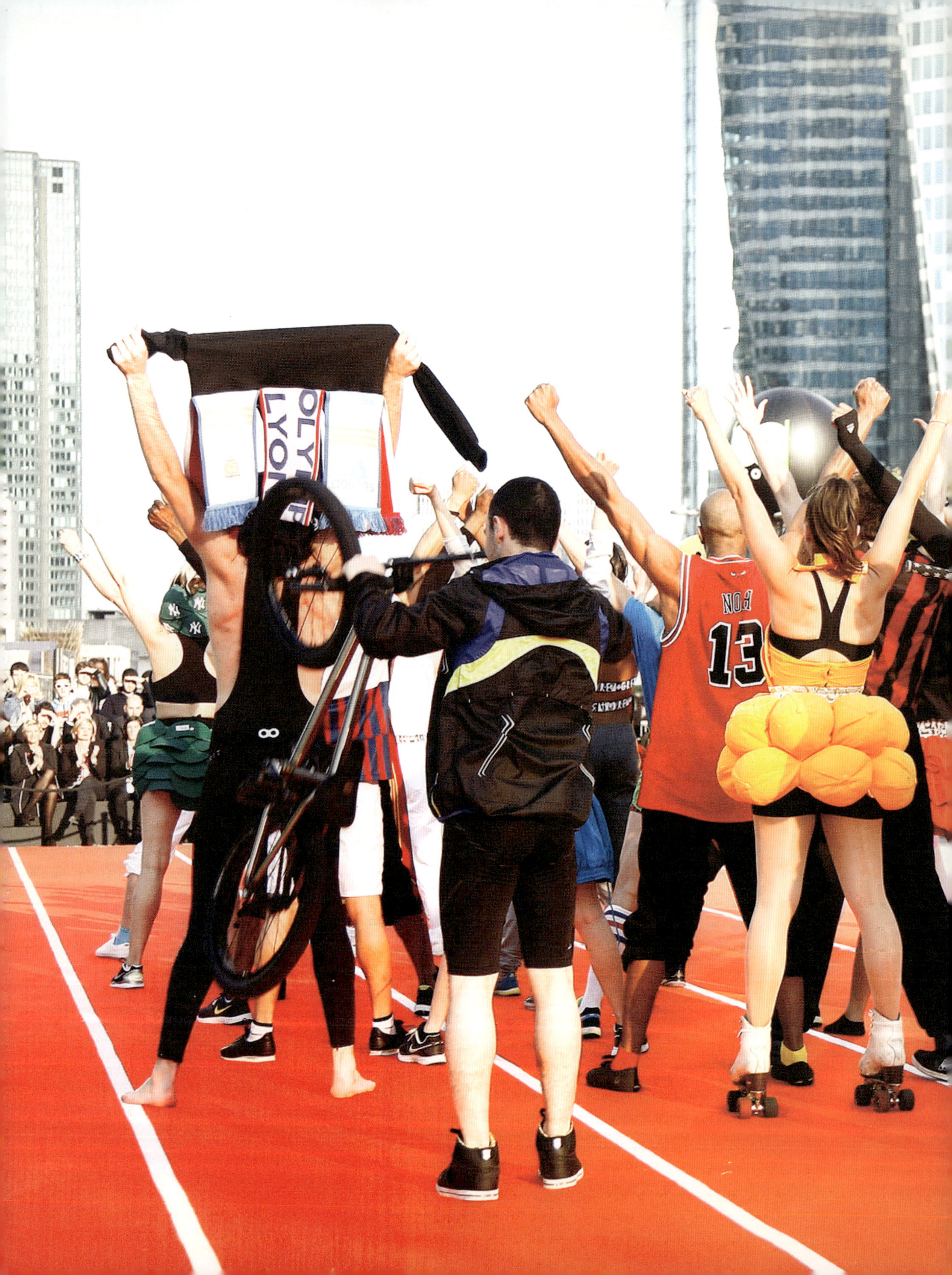
LYON
13

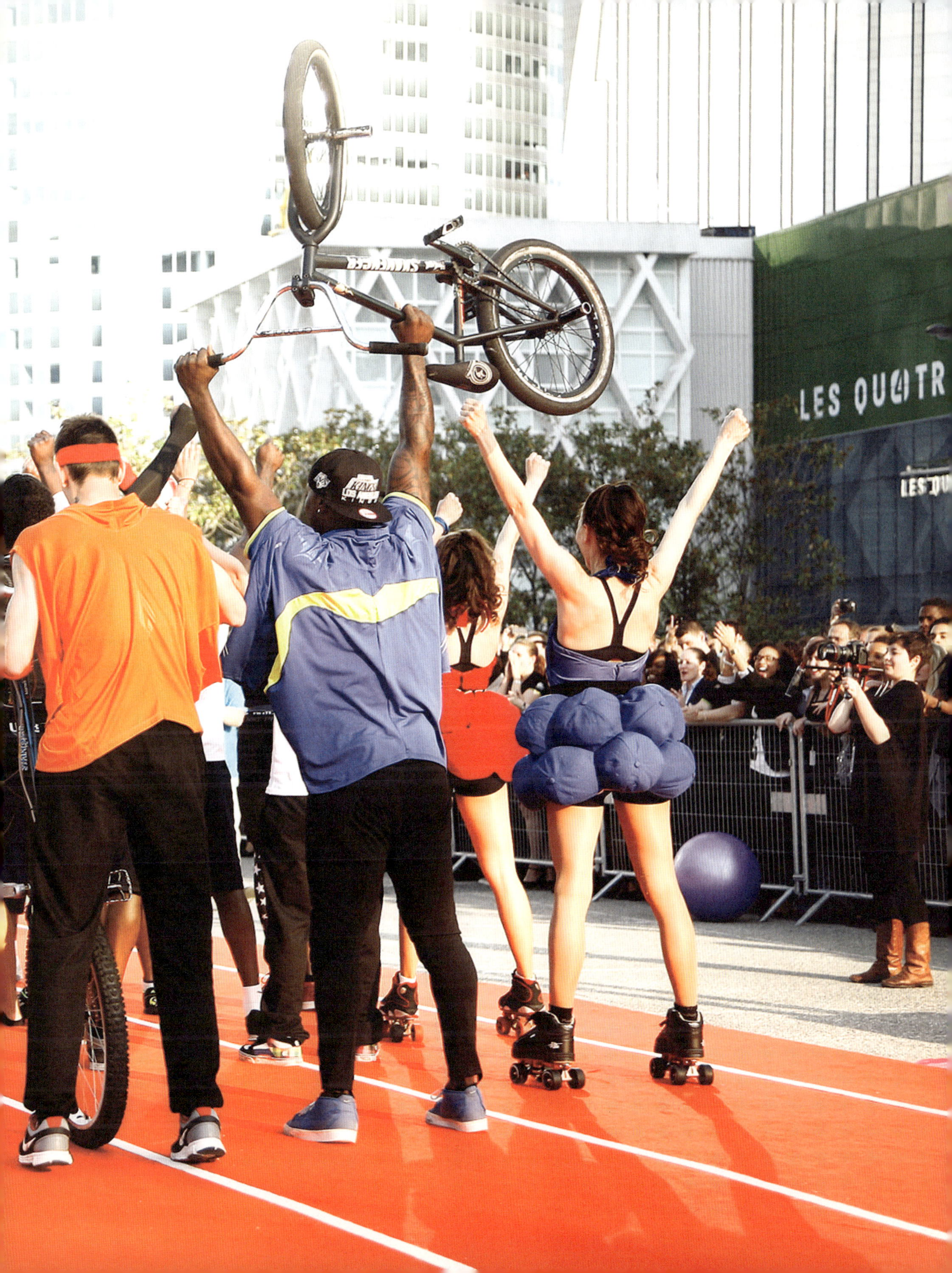
LES QU4TR

previous
3 – **<u>Go Sport</u>, performance, Paris, 2012**

4 – **<u>Run Baby Run</u>, performance, Palais de Tokyo, 2007**

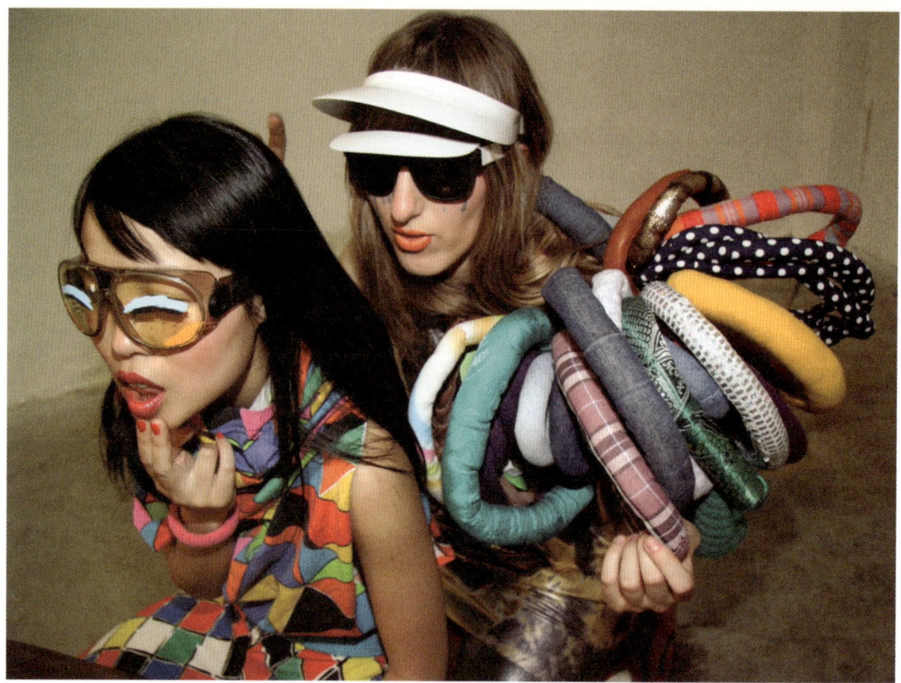

4

How important is each group member's individuality, both in terms of your artistic production and in terms of your relationship with the media? Does anonymity come into play?

We are all very different, but all we're all working on Andrea Crews, which is creative, free, and colorful. Working is a joy, a challenge, because we are building something that is not a fashion brand, but plays with that idea! We are "happy" activists—Andrea Crews is a fictional character; anybody who wears the mask can represent her spirit.

What is the relationship between your working methods and your art's "content"? In this sense, does technology tend to play more of a supporting role, or does it lead you in new directions?

Our content comes mostly from our history. For example, we just moved into a new studio from downtown to uptown, so our last collection is about that: what are the social codes in both area;, what does it mean to move and change neighborhoods; the attitude, the audience, the streets, and the lifestyle are so different. That creates not only the inspiration, but also the topic, and it's based on experience.

We recently discovered the Vine app and we've been very inspired by this media. We made our last show through Vine. As a statement, it was innovative, fun, and easy; in a time when we needed to do something light and strong to communicate, it was perfect. Lo-fi technology and deviant innovation are the essence of our inspirations; how to create universality out of our differences?

How does your collaboration relate to its cultural, institutional, and commercial contexts? In other words, how would you respond to those who call this a trend?

Andrea Crews is much more than a trend! Andrea Crews is a movement! A trend goes up fast and dies, Andrea Crews is very different: we are resistant, we grow organically, and even if we act quickly, we grow slowly and independently! We are hip for sure but strong and wild at heart. People respect our work and help it grow with them.

Who is your audience?

Worldwide, Dirty Fashion and Art People make our projects and wear our clothes, with a strong following in Asia, where the style is more graphic and sculptural than in Europe or the United States. Europe is turning old now in terms of creation and innovation for style; it is in crisis.

Does your engagement with one another translate into an engagement with the public? How so?

Actually we think that our story, in its particularities, is universal and should reach a maximum amount of people. The process of creation is intense, and even if we have some strong conceptual statement that takes it far from the mainstream, it's always free, and happy, and that's what we want to give to each other, to everybody. You can get it! Andrea Crews is a very generous project, one that tries to make a difference as well. And Andrea Crews has also always been a space where people meet and create; we are linked with our surroundings and their energies.

5 – Dance on the Beach, installation, Laonde, 2011

6 – Kitten Hologram summer lookbook, Paris, 2013

7 – La Generale, group portrait, Paris, 2008

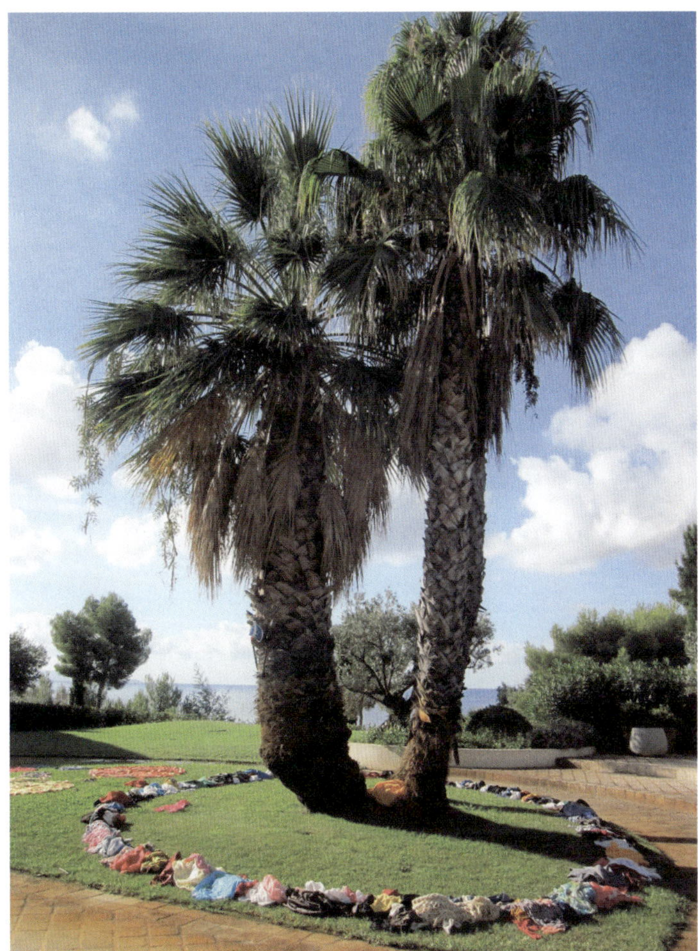

5

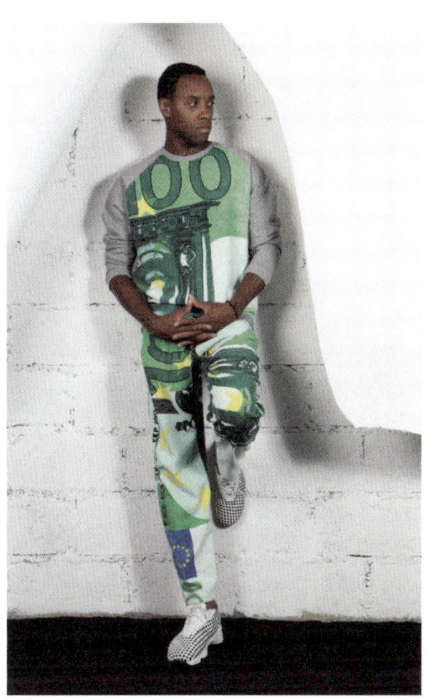

6

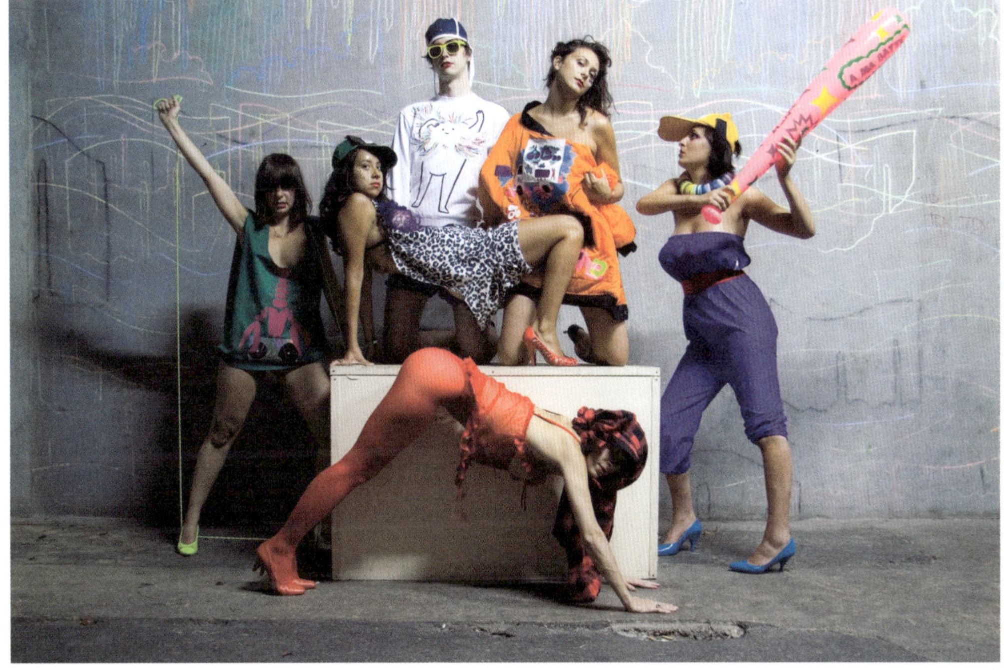

7

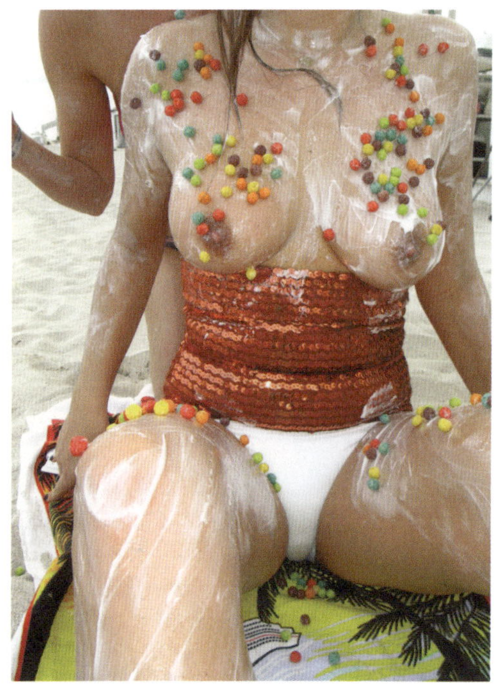

8

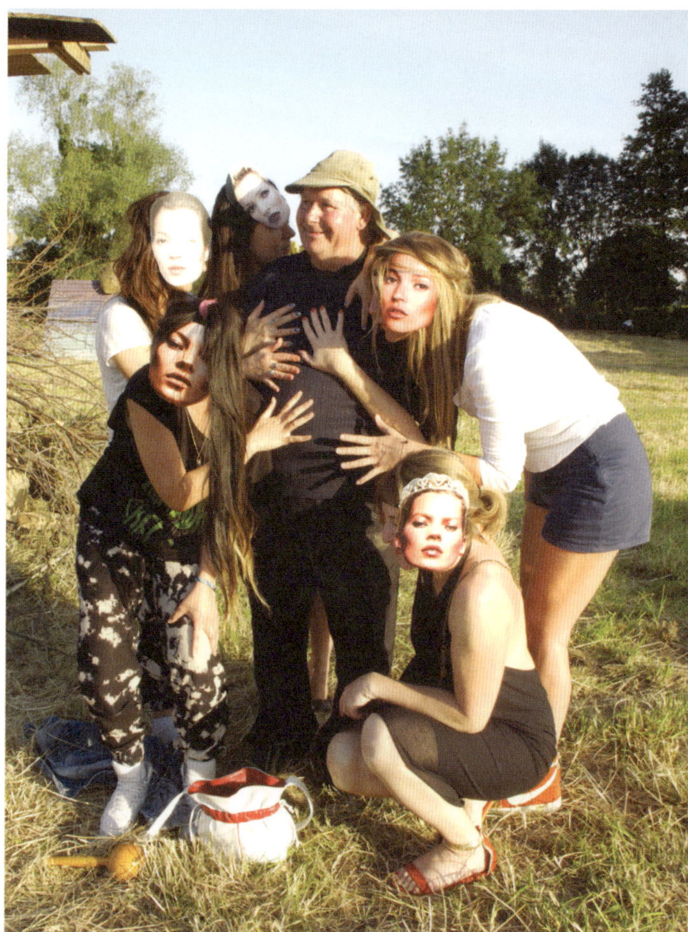

9

8 – Yummiami, performance, Miami Beach, 2009

9 – Burning Vogue, performance, Piacé le Radieux, 2012

10 – Dance On the Beach, performance, Laonde, 2011

opposite
11 – Damned Amsterdam, Upcycle Yourself workshop, Mediamatic Foundation, Amsterdam, 2008

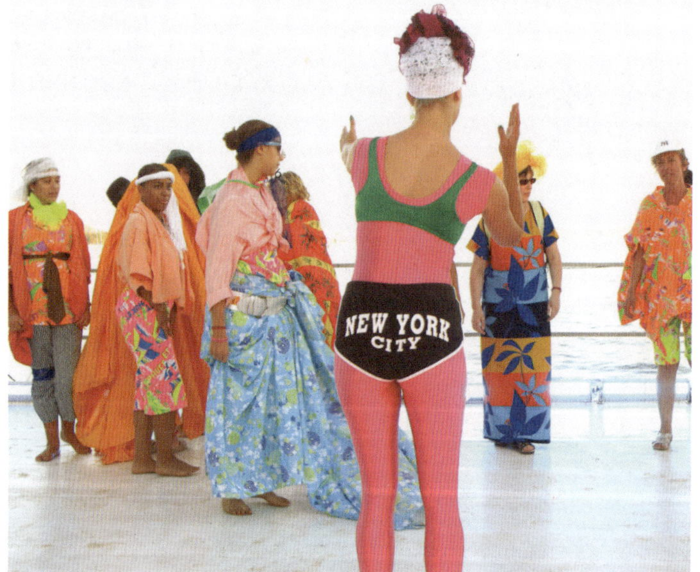

10

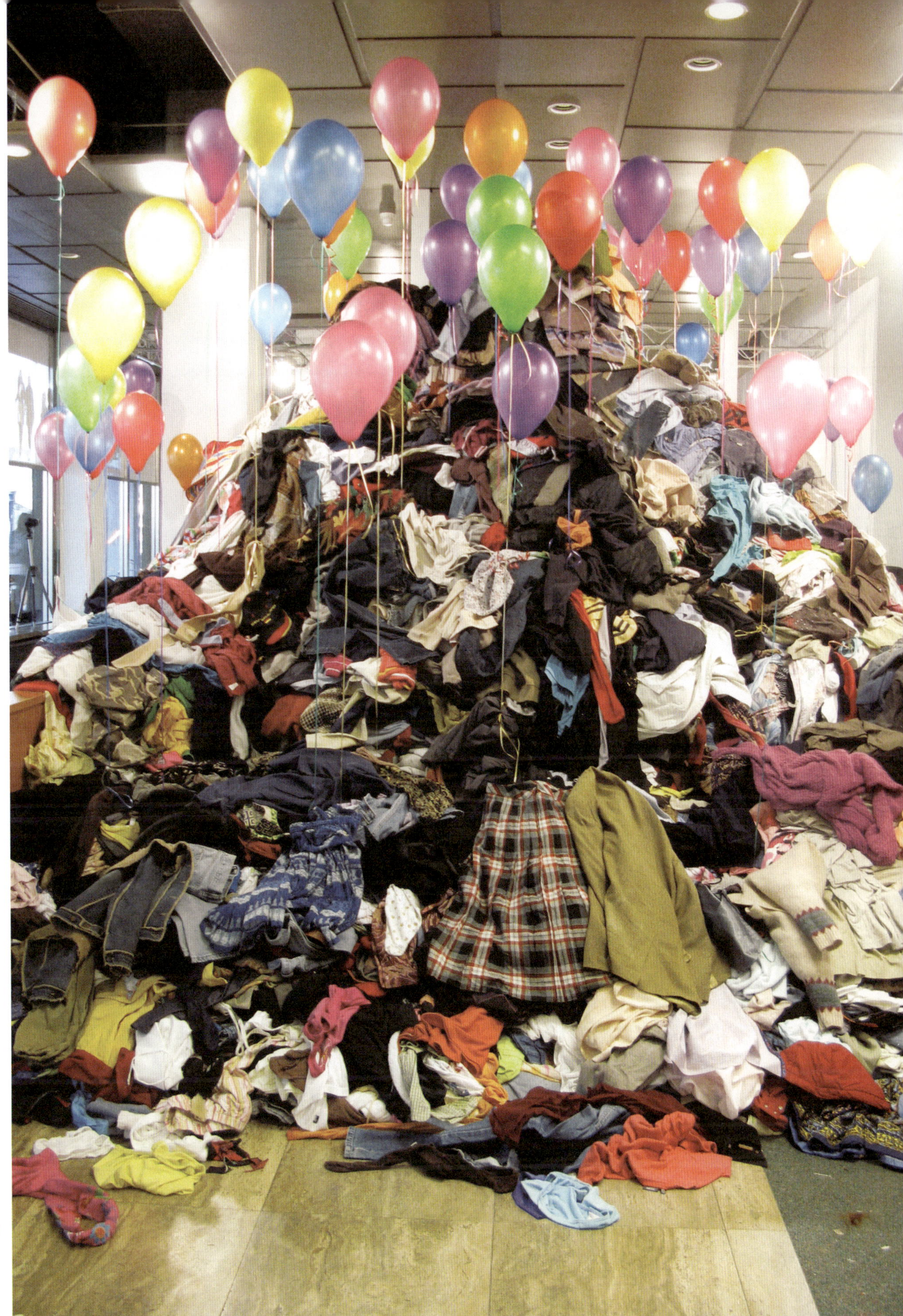

ACTIVE SINCE	CITY	WEBSITE
2000	New York, U.S. / São Paulo, Brazil / Paris, France	assumevividastrofocus.com

Assume Vivid Astro Focus

MEMBERS	ACTIVITIES	RECOMMENDED PUBLICATION
Eli Sudbrack and Christophe Hamaide-Pierson	Community Projects, Curating, Internet Art, Merchandising, Music, Painting / Sculpture / Installation, Public Performance, Publishing, Urban Interventions	ASSUME VIVID ASTRO FOCUS, Rizzoli, New York, 2010

Mixing graphic elements and symbols from Brazilian Tropicália and Californian psychedelia, Assume Vivid Astro Focus creates collages, installations, and performances that bring the audience into another dimension. Its events remind one of carnivals or raves, temporary autonomous zones of sexual, ethnic, and cultural liberation characterized by the use of Day-Glo colors, neon lights, and lysergic references to pop culture.

Why work collaboratively?

First, let me explain how it is for us to work collaboratively. We used to refer to ourselves as a "collective" but we stopped using this term in the past few years—now we say we are a "duo," which sometimes morphs into a "collective," depending on the project we are working on at that moment. Initially, we didn't want to make this clear because we were more concerned about hiding our identities (and the collaborators') under the AVAF moniker (just recently we relaxed about this and came to the assumption that we are indeed a duo with occasional collaborators).

The AVAF acronym is somehow a call to action—our utopian idea is that people can "assume" Assume Vivid Astro Focus and start making AVAF works on their own (without us even knowing) and thus, in our view, becoming collaborators.

How do you determine membership? Does physical location matter in this regard?

AVAF is me (Eli Sudbrack) and Christophe Hamaide-Pierson. Christophe is a long-time friend of mine who I met right when I moved to New York fourteen years ago in 1998. Christophe used to live in NYC but moved to Paris in 2000. We only started working together in 2005 (on the occasion of our Homocrap installation at MOCA, L.A.) and since then he is the only other person who has been involved in every aspect of our work and in every single project.

We never lived in the same city since we started working together. For this reason physical location has never been an issue for us (and this is true also for other collaborators we have worked with in the past). Christophe and I have some peculiarities in our "working together but being apart" process—we never talk on the phone, we never Skype, but we exchange emails about our ideas and stuff we are working on all the time.

If considered separately, how do your individual artistic practices contribute to or detract from your work as a group?

Everything we do as individuals is done as a team. Our working process has several similarities with a curatorial process. Choosing collaborators we will work with depends, first and foremost, on some sort of emotional connection with them—that is why we only work with people we are friends with. Certainly the collaborators' skills also determine how we will be working together and for which exhibition. We choose collaborators on a projec-by-project basis.

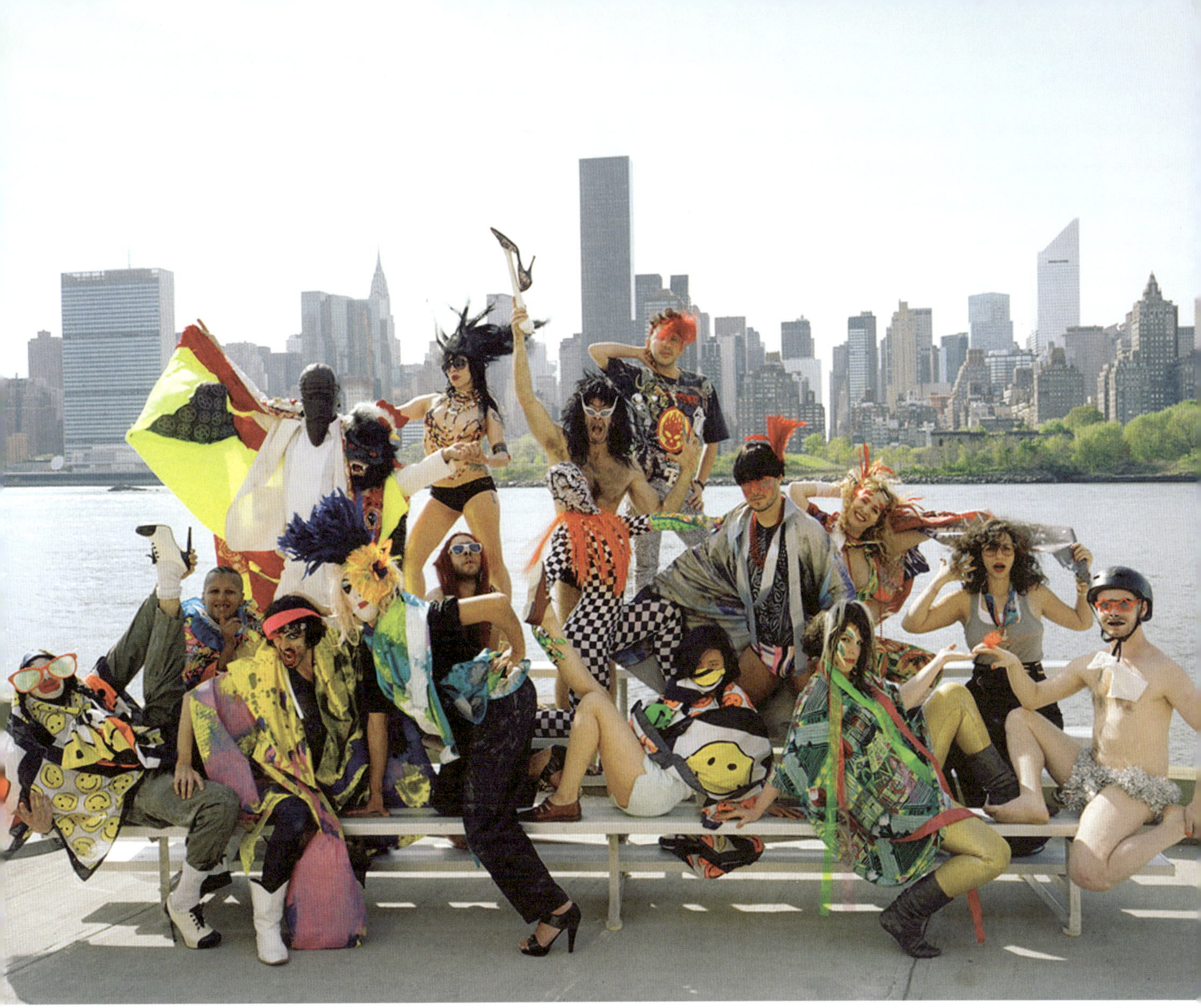

1

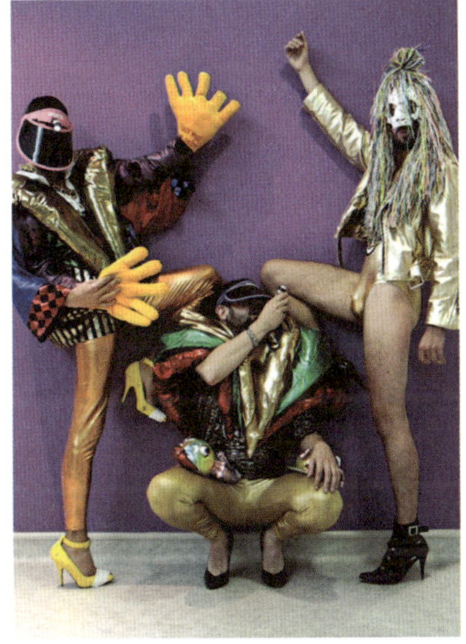

2

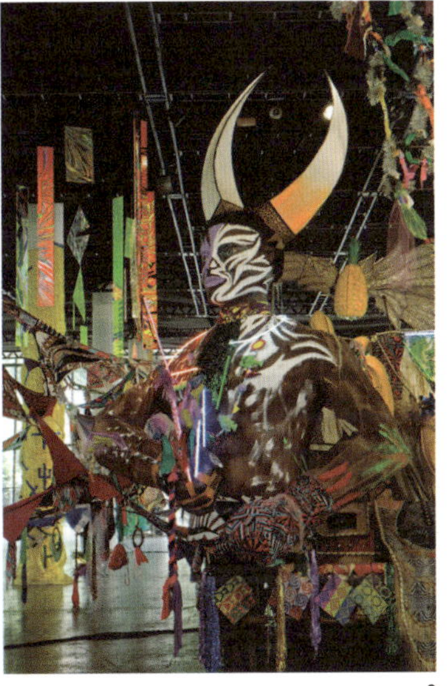

3

1 – Absolutely Venomous Accurately Fallacious (Naturally Delicious), group portrait, Deitch Projects, Long Island City, New York, 2008

2 – Shad Shada La Chatte, one-night performance with La Chatte for Noche en Bianco, Matadero, Madrid, September 22, 2007

3 – Axé Vatapá Alegria Feijão, installation, 28th Bienal de São Paulo, São Paulo, 2008

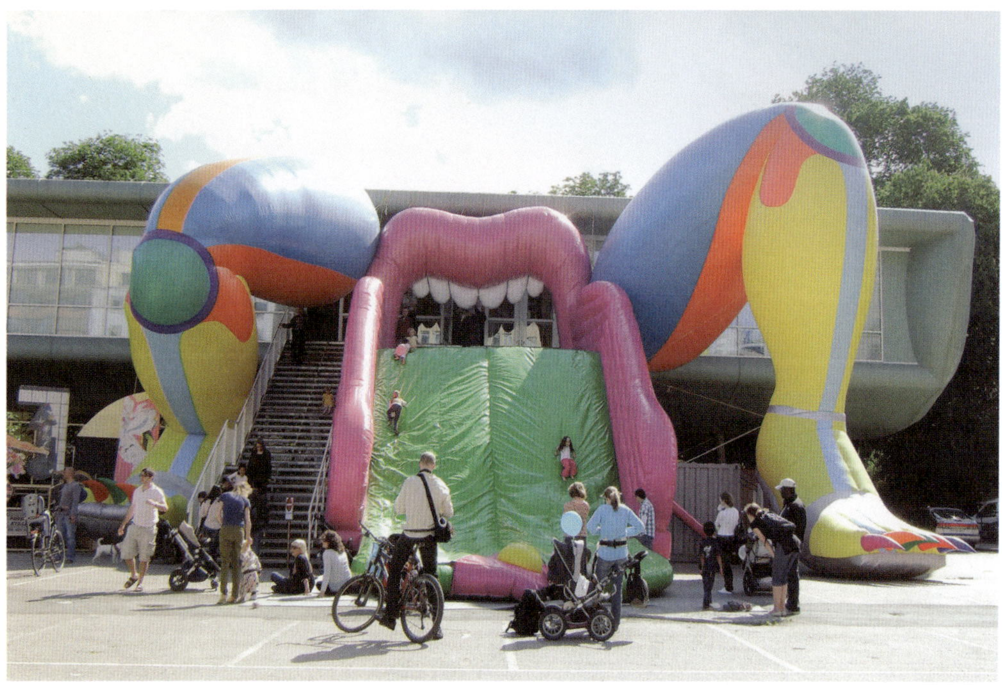

4

And it is us (Christophe and I) who decide how that person will be participating. This is when the curatorship aspect in our work becomes more apparent. In general, the first step is to present our ideas and concepts for a specific show to a collaborator. We often talk about how we are occupying the space, which other collaborators we will be working with, the connections between the different works, what we expect from the collaborator's contribution. From that point onward we have basically three forms of working with other artists. The first kind is when we work hand in hand with the collaborator—that of course depends on all of us being physically present during the production of the piece (which is not so common). Another kind is when we contaminate the collaborator with our ideas, and he or she reacts to these ideas and develops a work that fits in the general context. The third kind is when we choose an artist's existing work and curate it in the show along with other works.

How are decisions made?

We exchange emails on a daily basis. We meet only when there is an installation in progress, which is one of the rare moments we are physically working together (sometimes we spend a year without seeing each other). We are the only ones who deal directly with curators, galleries, museums, press, manufacturers, etc.

We like to suggest new directions to the collaborators and often propose challenges for their practice. This represents some sort of interference in their work and I guess it is the reason why we hardly ever collaborate with established artists (Kenny Scharf is the only exception, as far as I remember).

Does each of you have a clearly defined role? If so, what are some of each member's distinct responsibilities?

I could single out my role in AVAF as the igniter and the voice. I'm the one speaking in lectures, giving interviews, writing statements, etc. I'm more often in charge of production and the one who is dealing directly with the manufacturers. In general I'm the one who sets things in motion.

How important is each group member's individuality, both in terms of your artistic production and in terms of your relationship with the media? Does anonymity come into play?

Because of the way we "separately work collaboratively," both of us often work on our own, in our studios. In my case, at least, all the work that I individually make is AVAF; I make no distinctions. We want people to focus on the work and not on an individual's personality. This is one of the reasons we started distributing custom AVAF masks in our events/openings/performances—not only to fuse viewer and environment together, but also to avoid singling out people for who they are or what they have done. We want the installations to be inclusive and not exclusive. We want the work to be experienced fully and free from as many preconceptions as possible. We want engagement and deliverance—anonymity has always been one of our tools to set this in motion in our projects.

opposite
4 – affektert veffmaleri akselererende faenksap, inflatable installation, National Museum of Art, Architecture and Design, Oslo, 2009

5 – Cyclop Trannie #55 (Shqueefa Jabrina), collage, Cyclops Trannies, the Suzanne Geiss Company, 2011

6 – Crawl Girl from aqui volvemos adornos frivolos, collage, Peres Projects, Berlin, 2008

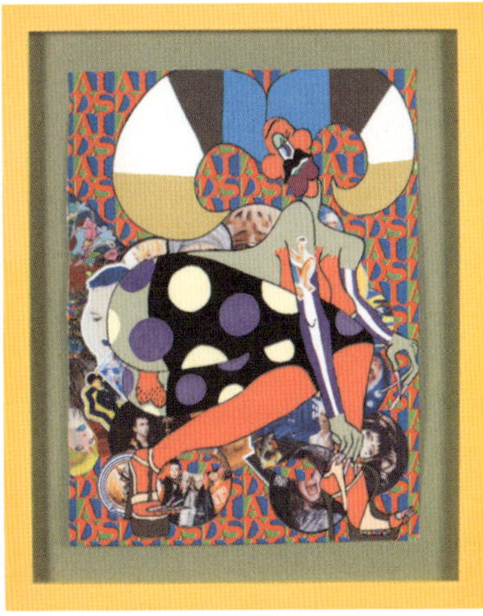
5

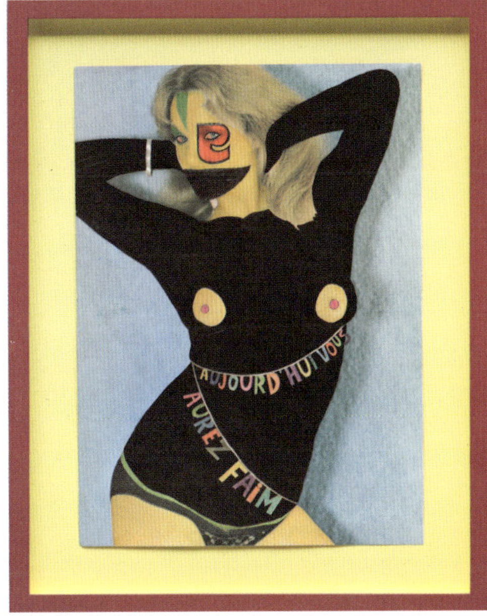

6

What is the relationship between your working methods and your art's "content"? In this sense, does technology tend to play more of a supporting role, or does it lead you in new directions?
It is important for us to blend together the works by the different collaborators so everything becomes one cohesive installation—and Christophe and I create the connecting thread. I could say that this is our most basic function in this collaborative process: we are the connectors. Connecting is, for us, one of the most gratifying elements of working collaboratively and definitely one of the reasons to do it. And, of course, the Internet plays a fundamental role in creating this connection, first between us and then betweenus and our collaborators.

How does your collaboration relate to its cultural, institutional, and commercial contexts? In other words, how would you respond to those who call this a trend?
For many years now, most of the work we have produced on a daily basis has been for a specific, upcoming project so we always create for its specific cultural, institutional, or commercial contexts and we morph accordingly. The flexibility of our practice provides us with a smooth transition between different contexts most of the time.

Nowadays it is very common and easy for people to connect and work together virtually. So I wouldn't call collaboration a trend in the "hype" sense of the word. In my point of view, collaboration is a much more spontaneous consequence of the tools (communication, production tools) that are out there today.

Who is your audience?
I wish our audience was broader and more varied. Unfortunately, most of the time we reach people who are at least interested in the art world, if not already inserted in it in one way or another.

Does your engagement with one another translate into an engagement with the public? How so?
There is a "classism" about the art audience that bothers us. It is harder to reach people who are not expecting to be reached. The environments in galleries and museums are also contrived and demand an obedience that doesn't really fit in our projects (and we often have trouble with institutions because of their safety rules, for instance). On the other hand, every single project we have done in the public sphere has been the most fulfilling. In these cases we are able to reach out to people who otherwise would never be exposed to us. The public sphere brings an otherworldly character to the unexpected. And at same time, you need to transmit confidence to people to guarantee their participation, engagement, and deliverance. This viewer doesn't necessarily know who you are, where you come from, what you usually do, and nevertheless they are there bringing your piece to life: the power of providing unexpected trust.

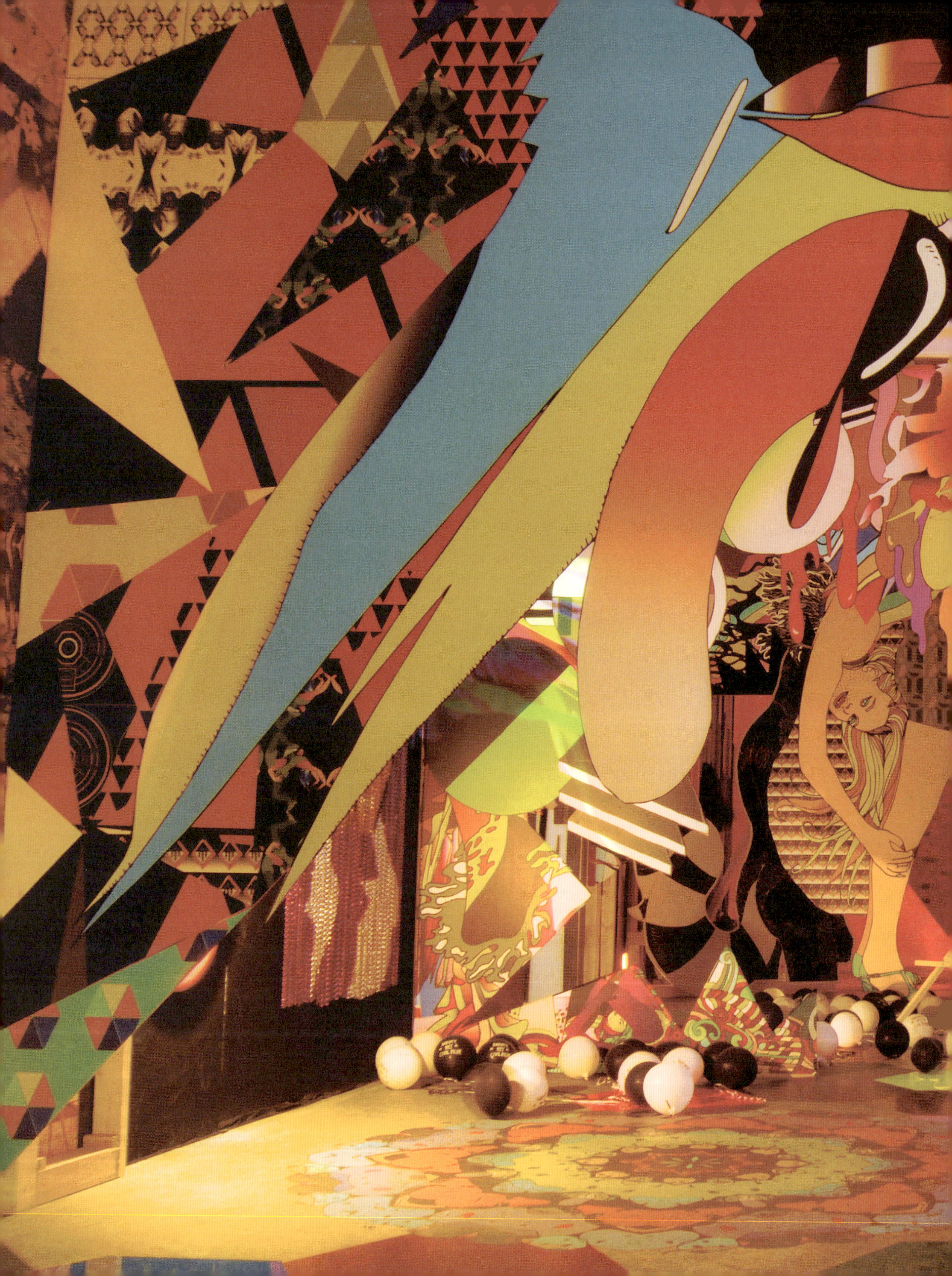

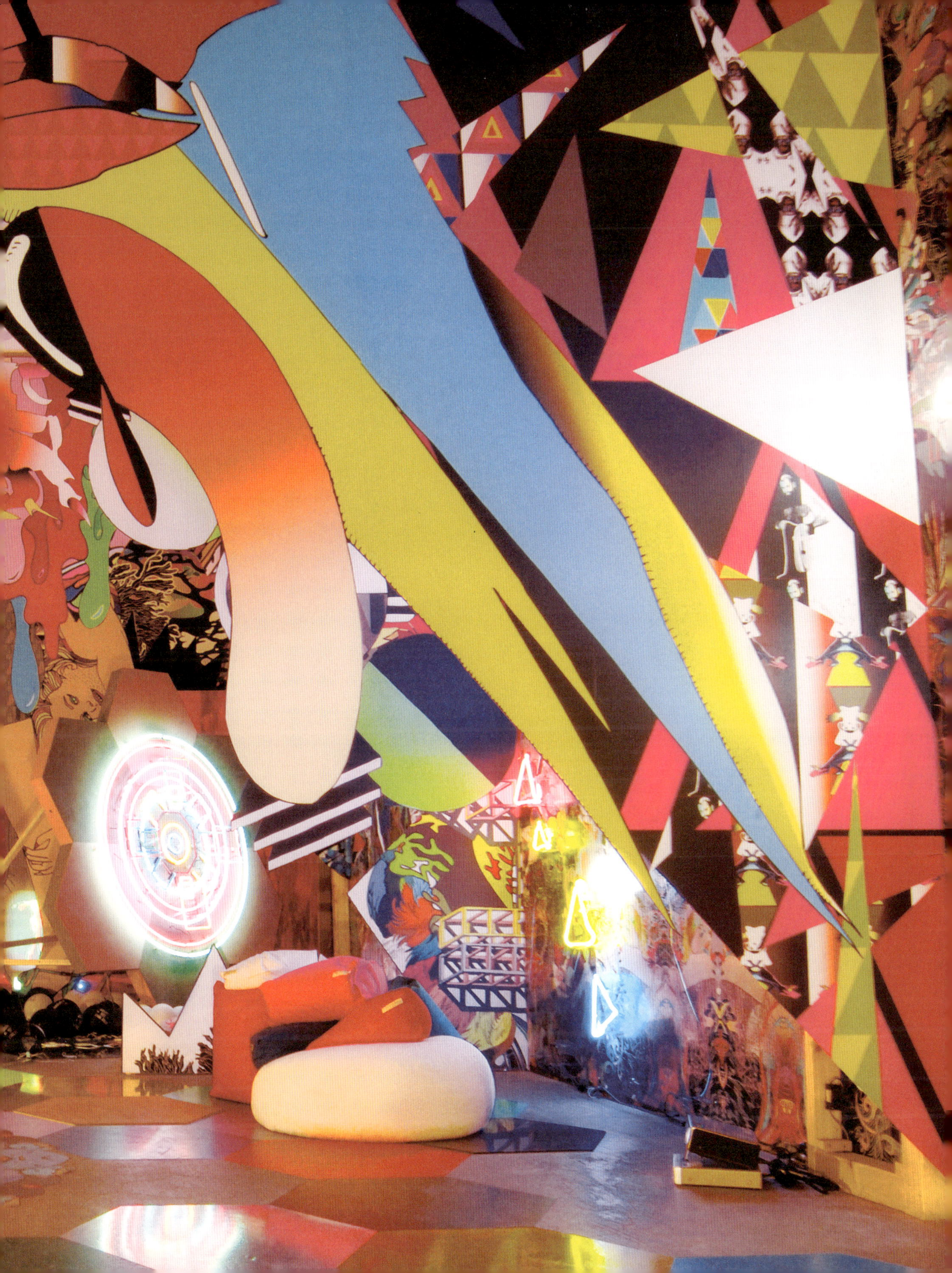

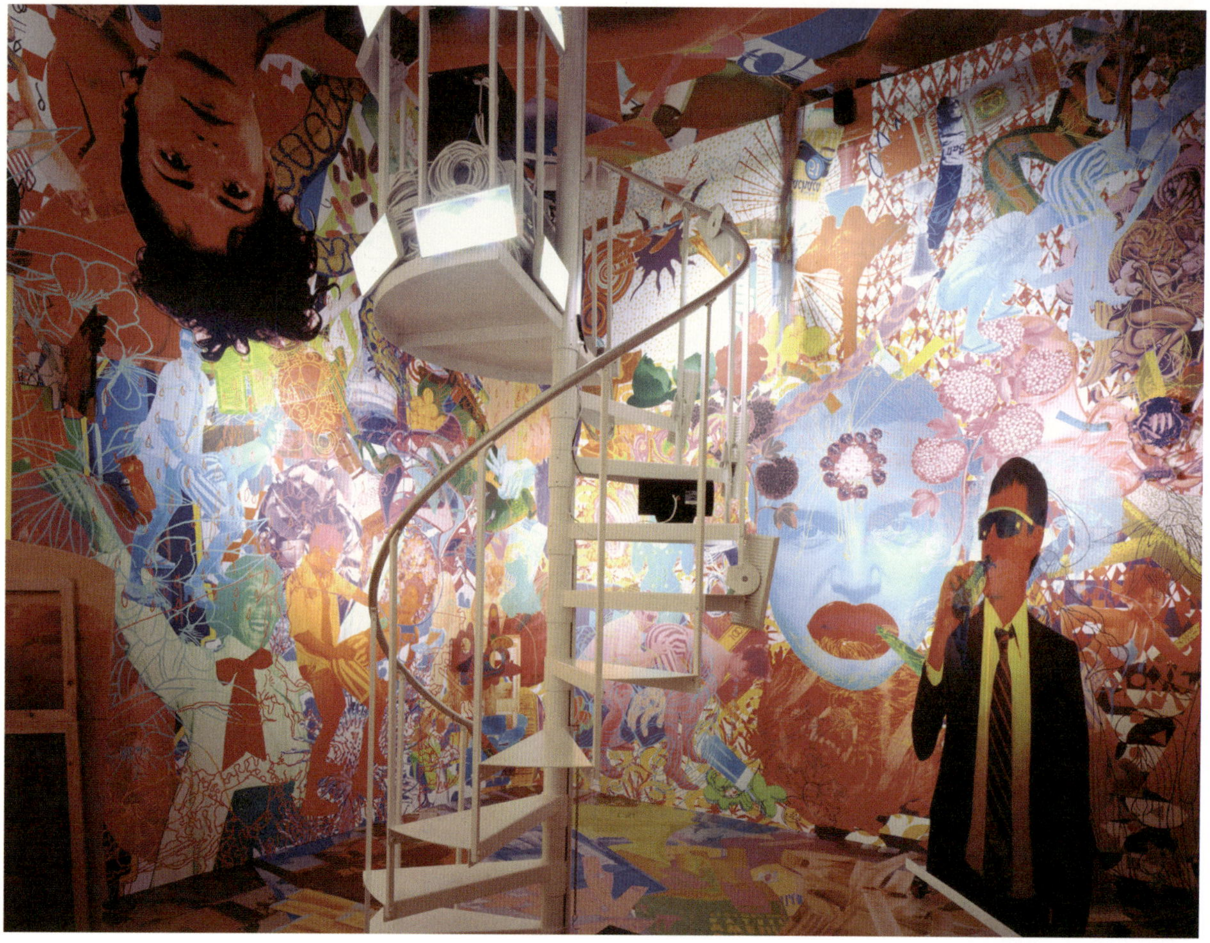

8

previous
7 – Absorb Viral Attack Fantasy, installation, Hiromi Yoshii, Tokyo, 2006

8 – Assume Vivid Astro Focus VIII, installation, Whitney Biennial, Whitney Museum, New York, 2004

9 – Assume Vivid Astro Focus VII wallpaper, Deitch Projects, New York, 2003

opposite
10 – Invitation for the Suzanne Geiss Company's Labyrinth, Wynwood Walls, Miami, 2010

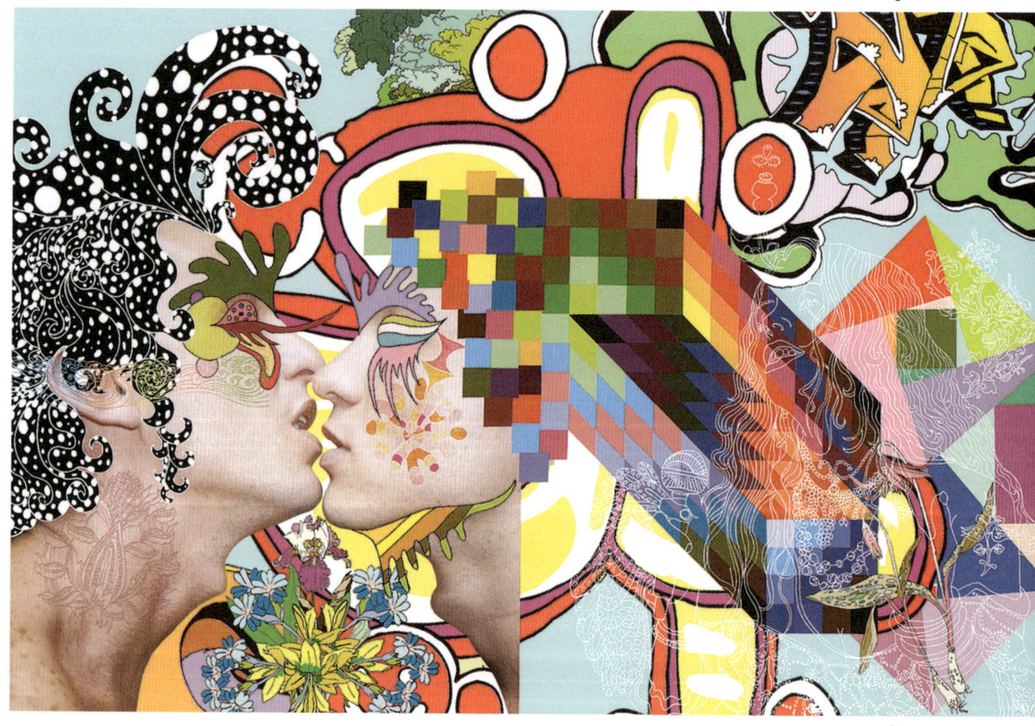

9

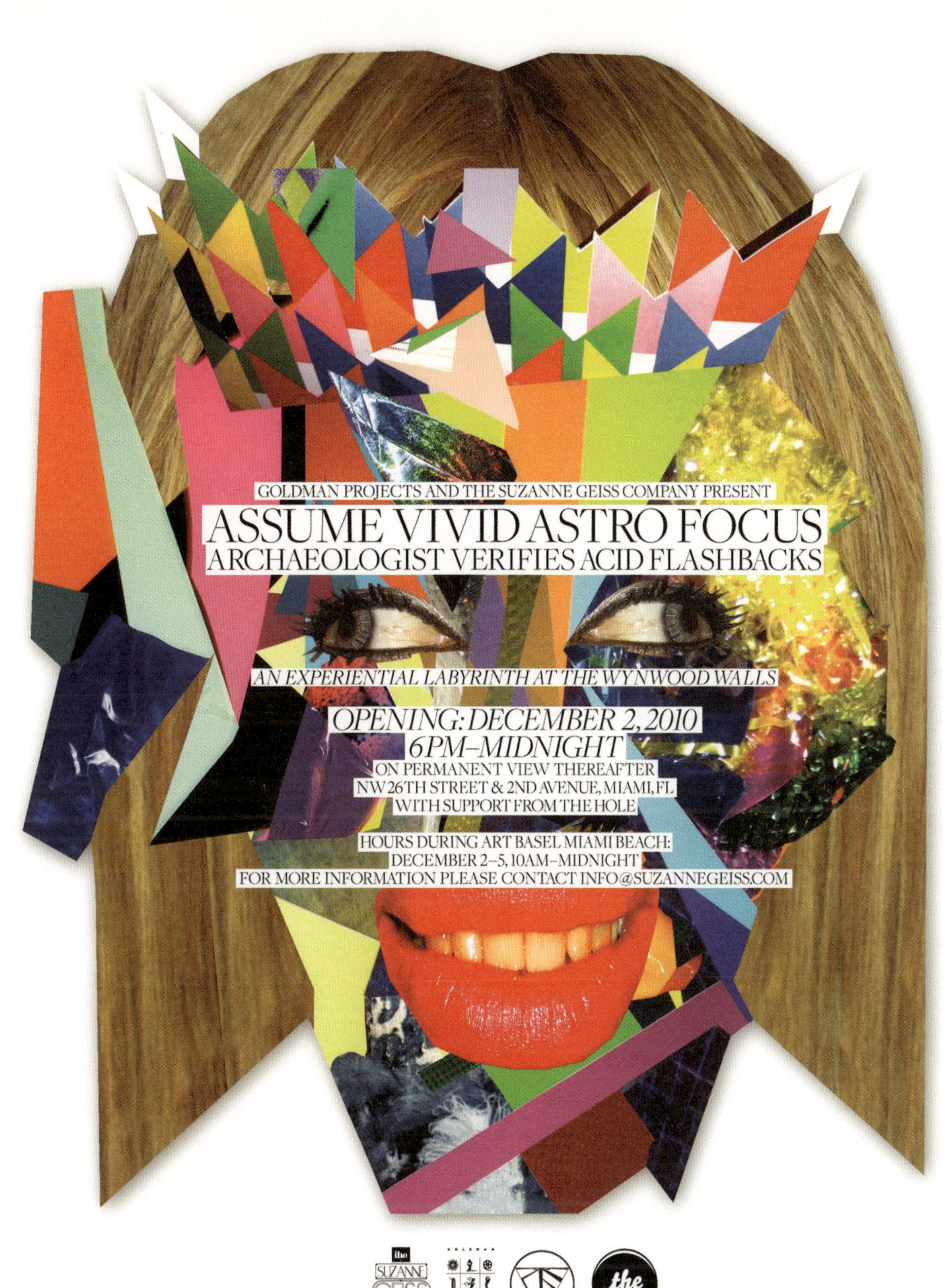
GOLDMAN PROJECTS AND THE SUZANNE GEISS COMPANY PRESENT
ASSUME VIVID ASTRO FOCUS
ARCHAEOLOGIST VERIFIES ACID FLASHBACKS
AN EXPERIENTIAL LABYRINTH AT THE WYNWOOD WALLS
OPENING: DECEMBER 2, 2010
6PM–MIDNIGHT
ON PERMANENT VIEW THEREAFTER
NW 26TH STREET & 2ND AVENUE, MIAMI, FL
WITH SUPPORT FROM THE HOLE
HOURS DURING ART BASEL MIAMI BEACH:
DECEMBER 2–5, 10AM–MIDNIGHT
FOR MORE INFORMATION PLEASE CONTACT INFO@SUZANNEGEISS.COM
the SUZANNE GEISS COMPANY
the

10

ACTIVE SINCE	CITY	WEBSITE
2000	decentered, mostly U.S., mostly SF Bay Area	tacticalmagic.org

Center for Tactical Magic

MEMBERS	ACTIVITIES	RECOMMENDED PUBLICATION
N/A	Community Projects, Convergent Media, Painting / Sculpture / Installation, Public Performance, Tactical Media, Urban Interventions	Secret Pockets, an interview by Gregory Sholette with CENTER FOR TACTICAL MAGIC, Art Papers, Winter 2007, pp. 16–19.

With references to the world of magic, illusionism, and escapism, the Center for Tactical Magic organizes public interventions and community-based projects that reflect on issues like private property, assistance, and propaganda. The collective's playful use of disappearance and ancient mystic beliefs become the tools to make the audience aware of its power as agent of social change.

Why work collaboratively?
The Center for Tactical Magic started in 2000 as a rather academic exercise exploring ideas of "power" on individual, community, national, and transnational levels. Initially, the plan was to survey a series of individuals who had unique insights into power relations—a private investigator, a magician, and a ninja—but this plan fell apart almost immediately. Each person could not effectively explain his skills without performing his knowledge. In the end, all three "interviews" became apprenticeships of sorts.

Out of this early set of relationships it became clear that a critical investigation could be active, immersive, and engaged, rather than isolated or distanced from the subjects being explored. So the CTM formed as a collective identity that could maintain a collaborative structure even if the collaborators changed from project to project.

How do you determine membership? Does physical location matter in this regard?
The CTM is neither a nonprofit organization nor a rock band type of collective in which a core group works on all of the projects. However, nearly all of the Center for Tactical Magic projects have involved collaborations with 2 to 120, or more, individuals. Some people have worked on several CTM projects while others have worked on single projects. The CTM shares authorship, assumes authorship, or releases authorship depending on the project and the goals of the collaborators. In some cases we have anonymously assisted other groups with their projects. At other times, projects have developed out of collaborations with individuals who have only ever met via telephone or email. As an entity, the CTM is perhaps best described as a "collective identity" that cloaks a shape-shifting form of organization, involvement, and engagement.

If considered separately, how do your individual artistic practices contribute to or detract from your work as a group?
One can simultaneously be an artist, educator, gardener, brother, sister, lover, cyclist, anarchist, mechanic, etc., without compromising one's integrity or conviction. Essentially, an arts context often functions as a sort of passport for transdisciplinary collaboration in which individuals can apply their skills in a nonquotidian manner.

How are decisions made?
Our collaborative process shifts depending on the task at hand. At times the collaborators build the project

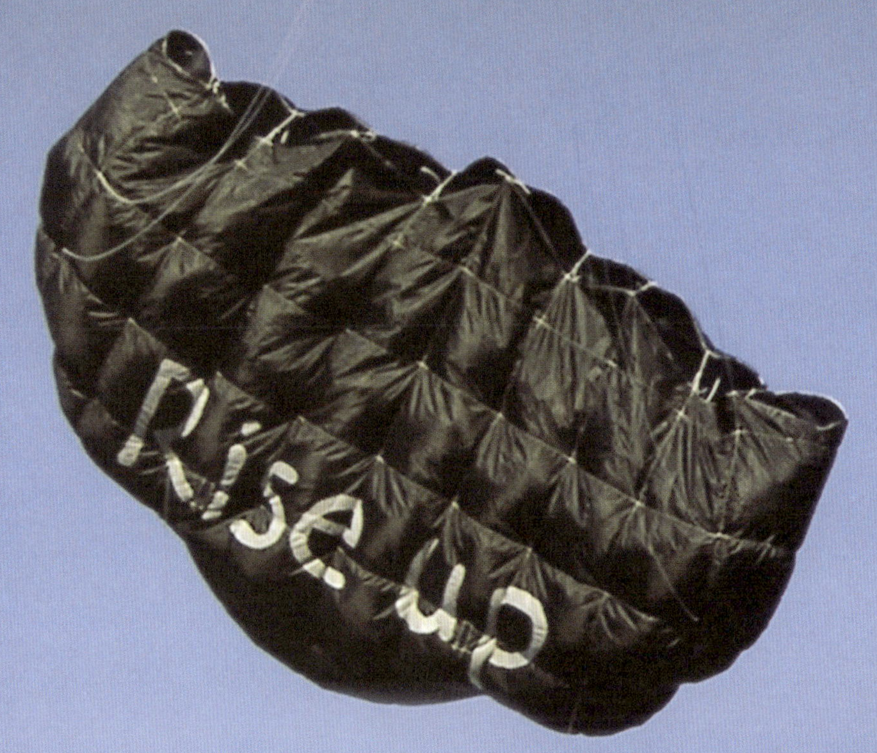
Rise up

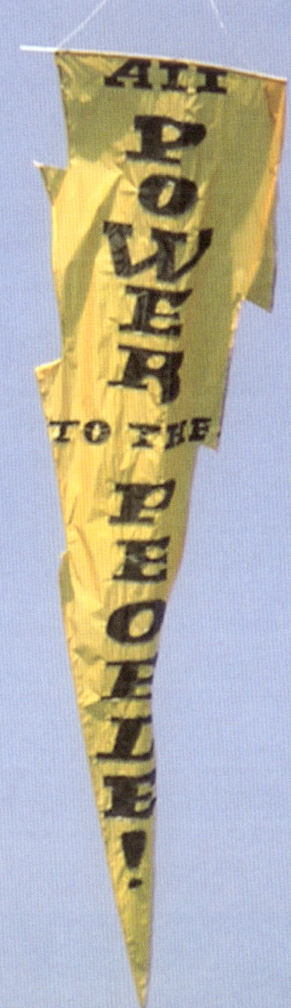
ALL
POWER
TO THE
PEOPLE!

previous
1 – Uprising! (detail), community kite-making project, Huntington Beach Art Center, Huntington Beach, CA, 2005

2 – Tactical Ice Cream Man (from the Tactical Ice Cream Unit), publicity photo, 2005

3 – Citizen Survey, public survey, San Francisco, Chicago, Oakland, CA, 2000

4 – Transporter: A Social Witches' Cradle, public installation, Beloit, WI, 2009

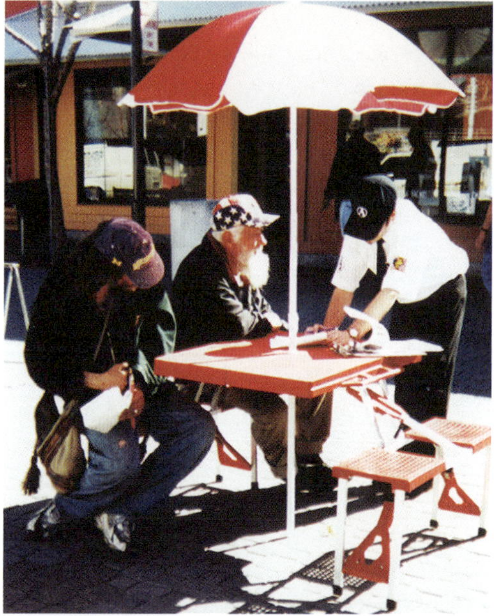

3

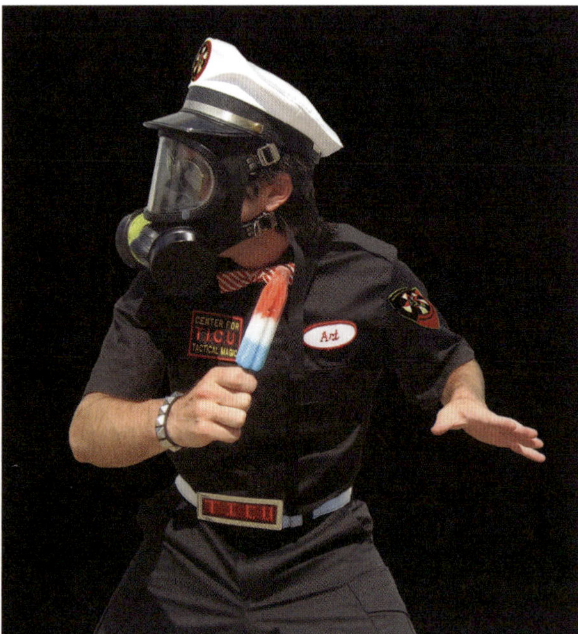

2

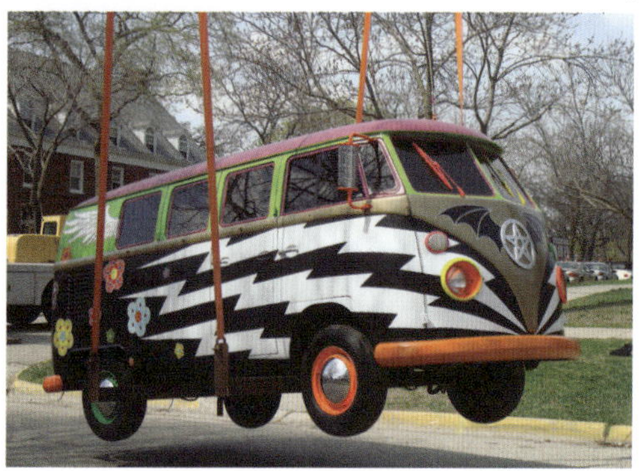

4

democratically from cradle to grave, while in other instances, a single person spearheads an idea and delegates specialized tasks to individuals. Still, the CTM membership structure is consistently growing as more and more folks contact us and ask how they can get involved. Ultimately, we've always acknowledged that the Center for Tactical Magic is rather decentered, and "center" should be thought of as a verb. And the number of people that are in the Center For Tactical Magic depends on the scale of activity and the desire to participate.

Does each of you have a clearly defined role? If so, what are some of each member's distinct responsibilities?

In 2005 the Center for Tactical Magic began work on the Tactical Ice Cream Unit, a mobile, interventionist command center that looks like the unlikely, bastard lovechild of an ice cream truck and a SWAT van. In addition to distributing community-based propaganda alongside free ice cream, the TICU also comes equipped with a rooftop stage, a public-address system, free Wi-Fi, sixteen channels of surveillance video, and a host of supplies to support rallies, protests, or other community endeavors. The project was supported by a nonprofit arts space with in-house fabricators, but also required the collaboration of a design team, an expert in mobile power systems, legal support, outreach coordinators, and countless volunteers who assisted in operations and upkeep as the TICU traveled to Mexico, to Canada, and across the United States. However, the collaborative scope of a project like the Tactical Ice Cream Unit is not limited to production and operation. The TICU often teams up with local organizations, institutions, artists, and activists for various events, performances, and exhibitions. Acting as a vehicle both literally and metaphorically, the TICU conveys meaning through action and therefore requires the active involvement of many collaborators.

How important is each group member's individuality, both in terms of your artistic production and in terms of your relationship with the media? Does anonymity come into play?

In some cases, the Center for Tactical Magic becomes a broad identity through which projects can be authored while maintaining the anonymity of individuals involved in the endeavor. For example, our Bechtel Predator Drones project (a.k.a. Unmanned Protest Drones), which used remote-controlled vehicles to distribute protest materials and sabotage manuals, involved collaborators who wanted to remain anonymous for fear of legal retaliation. At other times, collaborators want to maintain their individual identities and projects are authored as the "CTM in collaboration with." For instance, our Black Panther Historical Marker in Oakland, California, is authored as "Center for Tactical Magic in collaboration with artist Jeremy Deller and former chief-of-staff of the Black Panther Party David Hilliard." Because the somewhat amorphous nature of the Center for Tactical Magic occasionally presents challenges when working with institutions, agencies, and news media, we rely on a spokesperson (currently Aaron Gach, cofounder and director of operations) to provide a public face for the CTM.

What is the relationship between your working methods and your art's "content"? In this sense, does technology tend to play more of a supporting role, or does it lead you in new directions?

The Center for Tactical Magic is dedicated to exploring unconventional uses of technology; however, we fully recognize that emerging technologies are frequently fetishized both within and outside of contemporary art. Arthur C. Clark is famous for saying, "Any sufficiently advanced technology is indistinguishable from magic." Rather than simply using technology for technology's sake, we like to complicate this perspective further by using technology to examine our collective relationship to magic, and vice versa.

How does your collaboration relate to its cultural, institutional, and commercial contexts? In other words, how would you respond to those who call this a trend?

In the fall of 2012 we initiated a crowdsourcing project called the Bank Heist Contest that offered a $1,000 prize for the best scheme to steal money from a financial institution. The BHC functioned as a participatory cultural endeavor designed to revisit the historic, cultural narratives of the bank robber in relation to enduring economic and social crises. Although the crowdsourcing nature of the project relies on a model of disconnected communal collaboration to produce the final array of proposals, the BHC also featured two installations, a workshop, and a public program that included the participation of a former bank robber, a corporate security expert with a background in military intelligence, the staff of a nonprofit art space (Southern Exposure in San Francisco), and members of the Center for Tactical Magic. Because the themes of the project are so insinuated in cultural, institutional, and economic contexts, the collaboration necessarily occupied cultural, institutional, and economic forms. Although crowdsourced projects are regarded as something of a novelty in the current environment of cultural production, it's important to recognize that collective creativity has been performed for thousands of years.

Who is your audience?

There's rarely a single audience for any one of our projects; rather, there are multiple, specific audiences including those who will interact directly with the work in a "live" context and those who will engage with it discursively either during or after its initial public presentation. Additionally, we believe in providing multiple points of access and rewarding specialized knowledge. As such, those with a background in contemporary art will experience a project differently than someone with a background in martial arts, magical arts, or activism.

Does your engagement with one another translate into an engagement with the public? How so?

The Center for Tactical Magic has consistently worked toward integrating audiences as participants within our activities. On the one hand, this is a reaction against the passivity that is implicit within much of the Western tradition of art; on the other hand, it is also an embrace of longstanding non-Western traditions of immersive creativity in rituals, ceremonies, and festivities. When viewed in this context, it is easy to see how and why the modernist tradition of a unique author, separate from the audience, is reified in much of contemporary art. Conversely, it is hard to imagine how one could effectively engage varied communities without a structure of collaboration to draw on diverse talents and provide multiple points of entry to encourage a culture of active participation. At its best, this is what we hope the Center for Tactical Magic accomplishes—a creative praxis that actively and critically engages with the substance of our investigations.

5 – Unmanned Protest Drone, public intervention, Bechtel Headquarters, San Francisco, 2004

6 – Corporate Curse (sticker hex) from Free Occult Services, 2001

7 – Black Panther Historical Marker (in collaboration with David Hilliard and Jeremy Deller), public sign, Oakland, CA, 2002

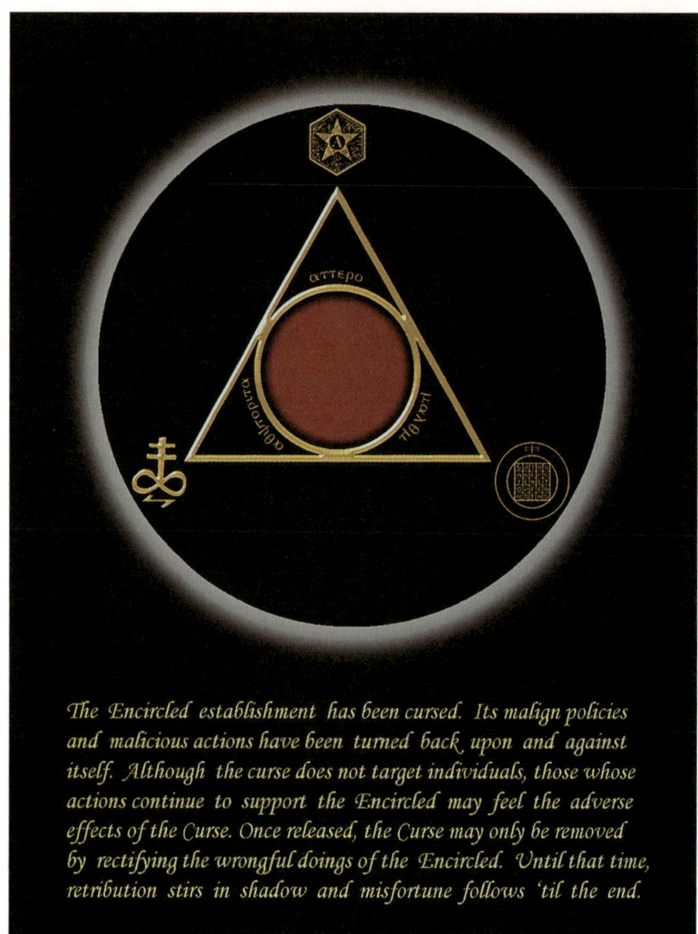

6

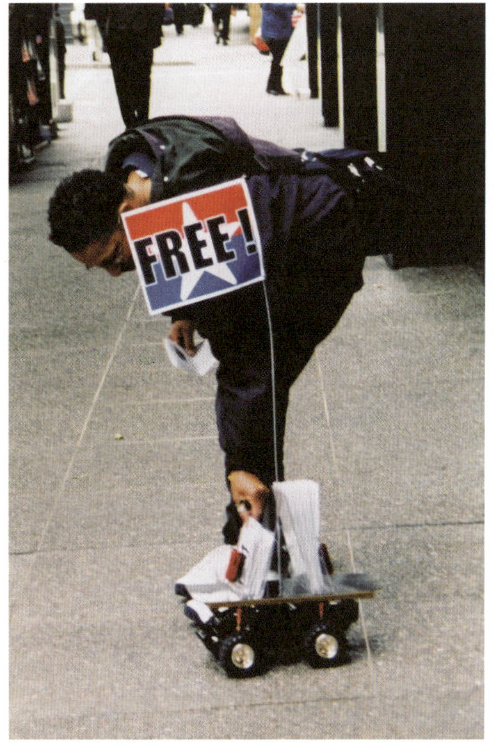

5

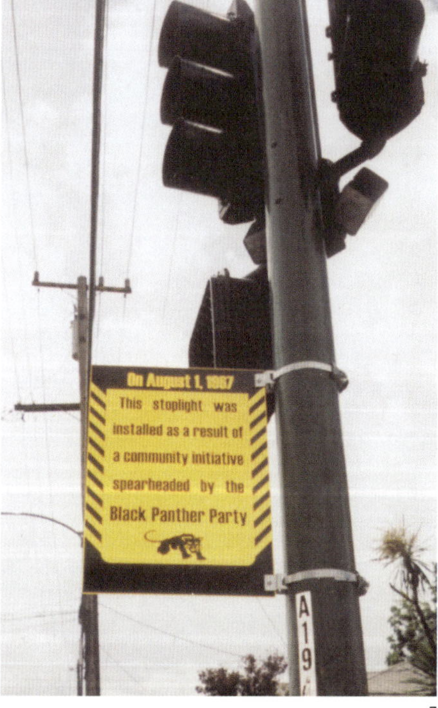

7

8 – Witches's Cradles (In the heart of a dark star), performance, Toronto, 2009

9 – The Ultimate Jacket (ad poster), 2002

10 – The Ultimate Jacket (display), installation, Massachusetts Museum of Contemporary Art, North Adams, MA, 2004

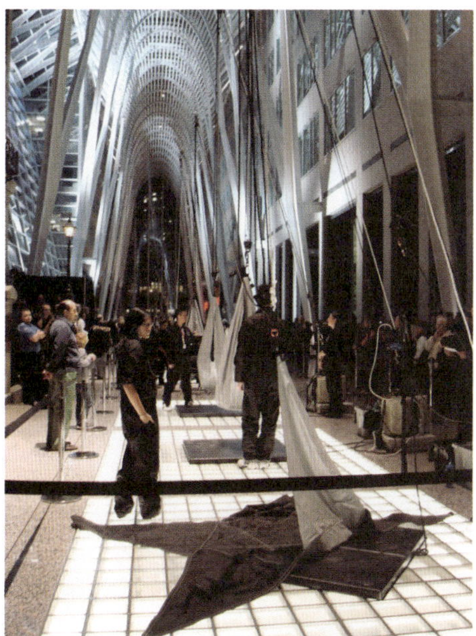

8

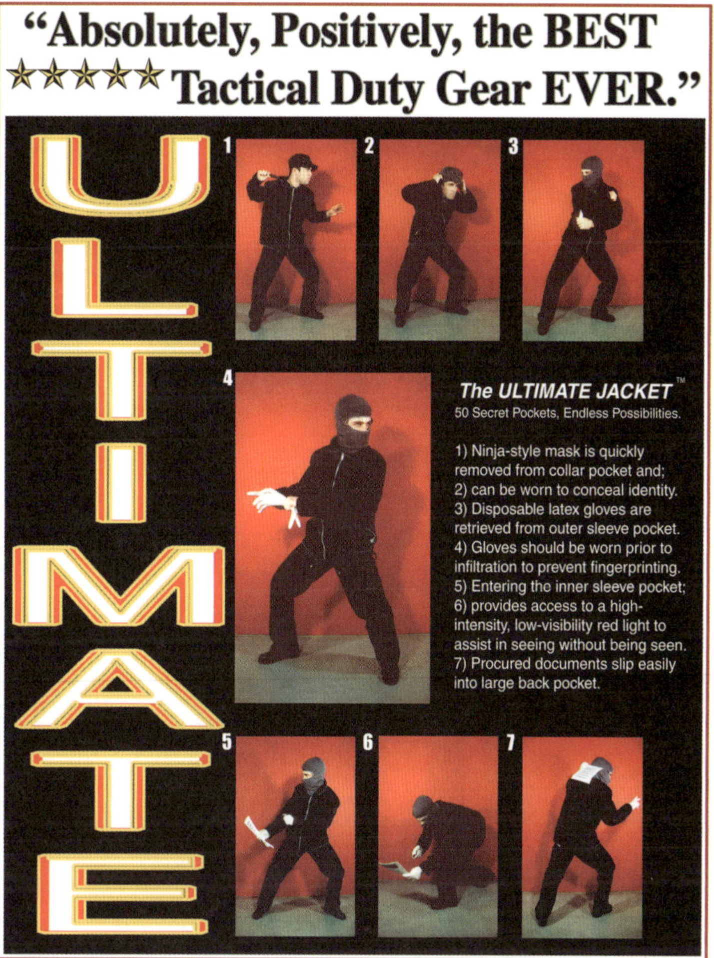

9

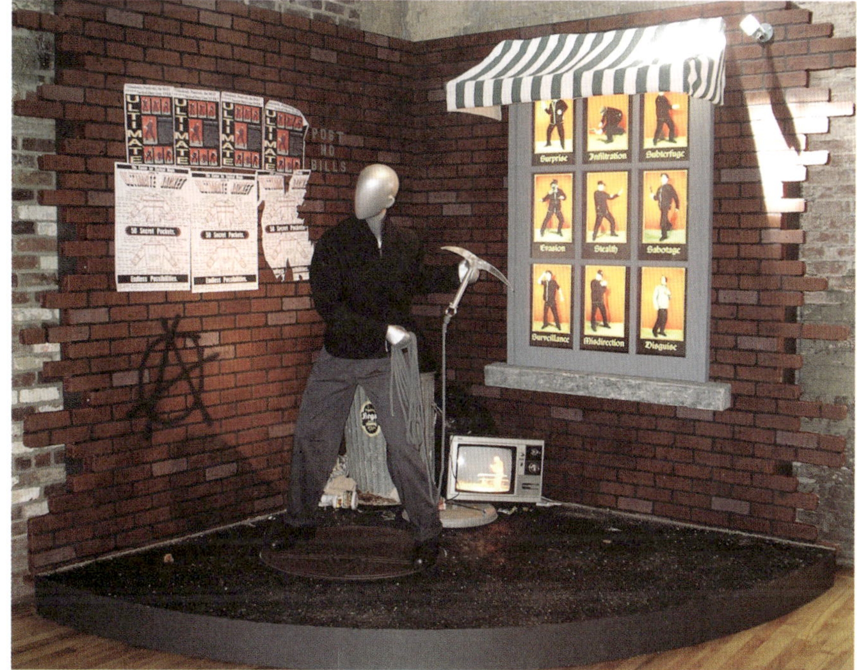

10

ACTIVE SINCE	CITY	WEBSITE
2003	Saint Petersburg / Moscow, Russia	chtodelat.org

Chto Delat

MEMBERS	ACTIVITIES	RECOMMENDED PUBLICATION
Tsaplya Olga Egorova, Artiom Magun, Nikolai Oleinikov, Natalia Pershina / Glucklya, Alexander Skidan, Alexei Penzin, Oxana Timofeeva, David Riff, Dmitry Vilensky, and Nina Gasteva	Curating, Films, Learning Community Projects, Learning Plays, Murals / Sculpture / Installation, Music, Musicals, Public Performance, Publishing, Seminars, Urban Interventions	Chto Delat?, Baden-Baden: The Lessson on Dis-Content, Staatliche Kunsthalle Baden-Baden, Verlag der Buchhandlung Walther König, Cologne, Germany, 2012

Chto Delat is composed of artists, philosophers, and writers. Through plays, publications, installations, and public performances, the group reflects on the utopian dimension of theatricalized life under socialist regimes. The group raises issues such as the need for collectivism and a reconsideration of the power of art in our society to disclose the fictional structures that lie behind politics.

Why work collaboratively?

Because it gives another power and quality to our work, allowing dialectical methods of self-questioning that are impossible when alone.

How do you determine membership? Does physical location matter in this regard?

The core group's membership was established and fixed in the early years of working together on the newspaper and other collaborative art projects. Many projects since then have involved broader collaborations, but the core group has remained relatively fixed, with one departure and one new addition over recent years.

If considered separately, how do your individual artistic practices contribute to or detract from your work as a group?

The group is consists of nine people with very strong personalities and elaborate individual practices; some are academic philosophers, others are artists, others still come from literature and dance. Different viewpoints collide, and that is an invaluable contribution. It prevents one-sided thinking.

How are decisions made?

Any three members can act in the name of the collective unless vetoed by another three. In editorial or collaborative processes, intense group discussions transform the collective into an executive committee whose decisions are reached and resolved through discussion rather than voting.

Does each of you have a clearly defined role? If so, what are some of each member's distinct responsibilities?

There are areas of expertise and principles of delegation, but then again, roles can be quite flexible, as members intervene in collective processes. Distinct responsibilities are self-imposed and voluntary, and over ten years, have involved different gravitational phases and levels of involvement.

How important is each group member's individuality, both in terms of your artistic production and in terms of your relationship with the media? Does anonymity come into play?

Individuality is paramount; we think of ourselves as an ensemble of singularities whose role in the collective is permanently questioned and negotiated in a process of collective work. We reject the idea of anonymity because it does not allow a chance to celebrate the unique value of each participant.

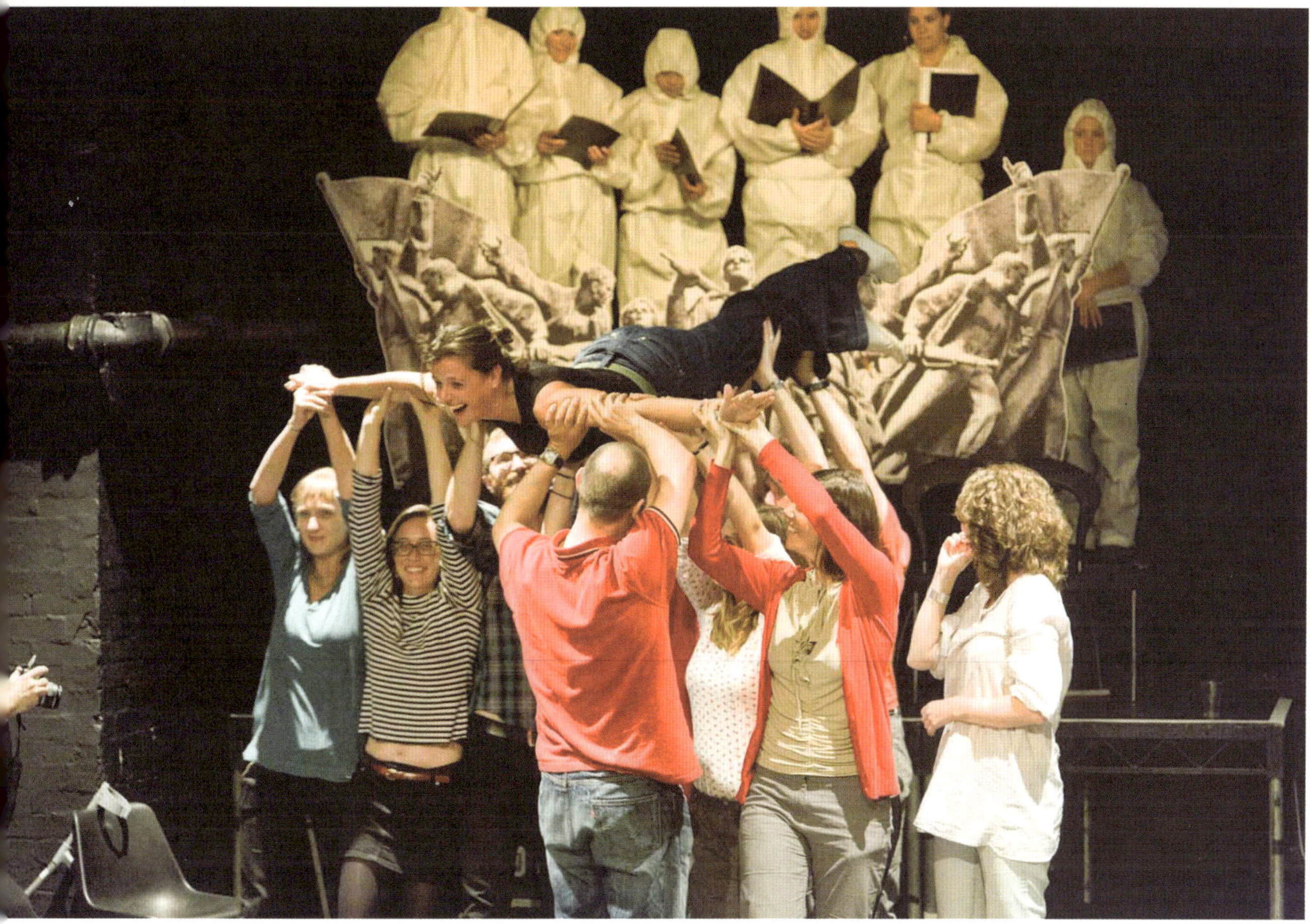

1

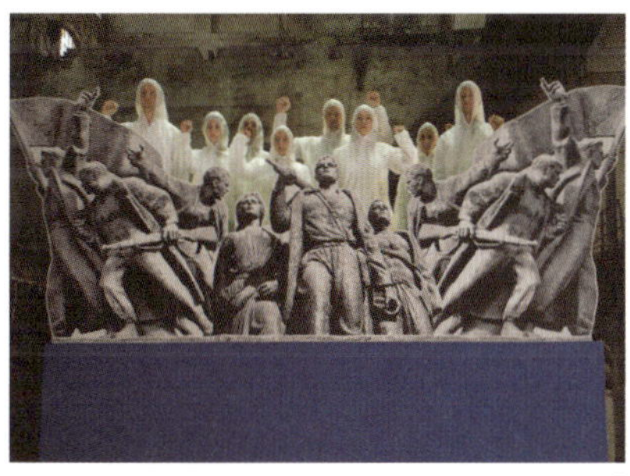

2

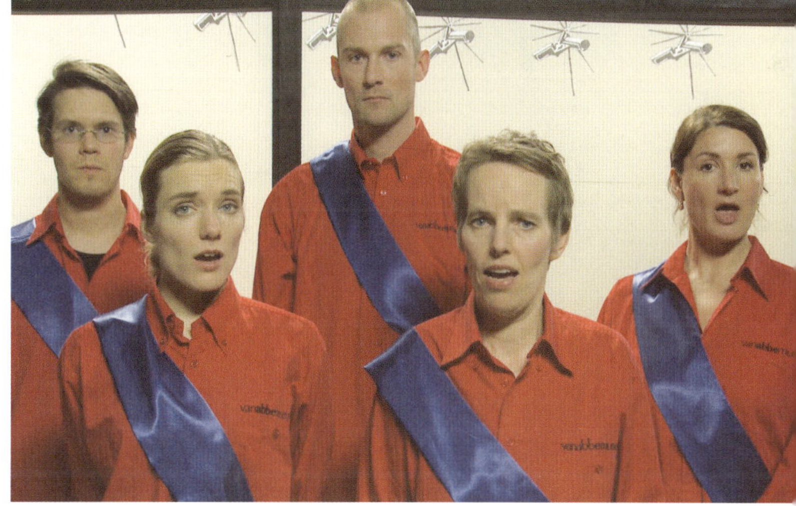

3

1 – Learning Play: What Struggle Do We Have in Common?, musical, Institute of Contemporary Art, London, 2010

2 – Partisan Songspiel production shot, 2009. Film by Chto Delat, director Tsaplya Olga Egorova, set Vladan Jeremic and Dmitry Vilensky

3 – Museum Songspiel: Netherlands 20XX film still, 2010. Film by Chto Delat, idea and realisation Dmitry Vilensky and Tsaplya Olga Egorova (director)

4 – Chto Delat? newspaper, special issue cover, November 2008. Graphics by Dmitry Vilensky

5 – Chto Delat? newspaper, no. 01–25 cover, March 2009. Graphics by Dmitry Vilensky

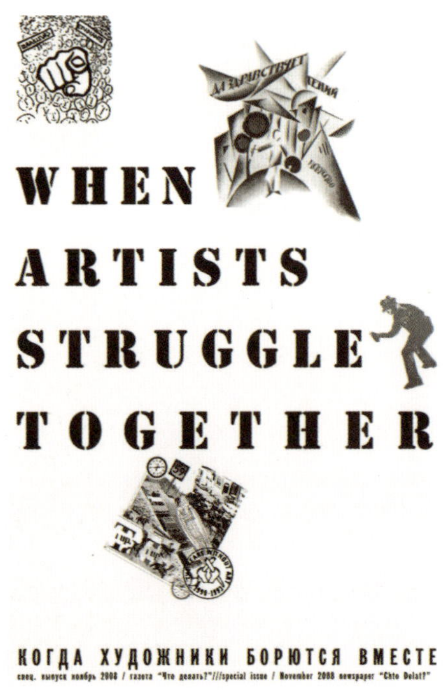

4

What is
the use
of art?

О ПОЛЬЗЕ ИСКУССТВА
газета "Что делать?" / выпуск 01-25 / март 2009 /// newspaper "Chto Delat?" / issue 01-25 / March 2009

5

What is the relationship between your working methods and your art's "content"? In this sense, does technology tend to play more of a supporting role, or does it lead you in new directions?

We do not build any separation between methods and matter. The ongoing publication project of the newspaper has been crucial in shaping the group on an organizational level; like Lenin said, it is not just an organ of collective agitation, but a collective organizer. Other formats—such as urban investigations, musical film, or theater—have opened the group to new possibilities, in terms of both content and collaboration with other individuals and initiatives.

How does your collaboration relate to its cultural, institutional, and commercial contexts? In other words, how would you respond to those who call this a trend?

Our work has transversal character. When everyone thinks that we are just producing intellectual publications, we are actually making a new film; when everyone believes that we are filmmakers, we make aninstallation; when everyone is sure that we only exist in an institutional landscape, we participate in social movements. We hope that this allows us to permanently escape easy commodification and stops us from becoming victims of our own trends.

Who is your audience?

We strongly reject the concept of the audience and prefer to speak about active or passive (frozen) participants. To reach this goal—to speak to the broadest possible number of people—we are trying to develop a multiplicity of languages inside one project, allowing anyone different levels of access to the same work.

Does your engagement with one another translate into an engagement with the public? How so?

Somehow, we hope that each collective is an open model for society at large as an example of an (im)possible community and a mode of production. So the big part of our work is opening up the structures of our collective to be self-analyzing and self-critical. The question of how far our public could engage into it should be addressed to them first of all.

6 – What is to be Done Between tragedy and Farce?, reading room at SMART Project Space, Amsterdam, 2011. Architecture by Dmitry Vilensky

7 – The Urgent Need to Struggle, installation, ICA, London, 2010

8 – Activist Club, installation, Plug-in 51, Van Abbemuseum, Eindhoven, 2008. Project of Chto Delat (realized by Dmitry Vilensky)

9 – Museum Songspiel: Netherlands 20XX film set installation, Van Abbemuseum, Eindhoven, 2011. Set Natalya Pershina and Dmitry Vilensky

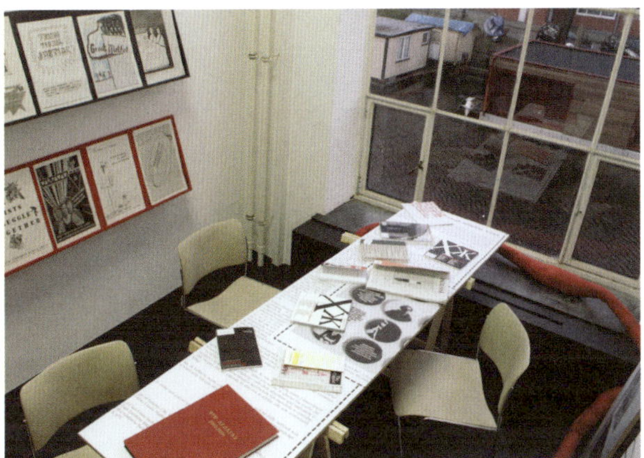

6

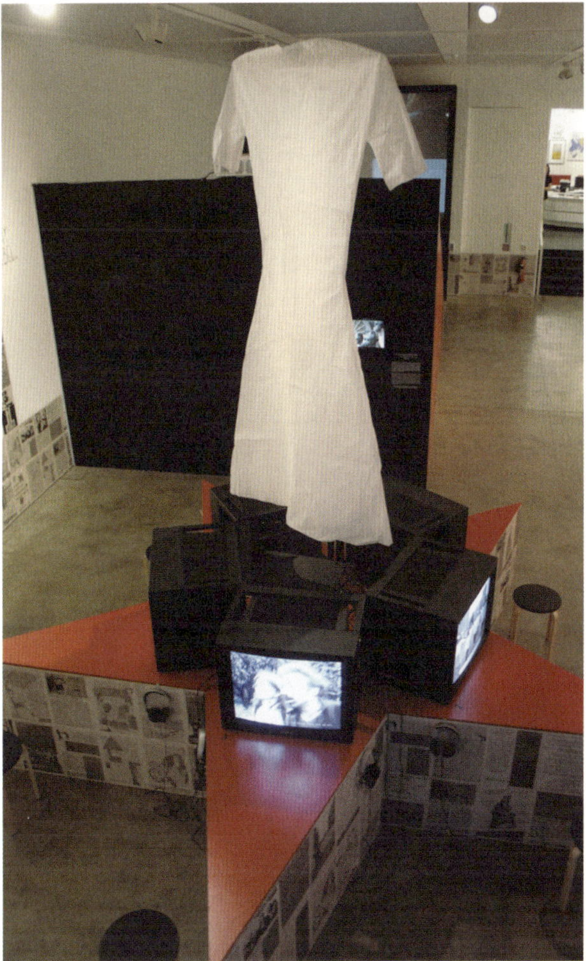

7

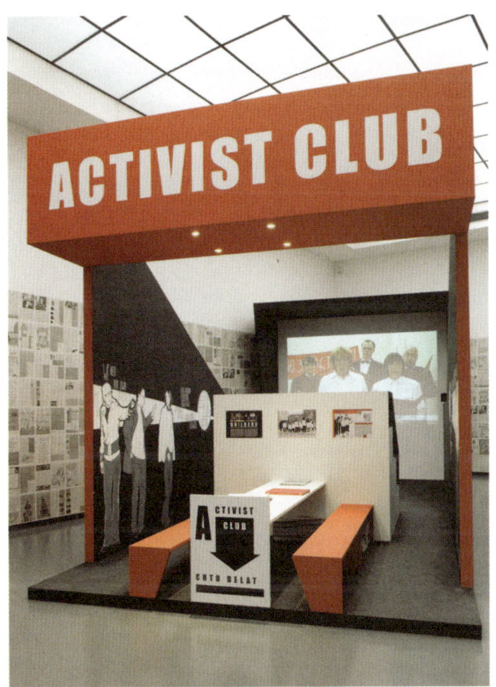

8

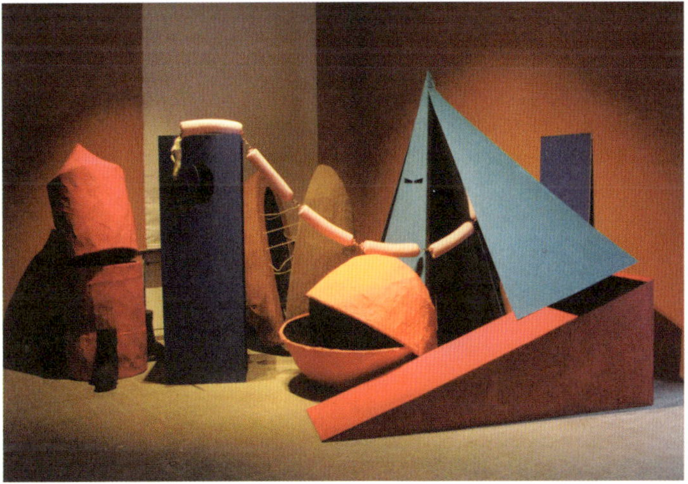

9

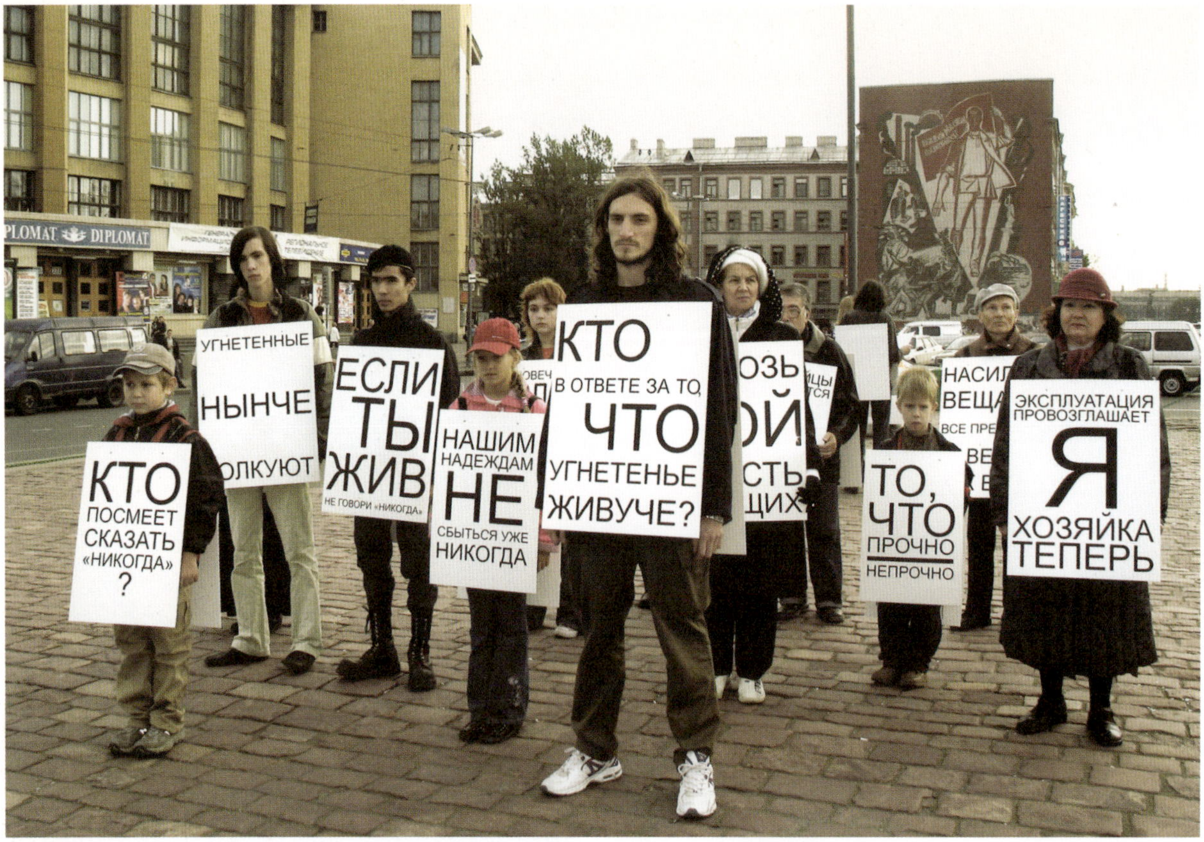

10

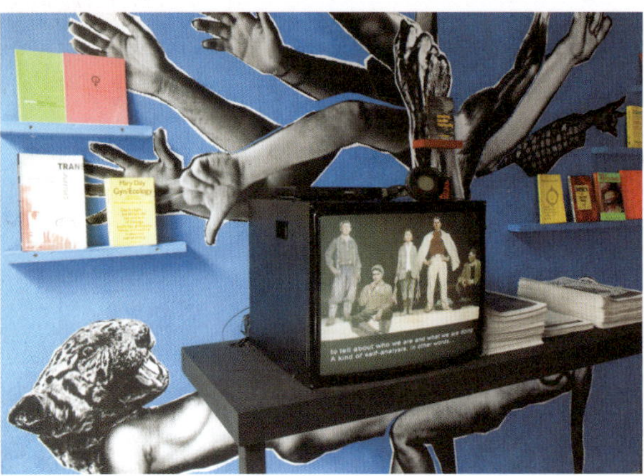

11

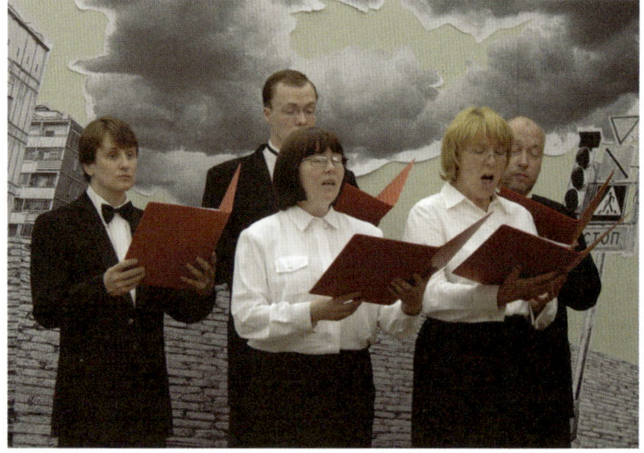

12

10 – Angry Sandwich People or In a Praise of Dialectic video still, 2006 from Chto Delat project realized by Tsaplya Olga Egorova, Nikolay Oleynikov, and Dmitry Vilensky

11 – Study, Study and Act Again, installation view, Moderna Galerja, Ljubliana, 2011. Project of Chto Delat, graphics by Nikolay Oleynikov

12 – Perestroyka Songspiel or A Victory Over the Coup production shot, 2008. Film by Chto Delat, director Tsaplya Olga Egorova, set by Nikoalya Oleynikov and Dmitry Vilensky

opposite
13 – Tower Songspiel production shot, 2010. Film by Chto Delat, directed by Tsaplya Olga Egorova, set by Natalya Pershina and Dmitry Vilensky

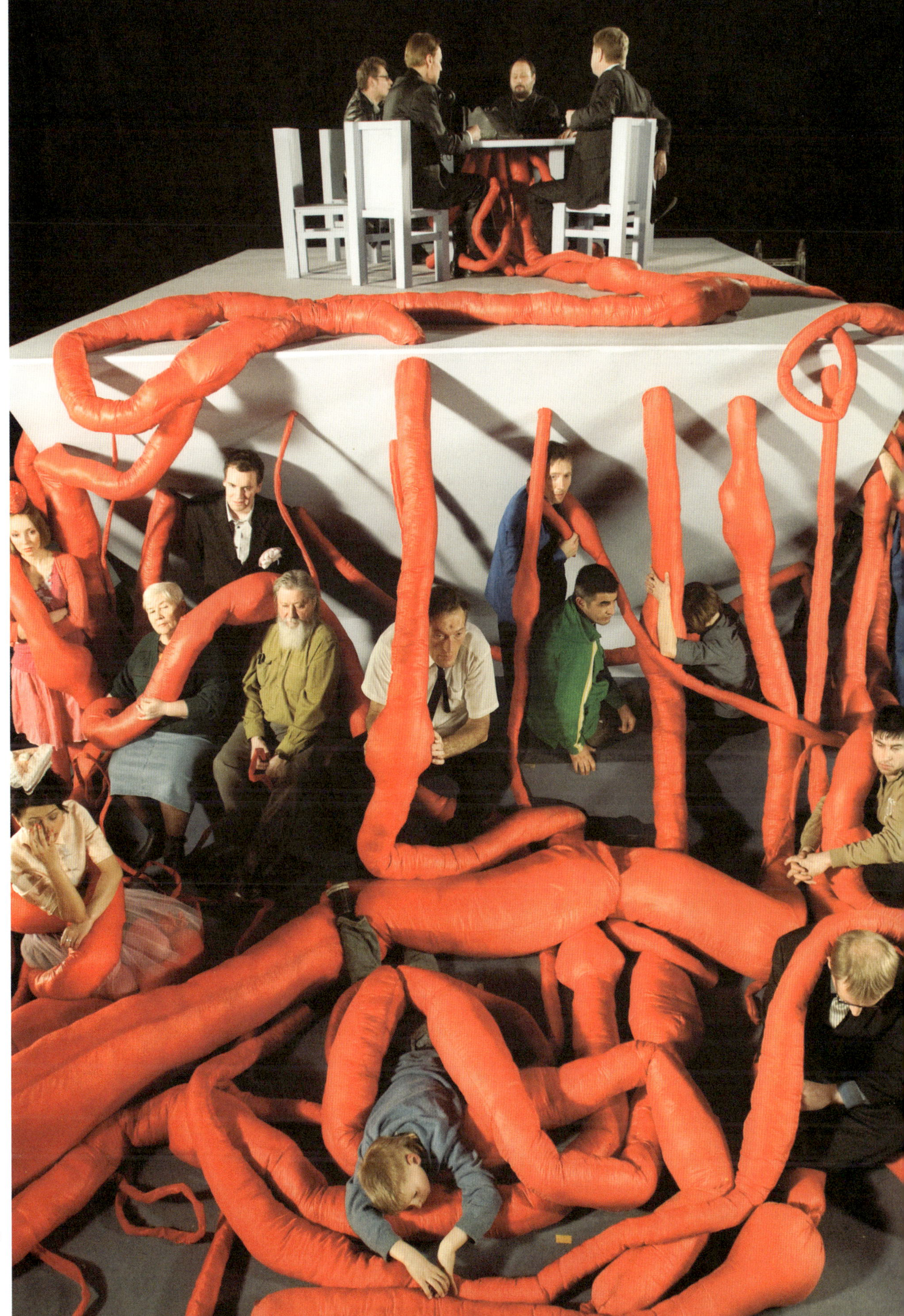

ACTIVE SINCE	CITY	WEBSITE
2000	Berlin, Germany	clubreal.de

Club Real

MEMBERS

Permanent members: Thomas Hauck, Marianne Ramsey-Sonneck, and George Reinhardt
Associate members: Sebastian Mauksch, Tuire Tuomisto, Christoph Theussl, Mathias Lenz, and Patrick Hanbaba

ACTIVITIES	RECOMMENDED PUBLICATION
Community Projects, Public Performance, Urban Interventions	Swantje Karich, CLUB REAL: Portrait, Goethe Institute, 2011

With backgrounds in architecture and theater, Club Real organizes community-based projects and public performances that deal with issues like ecology and mythology. While they develop a critique of the role of monuments in our cities, their group's collapsible installations made of cardboard and props suggest an alternative use of streets and parks as places of both congregation and discussion.

Why work collaboratively?

Because we believe it is valuable to know each other, trust each other, and support each other. Because concepts that have been discussed intensely and developed within our group have a good chance of convincing our partners, audience, and supporters. Because we work within societies and with ideas of social and cultural processes. Therefore we believe we should have a social conception of our work as well as an artistic one.

How do you determine membership? Does physical location matter in this regard?

At the beginning of our collaborative work, membership was determined by our friendship, our mutual experiences in projects before Club Real, and the time we spent together working and developing projects. Over the years we have started to cooperate more with associated members, who live partly in other cities/countries. It has become rather normal to have conceptual discussions via the Internet. But personal meetings are vital for the functioning of the collective. Our associated members are also working in other art collectives. This makes it easy to collaborate with other groups. Since 2007 we have worked with the Finnish group Todellisuuden Tutkimuskeskus on several projects.

If considered separately, how do your individual artistic practices contribute to or detract from your work as a group?

Although our individual artistic practices (landscape design, drawing, mask making, performance, music, lectures) are important in our collective work, we all engage in mutual practices, which means—even if we are not all visual artists or architects—we often work together as carpenters, builders, or painters. Sometimes we hold drawing sessions to develop ideas. And if performance is a part of a project, we usually all perform. We believe that it is important to keep a spirit of enthusiastic "amateurism" in the whole process.

How are decisions made?

Normally one of us makes a proposal, then we discuss it. If we can't agree, each of us tries to make a proposal to which we can all agree. All the important decisions are consensus decisions. It is very important to use some time for conceptual meetings outside the framework of funding deadlines and specific projects.

Most decisions are made in the regular meetings of the three founding members. Decisions that are connected to specific projects are made in the meetings of the project working group. For every project we choose one of us to be the organizational director.

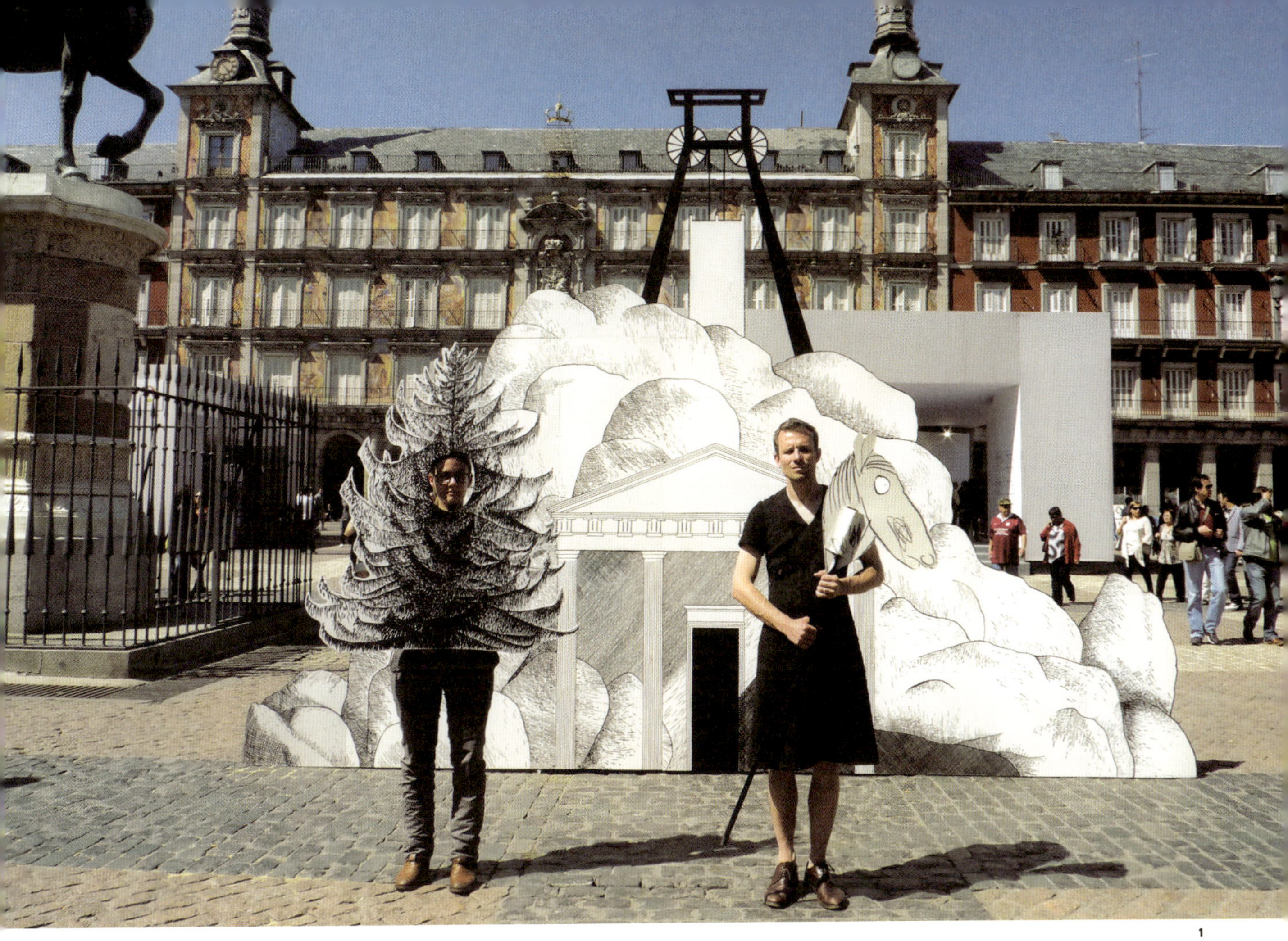

1

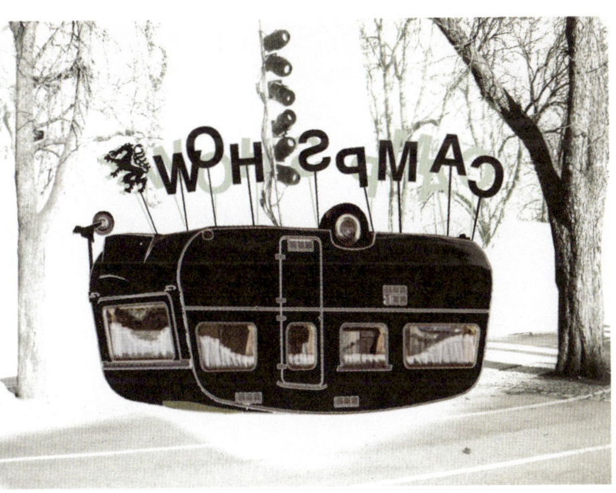

2

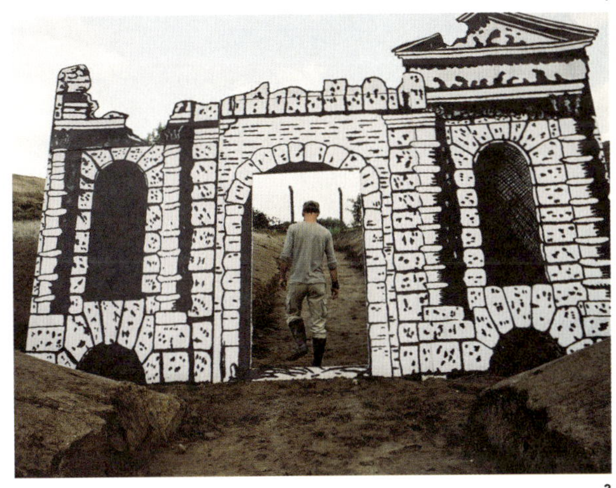

3

1 – <u>La Profundidad Alemana</u>, public installation and performance, Madrid, 2011

2 – <u>Camphshow Styria</u> graphics, Steirischer Herbst, Graz, 2006. Design: Thomas Hauck

3 – <u>Porta Tartarica</u>, public installation, Airport Leipzig/Halle, 2008

Does each of you have a clearly defined role? If so, what are some of each member's distinct responsibilities?

The roles are connected to the projects and to the amount of time that each of us has. The organizational director is often the one who had the idea for the project. The rest of the responsibilities are decided in the collaborative working process. Conceptual meetings, rehearsing, building, performing, and communication with local partners are the main group processes. The funding and financial work is always done by one of us alone.

How important is each group member's individuality, both in terms of your artistic production and in terms of your relationship with the media? Does anonymity come into play?

For the media we appear as a group and do not discuss our individual contributions very much. For the functioning of our group it is important that each of us gives his or her ideas into the process. We are not split into a creative and an organizational faction. It is sometimes complicated and takes time but it is also very productive that each of us has a different perspective and background when we discuss and work together. The differences are not only intellectual/emotional, they are also economic, because some of us have less money and are more politically oriented than others. The group process is a small-scale society process.

What is the relationship between your working methods and your art's "content"? In this sense, does technology tend to play more of a supporting role, or does it lead you in new directions?

Technology can be organized in a collaborative process too, a process that invites people to look at what is happening and even join the working process, for example, when we build an installation together with guests, passersby, and local inhabitants. That is often our aim.

In our project Quien es? (2010), in Havana, Cuba, we composed a life montage of local inhabitants with their vision of a mythological/fictional person they would like to be and, being that person, what they would change in their neighborhood. In our recent initiative The Good People: From Disease to Politics (2013), we are working with social technologies to find out how art can contribute to the evolution of social culture.

How does your collaboration relate to its cultural, institutional, and commercial contexts? In other words, how would you respond to those who call this a trend?

Our collaboration is not strategic. We think dialogue and dignity should be the basis for work, not competition and merit. It would be good if that became a trend. Right now it still seems that it is usual to collaborate for survival in competitive circumstances. The decision to work collaboratively without hierarchy is not unusual for art groups but it is also very important—and this aspect has only recently become more important for us—to stop the competitive game between art groups, organizations, and institutions. A way to solve this problem can be that art groups collaborate more with each other and with local self-organized networks. For this process it is also important to redefine success in art away from individual, monetary success and stardom toward collective success and cultural progress.

Who is your audience?

We work in very different contexts, but as a general experience, it's often old people, children, drunkards, the unemployed, and homeless people who have more time and openness to join into processes that are outside the well-known daily routine. In general, we avoid the description "audience" because we work with forms that make our guests participants/partners. In our project, The Cry of Wedding (2011), we photographed seventy locals of a district of Berlin while they were shouting the name of their district and used the pictures for paper lanterns that lit a public square for eight weeks in winter.

Does your engagement with one another translate into an engagement with the public? How so?

If the mutual process is successful, the experience becomes as important for them as for us. We try to involve/create dialogic forms and everyday life cultural practices that have a chance to continue after our projects are over. In our project Ancestors Adoption Agency (2008), our visitors had the possibility to take an old photograph of a deceased person without any living or caring descendants home with them as an "adopted ancestor." In our project The Good People: From Disease to Politics, 2013, participants can build a small black paper shrine with us and dedicate it to an important disease and its cultural representation.

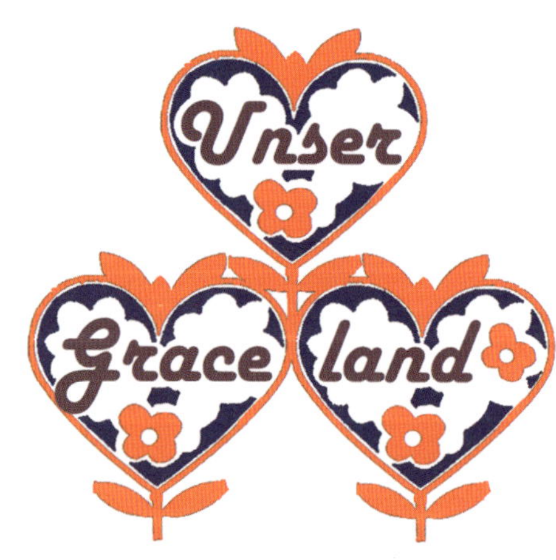

4

opposite
4 – Our Graceland graphics, 2002. Design: Thomas Hauck

5 – Our Graceland, public event, Berlin, 2002

6 – Fiedwitz by the Riverside film still, Germany, 2009

7 – Ancestors Office, installation, Berlin/Vienna/Linz, 2005–2010

8 – The Mountain, installation, Berlin, 2005

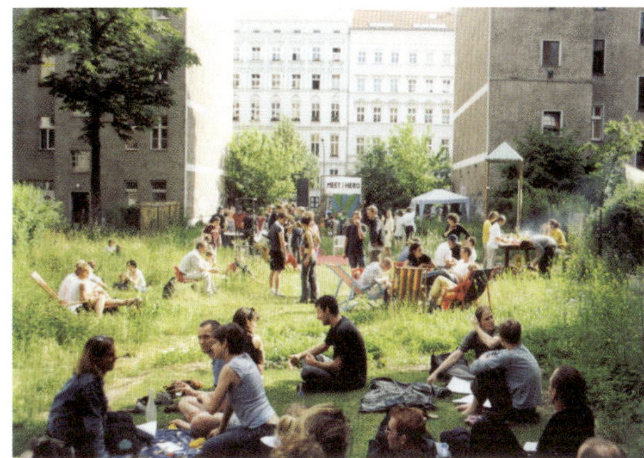

5

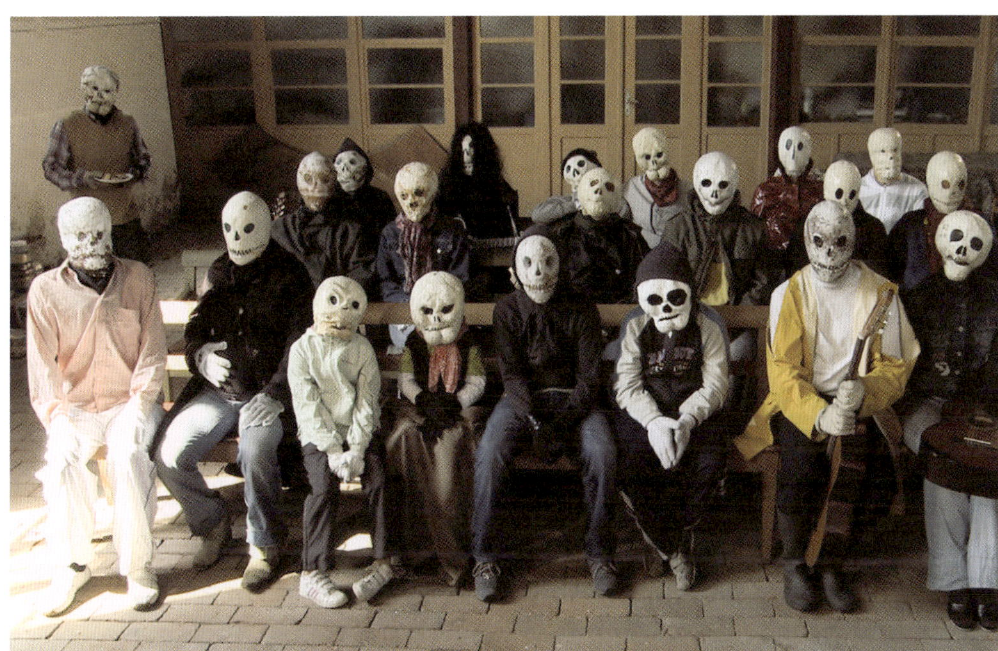

6

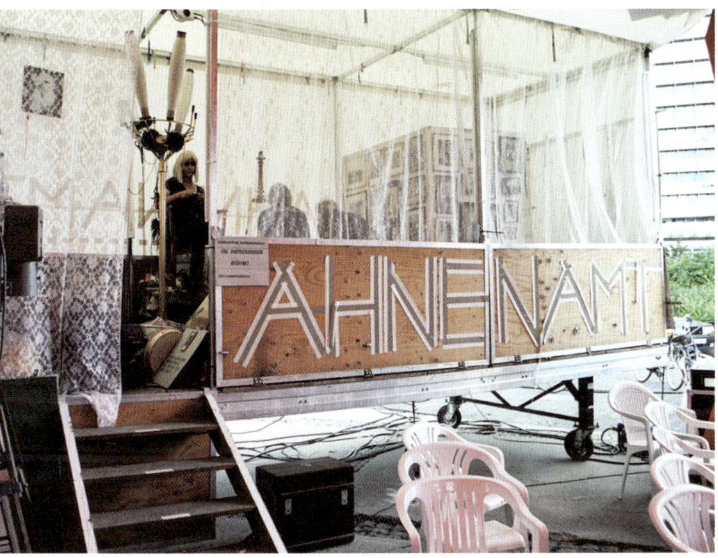

7

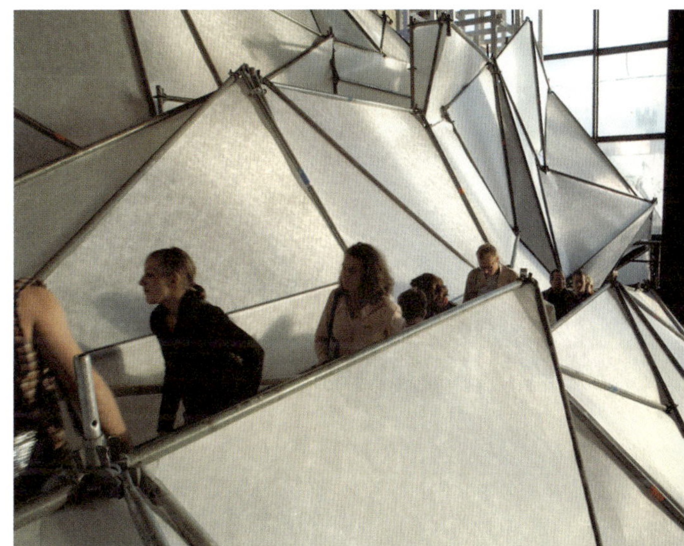

8

9 – Viennese Songs from All Over the World, public performance, Berlin/Vienna, 2001–2002

10 – May 1st Garden Performance, public performance, Berlin, 2002

11 – The Call of Berlin Wedding, public installation, Wedding district, Berlin, 2011–2012

12 – Refuge Future: Berlin/Halle-Neustadt, performance, 2003–2004

opposite
13 – Winter Olympic Games for Stuffed Animals, installation, Berlin, 2002–2006

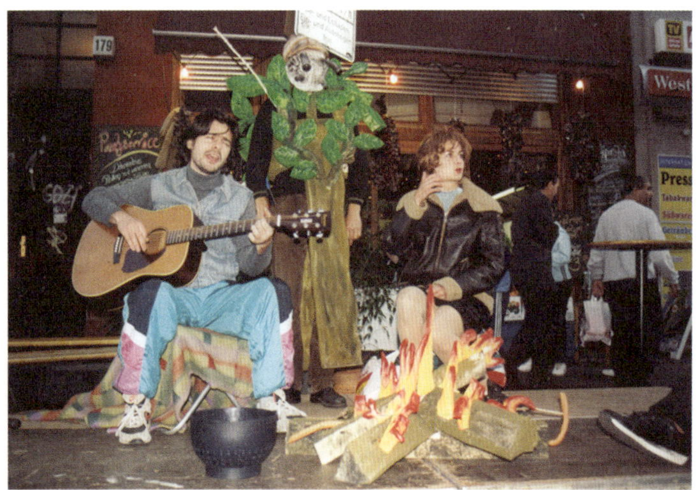

9

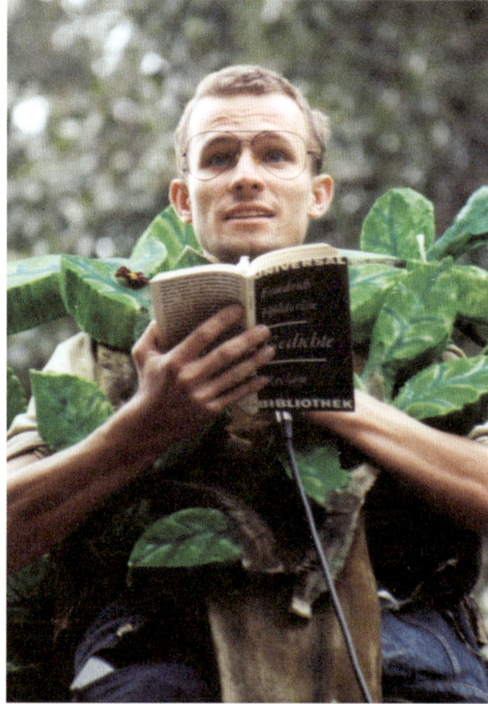

10

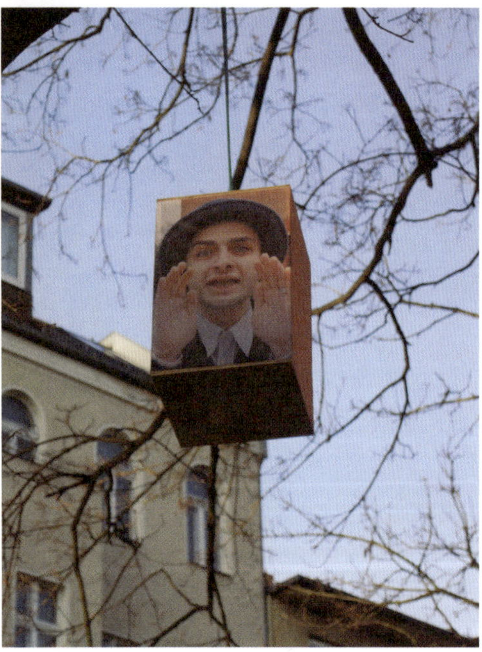

11

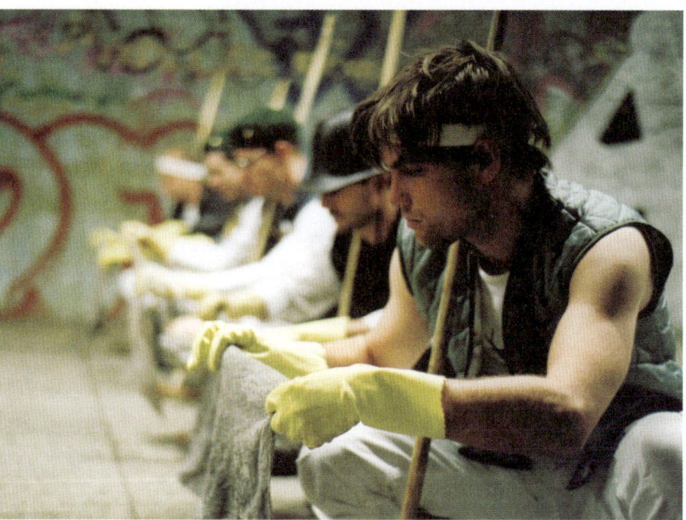

12

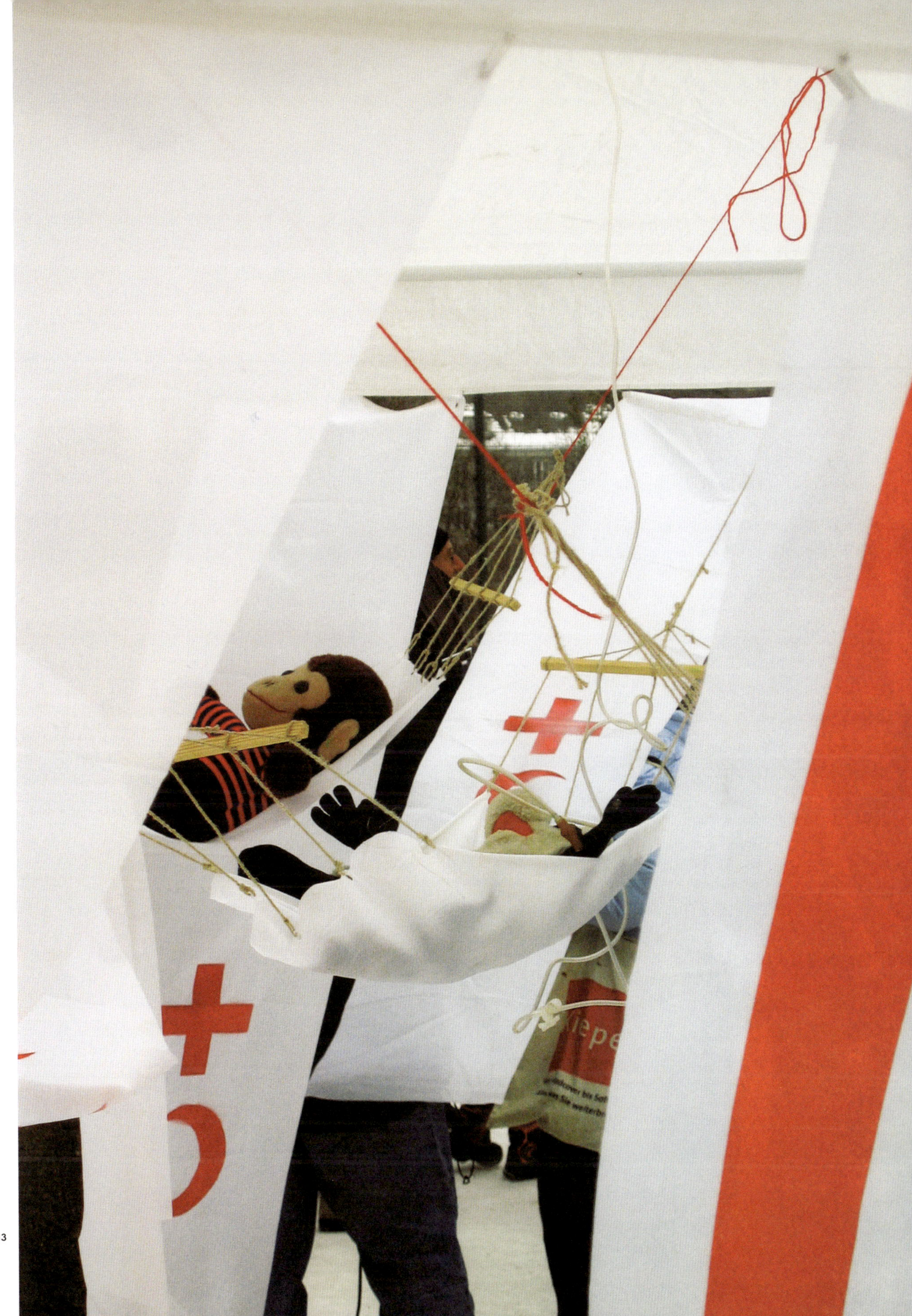

ACTIVE SINCE	CITY	WEBSITE
2007	New York, U.S.	N / A

DAS INSTITUT

MEMBERS	ACTIVITIES	RECOMMENDED PUBLICATION
Kerstin Brätsch and Adele Röder	Ephemeral Abstraction	DAS INSTITUT, Triennial Report 2011–2009, JRP Ringier / Christoph Keller Editions, Zurich, 2012

Proudly registered as a LLP, DAS INSTITUT investigates how information and products are built and distributed. In the duo's prints, paintings, fabrics, and installations, it is hard to distinguish what is created by hand and what is by machine. What emerges is a use of abstraction as a powerful tool to comment on mass media, the Internet, marketing, and how within these realms symbolic values are associated with images.

Why work collaboratively?

A massive multiplication—and so creation, obfuscation, and perpetual annihilation—of the self. Also: a distribution of responsibility, blame, consequence. For every addition to every crowd, so too a drop of madness. Of course, there are design trade-offs. When you're working alone in a studio practice, you spend time alone with the work. This changes both you and the work in the process. But when you work with others in a serious or engaged way, the work spends much more time by itself. It isn't privy to the conversations and email correspondences that decide its fate. It's a lonelier work, in some sense.

How do you determine membership? Does physical location matter in this regard?

I think at a most basic level, our practice is founded on a friendship. DI is Röder and Brätsch. However, the legal layer immediately succeeding this is something like a limited liability partnership (LLP): we've structured most of our creative activities on the model of a focused professional unit. It's an organizing structure often used in the United States by lawyers, accountants, architects, and others working in highly guarded or legislated professional fields. In an LLP, one partner isn't responsible or liable for another partner's misconduct or negligence. This is an important word to spotlight here because our production is very much oriented on the concept of "misconduct." That is, we create highly functional structures and design patterns for producing work from varied input, and later fill those structures with highly dysfunctional content. It personifies the partnership in many ways; it gives the union a silhouette. I guess you could think about it like introducing disorder into an ordered system.

If considered separately, how do your individual artistic practices contribute to or detract from your work as a group?

In the world of art, your name is the first layer of your brand as an artist. This is an unfortunate fact, perhaps—for most of us, our names are almost always working against us. If you look at the history of twentieth-century art, you'll see that for many collectives, working together wasn't so much about consolidating resources as unencumbering individuals from their identities. You could also think about early nineties Internet culture in that regard. Today, the Internet projects your material presence across time and space; it indexes your name and your activities. But when people were first going online twenty years ago, they were playing with new identities; they were making up new names for themselves. Today, this practice is mostly relegated to the world of online gaming.

How are decisions made?

Today, an entire class of management consultants steer corporate clients toward increasingly leveraging the decision-making power of crowds. This is happening to an absurd degree—companies and collectives are encouraged to be agile, flexible, open to revising or restructuring the very essence of their activities in response to market conditions or customer demand. In the past we've adopted similar

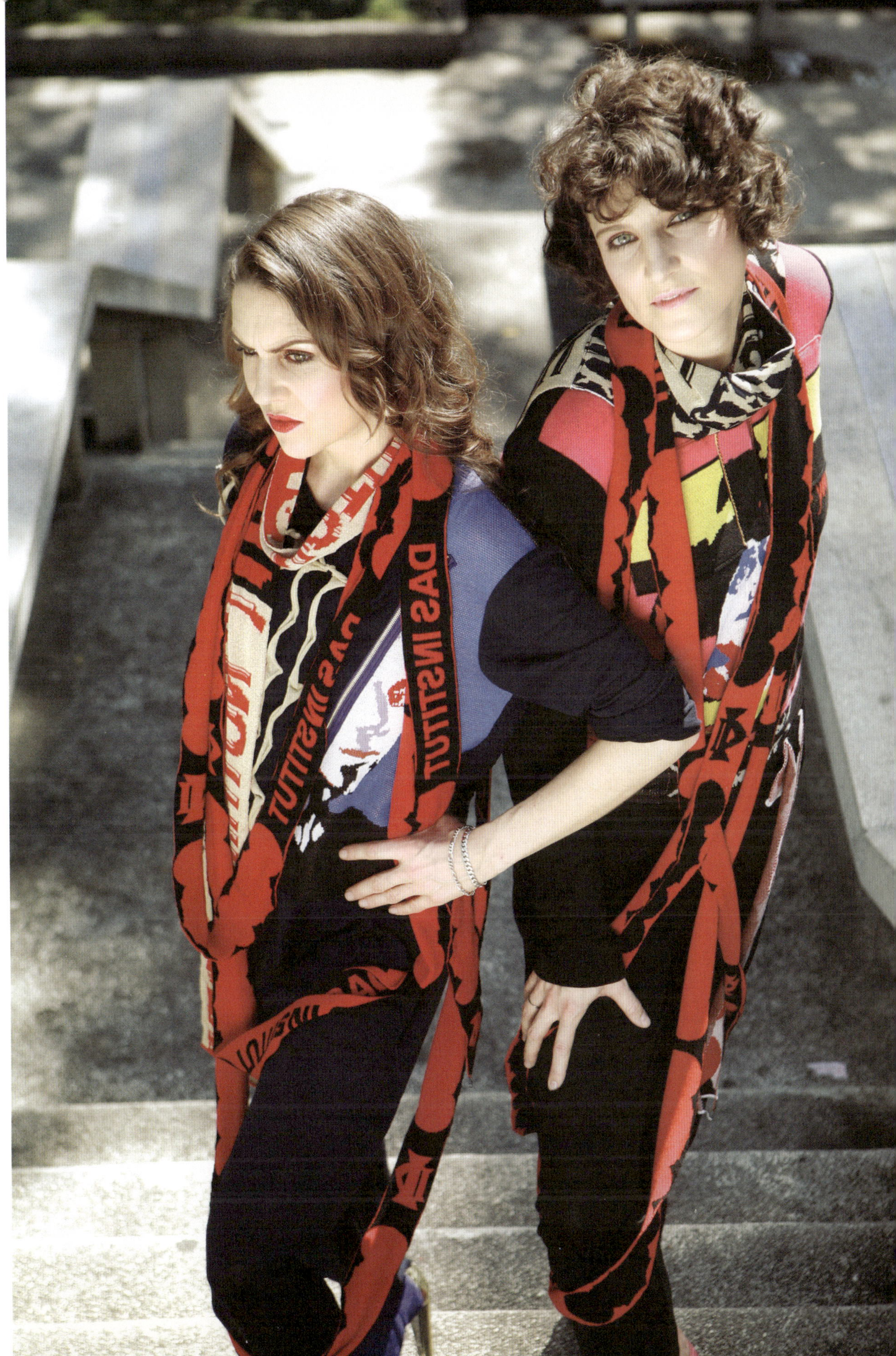

1

methods with a radically different end goal. While crowdsourcing alloys collective consumer or market demand into an anonymous wind that fills an organization's sails, we try to involve as many responsive friends and colleagues as possible when working or making decisions. We do this to highlight, frame, and contextualize their own work rather than simply fold it into our own.

Does each of you have a clearly defined role? If so, what are some of each member's distinct responsibilities?

We try to spend time in different time zones simultaneously: it helps with a broader coverage and faster response time for email. Email is probably the most important thing when running a cultural partnership. It's a very fluid medium: you can turn emails into writing; you can use them to transport other kinds of media; you can send reminders to yourself.

How important is each group member's individuality, both in terms of your artistic production and in terms of your relationship with the media? Does anonymity come into play?

Anonymity is quite a nostalgic thought these days. We don't mind, though. That's why we put ourselves in so much of our own work: better to succeed at increasing the speed and proliferation of your own image than be shamed by your failure to stop or control it. The other thing about proliferation and branding that you have to remember is its destructive capacities. If I try to suppress an image or some piece of writing on the Internet, I'll fail. But if I flood those same distribution channels with duplicates, forgeries, counterfeits, remixes, mislabeled copies—well, interesting things sometimes happen. Personal identity online can work in similar ways.

What is the relationship between your working methods and your art's "content"? In this sense, does technology tend to play more of a supporting role, or does it lead you in new directions?

"Content" has become a dirty word in some circles. Serious online publishers use it to deride the rise of the "content mill" businesses model—Internet properties requiring minimal assembly and maintenance, farming out content production to produce evergreen and traffic-generating web material—so as to mine a kind of sustained trickle of advertising dollars. Imagine what television in the eighties would have looked like with the Internet economy of today: millions of channels to flip through in order to find a sliver of quality programming you'd actually like to watch. But pause for a moment and elaborate this fantasy. With so much boring shit on TV, why not put the thing on mute and invite some friends over to throw a party? Content can be illuminating too. It can be an ambient and ever-shifting light source in the room, continuously throwing new color on everything inside it.

How does your collaboration relate to its cultural, institutional, and commercial contexts? In other words, how would you respond to those who call this a trend?

Trends are the original social network, aren't they? Expression is what one does for her own sake, regardless of who sees it or doesn't. But communication and culture are different. That requires reception and repetition. If you release a single, foreign sound into the night, it's an incident. But as soon as you repeat it, it's a thing that can be picked up by someone else and repeated again. You might say trends are the same: being aware of what others are doing, repeating what you see, and finally differentiating yourself—being a trend maker. This is the importance of trends: the possibility of being copied, of being imitated. That's why we'd be reluctant to accept the word "trend" as a purely negative or pejorative thing. How else to change the world but create alternate models for its inhabitation, and likewise the conditions for those models to be taken up by others, copied, revised, elaborated? The nature of working with someone rather than simply working alone helps us design projects with a fundamental orientation to this kind of sociability.

Who is your audience?

We try and think of audience in terms of epochs. How to make a book or a design object that could potentially be rediscovered and recirculated a decade from now. Planning the afterlife of a work: there is nothing more sincere or generous you could do!

Does your engagement with one another translate into an engagement with the public? How so?

I'd like to believe our friendship would endure the erosions of time, the uncertainty of reach.

previous
1 – Thoi Trang Tre, March 2010, magazine/artists' book, photo shoot with digitally knitted jumpsuits JRP Ringier, Zurich, 2011

2 – DAS INSTITUT with United Brothers and Nhu Dong, Blacky Blocked Radiants Sunbathed photo shoot, Halle für Kunst, Lüneburg, 2011

3 – DAS INSTITUT and Lucas Knipscher, Simultaneous Studios photo shoot, Gio Marconi Gallery, Milan, 2012

4 – DI WHY Relax! Raincoats, series of ten raincoats with aqua refreshment spray, silkscreen on PVC, limited edition for New Jersey, Basel, 2010

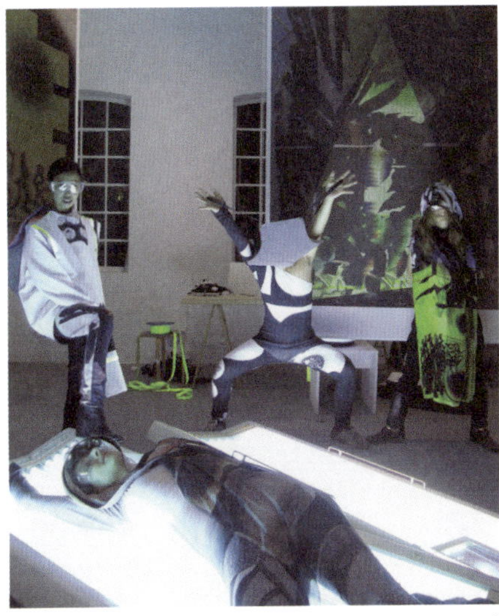

2

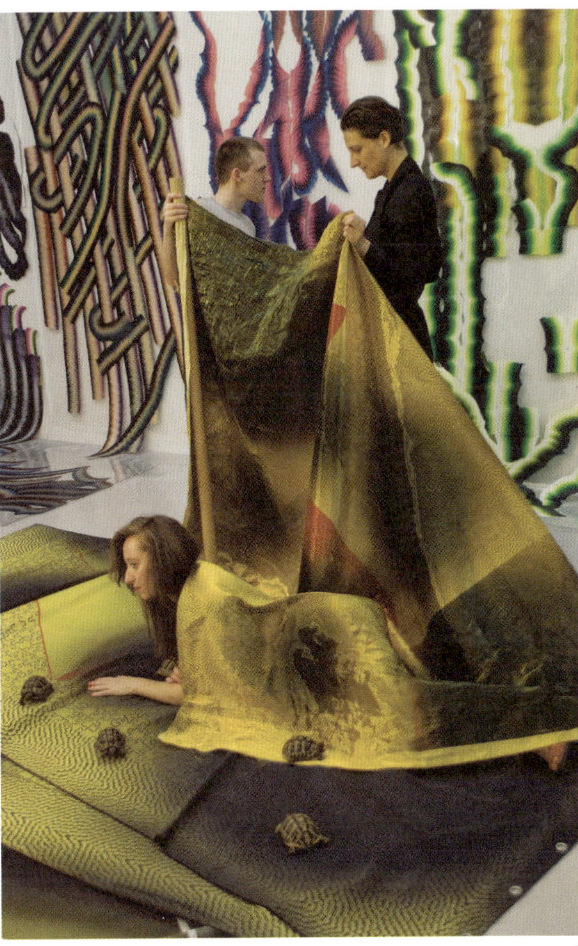

3

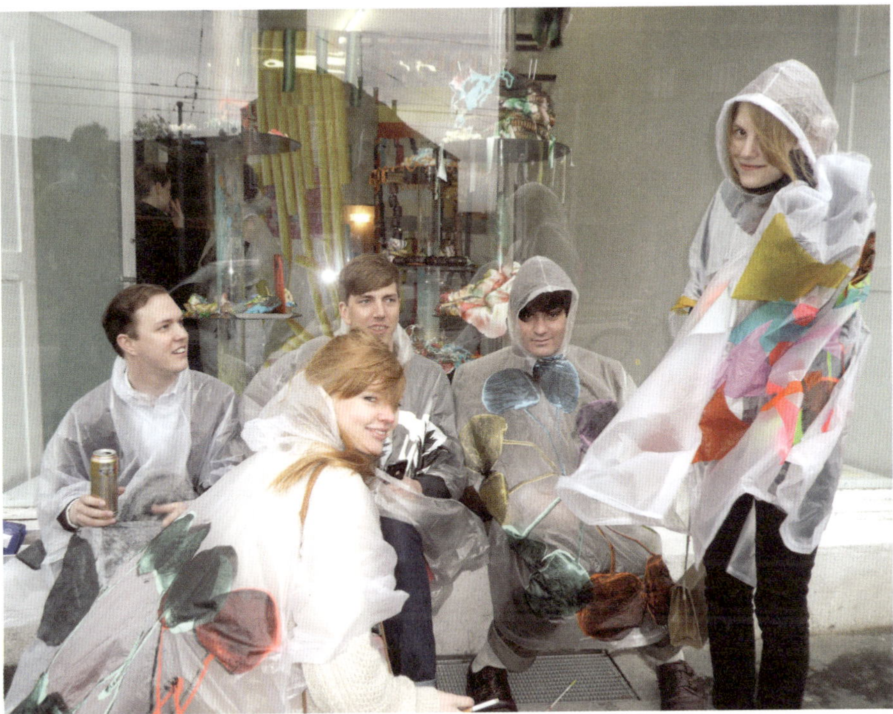

4

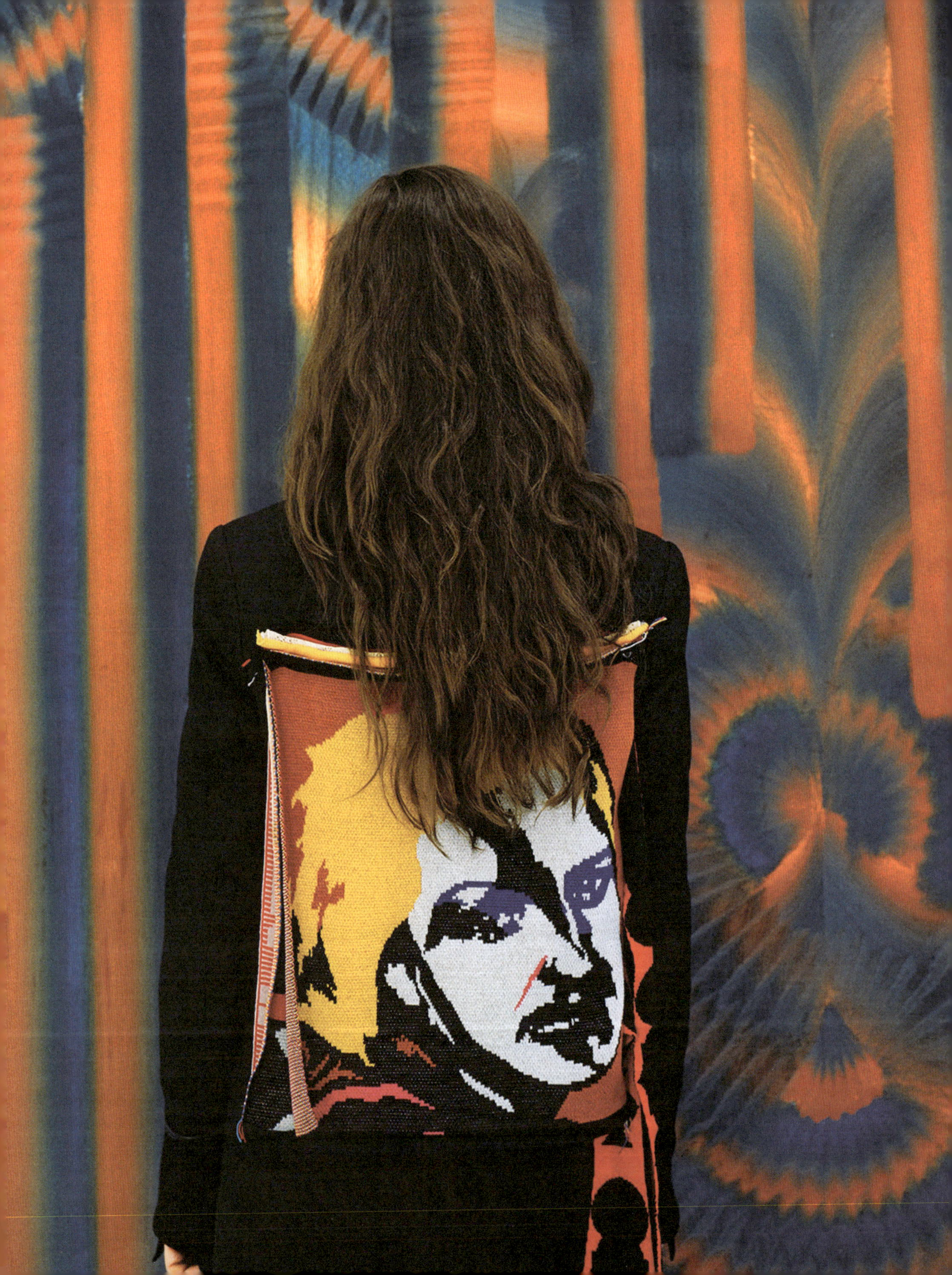

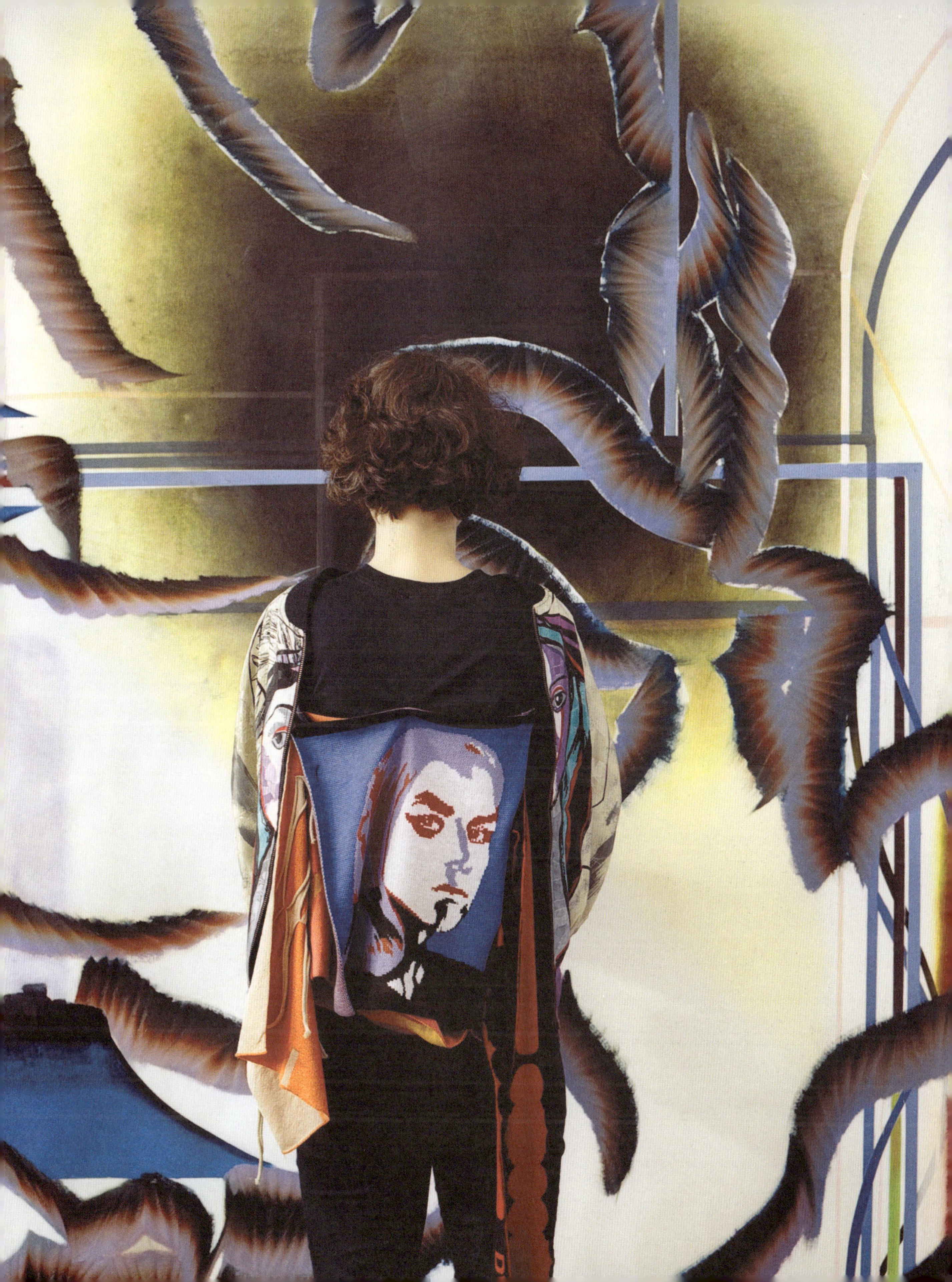

previous

5 + 6 – **Albrecht Fuchs with DAS INSTITUT, Painting Parasite, photograph, 2011**

7 – **My Life As Frau Cow Will Show You How To Chew The Leftover Grass On The Field, poster, 2009**

8 – **Who's Kerstin Brätsch?, poster, 2010**

9 – **DI WHY Relax! Campaign: Good Morning, flag design for Quartier des Bains, Geneva, 2010**

opposite

10 – **Treat Your Own Neck, performance and installation view, Deste Foundation, Athens, 2011**

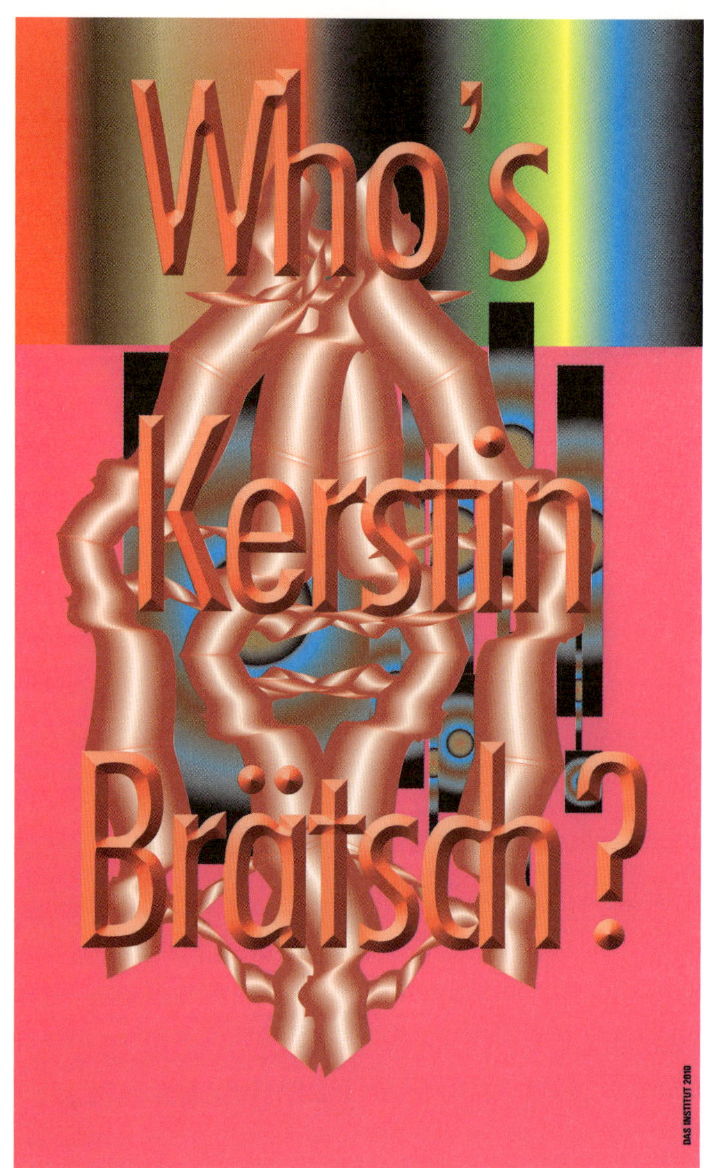

8

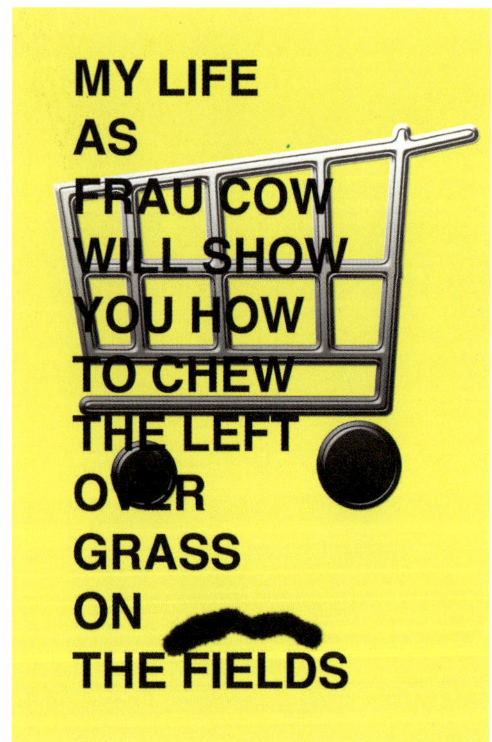

7

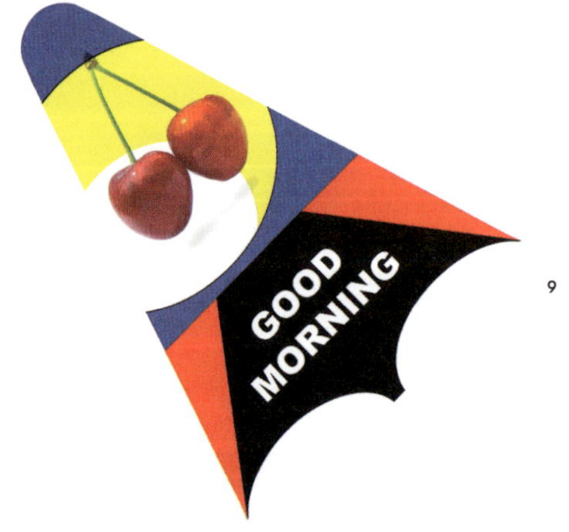

9

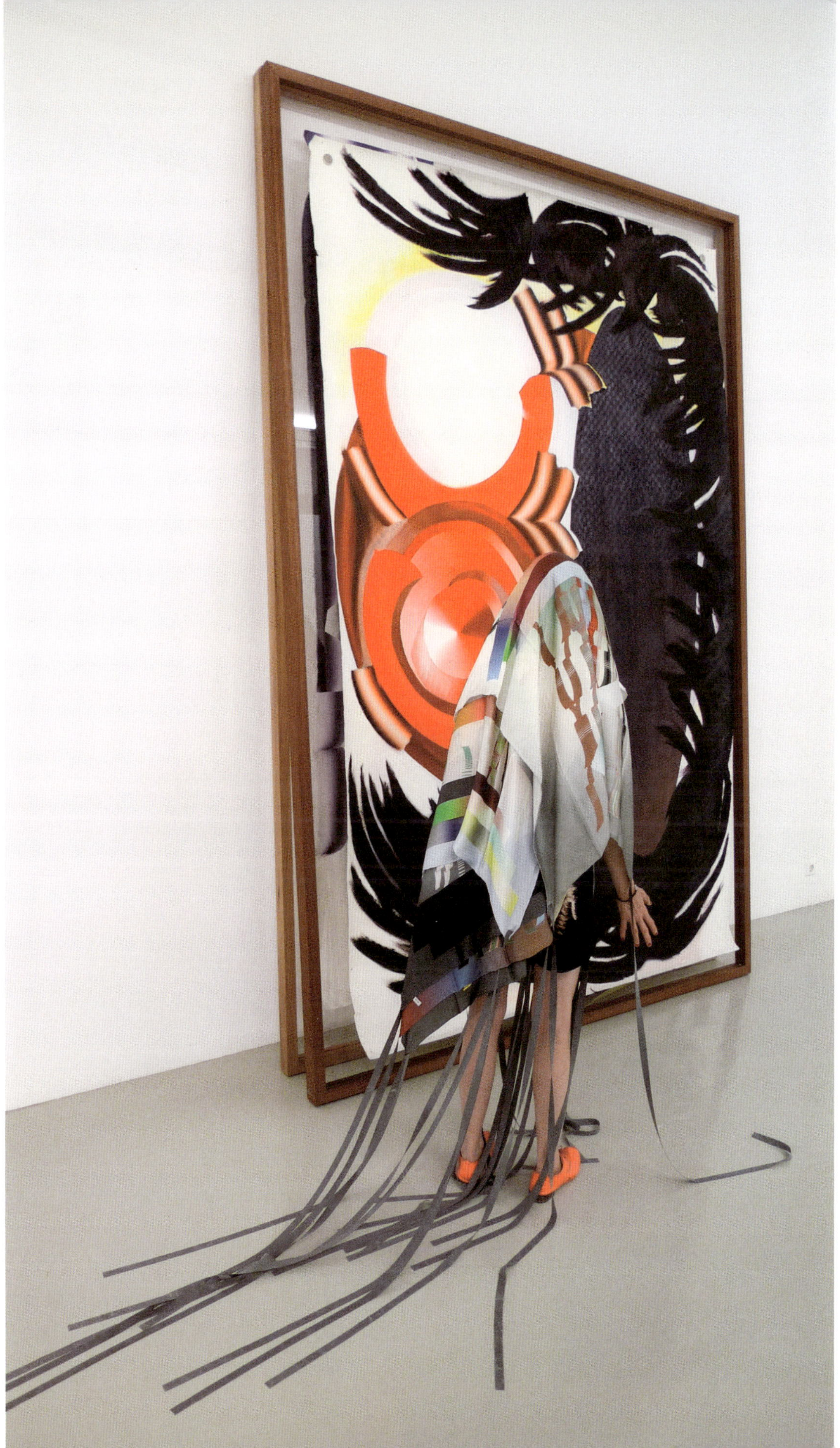

ACTIVE SINCE	CITY	WEBSITE
2002	Virginia Beach, U.S.	dearraindrop.org

Dearraindrop

MEMBERS	ACTIVITIES	RECOMMENDED PUBLICATION
Laura Grant, Billy Grant, and Joe Grillo	Curating, Happenings, Music, Painting / Sculpture / Installation, Video	DEARRAINDROP, Off / On, Deitch Projects, New York, 2005

Inspired by outsider and underground arts, Dearraindrop's production is symptomatic of the downtown art scene that emerged in New York in the 2000s. Uncanny heroes of cartoons and comics are revived in the collective's colorful and psychedelic paintings, sculptures, and installations. Modeled after the Independent Group—the British collective that initiated pop art in the 1950s—Dearraindrop, uses art to explore a mediascape the group struggles to identify with.

Why work collaboratively?

We never set out to be an actual collective; it just happened. And it happened when we were really young. Laura was seventeen, Joe was eighteen, and by the time Billy joined, two years later, he was sixteen.

We were big fans of past art collectives such as Chicago's The Hairy Who, from the late 1960s, and Ann Arbor, Michigan's Destroy All Monsters, from the mid-1970s, so we wanted to work in the same realm as those groups. Later on, we became obsessed with the Independent Group, featuring our favorite artist and the true godfather of pop art: Eduardo Paolozzi.

Our collaborative paintings feel innovative, fun, and experimental in their execution. The results of the collaborations are weird. Weird can be achieved more quickly and more thoroughly when we collaborate. Because we are such good friends, we grew up in the same town, and were all born within five years of each other, we have many shared experiences. We also have a shared competitive energy that is really motivating. The art we are interested in making takes a lot of dedication and long hours in the studio. It can be very lonely concentrating on a project this intensely. Collaboration makes this aspect of making art much more tolerable; it can be some of the best quality time you can ever spend with a friend. In turn, the fun/productive energy that can develop is like a magnet for people and opportunities. There are definitely some personality types that benefit more than others from working this way. Ultimately, the decision boils down to whether or not you have chemistry with a group of people that results in making art that you like.

How do you determine membership? Does physical location matter in this regard?

We lived together like a big weird family from 2004 to 2010. Our relationship was obviously demented but it created some demented paintings too.

If considered separately, how do your individual artistic practices contribute to or detract from your work as a group?

Eventually, it became apparent that everyone wanted to pursue their own strengths as individuals. In 2010 we took a break from painting together on large paintings for a while to pursue individual interests and decided to all live separately, although we are currently painting together now.

How are decisions made?

We brainstorm ideas for paintings together. Sometimes we flesh out themes sometimes we just go at it. Then we each individually sketch concepts or just add to what is already there. We often go for layering to bring everything together spatially. We use a sense of composition to guide us. There is never a lot of discussion. Our collaborations are very natural and fun, without any rules except "no rules." Our art-making decisions are largely autonomous. We rely on our practice of sharing art supplies and inspirations to bring cohesion to the chaos. We all contribute to the whole and whatever the qualities are that emerge from this process is our goal.

1 – **Self-portrait with installation pieces, Tokyo, 2004**

2 – **Riddle of The Sphinx, installation, Deitch Projects, New York, 2004**

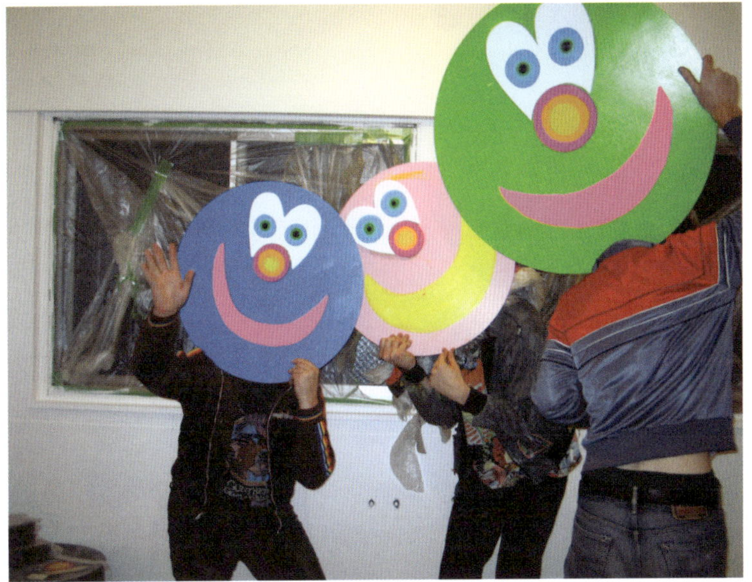

1

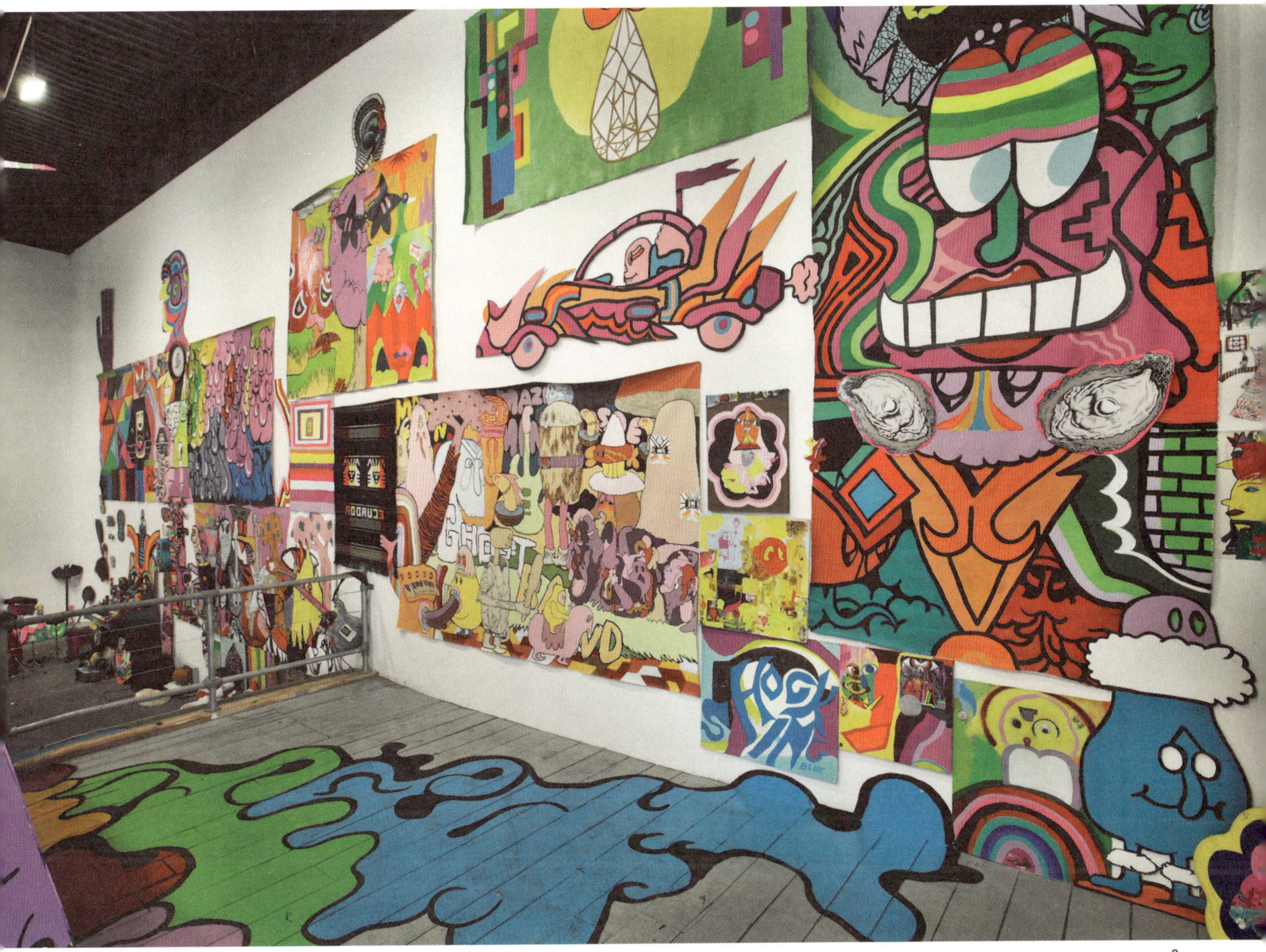

2

Does each of you have a clearly defined role? If so, what are some of each member's distinct responsibilities?

We definitely each have our own strengths. Billy is best at the computer. Laura is the most energetic. Joe is best at locating opportunities. Artistically, Billy has a steady liquid black line and an amazing use of symmetry. Joe's prolific obsession with making art is coupled by his left-handed personal style. Laura's tradition reflects a rounded form and love of color.

How important is each group member's individuality, both in terms of your artistic production and in terms of your relationship with the media? Does anonymity come into play?

Anonymity allows us to feel more liberated and experimental. On a personal level, individuality is very important to each of us. As a group there is a sense of working on something bigger than each of us. We are individuals living a shared lifestyle and that can be hard to decipher from the outside looking in. We are well aware of this although we never feel it to be crucial to be completely understood. Being free of individual recognition encourages us to share and experiment with each other in a very honest way. Flexibility is the greatest asset an artist can attain.

What is the relationship between your working methods and your art's "content"? In this sense, does technology tend to play more of a supporting role, or does it lead you in new directions?

With painting being our main form of collaboration, we feel we are following a historic precedent and adding a new twist on it by working together unilaterally. We are able to achieve larger projects more quickly together. There is a major lifestyle component to our art, which involves a long-term accumulation of collections. Living among the shared collections takes on its own meaning to us and we try to translate this cluttered imagery life feeling into most of our productions. We all really appreciate the synthesis of ideas that comes from collage practices. Collage provides a way forward for our approach. We were a collage of painters.

How does your collaboration relate to its cultural, institutional, and commercial contexts? In other words, how would you respond to those who call this a trend?

Although other collaboratives like CoBrA did work together on paintings, we feel that we are doing something new and experimental and high energy in a very business-oriented time for art. We feel our practice is authentic in that we didn't just hire someone to paint it for us. There is a deep appreciation for the skill and artistry involved in controlling the brush. It's a badass skill. It's not tough to trace or collage with Photoshop. You can see and feel the aura of authentic painting that's straight from the hand. You wouldn't say someone is a good skateboarder if he or she hired someone else to skateboard for him or her, but you might buy a skateboard T-shirt from a company that hires a good skateboarder to skate for it. In response to those who would call collaboration a trend, we would argue that that is a narrow view of the practice. In a commercial context, what isn't a trend? Collaboration seems at least as acceptable as an artist employing assistants. The only thing challenged by collaboration is the business model of the art market. Otherwise it seems to be a natural outcome of artists hanging out a lot. In fact, the history goes back to the beginning of art making itself.

Who is your audience?

Our work appeals to people of all ages. Young to old! Children are very drawn to our work because of the bright colors.

Does your engagement with one another translate into an engagement with the public? How so?

We have made many interactive works and worked with the electrical engineers Owen Osborn and Chris Kucinski (Critter and Guitari). We are very interested in creating total environments. We were focused on this more initially with works like Riddle of the Sphinx in which the viewer could enter and touch its walls and hear prerecorded sounds. Our love of painting overshadowed this interest for a long time. However, we do try to work in sound elements and interactive elements in a lot of our shows. We would love to think bigger about all-encompassing environments in the future. This is another reason public art is so appealing to us.

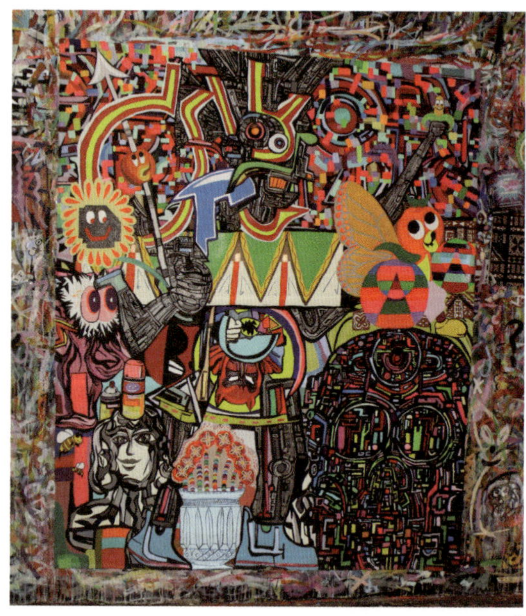

3

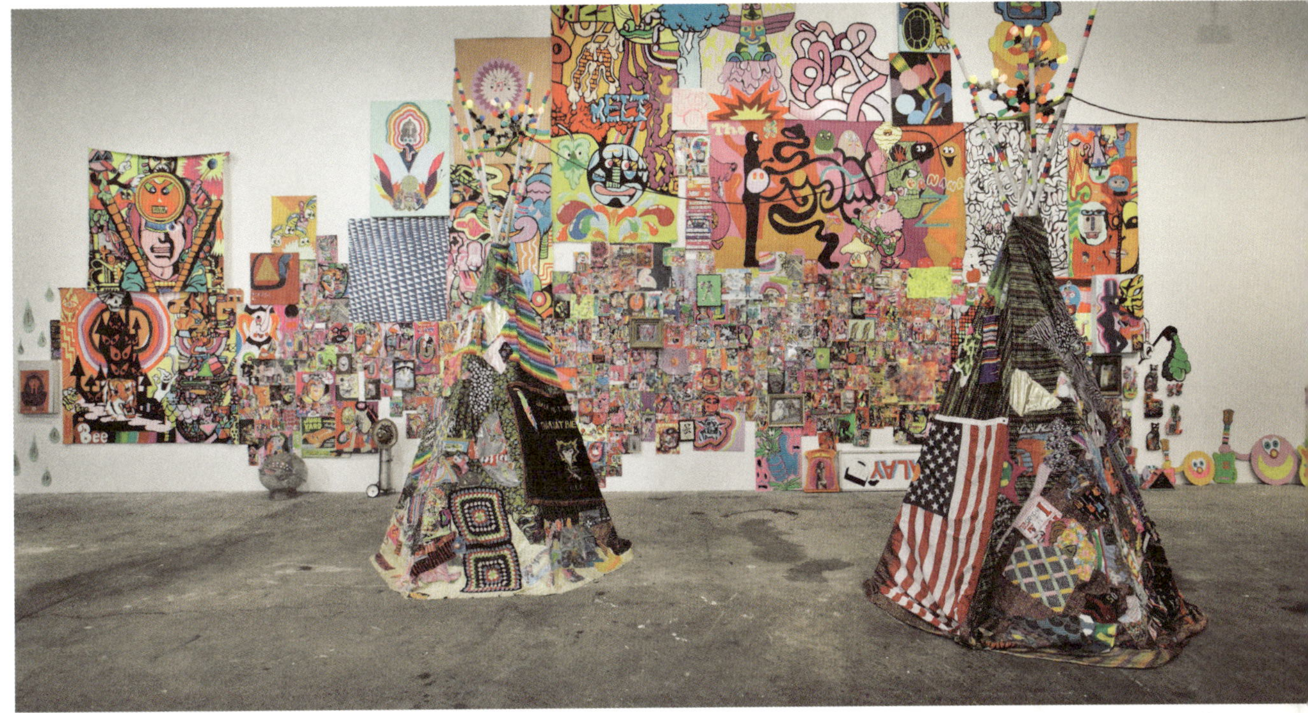

4

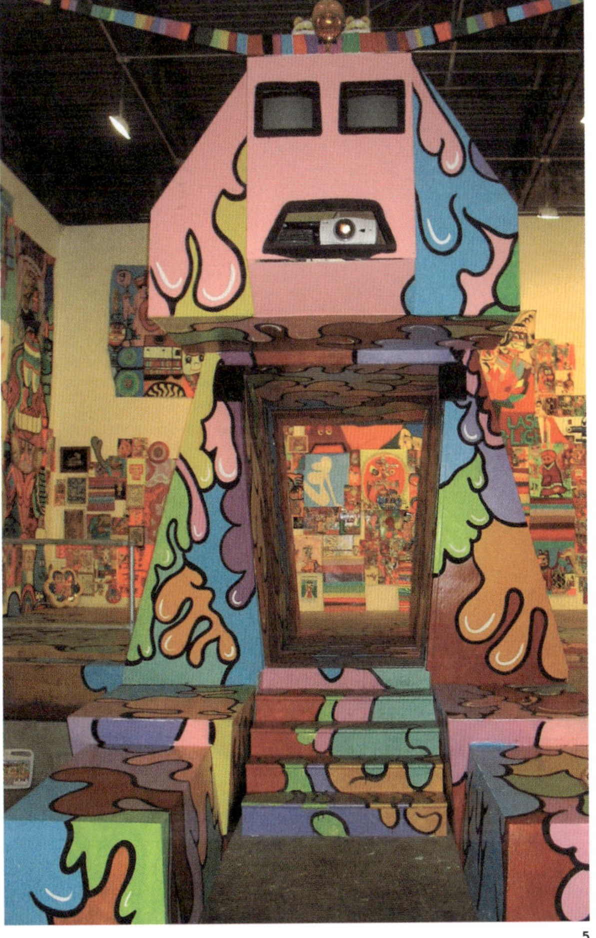

5

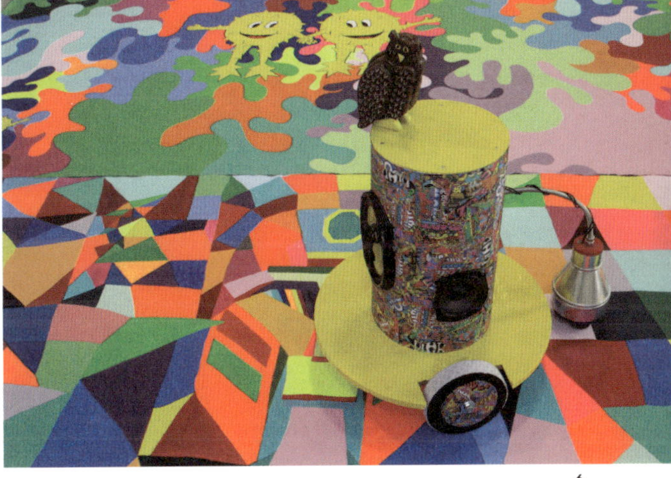

6

3 – Ballad of Baby Corn, installation, V1 Gallery, Copenhagen, 2010

4 + 5 – Riddle of The Sphinx, installation, Deitch Projects, New York, 2004

6 – Magic Brain: Color Reading Robot Reading 3 Paintings on the Floor, installation, Perugi Arte Contemporanea, Padova, 2006

7 – Concrete Trees, Glass Grass and Cream-Filled Stones: Color Reading Sound Wheels, installation, Loyal Gallery, Stockholm, 2007

8 – Dearraindrop logo, 2003

9 – Instruments and gourds by Owen Osborn painted by Dearraindrop, installation, 2006

10 – Members of the Island, vinyl record, side A, 2005. Produced by Diesel Denim Gallery, New York

opposite
11 – Portrait of Dearraindrop's member Joe Grillo, 2002

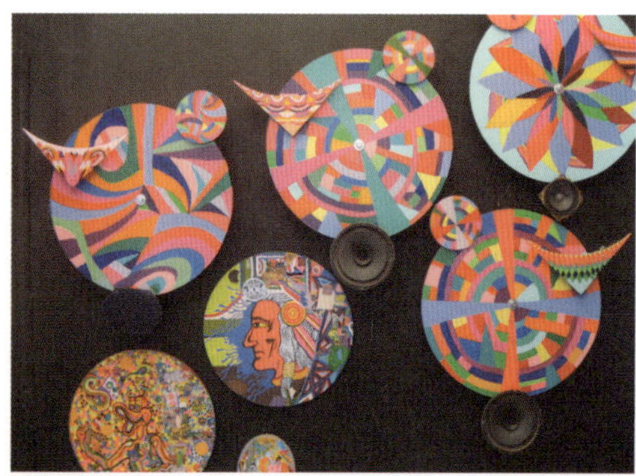

7

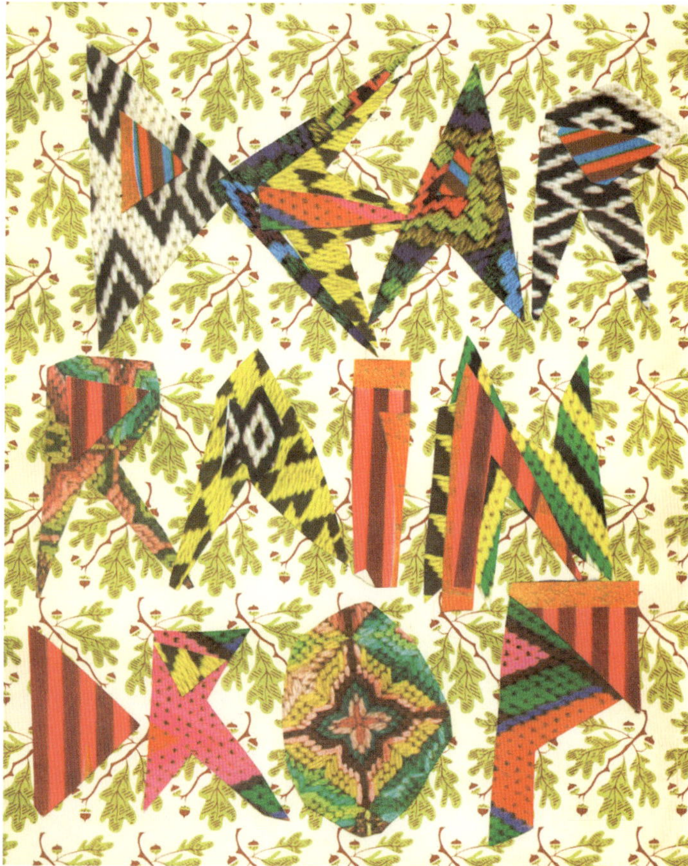

8

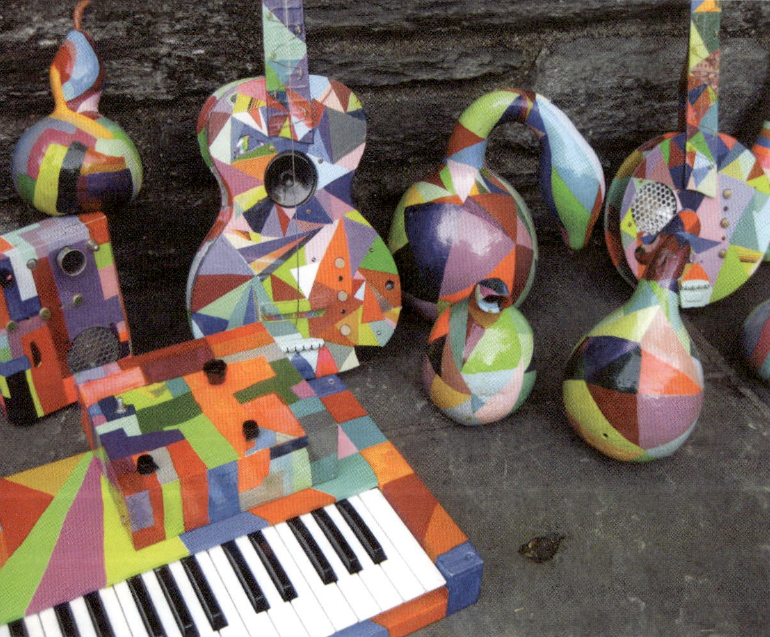

9

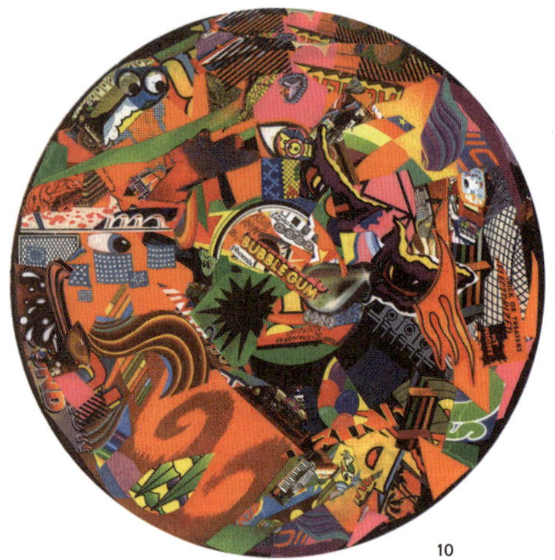

10

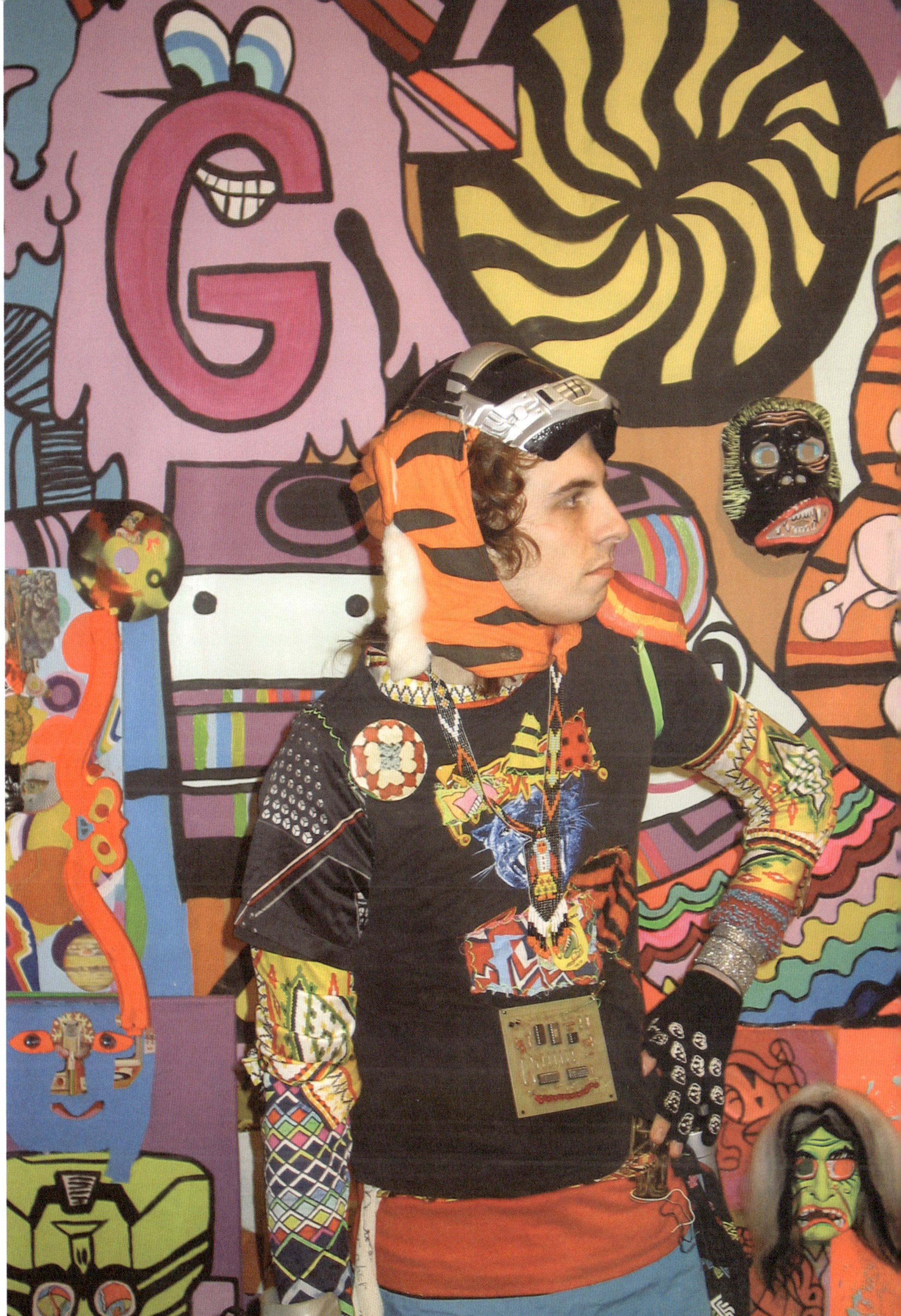

ACTIVE SINCE	CITY	WEBSITE
2010	New York, U.S.	dismagazine.com and disimages.com

DIS

MEMBERS

At the core of DIS is the collective of Lauren Boyle, Solomon Chase, Marco Roso, and David Toro. DIS Magazine was additionally cofounded by current editor Nick Scholl and editors-at-large Patrik Sandberg and Samuel Adrian Massey

ACTIVITIES	RECOMMENDED PUBLICATION
Internet Art, Performance, Photography, Red Carpet Services, Video	Kevin McGarry, OPEN UP: THE MUTATING ACTIVITIES OF DIS by Kevin McGarry, Frieze, April 2013

DIS is a multimedia collective and a metacommercial enterprise that operates through a website and a creative agency. It generates still and moving images that comment on marketing strategies, social networking, and digital fiction. Most of its works are products that seem destined for the commercial market or for entertainment, but in fact are dysfunctional and push us to think about what role constructed images play in our life.

Why work collaboratively?

It's a question of having elective affinities and a mode of production that combines individual skills to produce in a faster, more dynamic way. It reflects an inescapable current reality. Even the solitary worker/artist/producer is working in a collaboration, whether with manufacturers, solicitors, technology, reference materials, family, peers. It seems that an active collaboration is the only way to understand our situation. At times, it's about distribution of labor; more nodes, more modes. Other times, it's about antagonism; how does the individual relate to the group? Or it's about camaraderie and mutual support, mobilizing our talents, our desires, our shortcomings. We feed on each other, and through conversation, we make our ideas stronger and dilute the concept of authorship.

How do you determine membership? Does physical location matter in this regard?

Actually, most of us live within a two-block radius of one another. This and other circumstances, such as temporary unemployment, led to the formation of DIS.

If considered separately, how do your individual artistic practices contribute to or detract from your work as a group?

They definitely contribute. All of us have broad backgrounds connected to art or the arts. We're all involved with fashion to varying degrees. But we weren't pursuing art careers when we got together so we don't have that pressure to create artworks individually, which is probably to the benefit of DIS. One of our interns likes to save his best Tweets for his own Twitter (instead of using the @DISintern account); it's a nice analogy, because we don't have that problem: we give it all to DIS.

How are decisions made?

Micro facial expressions of approval or disapproval, endless email threads, and laughter generally get us somewhere. If not, majority rules.

Does each of you have a clearly defined role? If so, what are some of each member's distinct responsibilities?

The division is fairly murky, but we each excel in different areas. We all divide the labor of editing DIS Magazine, and then break down production, writing, styling, and photography among us.

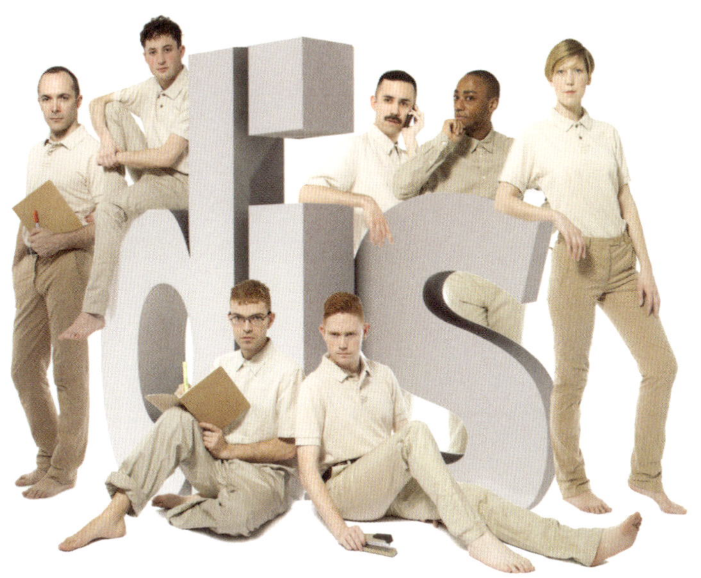

1

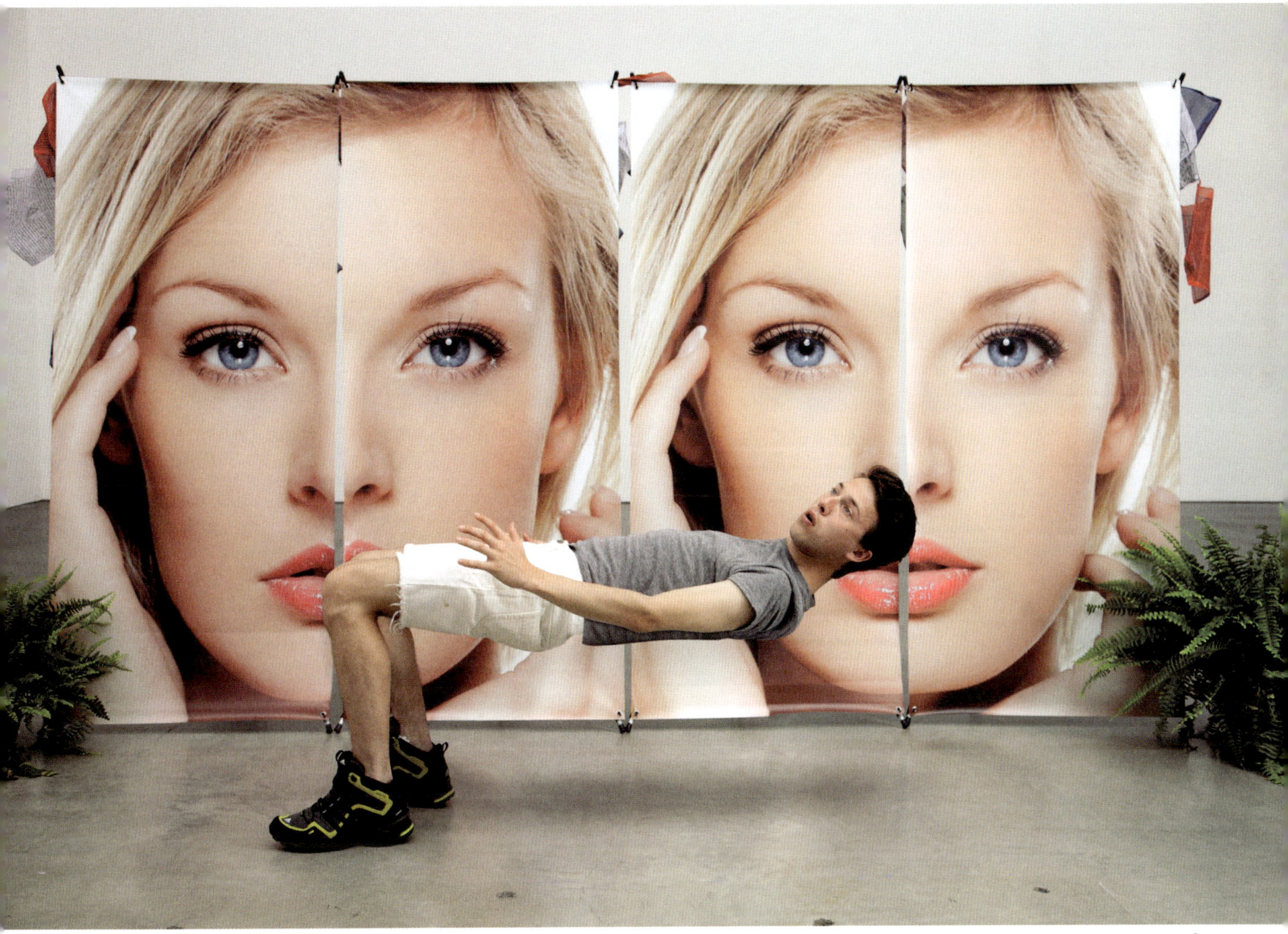

2

1 – Early portrait of DIS Magazine team, photograph, 2010

2 – Competing Images, photograph within the installation by Timur Si-Qin, The Struggle, 2012

overleaf
3 – Global Denim Community, photograph, 2010

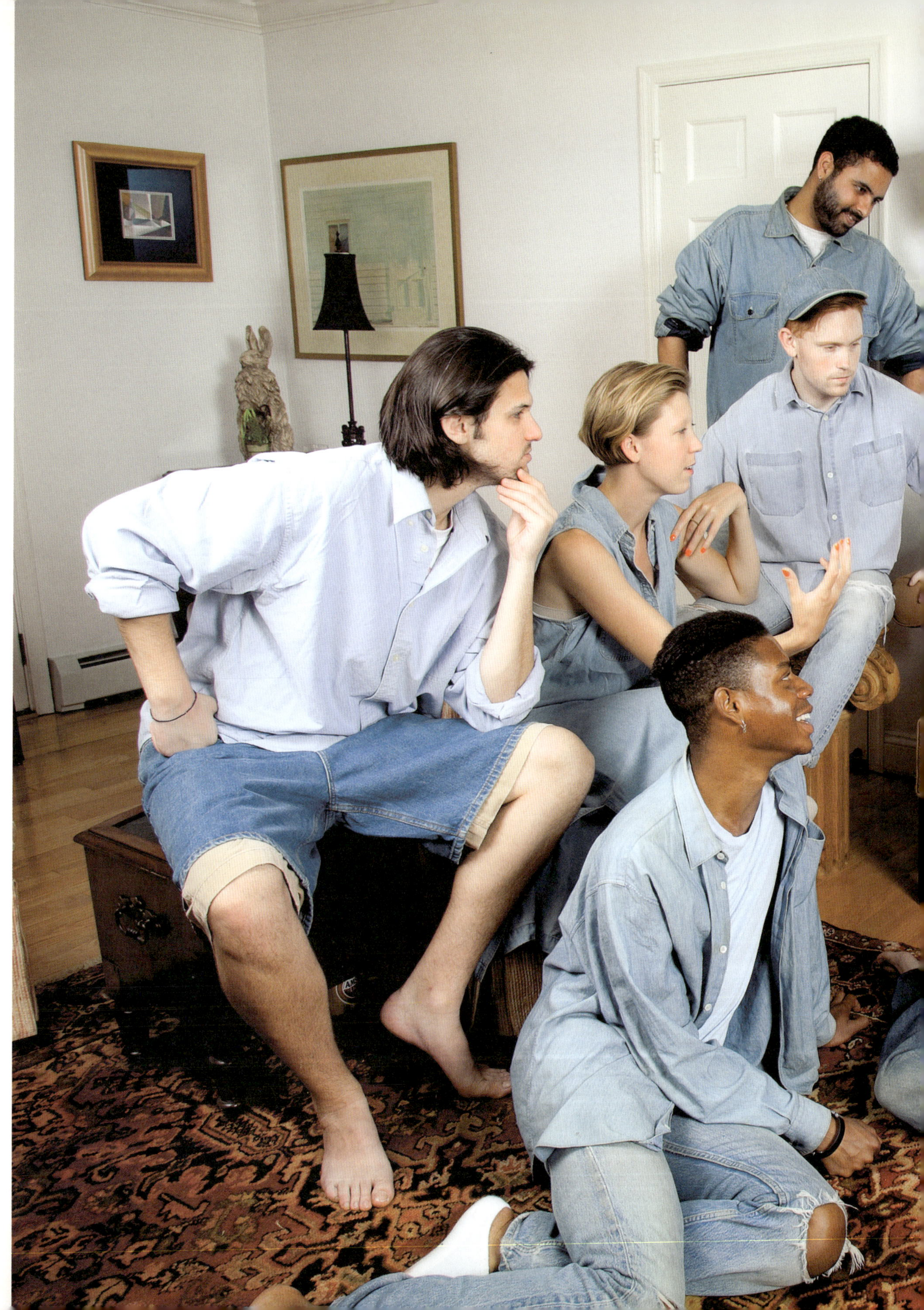

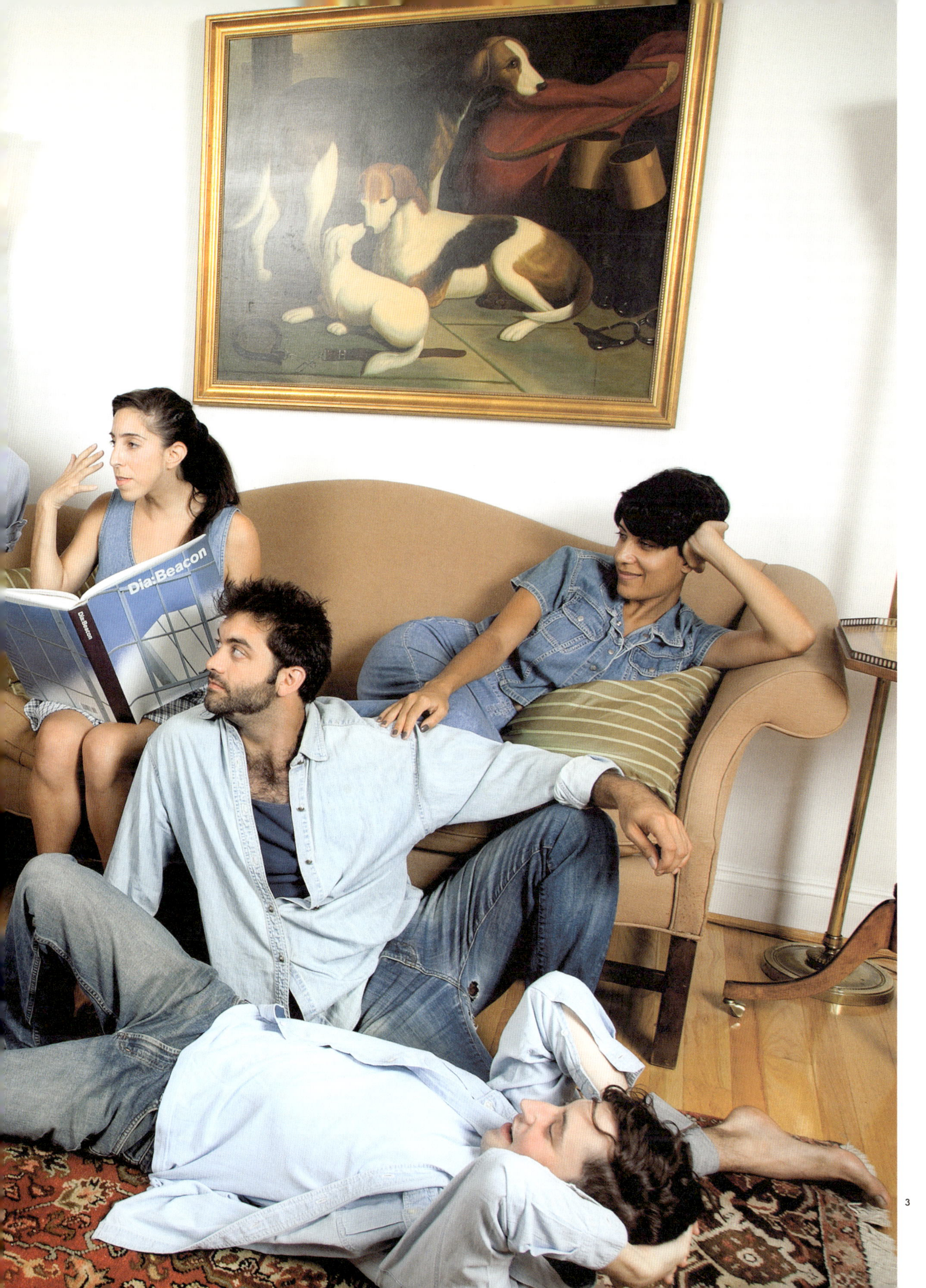
Dia:Beacon
Dia:Beacon

How important is each group member's individuality, both in terms of your artistic production and in terms of your relationship with the media? Does anonymity come into play?

We operate as an entity rather than a group of individuals. In a way, that frees us to think differently. DIS has its own kind of ethos. It sort of represents a twenty-first-century endgame of counterculture, depicting a world in which there is no "alternative" and not a drop of irony. Art as a lifestyle brand and fashion photography as a form of conceptual art. In our work we like to have a nonartlike quality that can inspire some curiosity in both art and nonart contexts. Shoes in Shoes (2011) is a good example. Ryder Ripps said, "This is a funny image first and an art piece second." That's pretty much how we see the majority of our work.

We probably do hide behind the anonymity of DIS. We like that most people don't know who's behind it. Sometimes people ask: Do you work for DIS? And we say yes. We work for DIS.

What is the relationship between your working methods and your art's "content"? In this sense, does technology tend to play more of a supporting role, or does it lead you in new directions?

Technology becomes a permanent soft pressure via the computer and social media. But most of the time technology has a supporting role; once in a while it really drives a concept. #Artselfie (2012) is a good example of that. The selfie genre's meteoric rise on Instagram revealed a new kind of social network, a phone/mirror hybrid. Taking selfies with art is a way of sharing and experiencing what you're looking at. The idea was simply, take a selfie with an artwork, tag it #artselfie, and it instantly populates a gallery on DIS Magazine.

The concept was derived from our ongoing exploration of the anthropological quality of art consumption. For the first of our DISimages project, we captured much of the work presented in the New Museum's Free exhibition (2010–2011). But rather than propagating the notion of the museum as a rarefied setting for artworks in various stages of their commodity-life, we essentially flattened that aspect and chose instead to invigorate the institution—both of the museum and of artwork documentation—by operating in and around the codes of stock photography. There is admittedly a kind of beauty to the life of art when it hangs on pristine walls, in a controlled environment with no visitors. But what about the life around the art under quotidian circumstances? That's the question we posed with New in Stock (the museum as public institution/interface), with Competing Images (2012) (documenting art in an attention economy), and at Frieze with Fair Trade (2012), where institution, commodity, social roles, and site/context are enmeshed in a fascinating and problematic way.

We were interested in what happens to the documentation of art when it also includes the people whom it is supposed to reflect, who gather to engage it and to manage it, and who themselves have a multitude of representations, concerns, distractions, agendas, and allegiances.

How does your collaboration relate to its cultural, institutional, and commercial contexts? In other words, how would you respond to those who call this a trend?

We work with any structure of diffusion available, from the Internet to art galleries, museums, art fairs, T-shirts, and commercial commissions. The context or site sometimes becomes the medium, or the place of production, and other times we become the middleman. But DIS Magazine is our preferred platform. It's where we are fully free of institutional and commercial politics. It's where we best amplify our voice and we are most committed to not conforming to the status quo.

We created DISimages.com (2013)—a fully functioning stock agency—because we saw how influential stock photography is on our culture. It's not only used in advertising and editorial; it's used as a reference material for new advertising and editorial. The effects are compounded and perpetuated. If we can penetrate the market with new stock options, we will contribute to culture in a broader way. We're interested in manipulating the idea of a stock image being "a code without a message" by allowing messages to seep into the equation while still maintaining its status as a multipurpose image commodity. We're less concerned with the mode of production than with the conditions of circulation, which in our case is hopefully wide reaching.

Who is your audience?

Our audience is a perplexing crossover of tweens, art students, academics, pregnant women, Internet addicts, and culture industry professionals. DIS has generated a lot of loyalty, and many people have adopted a sense of DIS into their outlook. We love that. But as a web-based entity, our work proliferates on Google Image, garnering out of context and unsuspecting visitors daily.

Does your engagement with one another translate into an engagement with the public? How so?

Absolutely. When we launched, we realized very quickly that if an idea was interesting to the four or five of us, then probably it would be interesting to other people. Working alone, you don't have that certainty that your ideas are going to be of any interest to someone else. We also realized that we're not always right.

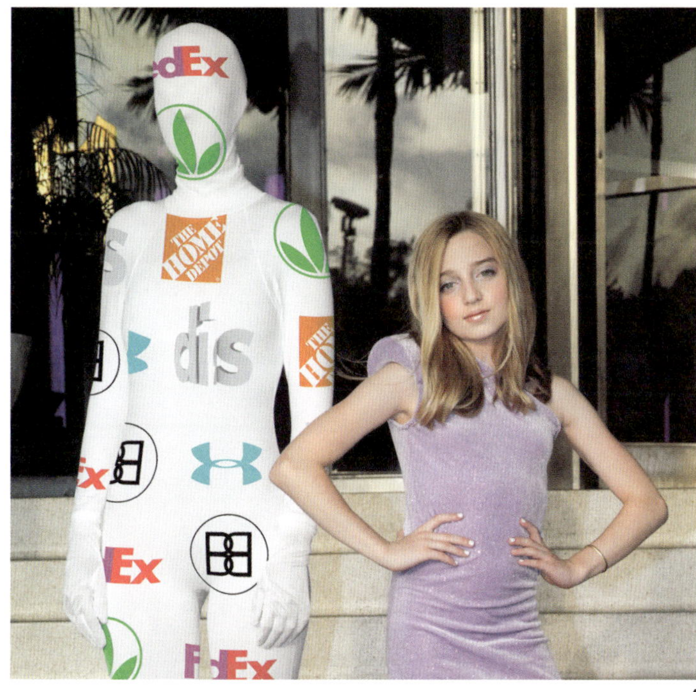

4

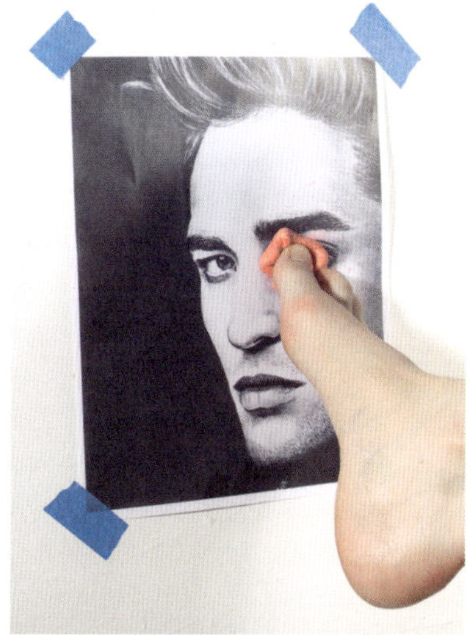

5

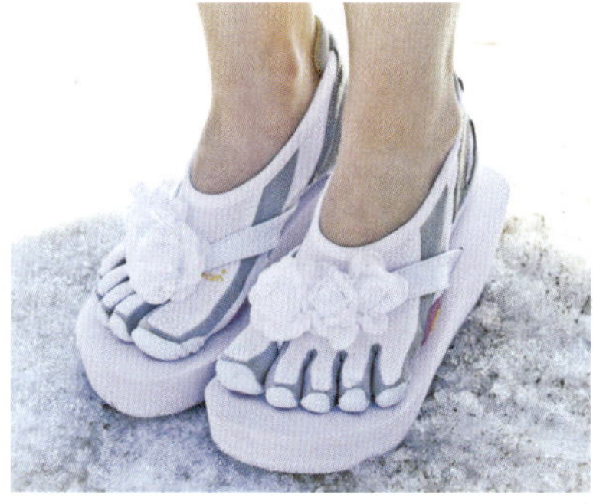

6

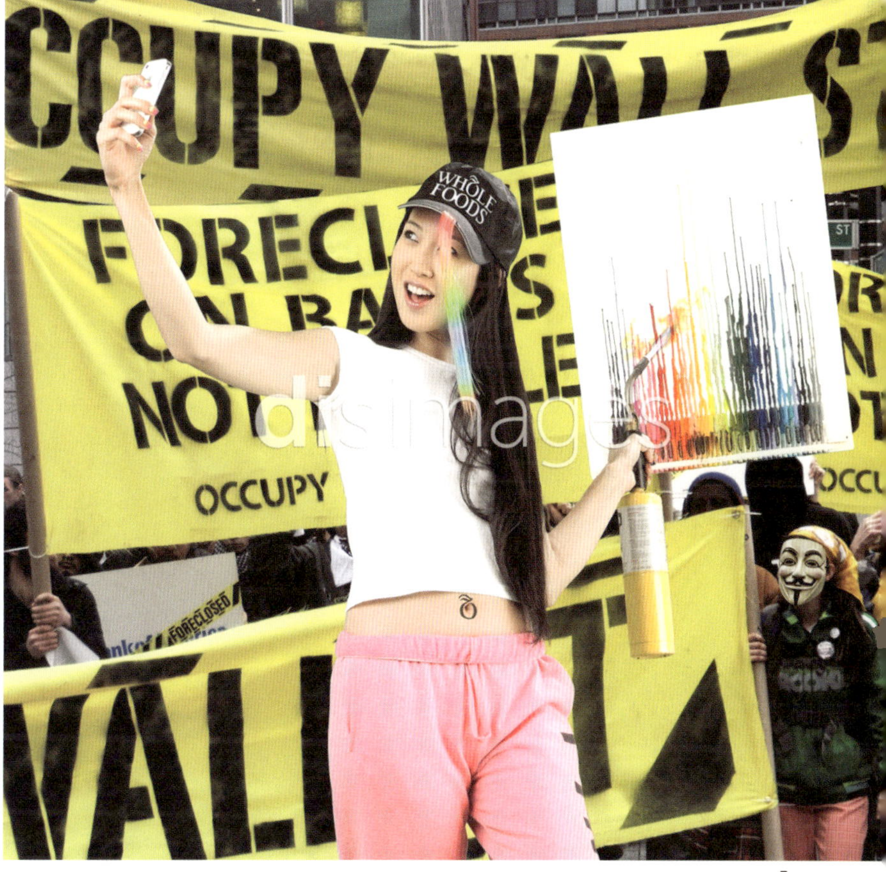

7

4 – Best Trends Forever, photograph, 2011

5 – DISability, photograph, 2012

6 – Shoes in Shoes, photograph, 2011

7 – DISimages: Gallery Girls by Jogging, photograph, 2013

8 – New in Stock, photograph, 2010

9 – DISimages: Gallerinas, photograph, 2013

10 – DISimages: Smiling at Art, photograph, 2013

opposite
11 – Wear to Bed, photograph, 2010

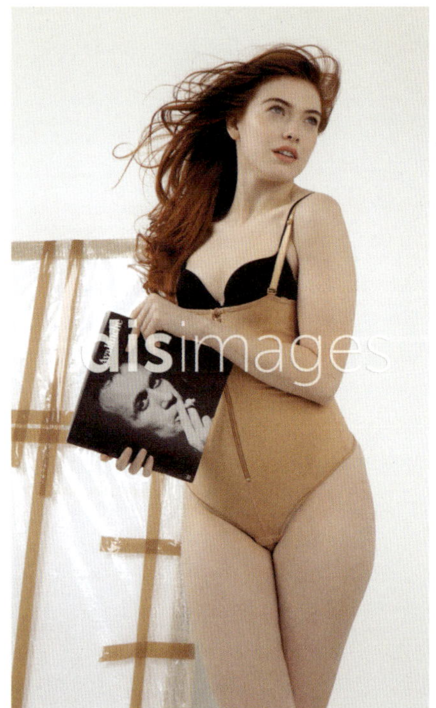

8

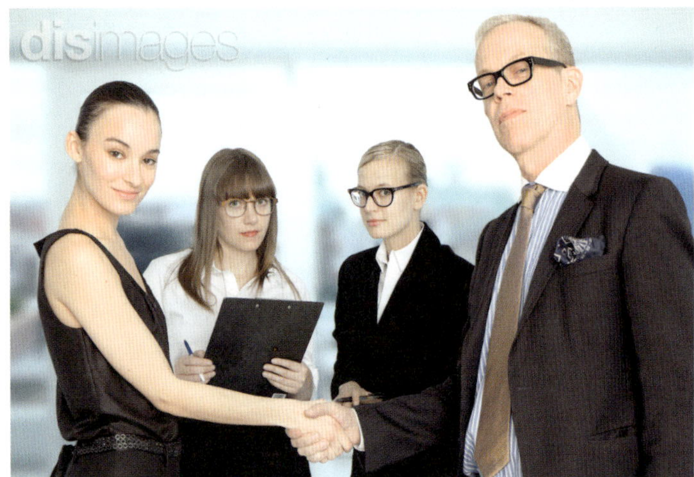

9

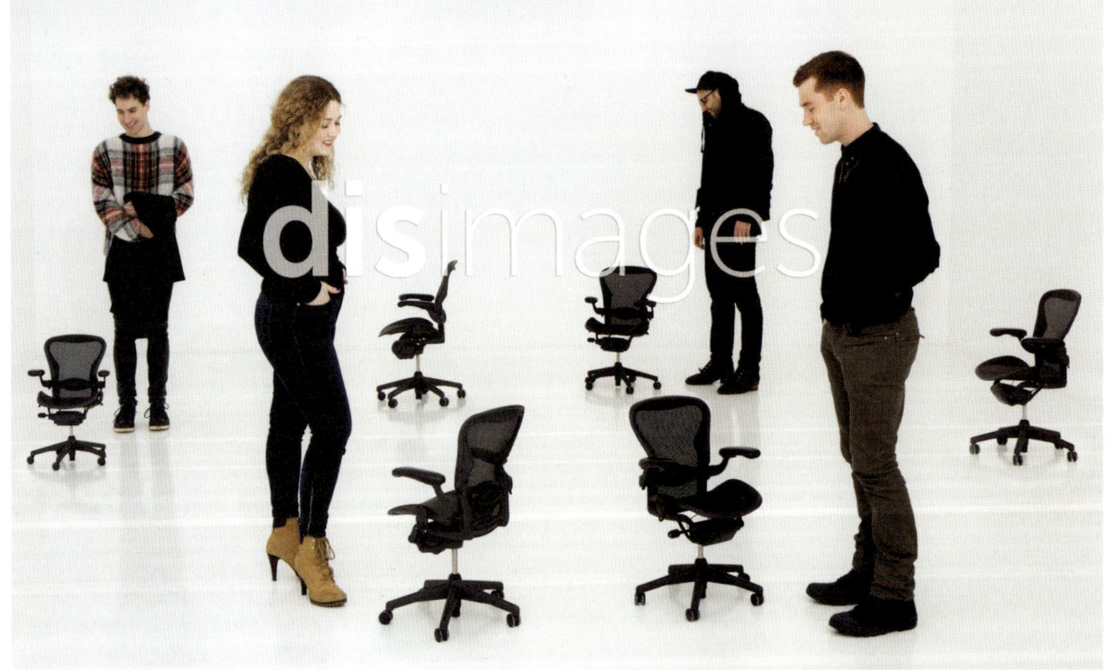

10

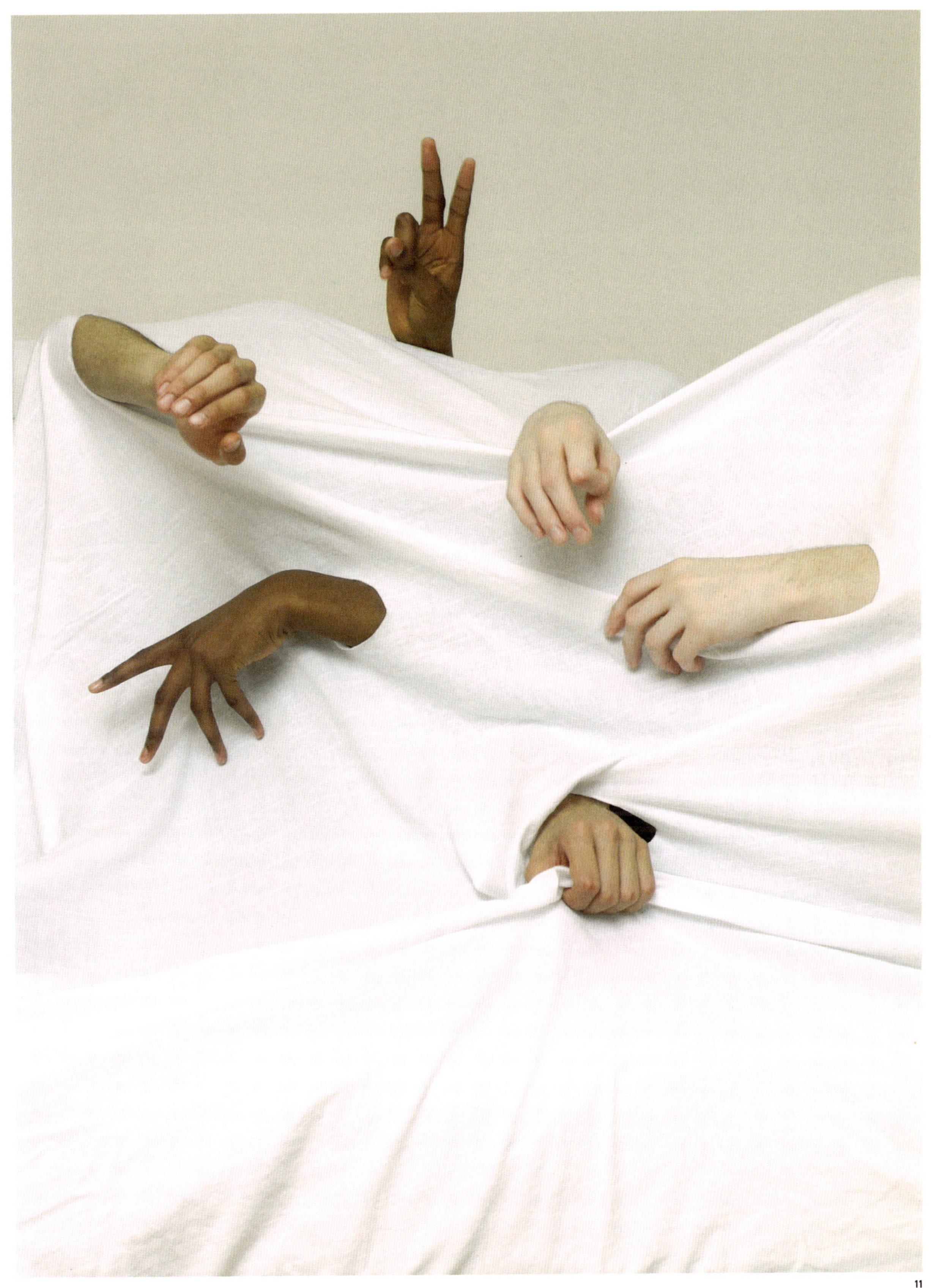

11

ACTIVE SINCE	CITY	WEBSITE
1998	Berlin, Germany	discotecaflamingstar.com

Discoteca Flaming Star

MEMBERS	ACTIVITIES	RECOMMENDED PUBLICATION
Cristina Gómez Barrio and Wolfgang Mayer	Performance, Public Performance, Painting / Sculpture / Installation	DISCOTECA FLAMING STAR, Mil Veras Mil Prinzessinnen Mil Centralias, Centro de Arte Dos de Mayo, Madrid, 2008

Mimicking a music band, Discoteca Flaming Star borrows symbols and rituals normally associated with glam and punk rock. The group's performances, fabrics, and installations are all aimed at the definition of a democratic open stage where the members can explore the mechanisms of aggregation and identification typical of youth subcultures.

Why work collaboratively?

We feel art is always made by more than one person, more than one gender, at more than one time; it is based on a dialogue with the world and the people around us, as well as the present, the dead, and the absent. We have the opportunity, the pleasure, and the excitement, which generates a stronger and bigger and different result than the simple joining of single parts or the input from the individuals participating in the collective.

This said, one should not idealize working in a collective—it has also an aspect of alienation. One has to continuously negotiate one's own individual longings in relation to the dynamic and needs of the collective process.

How do you determine membership? Does physical location matter in this regard?

DFS has no fixed concept of "membership." We think of this word in terms of a link, a body part, a fragment of a space. In our performances, this common space materializes temporally, enabled by artists, dancers, musicians, architects...

We understand our role in this structure as being one that keeps its possibilities alive, holding and losing control over it—it's a way of writing love letters to thousands of artists.

Within that structure and the experiences we make there, the two of us develop banners and "alfombras" (carpets) that expand and condense the existence of DFS.

The banners are pieces of fabric with painted text. They serve as backdrop curtains for many of the performances, as transformations within which disorders are formed into words. The texts are references—cryptic thoughts—we carry around for months. They represent concepts that reflect the relation of our art to the different layers of daily experience of artists and spectators.

The alfombras are spatial transformations that capture disorders and words. Grown out of the experience of performing, they are a scenography—a scenography of the writing that reflects its slippery, fragmentary essence. A space to stand on/in with the text: lyrics for found rugs, reading, lost in thoughts and memories, closer to the floor, woven among and in the ornaments.

If considered separately, how do your individual artistic practices contribute to or detract from your work as a group?

Our individual practices form the place from where we speak—also nonverbally. They mark the point of departure of our arguments, experiences, and desires within the collective.

It is difficult to say where the individual practice ends and the duet begins, where the duet falls silent and the collective arises.

How are decisions made?

Trusting each other and embracing the loss of control, either through conversation or silence, meeting live or via digital media.

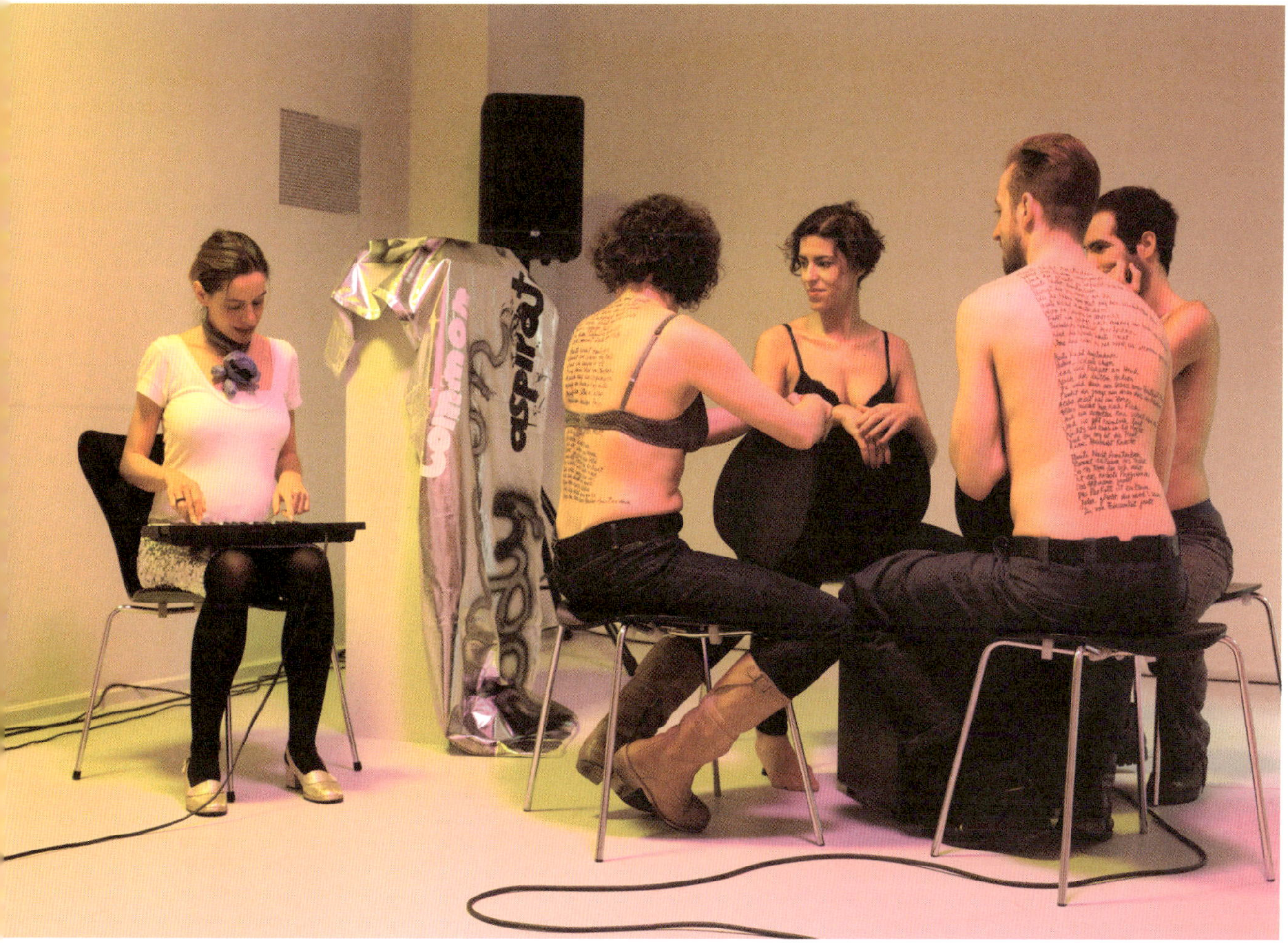

1

1 – 12x Alissa, Actually, performance, n.b.k., Berlin, 2010

2 – La Mano Gigante, musical, Basso, Berlin, 2011

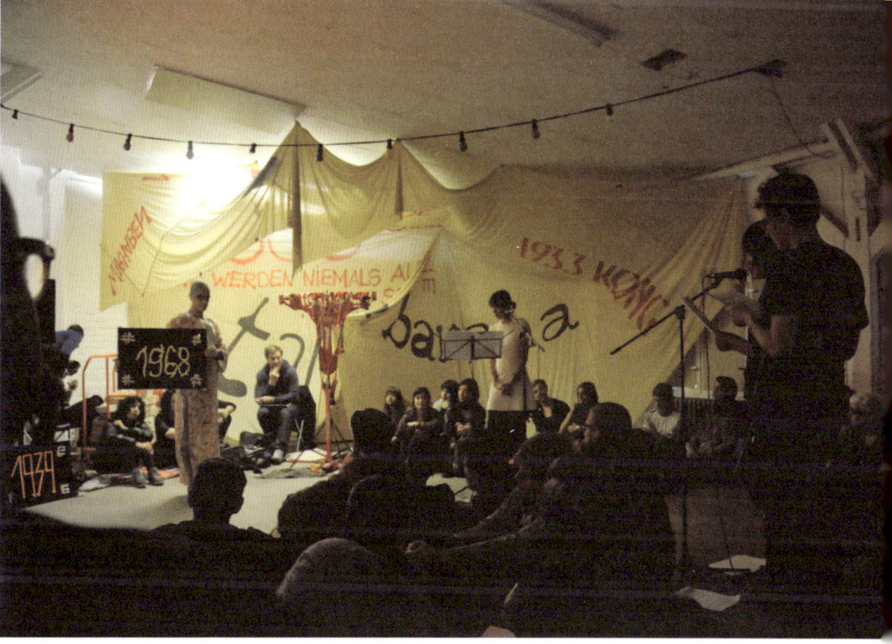

2

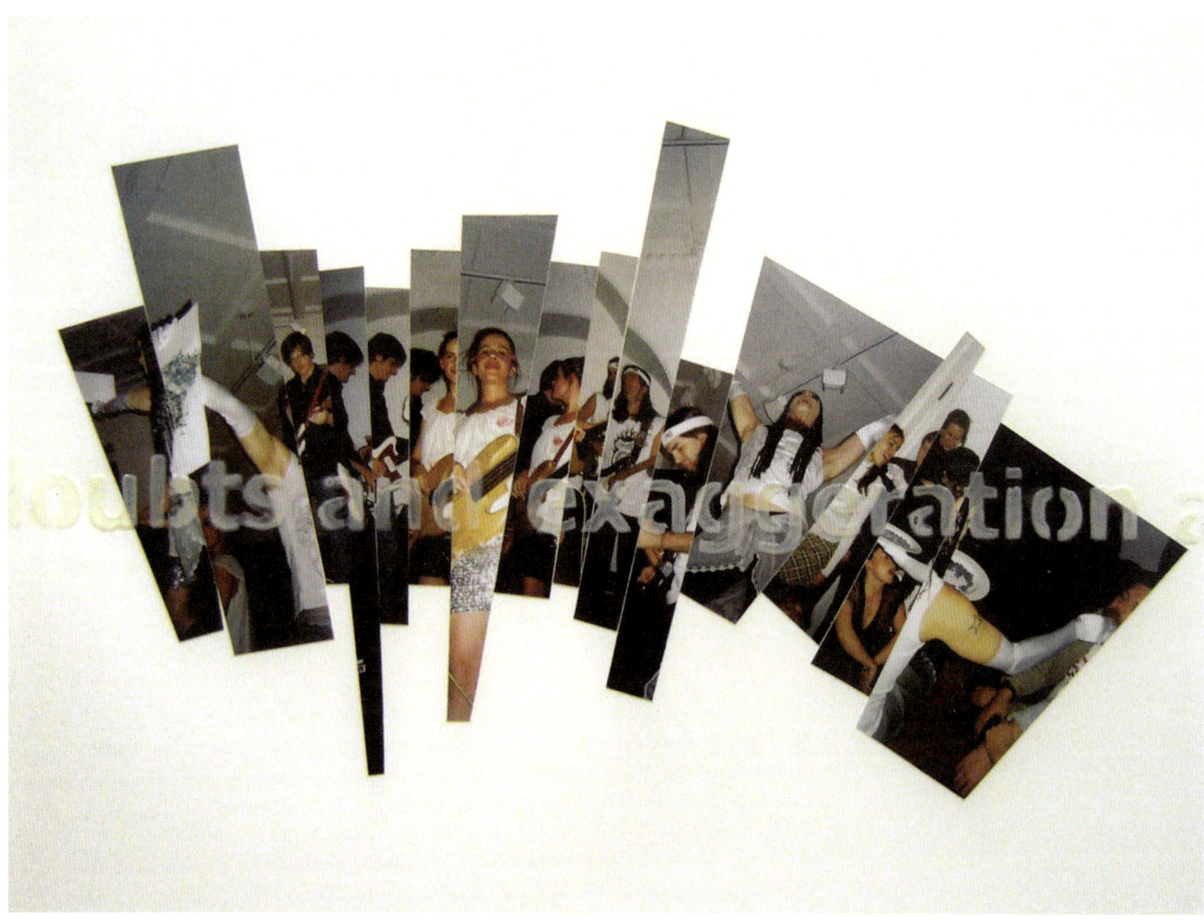

3

Does each of you have a clearly defined role? If so, what are some of each member's distinct responsibilities?

No. (*See question number two.*)

How important is each group member's individuality, both in terms of your artistic production and in terms of your relationship with the media? Does anonymity come into play?

There is an aspect of alienation involved in collective work, but it is more complex than taking the position of the individual within the collective or pitting individualism against collectivism.

This has been expressed so well by the artist Ulrike Müeller, a friend of ours, in the LTTR V Bulletin, 2006: "I feel anxious energy rushing through my body. I want to do meaningful things. My world is this stage. I will seek allies among the dead, the absent and fictitious. I'll embrace the absurd and the horrible. I'll propose yet another model and I'll push it further. I won't look away, and I insist for you to look at me. And I'll have to finally accept my need for recognition, because there is no way I can do this alone. Thanks for your companionship so far."

What is the relationship between your working methods and your art's "content"? In this sense, does technology tend to play more of a supporting role, or does it lead you in new directions?

By avoiding the idea of projects and project management, we do not materialize ideas, but work from/with the materials, the media, and the process itself. We think through them—filtering and contaminating one through the other. We might work on a performance following the parameters of filmmaking, and go back to where we began, always working with the knowledge and unknowledge of those involved. The process is based on trust and support of each participant—coordinated through very simple techniques of improvisation and notation. Content and method impregnate one another. DFS gravitates around a struggle to make something possible that seems impossible.

The revitalization of previous works or parts of them is one strong element, in the same way a singer works with a repertoire. We do so by simple operations of new layerings or reactivations of the existing work in another media or in other combinations. With this aspect of our work we want to insist in other chronologies further than those established

opposite
3 – La VERA: Favorite Performances 2001–2008, collage, 2008

4 – La Mano Gigante film still, 41 min., 2011

5 – La VERA: Wurfbanner 1, installation, 2008

6 – P P Piero und Was Dazwischen, installation, MACBA, Barcelona, 2009

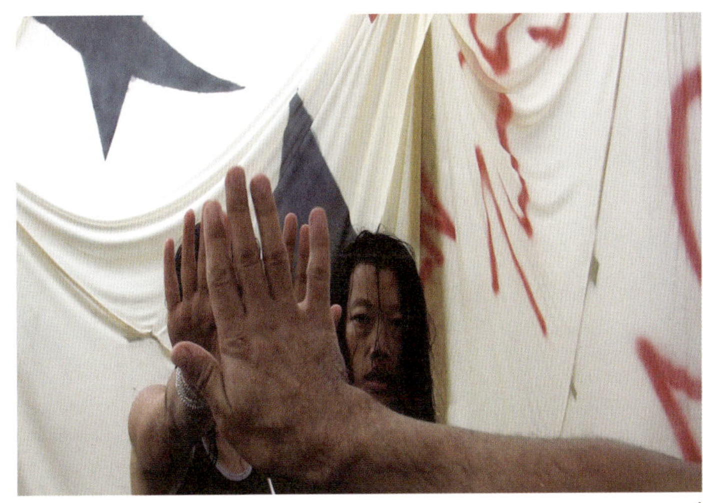

4

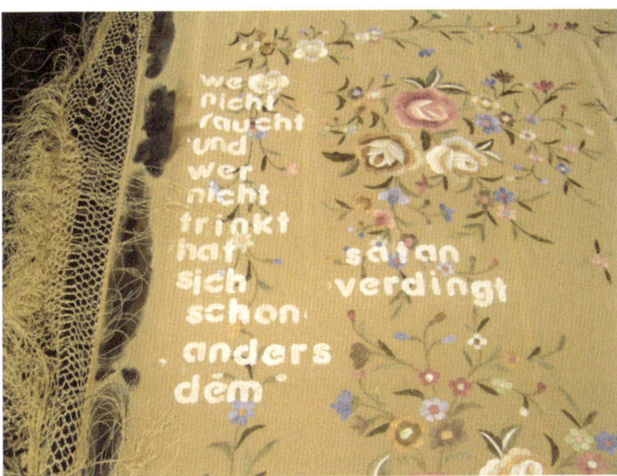

5

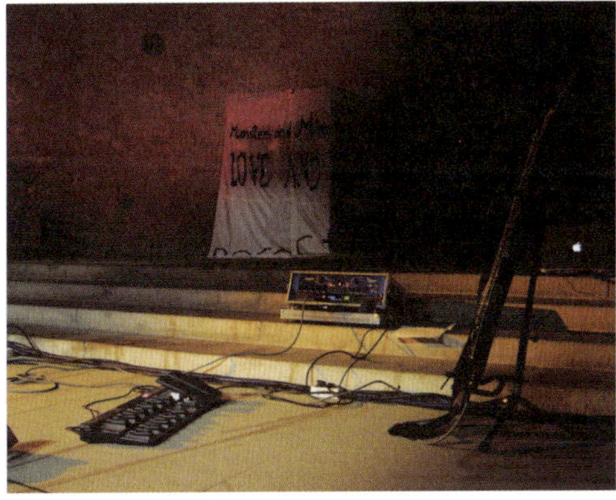

6

by seasons, by the need of the "latest." In this sense, the work of filmmaker Gregory J. Markopoulos has been very important and inspiring to us.

How does your collaboration relate to its cultural, institutional, and commercial contexts? In other words, how would you respond to those who call this a trend?

Your questions point toward the branding of collective work forms as an external imposed definition, which pushes it toward its commodification. All artistic practices are confronted with this, not only the collective ones. Our attempt in the face of this imposition is the insistence: "I am we are doing what I am we are doing while doing it"—an enunciation that our friend Gregg Bordowitz, a filmmaker, once formulated. With this, we want to insist on the legitimacy of every aspect of critical thinking and artistic ways of working beyond the material or immaterial product that might be the ultimate outcome.

This dilemma is very complex and very substantial to the system; every attempt to understand where we stand in these relationships is necessary and worthy. Our strategy includes fragility, accumulating layers of confusion, and insisting, insisting, and nevertheless insisting.

Who is your audience?

People who are interested in the world of contemporary visual art, queer thinkers, sexy desperates, poetry lovers, camp problems, Mrs. Contradiction, can't solve it, believe in it so you can dance to it, struggle and angel, toddlers, violets, etc.

Does your engagement with one another translate into an engagement with the public? How so?

We dearly hope so! In our field, artists are very often the audience of other artists. We try to work from this awareness and articulate it in the structure of the collective by being passionate and vulnerable, full of love and thoughts. We admire our audience and enjoy our dependency on them, hoping to seduce and estrange them. The spaces we try to create become complete only through our audience.

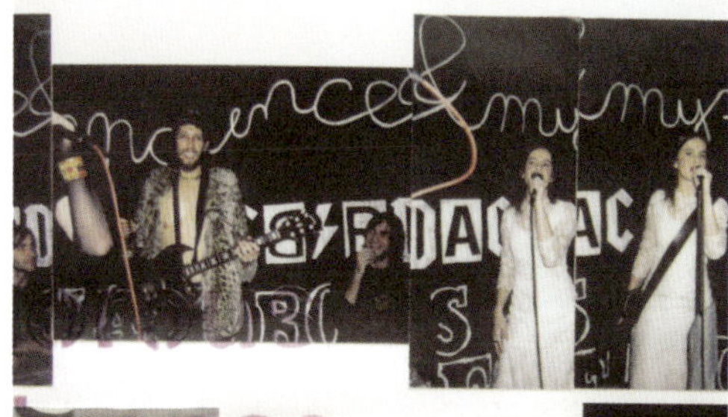

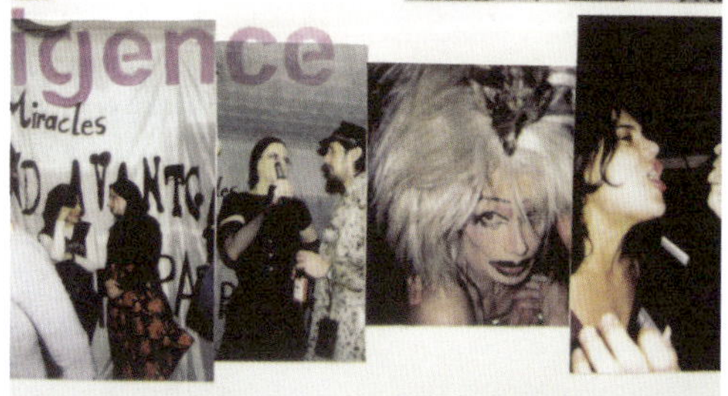

7

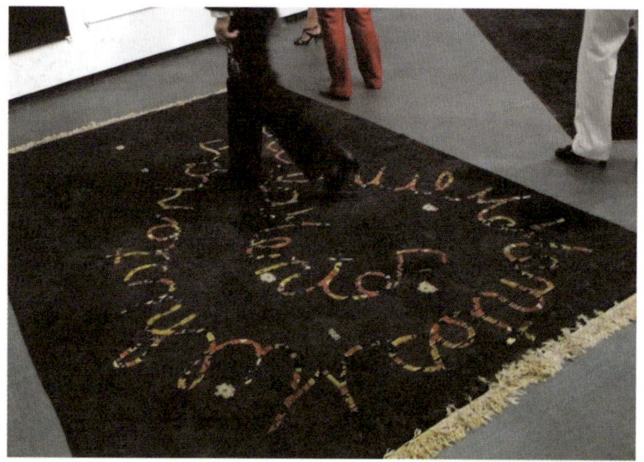

8

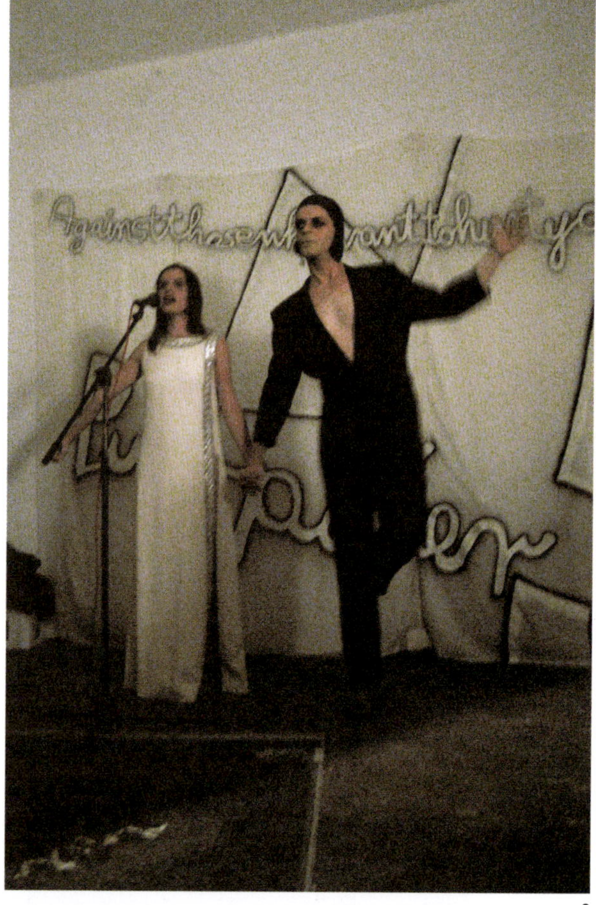

9

7 – Hardcore Karaoke: Favorite Performances 2001–2008, collage, 2008

8 – Alfombra #20, rug installation, Centro de Arte Dos de Mayo, Madrid, 2008

9 – Duett #1, performance, General Public, Berlin, 2006

10 – Banner Puto Poder (detail), banner, 2005, and Kronprinzessin Luise und Prinzessin Friederike, Film projection, 2004, Installation, Centro de Arte Dos de Mayo, Madrid, 2008

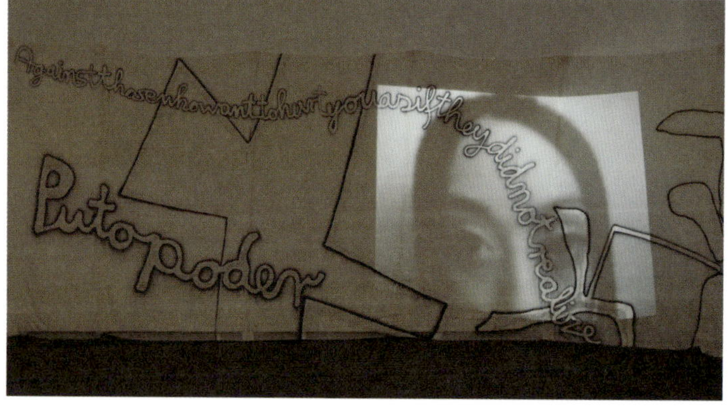

10

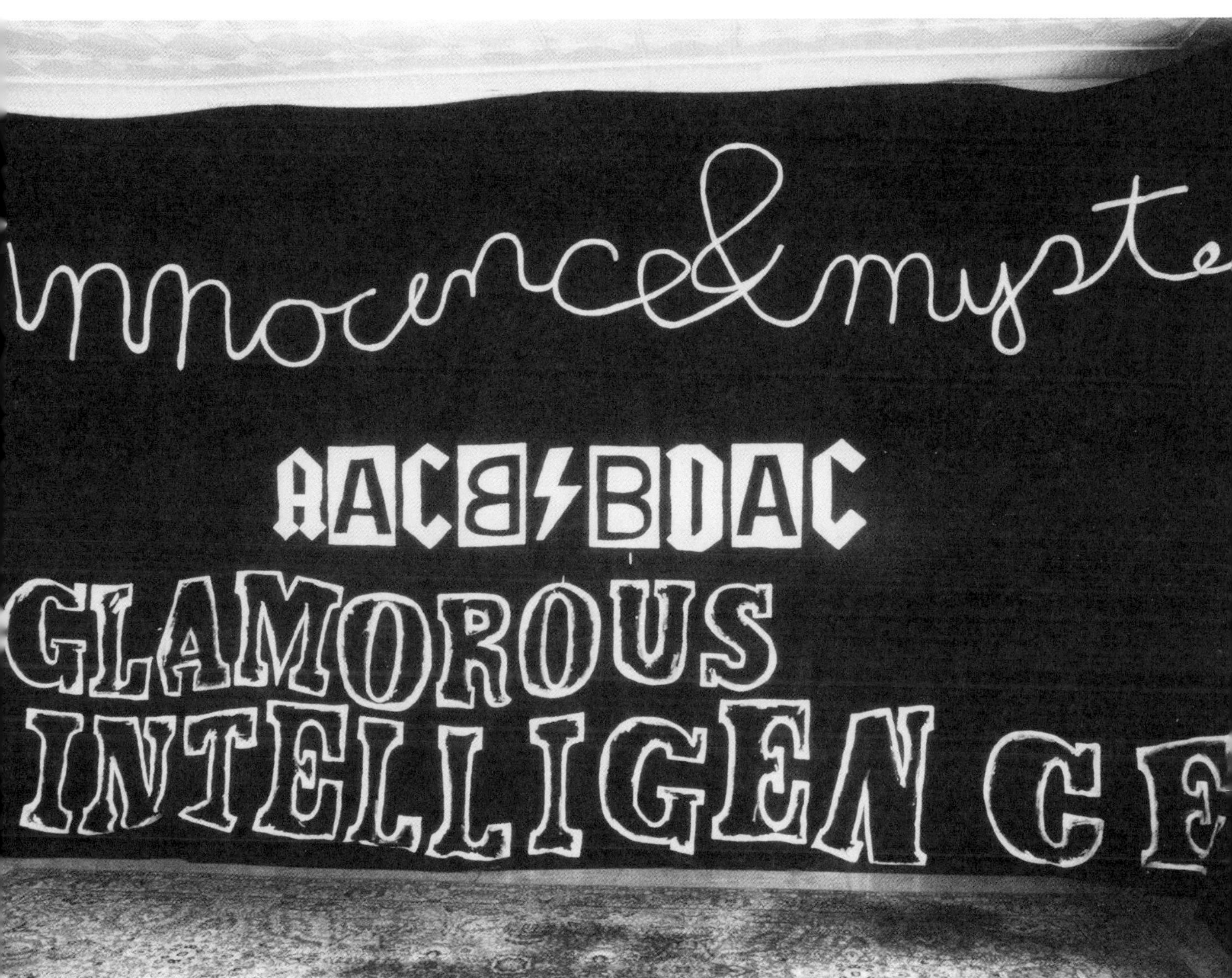

11

11 – Black Banner 1, banner installation, Parlour Projects, New York, 2003

ACTIVE SINCE	CITY	WEBSITE
1997	Buenos Aires, Argentina	facebook.com/grupoetcetera

Etcétera...

MEMBERS	ACTIVITIES	RECOMMENDED PUBLICATION
Variable depending on the time, the context, and the activity	Art in Demonstrations, Community Projects, Curating, "Escraches," Painting / Sculpture / Installation, Public Performance, Social Readymade, Urban Interventions	Jennifer Flores Sternad, Rhythm of Capital and the Theatre of Terror: The Errorist International, ETCETERA, in Lieven De Cauter, Ruben De Roo, and Karel Vanhaesebrouck (eds.), Art and Activism in the Age of Globalization, Nai, Rotterdam, 2011

Borrowing signs and symbols from past and contemporary forms of rebellion, Etcétera... builds installations and organizes cabarets around the concept of errorism, based on the provocative idea that "error" is the principle of order of reality. Investigating the role of protest and guerrilla activities in South America, collective's aim is to provoke immobile viewers to become aware of their social status and act, both in the art world and in the public sphere.

Why work collaboratively?

Etcétera...

Needs no definition...
Just imagine what comes after...
Etcétera... is the word that shatters language
Etcétera... closes and opens all speech
Etcétera... is in every language
As such, it's an ally anywhere in the world
Etcétera... is the present
Its members are without number
Etcétera... is singular and plural, feminine and masculine
Etcétera... adds subtracts divides and multiplies

For Etcétera... the collective work comes from the need for social representation. Etcétera... was born in the streets of Buenos Aires in the late nineties, when the global neoliberalist culture imposed a social scenario of individualism, social fragmentation, and competition. Toward the end of 1997, several artists, most around twenty years of age, all of whom were just beginning to work in poetry, theater, the visual arts, and music, all began to feel a desire to form a group, to be part of a movement. A movement that would bring them into contact with other social spheres and would bring art to the streets, into the spaces of social conflict, thereby moving these conflicts into areas where they had been previously silenced (the cultural institutions, the mass media, or the spectacles created by the culture industry).

How do you determine membership? Does physical location matter in this regard?

Collective membership occurs organically. In the past fifteen years, the core group (those who organize the actions) has been composed of about thirty people and more than a hundred around the periphery of the group (those people who are added or accompany the actions).

Not the "physical location," but the context and social circumstances are those that require the existence of the group. We say that Etcétera... enacts a "contextual practice," which means that its actions, works, or manifestos cannot be separated from the sociocultural context in which they arise. Each of the experiments carried out by the group arises from the same need: to put into question the very models of representation.

If considered separately, how do your individual artistic practices contribute to or detract from your work as a group?

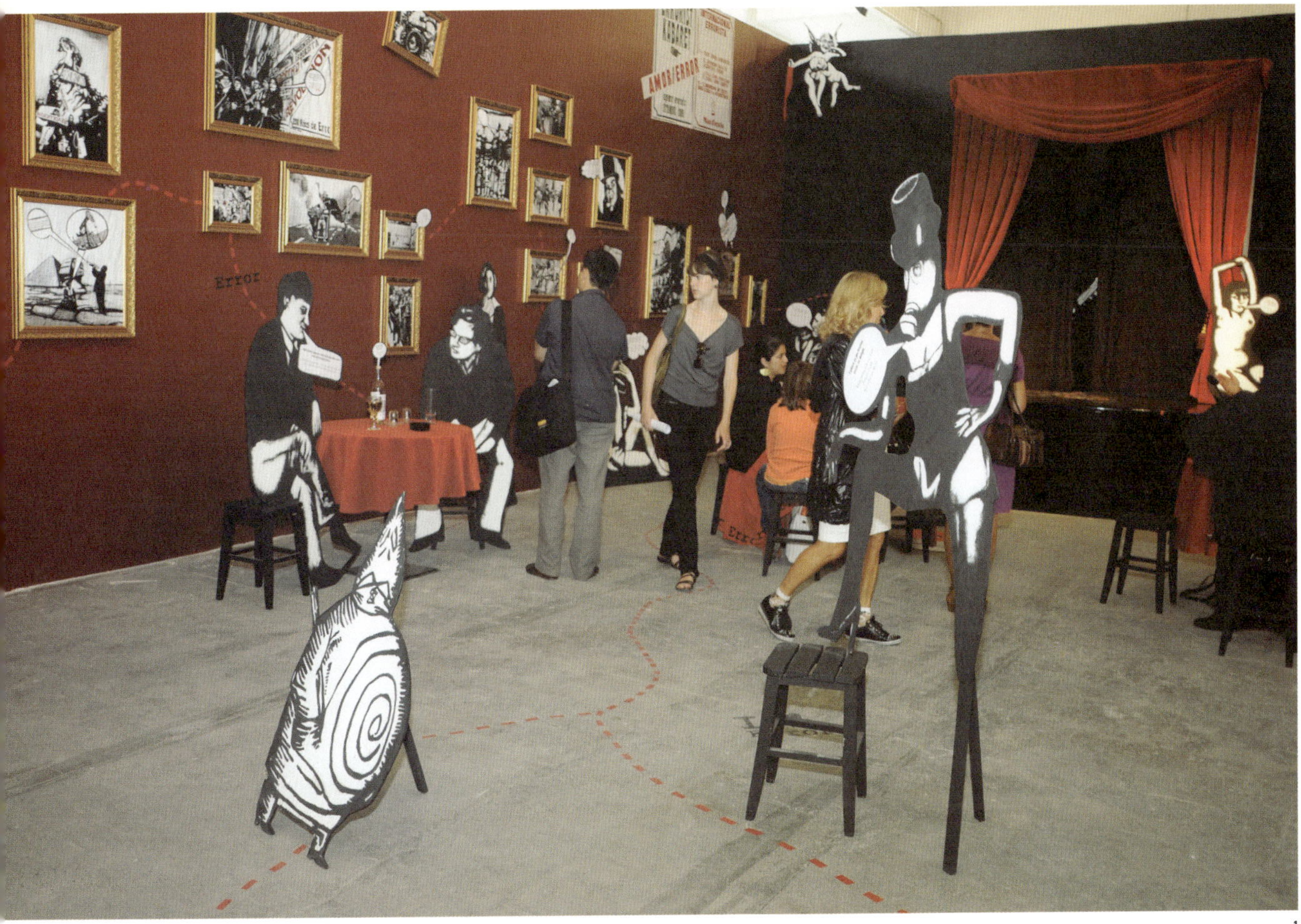

1

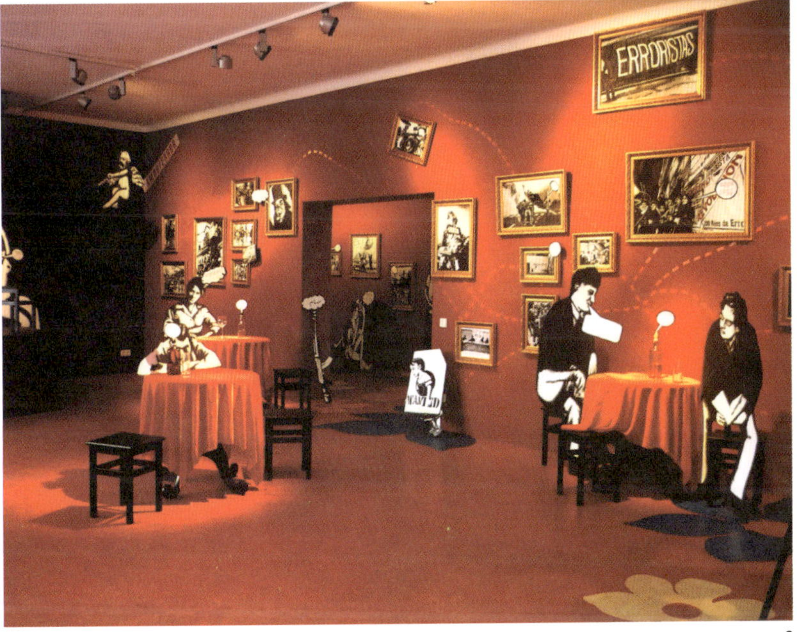

2

1 – Errorist Kabaret, installation, 11th Istanbul Biennial, Istanbul, 2009

2 – Errorist Kabaret, installation, 11th Istanbul Biennial, Istanbul, 2009

3 – Urban Errorist Cartography: Palestine and Estado de Israel Streets, street action, Buenos Aires, 2009

opposite
4 – Campaña Bicentenario Errorista, street action, Buenos Aires, 2010

opposite
5 – Con-Trabajo o (sin) Fonia, street action, Buenos Aires, 2005

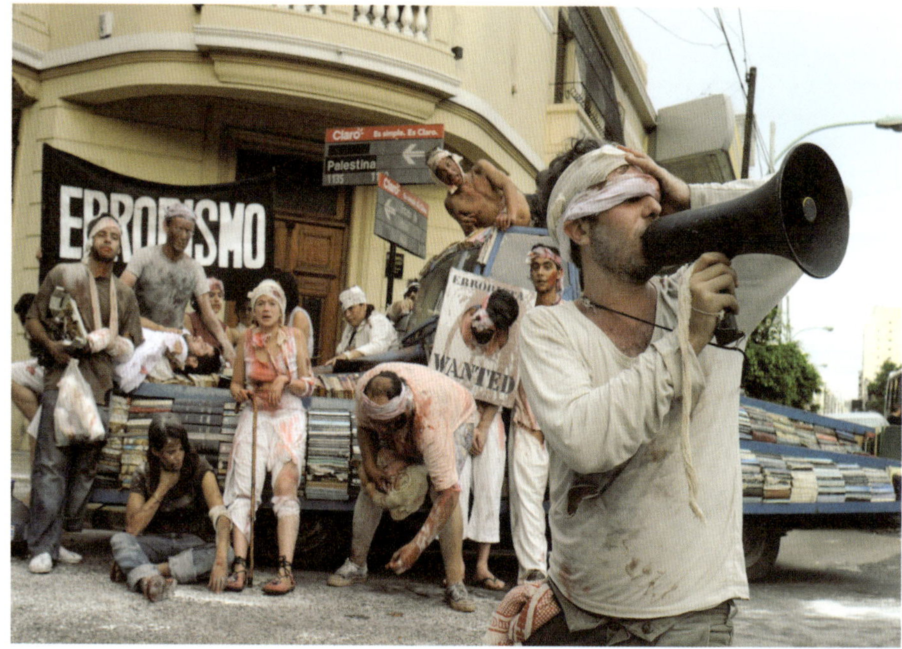

3

Etcétera . . . is a multidisciplinary group. For this reason precisely, each of the members who have passed through the group has provided different materials, techniques, and ideas: from philosophy to direct action, from poetry to theater, from contemporary art to the field of politics. The projects of each, as well as the personal development of each in his or her own field, is the basis of what we mean by "collective."

How are decisions made?

The decisions and representation models that have operated within the group have gone through different stages over time. At the beginning, in the late nineties, all decisions were based on the collective desire. More than "activists," our struggle was against social passivity.

Then Etcétera . . . went through a phase of organic militancy inside the human rights movement, participating in group discussions, assemblies, and all kinds of meetings. Later the group joined the organization Sons and Daughters of the Disappeared People (HIJOS), but the group had to explain and justify each action before an assembly of the human rights movement so it left the HIJOS.

In December 2001, there was the economic crisis (and resultant protests and riots arrived in Argentina). We used our distance from the organic militancy praxis to jump directly into the amazing autonomous experiences that the social movements started as a reaction to the economic crisis (and the crisis of representation).

Does each of you have a clearly defined role? If so, what are some of each member's distinct responsibilities?

The roles of each of the members have varied depending on the time, the mission, and the context. Of course, there are personal skills, and the idea of the collective is to enhance those skills. The defined roles have then emerged from the characteristics and interests of each member, but the idea is that everyone can teach and learn from the other comrades.

How important is each group member's individuality, both in terms of your artistic production and in terms of your relationship with the media? Does anonymity come into play?

In this sense, our works or actions may not often carry a personal signature, but rather a collective identity. Each of the members and former members has published books, exhibited, and performed in his or her own personal way. With the media, we often prefer to appear anonymous (if the idea is to be part of the social movement and not make personal profit from the struggle); in other cases we make it clear that the work is an Etcétera . . . action, but most of the time we choose surprise as our preferred method of action.

What is the relationship between your working methods and your art's "content"? In this sense, does technology tend to play more of a supporting role, or does it lead you in new directions?

We can't separate method and contents; we consider both part of the same unity.

We have developed a kind of "errorist" methodology for solving that issue, discovering that the content depends on the context, and the context is composed by the subjective effects of the objective social conditions.

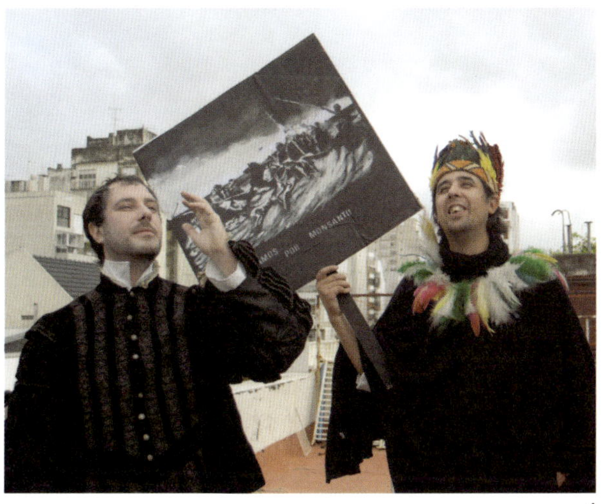

4

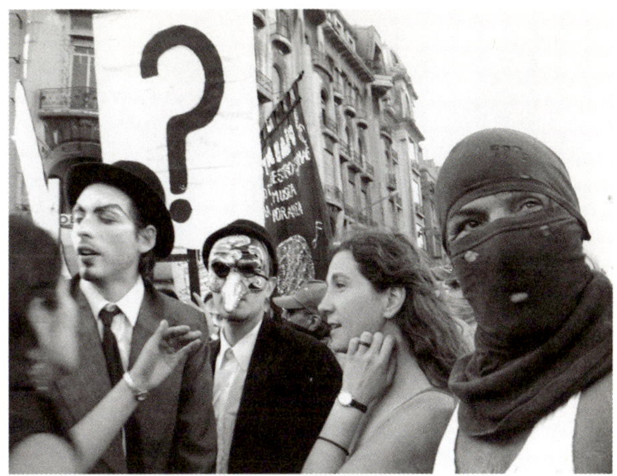

5

Etcétera . . . was founded in the analog era. We used cassettes and VHS and when the digital era arrived, the group adapted to the new technologies.

How does your collaboration relate to its cultural, institutional, and commercial contexts? In other words, how would you respond to those who call this a trend?

Since the beginning of its activity Etcétera . . . walks with one foot in the street and another in institutions (the first Etcétera . . . show inside an artistic institution was in 1998). Since then, the institutional participation has been constant as much as street activism. Etcétera . . . has participated in international exhibitions and biennials, and group and solo shows in independent alternative spaces, and also in commercial galleries. All this adds to the experience of militancy, activism, and street actions, making us stand in contrast to other groups that operate inside the institutional field.

Who is your audience?

Again, that depends on each context; if we make an action in a demonstration (there is not "audience"...), the public is thousands of people from different generations and social levels. If we make an exhibition in a gallery or museum, there will be the small (or sometimes large) audience who frequent such institutions. If we produce a scandal like the Mierdazo, the audience will be the thousands of people who watch it on the news or read about it in the newspapers. Many times we've felt bored in the mainstream visual arts where nobody cares about the audience. We don't like and don't feel comfortable working in that kind of bubble where the artists produce their works just for other artists, curators, and people involved in the same economic game or "club."

Does your engagement with one another translate into an engagement with the public? How so?

The commitment to various sectors, or social movements, revitalizes the artistic practice, transforms it into a relational art. These degrees of commitment are given based on ethics, a position of respect and support for each of these social subjects fighting for real change. Etcétera . . . uses our visibility and resources to spread a message that comes from other spheres of social life, looking for a collective participation in the construction of meaning. Social engagement for Etcétera . . . is how artists take an active role in the society in which they live. It's a call to change opportunism into accompaniment, individualism into collectivization and solidarity. Social engagement is to understand the role of the artist as a "congnitarian" worker inside the creative industry, and fight inside this own machine to change the relationships and to fight for better conditions.

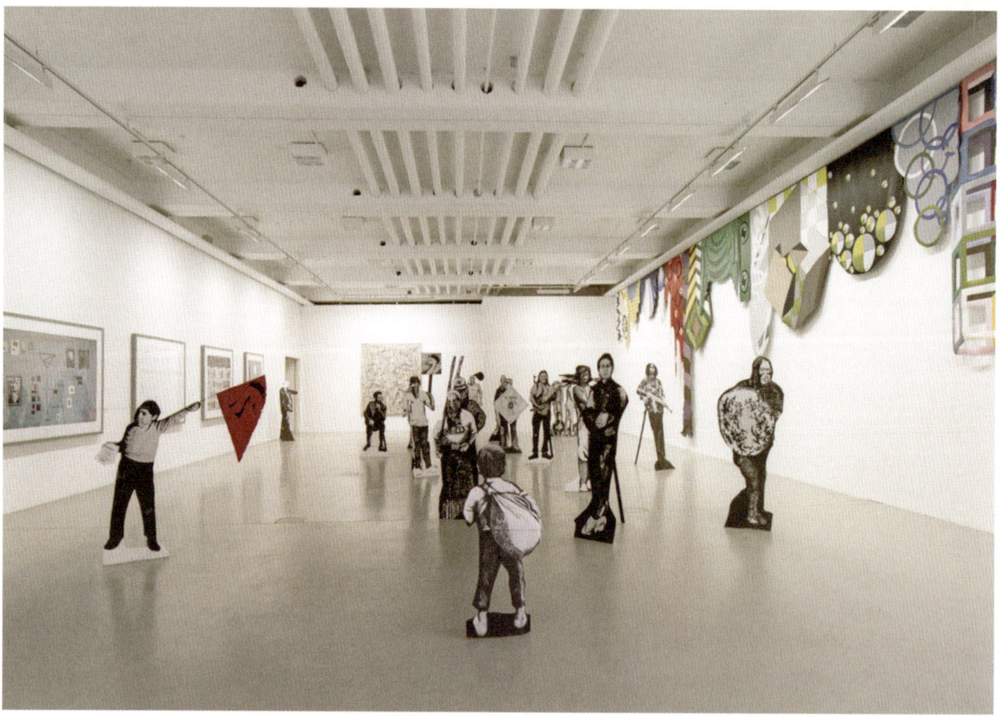

6

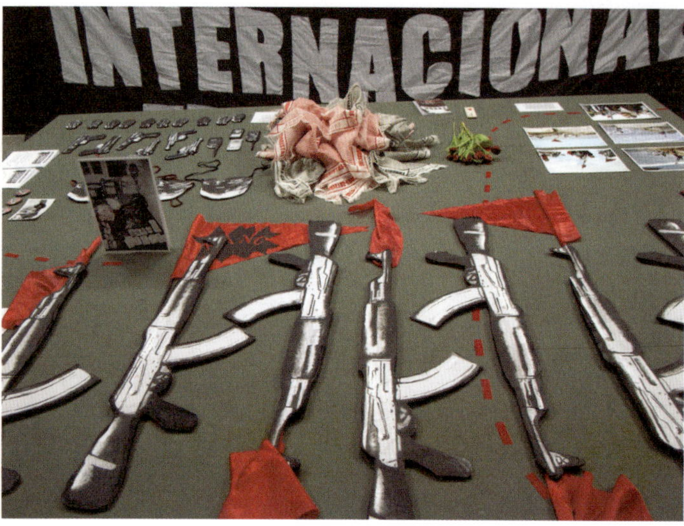

7

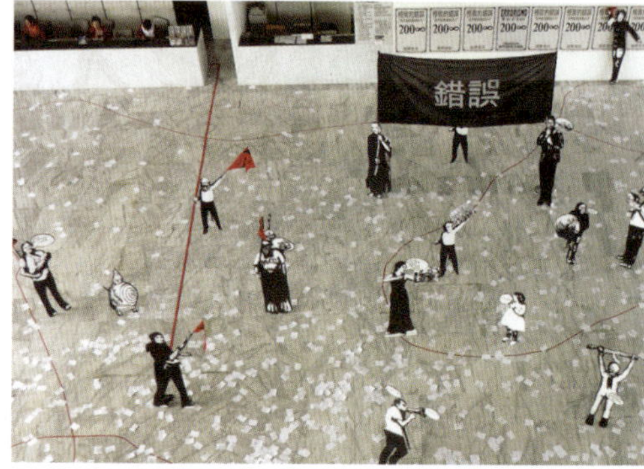

8

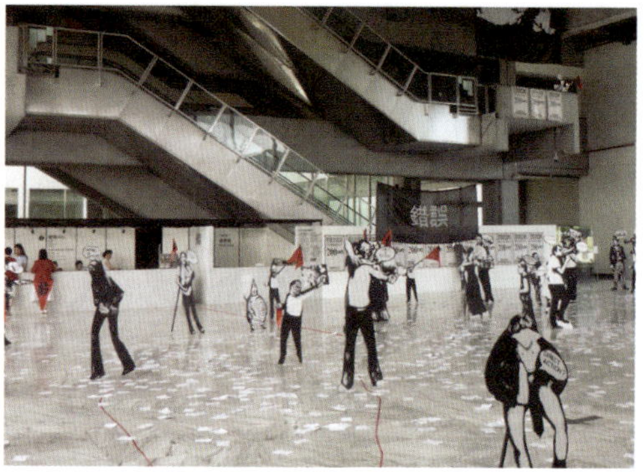

9

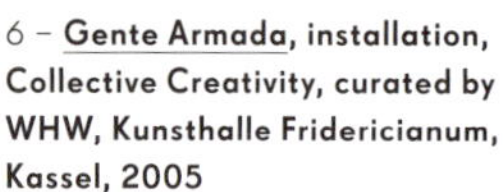

6 – Gente Armada, installation, Collective Creativity, curated by WHW, Kunsthalle Fridericianum, Kassel, 2005

7 – Error Arsenal: From the Relative Truth to the Absolute Error, installation, SMART Project Space, Amsterdam, 2011

8 – Todos Somos Erroristas, installation, Taipei Biennial, Taiwan, 2008

9 – Todos Somos Erroristas, installation, Taipei Biennial, Taiwan, 2008

opposite
10 – Gente Armada, public installation, Ludwig Museum, Cologne, 2004

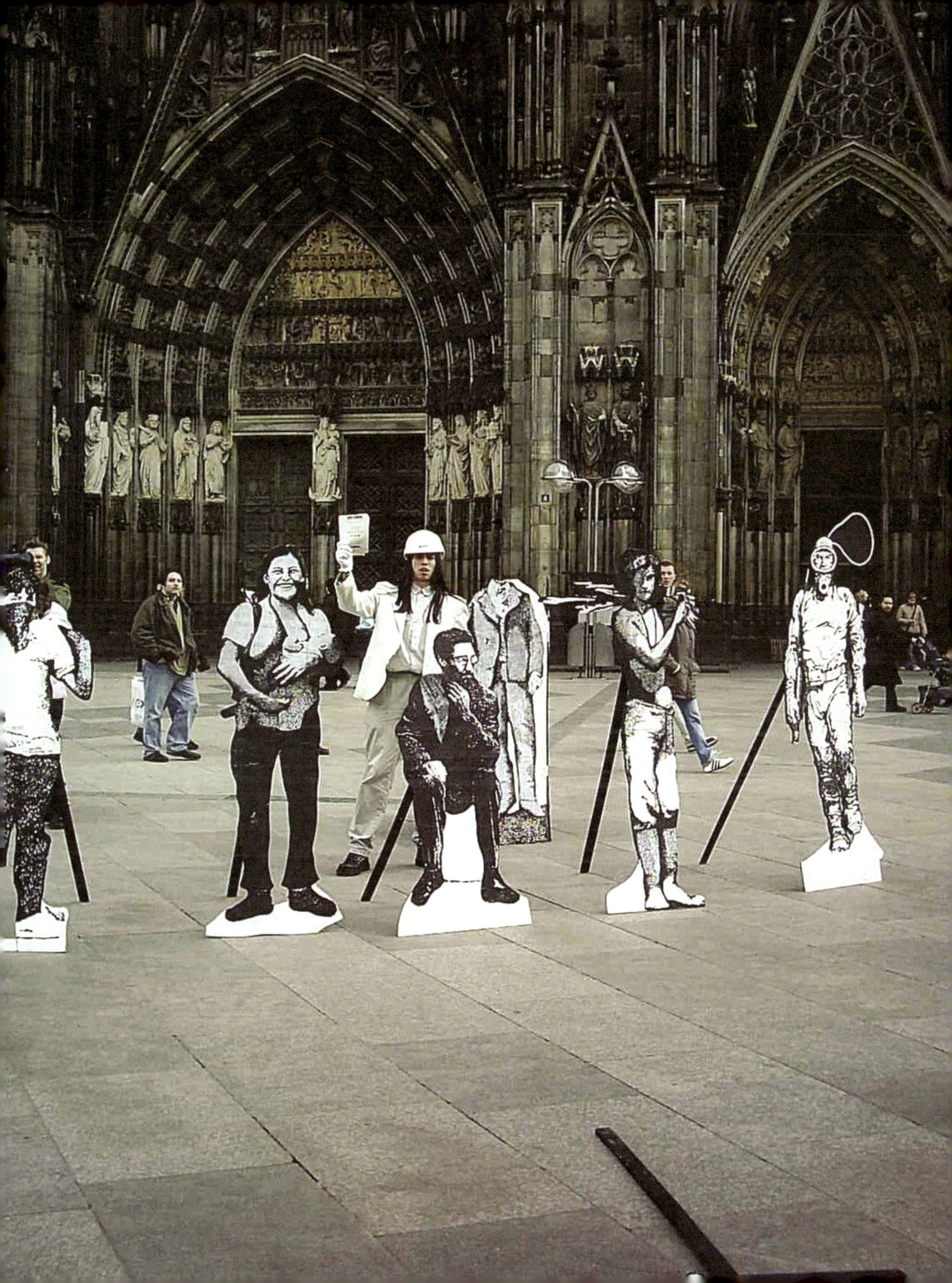

ACTIVE SINCE	CITY	WEBSITE
1995	New York, U.S.	010010111010101101.ORG

Eva and Franco Mattes

MEMBERS	ACTIVITIES	RECOMMENDED PUBLICATION
Eva and Franco Mattes	Internet Art, Urban Interventions	EVA AND FRANCO MATTES, Charta, Milan, 2009

Also known as 0100101110101101.ORG, this Italian duo develops critical research and productions based on anonymity and hacking. Its work comes to life both online and in the real world, through interventions, sabotage, and diversions that aim to overturn the power of corporations like Nike, cultural institutions like the Venice Bienniale, and religious institutions like the Vatican.

Why work collaboratively?

When we met we immediately started living together and traveling together; it felt natural to start working together. The first work we did is Stolen Pieces: a two-year performance in which we traveled around Europe and the United States stealing fragments of artworks from art museums.

How do you determine membership? Does physical location matter in this regard?

We're a couple; there is no membership. But most of our works are done collaboratively with the audience, though they may not be aware of it. Our last work, Emily's Video, compiles the reactions of random volunteers who replied to an online call to watch "the worst video ever." The original video has since been destroyed, so only these secondhand experiences are proof of its existence. So in a sense, the work is created by the audience rather than by us.

If considered separately, how do your individual artistic practices contribute to or detract from your work as a group?

We never work alone, so I don't know what I would do.

How are decisions made?

We must convince each other of the goodness of an idea, and it's harder than you'd think; we're more critical toward ourselves than toward others.

Does each of you have a clearly defined role? If so, what are some of each member's distinct responsibilities?

Everything is done pretty much by both of us.

How important is each group member's individuality, both in terms of your artistic production and in terms of your relationship with the media? Does anonymity come into play?

Neither of us has ever felt the urge to claim his or her individuality; we don't have huge egos.

What is the relationship between your working methods and your art's "content"? In this sense, does technology tend to play more of a supporting role, or does it lead you in new directions?

We use the Internet (as both a medium and a platform). The thing that immediately caught us is how on the Internet, given the right image, you could impersonate anybody; you could be an artist, a corporation, a serial killer, or the Pope. Since a lot of our works are based on impersonating others, it felt quite natural to use it.

For example, in one of our recent works, No Fun, I committed suicide in front of a public webcam-based chat room. I was hanging from the ceiling, in our apartment in Brooklyn, and random people could see the scene and react as they pleased. Eva was shooting a video with all the reactions.

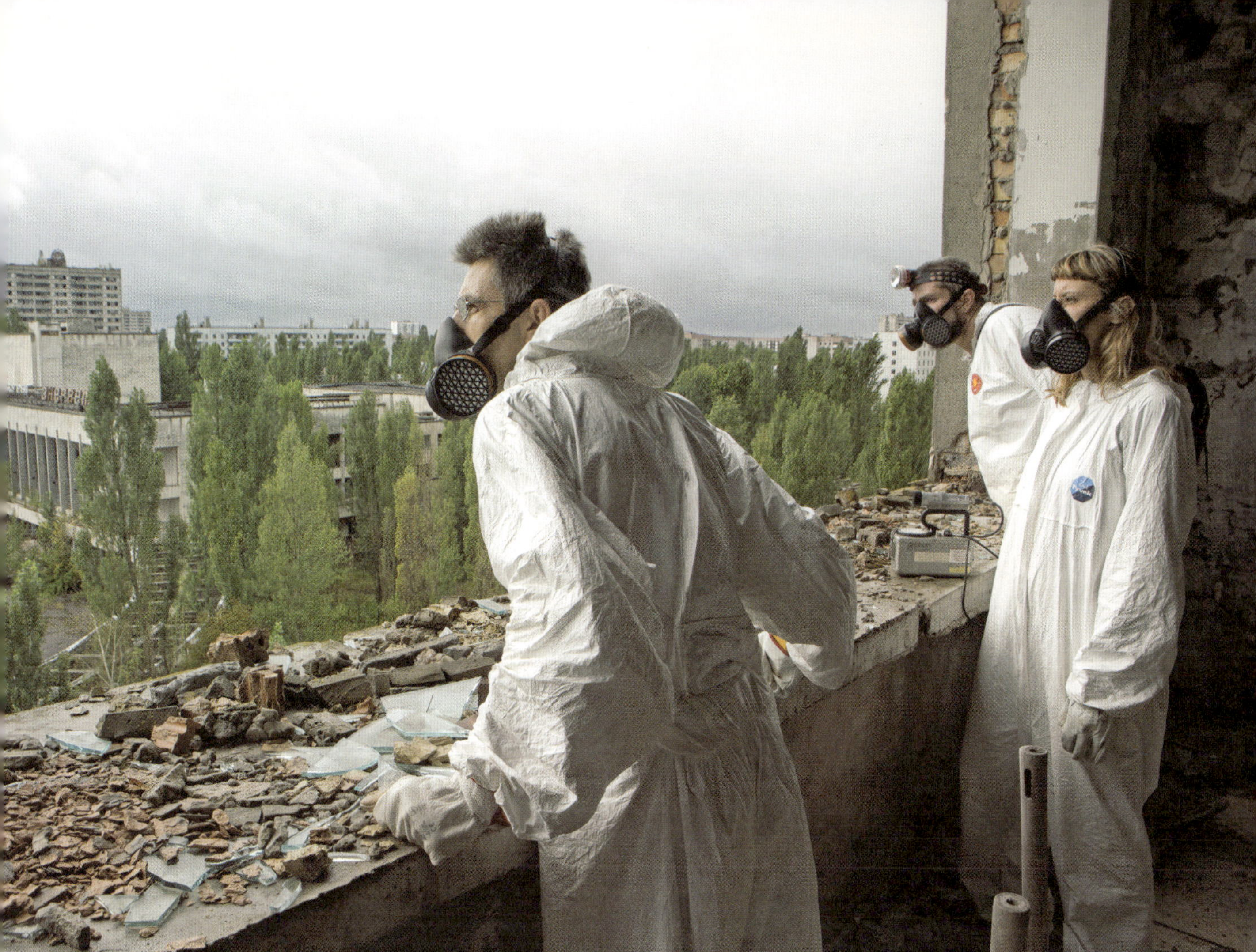

You could only realize such a work on the Internet, but on the other hand, I don't see it as a comment on technology; it's more about psychology.

How does your collaboration relate to its cultural, institutional, and commercial contexts? In other words, how would you respond to those who call this a trend?

Well, if it's a trend I think it's a good one, so let's hope it keeps trending.

Who is your audience?

Our ideal audience is our neighbor. A lot of our works require genuine reactions, so we try to involve people without them being necessarily aware of it. If you're walking down a street and see two guys in a garage shooting at each other, your reaction will be very different than attending a Chris Burden performance in a gallery.

Does your engagement with one another translate into an engagement with the public? How so?

In most of our works there is a first phase in which people are not aware they are part of an art piece; most of the time it involves some sort of impersonation, so they get involved in a very spontaneous way. We often incorporate their reactions in the final work. Once the piece is revealed, it's presented as an artwork and people became aware of its nature.

1 – Ryan C. Doyle and Eva and Franco Mattes, Plan C, public intervention, Chernobyl/Manchester, 2010

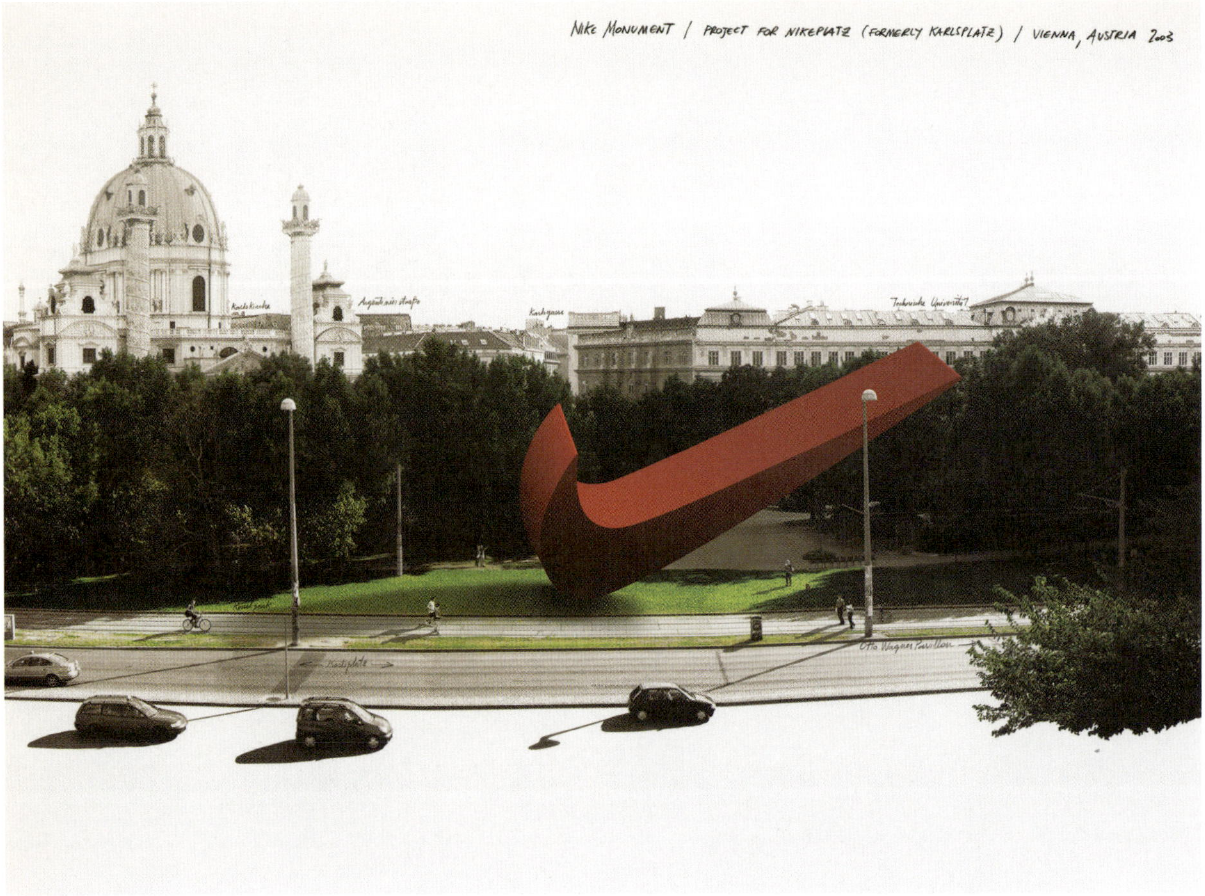

NIKE MONUMENT / PROJECT FOR NIKEPLATZ (FORMERLY KARLSPLATZ) / VIENNA, AUSTRIA 2003

2

2 – Project for the fake Nike Monument in Karlsplatz, print, 2003

3 – Fake Nike Infobox, installation view in Karlsplatz, Vienna, 2003

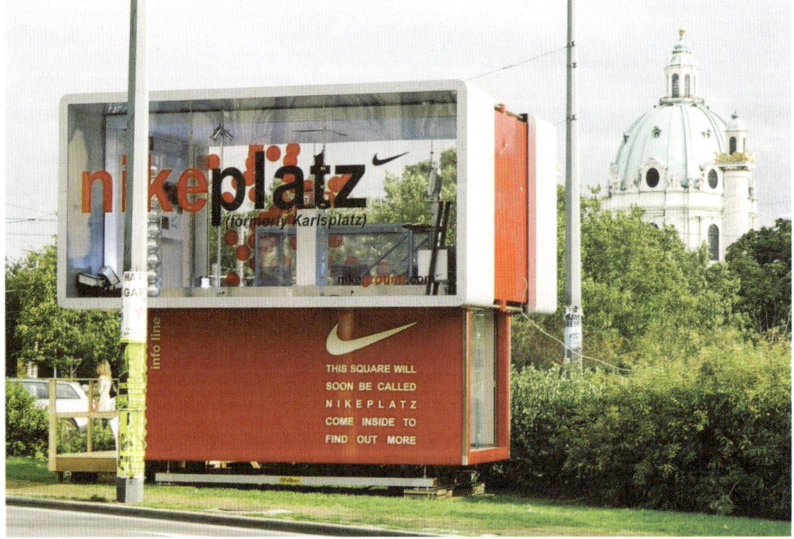

3

4 – No Fun, online performance/exhibition view, Carroll/Fletcher, London, 2010

5 – Perpetual Self Dis/Infecting Machine, custom-made computer infected with the virus Biennale.py, 2001–2004

6 – Copy of Jodi.org, website, 1999

7 – Colorless, Odorless and Tasteless, arcade game modified to fit an engine that emits carbon monoxide as the player accelerates, 2011

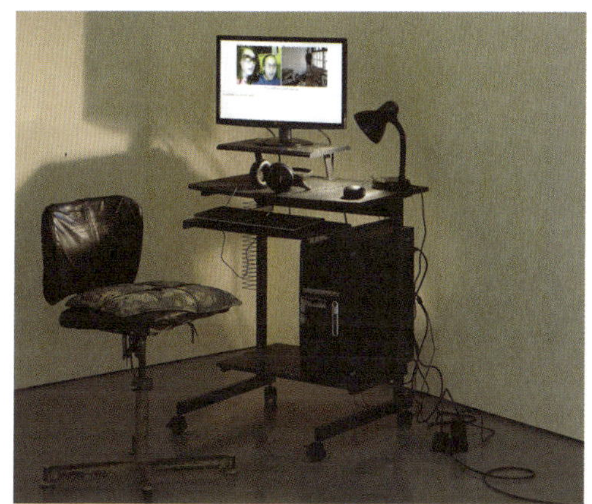

4

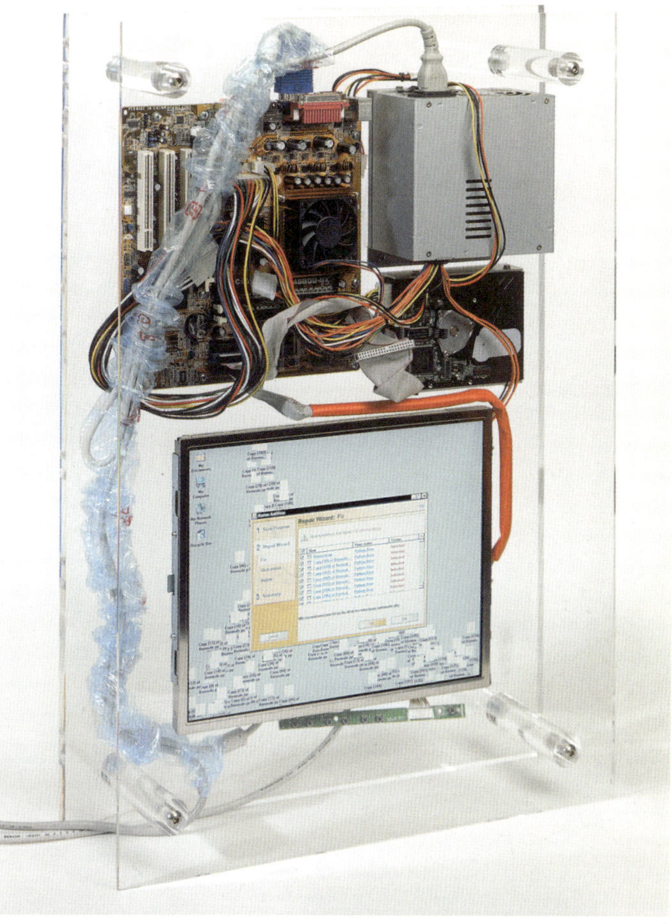

5

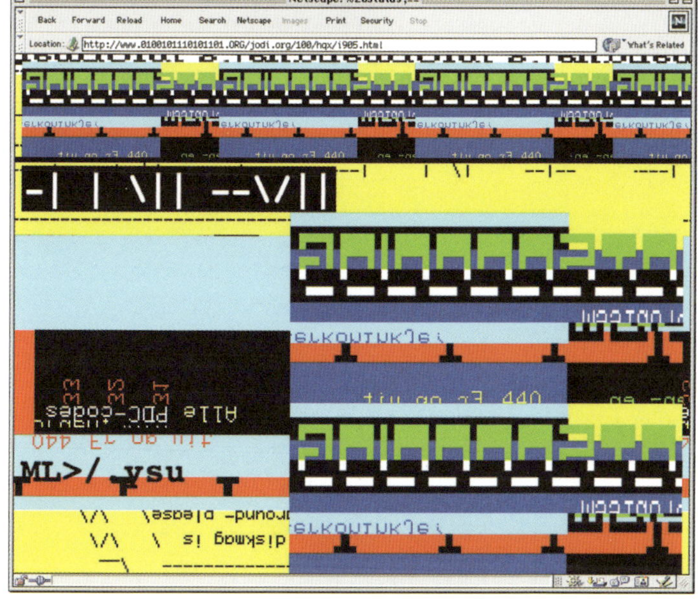

6

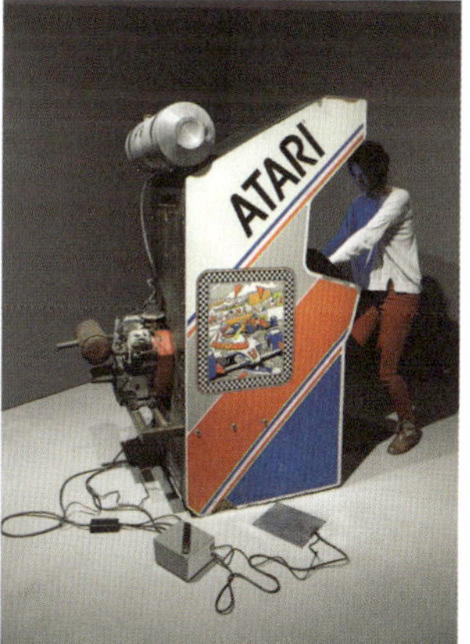

7

8 – <u>An Ordinary Building</u>, public installation, Viterbo, 2006

9 – <u>An Ordinary Building</u>, street sign, 2006

10 – <u>Bagless Canister Cyclonic Vacuum</u>, public billboard, Ljubljana, 2009

11 – <u>United We Stand</u>, public installation, Via Irnerio, Bologna, 2005

opposite
12 – <u>United We Stand</u>, poster, 2005

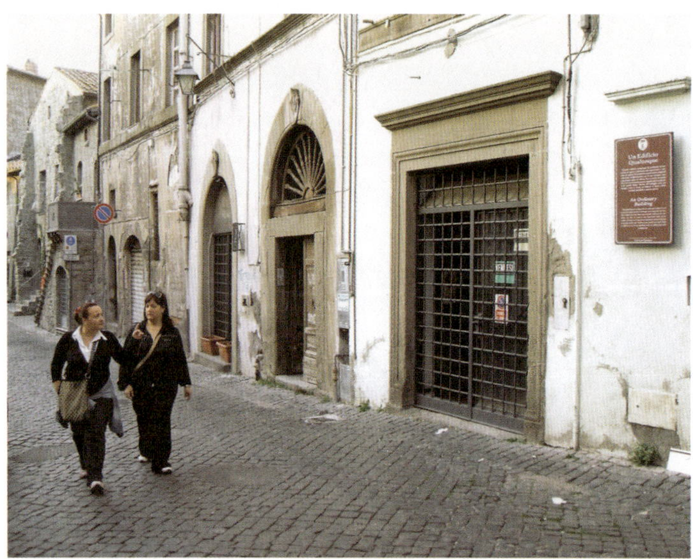

8

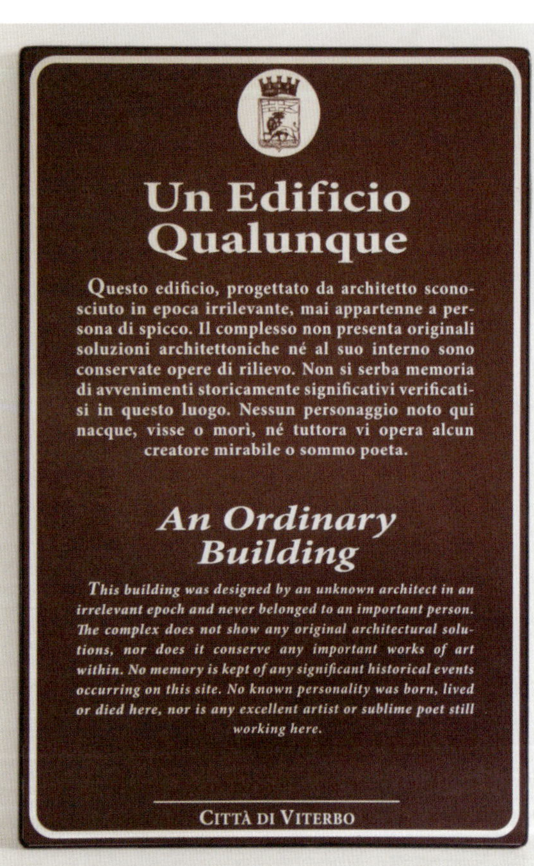

9

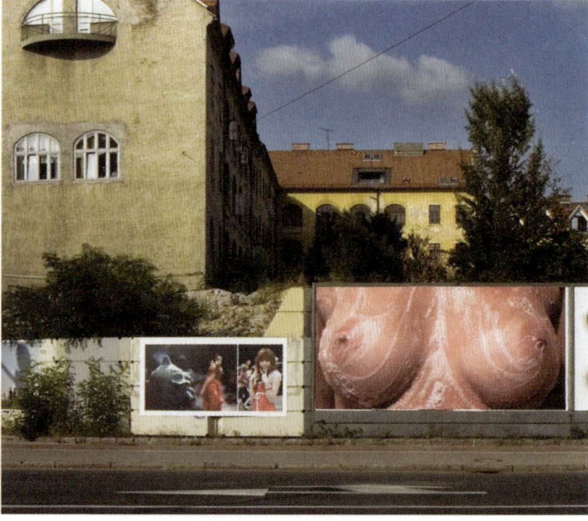

10

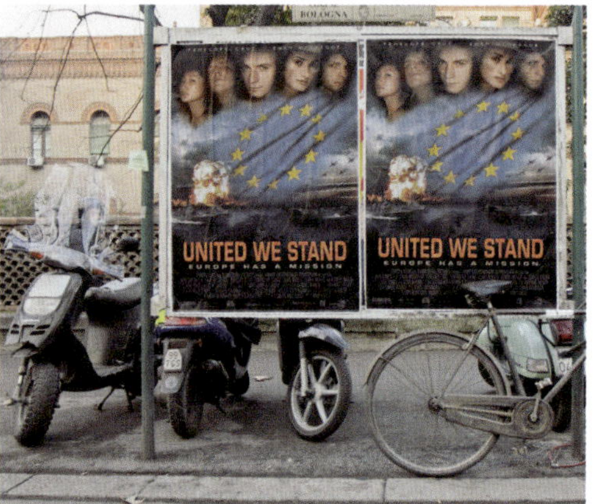

11

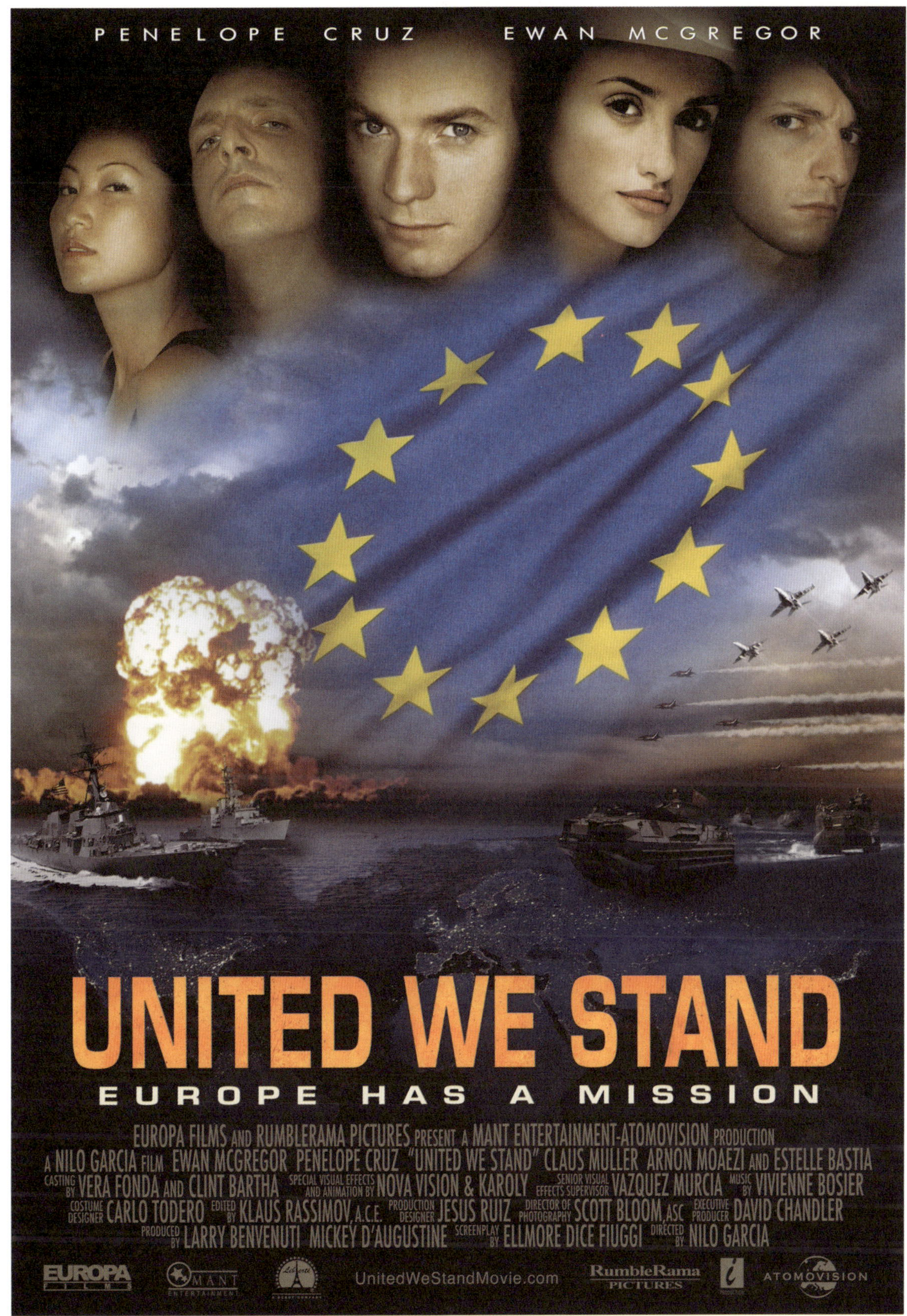
PENELOPE CRUZ EWAN MCGREGOR
UNITED WE STAND
EUROPE HAS A MISSION
EUROPA FILMS AND RUMBLERAMA PICTURES PRESENT A MANT ENTERTAINMENT-ATOMOVISION PRODUCTION
A NILO GARCIA FILM EWAN MCGREGOR PENELOPE CRUZ "UNITED WE STAND" CLAUS MULLER ARNON MOAEZI AND ESTELLE BASTIA
CASTING BY VERA FONDA AND CLINT BARTHA SPECIAL VISUAL EFFECTS AND ANIMATION BY NOVA VISION & KAROLY SENIOR VISUAL EFFECTS SUPERVISOR VAZQUEZ MURCIA MUSIC BY VIVIENNE BOSIER
COSTUME DESIGNER CARLO TODERO EDITED BY KLAUS RASSIMOV, A.C.E. PRODUCTION DESIGNER JESUS RUIZ DIRECTOR OF PHOTOGRAPHY SCOTT BLOOM, ASC EXECUTIVE PRODUCER DAVID CHANDLER
PRODUCED BY LARRY BENVENUTI MICKEY D'AUGUSTINE SCREENPLAY BY ELLMORE DICE FIUGGI DIRECTED BY NILO GARCIA
EUROPA FILMS
MANT ENTERTAINMENT
UnitedWeStandMovie.com
RumbleRama PICTURES
ATOMOVISION

12

ACTIVE SINCE	CITY	WEBSITE
2004	Los Angeles, U.S.	fallenfruit.org

Fallen Fruit

MEMBERS	ACTIVITIES	RECOMMENDED PUBLICATION
David Burns, Matias Viegener, and Austin Young	Community Projects, Public Performance, Urban Interventions	Matias Viegener, Fallen Fruit, Cabinet, no. 23, Fall 2006

Focusing on fruit to address wider ecological and social issues, Fallen Fruit organizes community projects, public interventions, and culinary workshops involving local communities. The idea is to use fruit, a universal language, as a symbol of aggregation and democracy and to develop in the audience the civic sense of protection, valuation, and respect of nature.

Why work collaboratively?

Fallen Fruit was founded by David Burns, Matias Viegener, and Austin Young as a result of a call for projects or ideas that was put forward by the Journal Of Aesthetics & Protest in 2004. We are friends and live in the same neighborhood and had previously worked on a couple of video art projects together. Fallen Fruit was meant to be a one-off art project that generated a manifesto text, a hand-drawn map, and a series of photographs about the idea of public space and public fruit.

We thought about the place we live and about what we had in common. We all knew about different fruit trees in the neighborhood and discussed if it was legal or illegal to pick this fruit in public space. Ultimately, we wondered what if the world was about sharing? What if every neighborhood was a communal garden and for a resource for the people who lived there (as much as the stranger or passerby)? What if we made a proclamation to the world that announced that the public is a resource that is overlooked? Could we create a collaborative public art project about radical inclusion?

Basically, Fallen Fruit is a collaboration that developed organically over time. Theses ideas sparked our imagination and we decided to continue developing this project. As a result, it changed the way we see the world.

How do you determine membership? Does physical location matter in this regard?

Everyone who participates is a collaborator. Fallen Fruit is a public art project in every expression of the idea we can imagine. We have always erased the artist/viewer relationship. For example, all of the Public Fruit Jams are coauthored; participants negotiate the jam recipes and never write them down. The combinations are determined by what people bring from their local streets or their own backyards. Meyer lemon, fig, and lavender. Grapefruit, mint, and lime. Bitter orange, kumquat, tangerine. There is no money exchanged in any Fallen Fruit project and everything needed is provided. The stranger and the passerby are equal participants with the grandmothers and neighbors from down the street. We believe everyone is an expert on the place they grew up. Everyone is an expert on the flavor of a strawberry. Everything is created by generosity and goodwill.

If considered separately, how do your individual artistic practices contribute to or detract from your work as a group?

A push and pull of opinions, personal philosophies, and a combining of our distinct practices has created a successful collaboration. We bring different perspectives, knowledge, and technical expertise to the group, and through the process of working together, these individual contributions become "Fallen Fruit."

How are decisions made?

As individuals, we have strong opinions. Basically we meet in person and throw around ideas. We argue for or against them. Often we work through this process deliberately to come to an agreement. It comes down to a two-thirds majority rule.

1 – City Hall / Fruit Protest, public action, 2005

2 – Street Bananas, public action, Los Angeles 2004

3 – Public Fruit Jam, community project, Los Angeles 2008

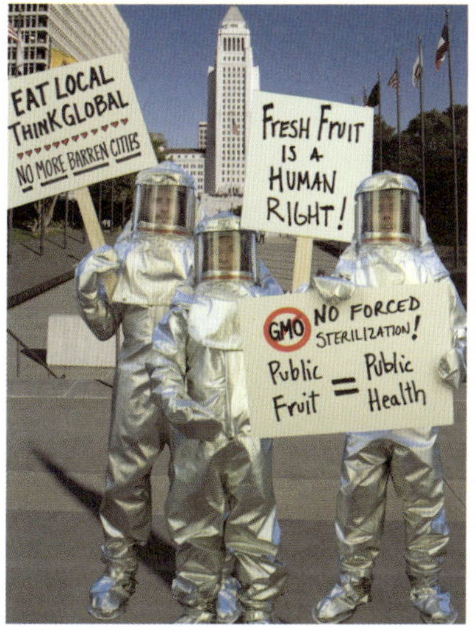

1

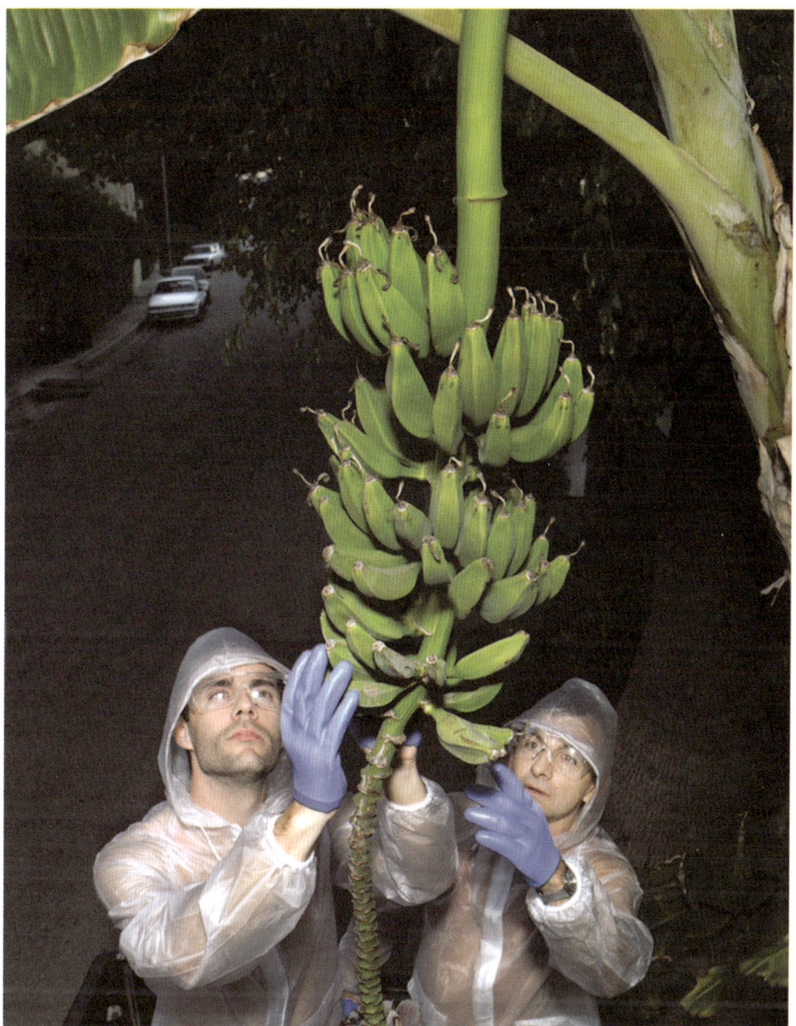

2

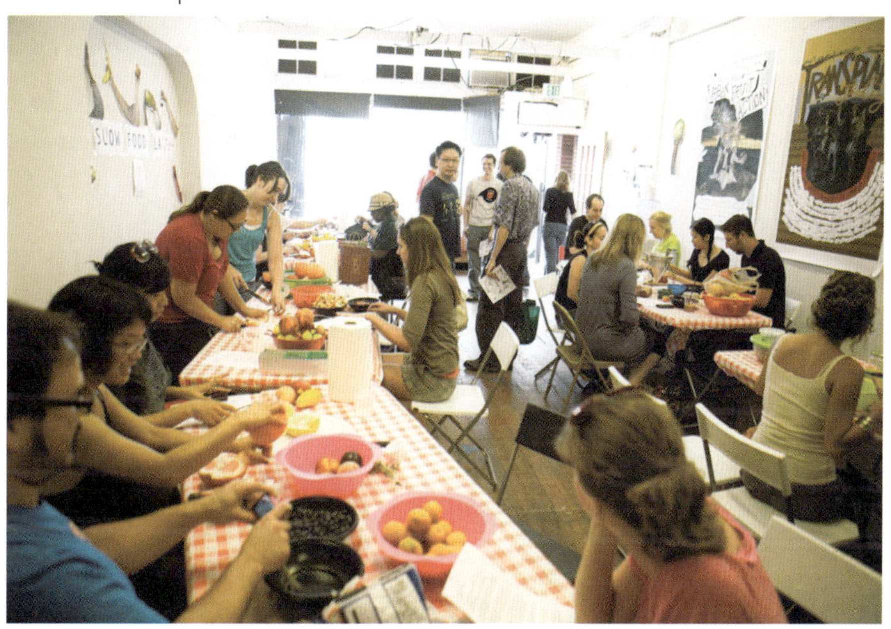

3

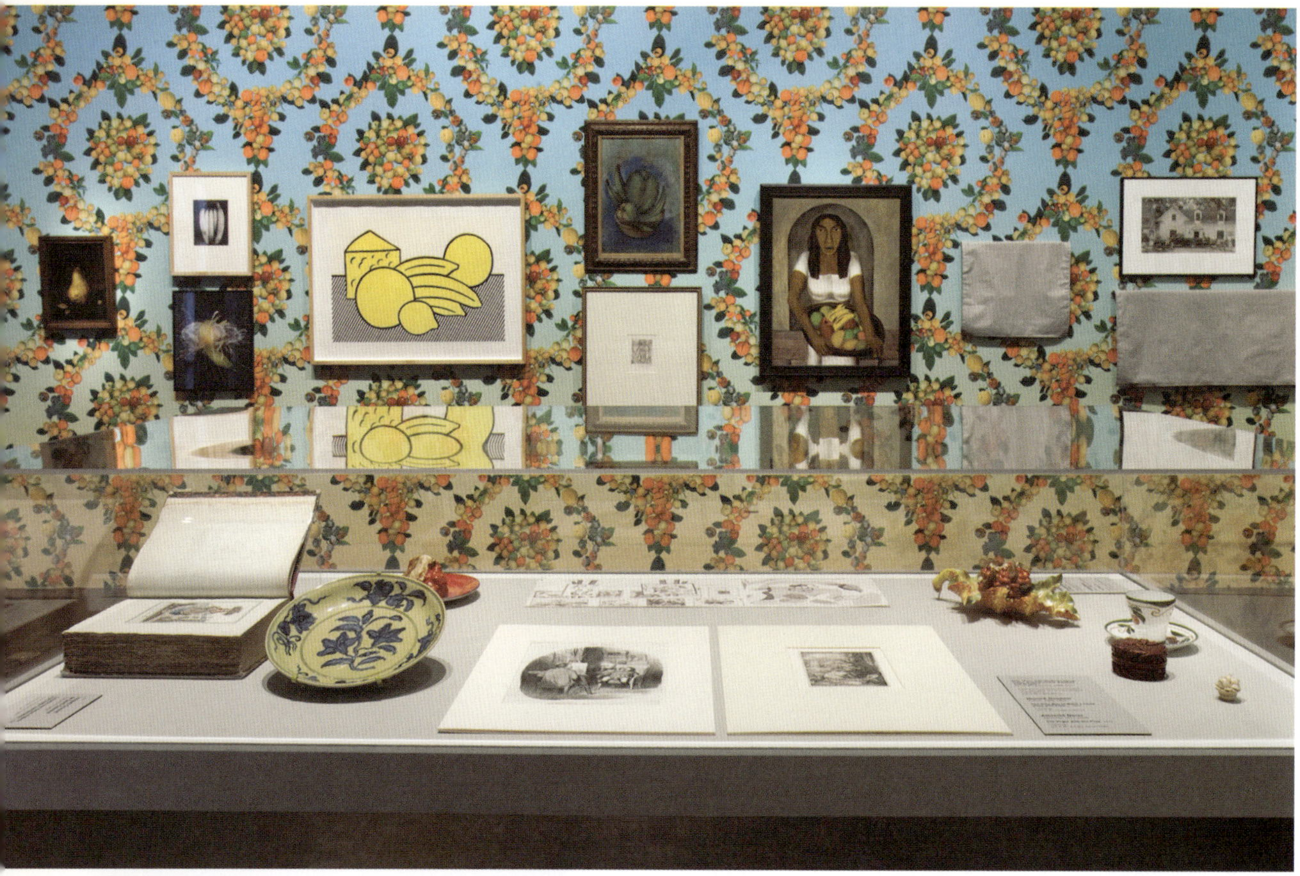

4

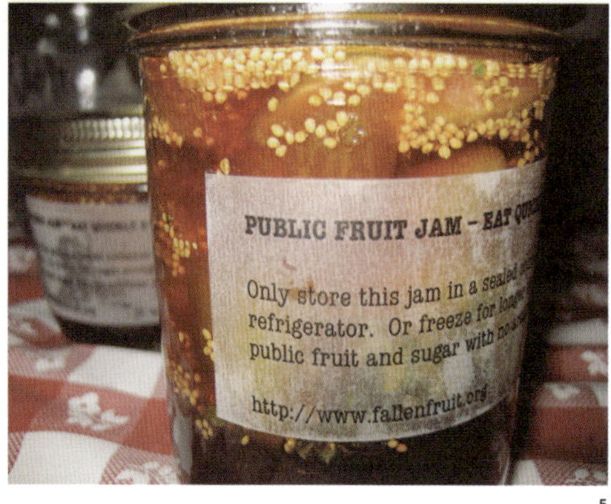

5

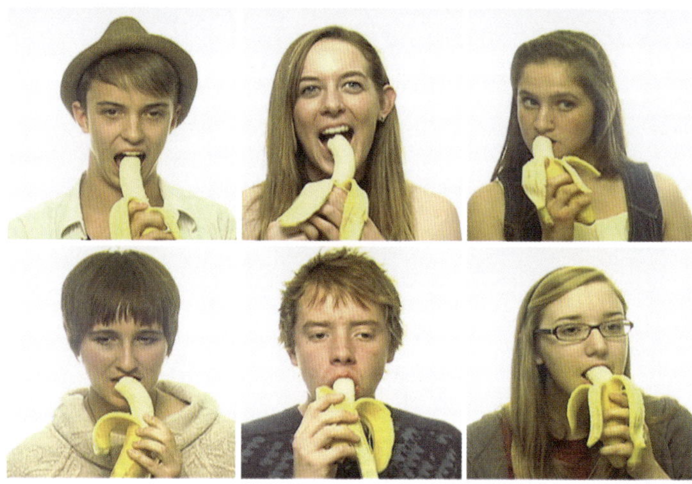

6

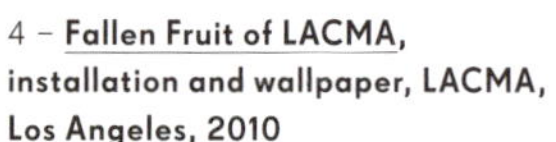

4 – Fallen Fruit of LACMA, installation and wallpaper, LACMA, Los Angeles, 2010

5 – Public Fruit Jam Jar, jam jar, 2005

6 – Banana Machine, video still, 2008

Does each of you have a clearly defined role? If so, what are some of each member's distinct responsibilities?

Fallen Fruit is a concept that has taken on a life of its own and over time developed conceptual parameters. It has a manifesto. It is bigger than us as individuals. The behavior of the group dynamic developed naturally; we take on defined roles within the group due to knowledge base or expert skills. Projects and work created are credited as "Fallen Fruit."

How important is each group member's individuality, both in terms of your artistic production and in terms of your relationship with the media? Does anonymity come into play?

Expressing our individuality within the group ensures that Fallen Fruit is always operating at its highest potential. Yet, we have never considered Fallen Fruit to be about individual authorship. In some cases there are Fallen Fruit projects that are without copyright, for example, the Public Fruit Maps and the Public Fruit Jams. Anyone can use a map, or reproduce one without copyright concerns, or perform a jam without permission. Ultimately, we collectively share credit on all Fallen Fruit projects regardless of whether there is individual leadership or individual skills required.

What is the relationship between your working methods and your art's "content"? In this sense, does technology tend to play more of a supporting role, or does it lead you in new directions?

We embrace technology as a tool of productivity—basically, digital tools and distribution are just part of the process for Fallen Fruit. Early on, people asked us why we don't "print the Public Fruit Maps and distribute them to people" and now, just a few years later, that notion would seem wasteful to most people. We think that our use of technology is really just part of the project; early on it became an essential part of the practice, and we mean this in a truly interactive and collaborative way, internally and with the broad public.

A lot of our work is created digitally, including images, maps, videos, and wallpaper. Our performances, including the Public Fruit Jam, Mediations, Fruit Tree Adoptions, etc., though, are intimate, immersive, and in real time. But they do rely on our use of Twitter, Facebook, Instagram, and our website.

How does your collaboration relate to its cultural, institutional, and commercial contexts? In other words, how would you respond to those who call this a trend?

We feel that trends are always in flux, emerging and waning and circling back again. Foraging fruit in neighborhoods has quickly become a part of contemporary culture. When Fallen Fruit started, the "green movement" had not really entered the collective consciousness but people were hungry for this kind of connection to the earth and our food. When the tidal wave of environmental thoughts about citizenship and righteous action hit mainstream culture, broadcast media like the BBC, NPR, CBS, and others embraced Fallen Fruit. Simultaneously, projects were created that radically challenged the ideas of authorship in a work of art or collaborative art practice. Fallen Fruit was in residency at LACMA in 2010 for a series of projects called EatLACMA that included eight commissioned works on site by other artists and performances commissioned by over fifty additional artists. The boundaries of curatorial practice and artistic production was more than blurred; in some cases the context was temporarily erased.

We believe the trend of rearticulating authorship is a merit of our time and certainly with our contemporaries within the Los Angeles art scene, like Machine Project. We've been rethinking language, syntax, and meaning. The public has many voices and many stories to share and together our voices are greater and our meanings more clear. The Public Fruit Jams are interactive and abuzz with storytelling about neighborhood fruit trees, family rituals, and childhood memories which led us to collecting "Fruit Stories" as an archive of these narratives. "Neighborhood Infusions" reimagines the "Nocturnal Fruit Forage"; instead of walking through a neighborhood, participants are prompted to describe the neighborhood where they grew up. Culture is fluid and currently we are focused on personal experience, childhood memory, and group dynamics as a conceptual component of every public participatory project and new opportunity.

Who is your audience?

We engage the broad transnational and cross-generational public and that is our audience. In terms of defining who is the broad public, it depends on context. We work with broadcast media and publications in hopes of engaging the imagination of people we will never actually meet in person. In terms of public practice or social practice this is essential, and very much at the core of Fallen Fruit's production. When we are doing a performance, our audience is varied: young and old. Men and women, artists, garden enthusiasts, foodies. When we did our exhibition "Fallen Fruit of Utah," we created a project that would engage Mormons and non-Mormons alike. Our projects create opportunities for radical inclusion and bridge communities. One thing we've realized through time is that fruit is an incredible equalizer. It's nonpolarizing. If you tell us about your favorite fruit from your childhood, we will probably nod in agreement and say, "We love that fruit too!"

Does your engagement with one another translate into an engagement with the audience? How so?

7 – Tomato Hootenanny, poster, 2010

8 – Accion Fruta Urbana, public billboard, Madrid, 2010

opposite
9 – Let Them Eat LACMA, picnic and opening invitation, LACMA, Los Angeles, 2010

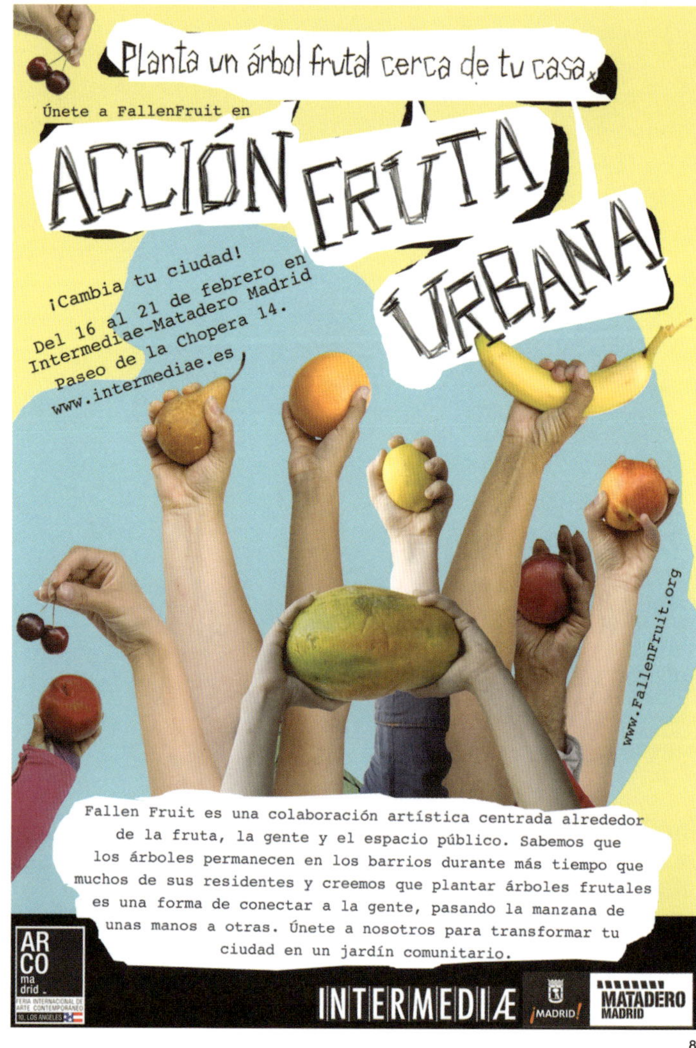

8

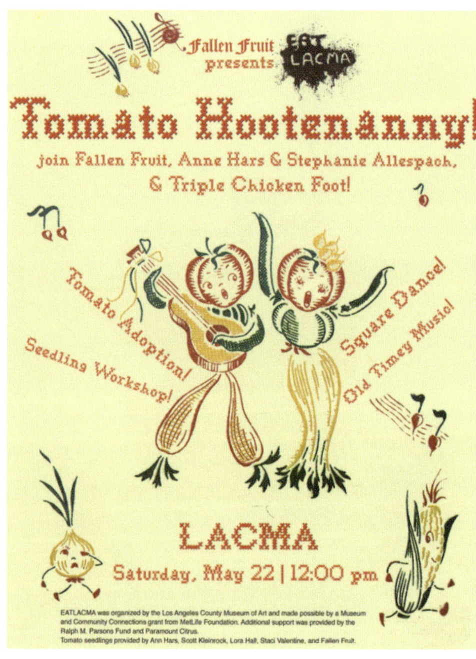

7

Fallen Fruit was founded on the idea of "radical inclusion." Everything we make is about capturing the imagination of the public. If you've never actively collaborated with us, perhaps we'll inspire you to collaborate in other ways, such as picking public fruit, neighborhood forages, planting public fruit trees, making jam, or making maps of other neighborhoods, etc.

We started this project with the understanding that fruit can be many things; it can be a subject and an object; at the same time, it is a symbol. It is transnational and crosses all class boundaries—the richest of rich and the poorest people on earth all eat the same bananas. Fruit is a symbol of goodness and generosity in almost all cultures in the world. It is most importantly cross generational; a young child is as much an expert on the taste of a strawberry as are the parents and grandparents.

We consider every project—including public participatory events, art objects, manifesto texts, blogs, and broadcast media, as well as corporate collaborations, museum installations, and civic interventions—a part of the whole concept of Fallen Fruit.

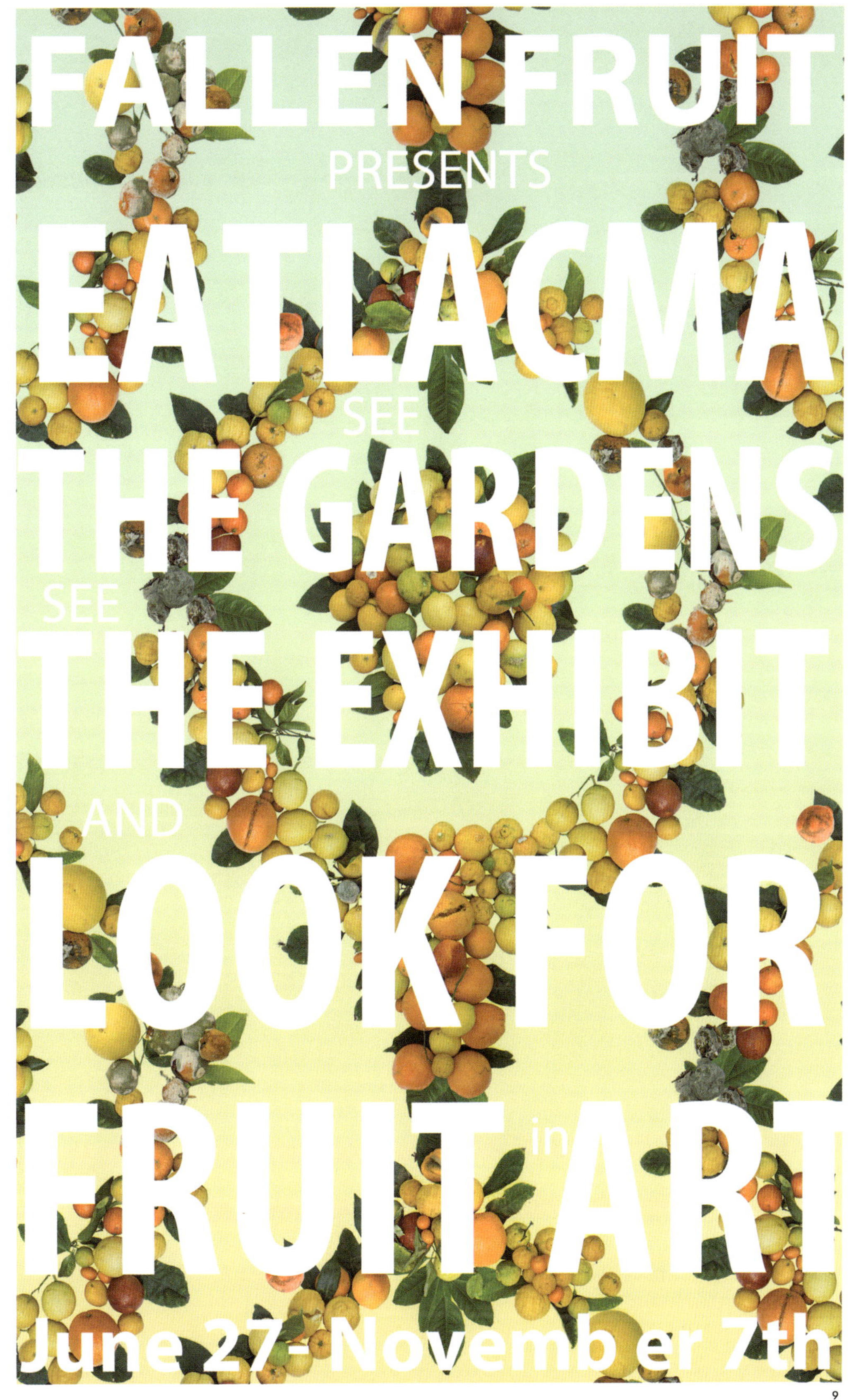
FALLEN FRUIT
PRESENTS
EAT LACMA
SEE
THE GARDENS
SEE
THE EXHIBIT
AND
LOOK FOR
FRUIT in ART
June 27- Novemb er 7th

9

ACTIVE SINCE	CITY	WEBSITE
2002	Los Angeles, U.S.	friendswithyou.com

Friends With You

MEMBERS	ACTIVITIES	RECOMMENDED PUBLICATION
Samuel Borkson and Arturo Sandoval III	Community Projects, Curating, Internet Art, Merchandising, Music, Painting / Sculpture / Installation, Public Art Projects, Public Performance	Kathy Grayson, "Laugh Often, Dream Big," I-D MAGAZINE, no. 315, September 2011

Friends With You is an art and design duo known for the creation of a childish universe populated by seemingly harmless and colorful creatures. Always smiling, these soft and round characters, born on paper or the screen, often become the mascots of inflatable installations, playgrounds, and parades that redesign cityscapes and malls, bringing kids as well as adults into a fun and surreal dimension.

Why work collaboratively?
We feel it is an organic option for our journey. It feels like a powerful endeavor when many minds are put to the same task in this spiritual sense. Once the artist can leave his or her ego behind to create something new, the new creation is pure, honest, and beautiful. We feel that many more people can then add their own emotions into the project and make it even brighter. We feel the next phase of art for us is a mission for social and spiritual change and exploration. It's a very exciting idea to us and we feel a lot of people are in need of what we are exploring, so through this process we are all healing ourselves. The vibration of this thinking results in happier people, which will have an exponentially good result in our world.

How do you determine membership? Does physical location matter in this regard?
Everyone is welcome to be involved. The point of it is to engage people in an impactful experience and empower them so they can carry out their own personal healing methods. It's about connecting to all people. We are working in Los Angeles now, but feel a great connection to artists all over the world and what they are expressing. People from all different parts of the world join us on our mission and it becomes something we are all a part of. Art is beautiful in that it can be experimental in its approach.

If considered separately, how do your individual artistic practices contribute to or detract from your work as a group?
I think we both possess very powerful tools that help us to create the work we do together. I think we choose to combine all of our energies in this project and we learn a lot from each other. We discuss the emotional aspect of each detail; our process can be lengthy at times. We are always in search of how we can better the work. I think both of our minds service different aspects of the overall picture, and it really is fun to play together and always be sculpting the overall message and ideas.

How are decisions made?
Decisions are made like emotions; they come in all shapes and sizes. We listen, we formulate, and we hypothesize on what would be the best solution. All ideas are heard and considered from all parties, and then we roll. Sometimes the decision is easy and sometimes it's very difficult.

Do each of you have a clearly defined role? If so, what are some of each member's distinct responsibilities?
I think it mixes a lot. We both like to get our hands dirty and contribute to each amazing project. Sometimes we will come to a quick consensus and then one of us will take the lead and roll with it.

How important is each group member's individuality, both in terms of your artistic production and in terms of your relationship with the media? Does anonymity come into play?

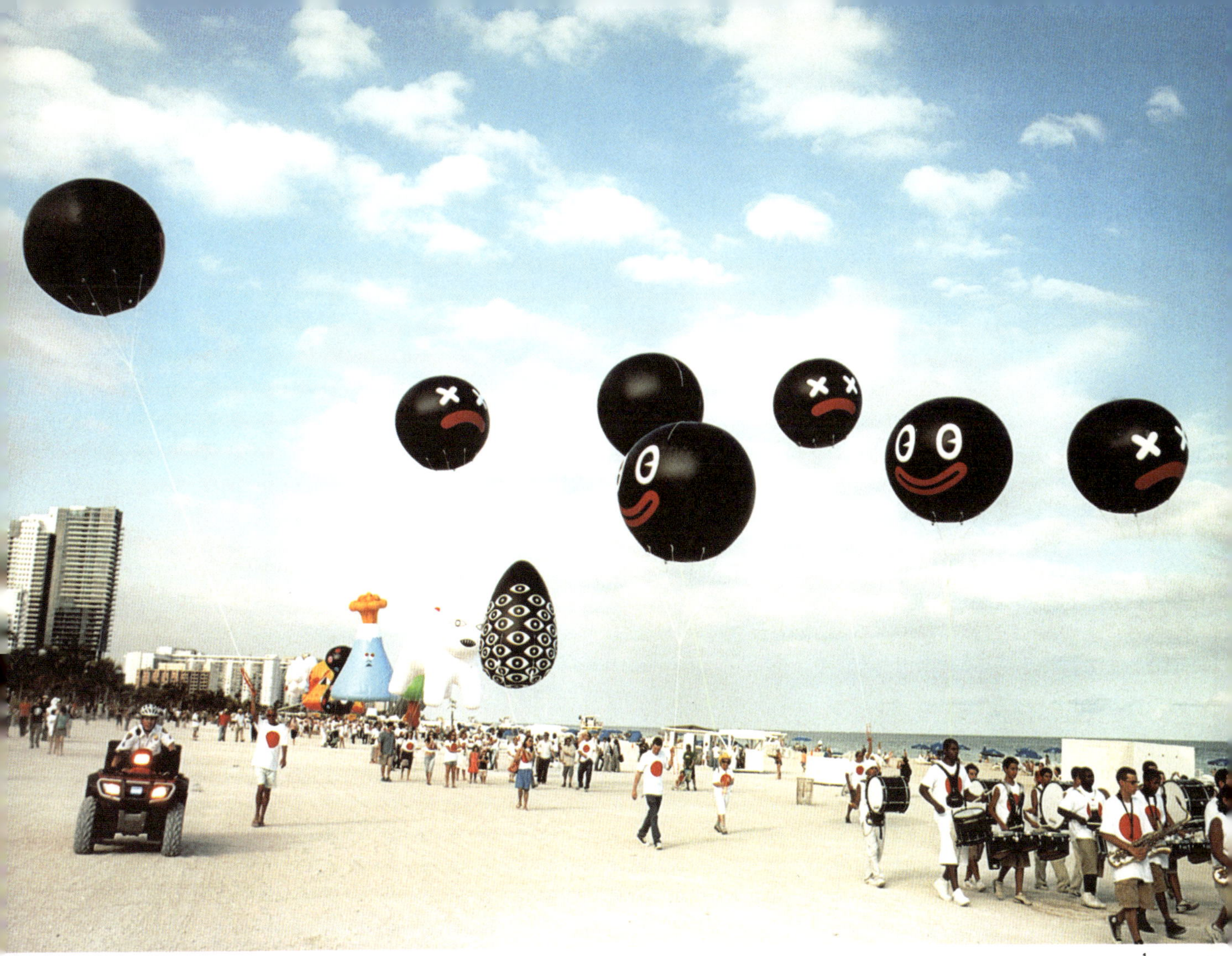

1

1 – Skywalkers, parade curated by Friends With You, Miami Beach, 2006

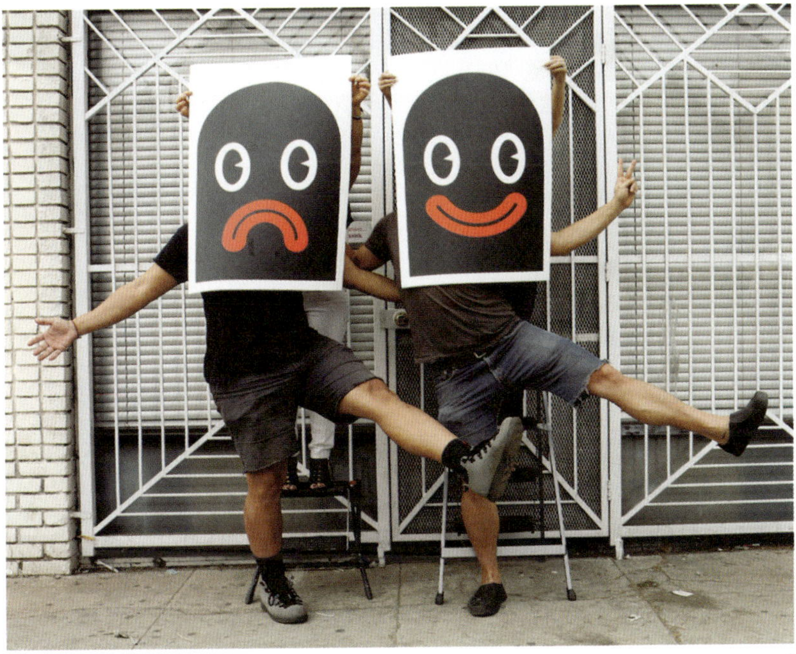

2

2 – I am Malfi and I am Malfi II, self-portrait with limited-edition prints, 2012

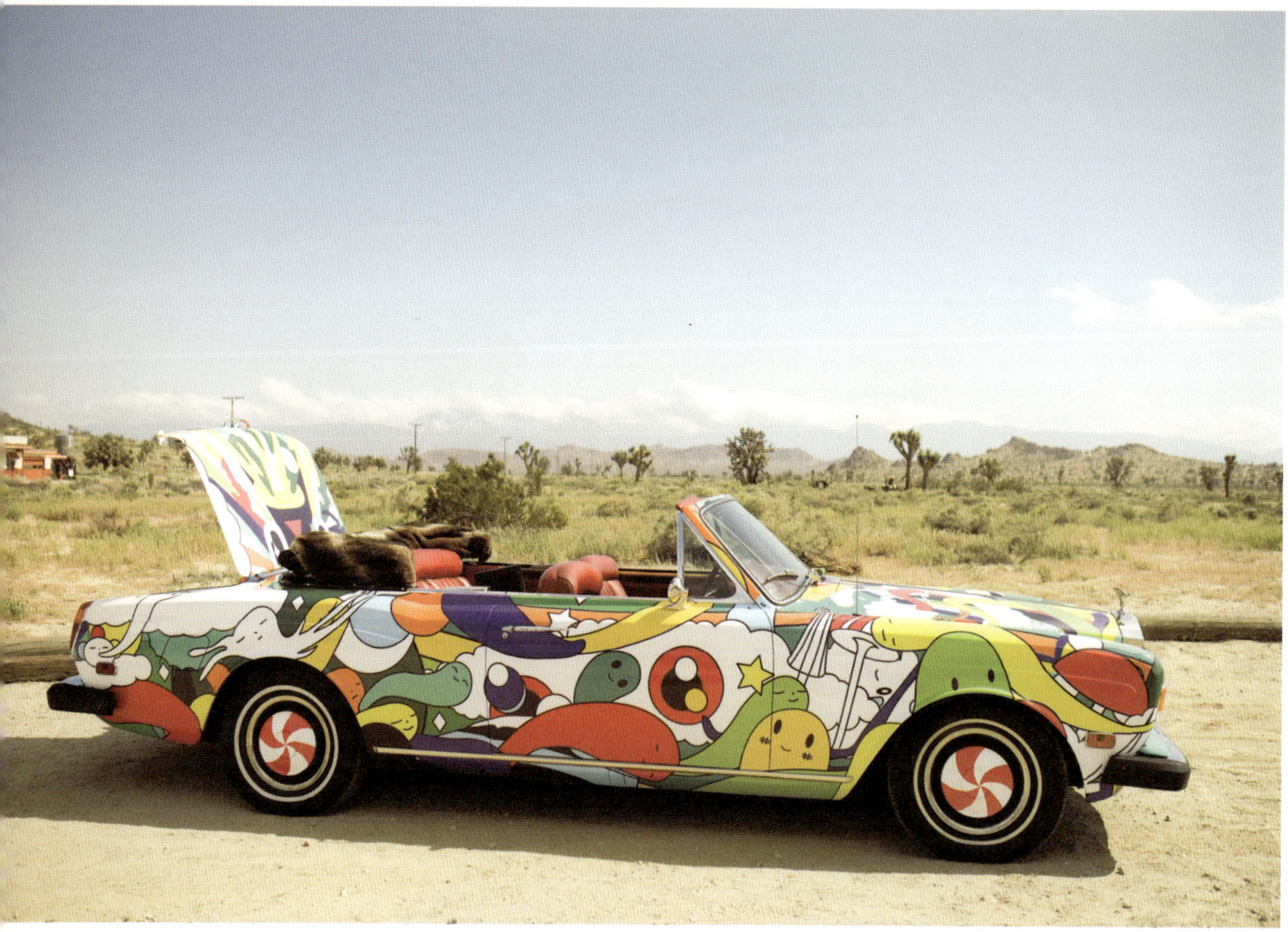

3

3 – Magical Explosions Car Wrap, painted car for Pharrell Williams's "Hot-n-Fun" music video, 2010

4 – Best Buddies International X Friends With You, jersey design for a benefit bike ride, Pacific Coast Highway, Carmel, 2012

opposite
5 – Rainbow King, performance in inflatable costume, Times Square, New York, 2011

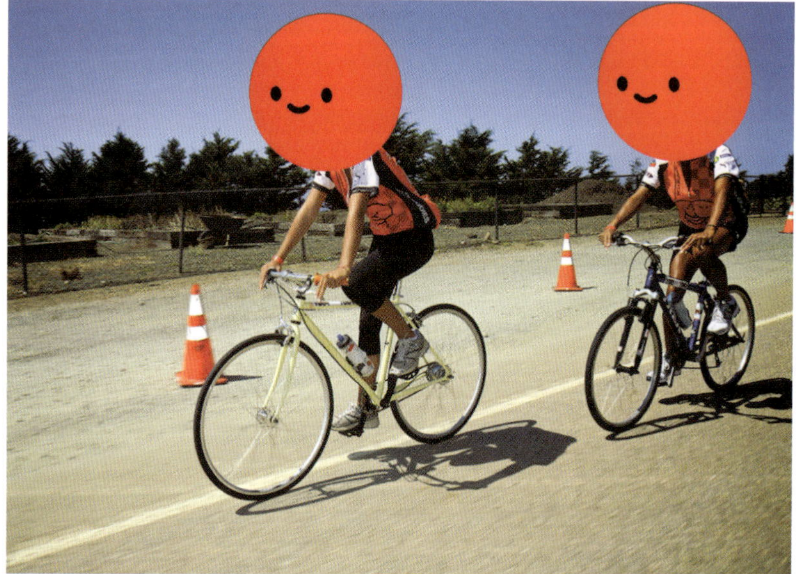

4

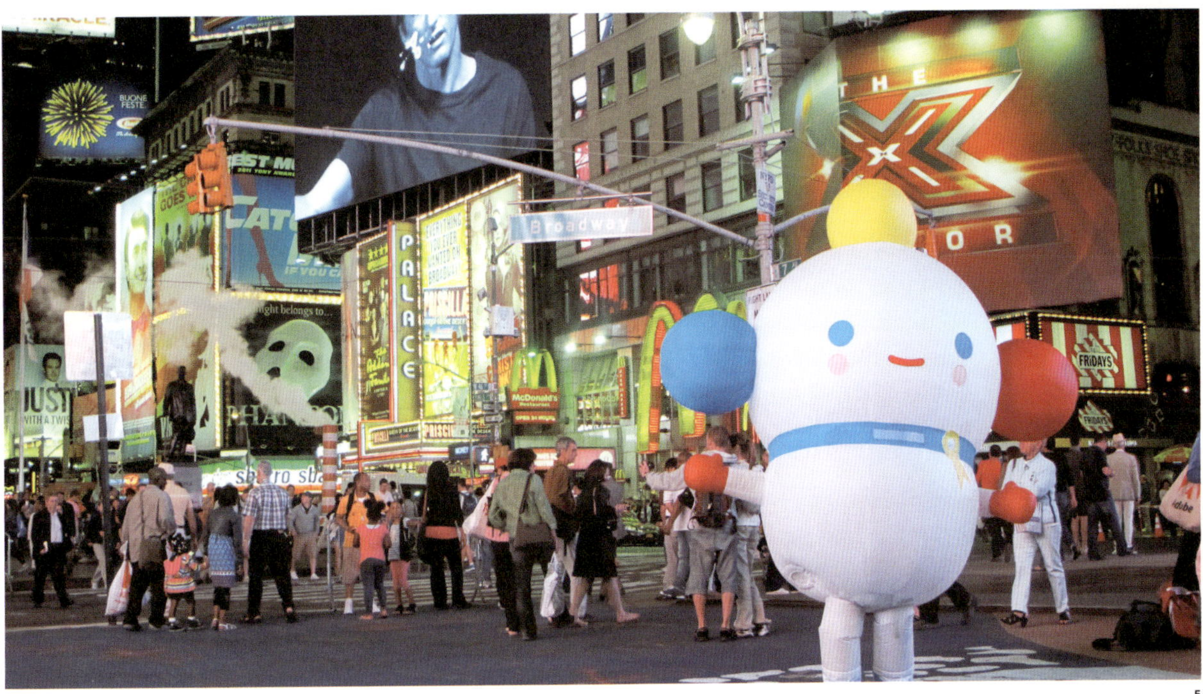

5

I feel that this is where the magic lies. Two separate people with two completely separate backgrounds meeting in the world and deciding that they share the same goals and vision. Each one of us brings hundreds of years of knowledge through our DNA and we are now learning together how to take the best of both individuals and make something divine. We act as one solid voice with combined ideas that we think and talk about. I feel we both celebrate happily who each of us is through our life adventure together. It's really cool to learn from each other and combine forces to make a great mission.

What is the relationship between your working methods and your art's "content"? In this sense, does technology tend to play more of a supporting role, or does it lead you in new directions?

Since we are born into this modern world, we think and create with these amazing technologies to our advantage. To be inspired by them and also to dream without limits. Reality is so expansive through our new world and all the evolutions of people and new information. Connectivity is a huge part of our process. We are working to impact people's lives and now more than ever that can happen on such a large scale. It is also a big help when it comes to our process. We don't have to be medium-specific. So we dream with all the tools and processes we wish to utilize. We find there are very little limitations and this lets us create very powerful works. Sometimes huge works. We are always inspired and pushing to learn about our own emotional process through every project.

How does your collaboration relate to its cultural, institutional, and commercial contexts? In other words, how would you respond to those who call this a trend?

Our main mission is to redesign spirituality and connect people to each other and themselves—we don't feel that this is a fad. We feel that we are mirrors of the current affliction and we feel it's a giant undertaking. We feel education and the art system is changing so much. Religion mostly divides people. We see art as the next step in cultural teachings of why we are different and why we are similar—and celebrating that to the fullest. We really want to be the happy virus inside the system and do everything we can to make a difference. As far as trends go, I think people always can encapsulate whatever they want into a trend. We make art so however people look at it is their own personal choice of where it fits and why. We don't think in those terms.

Who is your audience?

Everybody!

Does your engagement with one another translate into an engagement with the public? How so?

Yes, our working together is everything. Our process between two minds and two passionate artists always results in a clear and focused message. Every project that we both make has this quality inside. We love to see how people add to and interact with these ideas and how it grows from there. The message is soon everyone's message. We are about inclusivity and sharing this amazing life.

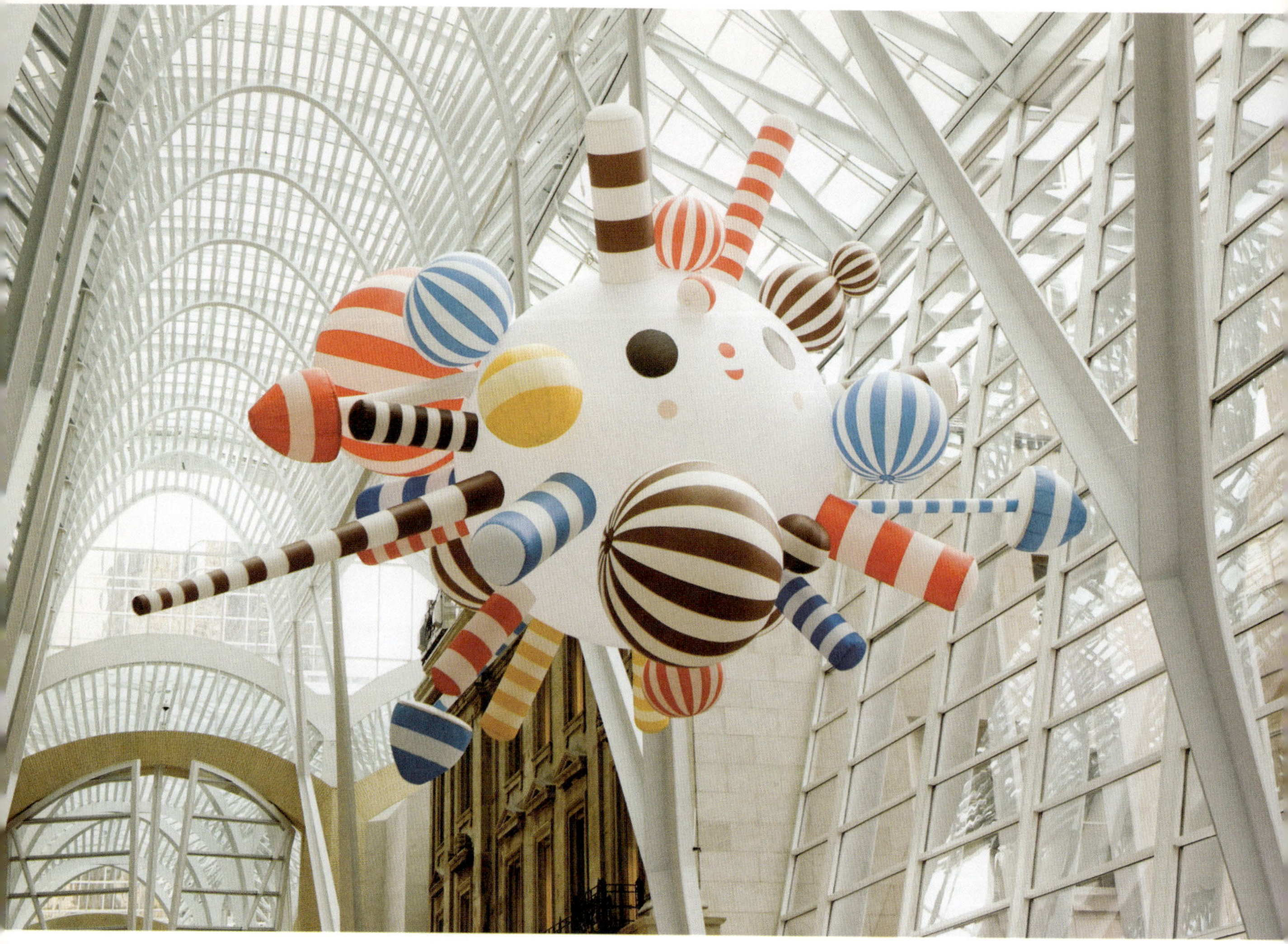

6

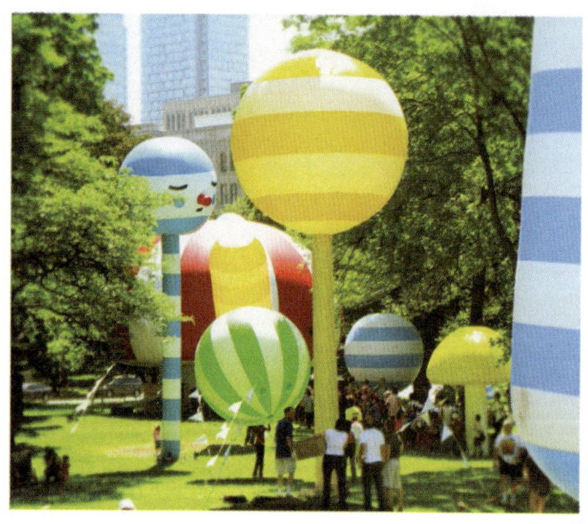

7

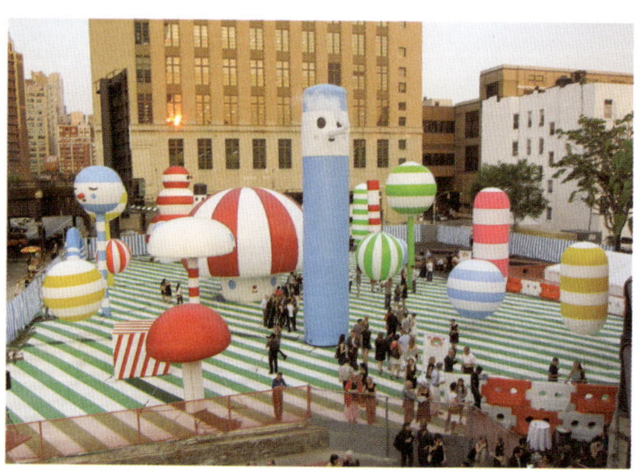

8

opposite
6 – Starburst, inflatable sculpture, Brookfield Place, Toronto, 2013

opposite
7 – Rainbow City, public inflatable installation, Queens Park, Toronto, 2010

opposite
8 – Rainbow City, public inflatable installation, p, New York, 2011

9 – Rainbow Valley, playground, Aventura Mall, Miami, 2006

10 – Happy Rainbow, playground, TMT Plaza, Hong Kong, 2012

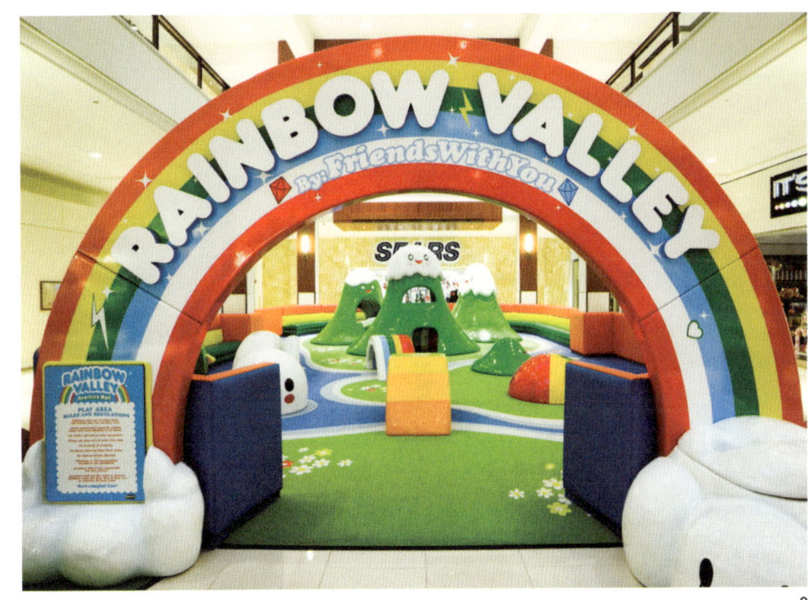

9

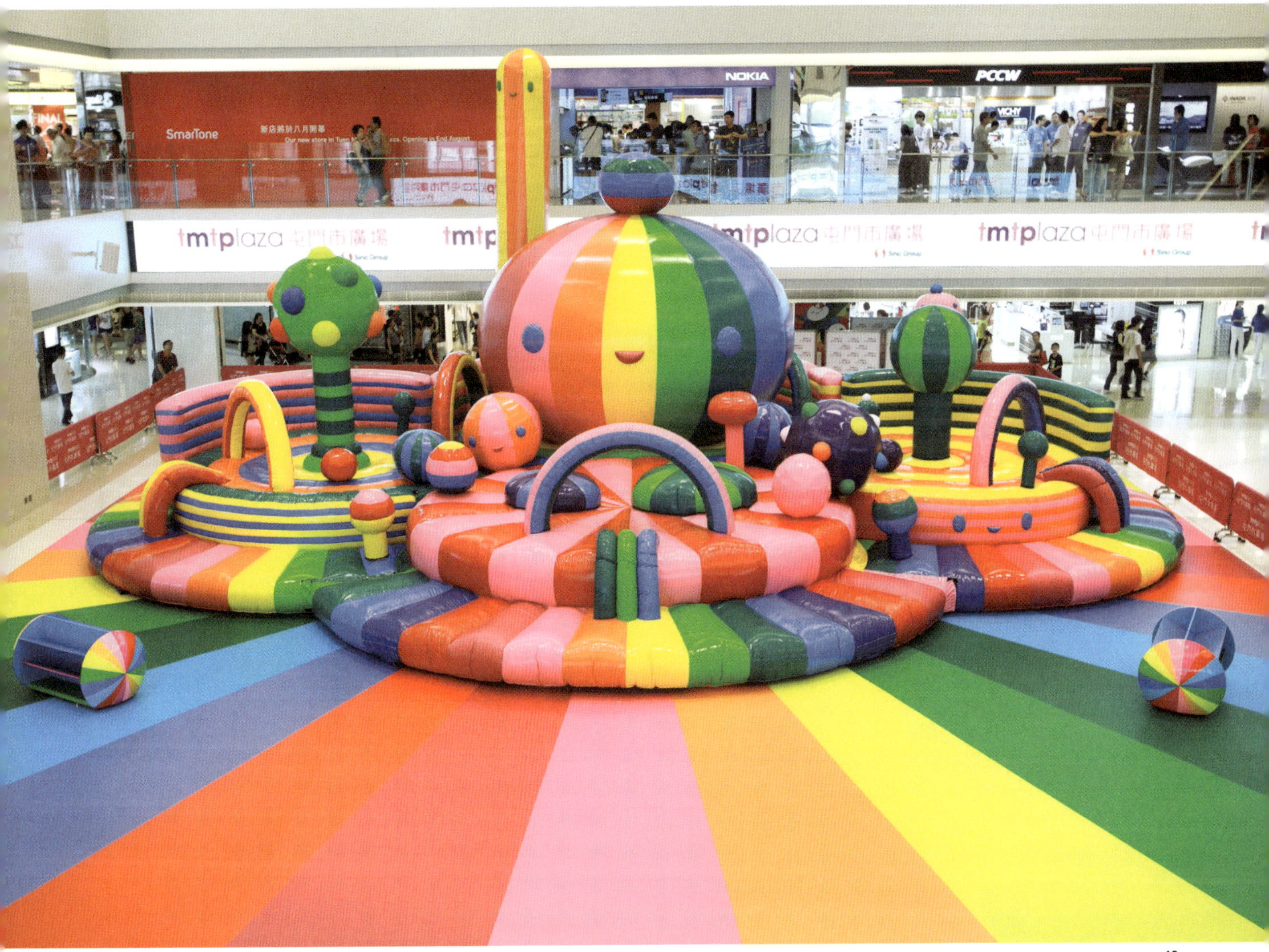

10

ACTIVE SINCE	CITY	WEBSITE
1998	Düsseldorf, Germany / London, UK	hobbypopmuseum.com

hobbypopMUSEUM

MEMBERS

Sophie von Hellermann, Christian Jendreiko, Matthias Lahme, Dietmar Lutz, André Niebur, and Marie-Céline Schäfer. Former embers and Guests: Markus Vater (1998–2003), Tine Furler (1998–2000), Thea Djordjadze (1998–2003), Nick Laessing (1999–2003), Olivia Berckemeyer (1998–2000), Björn Dahlem (1998–2000), Tatjana Doll (1998–2000), Andreas Reihse (1999–2000), Mike Silver (2000–2001), Detlef Weinrich (1999–2000), Kid Congo Powers, Khan, Little Annie, Karla Milosevich, Kota Ezawa, Craig Goodman, Gerald Corbin, Kevin Killian, SF Poets' Theater, Hannes Hellmann, Doris Schade, Lampros Boussakis, Adeline Morlon, Alexander Jasch, Mareike Föcking, H. G. P. Pahl, Andreas Gursky, Nina Pohl, Guido Münch, Jonathan Viner, Giles Round, Dan Fox, Tim Braden, Maaike Schoorel, Art Davis, Nat Mellors, Stefan Werni, Polly Coppolla, Mo Whiteman, and many more

ACTIVITIES	RECOMMENDED PUBLICATION
Curating, Internet Art, Merchandising, Music, Public Performance, Publishing, Painting / Sculpture / Installation	hobbypopMUSEUM, Werte schaffen, Verlag der Buchhandlung Walther König, Köln, 2004

Camps, bistros, tents, and sofas are recurrent elements in the universe of hobbypopMUSEUM, whose name alone sounds like a critique of the cultural institutions where it often takes shape. Instead of contemplation, indeed, the artists offer chances for discussion and exploration of the mechanisms of aggregation and conformity, using themselves, as members of a collective, both as medium and message.

Why work collaboratively?

We believe strongly that within artistic collaboration there lies something other than compromise, something very valuable.

As a group, we create site-specific installations. These installations can be seen as textures woven out of figures that are linked together by iconographic and formal criteria. The arsenal of figures spans from painting, drawing, photo, film, and sound to words, performance, sculpture, and architecture. Which form the figures will have depends on the basic idea and how this idea is developed by the group, while working on the site of the exhibition space.

We see our work as a journey with, each exhibition representing a station on this journey. This image is enhanced by the fact that we travel, meet up, disperse, and reconvene for our exhibitions all over the world. There is a definite thread of narrative running through the shows as well.

By melting our individual cores we will achieve a massive release of beautiful energy.

How do you determine membership? Does physical location matter in this regard?

hobbypopMUSEUM began as a space that we named thus. It was a huge empty room in an enormous, cavernous building in the middle of Düsseldorf. That was where we spent most of our days (and nights).

It wasn't so important who was a part of the group and who wasn't. Whoever happened to be there and took part was a part of it. It was an open process.

However, as time passed and demands on our time increased, it became clearer who was truly committed. So in 2003 a core group of six people formed hobbypopMUSEUM. hobbypopMUSEUM today is wherever we happen to get together, because it has been a long time since we have all lived in the same town.

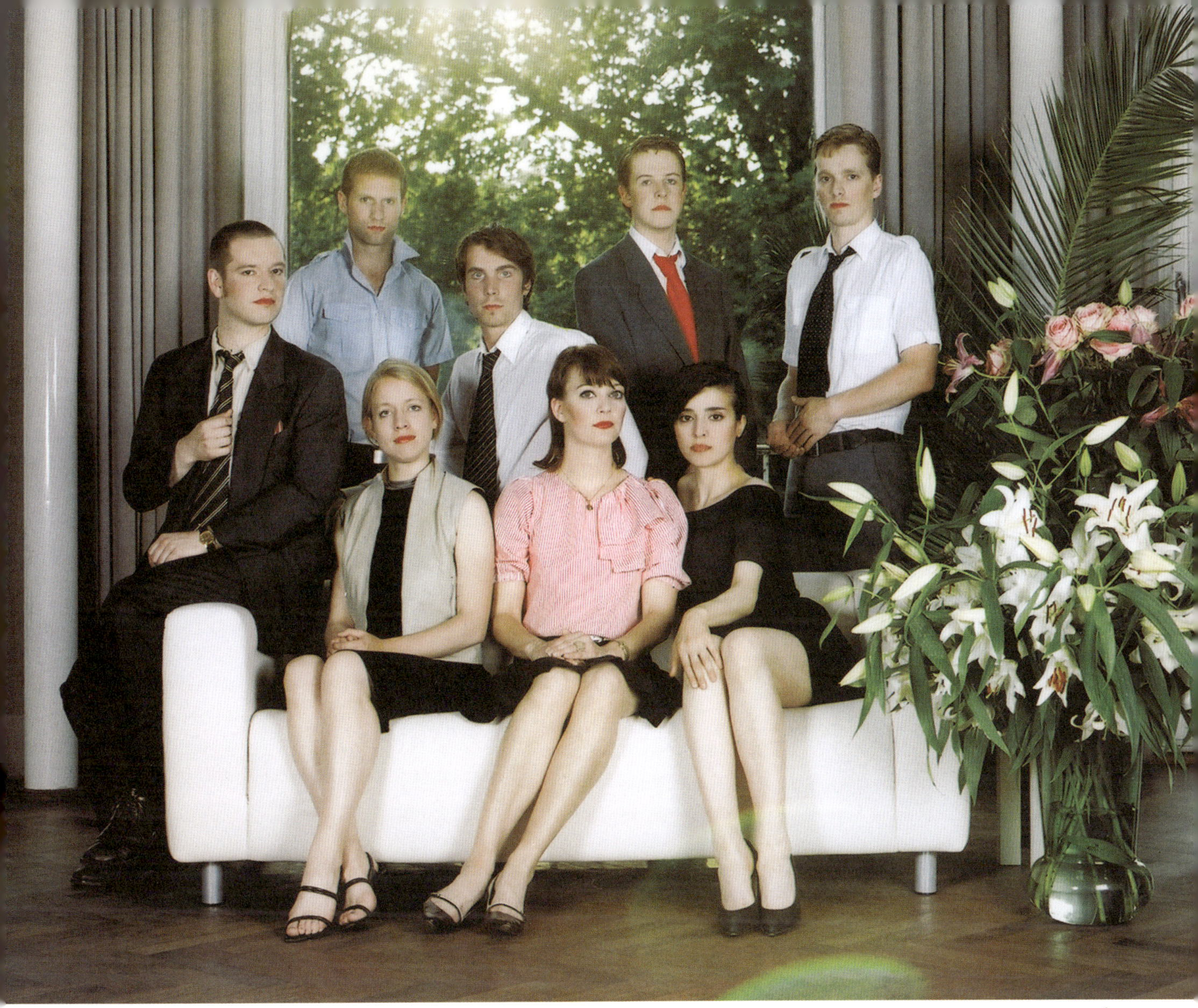

1

1 – <u>FOR PROMOTIONAL USE ONLY</u>
photo shoot, 2001

2 – <u>Neue Arbeiten auf Papier</u>, installation, Malkasten Düsseldorf, 2001

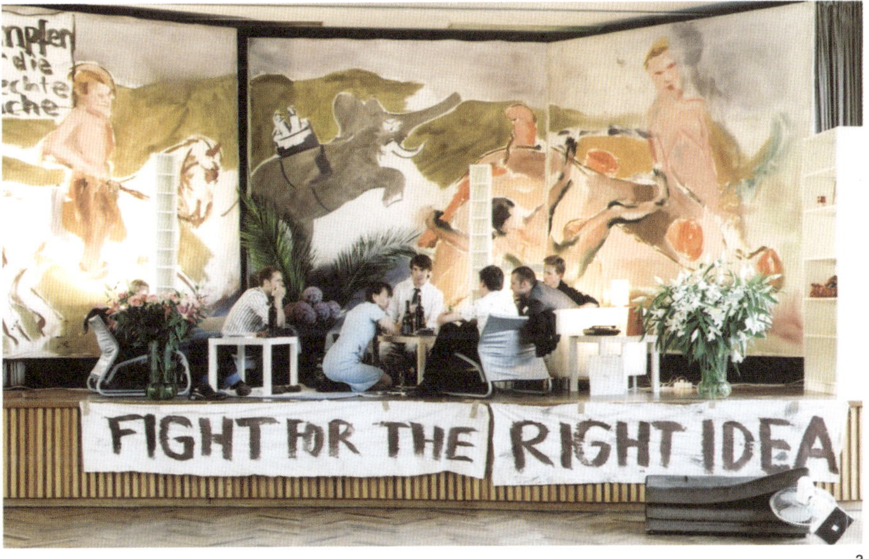

2

If considered separately, how do your individual artistic practices contribute to or detract from your work as a group?

You cannot separate the two. Our individual practices inform the collaborative practice and vice versa.

How are decisions made?

We set a process in motion, a sort of chain reaction, inside of which decisions are on autopilot. One idea and one execution of one idea therefore do not need to be in one person's hands, but can be passed from one to the other. Whoever fancies a particular idea can make something from it. One of us, or more, or all of us.

Does each of you have a clearly defined role? If so, what are some of each member's distinct responsibilities?

Naturally each of us has his or her specialty, a specific role and task within the group, but it is not set in stone, and we like to play with that. Moreover, it is entirely possible not to contribute anything tangible at all and still be part of the making of a hobbypopMUSEUM show (a physical Would you like some tea? presence does help but isn't necessarily required either).

How important is each group member's individuality, both in terms of your artistic production and in terms of your relationship with the media? Does anonymity come into play?

We do not work anonymously. Each member of the group is well known.

hobbypopMUSEUM is the only author of any hobbypopMUSEUM work.

For example, early in 2004, a member went to the Caribbean, and through a telephone conversation, we decided that a chapter of the book we were working on (Werte Schaffen) should be written there: "Welcome to Normal." So we produced a sign in Martinique, with a casing of handwoven palm leaves, and whether they liked it or not, everyone back in Europe became a coauthor.

However, it is interesting how any individual leaps of faith can psychologically be justified because hobbypopMUSEUM is bigger than all of us.

What is the relationship between your working methods and your art's "content"? In this sense, does technology tend to play more of a supporting role, or does it lead you in new directions?

Technologywise, we always use whatever is at hand and that won't distract us from what we are trying to achieve.

It is always great when new places and new contacts offer new possibilities, like for example at our production of Aeschylus's The Persians at the Kammerspiele theater in Munich. We got to work with trained actors and musicians and were able to compose music for them to perform as well as write the script for the play, and alongside our works they became elements of the whole installation.

How does your collaboration relate to its cultural, institutional, and commercial contexts? In other words, how would you respond to those who call this a trend?

There is an understanding that has become prevalent in many disciplines and has grown with the internet revolution of neural networks and the acceleration of ideas through sharing.

When we first started working together this was of interest to us, but since then it has become interesting to work against the trend that the market expected us to follow, namely that of collaborating and sharing when you're young and in need of support of the group, and then assuming the solo practice when a support network outside the group is established. Most confusing for outsiders seems to be the fact that we continue to do both.

Who is your audience?

The audience changes with the places where we exhibit, being geographically as well as socially different. Friends and family of the artists who invited us to exhibit in their tiny window space in the Mission district of San Francisco, theatergoers in Munich, a wide gallery audience at Deitch Projects in New York, supporters of a small Kunstverein (art association) in Enschede. Then there are the people who buy our books and those who Google us. Whoever looks, wins!

Does your engagement with one another translate into an engagement with the public? How so?

Our works are almost always openended and only feel finished when the viewers engage with them.

We have often asked them to participate and interact with the works, or moreover just provided a setting for the audience to perform in, albeit with some direction from us. Most shows in our fixed abode 1998–2000 in Düsseldorf worked like that.

3 – Wind is When Empty Coke Cans Start Singing, public performance, 2001

4 – Dead Sea, photo shoot, 2007

5 – Welcome to Normal, public sign, 2004

6 – Studio Apartment, album cover, Flesh Records, London, 2002

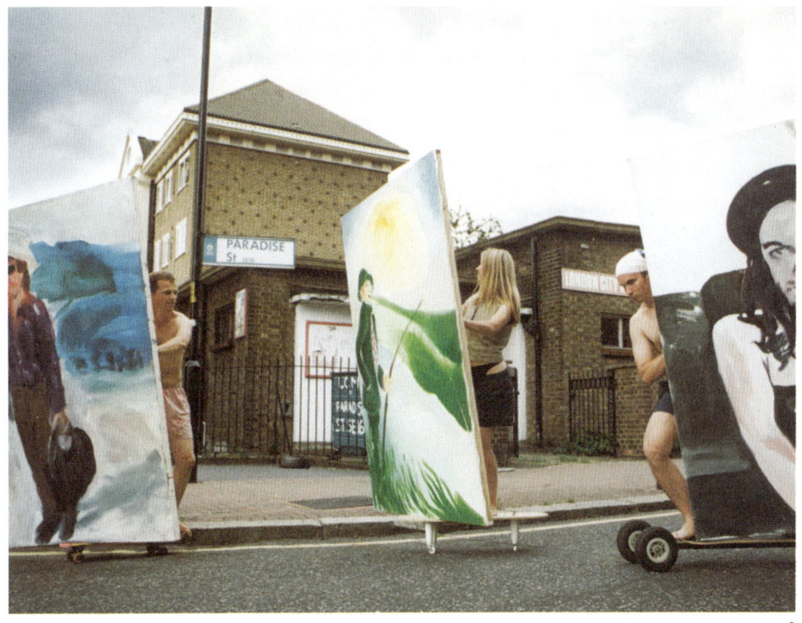

3

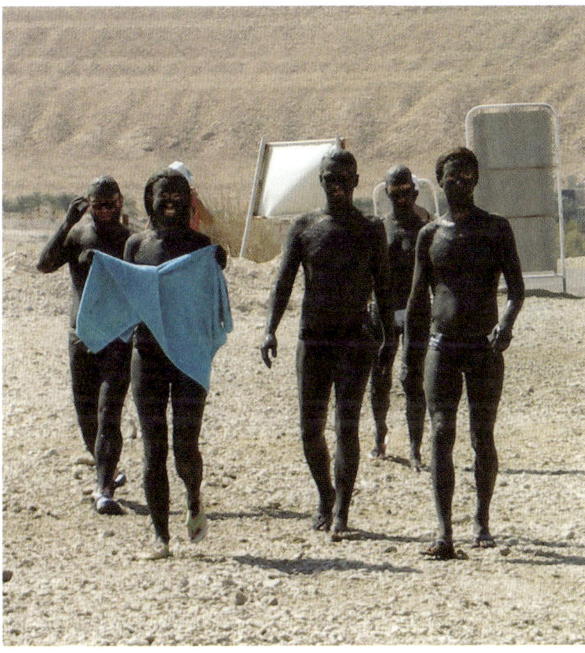

4

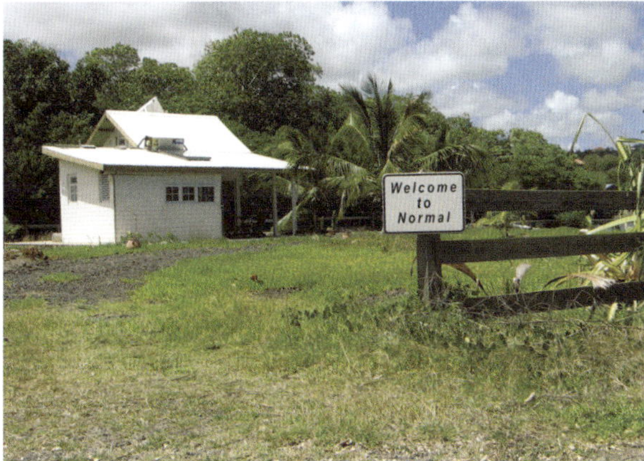

5

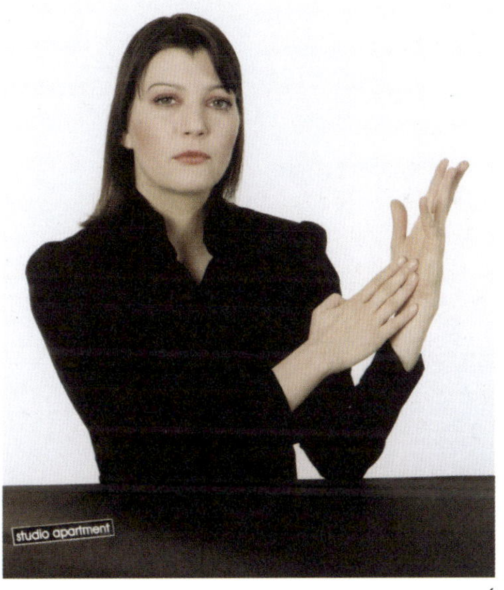

6

7 – Cmp Inc., installation, hobbypopMUSEUM, Düsseldorf, 1999

8 – Neo Psychico, installation, hobbypopMUSEUM, Düsseldorf, 2005

opposite
9 – Taking the Air, installation, Right Window, San Francisco, 2010

opposite
10 – Bistro Forever, collage, 1999

opposite
11 – Intelligent Design, public installation, 1st Athens Biennial, Athens, 2007

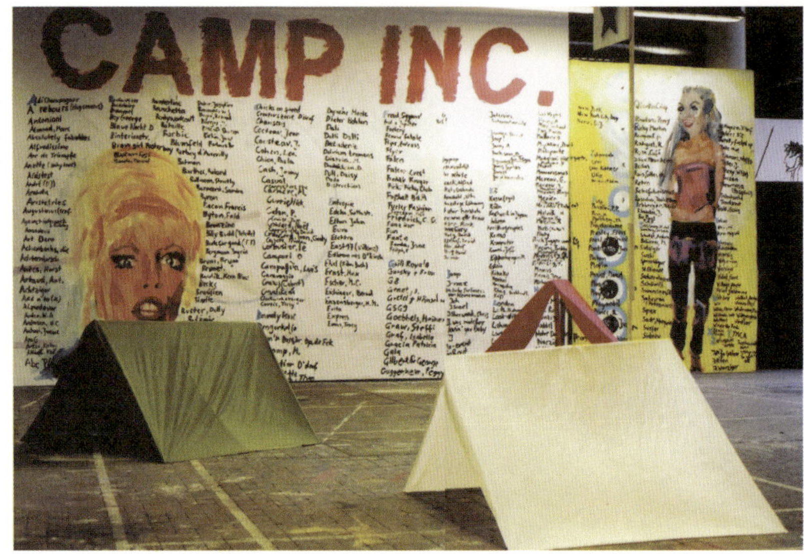

7

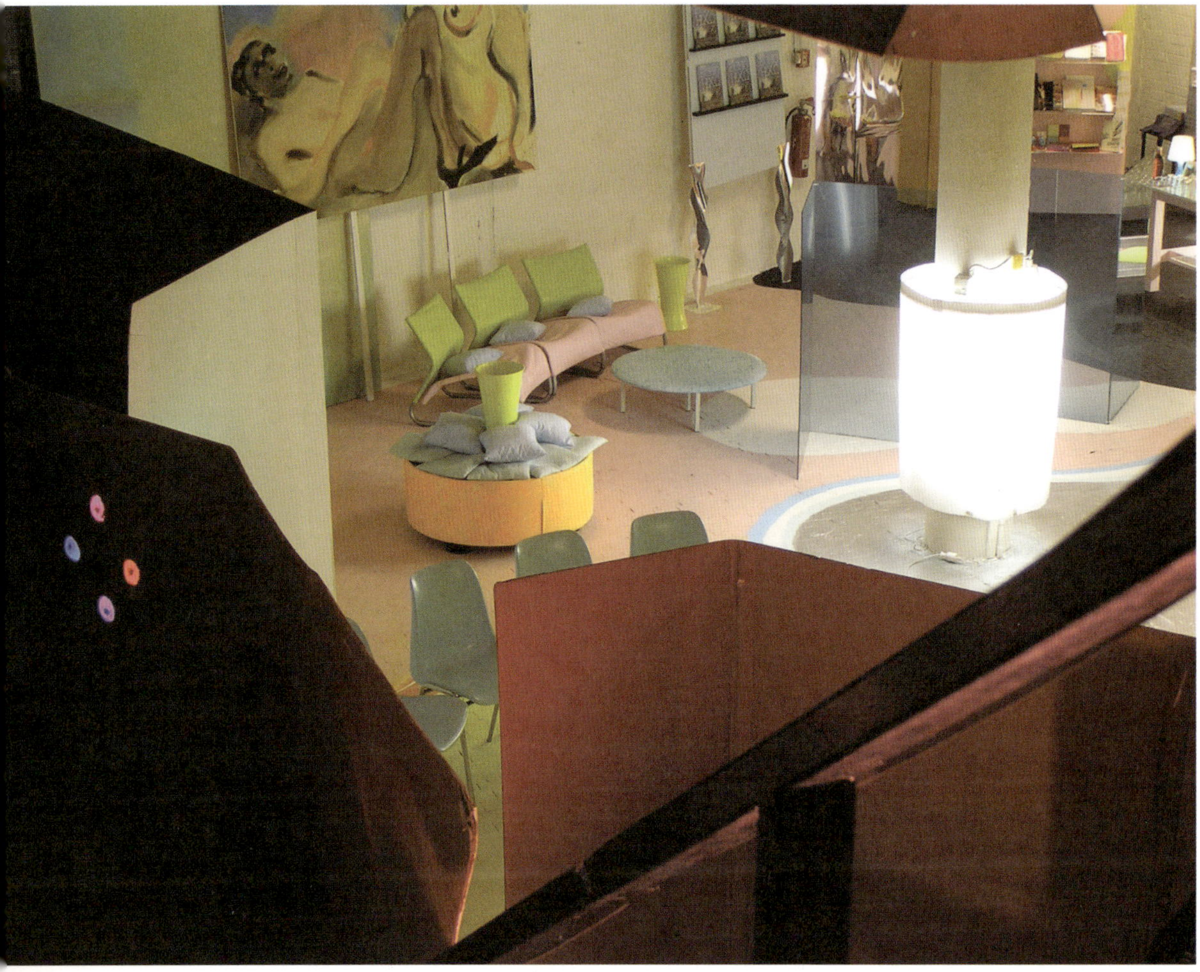

8

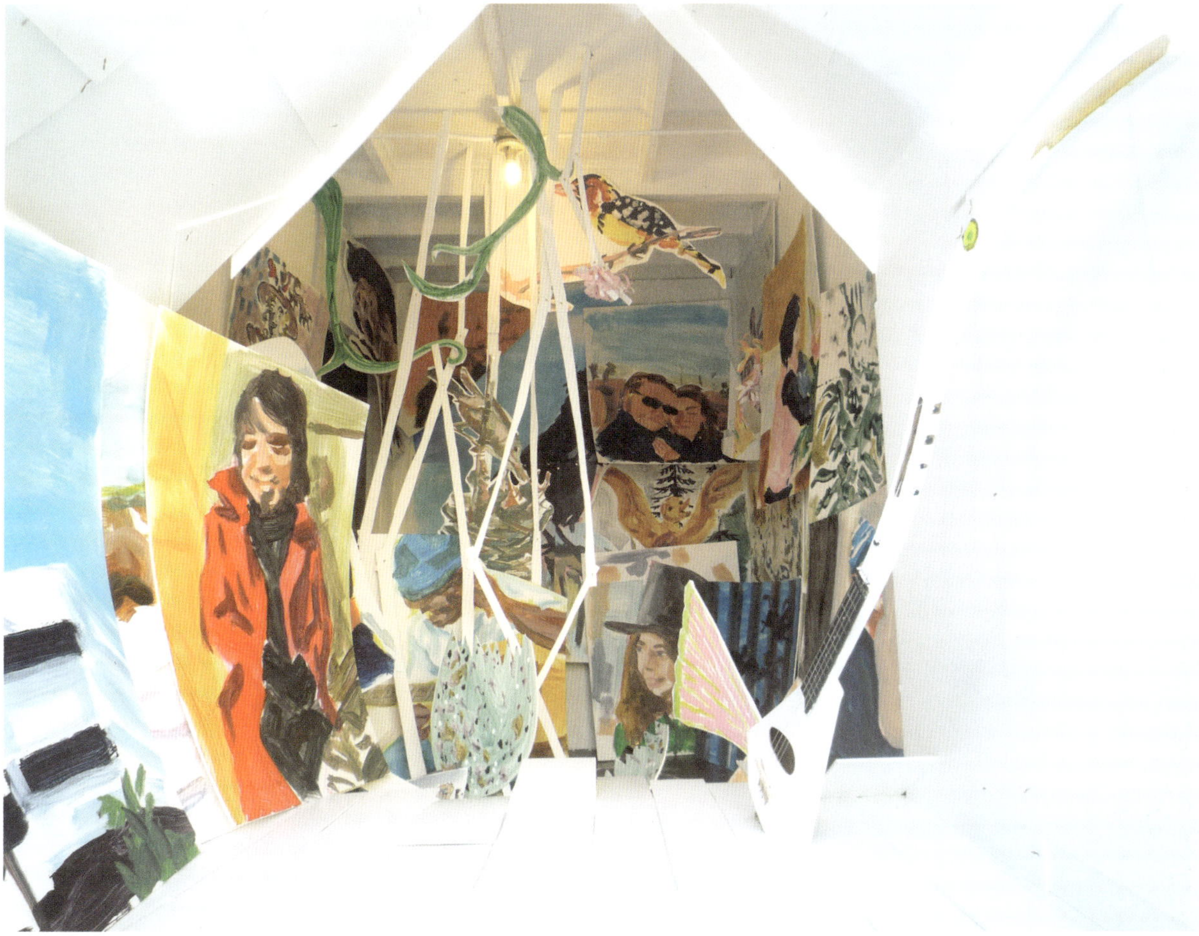

9

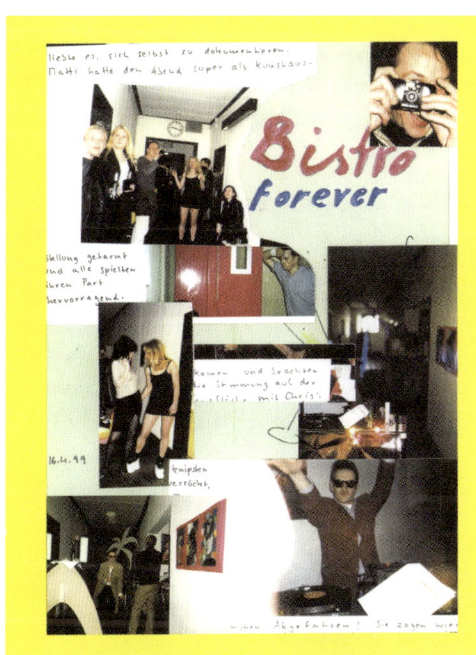

10

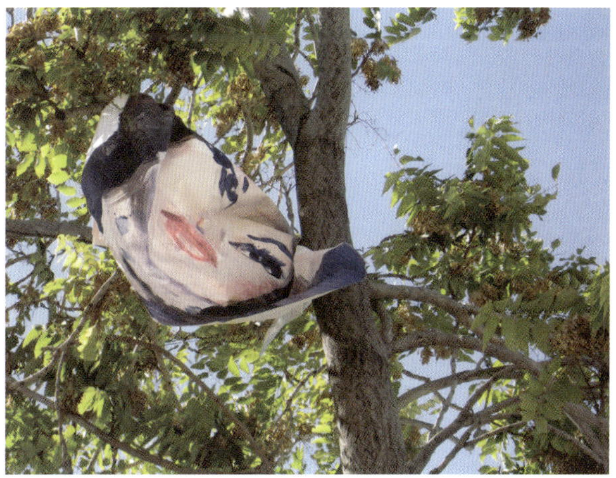

11

ACTIVE SINCE	CITY	WEBSITE
1996	Reykjavík, Iceland	ilc.is

The Icelandic Love Corporation

MEMBERS	ACTIVITIES	RECOMMENDED PUBLICATION
Eirún Siguroardóttir, Jóní Jónsdóttir, and Sigrún Hrólfsdóttir	Curating, Performance, Public Performance, Painting /Sculpture / Installation	THE ICELANDIC LOVE CORPORATION, The Reykjavík Art Museum, Reykjavík, 2007

The Icelandic Love Corporation multimedia practice spans from sculpture to fashion, from video to performance, from installation to publishing. Nature plays an important role, both as context and content. Often immersed in the vastness and glacial scope of the Icelandic landscape, the group explores issues related to femininity, crafts, family, and youth. Handmade clothes and the use of music suggest a surreal dimension where the group becomes a safe escape from the real world.

Why work collaboratively?

We started working together in 1996, when we were still in art school. We felt that the collaboration really accelerated the process, both practically and conceptually. We started making performances together because we shared the urge to get a direct reaction from the audience and we felt that as a group we had more power. Now we work in all different media but performance is a very strong root in all of our work. In the beginning we would make things very fast. We might get an idea on a Tuesday and then it would be all done by Saturday. This has changed and we like to give things more time to develop. But it is still very clear to us that collaboration brings us to places and ideas that we would not get to as individuals.

How do you determine membership? Does physical location matter in this regard?

The three current members started the group and are still the only members. In the late nineties when the internet was really taking off, we were living in NYC, Berlin, and Copenhagen, respectively, and we would exchange ideas over email and chat, and we felt that we were really connected, even though this technology was nothing close to what it is today. We feel that the internet made a big difference in our work at the beginning. The whole idea of globalization and communications technology was really enchanting. Now we all live in close proximity to each other in Reykjavík but make trips to the mainland every now and then.

By definition a corporation is a group of people who are authorized to act as a single entity. This is how we see The Icelandic Love Corporation (ILC). We created a logo and slogans for the group and used all kinds of branding techniques to create an identity, and with time the group has taken on its own identity. We are its caretakers and must make sure that it prospers. ILC is like a baby that needs to be taken care of, or a Frankenstein.

If considered separately, how do your individual artistic practices contribute to or detract from your work as a group?

Everyone in the group also has an individual art career. So far, this has been working very well. We organize ourselves around ILC and feed on it. The individual work fuels the group work as well as letting off pressure, and the group work also gives energy to the individual work and empowers us. It is clear that the ego of each and every one needs nurturing. It can sometimes be very claustrophobic to work in a group, so there have to be defined "emergency exits." But the individual work is not just a result of having to flee the group. This is all kind of complicated but still very simple.

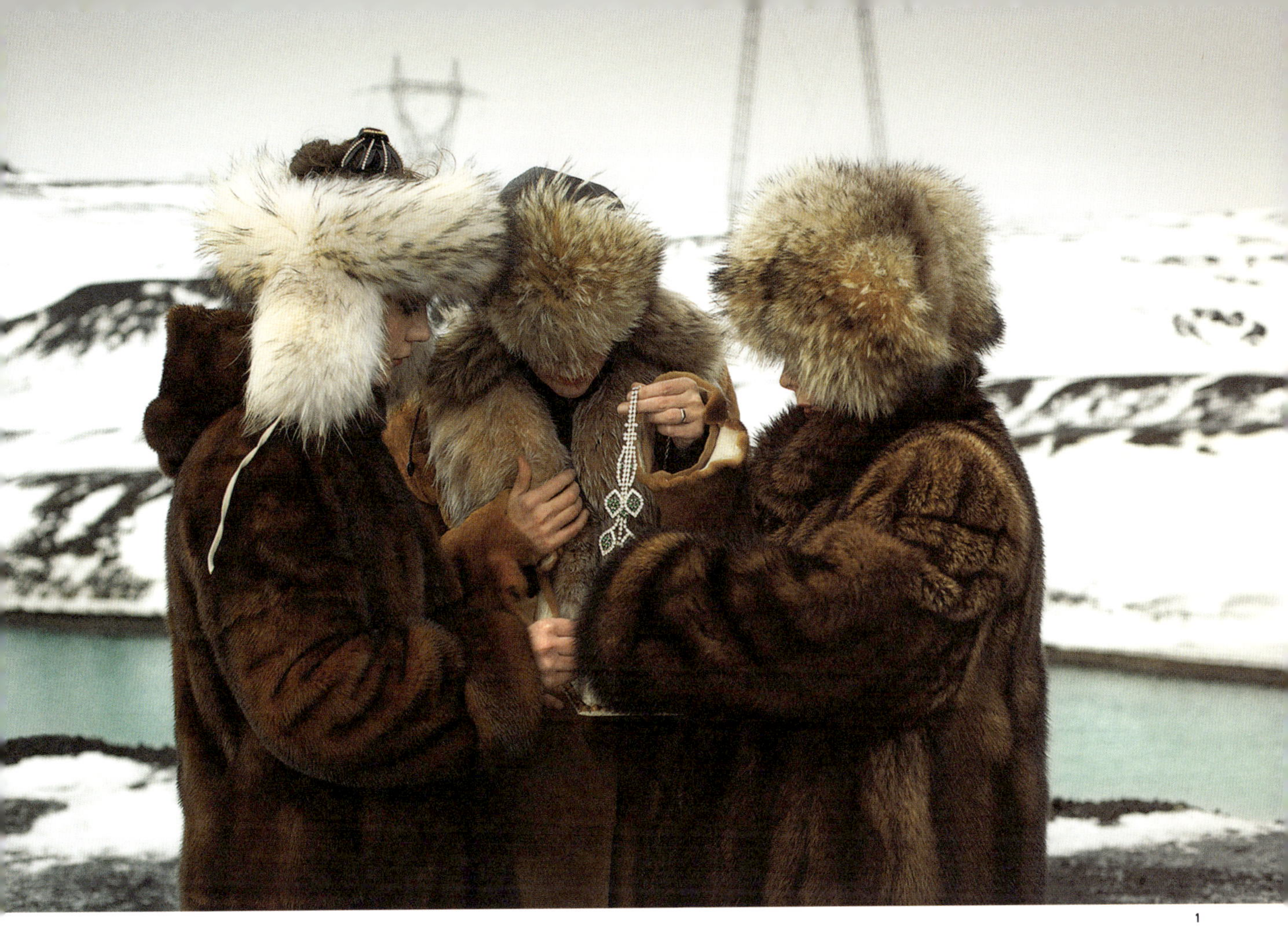

1

THE ICELANDIC LOVE CORPORATION

2

1 – Dynasty film still, from a performance shot in the Icelandic highland, 2007

2 – Logo by The Icelandic Love Corporation, 1996, and special ILC font Crochet, by Gunnar Vilhjálmsson, 2007

3 – Where Do We Go From Here?, performance, Iceland, 2001

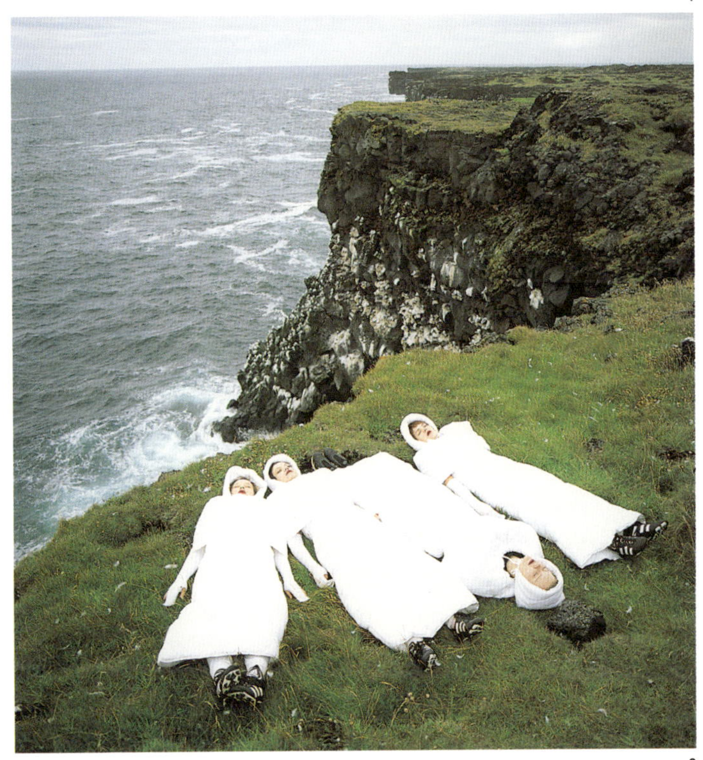

3

How are decisions made?

We discuss everything and everybody has to agree on everything. Majority does not rule. Discussion usually leads us to a good solution to all challenges.

Does each of you have a clearly defined role? If so, what are some of each member's distinct responsibilities?

No, we do not have such roles. We have two rules that we set in the beginning and have never strayed from: If an idea is verbalized within the group, it belongs to the group. So we do not say who owns this or that idea, and it is, of course, unclear most of the time whose idea it was in the first place. Rule number two is that we do not say who does what.

How important is each group member's individuality, both in terms of your artistic production and in terms of your relationship with the media? Does anonymity come into play?

Anonymity does not come into play. We feel that it is very important that people know who the members of ILC are and we state our names when appropriate. But all works that we make as a group belong to ILC as a group. We think that it is extremely important that our work is the result of three distinct persons, without a leader or a governor. Our power structure is flat and we feel that there is redemption in that, in the notion that we can make it work. This goes to show that people can work together, and there should be a way to deal with conflict in a positive way.

What is the relationship between your working methods and your art's "content"? In this sense, does technology tend to play more of a supporting role, or does it lead you in new directions?

Normally it is the idea that leads us to the choice of technique and material. But of course ideas also spawn from materials, techniques, and situations. So we cannot state clearly what comes first. Now that we have been working together for a long time, we have created certain patterns, and every time a new work is created, it in some sense stems from an older piece. The works are all intertwined and the body of work keeps growing on its own terms.

How does your collaboration relate to its cultural, institutional, and commercial contexts? In other words, how would you respond to those who call this a trend?

People have been working in groups since before the Neanderthals. And people have always been working in groups within the art world. It is a double-edged thing to form a group,because you have to let go of certain egotistic tendencies to make the group flourish, but on the other hand the group can be a great source of power. We think that collaboration should be endorsed in all stages of life. "Collaborate or die" are the key words for humanity.

Who is your audience?

The general public, people within the art world.

Does your engagement with one another translate into an engagement with the public? How so?

It is very clear who is a part of the group. In our works we often wear uniforms to distinguish us from the audience. But we still invite people to enter the work. Of course, all works of art depend on the engagement of an audience, so there is a certain contradiction in our ideology. We want everyone to accept our terms and invite them to take part in our activities, but they are never really allowed to make any decisions. There is no democracy. But doing this within the art context hopefully inspires people to take matters into their own hands in their own lives.

Our first slogan was Love conquers all, without a doubt! We would stand on rooftops and blare this statement through megaphones in a very fascistic manner. The contradictions in our operation are maybe crystallized in this early performance. This was really our manifesto.

The Icelandic name of our group is Gjörningaklúbburinn, which basically means "Performance Club." But it has connotations of the term "sewing circle," a very private and close-knit party of women, and of witchcraft, which is of course just a name for females trying to take control in a male-dominant world. The Icelandic word "gjörningur" means both act and craft in relation to witchcraft. We want to attract attention and have influence, but we are also very clearly a closed group or a gang, one that is not open in any way. The English title The Icelandic Love Corporation expands this idea to a global scale.

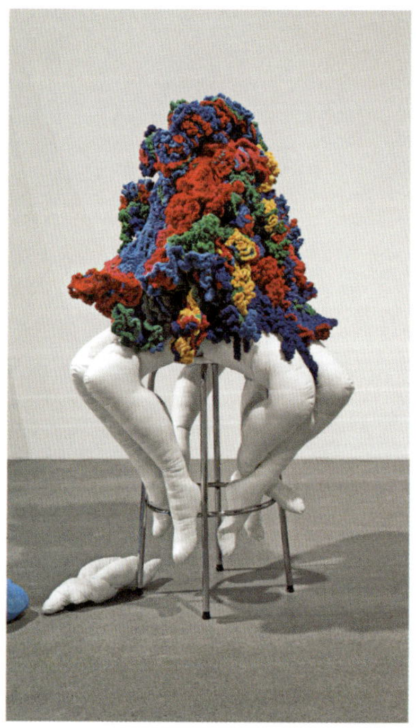

4

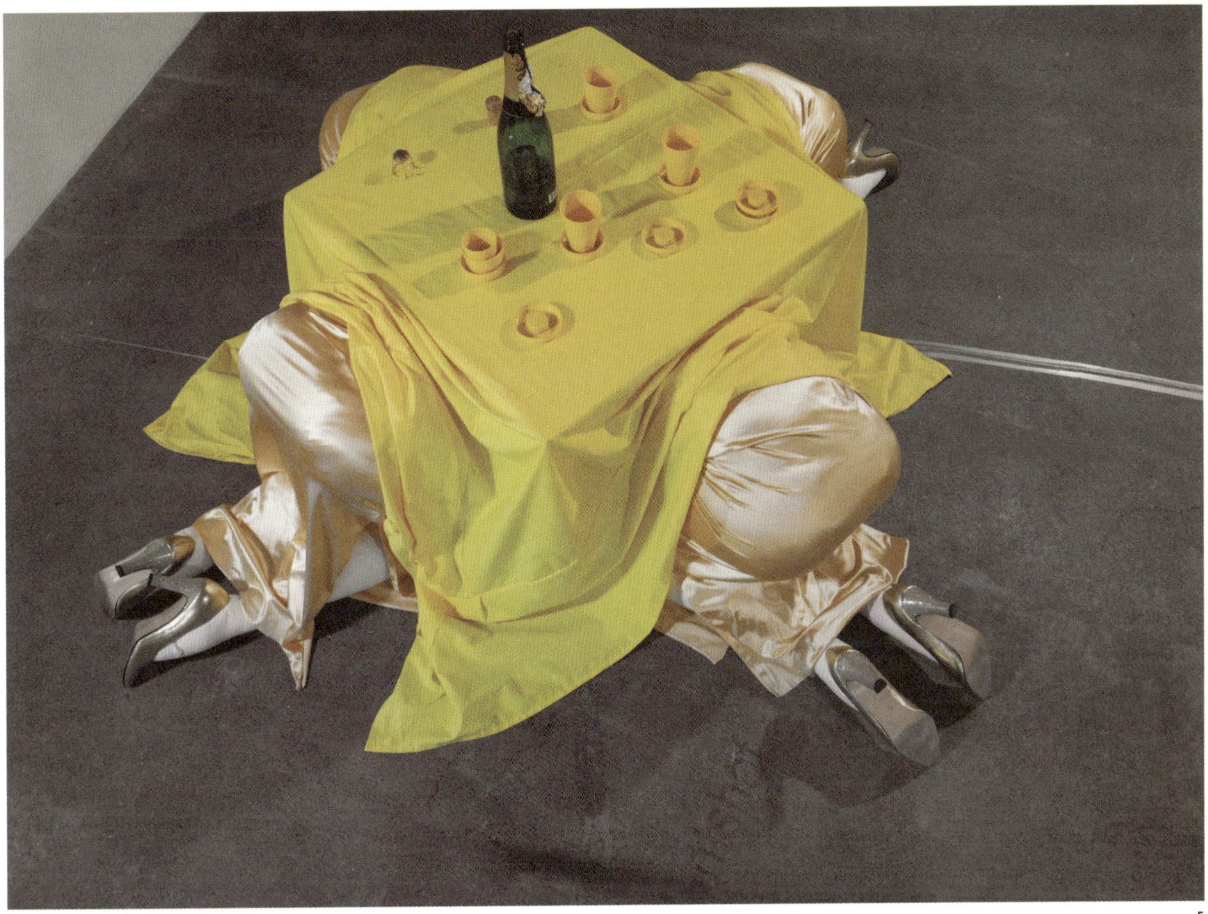

5

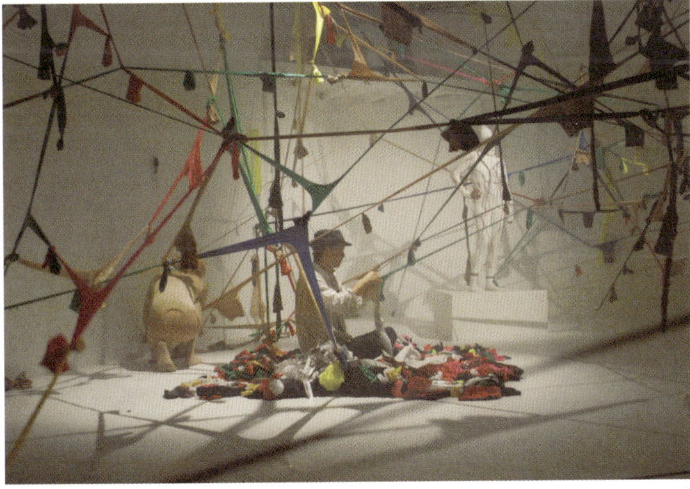

6

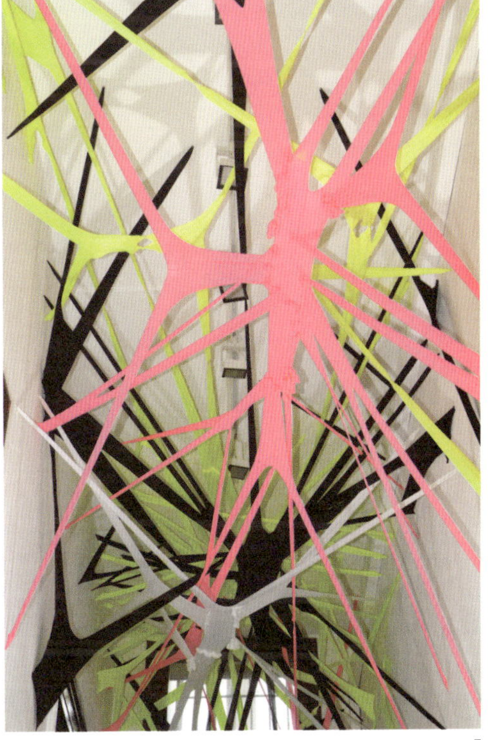

7

opposite
4 – Self Portrait, sculpture made of yarn, fabric, and steel, 2009

5 – Higher Beings, performance as sculpture, Midnight Walkers and City Sleepers, Amsterdam, 1999

6 – Think Less – Feel More, performance, Lilith Performance Studio, Malmö, 2011

7 – The Third Dimension, installation, Palazzo Bembo, Venice, 2013

8 + 9 – Intimacy Circus, performance, McCarren Park, Brooklyn, 2004

10 – Crystal Rain, performance in collaboration with Ragnar Kjartansson, Hamburger Bahnhof, Berlin, 2004

11 – Faces, self-portrait, 2010

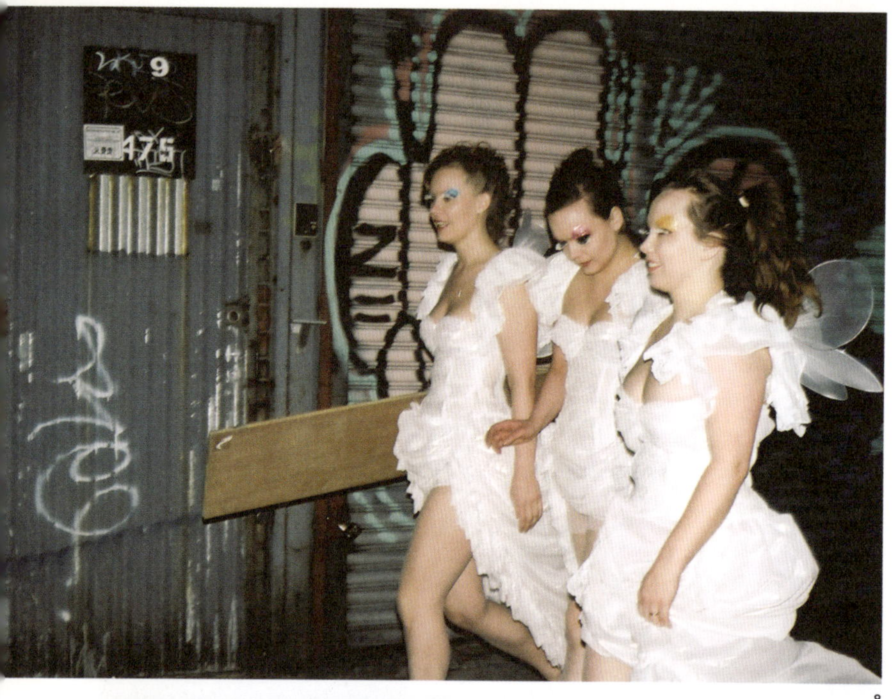

8

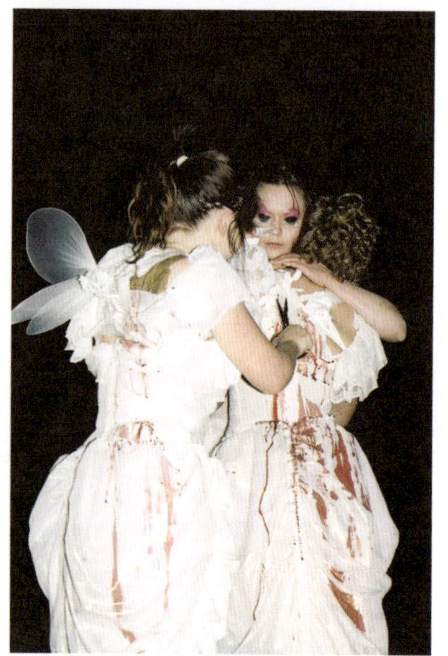

9

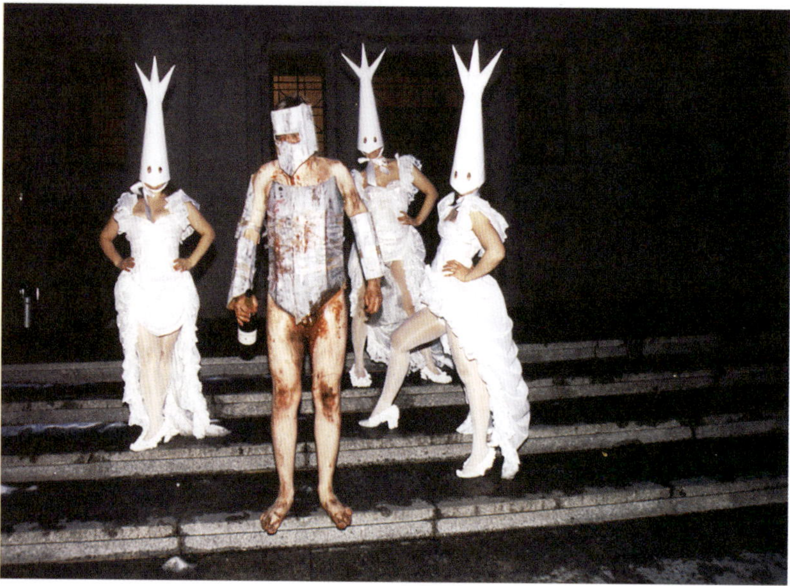

10

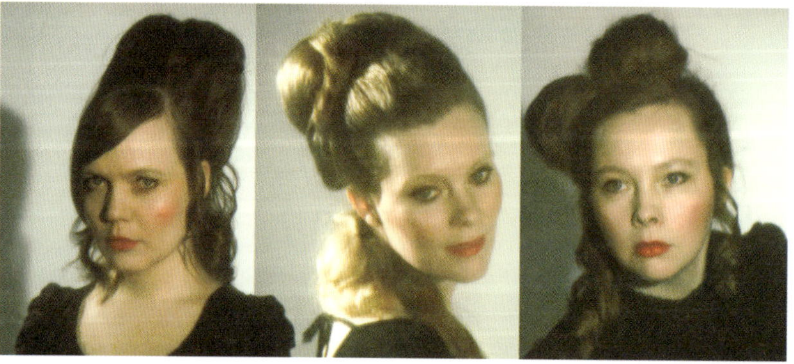

11

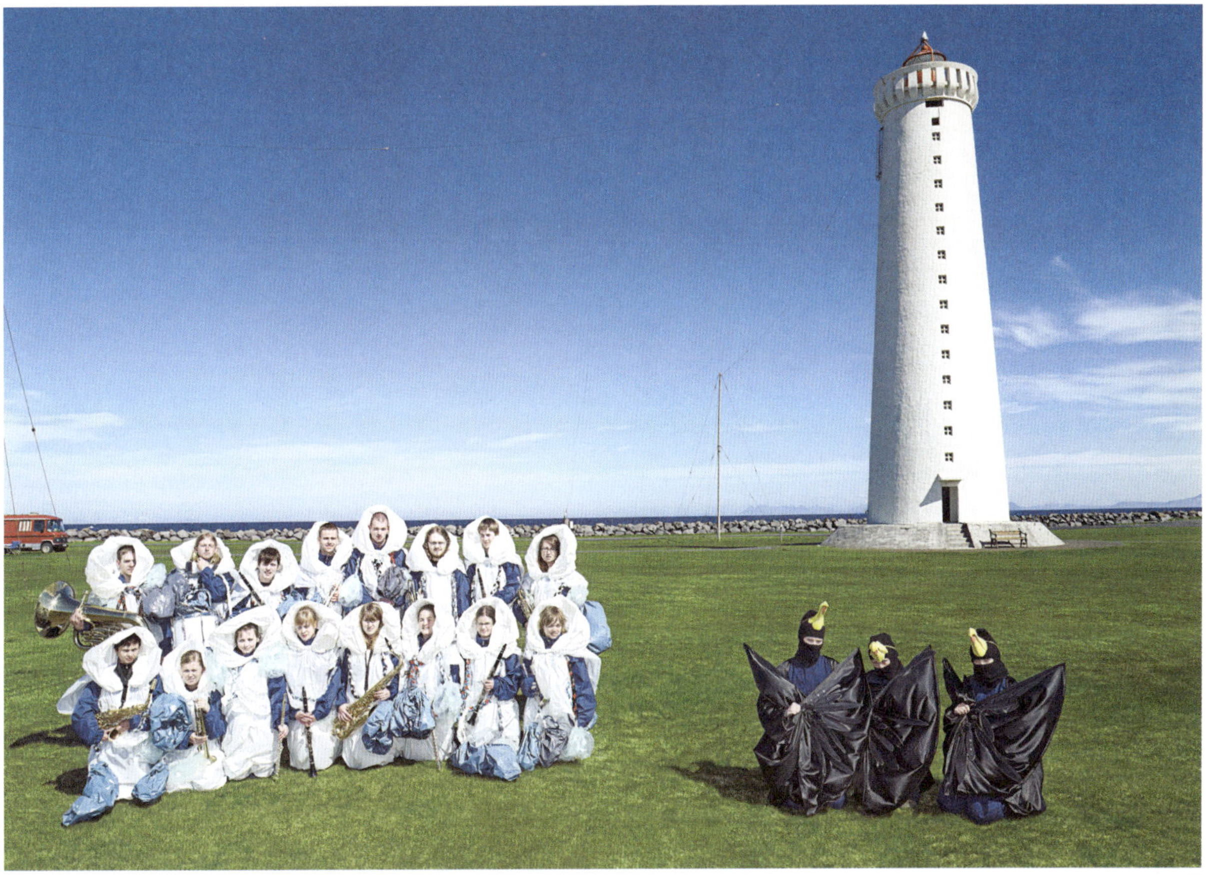

12

12 – Indeed, Of Course!, performance, Gardskagi Lighthouse, Reykjavík, 2009

13 – Ashford Castle, performance, Ashford Castle, Ireland, 2006

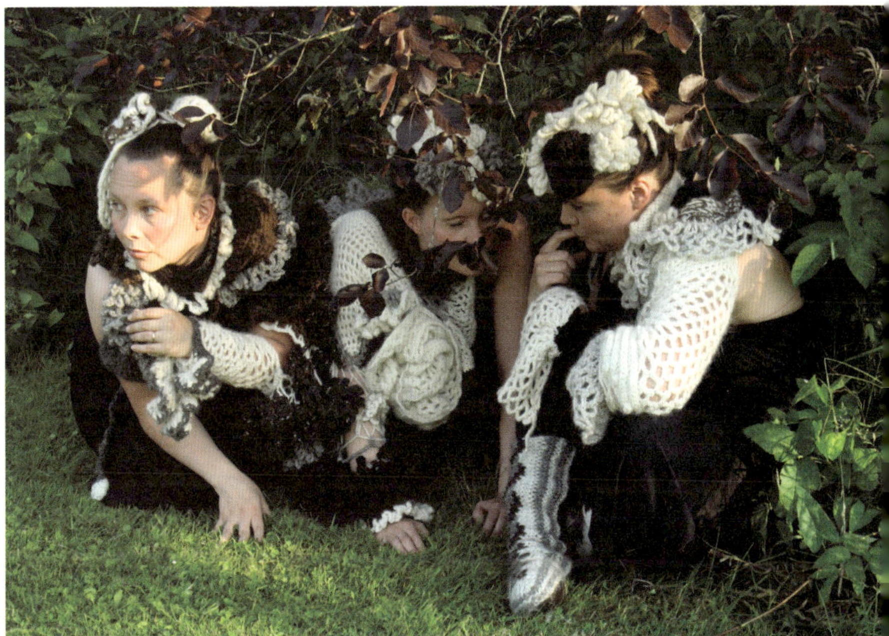

13

ACTIVE SINCE	CITY	WEBSITE
2001	New York, U.S.	improveverywhere.com

Improv Everywhere

MEMBERS	ACTIVITIES	RECOMMENDED PUBLICATION
Tens of thousands	Public Performance, Urban Interventions	Charlie Todd and Alex Scordelis, Causing a Scene: Extraordinary Pranks in Ordinary Places with IMPROV EVERYWHERE, Harper Collins, New York, 2009

Led by Charlie Todd, Improv Everywhere is one of the largest collectives ever. Its actions take place in the public sphere—streets, parks, plazas, subway stations, supermarkets—and may involve thousands of people, gathered through social networks and digital media. The aim is to turn viewers into participants, choreographing entertaining events that temporarily change the use of the non places of contemporary cities like New York.

Why work collaboratively?

The internet has given us the power to work with crowds in new and exciting ways. I can send one email to my list and have thousands of people show up in the right place at the right time, wearing something specific and with specific props in hand. The web also gives you the power to crowdsource ideas. While the majority of our Improv Everywhere projects have either been my idea or a collaboration with a close colleague, more than a few have been born out of suggestions emailed in by a random stranger.

How do you determine membership? Does physical location matter in this regard?

Physical location matters for Improv Everywhere. We do not stage projects that are online only, but rather use the internet to organize things that happen in the real world. We stage a few projects every year that are open to the public. For the smaller projects, I cast friends and longtime members of the group. Most members have a background in improv comedy performance.

If considered separately, how do your individual artistic practices contribute to or detract from your work as a group?

I run the group so all of the creative choices are funneled through me. However, I'm lucky to work with a team of people who are far more talented than me in areas like photography, videography, editing, songwriting, and music composition. I know my strengths and I know the aspects of our projects I need help with.

How are decisions made?

Ultimately the buck stops with me. All creative decisions are ultimately mine. I don't like making decisions in a vacuum though, so I'm constantly having conversations with my documentation team and other longtime collaborators about the choices I make.

Does each of you have a clearly defined role? If so, what are some of each member's distinct responsibilities?

Those in the group who have a defined role are the ones on the technical side—video, photography, music, etc. There is also a stable of actors I work with who I know I can count on when particular performance needs arise.

How important is each group member's individuality, both in terms of your artistic production and in terms of your relationship with the media? Does anonymity come into play?

I've been lucky to work with a huge number of collaborators over the years. Our lineup changes as people come and go from the city. We have a great team now and it includes many people who have been with the group for over a

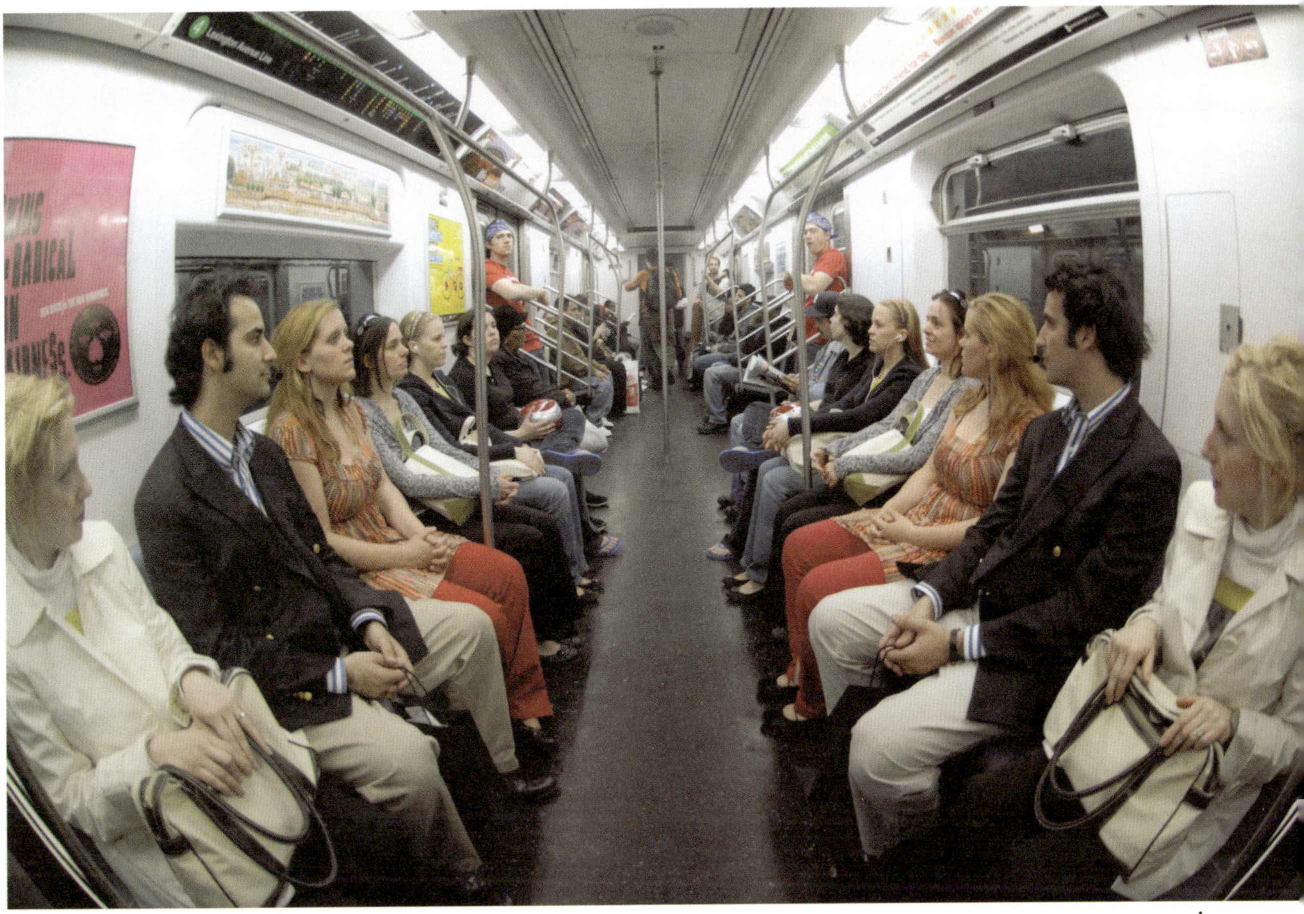

1

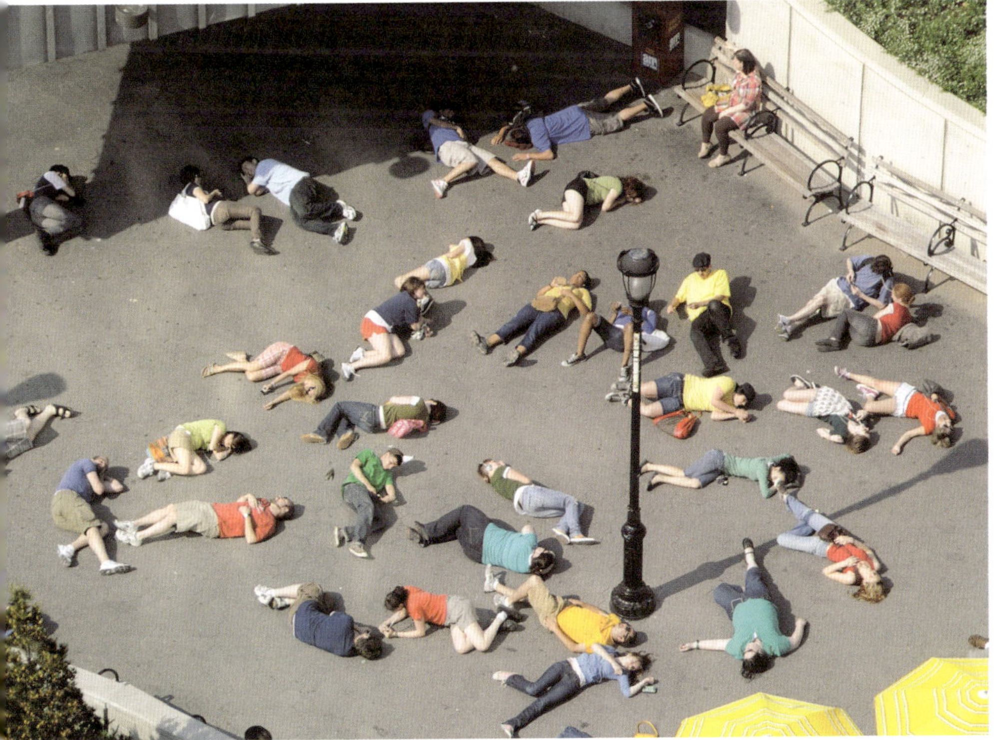

2

1 – Human Mirror, public performance, New York, 2008

2 – The Mp3 Experiment Six, public performance, Roosevelt Island, New York, 2009

3 – The Mp3 Experiment Four, public performance, New York, 2007

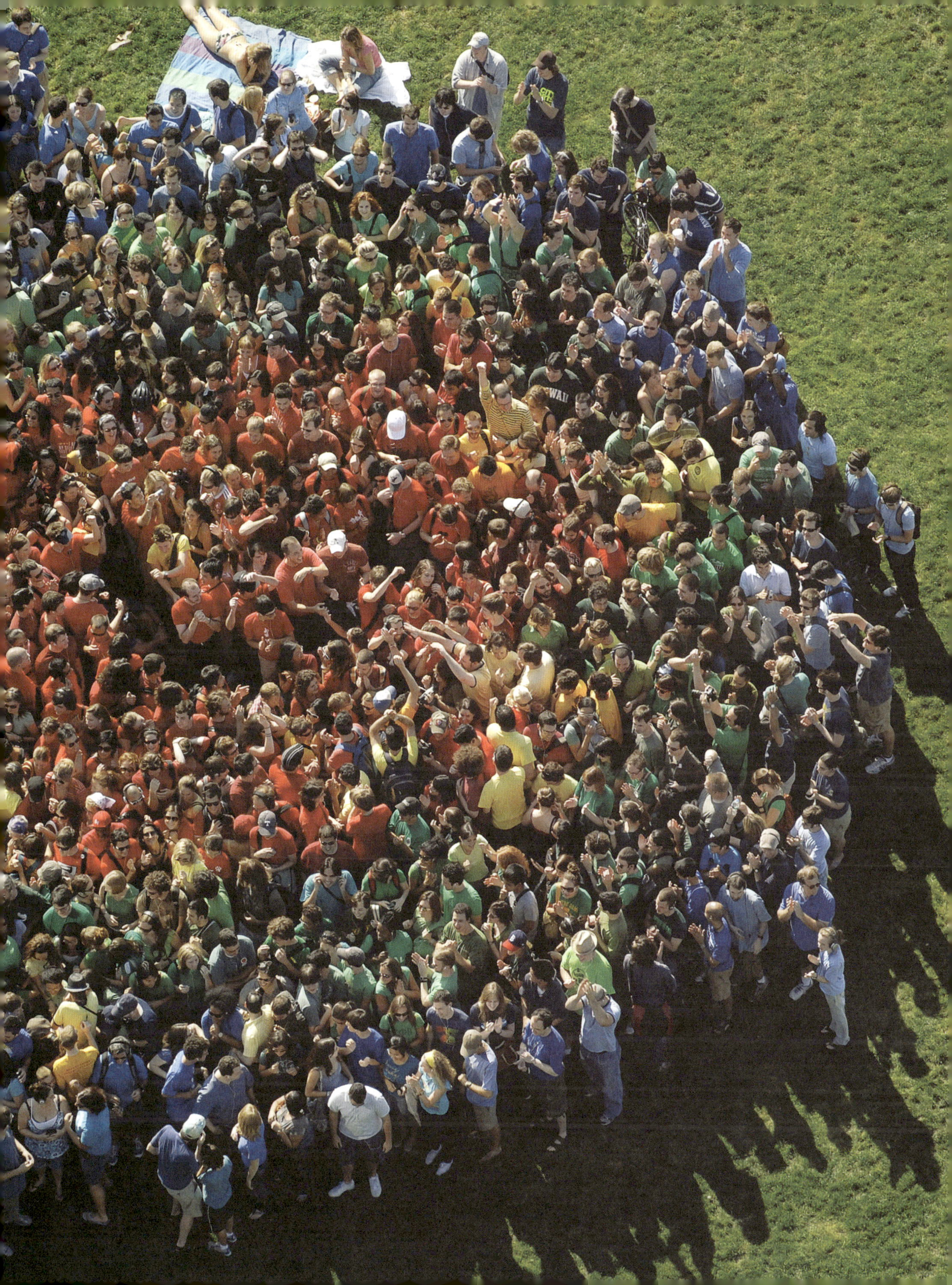

4 – Look Up More, public performance, Union Square, New York, 2005

5 – Best Funeral Ever (April Fool's 2009), public performance, New York, 2009

6 – I Love Lunch! The Musical, public performance, Trump Tower Atrium, New York, 2009

7 – Subway Art Gallery Opening, public performance, New York, 2009

8 – Best Buy, public performance, Twenty-third Street, New York, 2006

opposite
9 – The Mp3 Experiment Eight, public performance, Nelson Rockefeller Park, New York, 2011

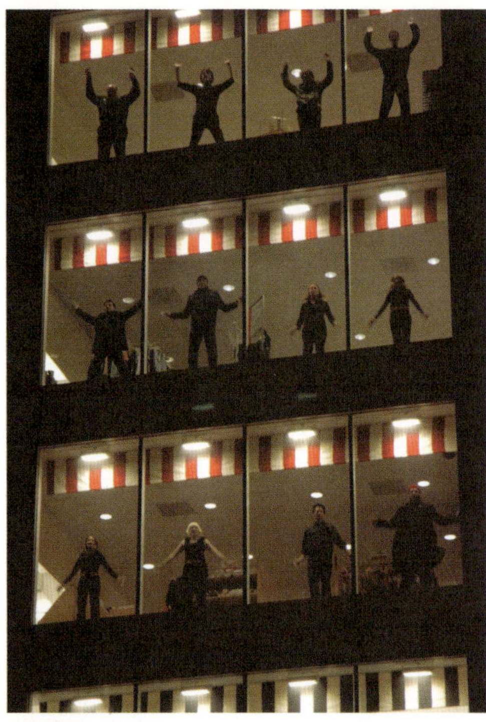

4

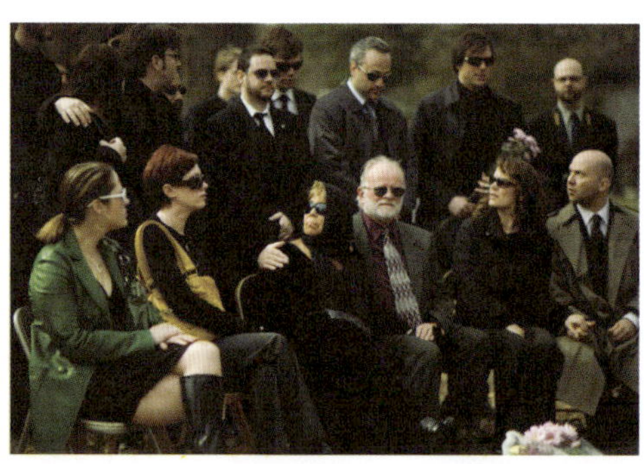

5

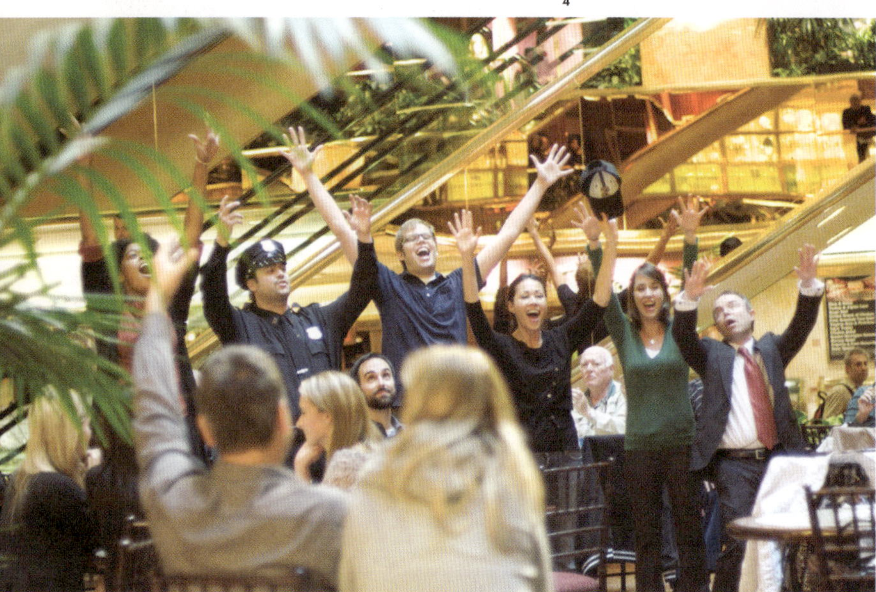

6

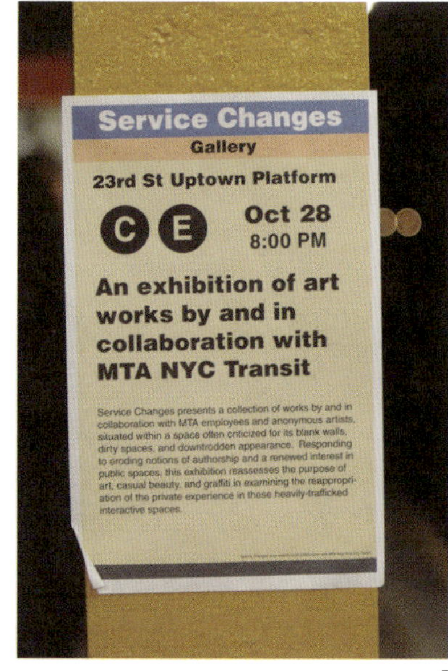

7

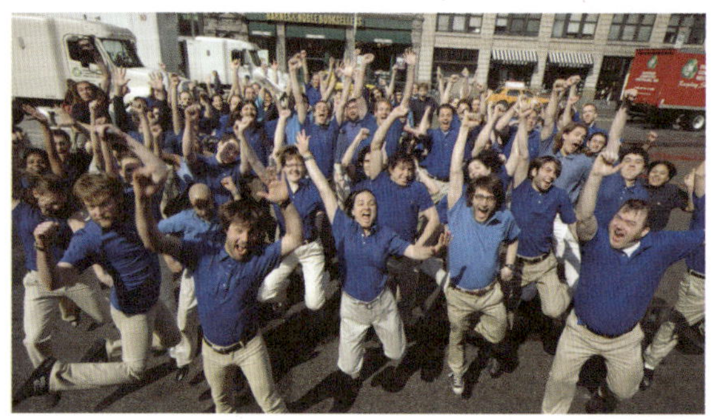

8

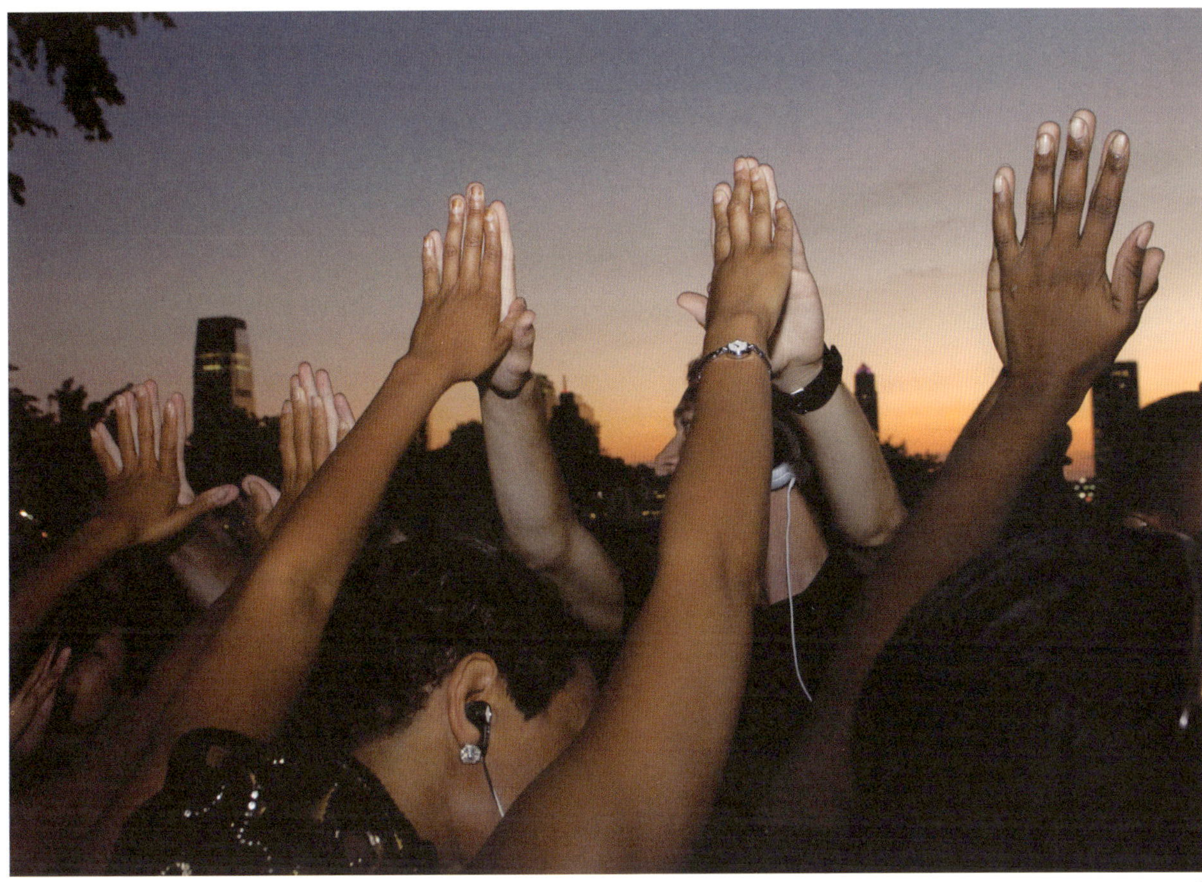

9

decade. I would say that the team is very important to me and there are several key people who contribute great amounts individually to our production. In terms of the media, I handle most media requests. Anonymity doesn't come into play.

What is the relationship between your working methods and your art's "content"? In this sense, does technology tend to play more of a supporting role, or does it lead you in new directions?

Technology plays a very important role in our process. We started in 2001 and things have changed so much in the past thirteen years. We are able to document and distribute our work in ways that would not have been possible back then. In terms of the projects themselves, we use technology to our advantage whenever we can, whether it's using 270 LED flashlights or getting four thousand people to listen to the same MP3 file.

How does your collaboration relate to its cultural, institutional, and commercial contexts? In other words, how would you respond to those who call this a trend?

We are linked to the flash mob trend although I never use the term and do not feel a connection to the trend, largely because we predate it by a few years. Obviously some of our projects are similar to flash mobs. I understand how 200 people frozen in place in a train station is in the style of a flash mob. I've personally never been interested in having our work tied to a buzzword or trend. I'd rather have it stand on its own.

Who is your audience?

We have two audiences—those who witness our work by chance (and perhaps without knowing) in public spaces in New York City, and the millions of people who see our work on YouTube. It is a balancing act to keep both of these in mind. The live audience is the most important, but the YouTube audience is exponentially larger.

Does your engagement with one another translate into an engagement with the public? How so?

Our work is centered on engaging with our audience. The whole point of Improv Everywhere is to cause a scene that elicits an unexpected, positive response from random strangers.

ACTIVE SINCE	CITY	WEBSITE
2000	Vancouver / Toronto, Canada	instantcoffee.org

Instant Coffee

MEMBERS	ACTIVITIES	RECOMMENDED PUBLICATION
Jinhan Ko, Kelly Lycan, Khan Lee, Cecilia Berkovic, Kate Monro, and Jenifer Papararo	Curating, Music, Painting/ Sculpture / Installation, Public Art, Public Performance, Publishing, Services (e.g., a weekly Listserv announcing exhibitions, calls, lectures, jobs, residencies, etc.)	Rosemary Heather, INSTANT COFFEE: Disco Fallout Shelter, The Party's Over, Toronto Sculpture Park, Toronto, 2009

Exploiting the social dimension of the cafe, Instant Coffee produces posters, installations, and workshops that posit coffee as a universal symbol of collective endeavor. It is less interested in contents than in the structures where ideas and discussion take form, offering the audience the stimulus and the tools to socialize.

Why work collaboratively?

One Is Never Enough.

Although we have been asked this question many times, we haven't theorized it, choosing not to evaluate why we've come to work together much beyond surface responses. In the past we've stated that working collaboratively gives each of us a ready-made audience—we've spoken about the privilege of having immediate feedback. How that immediacy accelerates process and offers confidence. We've flippantly talked about the role of codependence and how admitting an outright reliance on others is a viable strategy for making art. We've named our suspension of isolated studio practices—the lone genius-maker working in seclusion has reason enough to work collaboratively. We've used pat critiques of authorship as a significant motivation. There is no sole reason and not a singular trajectory as to why we've decided to work collaboratively. But in a general sense and in Canadian terms, it is part of our history. All of us have been influenced by the collective history of artmaking in Canada—the major role of artist-run centers in the latter half of the twentieth century in the production, exhibition, and distribution of art. It is as if we came to it by rote. Working collaboratively wasn't necessarily an active choice so much as an assumption.

How do you determine membership? Does physical location matter in this regard?

We Want More Than We Can Give.

We started in Toronto in order to address a general set of concerns that we tested out locally. We felt there was a loss of meaning, emotion, and energy in the transition from studio to the gallery and we wanted to see if we could find a different way to engage with art that was public but not confined by the formal characteristics of gallery exhibitions. Membership was fairly loose at the beginning. It started with four members: Jinhan, Kate, Jenifer, and Stephan Crowhurst, but then expanded quickly to include Cecilia, with other members joining as projects unfolded. Timothy Comeau, Jon Sasski, and Emily Hogg all contributed to various artworks from 2001 to 2004. When several members moved to Vancouver we gained Kelly Lycan and Khan Lee. Our studio is based in Vancouver and most of the production happens there.

If considered separately, how do your individual artistic practices contribute to or detract from your work as a group?

What Do We Do When We Can't Be Together.

Most all of us have bifurcated practices, except for Jinhan, whose primary activity is Instant Coffee. He is always we. The rest of us either have art, curatorial, publishing, or design practices parallel to Instant Coffee.

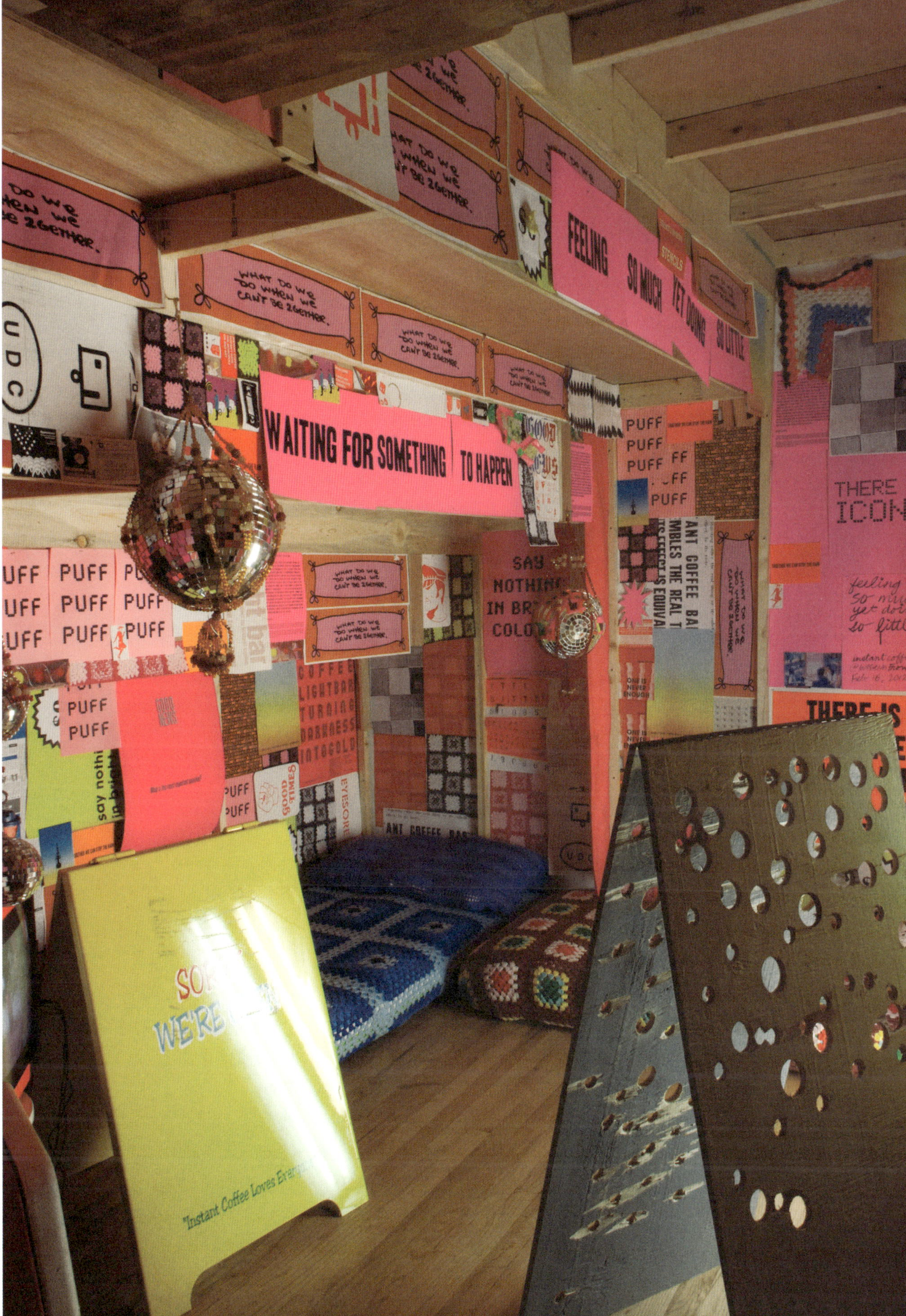
WHAT DO WE DO WHEN WE CAN'T BE 2GETHER.
WAITING FOR SOMETHING
TO HAPPEN
FEELING
SO MUCH
YET DOING
SO LITTLE
PUFF
PUFF
PUFF
SAY
STENCILS

1

How are decisions made?

It Doesn't Have To Be Good To Be Meaningful

It varies from project to project. There are shifting heads. But generally if a member can rally the interest and support of enough of the other members, then the project is a go. Not everyone works on everything and not everyone has to agree on everything.

Does each of you have a clearly defined role? If so, what are some of each member's distinct responsibilities?

Waiting For Something To Happen.

Of course we each have our unique offerings, but nothing is clearly defined or assumed.

How important is each group member's individuality, both in terms of your artistic production and in terms of your relationship with the media? Does anonymity come into play?

There Is No Romance In Taking A Risk.

Maybe it isn't so important to speak about individuality in this context. We acknowledge our relations to the collective as a part of it. This is not to say that each of us doesn't retain value. We all factor in, but always and only as pieces, and as pieces we have to be perceived within a larger whole.

What is the relationship between your working methods and your art's "content"? In this sense, does technology tend to play more of a supporting role, or does it lead you in new directions?

Feeling So Much Yet Doing So Little.

Generally we don't separate form and content. We use a lot of fluorescent orange/pink in our work not simply because we're drawn to it but because we're interested in exploiting its vernacular uses in advertising and as a utilitarian safety measure. In past installations, we used a lot of woven afghan blankets typical of North America in the seventies. We used them because they were colorful and easily commanded an aesthetic presence, but we were also interested in their economy as a laborious craft and their ready availability in secondhand stores.

And yes, how we work is an important part of the content. As a collective, we are dependent on the work of others. We often invite other artists to work with us, staging scenarios in order to incorporate their work with ours. Many of our exhibitions have functioned as venues for us to program music, performances, lectures, and screenings by other artists.

How does your collaboration relate to its cultural, institutional, and commercial contexts? In other words, how would you respond to those who call this a trend?

We Can Not Be Moved.

As we mentioned in our first response, we come from a long history of collaborative practices. It is a common means of working in Canada and we can draw a longer line through broader art history, naming arts and crafts movements from the Bloomsbury group to the artists working in Worpswede, Germany, in the early twentieth century. We could stretch our thinking to include the Constructivists and Dada, but if we look locally and nationally we can talk about Image Bank, the Western Front, and General Idea, all of whom have had an impact on us. We like to situate ourselves in this lineage.

Who is your audience?

Instant Coffee Loves Everyone Plus You

Does your engagement with one another translate into an engagement with the public? How so?

We did state earlier that we are our own audience and this is true, but of course we're interested in engaging more than ourselves. In the beginning we'd hold large events that incorporated work by sometimes up to seventy artists. In these instances the artists we invited were both content providers and audience members. We were interested in leveling producer and audience as equal participants. Lately we have been working in the public art realm with a wide and mostly anonymous audience. We're happy moving between these two extremes, from insular to unfathomable.

With wavering clarity we understand that what we do is confined to the limitations of representation and we're okay with that. This understanding is in the name Instant Coffee. As a product Instant Coffee is an effective substitute. It mimics the real thing without the pretence of being better. It isn't that much easier to make, but that much is reason enough to justify its particularities. Taste is a factor, and to those with taste is an important difference used to mark quality and define preference.

BUT QUALITY IS TOO PARTICULAR AND PREFERENCES CHANGE.

They are superfluous really, misnomers that distract from the fundamental reasons for ingesting either the real thing or its substitute. Value is in their effect. In its taste.

INSTANT COFFEE BARELY RESEMBLES THE REAL THING, BUT ITS EFFECT IS EQUIVALENT.

Regardless of taste it still works. Quality is beside the point. And in this disregard Instant Coffee becomes a medium to be used.

INSTANT COFFEE MANIFESTO

2

previous

1 – Feeling So Much Yet Doing So Little, installation, Western Front, Vancouver, 2012

opposite

2 – Instant Coffee Manifesto printed for MDE07 Encuentro internacional, Casa del Encuentro, Medellin, Colombia, 2007

3 – It Doesn't Have To Be Good To Be Meaningful, installation, Art Gallery of Greater Victoria, Victoria, 2009

4 – Year of Perfect Days, installation and series of events, Sparwasser HQ, Berlin, 2005

5 – When Bored We Reserve the Right to Do Nothing, installation, New Forms Festival 11, Vancouver, 2011

6 – Wrong Gallery Edition #125 poster, Lobby Gallery, Vancouver, 2006

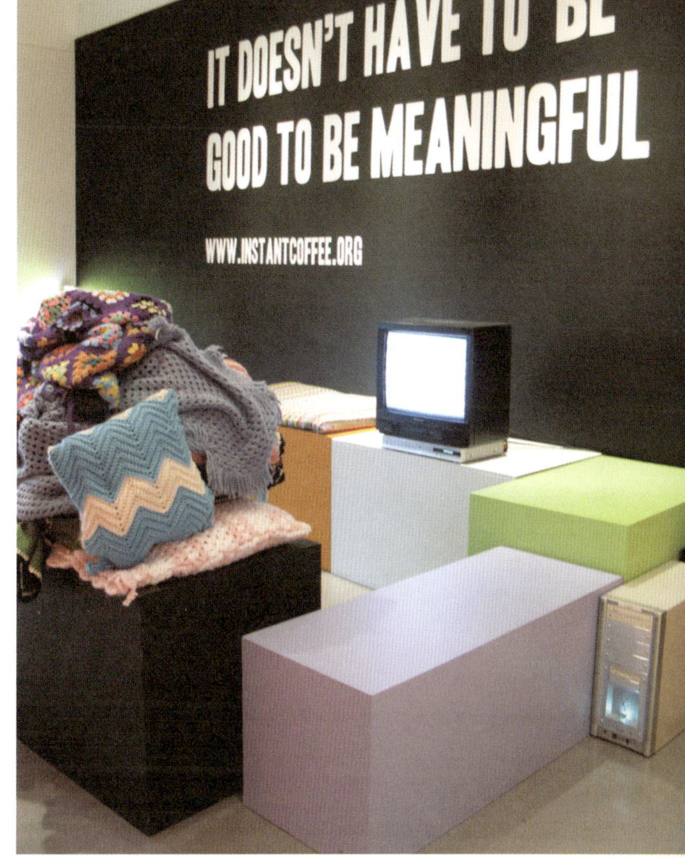

3

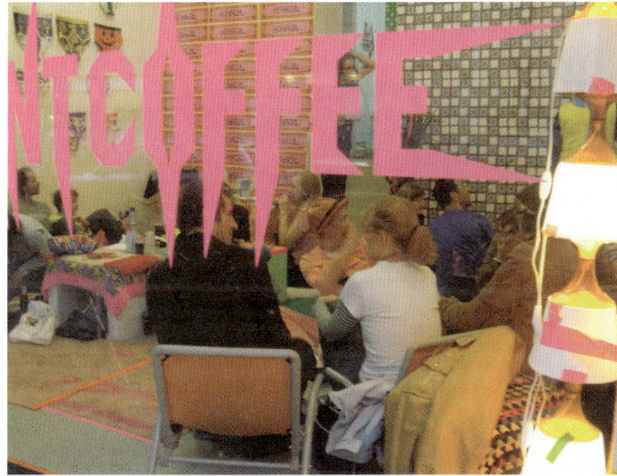

4

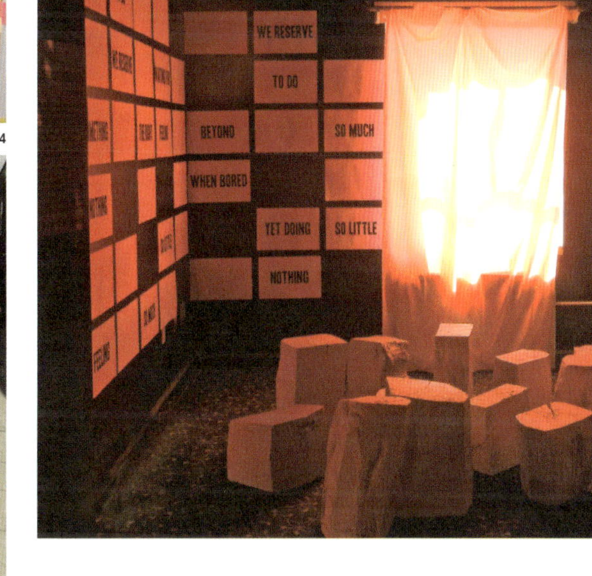

5

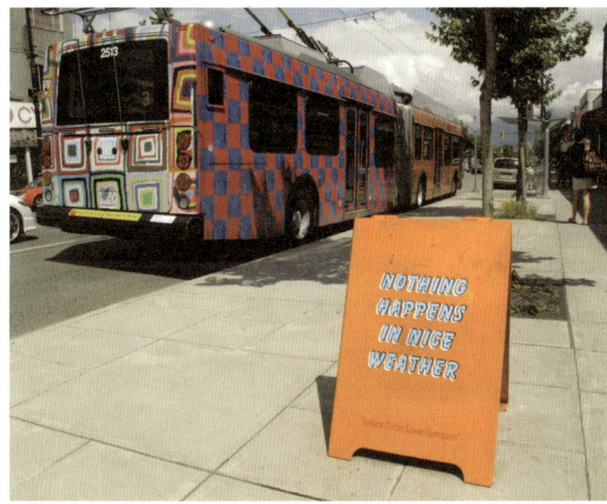

6

ACTIVE SINCE	CITY	WEBSITE
2008	London, UK	luckypdf.com

LuckyPDF

MEMBERS	ACTIVITIES	RECOMMENDED PUBLICATION
James Early, John Hill, Oliver Hogan, and Yuri Pattison	Broadcast, Curating, Internet Art, Merchandising, Media Interventions, Music, Painting / Sculpture / Installation, Public Performance, Publishing	Frieze Projects 2011: LuckyPDF Interview with Sarah McCrorm, Frieze Art Fair Yearbook, London, 2011–2012

Using photography, video, performance, and installation, LuckyPDF's work focuses on the power of mass media to create stereotypes. Most of the group's activities play with the idea of TV productions—talk shows, musicals, and other forms of entertainment—in which members of the group and friends take imaginary roles and the line that separates real life from fiction gets narrower.

Why work collaboratively?

We view LuckyPDF as a form of emergence; when done right the whole is greater than the sum of its parts.

LuckyPDF itself isn't always a straightforward collaboration between core members; projects often involve many other artists, brought together under the LuckyPDF umbrella. Collaboration is a great way to propose new ways of working, challenging artists to step out of their practice or predefined roles and produce things in new ways with new people.

Proposing systems within which to collaborate creates a fertile territory for ideas that might not otherwise be conceived or realized by a single practitioner. The structures we work within, such as live Internet TV shows, are designed to provide inspiring parameters/focus to the work process. We view collaboration as a useful leveling of audience and participant in a way that reflects wider engagement with network technology and media in society.

How do you determine membership? Does physical location matter in this regard?

We started with a specific location, both in terms of membership and audience. Originally membership was more fluid, with less distinction between who's a "member" and who we were working with. At this early stage, LuckyPDF was situated within the South London art scene, consciously separate from the more established (grown-up) East London art scene. Membership became fixed in 2011 for our first major TV project; at the same time the artists we work with, and the audience, became more diverse. We now actively try to work with artists and develop audiences all across the world.

If considered separately, how do your individual artistic practices contribute to or detract from your work as a group?

We can develop greater projects in collaboration; we have aspirations that exceed what's possible as an individual. As individuals, we are all interested in collaboration generally, sometimes collaborating outside of our nucleic group if necessary to realize specific desires. LuckyPDF is the space where some of our individual artistic aspirations are served; these are not always the same aspirations; we try to make work that serves the multiple wants of our own and those we collaborate with. As individual practitioners we are all interested in expanding practice into a social activity; this requires flexibility in where we exist as individuals within projects.

How are decisions made?

We don't have a fixed process although we try to reach unanimous, mutually beneficial decisions that satisfy all parties. Decisions are made by discussion; we value conversations as it's through this that we develop ideas. We believe that ideas are improved by incorporating multiple opinions to create universal outcomes and through collaboration we will create better projects. Although we

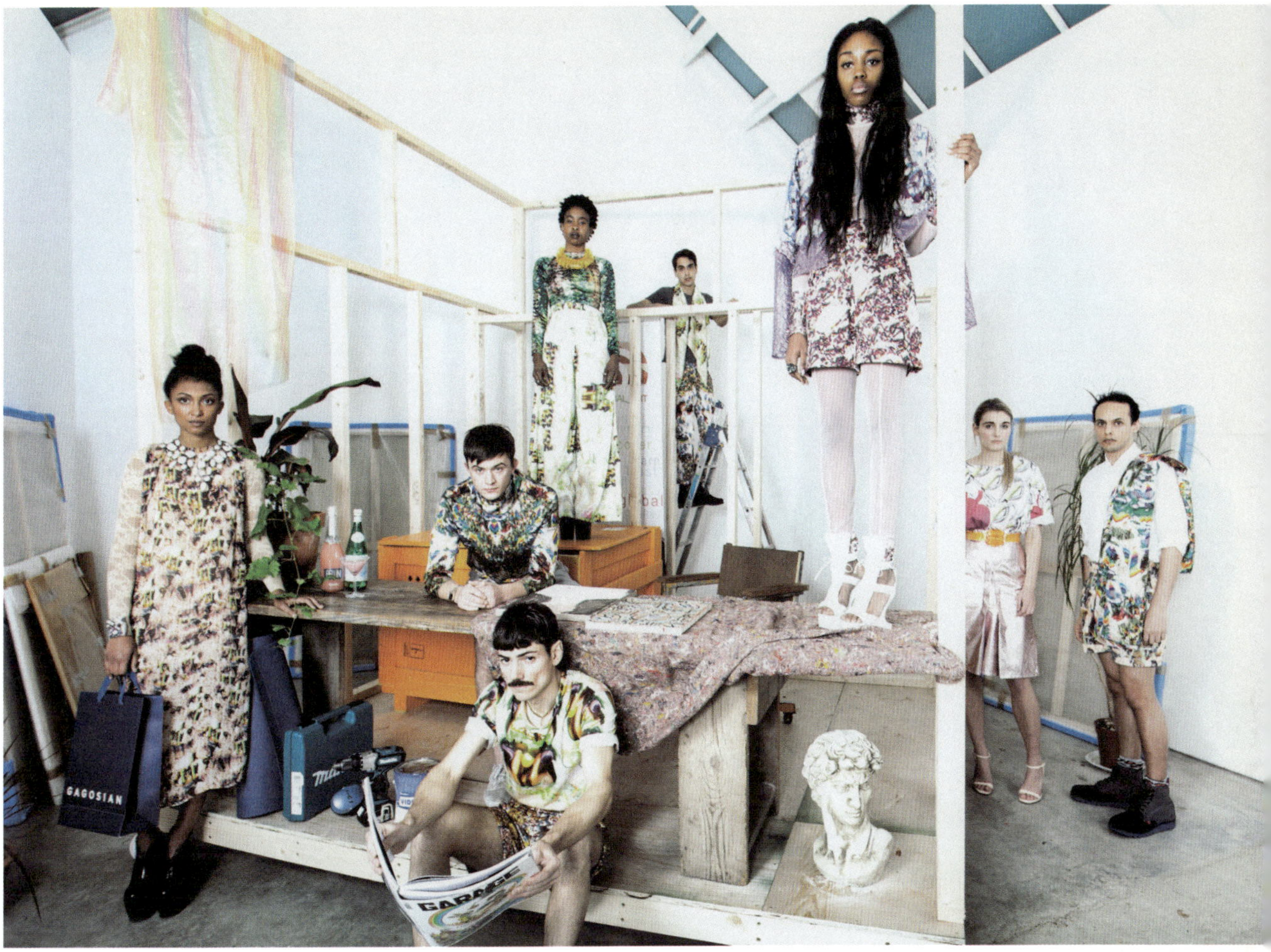

1

1 – LuckyPDF, PDF S/S 2013, group portrait, 2013

2 – Lucy Beech and Edward Thomasson (performance), Adham Faramawy (set) for LuckyPDF, From LuckyPDF TV: This is Frieze Art Fair, installation and performance, Frieze Art Fair, London, 2011. Commissioned by Frieze Foundation for Frieze Projects, curated by Sarah McCrory

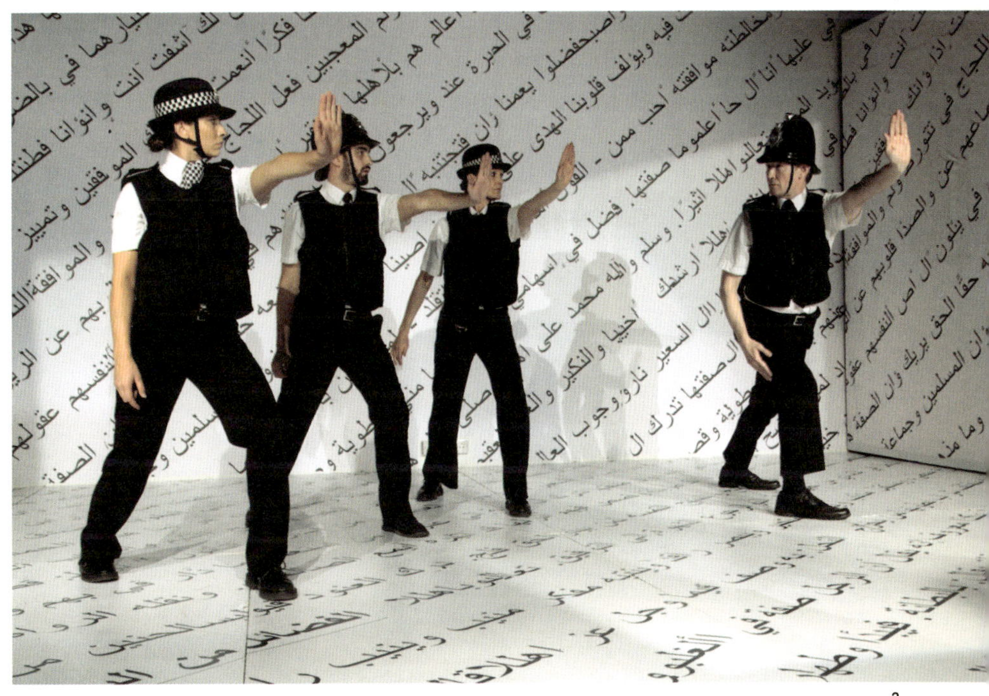

2

may differ on strategy, we have shared aspirations and want roughly the same thing; we sometimes compromise individual wants because the shared reward is greater.

Does each of you have a clearly defined role? If so, what are some of each member's distinct responsibilities?

Different people take leads on different projects, or parts of projects, and responsibilities follow. Our wider collaborations are initiated and developed through personal relationships, so it's likely that one of us will work with each artist who contributes to a project, but it's flexible and practical. We have different skills, whether they be technical, practical, or social, and so some things will generally appeal or default to one of us but we always keep things interesting in order to keep interested.

How important is each group member's individuality, both in terms of your artistic production and in terms of your relationship with the media? Does anonymity come into play?

Like in any four-piece boy band, there's a member of LuckyPDF to suit every taste. No one is expected to subscribe to an ideology, and we rarely make group statements. Things written with one voice are amalgams rather than coauthored, and there's no on or off message.

We develop projects that have a polyphony of voices. Although production strategies manifest in singular outcomes, most of our projects act as vessels for the work of others and are vehicles for many ideas; we want our projects to have space for multiple people to exist within them. A collective brand creates an umbrella under which multiple people can exist and this extends to the people we collaborate with. A group name can allow individuals certain freedoms, a mask to hide behind. We can be adventurous with our projects without jeopardizing perceived personal reputations and because we are somewhat self-institutionalized, we have a perceived mandate. As a group, our presence in life and on social media can be relentless and more international. As individuals, we are spokespersons for the brand; we try to talk candidly about our individual experiences within the group. When our opinions differ in public it ingratiates the audience to us and it's an insight into the human functionality of the group.

What is the relationship between your working methods and your art's "content"? In this sense, does technology tend to play more of a supporting role, or does it lead you in new directions?

We always aim to learn something from the process, self-teaching through practice. The process often is the content; we measure the outcomes of a project in social terms.

How does your collaboration relate to its cultural, institutional, and commercial contexts? In other words, how would you respond to those who call this a trend?

There's a popular understanding of the world as a network of networks. Mobile phone companies probably did most to make us imagine networks as real, tangible things with positive, aspirational connotations. LuckyPDF is a network of networks, a service provider of sorts.

The more people involved in a project, the greater its potential for wider cultural relevance. As an institution ourselves, we can negotiate better working relationships with other institutions and because we have knowledge of working with others, we understand that relationship better. Commercially, we have four times the marketing and production firepower, although we must also split the spoils. Thus far we have limited commercial output in the traditional art-world model, so exploring new strategies is part of our practice; we try to find ways that being a group is an advantage. Artists have always collaborated; motivated people who are interested in culture want to push things forward at large; this means getting involved with others.

Who is your audience?

LuckyPDF projects aim to push new ways of displaying art and the physical and social spaces it can exist in: market-testing strategies to deliver art to the widest possible international audience, hence our interest in TV, schools, fashion, advertising, and the Internet. We believe it is the responsibility of the artist to serve his or her ideas by trying to expand his or her audience. We aim to bring audience into the production space.

Does your engagement with one another translate into an engagement with the public? How so?

LuckyPDF is the manifestations of conversations among ourselves and with others. We provide infrastructure that solo artists may find hard to maintain, and we formalize it. Because we have a social familiarity, we can act as a test bed. We create projects to help us engage in a meaningful way with new audiences, meeting new people that we can potentially collaborate with in the future. We've been afforded the opportunity to travel with our art and this has helped us to build international relationships and create a global network.

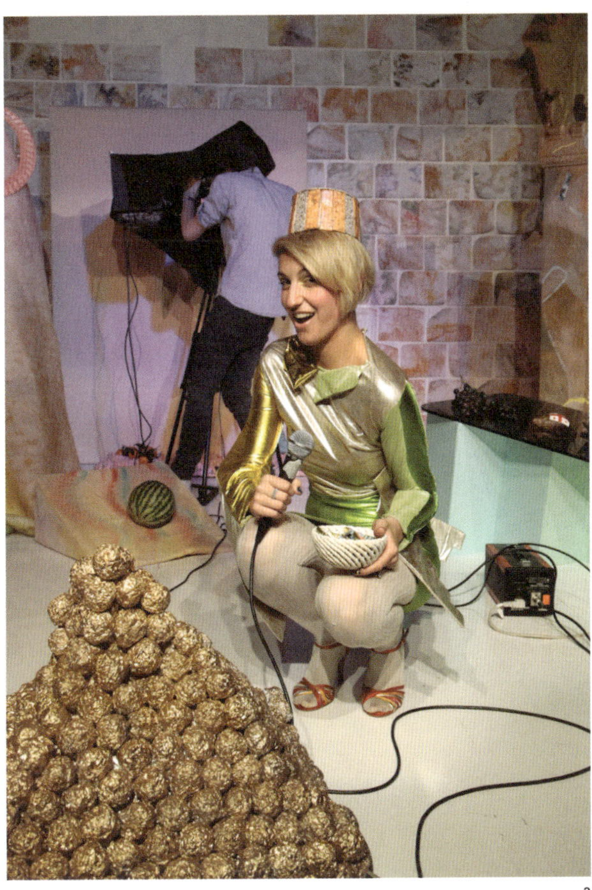

3

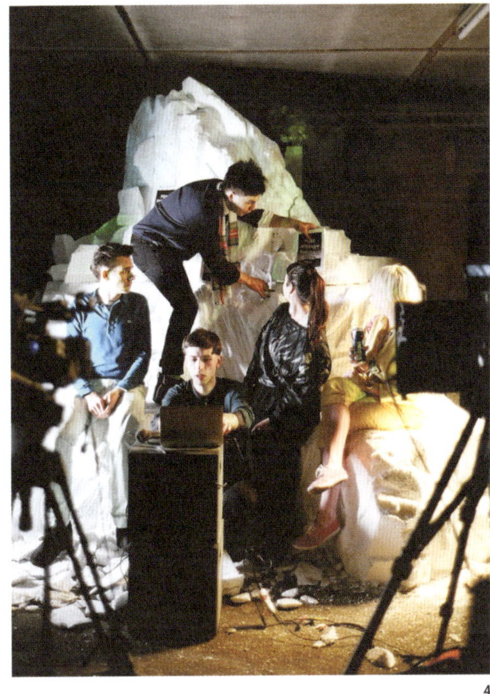

4

3 – Attilia Fattori Franchini (presenter), Samara Scott (set) for LuckyPDF, From LuckyPDF TV: This is Frieze Art Fair, installation and performance, Frieze Art Fair, London, 2011. Commissioned by Frieze Foundation for Frieze Projects, curated by Sarah McCrory

4 – This is LuckyPDF TV, BYOB London, 2011, installation and performance, The Woodmill, London, 2011. (Clockwise from top: Ollie Hogan, Nicky Carvell, Katja Novitskova, Ben Vickers, Rafaël Rozendaal)

5 – Helen Benigson, a.k.a. Princess Belsize Dollar (performance), Samara Scott (set) for LuckyPDF, From LuckyPDF TV: This is Frieze Art Fair, installation and performance, Frieze Art Fair, London, 2011. Commissioned by Frieze Foundation for Frieze Projects, curated by Sarah McCrory

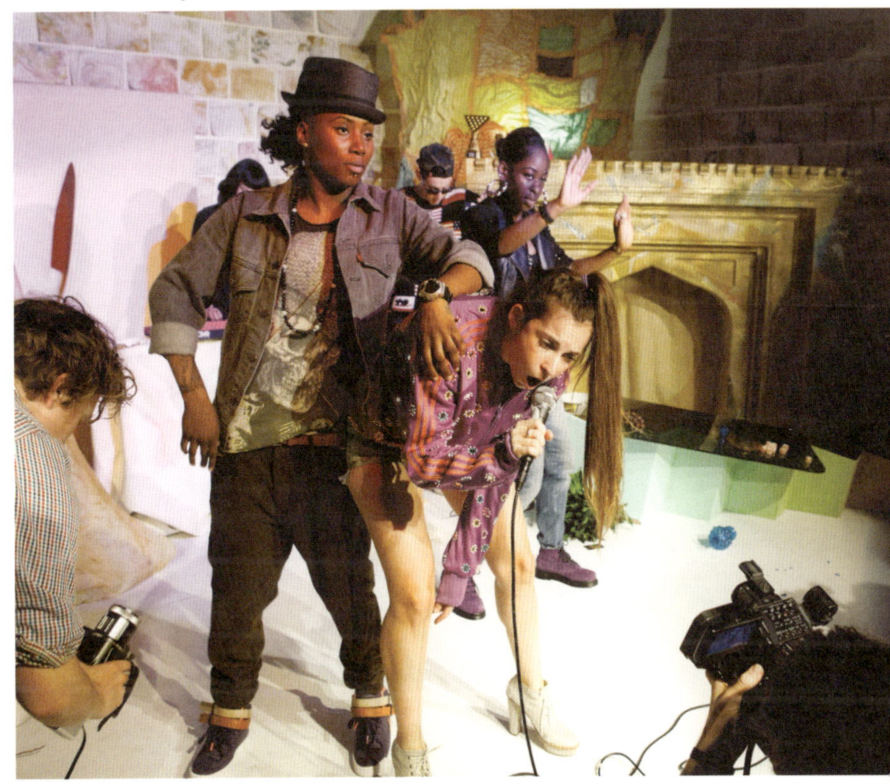

5

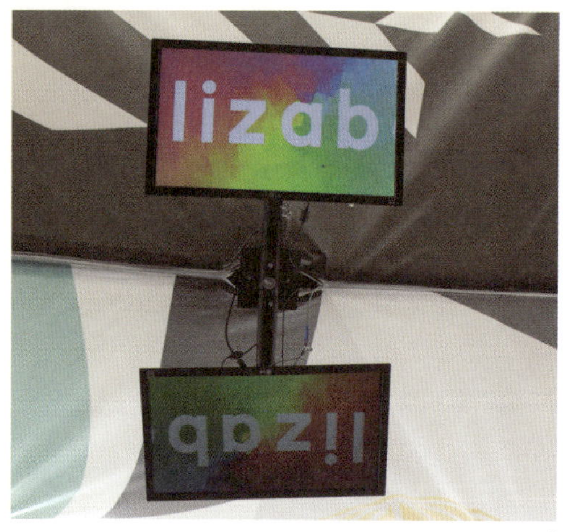

6

6 – LuckyPDF Promotional Art Fair Blimp, installation, Frieze Art Fair, London, 2011 Commissioned by Frieze Foundation for Frieze Projects, curated by Sarah McCrory

7 – Philip Li for LuckyPDF, The Conservatory, installation and performance, Barbican Art Gallery, London, 2011

8 – Dominik Salter-Dvorak/Your Body is a Temple for LuckyPDF, The Conservatory, installation and performance, Barbican Art Gallery, London, 2011

9 – Callum Hill for LuckyPDF, The Conservatory, installation and performance, Barbican Art Gallery, London, 2011

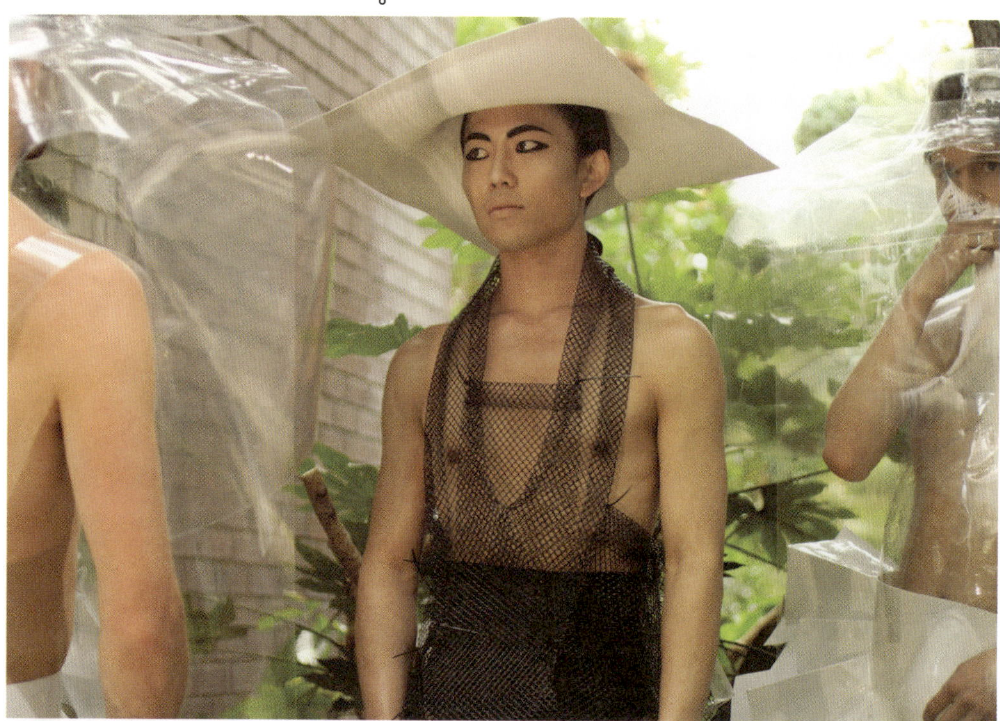

7

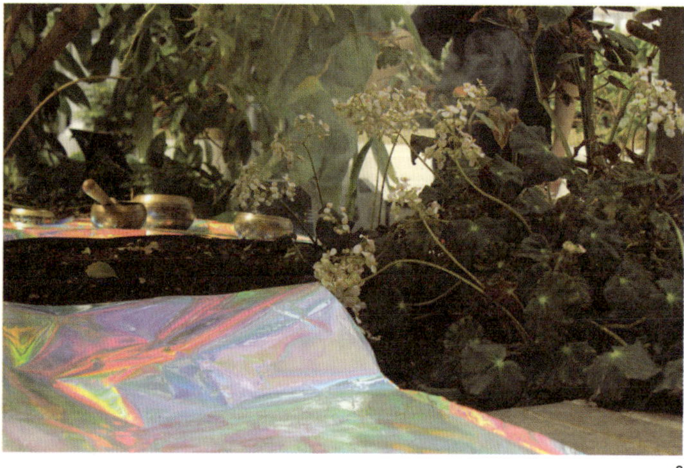

8

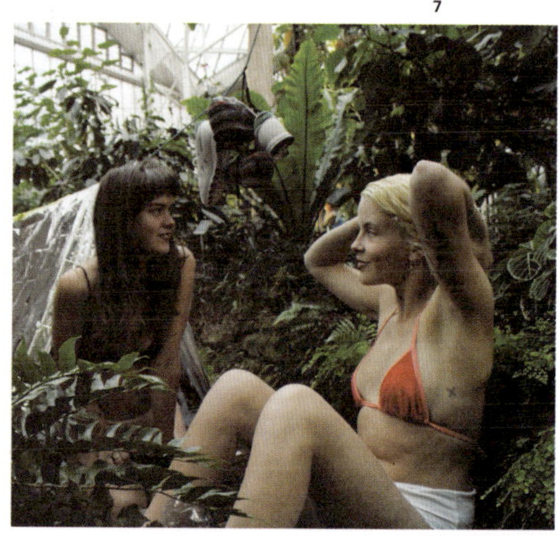

9

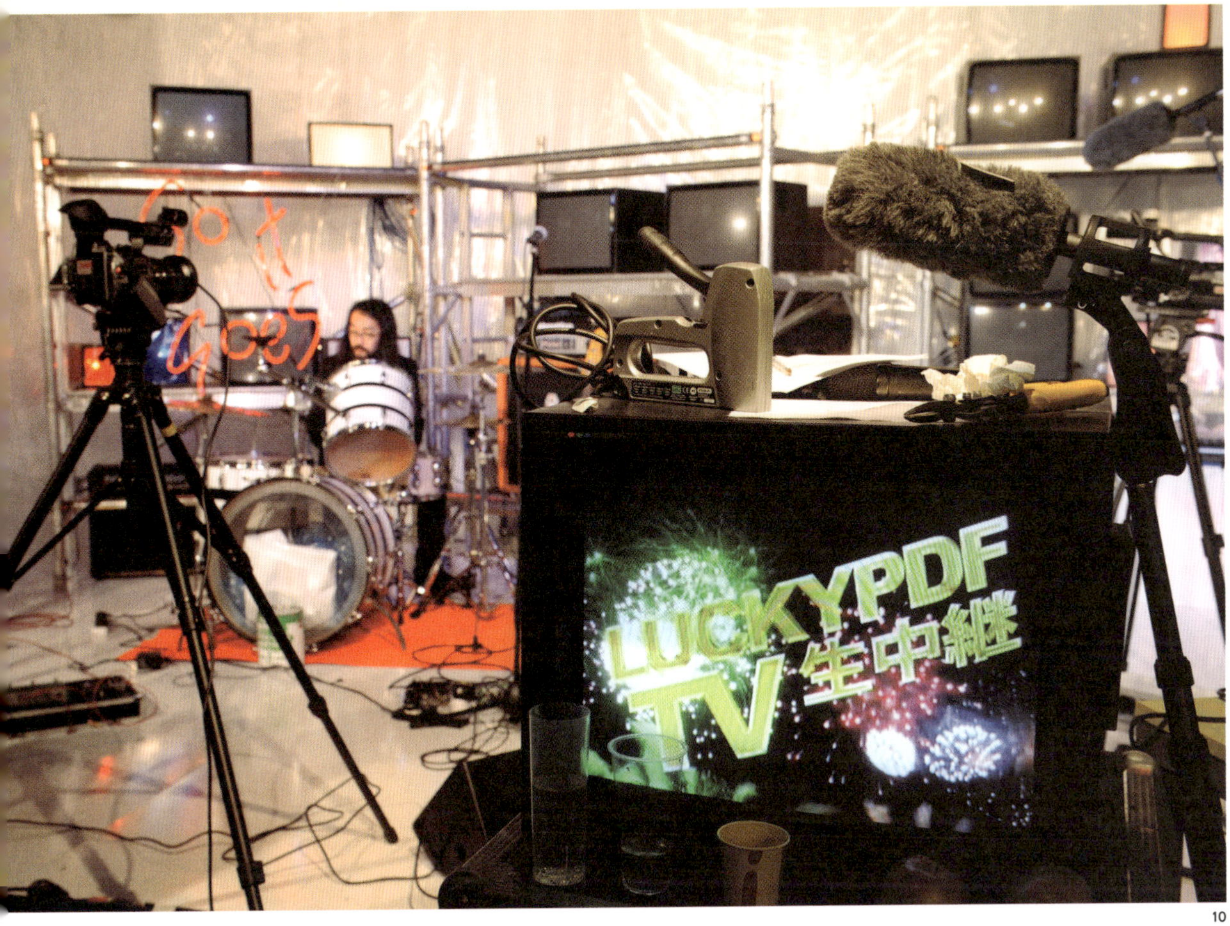

10

10 – Hannah Perry with LuckyPDF (set), Bo Ningen (band), and Daniel Swan (TV graphics) for LuckyPDF, From LuckyPDF TV: This is Frieze Art Fair, installation and performance, Frieze Art Fair, London, 2011. Commissioned by Frieze Foundation for Frieze Projects, curated by Sarah McCrory

11 – Hannah Perry with LuckyPDF, From LuckyPDF TV: This is Frieze Art Fair, installation and performance, Frieze Art Fair, London, 2011. Commissioned by Frieze Foundation for Frieze Projects, curated by Sarah McCrory

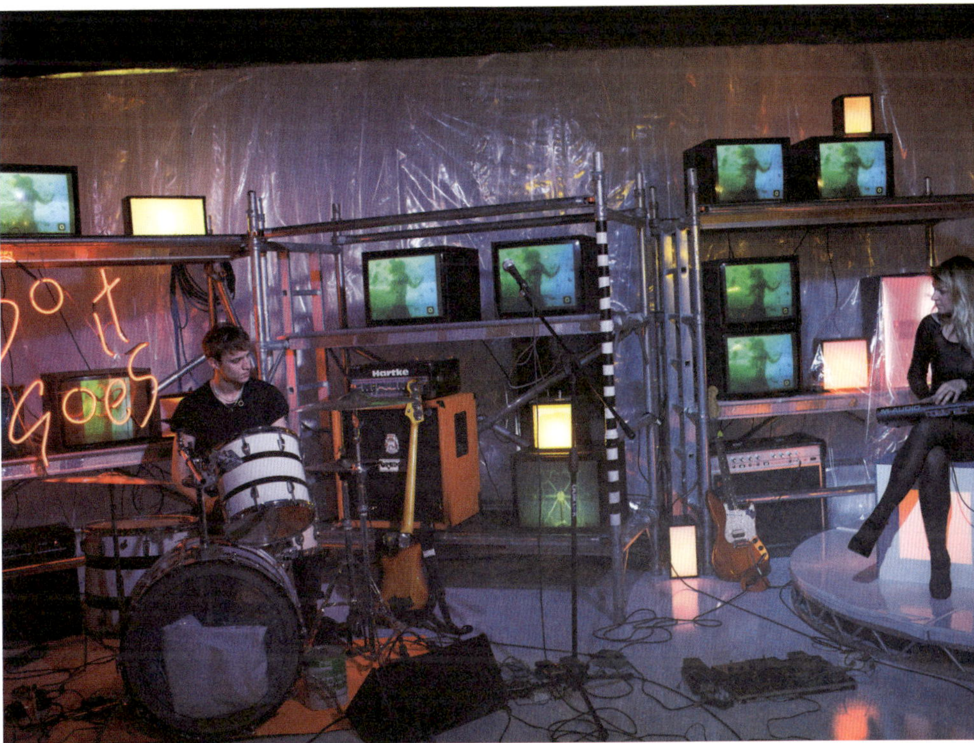

11

ACTIVE SINCE	CITY	WEBSITE
2006	Amsterdam, Netherlands	metahaven.net

Metahaven

MEMBERS	ACTIVITIES	RECOMMENDED PUBLICATION
Daniel van der Velden and Vinca Kruk	Design, Merchandising, Research, Strategy, Writing	UNCORPORATE IDENTITY, Lars Müller Publishers, Zurich, 2010, by Metahaven with Marina Vishmidt

Amsterdam studio Metahaven is involved in projects of research and production that span from publications to merchandising, from installations to digital interventions, from teaching to branding. Its attentions are focused on liberated spaces, such as micronations and websites like WikiLeaks. Borrowing from the language of governments and corporations, the studio's visual production investigates how information is generated and distributed through the media-scape.

Why work collaboratively?

We work collectively. There is a certain erosion of the traditional studio, in favor of more nomadic, "situationally agile," and networked forms; our practice holds the middle ground between the two. We are still aligned with the notion of the design studio, but obsessed with the possibilities of the network. The transition we face:

CONVENIENT ⟵	⟶ DISRUPTIVE
"bureau"	"network"
"firm"	"nonpermanent membership"
"studio"	"secret think tank"
dependent on financial model/ market/client base/etc.	depends on willingness and ability to work under "unconventional circumstances"
low situational agility	high situational agility
normally "easy to monetize," except during transitional or emergency circumstances	difficult to monetize

How do you determine membership? Does physical location matter in this regard?

Motivation matters more than physical location. It is nice, but not strictly necessary, to work from one place. We don't work with a strict determination of anything, so membership is not specifically defined, but over time the contour of what we consider to be Metahaven has emerged more clearly. For instance, we prefer to collaborate with the same people more often; we have had great people join for a few months who then return for a longer period. Overall, the two founders of Metahaven determine the direction of the work.

If considered separately, how do your individual artistic practices contribute to or detract from your work as a group?

We do not have practices besides Metahaven. We do teach, and that has an influence, definitely.

How are decisions made?

Decisions are made in various ways. One is through long lists of bullet points that can get a yes or no; another way of decision making is more impulsive, in a split second. There are always opportunities for criticism at every stage of a project, both from outside and inside. There is a constant back and forth between intuition and rational decision making. We have some unwritten rules; arguments "against" something should never by themselves hold a project back, and nothing is published publicly if one of us can't support the result, whether it is text or image.

Does each of you have a clearly defined role? If so, what are some of each member's distinct responsibilities?

We don't work with distinct responsibilities. It depends on the project and it depends on who is more available.

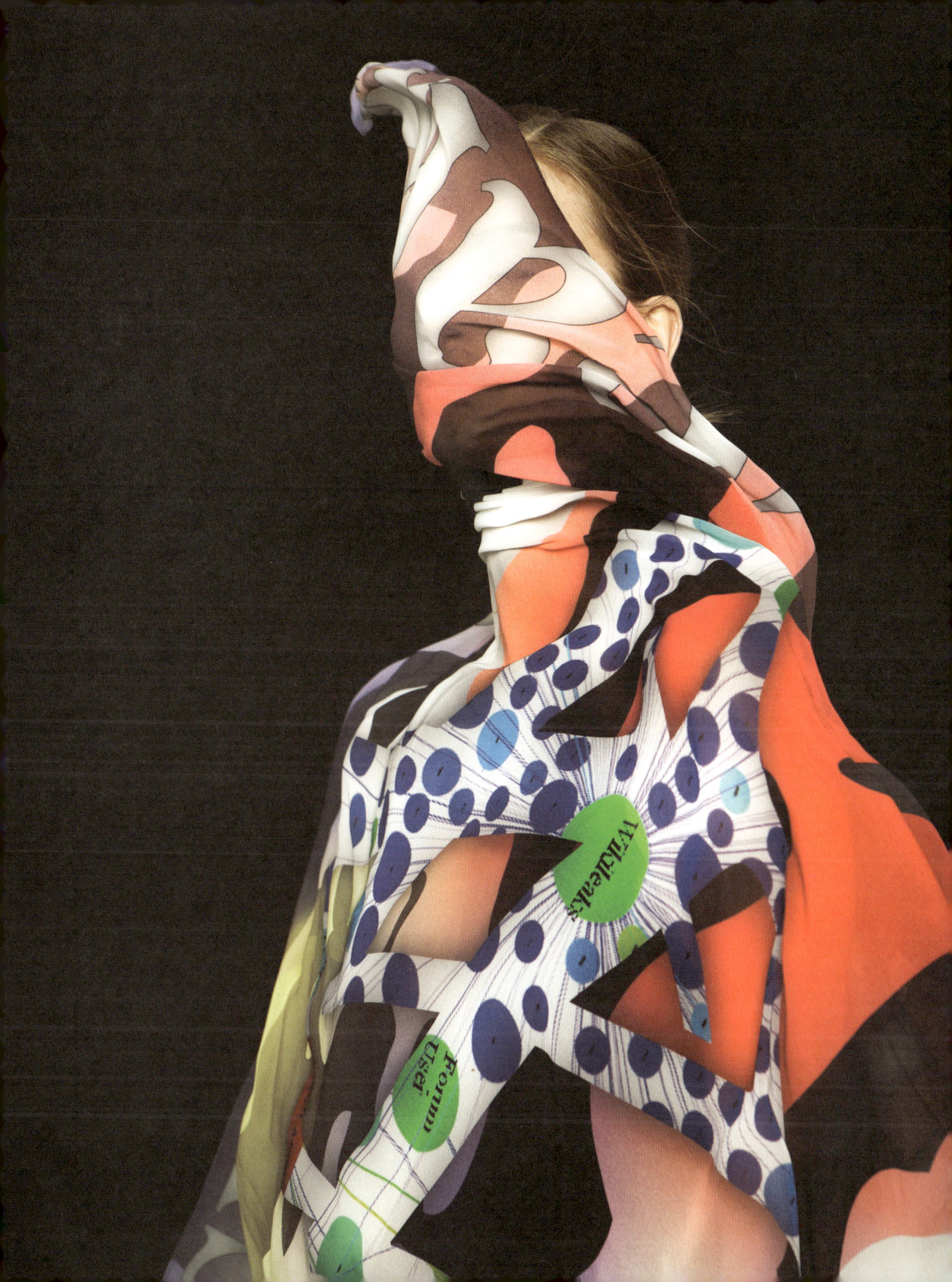
Wikileaks
Forum User

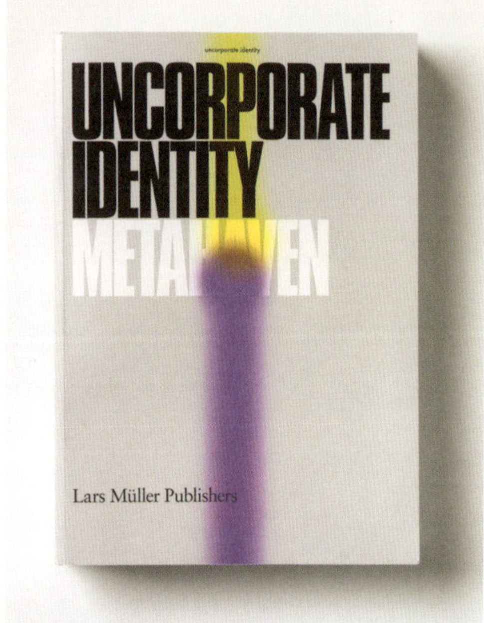

2

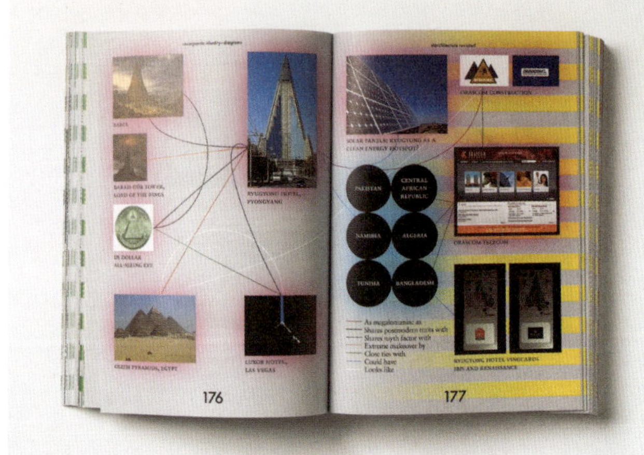

3

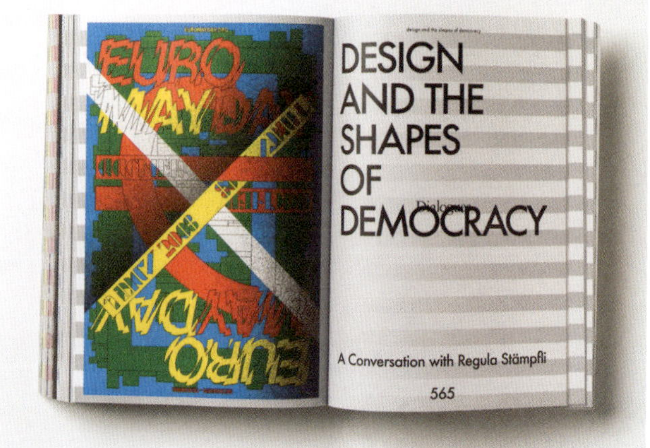

4

previous
1 – **Transparent Camouflage, WikiLeaks scarf, 2011**

2–4 – **Metahaven with Maria Vishmidt, Uncorporate Identity, cover of the book and spreads, Lars Müller Publishers, Zurich, 2010**

How important is each group member's individuality, both in terms of your artistic production and in terms of your relationship with the media? Does anonymity come into play?

It would be quite lovely to remain anonymous behind the Metahaven identity. That said, individuality is extremely important. There is space for everyone's personal ideas, and room to let those ideas change over time. There are individual preferences in terms of how public or private someone wants to be. There should be space for all kinds of different dynamics.

What is the relationship between your working methods and your art's "content"? In this sense, does technology tend to play more of a supporting role, or does it lead you in new directions?

Frankly, these questions feel like you are gathering "metadata" regarding practices rather than information about the practices themselves. Technology always plays on both ends; it is always both supportive and a catalyst. When making physical objects, not so much "technology" as much as "production" is important, as well as the "postproduction" of what is made in an iterative process, in which one thing leads to another.

How does your collaboration relate to its cultural, institutional, and commercial contexts? In other words, how would you respond to those who call this a trend?

It is not a trend; there is a definite shift in what organizations and institutions are, as well as in how they function.

Who is your audience?

You.

Does your engagement with one another translate into an engagement with the public? How so?

As designers we make things that can be useful or not. Any engagement with a viewer or a user happens through the objects we produce (and these include internet images, semifinished prototypes, texts, and lectures). What these things are, and what they stand for, determines the engagement.

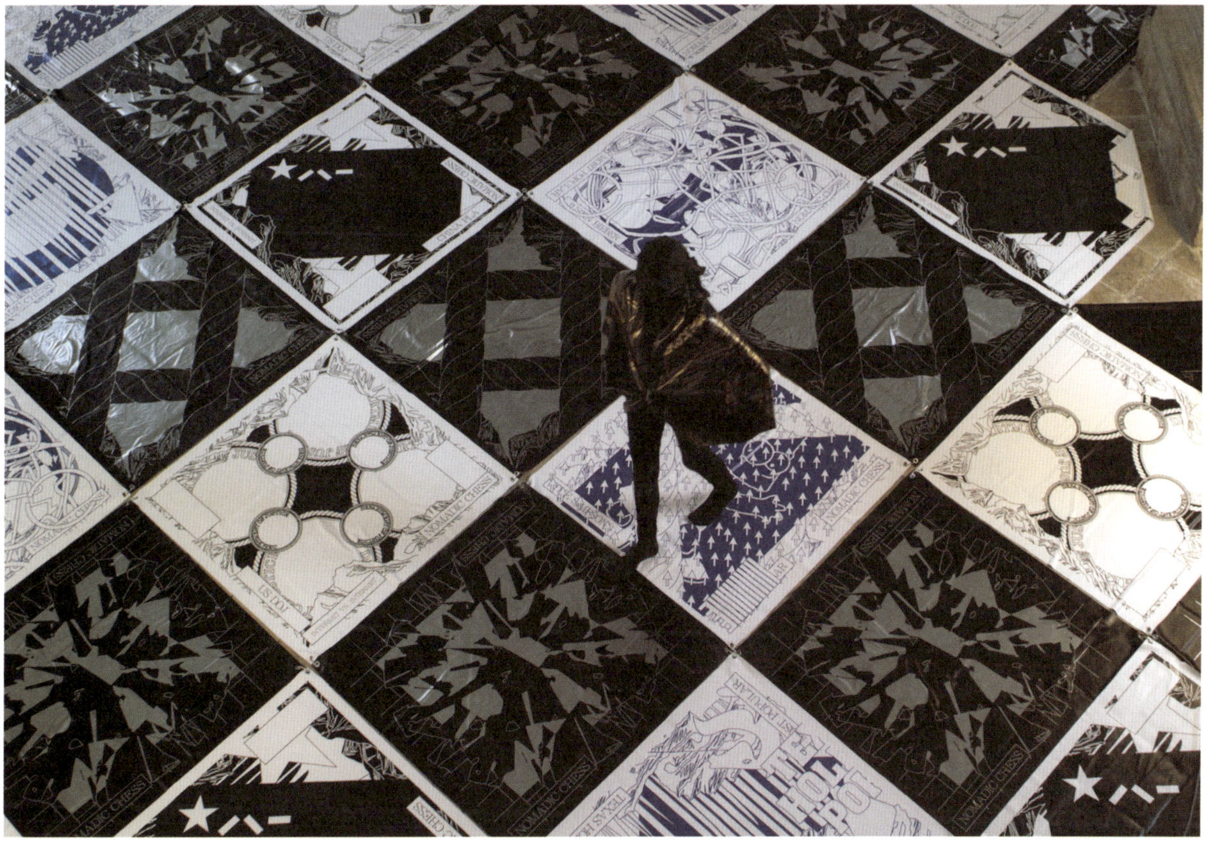

5

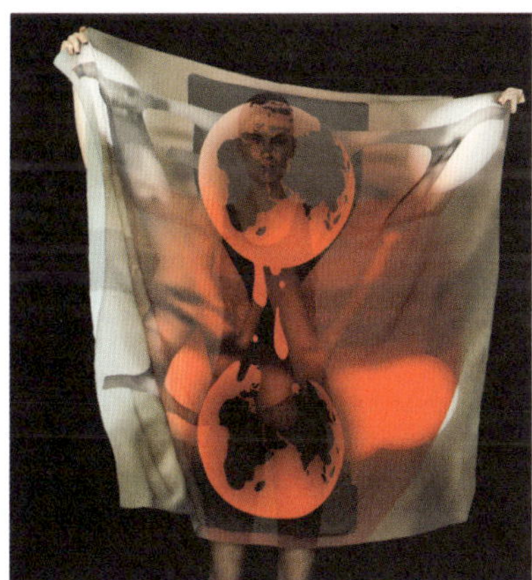

6

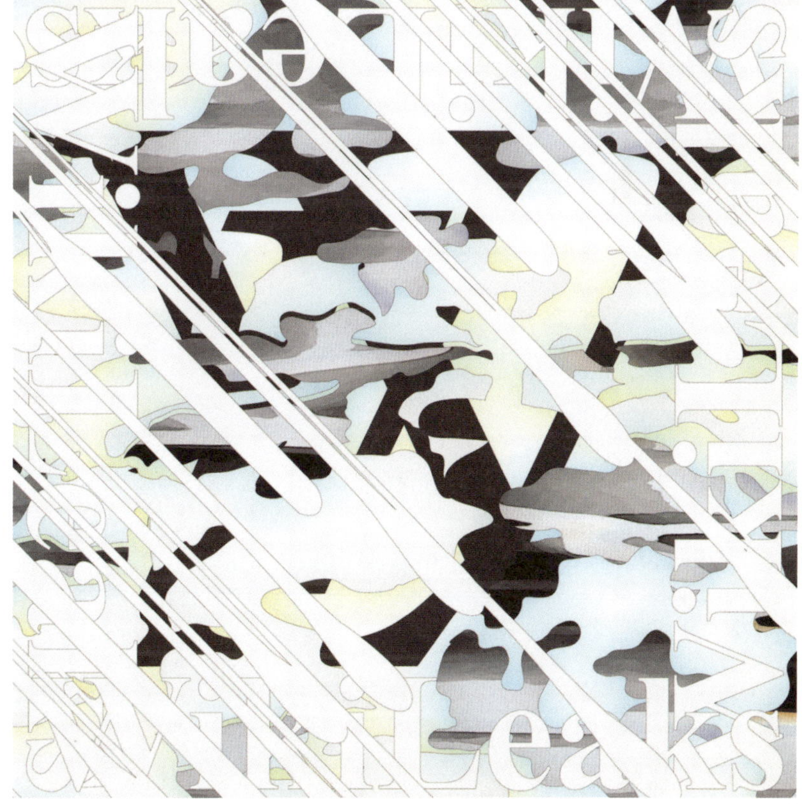

7

5 – <u>Nomadic Chess</u>, installation, La Chapelle des Jésuites, Chaumont, 2013

6 – <u>Transparent Camouflage</u>, WikiLeaks scarf, 2011

7 – <u>WikiLeaks Requiem Scarf</u>, scarf design, 2013

overleaf
8 – <u>Islands in the Cloud</u>, installation, MoMA PS1, New York, 2013

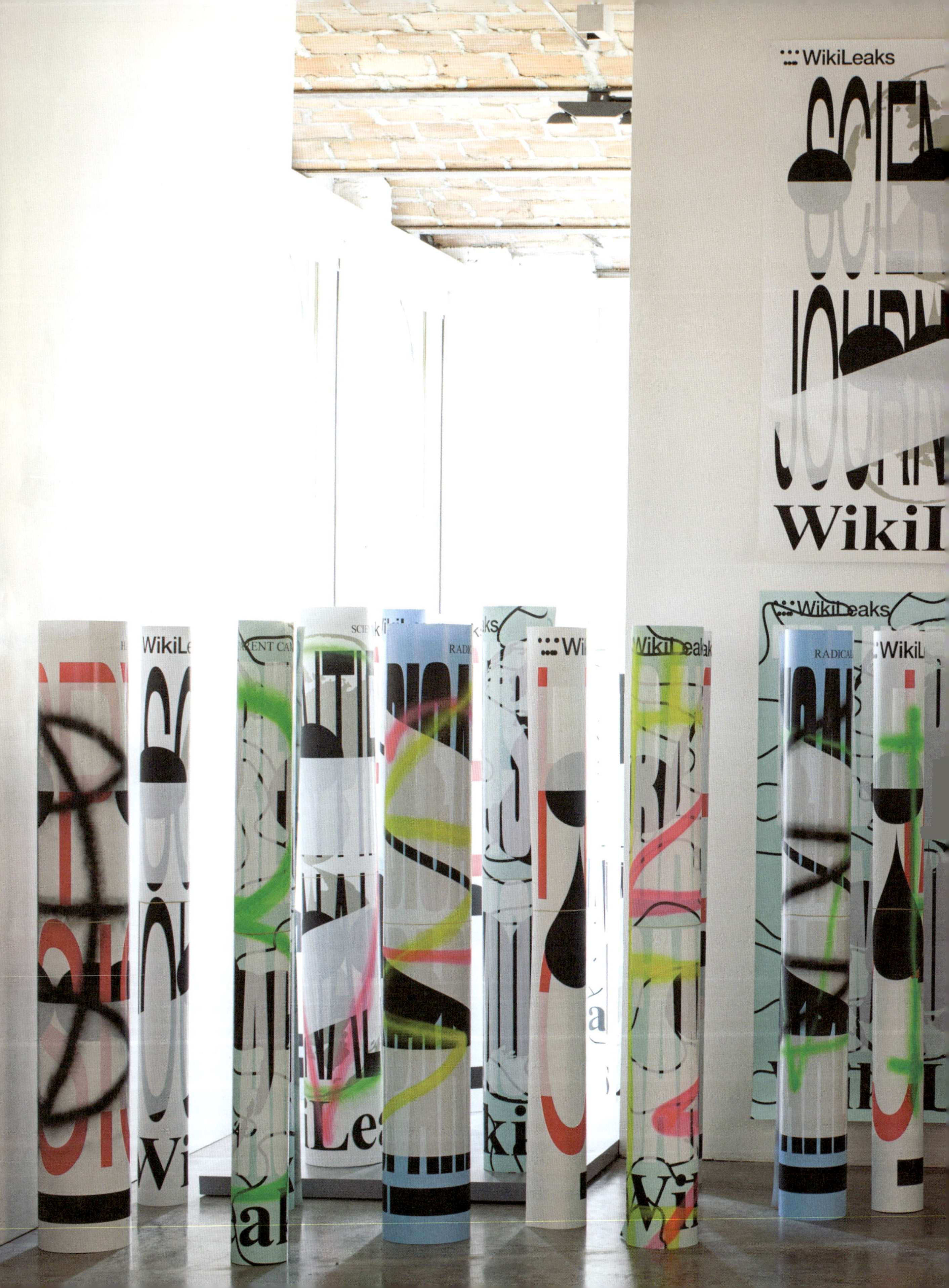

WikiLeaks
WikiLeaks
RADICAL

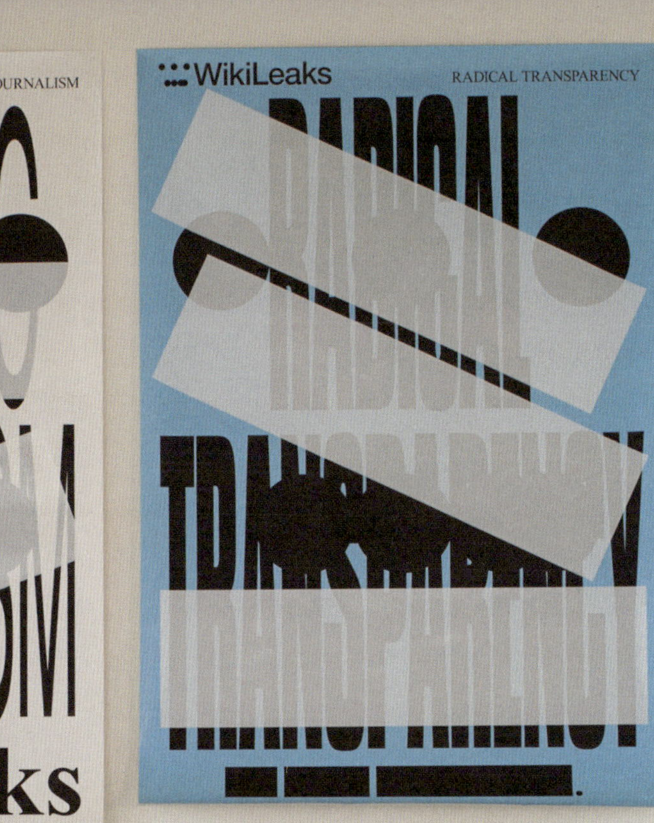
WikiLeaks
RADICAL TRANSPARENCY

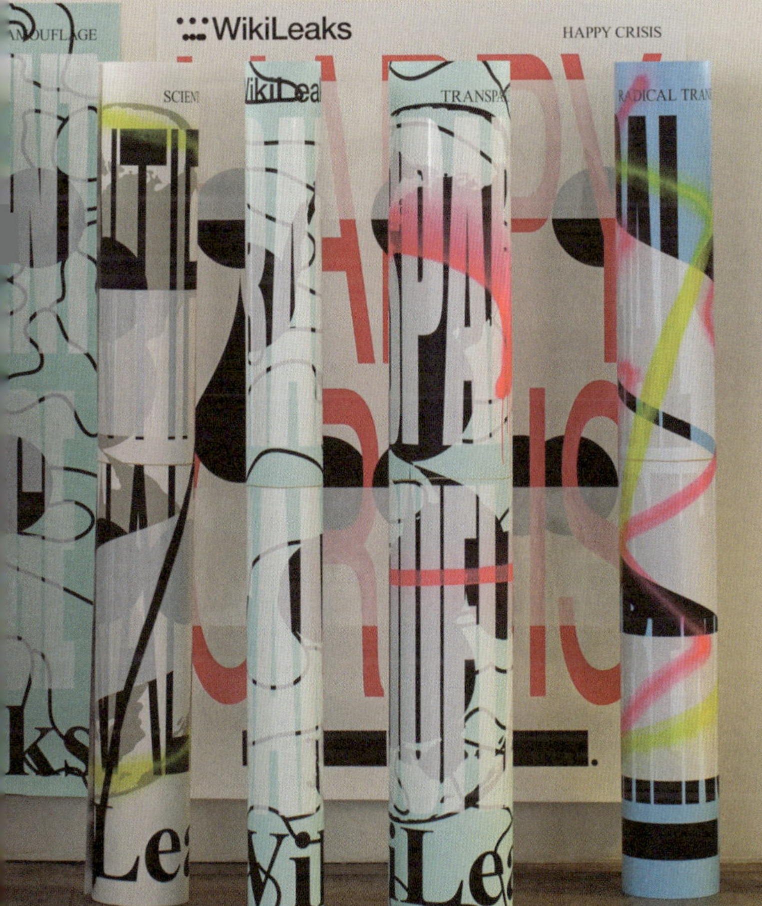
WikiLeaks
HAPPY CRISIS

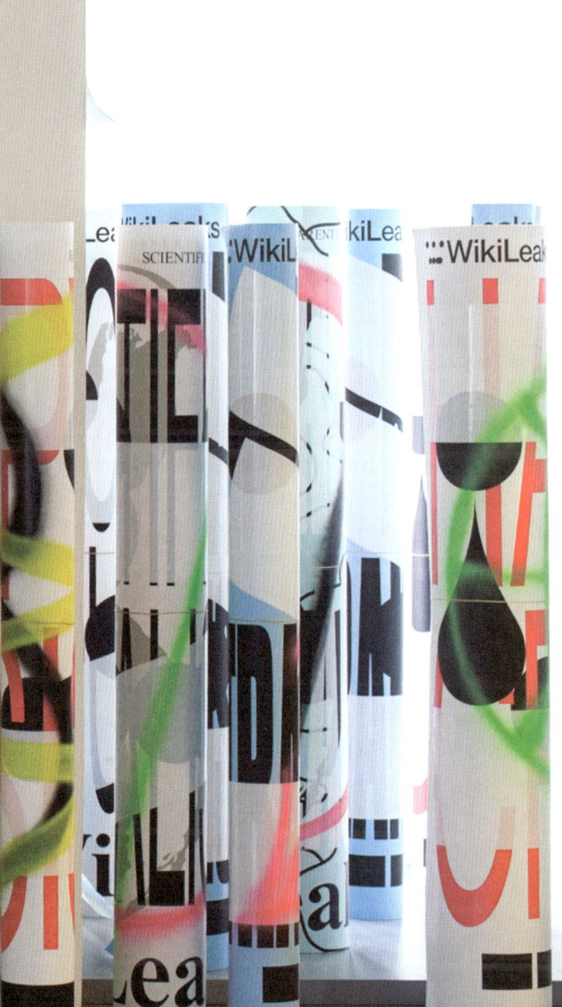

ACTIVE	CITY	WEBSITE
2001–2008	Boston / Pittsburgh / Easthampton / Providence, U.S.	paperrad.org

Paper Rad

MEMBERS	ACTIVITIES	RECOMMENDED PUBLICATION
Jacob Ciocci, Jessica Ciocci, and Ben Jones	Comics, Internet Art, Music, Painting / Installation, Performance, Self-Publishing / Distribution, Video	PAPER RAD, BJ AND DA DOGS, Picturebox Inc., New York, 2005

Representative of the postdigital underground scene of mid 2000s New York, the members of Paper Rad were authors of a lo-fi psychedelic universe, populated by imaginary creatures appropriated from old cartoons and video games. They worked with painting, installation, performance, comics, video, and music; they printed T-shirts, organized happenings and self-produced records and zines.

Why work collaboratively?

In the beginning working collaboratively simply came out of being friends with similar interests in a specific town at a specific time. Eventually the more we worked together, the more we realized working collaboratively allowed us to get much more done than we would have ever gotten done individually, and it made us work in ways we would have never worked individually. Working collaboratively also allows for projects to have an identity that is not tied to individuals but seems bigger, more inclusive, and perhaps more mysterious than individual attribution.

How did you determine membership? Did physical location matter in this regard?

Paper Rad came out of the experience of being in Boston in 2001—membership was never discussed—the process was much more everyday, informal, and fluid. Much later in the history of Paper Rad we determined who to reach out to for short-term collaborations based on shared goals, interests, and skill sets.

If considered separately, how did your individual artistic practices contribute to or detract from your work as a group?

At the beginning of Paper Rad it was very hard to separate individual artistic practice from shared artistic practice. That was a part of the point. Our ideas, creative strategies, and inspirations were affecting one another and shaping our output to the point that the work was no longer created by three people but by one group.

How were decisions made?

We made decisions probably like any actively engaged, critically thinking group of people make decisions: arguing, intuition, logic, chaos, love. We always tried to work within our means to create projects that pushed whatever medium was at hand (zines, T-shirts, websites) to the limit but still seemed "doable" by anyone who put his or her mind to it. The ethos of DIY was an important one.

Did each of you have a clearly defined role? If so, what were some of each member's distinct responsibilities?

There were no defined roles in Paper Rad. Individuals gravitated toward certain roles or responsibilities but those roles and responsibilities were always changing based on a project-by-project basis. We did whatever it took to get the project done until the roles became too rigid, then we stopped working together.

How important was each group member's individuality, both in terms of your artistic production and in terms of your relationship with the media? Did anonymity come into play?

There was a shared set of interests, approaches to image making, and overall conceptual framework that packaged each individual's own artistic identities within a larger vision. If you studied hard, you could uncover the particular styles or voice of each member's work, but the member's work always

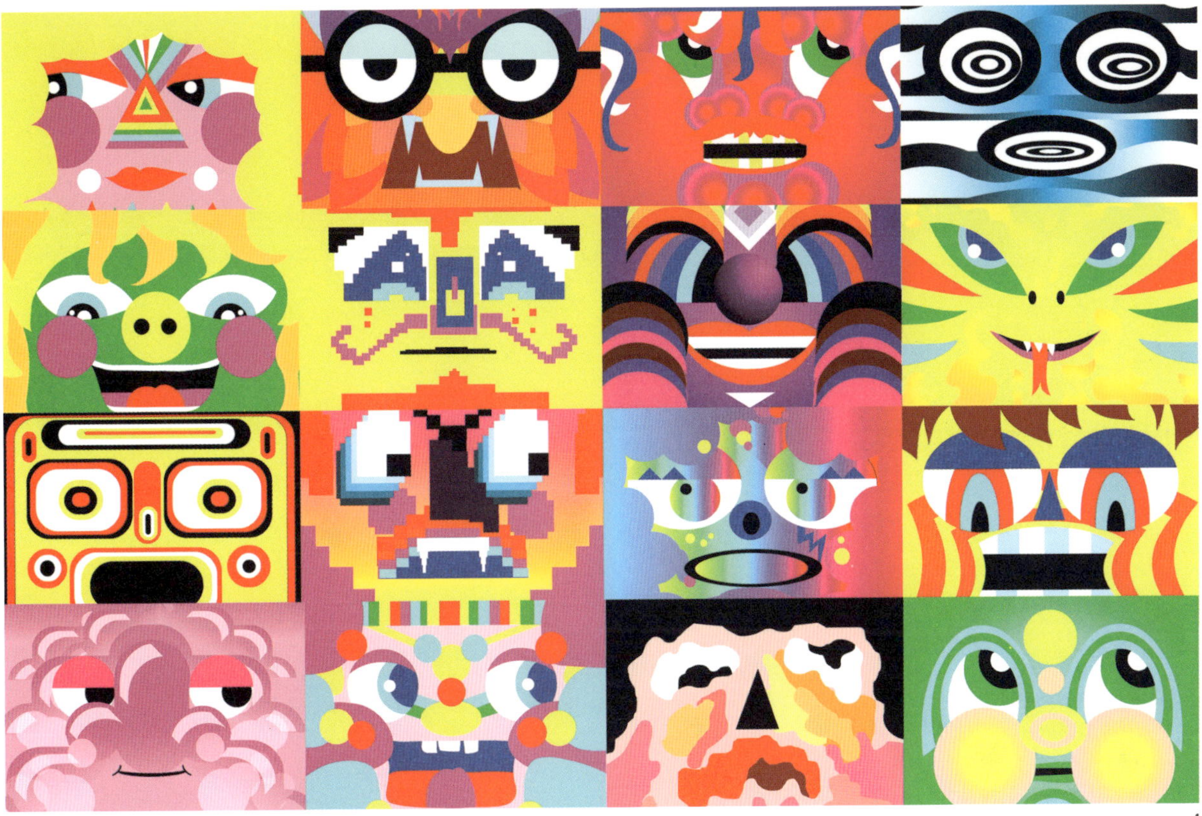

1

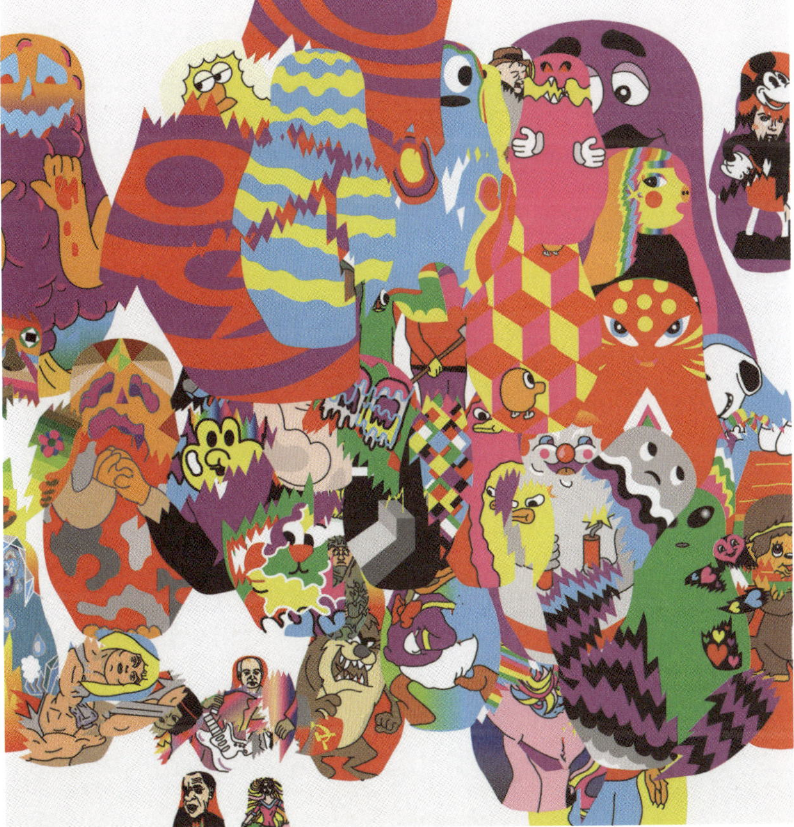

2

1 – Mirror Phazer, video still, 2006

2 – Untitled, digital print, 2007

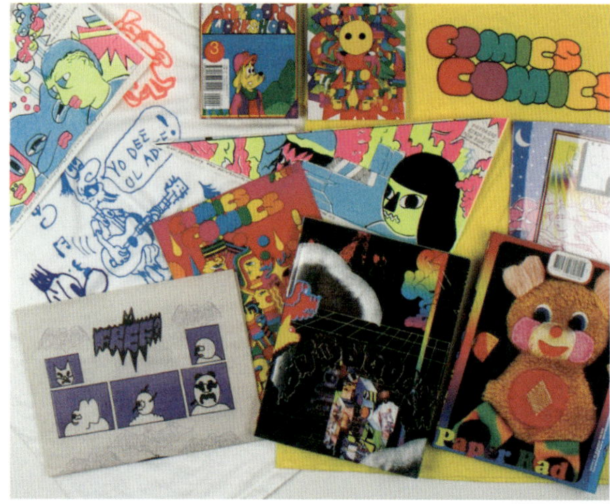

3

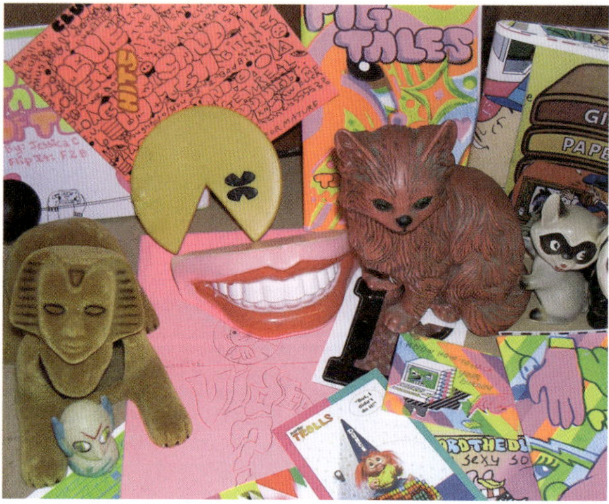

4

fit into the larger puzzle of Paper Rad. Anonymity worked to our favor on the web and in our zines—sometimes making it hard to tell if one individual or a group of twenty was producing the work. Anonymity also made it sometimes hard to tell if the work was "original" or simply sampled from an older source—another productive confusion that Paper Rad thrived on.

What was the relationship between your working methods and your art's "content"? In this sense, did technology tend to play more of a supporting role, or did it lead you in new directions?

Form, content, technology, and meaning are all intertwined and inseparable from experience. Pulling these terms apart and putting them back together in new ways to create new experiences is what artists do. We worked with whatever technologies were logical and easily available for us to use, and we figured out a way to express our shared, collective visions through this technology in simple yet evocative ways.

How did your collaboration relate to its cultural, institutional, and commercial contexts? In other words, how would you respond to those who call this a trend?

Collective activity is older than individual activity. The artist as individual is a relatively new model, when compared with the entire history of human creativity. Perhaps in the twenty-first century the model of the genius who works in isolation and is in total control of his or her work no longer makes sense. Our work was in constant conversation with (and sometimes synonymous with) other cultural, institutional, and commercial contexts. Superficially, we based our creative collaboration on the model of a "company" and branded ourselves within the identity of our company fully—we made T-shirts, books, videos, websites, dolls, and music—all of which were undeniably recognizable as Paper Rad. Eventually the Paper Rad brand began to creep beyond the creative output of the three of us and into the public domain, further blurring the line between media author and media consumer. Others began to mimic, copy, and appropriate the Paper Rad brand, thus continuing the conversation beyond the control of the three of us as individuals.

Who is your audience?

When Paper Rad began our audience was initially regional. We made hand-published magazines and distributed them in New England. Eventually we began going on tour and shared these magazines along with our videos across the United States. Once we began our website our audience instantly became international. When Paper Rad was at its peak our audience was a rare cross section of those interested in underground aesthetics, video art fans, other artists, musicians, comic book fans, and internet art aficionados.

Did your engagement with one another translate into an engagement with your audience? How so?

The work of Paper Rad oftentimes felt conversational—as if the three members were having a dialogue with one another through the work. This conversational tone carried across to our larger audience so that often a joke that began as one shared between three people became a joke shared between thousands. In addition, because our work embodied shared experience (because we sampled or referenced cultural tropes that others from our generation could relate to), it became very easy to have complex cultural conversations with our audience through simple gestures.

opposite
3 – **Various Paper Rad–related T-shirts and publications by PictureBox Inc., Brooklyn**

opposite
4 – **Various self-published Paper Rad–related publications, 2006**

5 – **Where Are They Now?, installation with video and wallpaper, Deitch Project's Live Through This exhibition, Miami Art Basel, Miami, 2005**

6 – **Untitled, installation, Reverse Engineers, Carnegie Arts Center, North Tonowanda, New York, 2005**

7 –**Mixtape Clubhouse, installation, Space 1026, Philadelphia, 2005**

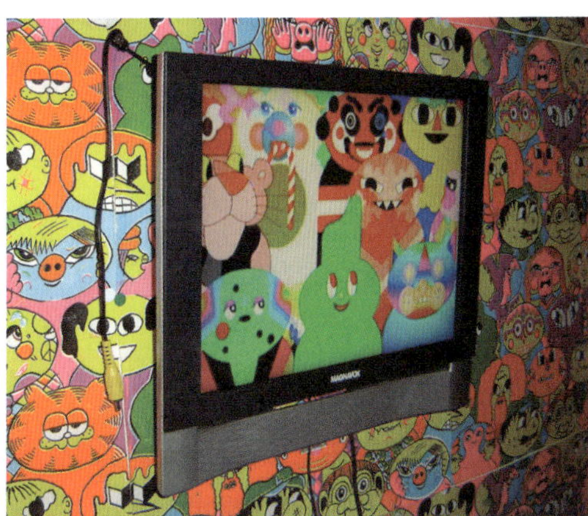

5

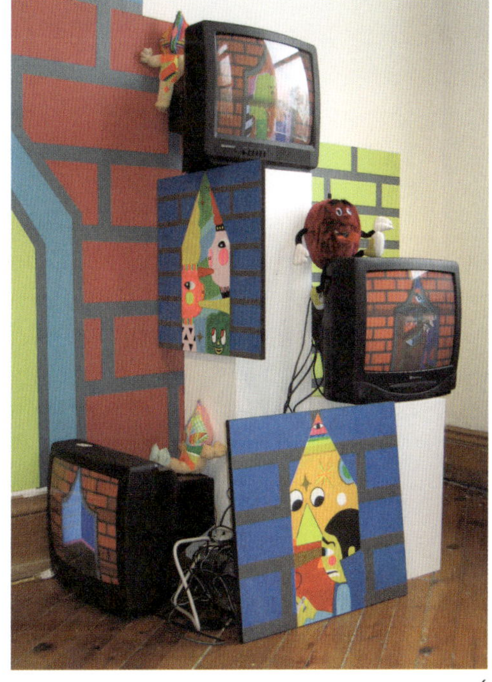

6

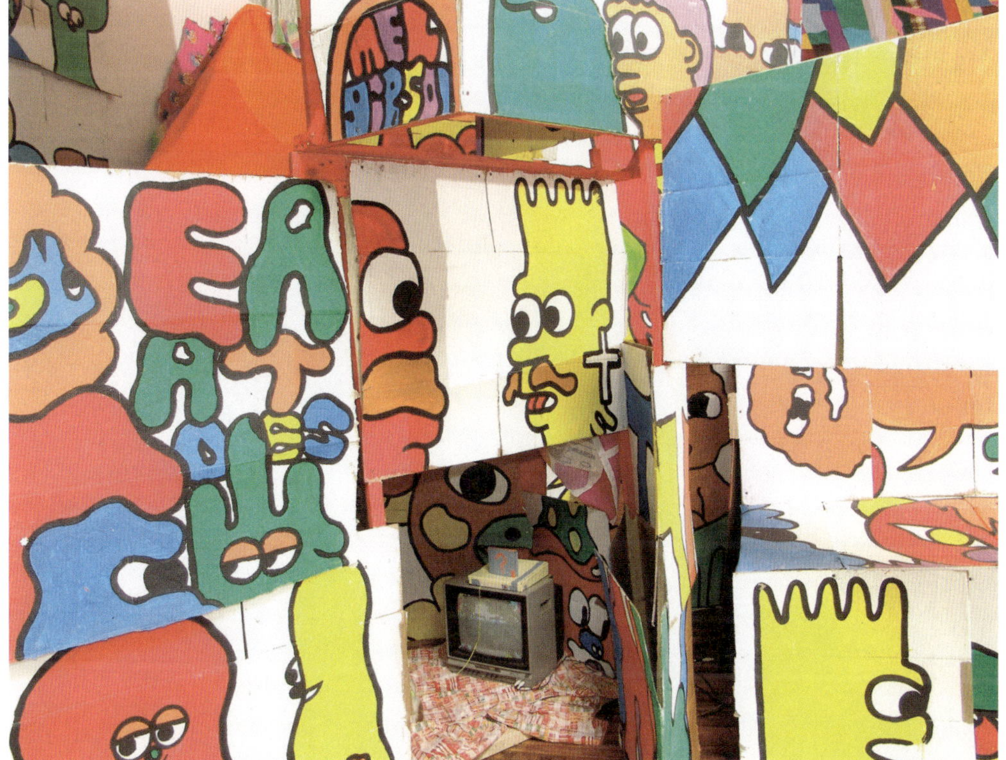

7

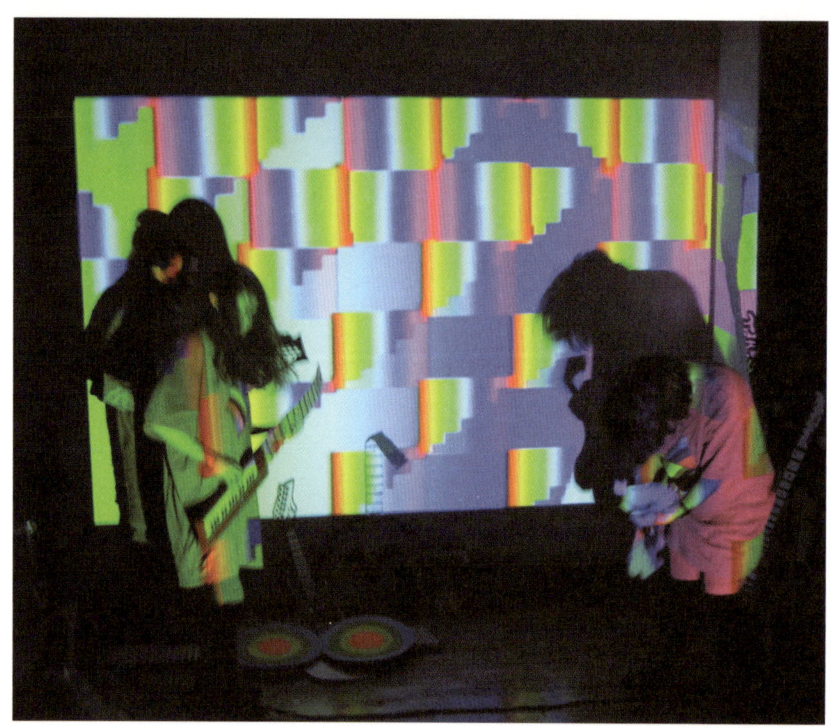

8

9

8 – Doo Man Group, performance, 2005

9 – Untitled, installation, Yerba Buena Center for the Arts, San Francisco, 2006

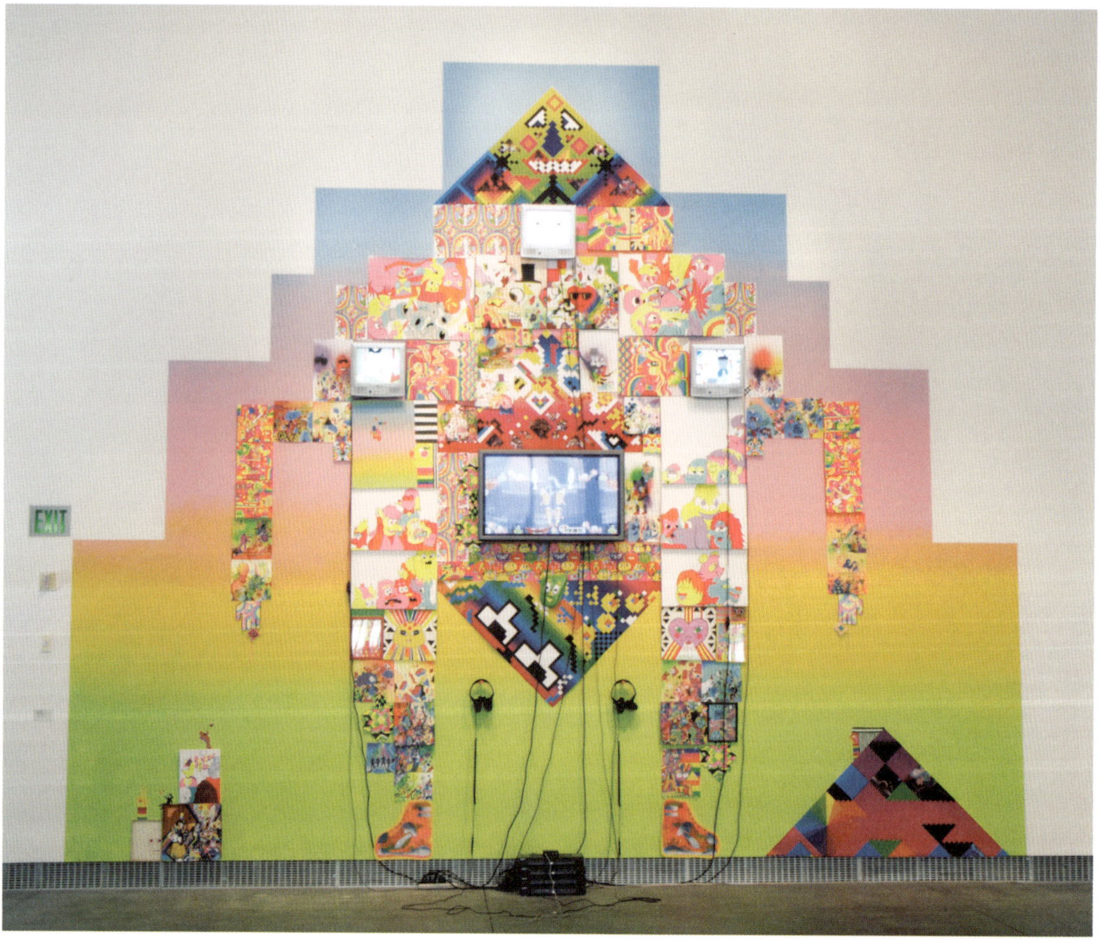

10 – <u>Free Music Videos</u>, performance and video installation in collaboration with Cory Arcangel, University of Pittsburgh, Pittsburgh, 2003

11 – <u>Welcome To My Homeypage</u>, video still, 2002

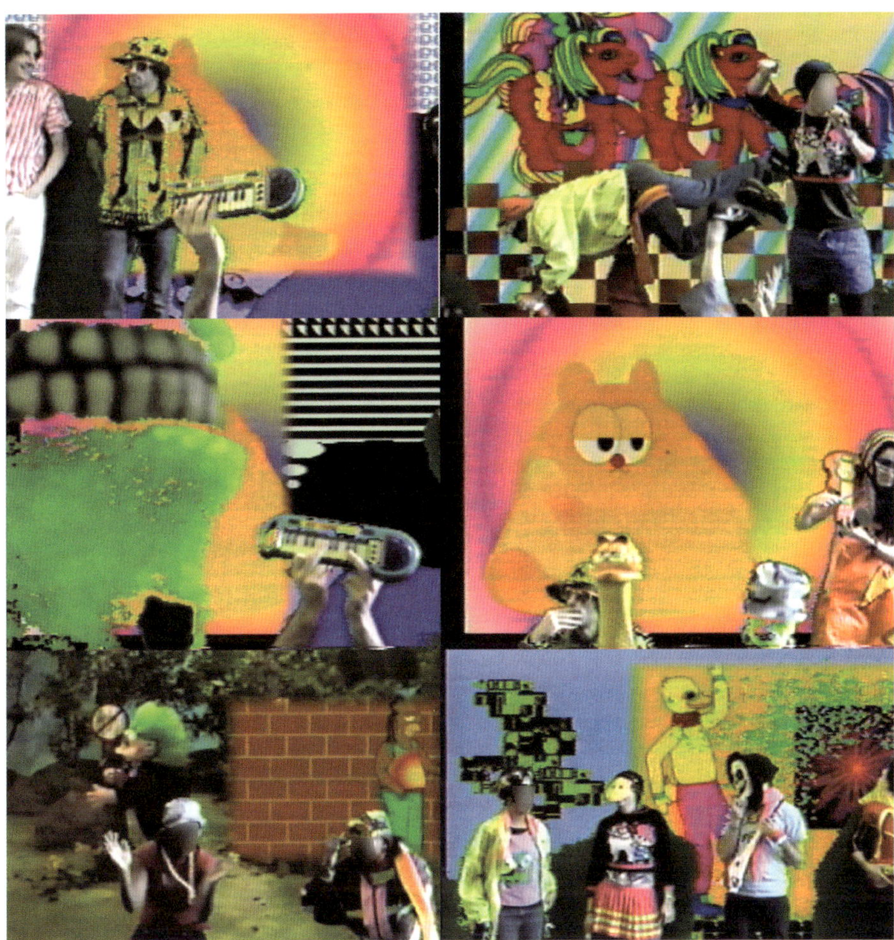

10

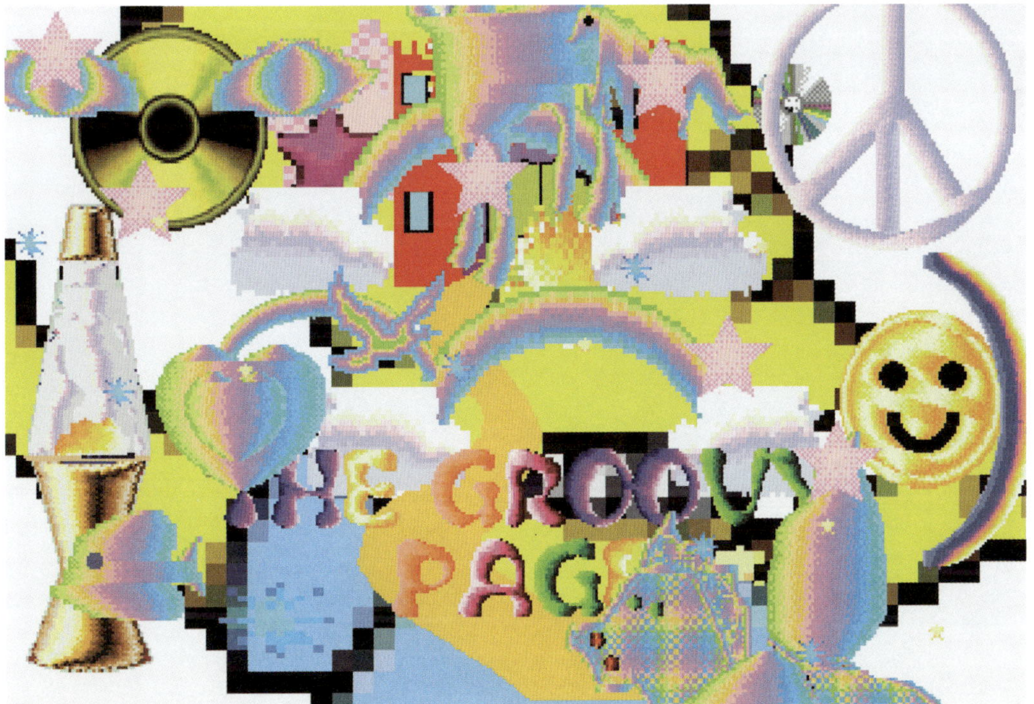

11

ACTIVE SINCE	CITY	WEBSITE
2004	New York, U.S.	projectprojects.com

Project Projects

MEMBERS	ACTIVITIES	RECOMMENDED PUBLICATION
Adam Michaels and Prem Krishnamurthy, founders; Rob Giampietro, principal; team includes Chris Wu, Aileen Kwun, Andrew LeClair, Kim Sutherland, Jonatan Eriksson, Won Choi, and Simon Lagneaux	Curating, Design, Editing, Performance, Photography, Publishing, Recording, Research, Teaching, Writing, Etc.	Kerry William Purcell, PROJECT PROJECTS, New York, U.S., Grafik no. 182, February, 2010

New York studio Project Projects is involved in operations of branding, identity, and design of cultural events and institutions aimed toward a relational and participative effect. Publications, social sculptures, reading rooms, seminars, wall stickers, and fill-in questionnaires are often at the core of the studio's activities like those they organize at P!, a space it runs in Chinatown, New York.

Why work collaboratively?

Design work is, by its nature, inherently collaborative. It involves the coordination and collaboration of multiple producers and agents. This synthesis of the needs and desires of a community produces work that is multiauthored and multivocal.

How do you determine membership? Does physical location matter in this regard?

While the work that we do is far ranging, we're structured as a traditional business: a limited liability company. We have employees, payroll, and other kinds of conventional infrastructure, including our studio space in Manhattan. Happily, for some years we've been able to provide health benefits, paid vacation, retirement funds, etc. A self-selecting community has built up around the studio, in which our work has attracted the involvement of similar-minded people from a range of locations. Physical location does matter, as we all converge upon our studio on a daily basis or close to it.

If considered separately, how do your individual artistic practices contribute to or detract from your work as a group?

Each of us brings to our design work different ideas and impulses from outside of the studio that ultimately feed back into the work done collectively. For example, publishing, curating, writing, and teaching are all activities that sometimes take place separately from Project Projects, but which inform the work here. Adam edits and publishes a series called Inventory Books with Princeton Architectural Press, with three books in the series so far. The most recent is The Electric Information Age Book, coauthored with Jeffrey Schnapp, which focuses on the dawn of the "experimental paperback book" in the sixties, and on the trio of radical thinkers Marshall McLuhan, book packager Jerome Agel, and graphic designer Quentin Fiore. Together they created a thoroughly challenging yet commercially successful paperback called The Medium is the Massage. Prem recently founded the experimental, multidisciplinary exhibition space P! in Chinatown, which actively mixes work from different contexts and time periods to look at the ideas that encapsulate and connect them. In addition, P! explores exhibition design and display—in an activated form—as a way to question the supposed neutrality of the gallery context. Rob's decade-long work as a teacher at RISD and writer for Dot Dot Dot, Eye, Emigre, and other publications are collected on his website Lined & Unlined. Together, these activities at the edge of Project Projects constantly

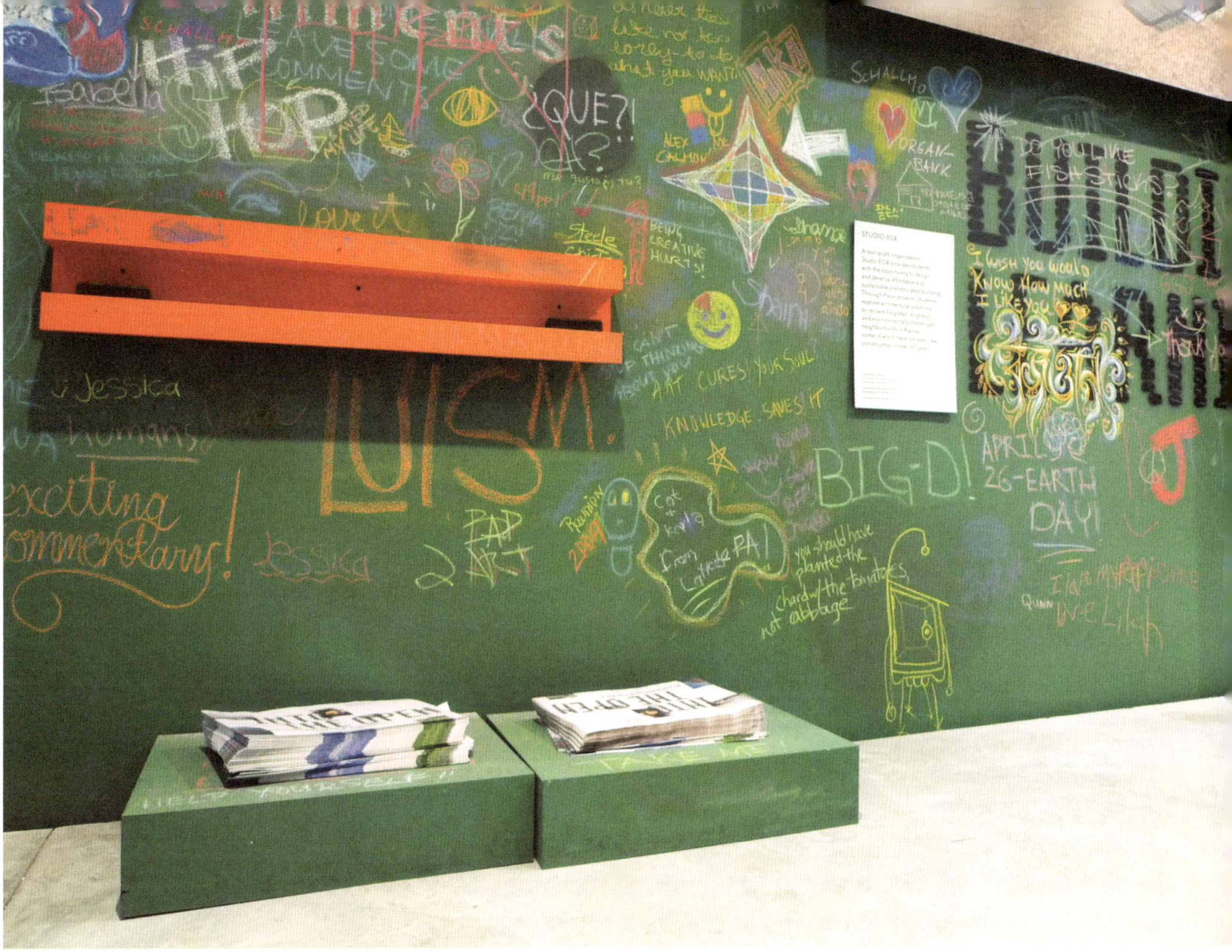

1

1 – Into the Open: Positioning Practice, exhibition design and graphics, Keller Gallery, Parsons School of Design, New York, 2008. The New York version of the U.S. Pavilion from the Venice Architecture Biennale 2008, curated by Aaron Levy and William Menking, and designed in collaboration with Saylor + Sirola

2 – Productive Posters, installation, Van Alen Institute, New York, 2008

overleaf

3 – Process 01: Joy, exhibition, P!, Chinatown, New York, 2012. Featuring works by Chauncey Hare, Christine Hill, and Karel Martens

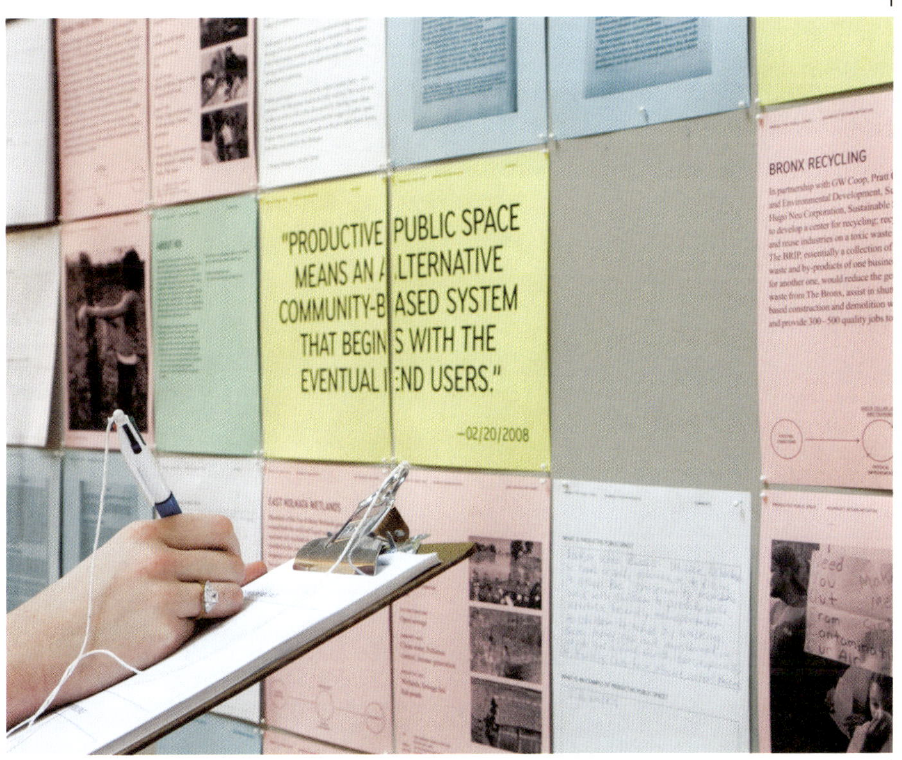

2

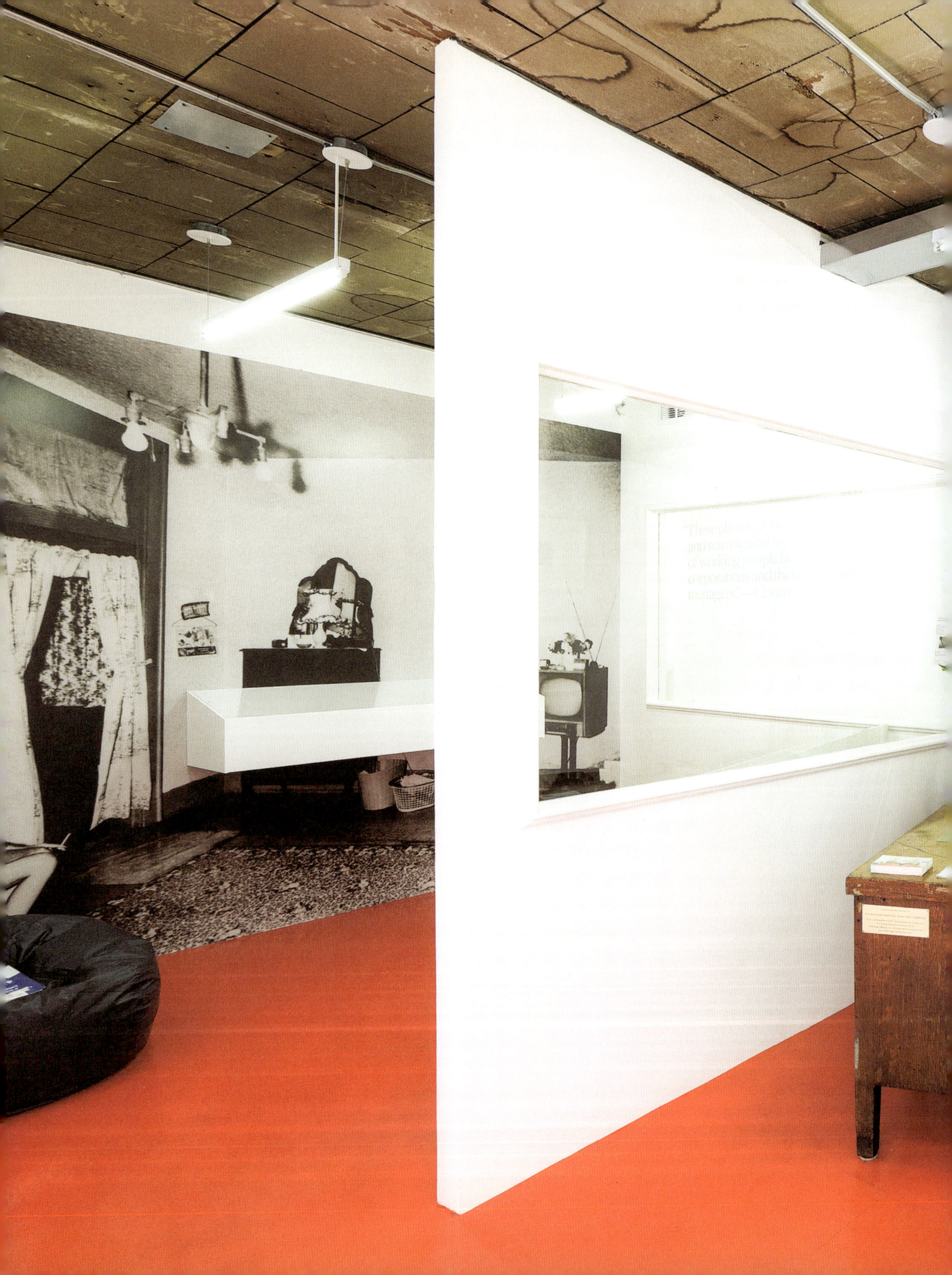
“These
and warn against
of working people
corporations and their
managers.” —

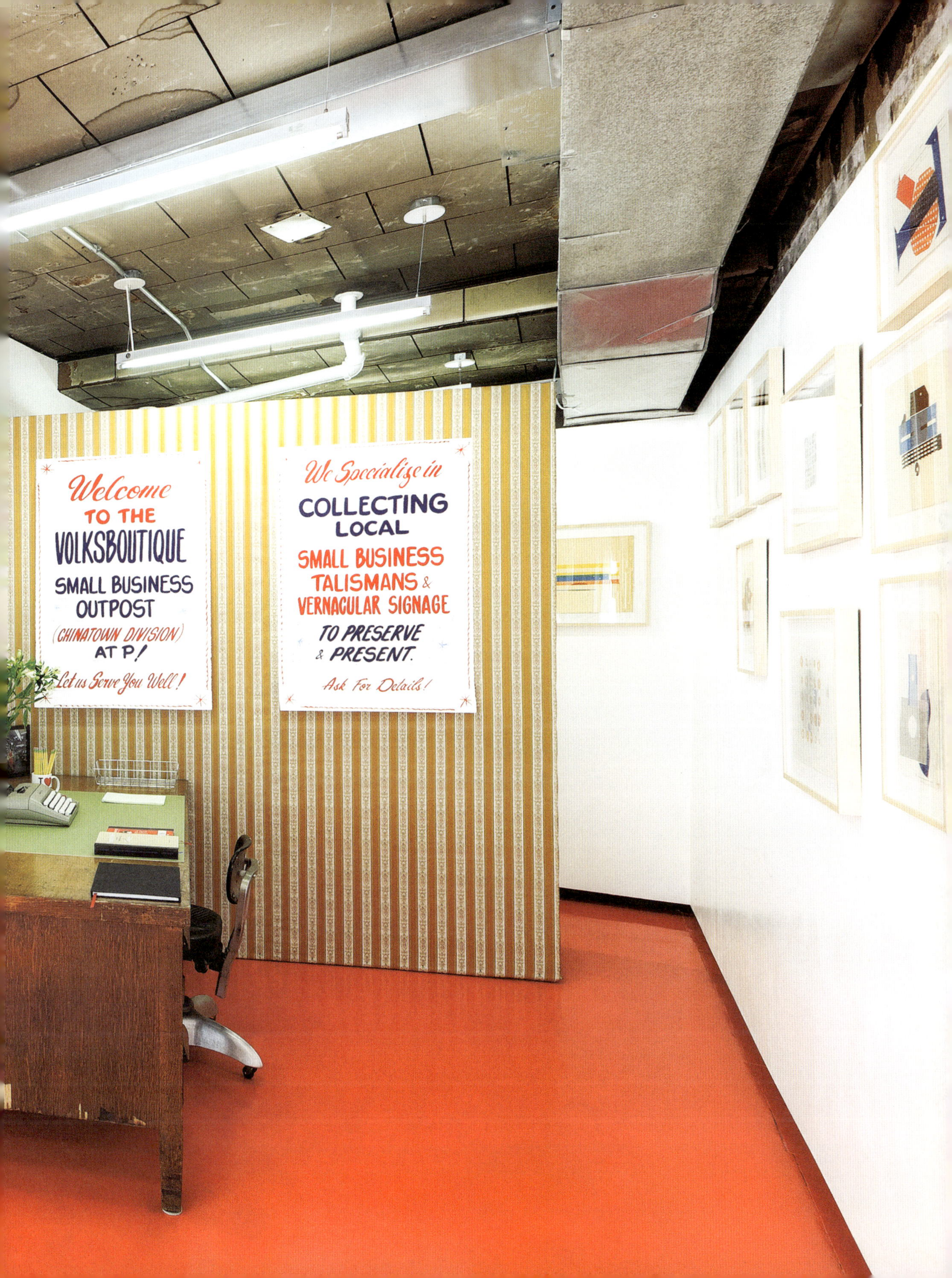
Welcome
TO THE
VOLKSBOUTIQUE
SMALL BUSINESS
OUTPOST
(CHINATOWN DIVISION)
AT P!
Let us Serve You Well!
We Specialise in
COLLECTING
LOCAL
SMALL BUSINESS
TALISMANS &
VERNACULAR SIGNAGE
TO PRESERVE
& PRESENT.
Ask For Details!

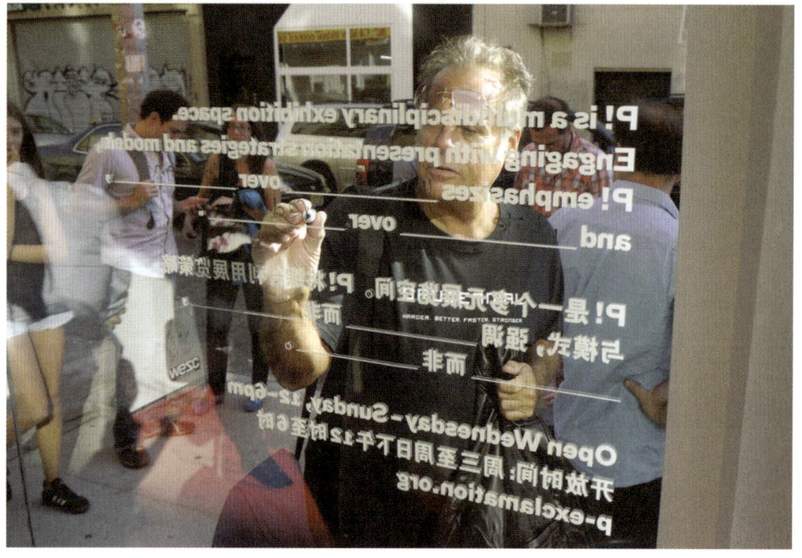

4

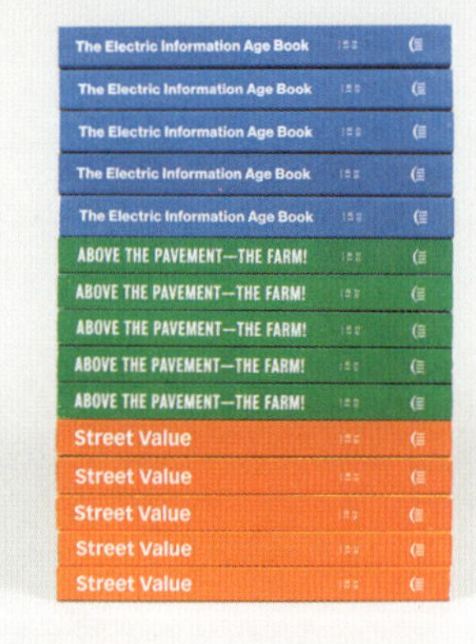

5

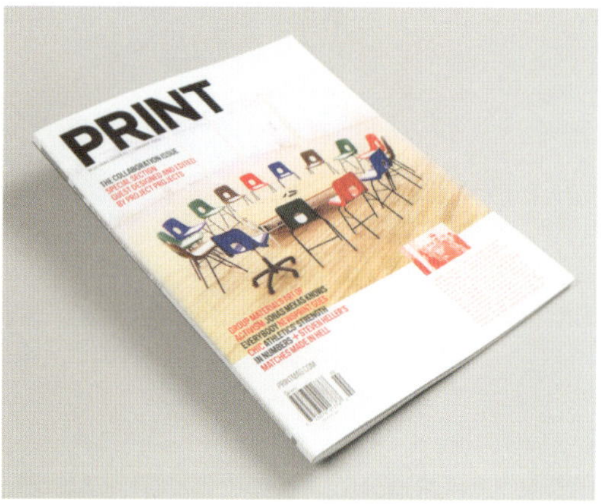

6

4 – **A visitor annotates the Mad Lib mission statement on the glass-front facade of P!, Chinatown, New York**

5 – **Inventory Books, a paperback series edited and designed by Adam Michaels and published by Princeton Architectural Press, 2010–ongoing**

6 – **Cover shot of Print magazine's collaboration-themed issue, guest edited and art directed by Project Projects in January 2011**

feed back into the design and commissioned work in ways that push our collective practice further.

How are decisions made?

It depends on the scale of the decision, and the number of other parties affected by a given decision. Accordingly, each of us has a good deal of autonomy for small-scale decisions (often pertaining to the production of design work); there is usually a more involved process of negotiation between the studio principals and staff when considering aspects of studio superstructure.

Does each of you have a clearly defined role? If so, what are some of each member's distinct responsibilities?

In the abstract, the idea is that anyone can do anything. In reality, we've each developed particular areas of interest and expertise over the years, and we each tend to focus in large part on those areas. It can be ideal to work with an emphasis on depth, without feeling like that causes an undue sacrifice of breadth.

How important is each group member's individuality, both in terms of your artistic production and in terms of your relationship with the media? Does anonymity come into play?

We value collectivity in the production of our work—the vast majority is attributed to Project Projects, not to individuals. We've never tried to cloak our identities through any sort of anonymity, however, and we've spoken publicly about our work on many occasions, both individually and as a group.

What is the relationship between your working methods and your art's "content"? In this sense, does technology tend to play more of a supporting role, or does it lead you in new directions?

Our work embraces interactivity on an increasingly integrated level, and we've found that the structure and logic of the database itself can help to inform our working methods and approach. The ability to think about books, exhibitions, and identities—forms not primarily associated with technology—in a forward-thinking manner that

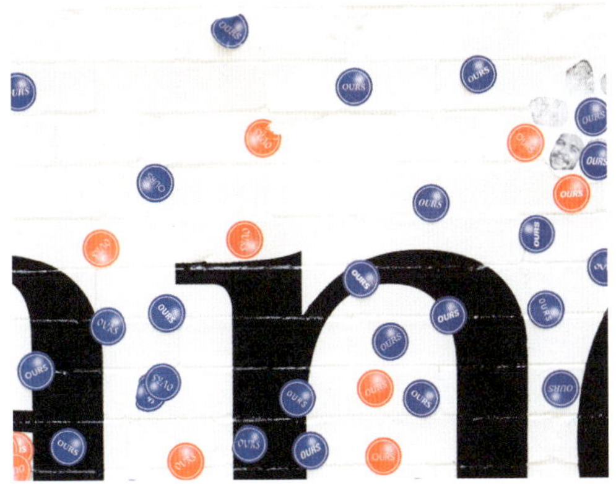

7

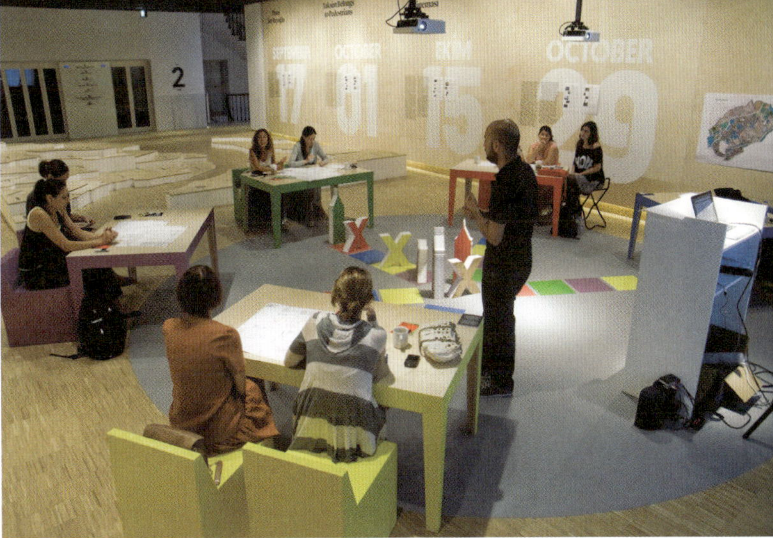

8

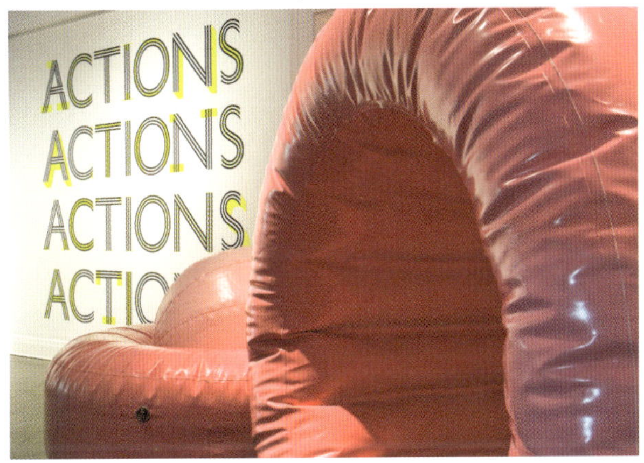

9

7 – OURS: Democracy in the Age of Branding, exhibition design, the Vera List Center for Art and Politics, The New School, New York, 2008

8 – Becoming Istanbul, exhibition, workshops, and events, SALT, Istanbul, 2011

9 – Actions, exhibition, the Canadian Centre for Architecture, Montreal, 2008

looks at how they will change in the future is a key part of our recent thinking.

How does your collaboration relate to its cultural, institutional, and commercial contexts? In other words, how would you respond to those who call this a trend?

Our studio and work has always been structured collaboratively. Graphic designers within a certain social and political context—Grapus, Pushpin, and Cyan, to name but a few—have used this form throughout the twentieth and twenty-first centuries, operating as a hybrid of a company and a collective. We see ourselves as within this tradition, while also creating our own studio model that fits the time and context of our work.

Who is your audience?

It's an aspiration of ours to invite as many people as we can to the party—broad inclusivity is a subtext found throughout much of our work. Accordingly, much of our practice occurs at perceived borders between disciplines or constituencies. We frequently work on projects involving a complex body of knowledge meant for a narrow audience, and then labor to make that knowledge understandable and useful to broader audiences.

Does your engagement with one another translate into an engagement with the public? How so?

We all come from different backgrounds and contexts; these differences are compounded through our engagement with our external collaborators and commissioners. The synthesis of multiple perspectives not only leads beyond individual ego in the production of work; we see it as leading to the creation of work that communicates to a range of audiences, pushing beyond existing, hermetic constituencies.

ACTIVE SINCE	CITY	WEBSITE
2006	Los Angeles, U.S./ Saigon, Vietnam	the-propeller-group.com

The Propeller Group

MEMBERS	ACTIVITIES	RECOMMENDED PUBLICATION
Phunam, Matt Lucero, Tuan Andrew Nguyen	Community Projects, Curating, Internet Art, Merchandising, Music, Painting / Sculpture / Installation, Public Performance, Publishing, Urban Interventions	Apsara DiQuinzio, SIX LINES OF FLIGHT: SHIFTING GEOGRAPHIES IN CONTEMPORARY ART, University of California Press, Berkeley, 2012

Divided between Vietnam and California, The Propeller Group members have backgrounds in film and visual arts. Their main focus is on how cultural, religious, and political ideologies and symbols become universal through mass media and advertising. Their videos, objects, and graphics borrow from traditional art forms like crafts, drawing, and murals, but put them in a commercial frame as if they were at the center of a marketing campaign.

Why work collaboratively?

We work collaboratively because each of us individually got tired of telling jokes to ourselves in the mirror. Telling jokes to yourself in front of the mirror is an audience of two, but with two other people you get an audience of six. Add more mirrors and you've just created a great media funhouse and you can pretend to be things like advertising agencies and big media companies.

It was ambition and urgency that drove us together. We discovered that there was no way we could attempt to engage the social/cultural structures we wanted to if we didn't work collaboratively. It's the coordinated collaborative effort from an organized team that allows us to attack these larger, more ambitious projects. Collaboration has become a medium to us and we explore different collaborations with different projects.

How do you determine membership? Does physical location matter in this regard?

Membership is fluid but it has been mainly structured around the three of us. In many productions we expand our team in order to carry out particular projects and there are also some projects in which other collectives and individuals join in. We work with creative people from different backgrounds, from architects to advertising agencies, designers, writers, and producers of culture who are engaging or attempting to engage communities.

Physical location is important to us conceptually but it's been less and less important in terms of logistics.

If considered separately, how do your individual artistic practices contribute to or detract from your work as a group?

Funnily enough, we all see this collective as a part of our individual practice. And we each mold this collective based on our own individual interests and concerns. So at any given time, Matt could say he's working on a piece called The Propeller Group, or Phunam could give a lecture about how The Propeller Group is part of his individual practice, or Tuan could hire an advertising agency to rebrand the image of The Propeller Group.

How are decisions made?

The decision-making process is always an adventure, sometimes strange and other times spectacular. Before we come to decisions, there is extensive conversation and research and more conversation and more research. There is no one set of rules on how we decide to move or not move on a particular project. We all contribute in different ways, and we allow the idea to shift, jump, and change all the time. Sometimes the result doesn't resemble the initial idea that spurred the project. Sometimes we consult with

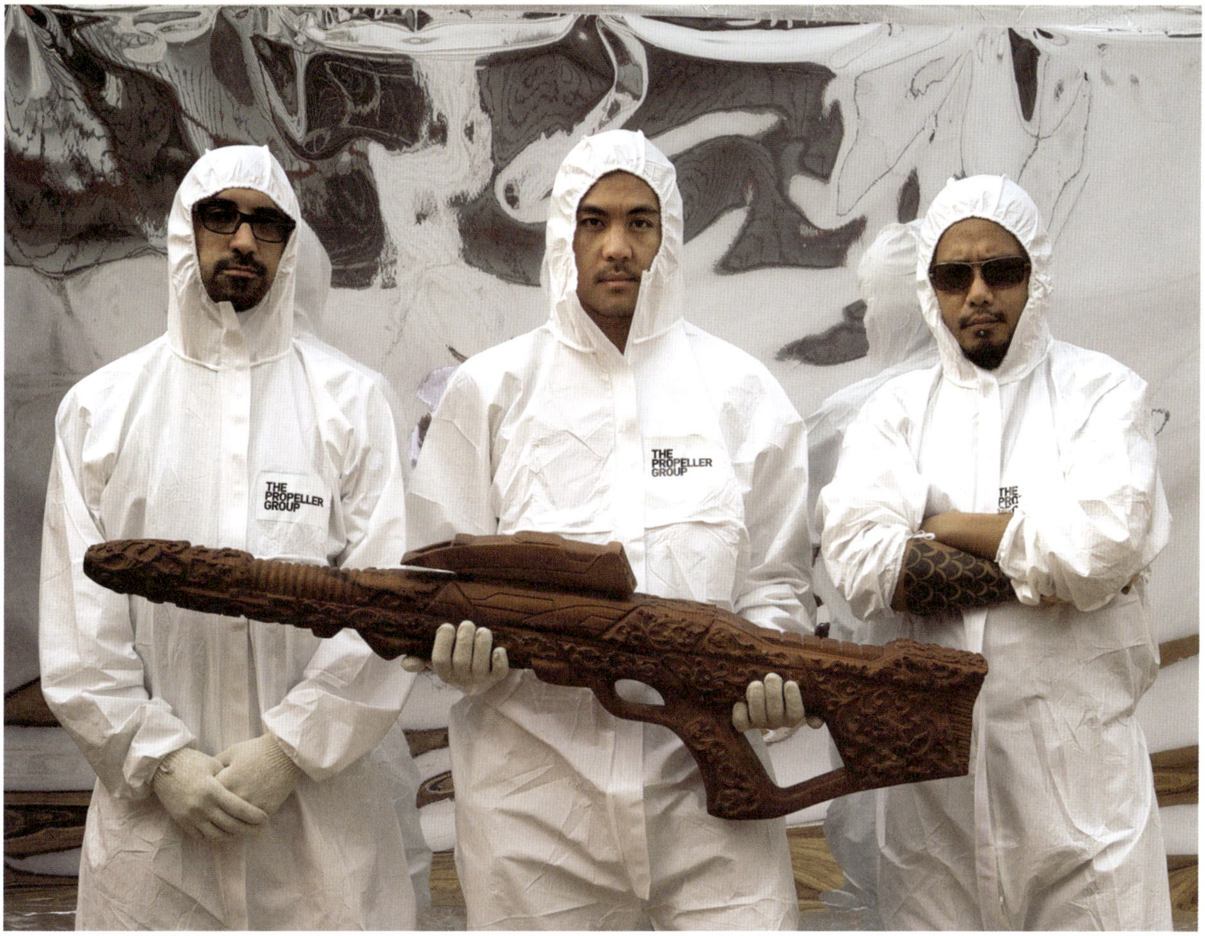

1

1 – Group portrait

2 – Viet Nam The World Tour, performance, 2010–ongoing. Kaba Modern Legacy (Ambitious Alex, Barry Goods, Trandrew, and Tony Transformer) freestyles for a crowd of tourists at Marina Bay in Singapore, 2010

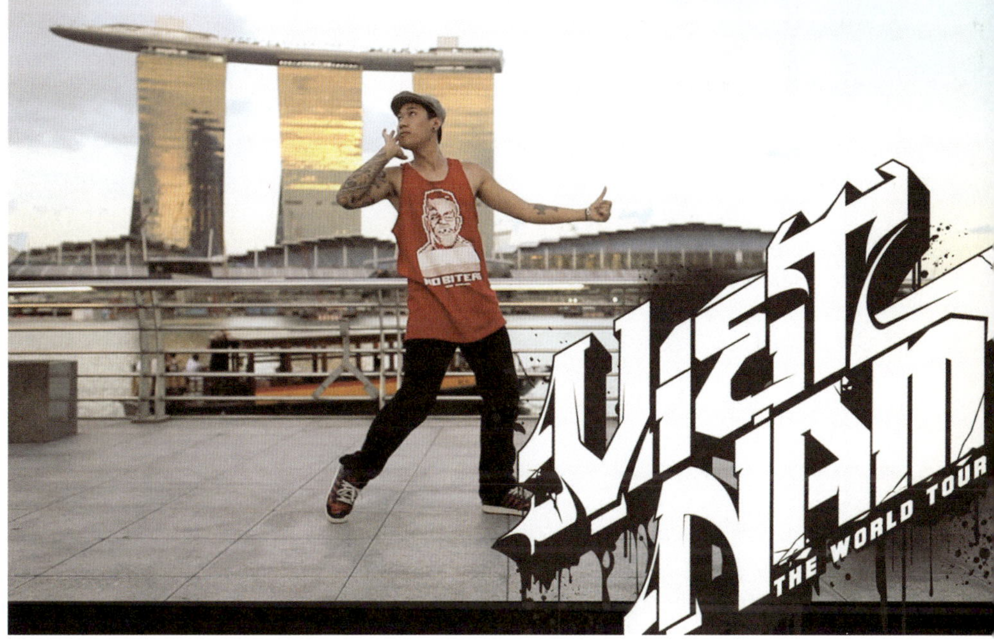

2

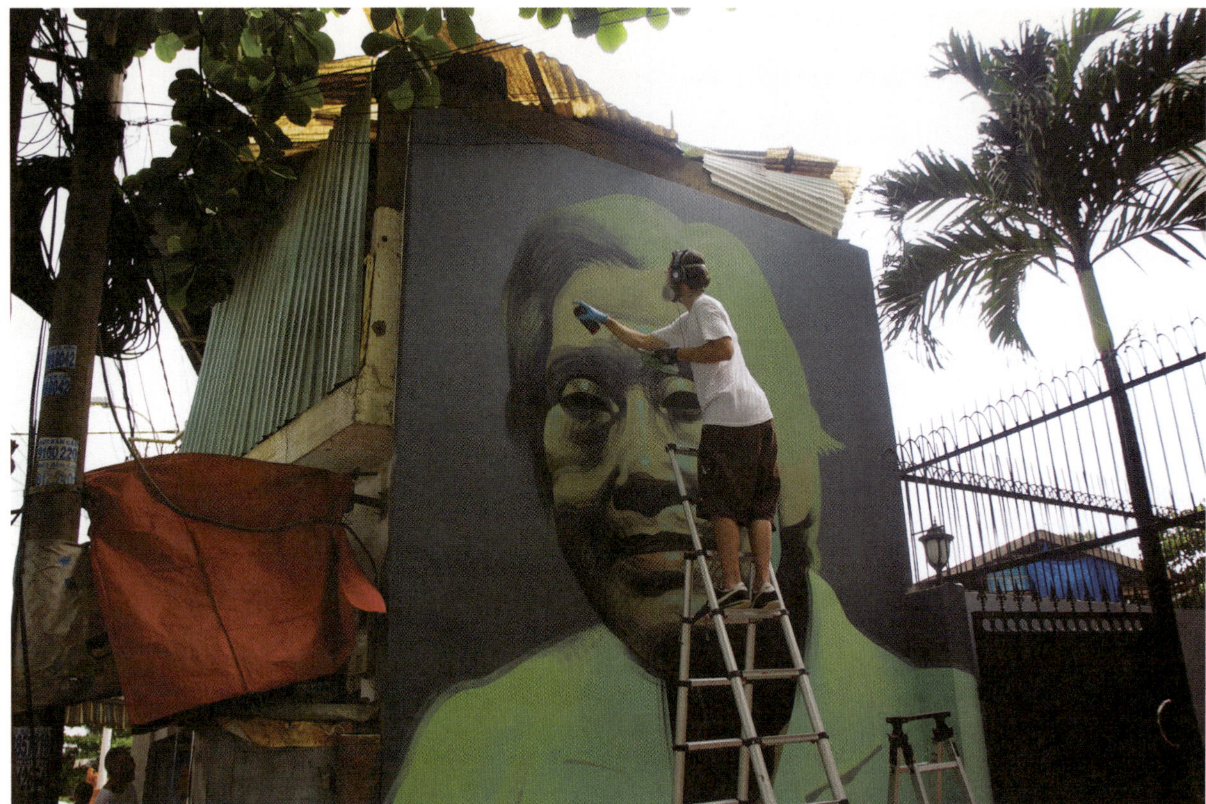

3

fortune-tellers and shamans. The I Ching is effective for this as well.

Does each of you have a clearly defined role? If so, what are some of each member's distinct responsibilities?

Matt: No. We have different responsibilities depending on the project and circumstance. We can shape-shift and mold ourselves to what is needed at any given time. We also open up roles for other groups and individuals to fill.

Phunam: Uh... Tuan and Matt do all the public speaking and I do all the writing.

Tuan: Yes, we most definitely have specific responsibilities. Matt is the snake charmer—strong in praying mantis style. Phunam is the afro-samurai—silent slicin' and dicin'. And I'm weapons fabricator—C4 to ya door no beef no more!

How important is each group member's individuality, both in terms of your artistic production and in terms of your relationship with the media? Does anonymity come into play?

We started a collaborative[s] in Los Angeles in the late 1990s, early 2000s. It was a natural coming together of close friends who all shared similar interests. We decided that with each project, we would take on another identity as a collaborative, with its own name and manifesto. After the project was completed, the collaborative would disband and another would form with another name and manifestation and a new project. From the beginning, we set out to fail and that became the point but at the same time we were able to explore the complex and mucky relationship between author and audience. Little has remained of the work that we did.

A great example of the complexities of anonymity is an art project called The Invisible Monument that was to be installed outside of one of the world's largest shopping malls in Guangzhou, China. It was the resurrection of a controversial monument called the Goddess of Democracy that stood ten meters tall facing the large portrait of Mao in Tiananmen Square, Beijing. It was destroyed by the Chinese government during the protest in 1989. In order to resurrect the monument, the artist had to strategically hide the content from everyone. The Goddess of Democracy became embedded inside another monument, which appeared to be an unassuming piece of modernist sculpture.

The Invisible Monument presented a situation where the public who sees the work might not have access to the original Goddess monument hidden inside. It left us with the question, what happens to the anonymity when the artist talks about the work and the art world becomes privy to the content but it remains anonymous to the public?

opposite
3 – **El Mac, Viet Nam The World Tour: Kosoom by the Mekong, mural, Ho Chi Minh City, 2010**

4 – **Viet Nam The World Tour, photo shoot, Singapore, 2010. Kaba Modern Legacy (Ambitious Alex, Barry Goods, Trandrew, and Tony Transformer) with the crew from Recognize Studios**

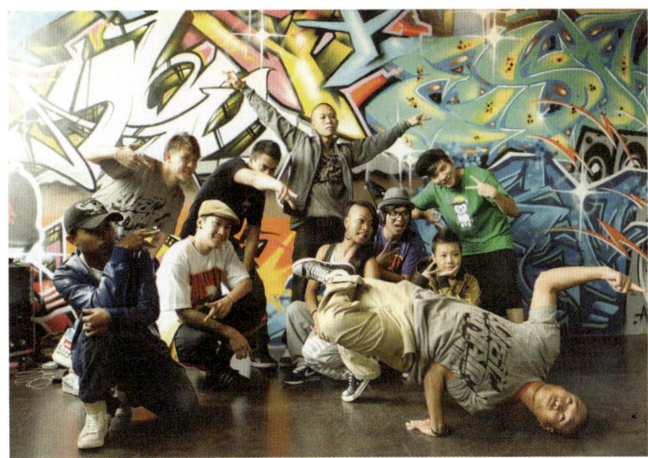

4

What is the relationship between your working methods and your art's "content"? In this sense, does technology tend to play more of a supporting role, or does it lead you in new directions?

We agree with McLuhan but don't believe that's the endgame anymore. We're interested in creating narratives that can at once collapse and expand the medium, using, for instance distributions channels and how the narratives get passed through those channels. The reconfiguration of the current methods of distribution of narratives is as important as the narratives themselves. There's a dimension of our work that exists beyond the artwork and how each specific work operates. Our practice and the development of our collective is a brand. The distribution of that brand is as important as the brand itself.

How does your collaboration relate to its cultural, institutional, and commercial contexts? In other words, how would you respond to those who call this a trend?

We have initiated a collaborative project with George Clooney and the band Fun to create the Save All Rhinos Of the World Organization, a nonprofit involved in shutting down the rhino-horn trade between South Africa and Vietnam. The organization would raise funds to create a feature film starring Clooney and Ben Affleck to bring the highest level of global awareness to rhino extinction and to reach the largest supporter base possible by setting its goal as an Oscar award–winning film and Grammy Award–winning soundtrack.

Who is your audience?

The notion of defining the audience has completely failed, becoming victim to vague and limiting ideas of demographics that are unable to take into consideration all the levels of experience and awareness that happen during and after viewership. We thought of this dilemma in relation to the experience of a film, in which the audience is always kept in on the joke, and the protagonists, antagonists, and supporting characters on-screen may not have any idea what is going on. The unawareness that there is an audience for the characters on-screen turns the spectator watching into a sort of metaaudience.

But there is another level of audience that is overlooked during the production of the film, when the actors perform for a potential audience and the director plays the role of the audience.

Does your engagement with one another translate into an engagement with the public? How so?

In our project Television Commercial For Communism, in which we work with a major advertising agency to rebrand the idea of communism, we engage with TBWA and present the concept. Once the agency starts working, we become the audience and are engaged with its work. When the commercial is made and we release it online, we then have a new base of viewers who become involved. Then it is shown in an art institution; the art world becomes enmeshed. And if the commercial would be broadcast during the Super Bowl, there would be yet another layer of engagement added. Participation between author and audience is now multilayered due to technology and different means of distribution. In a way, we, the authors, have become attentive to the audience in this engagement. We spend as much time reading and responding to YouTube comments on our video work as we do making the work itself.

Technology and modern methods of distribution have created a two-way mirror, set in front of all those logged in. This begs a question, who is your audience when you are performing in front of the mirror?

5–9 – Television Commercial For Communism video stills, 2010

opposite

10 – Daytona, February 14, 2012 (Nokia N95), drawing, 2012

11 – Static Friction: Burning Rubber, performance, Ho Chi Minh City, 2012

12 – Television Commercial For Communism production still, 2011

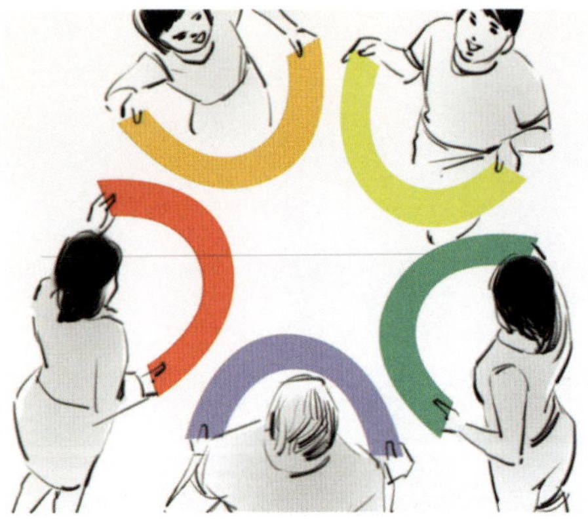

5

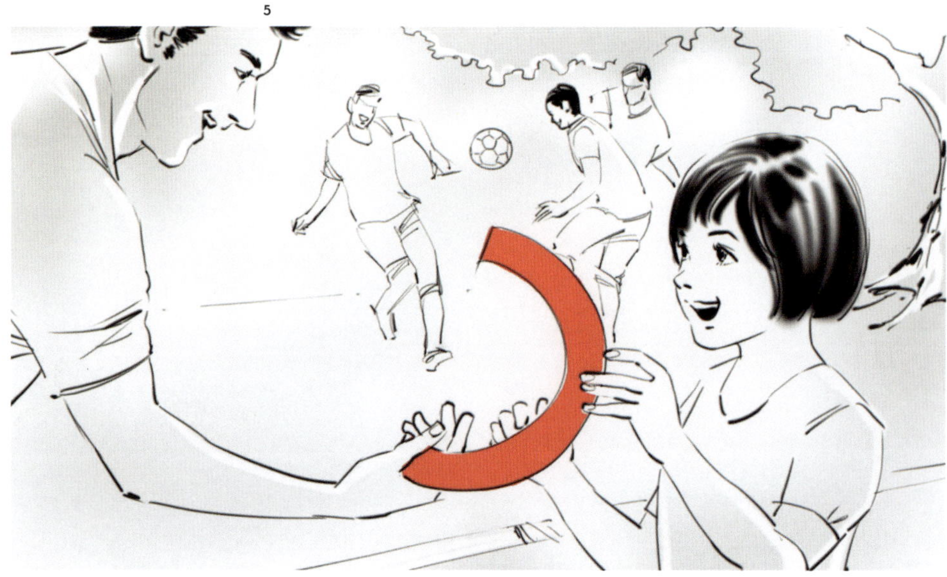

6

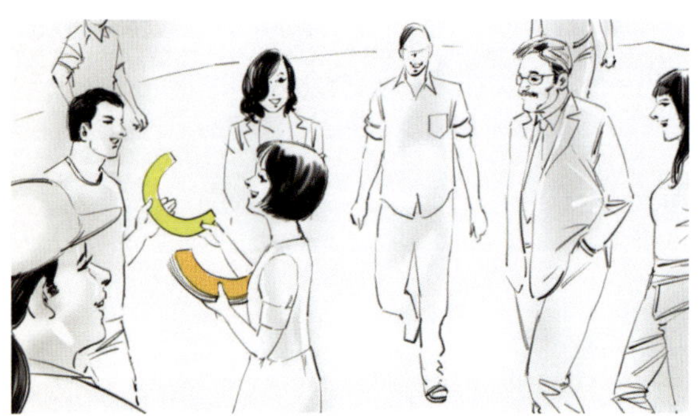

7

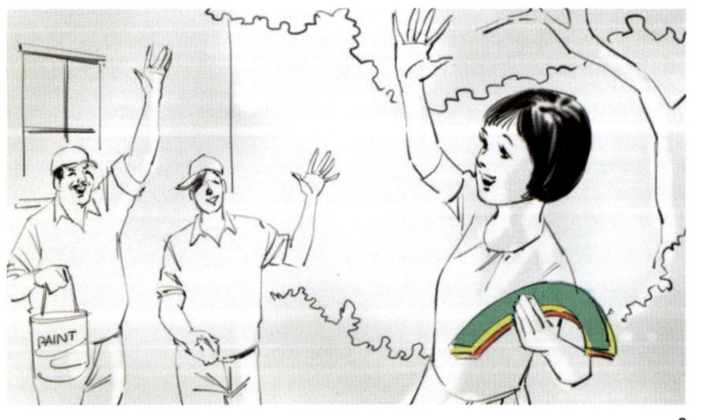

8

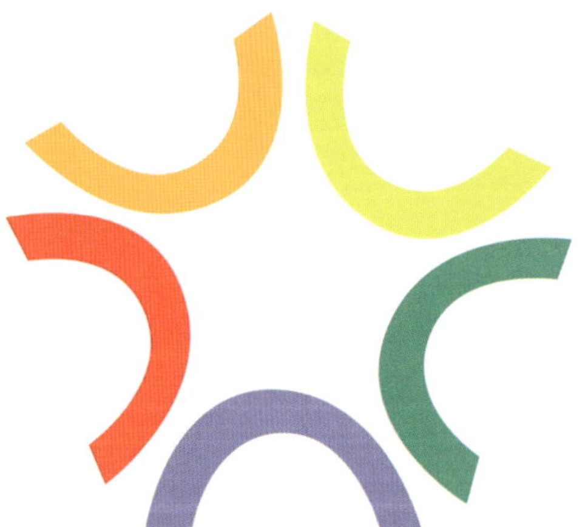

9

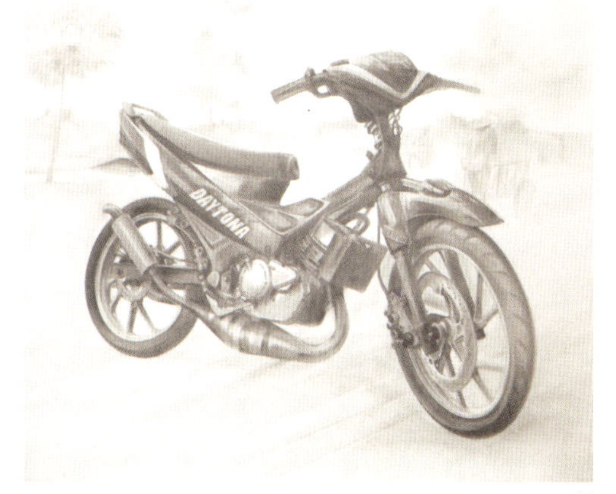

10

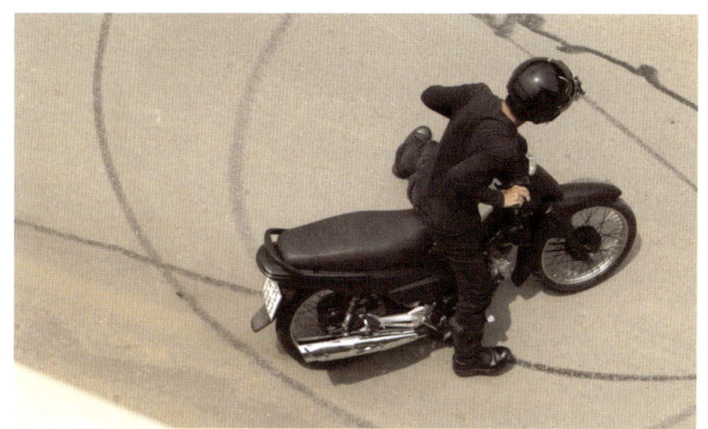

11

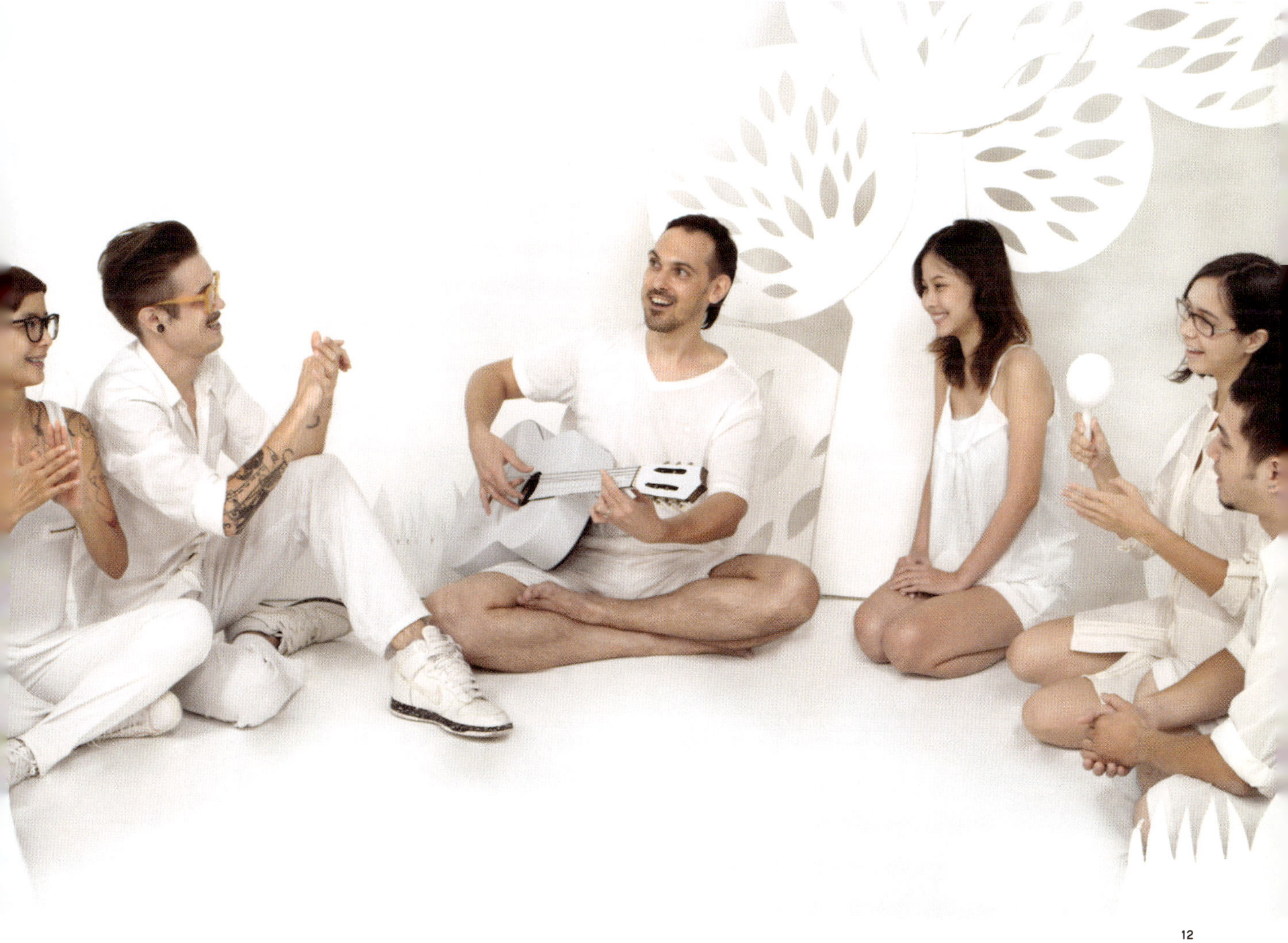

12

ACTIVE SINCE	CITY	WEBSITE
2003	Madrid, Spain / Berlin, Germany	psjm.es

PSJM

MEMBERS	ACTIVITIES	RECOMMENDED PUBLICATION
Cynthia Viera and Pablo San José	Curating, Internet Art, Literature, Merchandising, Painting / Sculpture / Installation, Public Performance, Publishing, Urban Interventions, Video	PSJM: A Critical Decade 2003–2013, Centro Atlántico De Arte Moderno, Las Palmas, 2013

PSJM produces graphics, installations, merchandising, and events structured around social, economic, and political themes, in relation to both society and art history. Globalization, the commodification of culture, and ecology are at the core of the duo's activities that borrow from the language of marketing and mass media to put into question the role of art in our society.

Why work collaboratively?

PSJM was established in 2003 by Cynthia Viera and Pablo San José. PSJM acts as a commercial cutting-edge art brand that raises questions about works of art in the market, communication with consumers, and the idea of function as an artistic quality. We make use of the communicative resources of spectacular capitalism to demonstrate the relevance of the paradoxes that its chaotic development produces.

The production of this kind of artwork requires a team, a company-like working structure in which tasks must be separated.

How do you determine membership? Does physical location matter in this regard?

In 1998 Pablo San José decided that his signature would become a brand and began a still-ongoing work that explores the idea of the artist's signature as a commodity. It's a project that constructs itself anew with each new piece executed. "The artist is the brand, the artwork is the product." In 2003 Cynthia Viera, a management graduate in International Business and Marketing, and the head of marketing services at a large telecommunications company, joined the project, turning the theoretical intention of working within the standard business model into a reality by helping to legally formalize the team as a commercial brand.

We moved from Madrid to Berlin in 2007, but we are still the same. Our work reflects on global socioeconomic problems; we could work from anywhere in the world.

If considered separately, how do your individual artistic practices contribute to or detract from your work as a group?

We do not develop separate artistic activities from the group. Our tasks, whether creative, theoretical, managerial, production, or promotions, always go toward the realization of PSJM's specific projects,or further building the overall brand value of PSJM.

How are decisions made?

Our raw material is information, dialogue, and communication. All decisions and statements are taken by common agreement. The PSJM brand is a company based on empathy.

Does each of you have a clearly defined role? If so, what are some of each member's distinct responsibilities?

Cynthia concerns herself with marketing, management, and administration work and Pablo takes charge of theory and creativity, both sharing production tasks.

How important is each group member's individuality, both in terms of your artistic production and in terms of your relationship with the media? Does anonymity come into play?

As individuals and workers we are 50/50 important for the team. An idea without management is useless. A promotion without an idea is nothing. So we need each other.

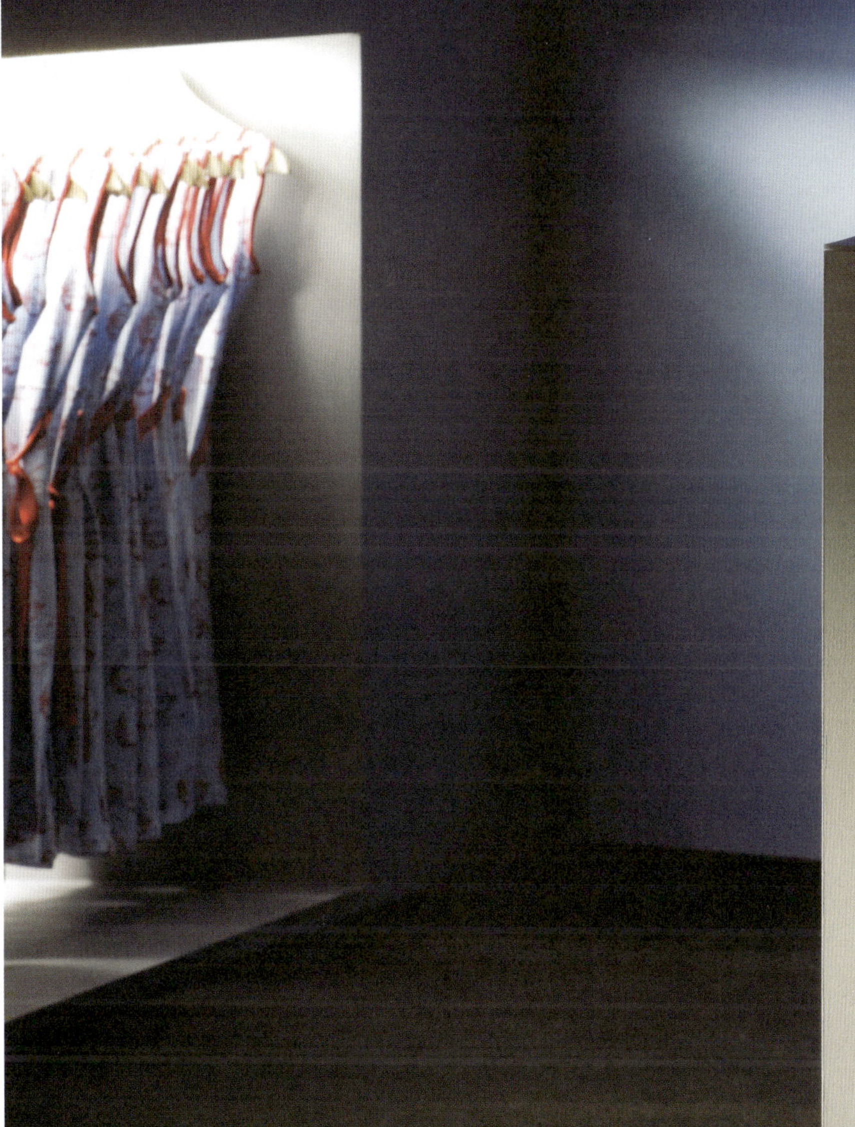
marx

HAZ COMO NOSOTROS,

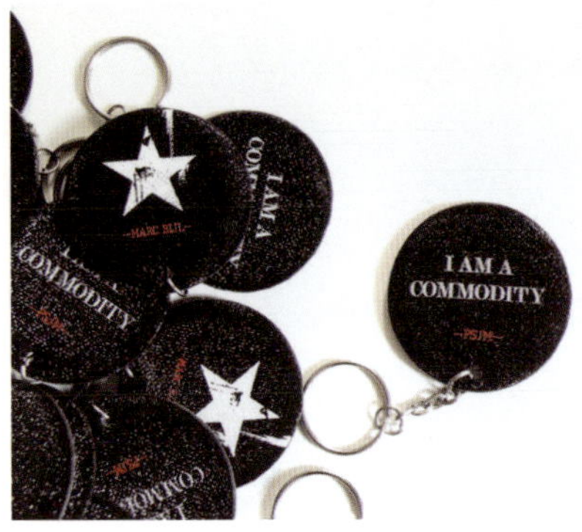

2

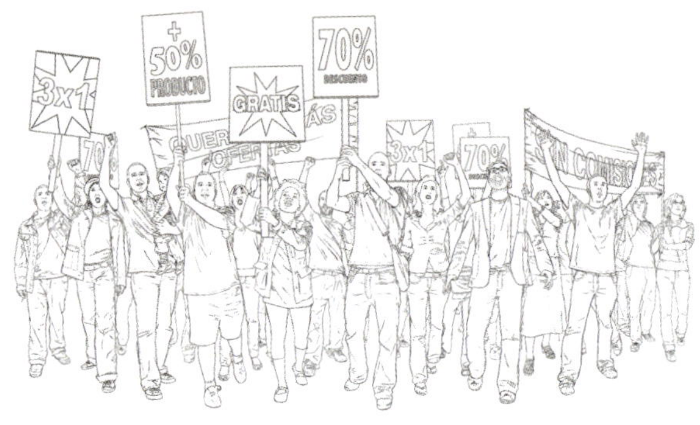

3

Regarding our relation with the media, Cynthia does arrange interviews and Pablo speaks (managerial/theoretical), but roles can eventually change due to specific situations. In any case, it is always PSJM who is speaking. Nevertheless we do not hide ourselves as persons—our logo shows our silhouettes beside the acronym; we are not machines: we are persons making art for persons.

What is the relationship between your working methods and your art's "content"? In this sense, does technology tend to play more of a supporting role, or does it lead you in new directions?

The correlation between our working methods and our artwork is really important. The team structure and procedures decisively affect the type of artwork that we execute. Our complex projects involve experiments with language and marketing technology in order to reveal their paradoxes and develop a critique accessible to the general public without neglecting the more nuanced intellectual concerns that these projects raise within the contemporary art world. At PSJM, we call it "experimental marketing," which does not seek economic profit as much as the exploration of new channels of artistic creation, always with an eye on the brand-dominated ideology of today's world.

How does your collaboration relate to its cultural, institutional, and commercial contexts? In other words, how would you respond to those who call this a trend?

Our collective work is a mirror of society. More than a trend, it is a sign of the times.

Who is your audience?

It is mostly a contemporary art audience, because this is our field of production. But as we use marketing, advertising, and design language to create a critical message in the art world, we reach a wider audience. The audience is considered seriously in our whole work; it is important for us that people can understand our artworks. We strain to obtain two reading levels, one for the individual unfamiliar with the codes of contemporary art and one for the art world itself. We reach the first level through global culture industry language, and the second by contributing to the current aesthetic debate.

On the other hand, when we make public interventions, like Capitalism R.I.P. (a capitalism death notice on Cuenca's advertising panels), the audience grows. The art world has limited audiences, and "critical activists" are like ants in front of the whole ideology spread by mass media. But there are gaps, narrow ways to act.

Another example is our project Corporate Armies, based on an article we read in the Guardian, in July 2007. Russia's parliament voted to allow the country's biggest energy monopolies, Gazprom and the state oil pipeline company Transneft, to employ and to arm private security units in order to "protect themselves from terrorist attack." Russia's interior ministry said that it would supply Gazprom with guns from its own army. This was the starting point of Corporate Armies, a project of "political fiction" in which we pushed to the extreme the possible sequels of the Russian proposal. Of course, our project has exclusively been shown in art spaces like ARCOmadrid '09, where thousands watched the video. But the media thought of it worthy of reporting, so they picked up our work and published it as news. Otherwise only the lefty Guardian would have exposed this issue.

Does your engagement with one another translate into an engagement with the public? How so?

This occurs in at least two respects: the ethical and theoretical one. We think ethics is the more important problem in this unfair system. So we try to behave ethically at work, within the group and with our suppliers. Similarly, with the public, by means of showing artworks that speak to the lack of ethics in global capitalism. On the theoretical side, the work of art is understood as a fact made collectively, not only by artists, but by all the actors involved in the art world: critics, curators, gallery owners, collectors, museum directors, suppliers of all kinds, and, of course, the audience. Without audience, the artwork is unfinished.

previous
1 – Marx®, boutique installation, Centro Atlántico ee Arte Moderno, Las Palmas/LABoral, Gijón, 2008

opposite
2 – I am a commodity, keychains edition, Freies Museum, Berlin, 2010

opposite
3 – Demonstration of consumers, mural design, Off Limits, Madrid, 2007

4 – Total Experience. Wagner's Legacy in the Global Cultural Industry, lecture-performance, ULPGC, Las Palmas, 2010

5 – This is a Work of Art, performance-survey, Zagreus Project, Berlin, 2009

6 – Out of Context, Inside the Market, performance, Art Forum, Berlin, 2005

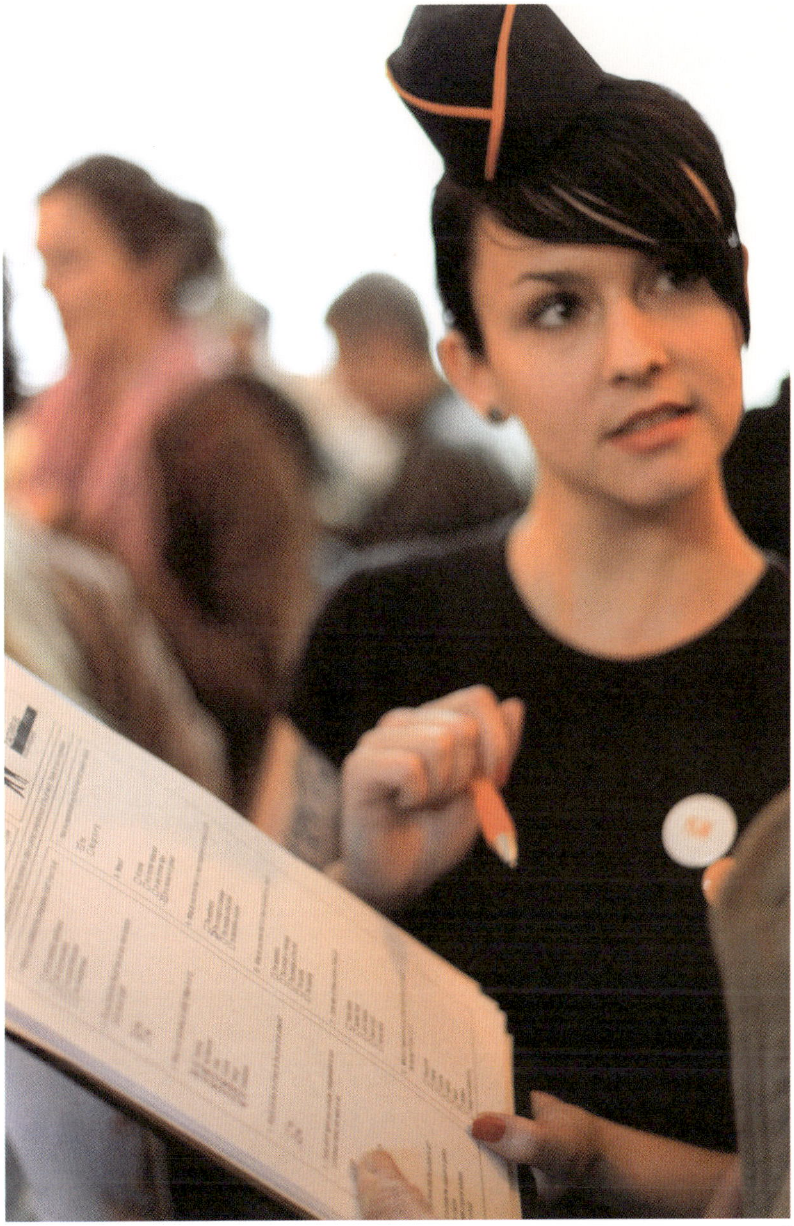

5

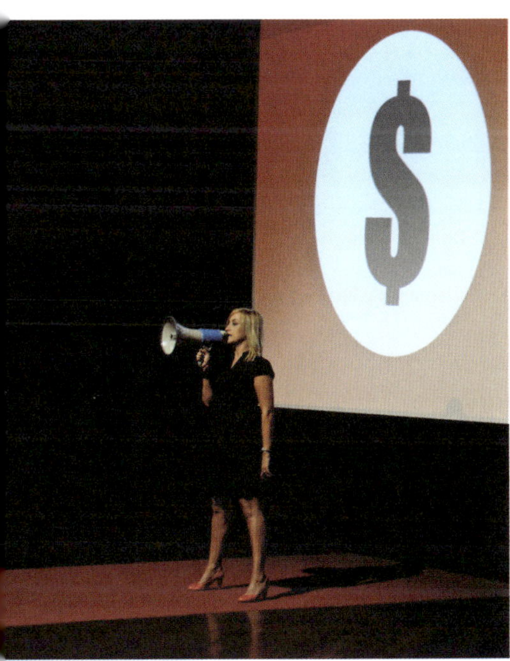

4

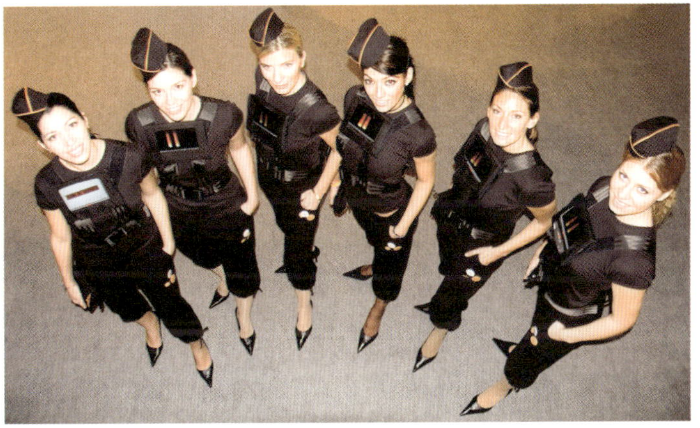

6

7 – Great Brands, logos for T-shirts, light boxes, and video, 2006

8 – Marx®, pattern design for wallpaper, 2008

opposite
9 – Capitalism R.I.P., public billboard, Cuenca, Spain, 2009

opposite
10 – Slogans, installation, Museo Barjola, Gijón, 2009

opposite
11 – Neutralized: Essays by Artists Who Write, cover of the book, PSJM (ed.), Empatía Ediciones, Madrid, 2010

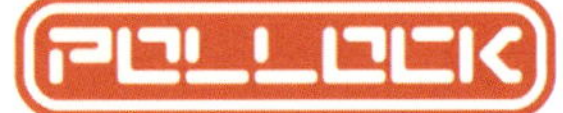

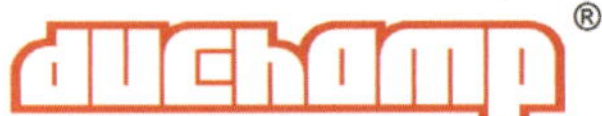

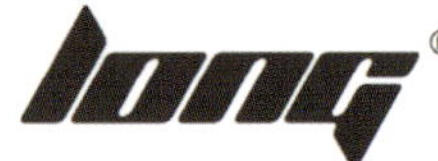

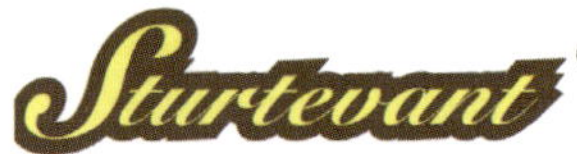

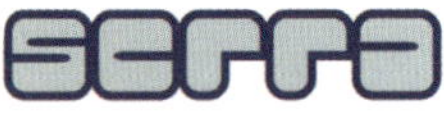

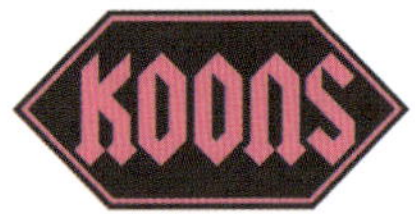

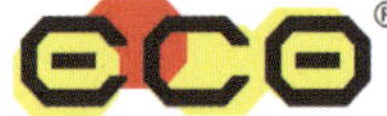

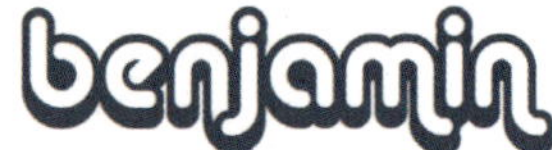

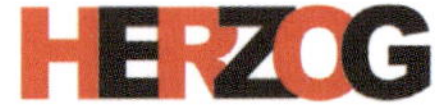

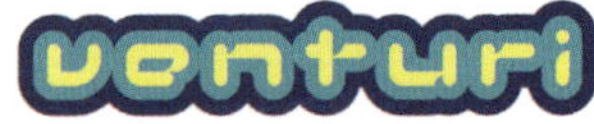

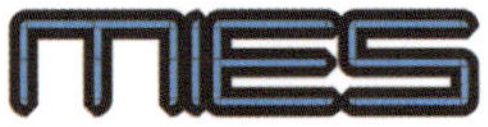

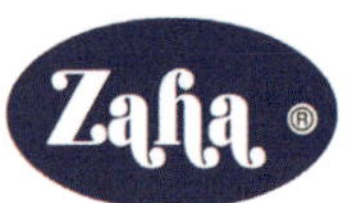

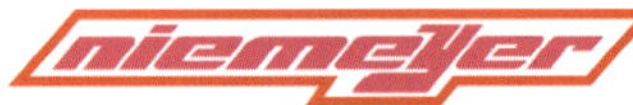

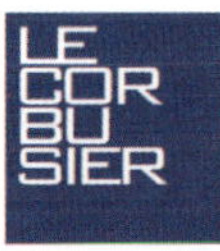

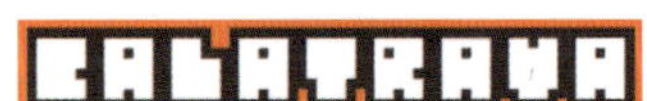

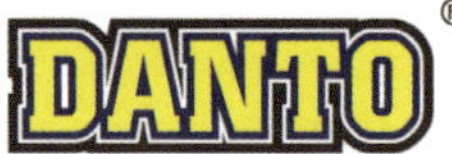

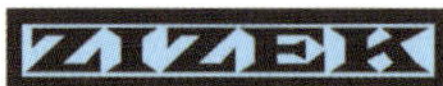

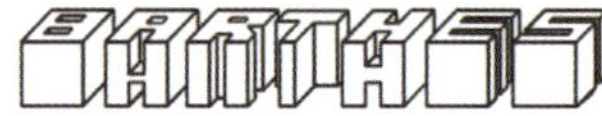

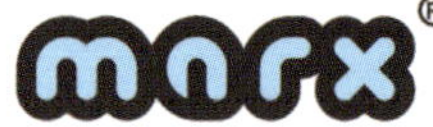

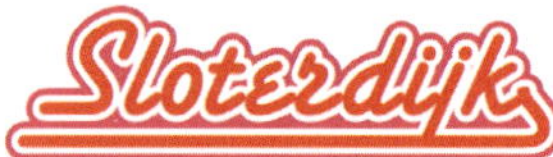

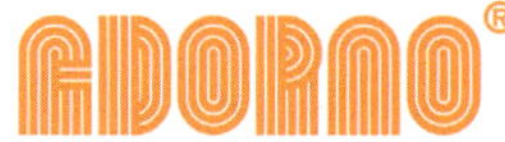

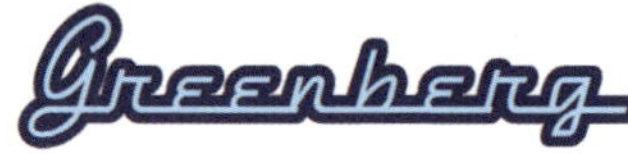

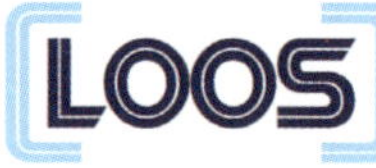

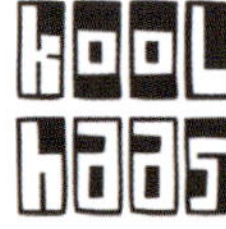

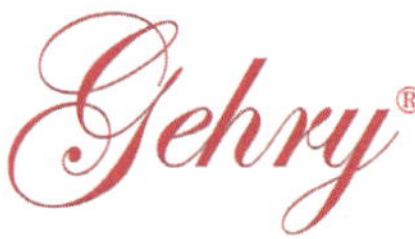

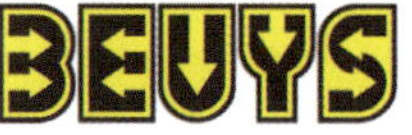

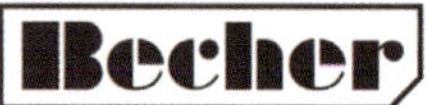

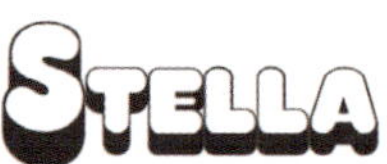

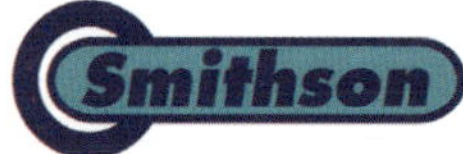

7

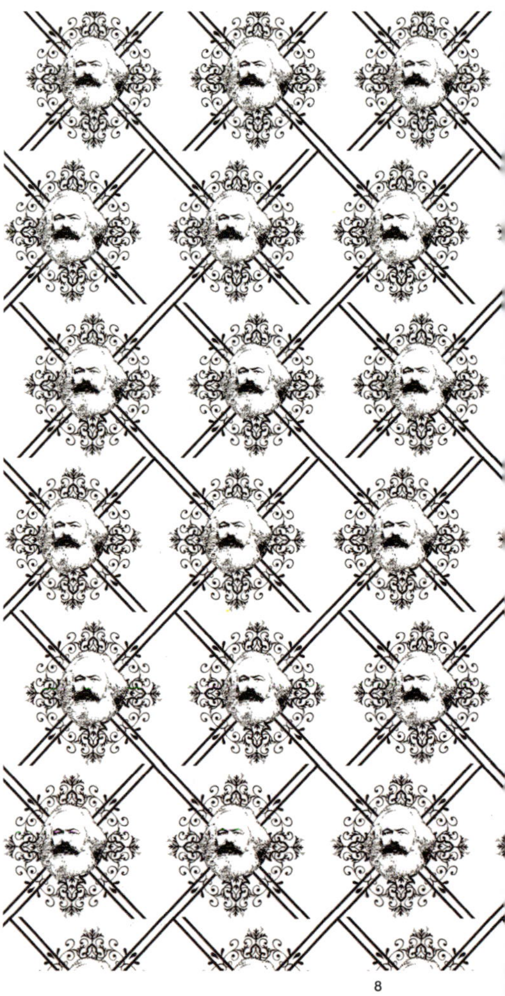

8

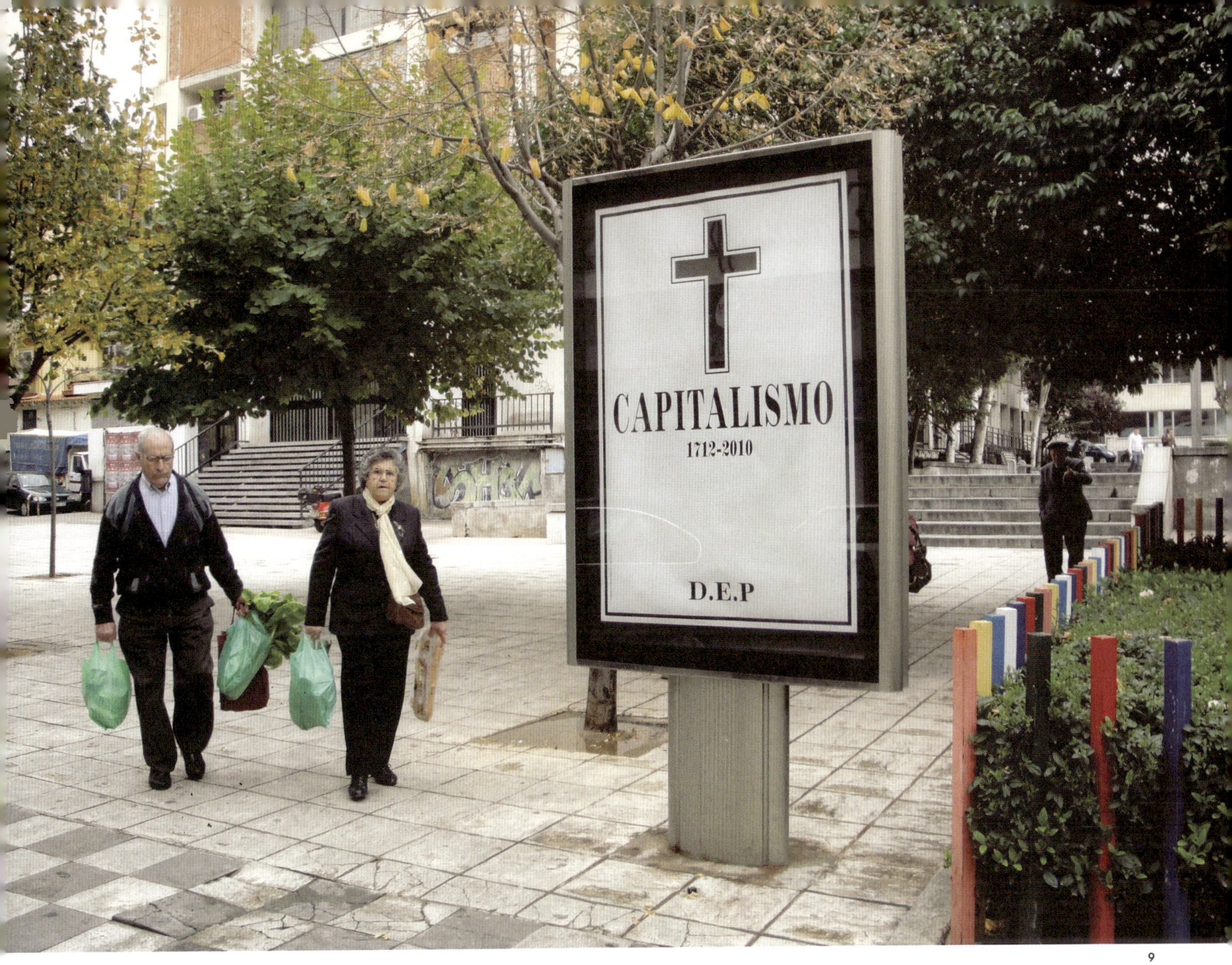

CAPITALISMO
1712-2010
D.E.P

9

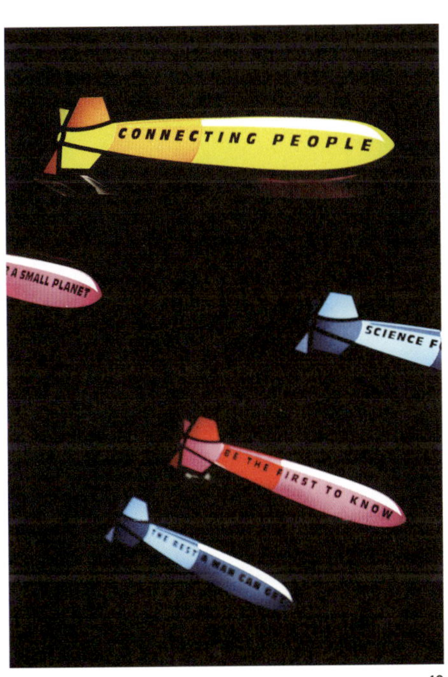
CONNECTING PEOPLE
A SMALL PLANET
SCIENCE F
BE THE FIRST TO KNOW

10

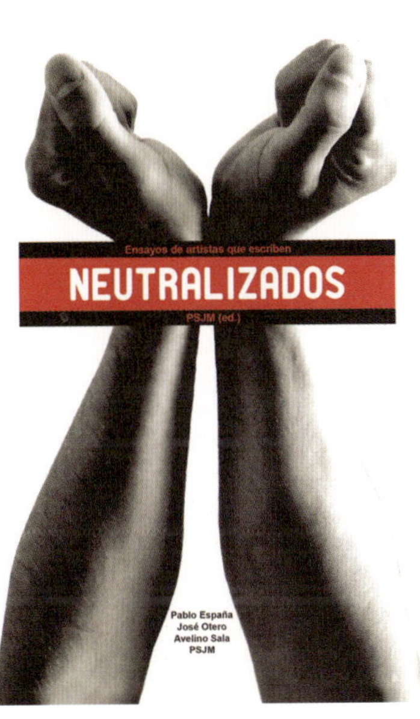
Ensayos de artistas que escriben
NEUTRALIZADOS
PSJM (ed.)
Pablo España
José Otero
Avelino Sala
PSJM

11

ACTIVE SINCE	CITY	WEBSITE
2006	Tel Aviv, Israel	publicmovement.org

Public Movement

MEMBERS	ACTIVITIES	RECOMMENDED PUBLICATION
Leader 1, Members 6	Public Performance	Ellen Feiss, Artists at Work: PUBLIC MOVEMENT, Afterall.org, November 4,2013

Led by Dana Yahalomi, Israeli collective Public Movement is one of the few in this book to be organized hierarchically. Its structure, however, is itself part of its exploration on how governmental structures produce consensus. Its choreographed public performances, often in collaboration with state institutions, simulate how governments act, involving the audience in the production of a collective awareness.

Why work collaboratively?

From its inception, Public Movement has been predicated on "working together," as both its method and the primary field of its engagements. It is a group of people in constantly shifting relations who deal with communal identities: national, religious, historical, and cultural. As a performance-based research body interested in the choreography of everyday public life, working in a group allows us to be both the subjects conducting the research and the objects being studied.

How do you determine membership? Does physical location matter in this regard?

Public Movement is based in Tel Aviv, where all the members live. We use to meet three times a week. In the first four years membership was determined by the leaders of Public Movement, Omer Krieger and Dana Yahalomi, who founded the Movement in 2006 and recruited its first group of members. In 2011 Yahalomi became the sole leader and new members were recruited by her and by older group members. There are also three agents of Public Movement who live outside Israel. An agent has a thorough understanding of Public Movement practices and contributes to their development over the years.

Not all Public Movement actions include members some of them are initiated by the leader and carried out with local participants, but those are not considered members but rather a second circle of Public Movement collaborators.

If considered separately, how do your individual artistic practices contribute to or detract from your work as a group?

We do public choreographies. Therefore, each member has a physical knowledge: from folk dance to Israel Defense Force combat tactics. We learned these skills in different ways: from being at the service of the state, or in an anarchist group or the Scouts. We teach each other.

How are decisions made?

Quite democratically. Anyone can make suggestions, and based on how persuasive the member is or how good the idea, we'll consider it together. There's no formal vote, rather shared conversation to work it out.

Decision making in the group has changed over time. Initially, it was the two leaders who brought ideas to the group and conducted the discussion. Since 2008, members have the opportunity to propose demands if they are in disagreement with the leader. Negotiating inner power relations became an inherent part of the life of the group. Public Movement was formed as a hierarchical group and is likely to remain so, but at present state it is a group with one leader and members who gradually grow in power and responsibility.

Does each of you have a clearly defined role? If so, what are some of each member's distinct responsibilities?

There are few fixed roles. Responsibilities are changing all the time. We can start with the voice who is answering

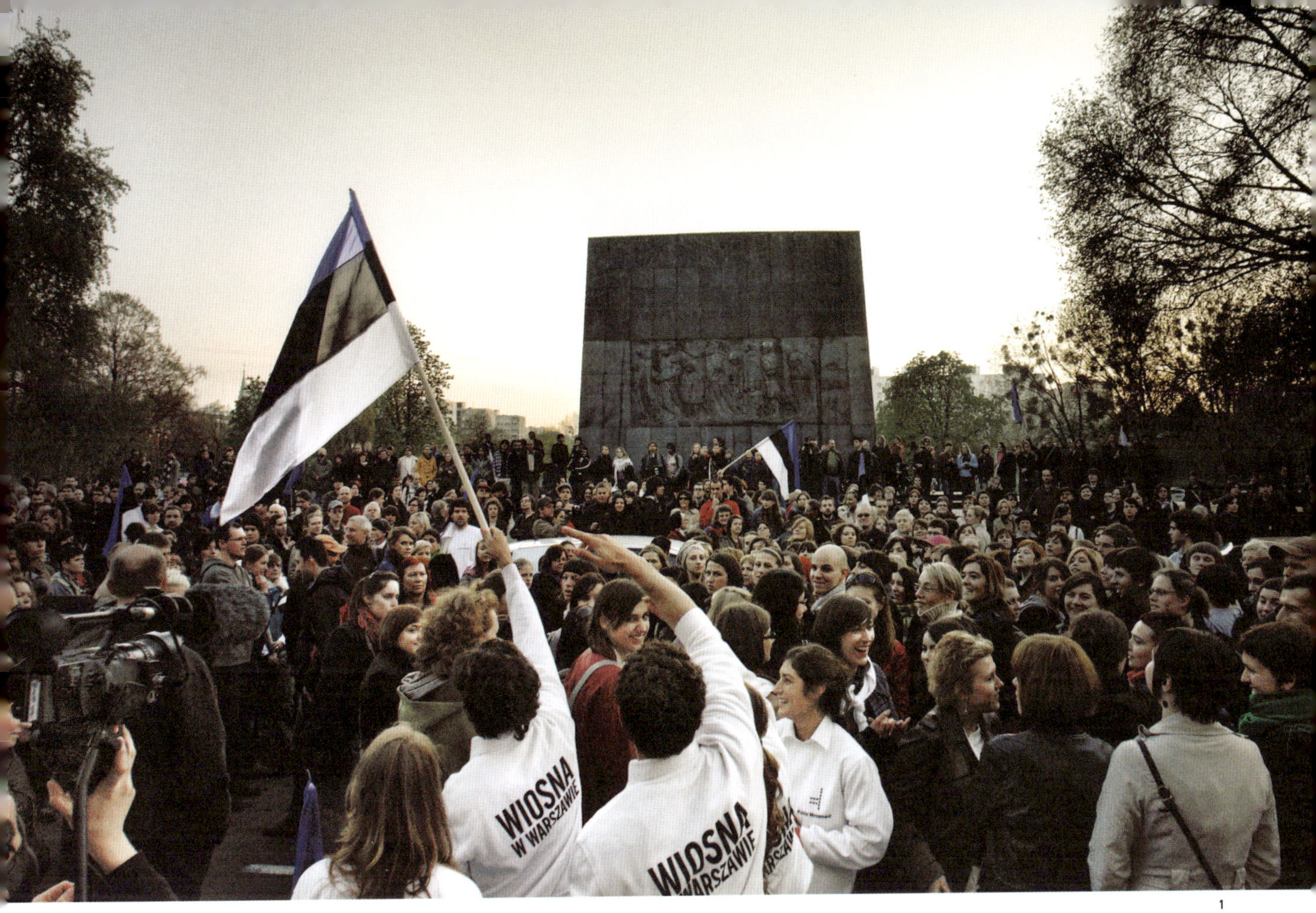

1

1 – Spring in Warsaw, public performance, Warsaw, 2009

2 – Performing Politics for Germany, public performance, Berlin, 2009

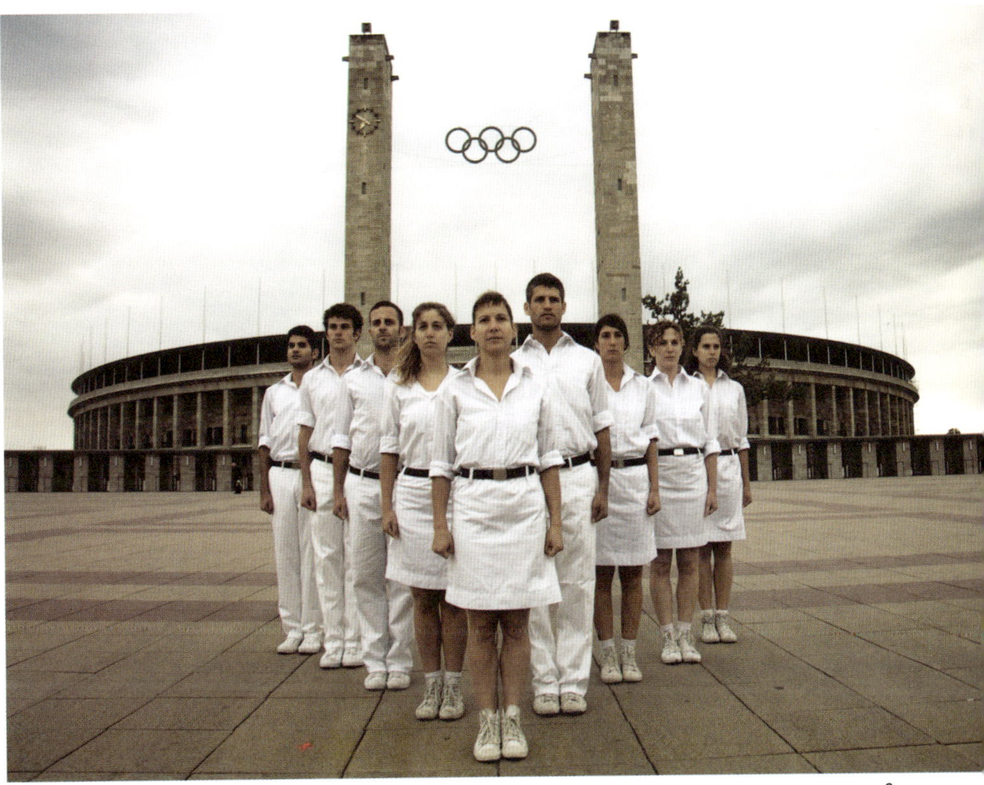

2

these questions: the leader, Dana Yahalomi. Hagar Ophir is currently the research manager and sometimes initiates independent Public Movement actions together with another member, Saar Szekely. Alhena Katsof is an agent living in New York City who has had many different roles in Public Movement actions—as a writer, strategist, and researcher. Lital Levin is an agent living in Tel Aviv, active as an editor and development consultant. Daniel Miller, a longtime consultant for the Movement, is based in Berlin.

How important is each group member's individuality, both in terms of your artistic production and in terms of your relationship with the media? Does anonymity come into play?

Members and agents bring in different qualities and knowledge, which influence the work of the Movement, but not in the sense that each is responsible for the creation of a piece based on his or her specialties. Members are selected into the group for skills that might not be the most important for their identity outside the group, but within Public Movement become an important resource. For example, Luciana Kaplun was a folk dancer in the Jewish community of Buenos Aires. Her knowledge of folk dancing and experience with teaching and leading others in dance became central for several Public Movement actions. Michael Rosman was a combatant in the Israeli military who taught us war strategies and combat moves. And so on.

What is the relationship between your working methods and your art's "content"? In this sense, does technology tend to play more of a supporting role, or does it lead you in new directions?

Our working method and the art's "content" are fully intertwined. Almost all our actions involve discourse, are place- and time-specific, and can rarely be repeated. A Public Movement action starts with several months of intensive research, a central part of which is building relationships with the community the work will involve. We act as civil servants: it is not about what we had planned but rather what, based on interviews, discussions, and overall immersion in local politics, we think has to be done by us as a group. Some react with suspicion to the hierarchical construction of Public Movement, expecting a group of artists to be based on equality. But everywhere power is institutionally structured into organizations. We are not in the art field to uphold certain values, neither in our performances nor in our conduct as a group. We are working with widely exercised power structures but then challenge them; thus we believe that art is a good arena for social concepts to emerge and new public choreographies to be invented and melt back into reality.

How does your collaboration relate to its cultural, institutional, and commercial contexts? In other words, how would you respond to those who call this a trend?

When the work Positions was acquired by the Van Abbe Museum for its collection, Public Movement worked with a lawyer to draft a contract in which acquisition is based not on exchange of goods but rather on a relationship between the museum and Public Movement, somewhat like a marriage agreement, transforming the museum into an agent of Public Movement.

The group agreed early on, due to the public nature of its works, not to cooperate with private galleries or sell projects to private collections, unless exhibited publicly. We're creating singular events catering to national, social, and political needs, and therefore feel obliged to invent new methods of working in the art field that challenge the habitual dependence on galleries, dealers, art fairs, and collectors.

Who is your audience?

Everybody.

Does your engagement with one another translate into an engagement with the public? How so?

The group formed through a series of works that involved training and collaboration with Israeli state institutions—police forces, military units, fire fighters, and representatives of government, involving them in our public performances: from a national ceremony or a vote in the parliament to anti-riot units on the street. Our aim is to offer an alternative to the official state events.

In many of our actions we create realms in which the public is invited to perform—in unity, in resistance, in obedience. Meeting the public as a group encourages them to experiment with the potential of "working together." The projects always transgress the passive role of the public and propose the artistic moment as one in which politics can happen.

For an action about freedom of speech at Heidelberg University, Germany, in 2010, we invited German riot police to rehearse and perform with us. Public Movement works in and through conflicts, inside the group and in relation to the place where it acts, out of a belief that conflicts are a productive means of shifting power. In enabling new movements and compositions to occur among people in public spaces, we hope to encourage audiences to accept or even perform a certain degree of productive violence, involving and a good amount both of disagreement and joined vision.

PUBLIC MOVEMENT

PERFORMING POLITICS FOR GERMANY.

3

PUBLIC MOVEMENT

EXERCISE IN CITIZENSHIP

7, 8, 9 DEC. 2010

ACTION IN THE TEL-AVIV UNIVERSITY

POWER MANIFESTATION / CEREMONY / DEMONSTRATION / RIOTS / MARCH / PUBLIC BEHAVIOR DRILL / LECTURE WITH CARUSELLA BAND AND DR. IGAL DOTAN

Meeting at 19:30 in Entin Square, Haim Levanon St. / Einstein St. Corner, Ramat Aviv

www.publicmovement.org

4

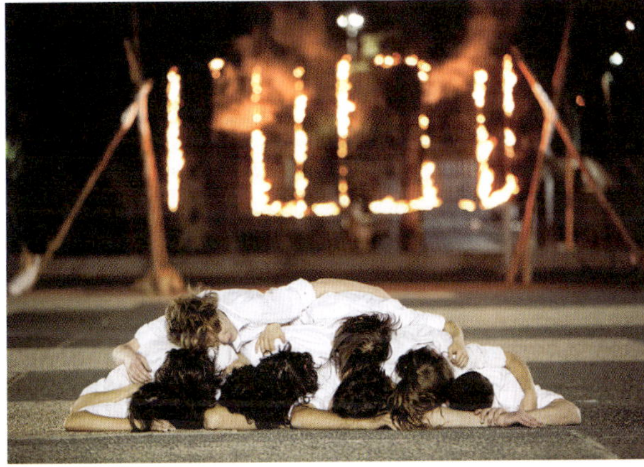

5

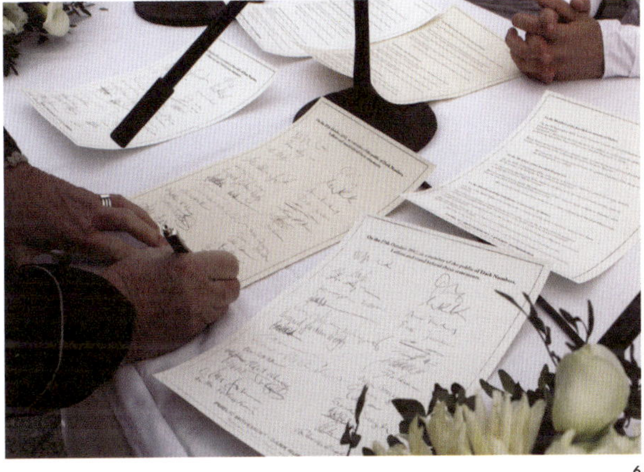

6

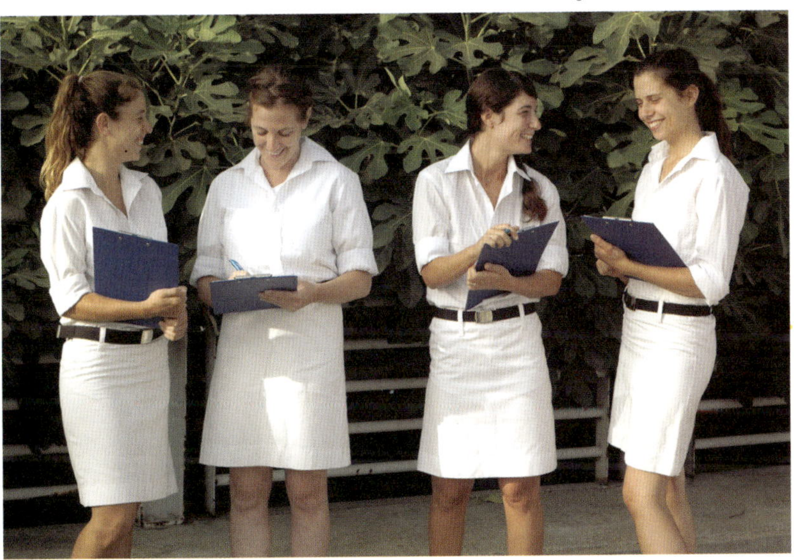

7

3 – Performing Politics for Germany invitation graphics, Berlin, 2009

4 – Exercise in Citizenship invitation graphics, 2010. Design: Yotam Hadar

5 – 5-Year Anniversary, public performance, Tel Aviv, 2011

6 – Dark Numbers, public performance, Malmö, Sweden, 2012

7 – Census, public performance, Tel Aviv, 2010

overleaf
8 – Group portrait, 2008

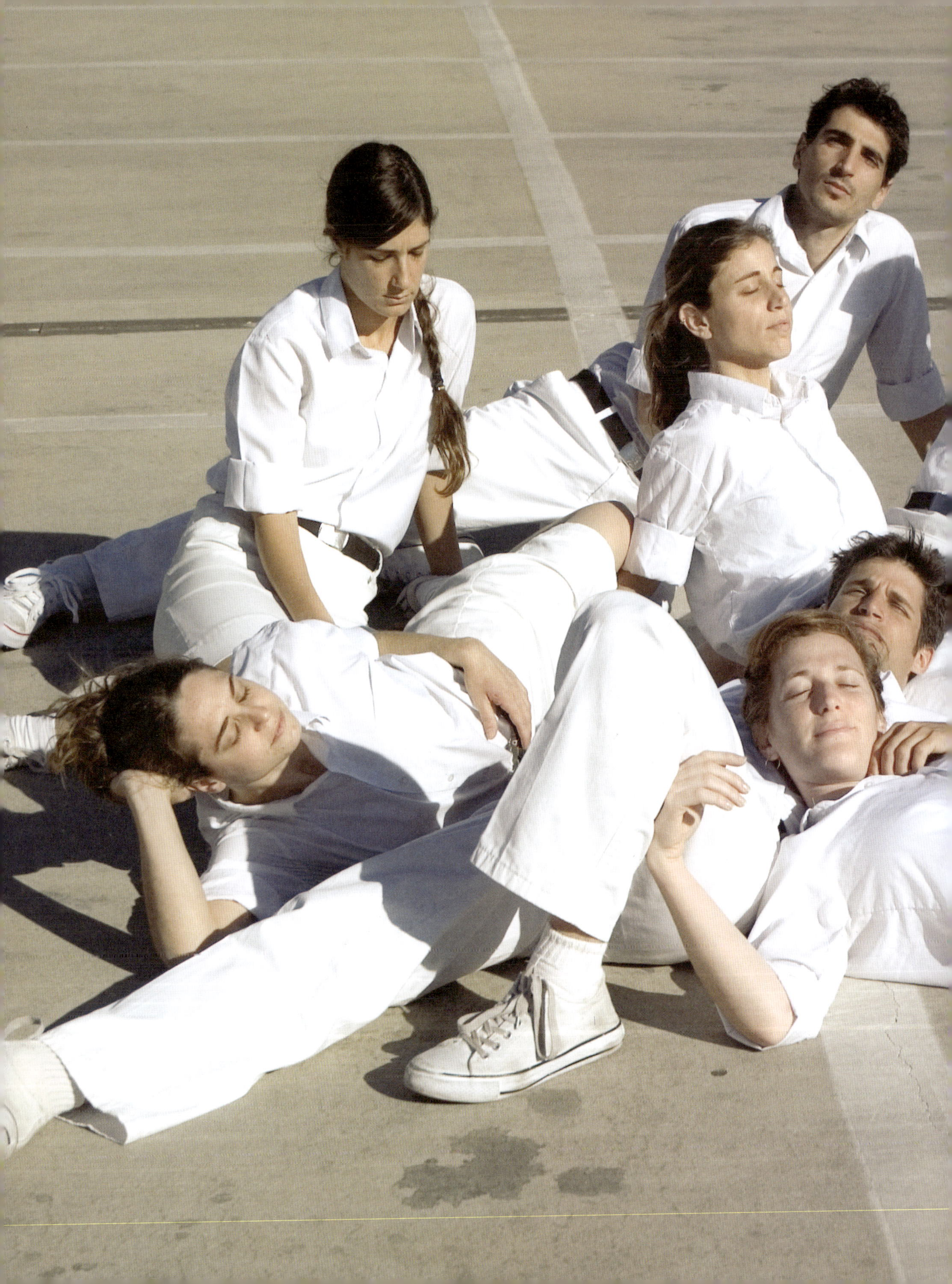

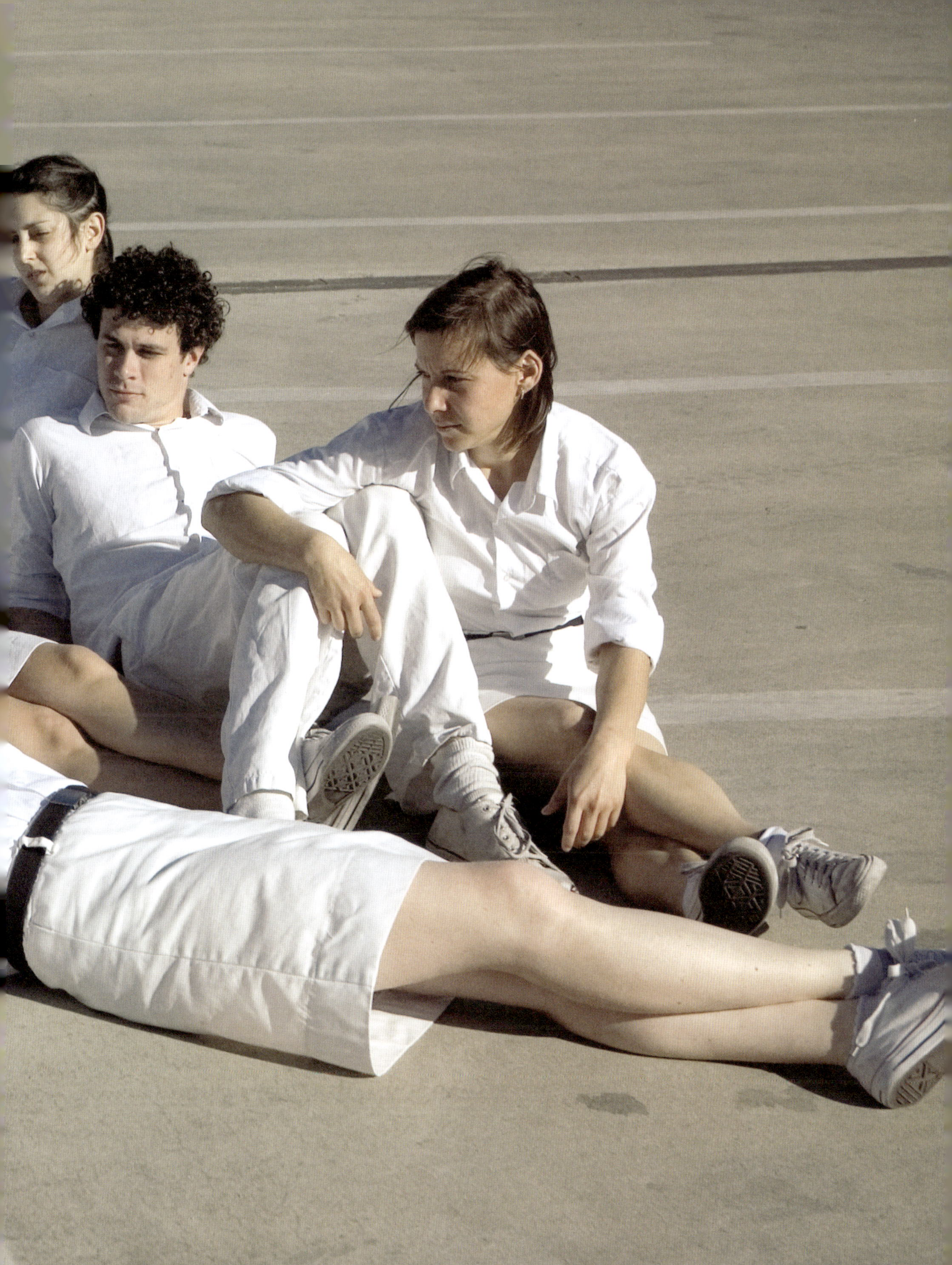

ACTIVE SINCE	CITY	WEBSITE
2000	Stockholm, Malmö, Tromsö, Rejmyre, Kalibukbuk, Mattmar, Sweden	raketa.nu

RAKETA

MEMBERS

Veronica Wiman, Cecilia Enberg, Åsa Lipka Falck, Camilla Schlyter Gezelius, Elisabet M. Nilsson, Mattias Sköld, Magda Lipka Falck, Lola Carlander, Macarena Dusant, Jann Lipka, Sofia Falck, Linda Hofvander, Amanda Eriksson, and Frank Heron (Roger Connah)

ACTIVITIES	RECOMMENDED PUBLICATION
Architecture, Community Projects, Curating, Internet Art, Merchandising, Music, Painting / Sculpture / Installation, Public Performance, Publishing, Urban Interventions	R A K E T A, Frank Heron & The Rocket Girls by N. Alice Challinor, R A K E T A Press, Stockholm, 2009

Through projections and wallpapers, R A K E T A merges metropolitan and natural landscapes, transforming streets and facades into sublime seas and woodlands typical of Northern Europe. Its "psychogeographical" temporary interventions offer passersby a chance to reconsider how they live and what is supposed to be their relationship with the environment.

Why work collaboratively?

R A K E T A is an opportunity for its participants to expand their work and its context. The interdisciplinary nature of collaboration creates an expanded network of associations and context. R A K E T A makes it possible to take on larger, more complex projects; working parallel in different disciplines. Possibilities and impossibilities. R A K E T A itself is a meeting place and an ongoing conversation, a dialogue over time. It is the courage to hand over, allow voices to blend and become part of a larger process. The courage to let go of control and allow process to show the way. The unpredictable. Chance.

How do you determine membership? Does physical location matter in this regard?

The people in R A K E T A are not referred to as members but as participants in a process. Initially, the physical location is important—the first meeting, the conversation. When someone is part of the process, the physical location is no longer important; the meeting and conversation are, but those can take place in either the physical or digital space. The ongoing dialogue is essential. The working process and the dialogue take place physically and digitally in an expanded geography. R A K E T A is working in the organized and the unorganized field. Anarchic model. The work is an exploratory process.

If considered separately, how do your individual artistic practices contribute to or detract from your work as a group?

A cannon of voices coincide as a song, a work, an event. Each voice adds its own color. The group dynamic is important; every change has an effect on the outcome. Since all the work is interdisciplinary with different inputs, every individual is very important for the outcome, effect, and event. In Sweden, R A K E T A is registered as self-authored, which means that the group is considered a non-physical entity. R A K E T A is singular, hence functions as an individual. R A K E T A is the author. In a physical sense, however, R A K E T A consists of a small or large group of individuals. All with their personal objectives and goals.

How are decisions made?

The project organically unfolds during the process.

Does each of you have a clearly defined role? If so, what are some of each member's distinct responsibilities?

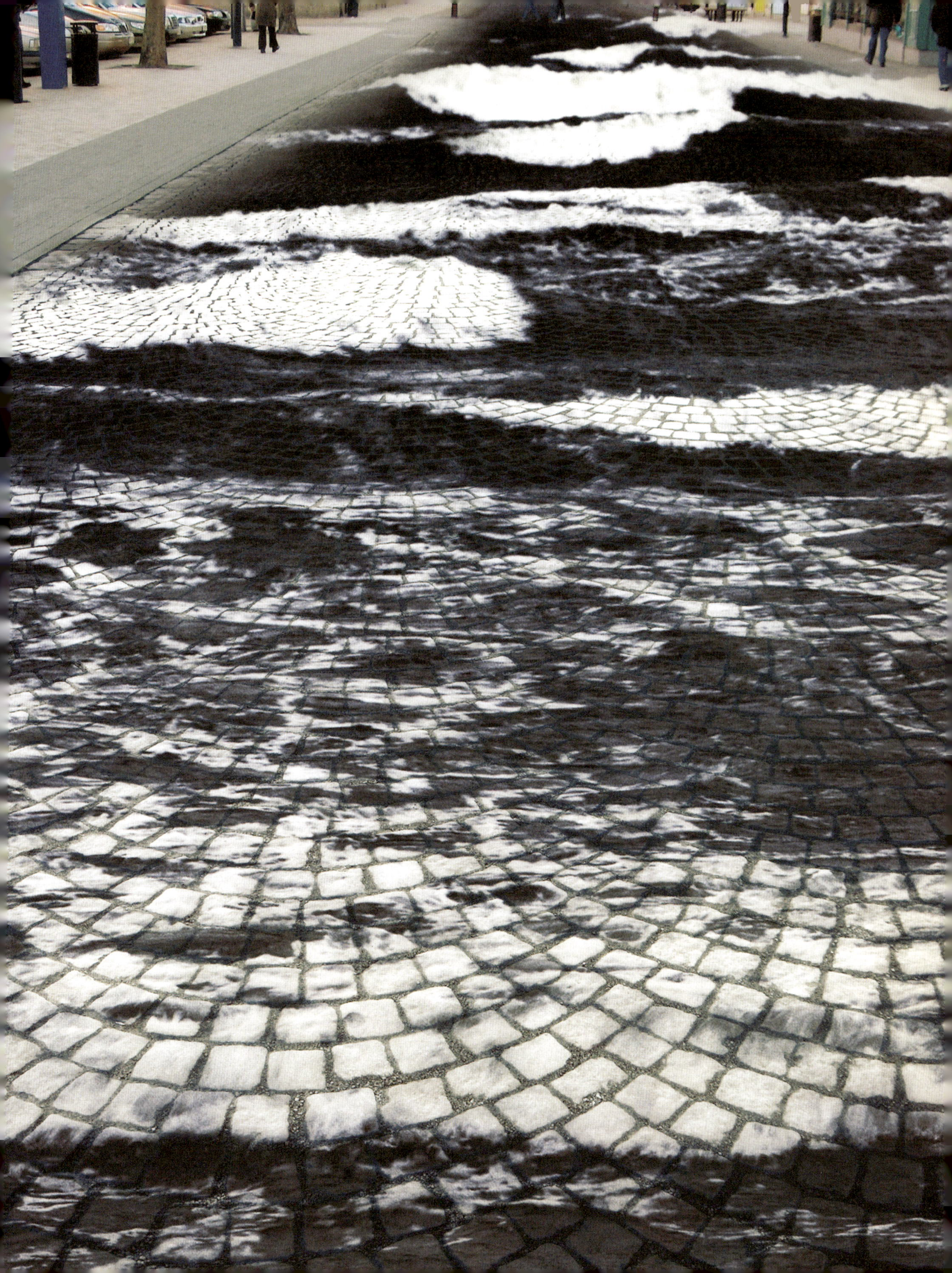

previous

1 – Where is the Ocean?, public projection, Kristianstad, Sweden, 2007

2 – Midori Mitamura, Art & Breakfast, installation, exhibition curated by R A K E T A, Stockholm, 2006

3 – What makes you happy? Fotoautomaten (Photo Booth), installation, Moderna Museet, Stockholm, 2010

4 – 27-barns-bana (27-children-path), installation, Haninge Kulturhus, Stockholm, 2013

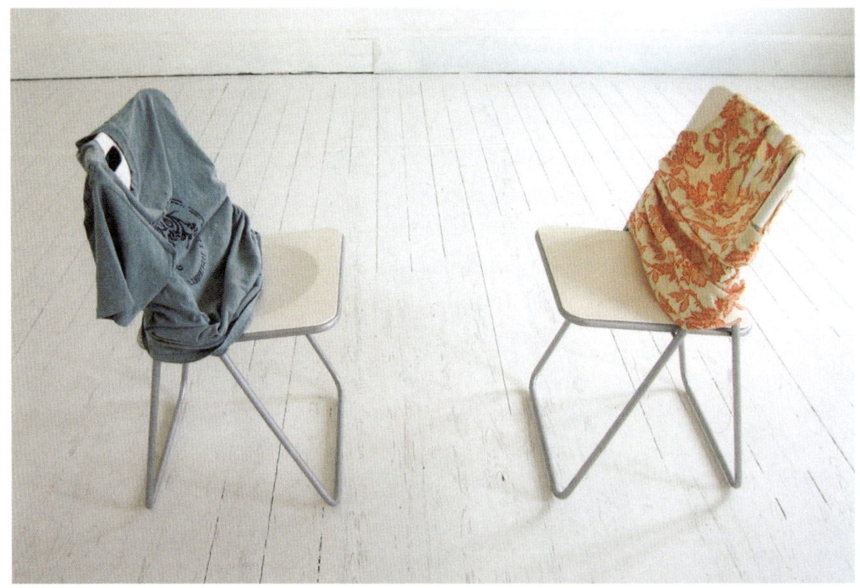

2

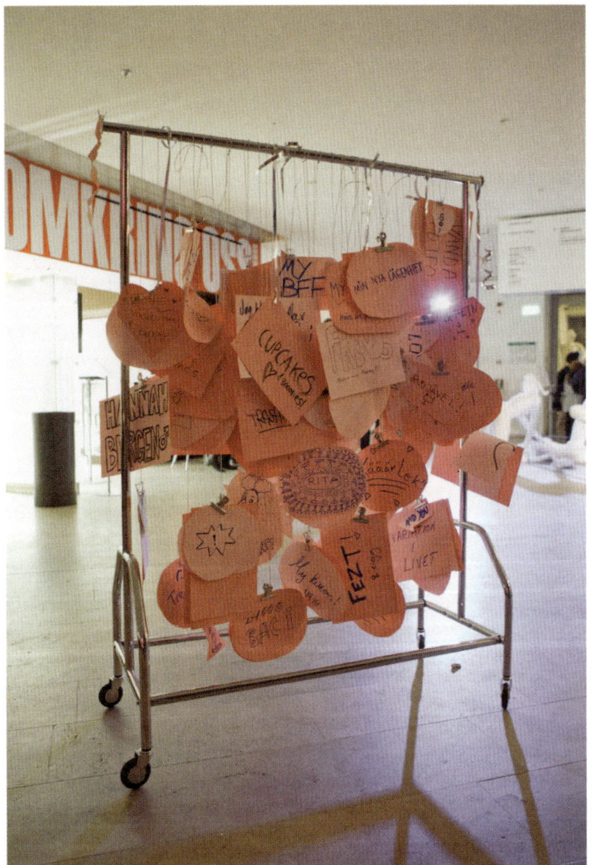

3

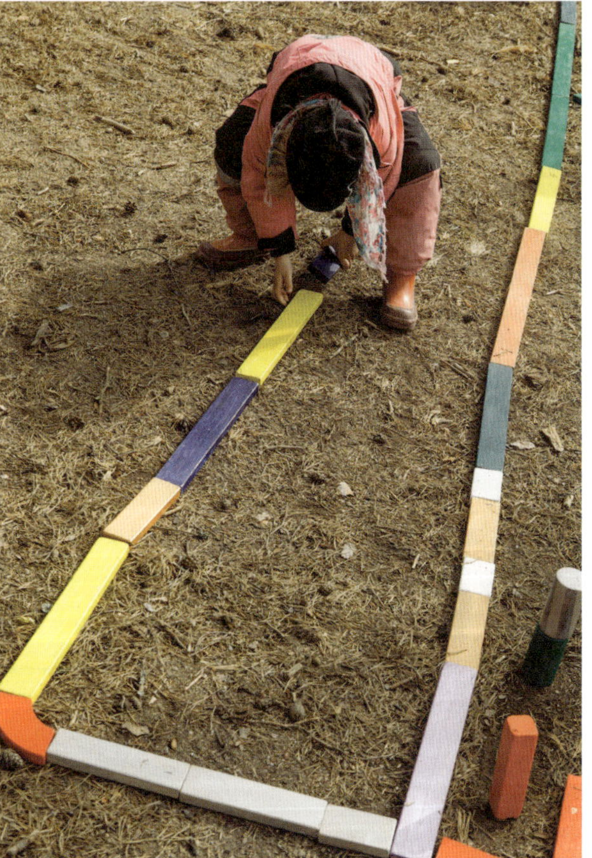

4

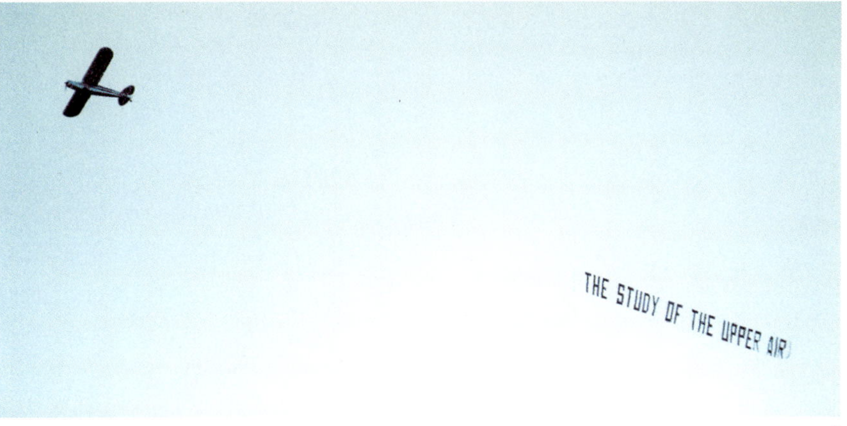

5 – The Study of the Upper Air, airplane banner, in collaboration with Alternative Nobel Dinner, 2001

Each has his or her own role. Everyone takes on what they want, depending on time, interest, and desires. Treasurer and signatory are two legal representatives who represent the nonprofit organization. This is the part of R A K E T A that is part of society's larger bureaucracy.

How important is each group member's individuality, both in terms of your artistic production and in terms of your relationship with the media? Does anonymity come into play?

Each individual plays an important role in the operation and the process. Everyone goes in and out of the process and projects depending on interest, time, geographic opportunities, finances, etc. Once projects are presented to the world, R A K E T A is the author and individuals are not important. This has changed over time, and different attitudes have been, and will be, tried out. This is an experiment and a process, and not intended to be static.

What is the relationship between your working methods and your art's "content"? In this sense, does technology tend to play more of a supporting role, or does it lead you in new directions?

The content and method are highly correlated with each other. R A K E T A is, in itself, an experiment and a lab: an investigation of a business, which takes off in the context of art. Placed and produced in a social context, it raises the question: How can we live together? Technique is communication and an expanded field, an alternative geography. The ongoing conversation and investigation is a journey, physically, digital and virtual. We are continuously drawing the map during our journey.

How does your collaboration relate to its cultural, institutional, and commercial contexts? In other words, how would you respond to those who call this a trend?

We see our business as part of the important global network, akin to the activities of NGOs in all parts of society. This is an ongoing process over a extended period of time. Collaboration and conversations with various parts of the political body is necessary: institutions of different types and fields. We are trying to open as many channels as possible to create conversations and collaborations. Is it possible to move forward in a new direction? R A K E T A has a very process-oriented attitude. Trends are not important to us. Only time will tell which direction is the right one. Sometimes going in the "wrong" direction can prove to be necessary for the process. We are obviously exposed to trends, for example when it comes to finances and funding, but we have chosen our way to work by necessity.

Who is your audience?

"There is a visitor but one we do not expect, one we do not invite, one which goes where we wish them not to go, does things we do not expect," From R A K E T A, Frank Heron & The Rocket Girls, by N. Alice Challinor, R A K E T A Press, 2009.

In R A K E T A's projects the audience is an active participant and pushes the project forward. R A K E T A is working in different contexts with a diverse "audience": schools, streets, museums, art galleries, football fields, forests, etc.

Who is our audience? Everybody?

Does your engagement with one another translate into an engagement with the public? How so?

Many projects can be reused at the same location and evolve over time along with the "audience." Parts of the "crowd" can even become part of R A K E T A. Overlaps are frequent.

Can the museum be a street? A wood a mountain an ocean?

Can we ever enter the past or the future? Can a database be a museum, which runs in two directions?

How?

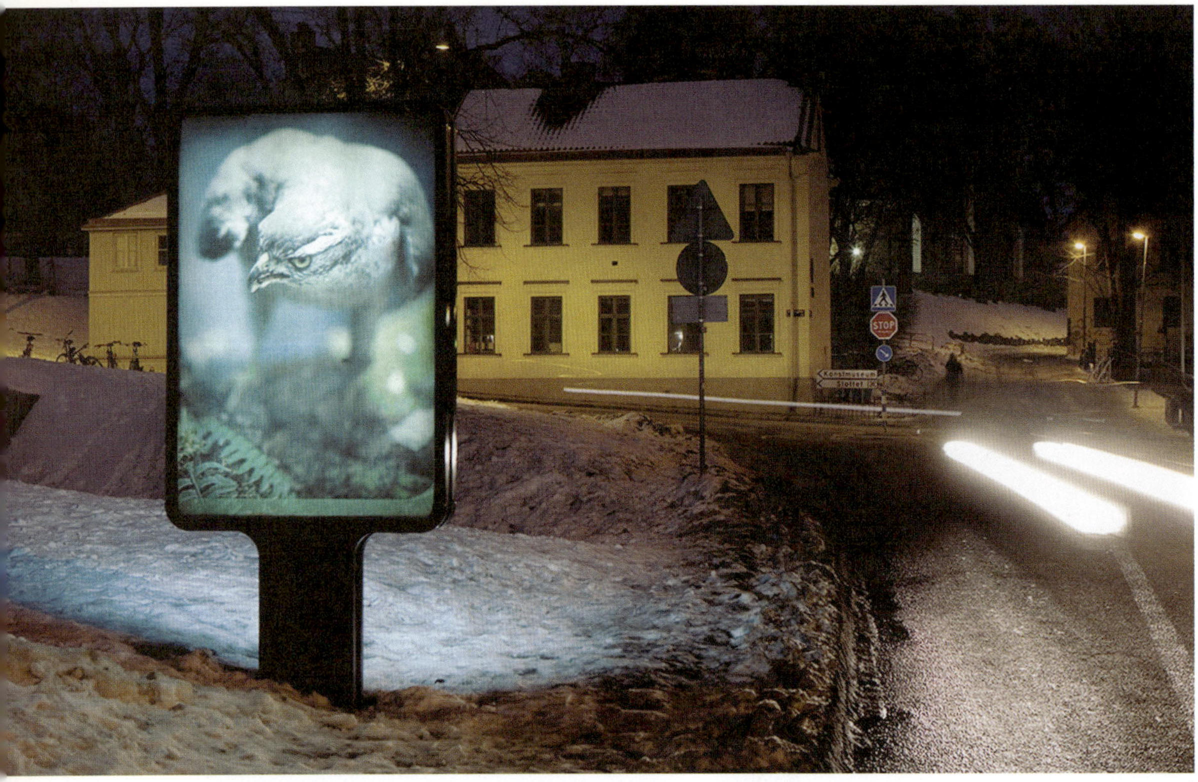

6

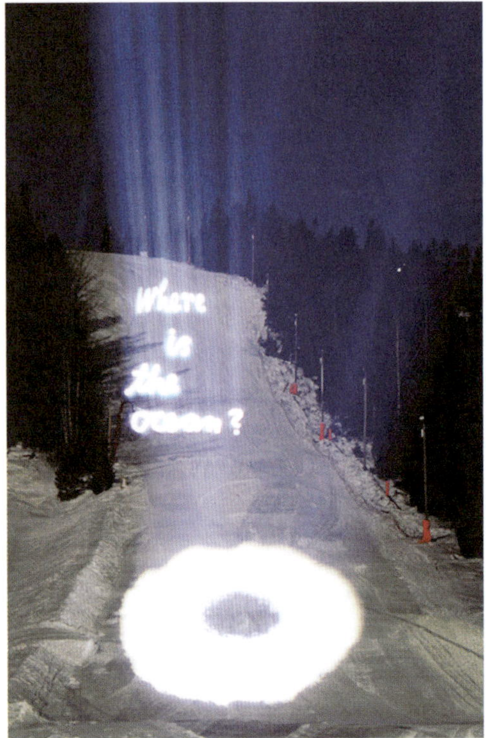

7

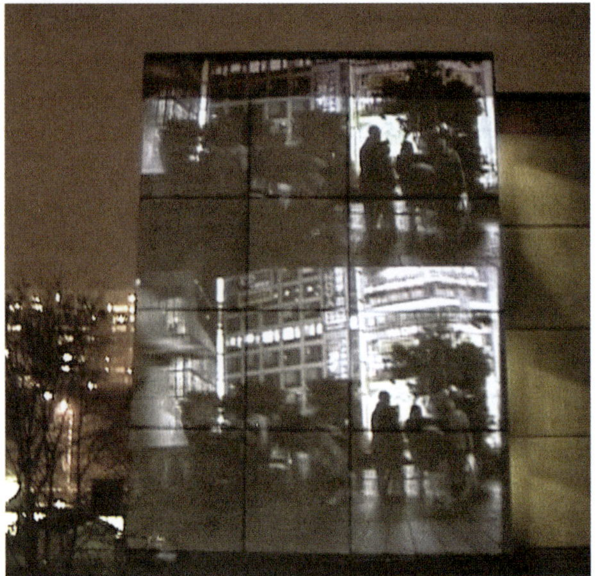

8

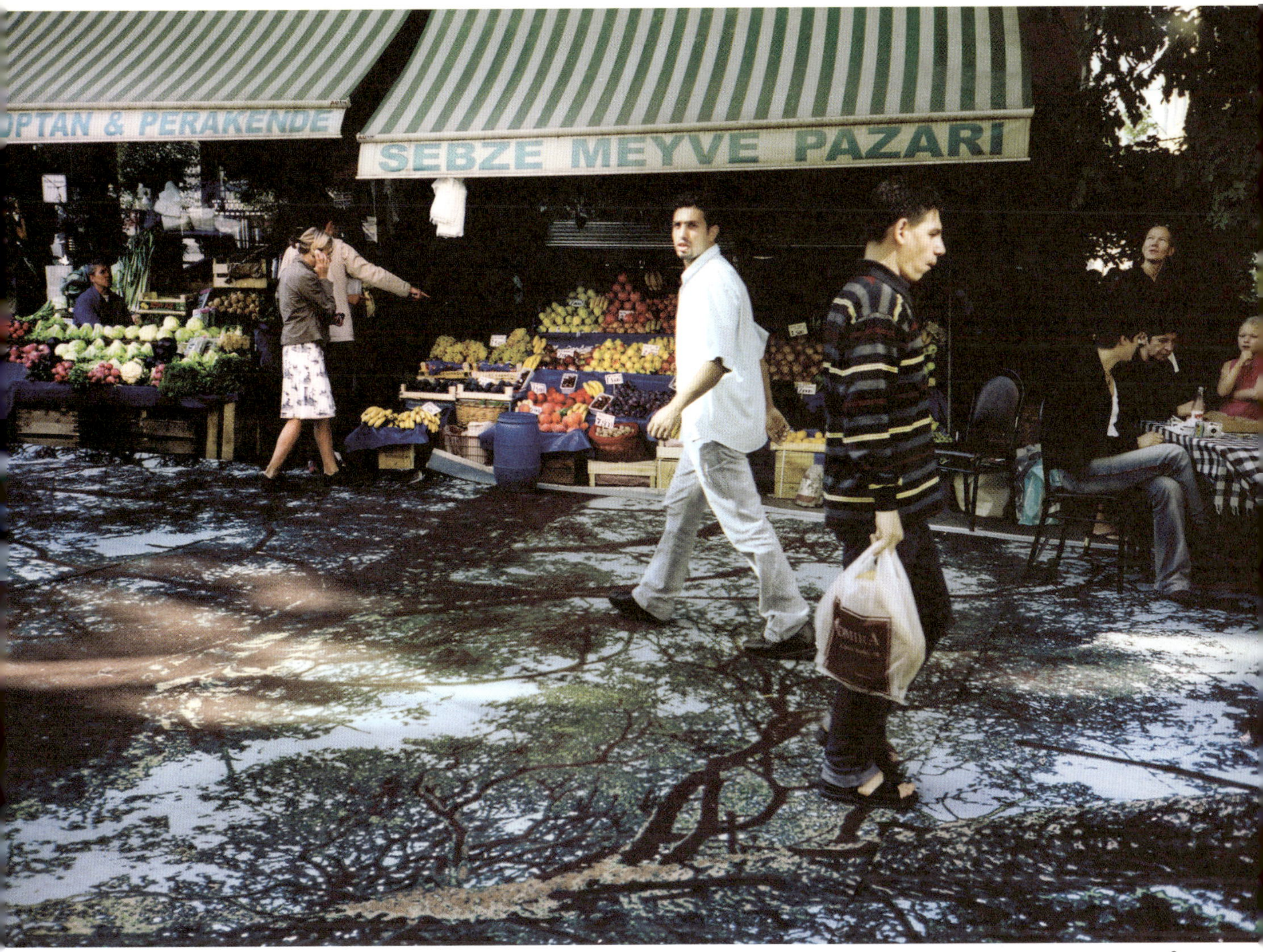

opposite
6 – **R A K E T A** & friends, The Visitors as part of How to Build the Mississippi River in your own Backyard, public billboard, Uppsala Art Museum/Biological Museum, Uppsala, 2007–2008

opposite
7 – Was it a dream. Was it a memory? (Where is the Ocean?), public projection, Bjästabacken, a ski slope close to the ocean in the north of Sweden, 2007

opposite
8 – Shibuya Crossing, public projections, Botkyrka, Sweden, 2000–2002

9 – Right of Common, public projection, Definitely Maybe, Istanbul, 2003

10 – 19840520 15:20 Art Volume, installation, Garden of San Lorenzo, Venice, 2001

9

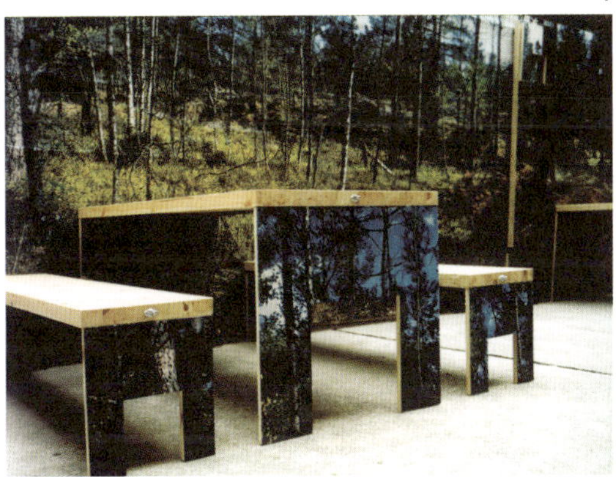

10

ACTIVE SINCE	CITY	WEBSITE
2002	London / Manchester / Nottingham, UK	reactor.org.uk

Reactor

MEMBERS	ACTIVITIES	RECOMMENDED PUBLICATION
Reactor is currently made up of two core members (Niki Russell and Daniel Williamson), one guest member (Stuart Tait), and an undisclosed number of secret members	Curating, Painting / Sculpture / Installation, Public Performance, Urban Interventions	REACTOR 2006–2011, DVD, Self-released, 2011

Like with other collectives in this book, a main focus for Reactor is collectivity itself. The group's carnival-like performances take place in the public sphere or post-industrial buildings. Borrowing symbols and rituals both from entertainment and secret societies, the group is responsible for multimedia interventions that address political and ecological issues, and often involve the use of props, costumes, and masks.

Why work collaboratively?

Reactor exists in the space between its members. We think about the combination of individuals within the group as the Reactor assemblage, and the collective will of the assemblage can be interpreted and enacted by those individuals. As such, Reactor operates in relation to the concept of a third mind as discussed by William Burroughs and Brion Gysin. When thinking about any given decision that needs making, we ask: what would Reactor do?

How do you determine membership? Does physical location matter in this regard?

Anyone can apply to be a member of Reactor. Interviews are held each year on Martinmas (November 11), and current members guide an applicant's preparations. The interview is a festive occasion that we all attend in costume, and combines ritual, "formal" interview, and celebration. If an applicant is accepted, he or she becomes a Secret Member for one year, and he or she is publicly revealed as a Core Member following the subsequent Martinmas.

Each Reactor member lives in a different city in the UK; however, the spiritual home of the group is Nottingham, home of Robin Hood and where it all started in 2002. During project development, physical studio meetings are held in Nottingham, where the group will spend time talking and working. This physical connection allows ideas to bounce, silences to occur, and key misunderstandings to develop in a way that a virtual meeting does not.

If considered separately, how do your individual artistic practices contribute to or detract from your work as a group?

Each individual member's specific interests and knowledge (rather than individual artistic practices) feed directly into the group. However, Reactor filters this information and anything not deemed relevant to Reactor is rejected. That said, the skill set of each individual is a key strength in undertaking Reactor's work, and this is ever growing, as Reactor does not allow the fact we have never tried, used, or practiced something before stop it from becoming a part of a project. We figure out a way to employ this new item, even if it is the wrong way, and this unconventional approach to using an item—that has another regular use—can become a key feature of a project.

How are decisions made?

The early stages of project development are like a collaborative editing process, with ideas rapidly generated, altered, lost, or purposefully removed. It's a survival of the fittest ideas through the evolution of the project. Somehow, certain ideas are more "sticky" than others and, even if they get dropped, they somehow work their way back in, caught up between the folds of the project. The final

1 – Big Lizard's Big Idea, public performance, Donau Festival, Krems, Austria, 2009

2 – Ivan's Dogs, We Provide the Smiles, happening, Nottinghamshire, 2006

3 – The Munkanon Centre, performance, The Knot, Berlin, 2010

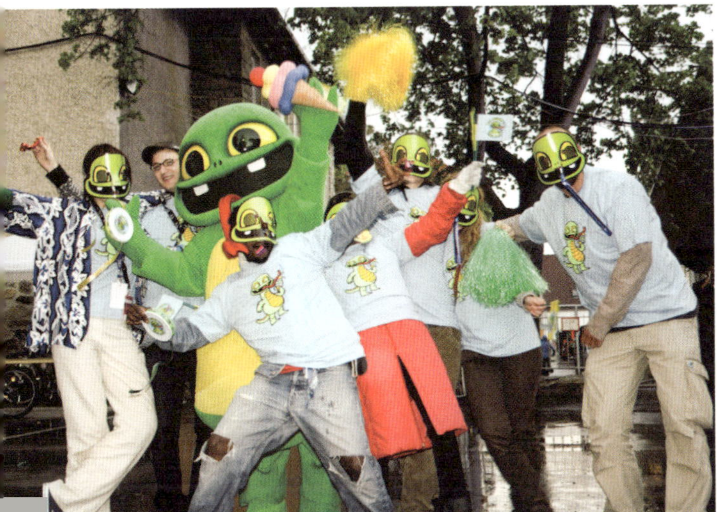

1

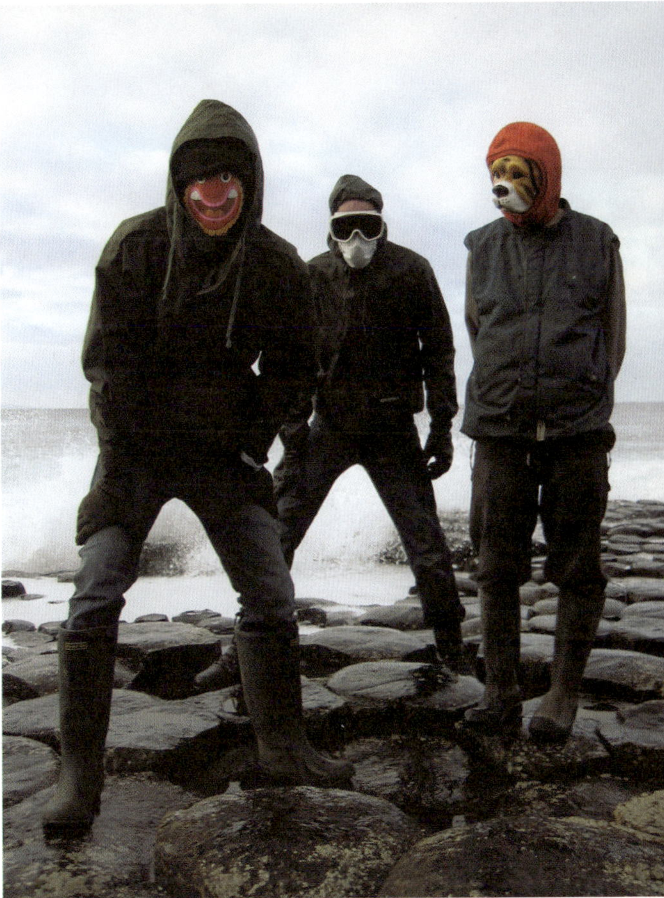

2

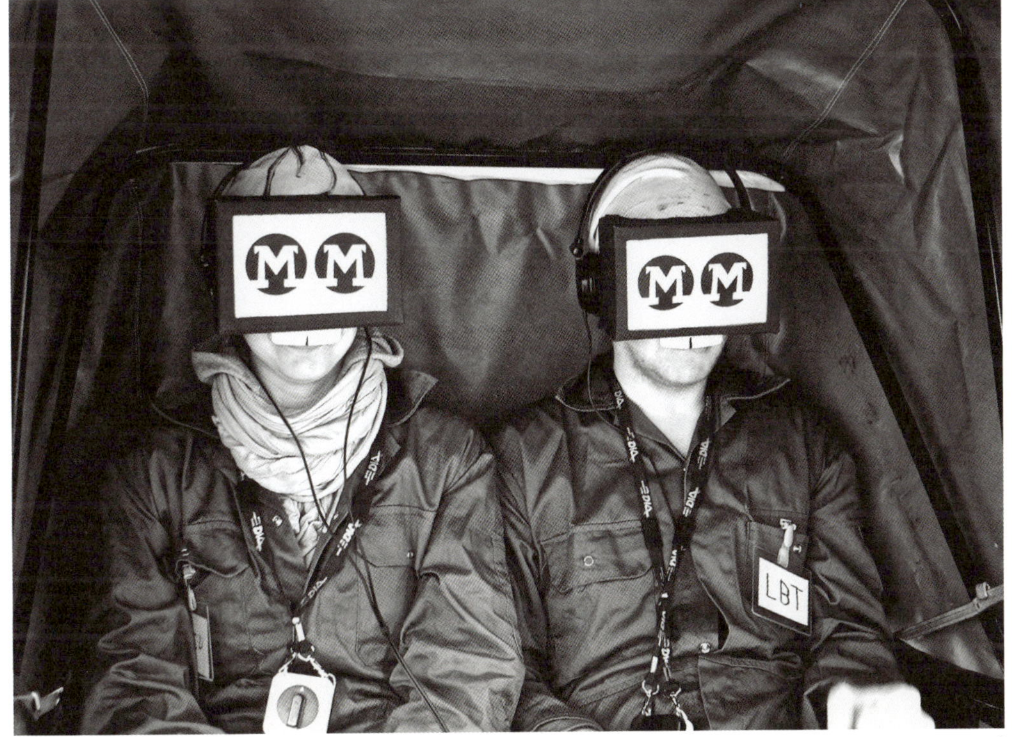

3

stages of project development reach coherence by achieving consensus on decisions that have to be taken for the work to function.

Does each of you have a clearly defined role? If so, what are some of each member's distinct responsibilities?

With the exception of certain specific administrative functions, there are no clearly defined responsibilities within the collective. Roles are fluid and subject to ongoing change, depending on people's availability, skill set, and disposition.

How important is each group member's individuality, both in terms of your artistic production and in terms of your relationship with the media? Does anonymity come into play?

Members' individuality is an important factor in determining the Reactor assemblage at any time. We are not worker units in a hive and changes in membership bring about a qualitative change in the assemblage. However, this individuality is not a public aspect of the work—elements are not attributed to individuals, but are presented as part of Reactor's work.

What is the relationship between your working methods and your art's "content"? In this sense, does technology tend to play more of a supporting role, or does it lead you in new directions?

We have discussed the transferability of roles within project development. This is often reflected in the performance of the work, where roles can be handed from person to person. Technology plays a part in project development due to the geographically dispersed nature of the group, but its integration into projects is purely pragmatic. As in MoMAMonarch (2013)—where we hijacked a class using pseudobrainwashing techniques, convincing students to build protective gear to stop an unnamed entity from getting into their heads—we used Skype as a facilitating technology. We needed to remotely deliver a workshop at MoMA in New York; therefore, geographical and financial constraints led to the development of a new strand of mediated practice.

How does your collaboration relate to its cultural, institutional, and commercial contexts? In other words, how would you respond to those who call this a trend?

Reactor does not consider itself to be part of a trend and doesn't understand how collective work can even be considered a "trend" when there are numerous art historical precedents.

Reactor does not seek to explicitly reference specific contexts, but the thematics of Reactor projects do utilize systems of signification associated with politics or the social sciences. There is a micropolitical dimension to the work, including how decisions are made within the group. The projects offer an opportunity to grasp how political "pragmatism" works on a small scale as an example of how wider political decisions and actions are motivated, without spoon-feeding a specific message to the audience.

Who is your audience?

Each Reactor project approaches and reconsiders what form the audience can take, and these different ideas of audience have changed alongside the group's evolution. Earlier in its history with projects such as Total GHAOS (2005)—which took the form of a fantasy totalitarian society built on a multileveled scaffolding structure—there was a militant expectancy for a fully participating audience, and it appeared that we would control this through the Reactor Party. More recently, in projects such as The Green Man & Regular Fellows (2011)—which took the form of a pub, complete with adjoining function room, and played with the traditions, regularity, and conventions of the "public house"—Reactor has taken a more a relaxed approach, building into the work less active positions that could be considered a watching audience. In addition, within certain Reactor projects we would say that there is no audience as such; rather there are coparticipants, or cocreators, responsible for the ongoing production of the work.

Does your engagement with one another translate into an engagement with the public? How so?

Language, quirks, jokes, and so on can translate from our in-group interaction to interaction with others, as they begin to learn the language of the work. Within particular projects we treat one another and our "audience" in the same way—we are just other people in the project that happen to have a more extended relation to it. This is partly to weaken the barriers to coparticipation but also to create uncertainty about the authorship of the work. Reactor considers it to be a success if we are inducted in an activity, or have become part of the microcosm we helped create, explained back to us by a coparticipant. This takes the work beyond our control and at times beyond even our awareness. Reactor is interested in moving toward initiating a complex microcosm that can then be left to run itself without the presence of Reactor.

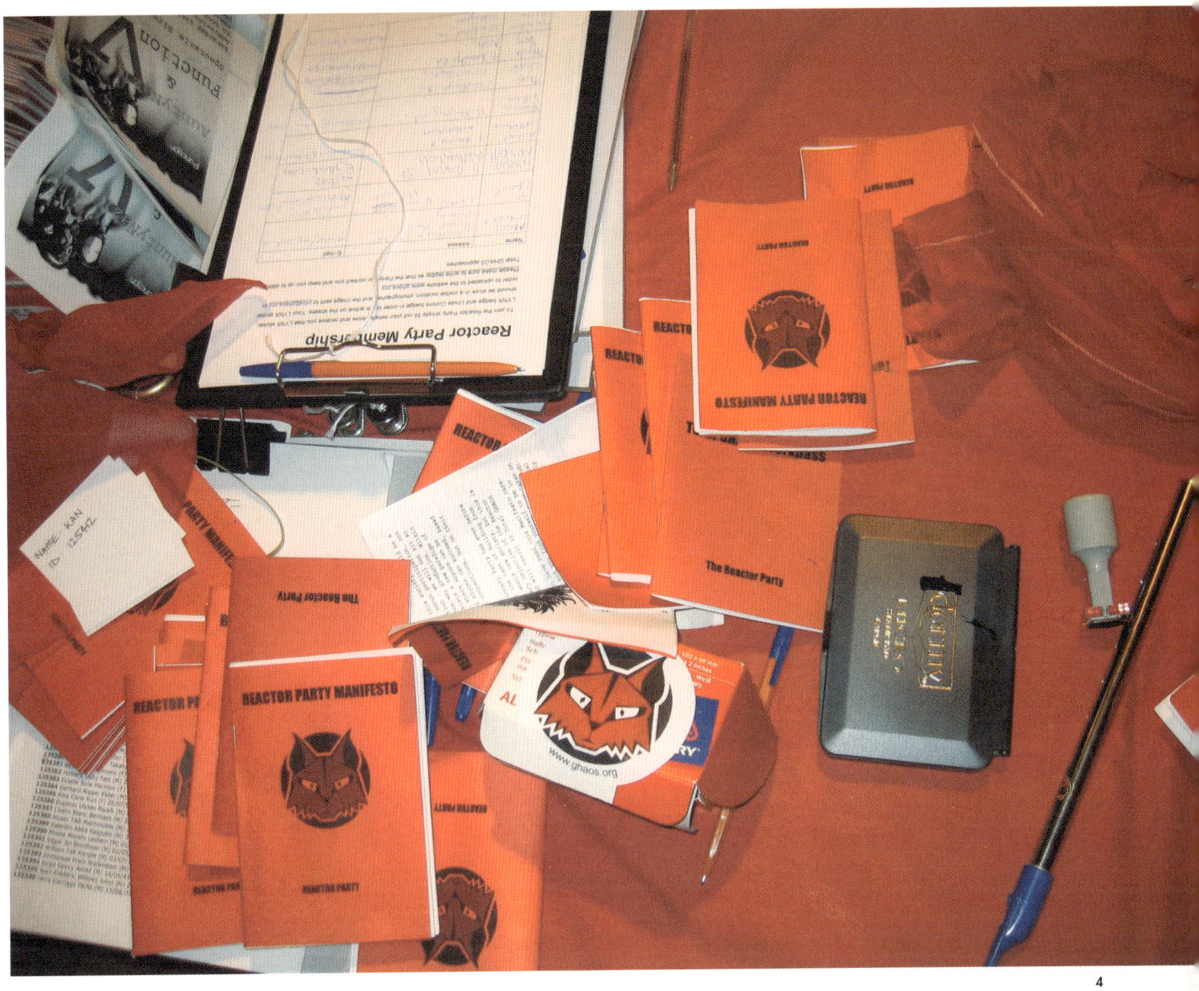

4

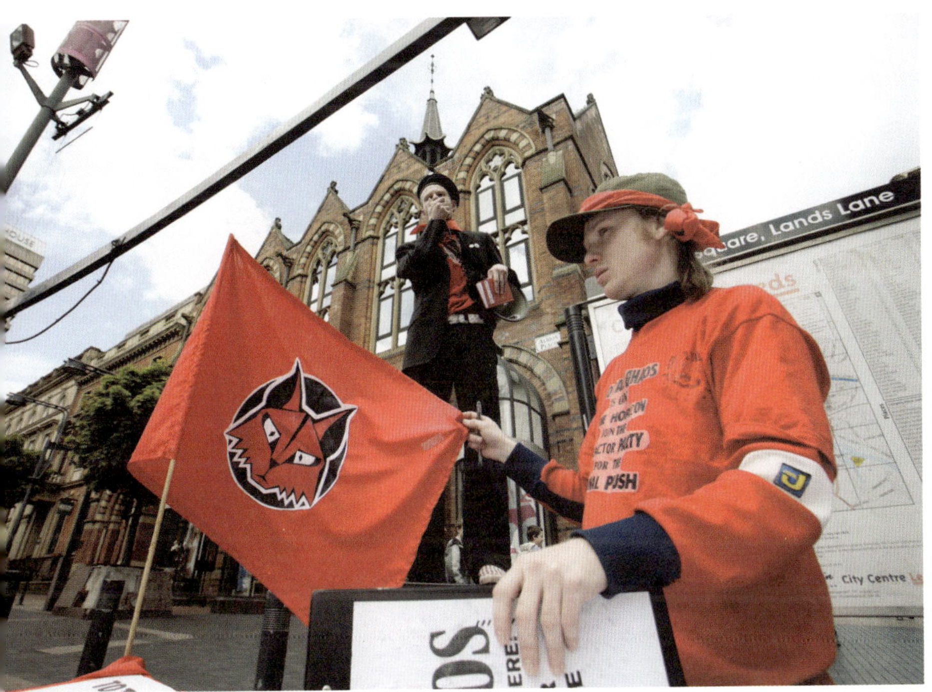

5

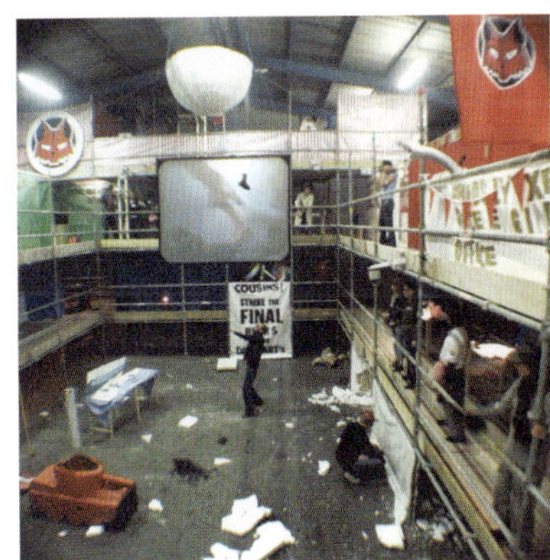

6

4 – Reactor Party Campaign membership documents, Nottingham, 2005

5 – Reactor Party Campaign, public performance, Leeds, 2005

6 – Total GHAOS, happening, Nottingham, 2005

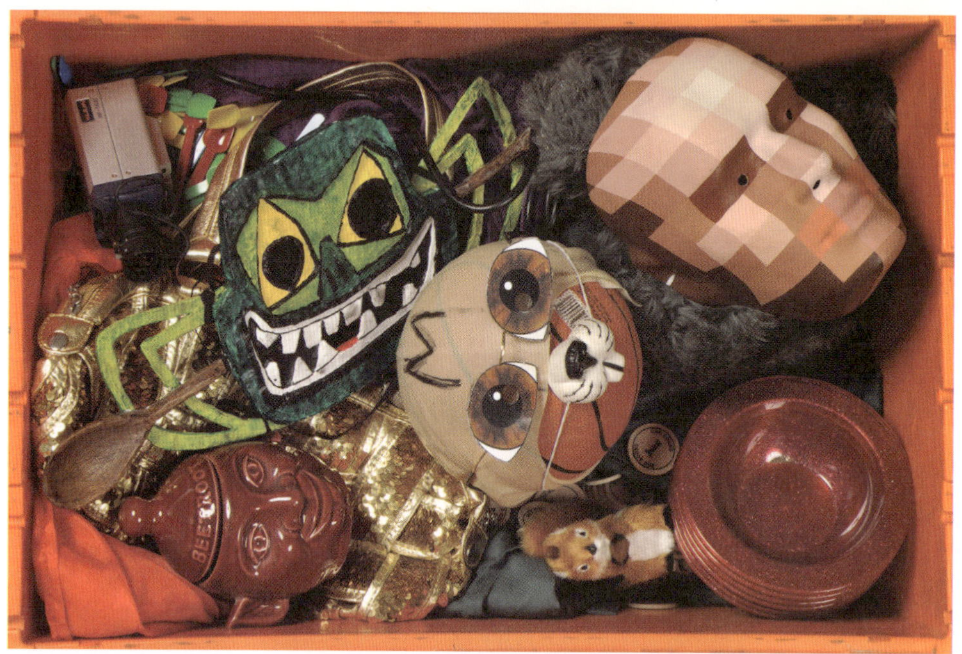

7

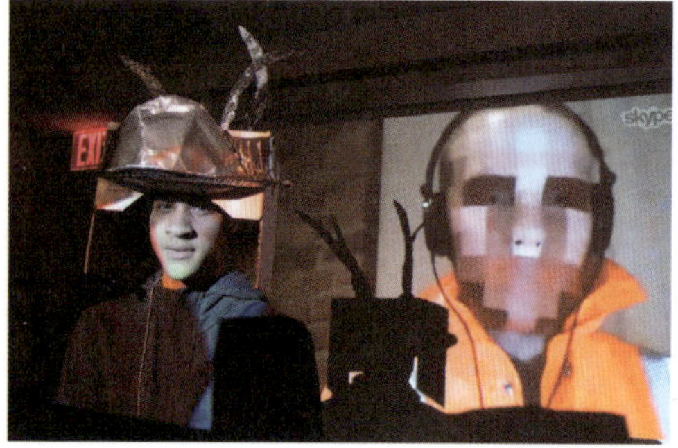

8

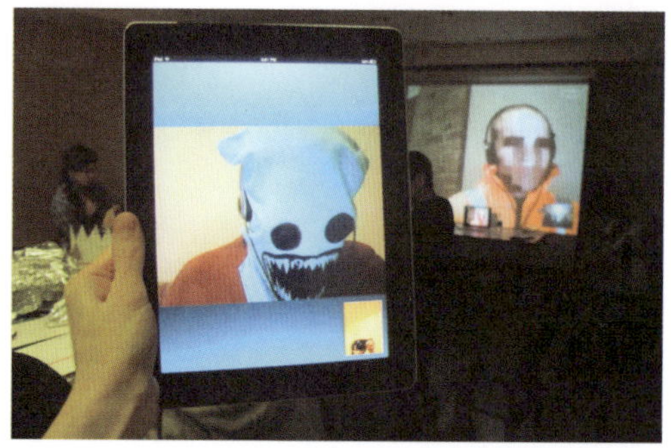

9

7 – Reactor 2006–2011, photograph inside the DVD packaging, 2012

8 + 9 – MoMAMonarch, multimedia performance, MoMA, New York, 2013

10 – Martinmas Interviews, initiation performance, 2012–ongoing

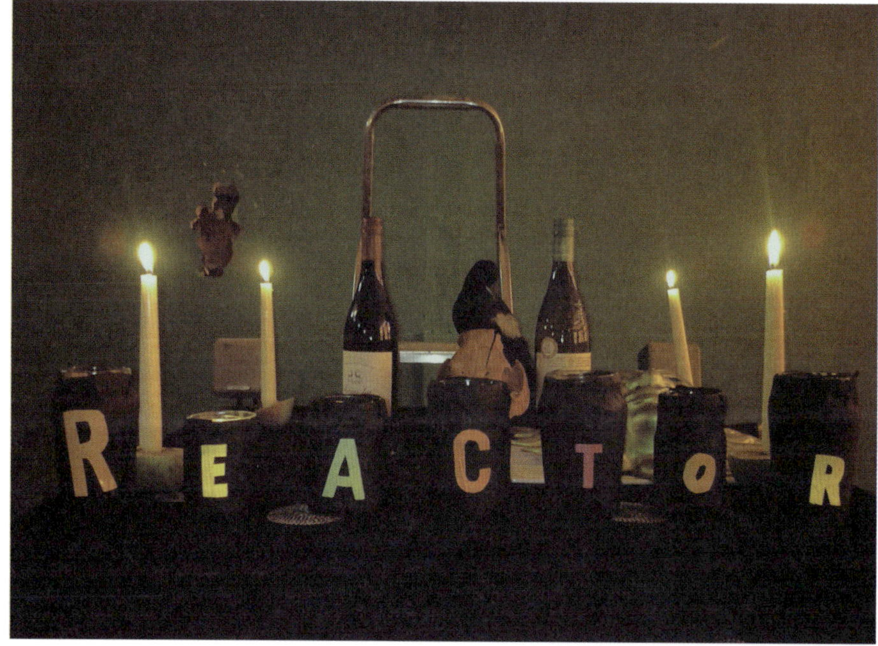

10

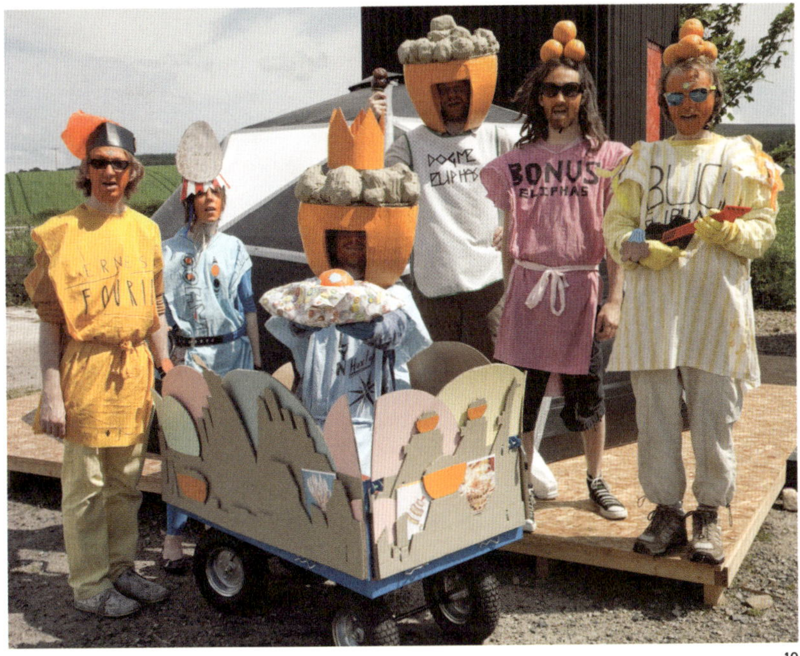

10

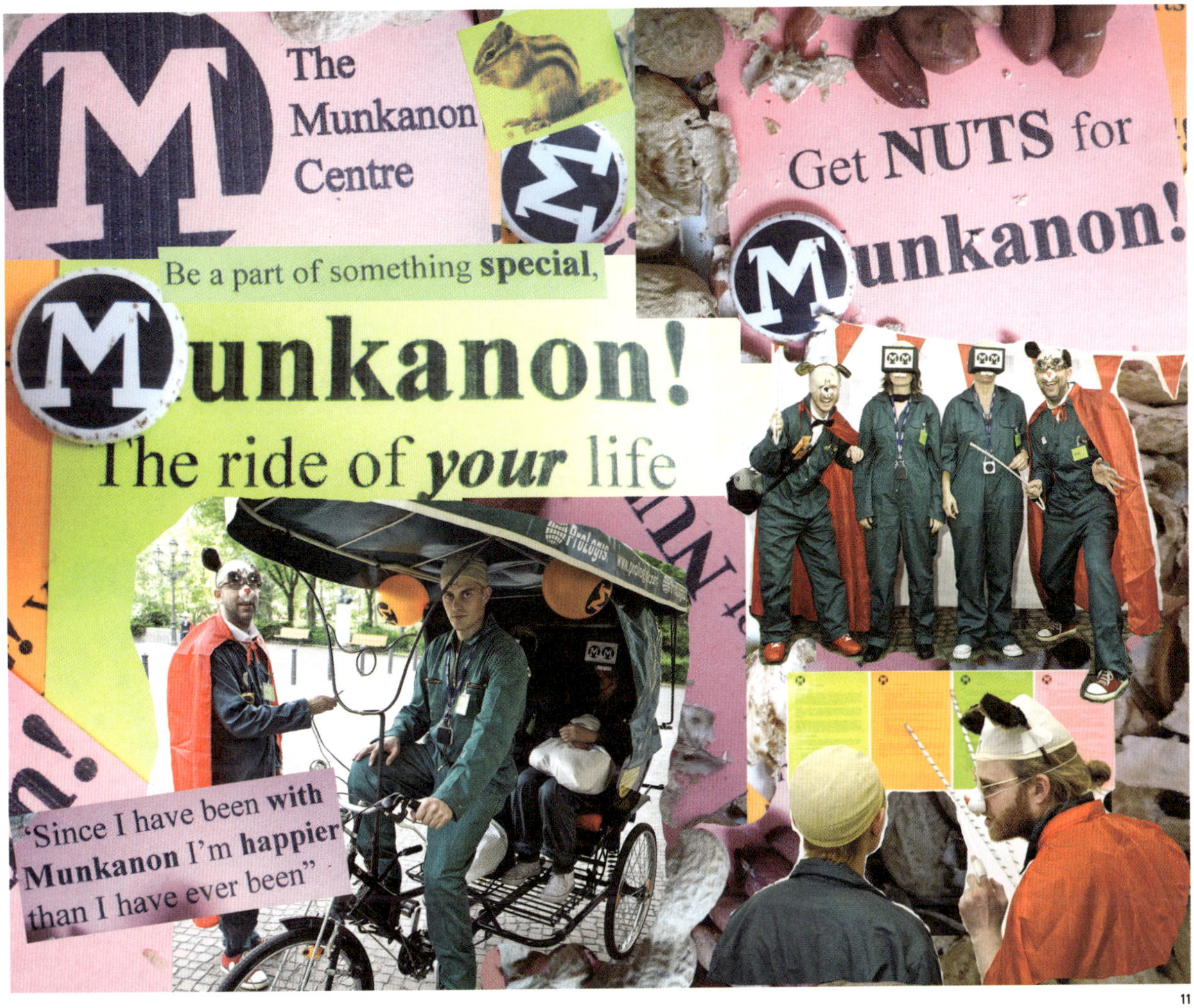

11

11 – The Geodecity Project, happening, Scottish Sculpture Workshop, Lumsden, Scotland, 2009

12 – The Munkanon Centre, performance, the Knot, Berlin, 2010

ACTIVE SINCE	CITY	WEBSITE
2000	Jakarta, Indonesia	ruangrupa.org

Ruangrupa

MEMBERS	ACTIVITIES	RECOMMENDED PUBLICATION
N/A	Community Projects, Curating, Installation, Merchandising, Music, Publishing, Urban Interventions	All for Jakarta. A Note on the Tenth Anniversary of RUANGRUPA: Decompression #10 in Mirwan Andan, Expanding the Space and Public, Journal of Inter-Asia Cultural Studies, Routledge, New York, 2011

A nonprofit organization and collective based in Jakarta, Ruangrupa organizes exhibitions, workshops, film, and music festivals encouraging the formation of an Indonesian art scene. Its activities show the importance of contemporary visual culture as propeller of local creative energies that may serve as a model of democracy and participation for other areas of social and political life.

Why work collaboratively?

Ruangrupa is an art collective and art space run by artists, researchers, accountants, musicians, architects, carpenters, etc. Collaboration is part of our daily activity, a way to exchange knowledge and experience and cross the boundaries between disciplines. Artists can no longer act passively or isolate themselves from other fields of knowledge; they have roles in the construction of many other discourses and social practices, both in terms of the community and the state.

How do you determine membership? Does physical location matter in this regard?

We work with people of different backgrounds and disciplines: from students to NGOs. We have never centralized ourselves. That keeps our position organic. People can come and go or stay as they like, according to the needs of a specific project. Physical space is important for us, but we adapt to whatever activities happen within our space. For us, the center doesn't hold autonomy in cultural production. Other areas have taken a major role in the creation of discourses about the city, identity, space, and local and global issues through a new level of work production and media.

If considered separately, how do your individual artistic practices contribute to or detract from your work as a group?

We all have different backgrounds: visual art, graphic design, cinematography, political science, architecture, photography, music, etc. We all contribute to every stage of the Ruangrupa creative process. We try to match and negotiate the personal vision to the collective dream. We're all passionate people with good senses of humor and many skills, and we are happy to be distracted by many things. We appreciate freedom and facilitate personal and collective ideas for creating spaces of their own.

How are decisions made?

The priority is that the decisions we make should accommodate our artistic practice and also help share our knowledge with each other. Discussion has strong relation to the structure of the group but we do not pay too much attention to the structure; we always let the content define its structure.

Does each of you have a clearly defined role? If so, what are some of each member's distinct responsibilities?

As an organization, yes, we have clearly defined roles and each of us has a specific responsibility. In conservative organizations, roles are very limited. In Ruangrupa, instead, sometimes the role is diverse. Each of us understands what to do and not to do, depending on the situation.

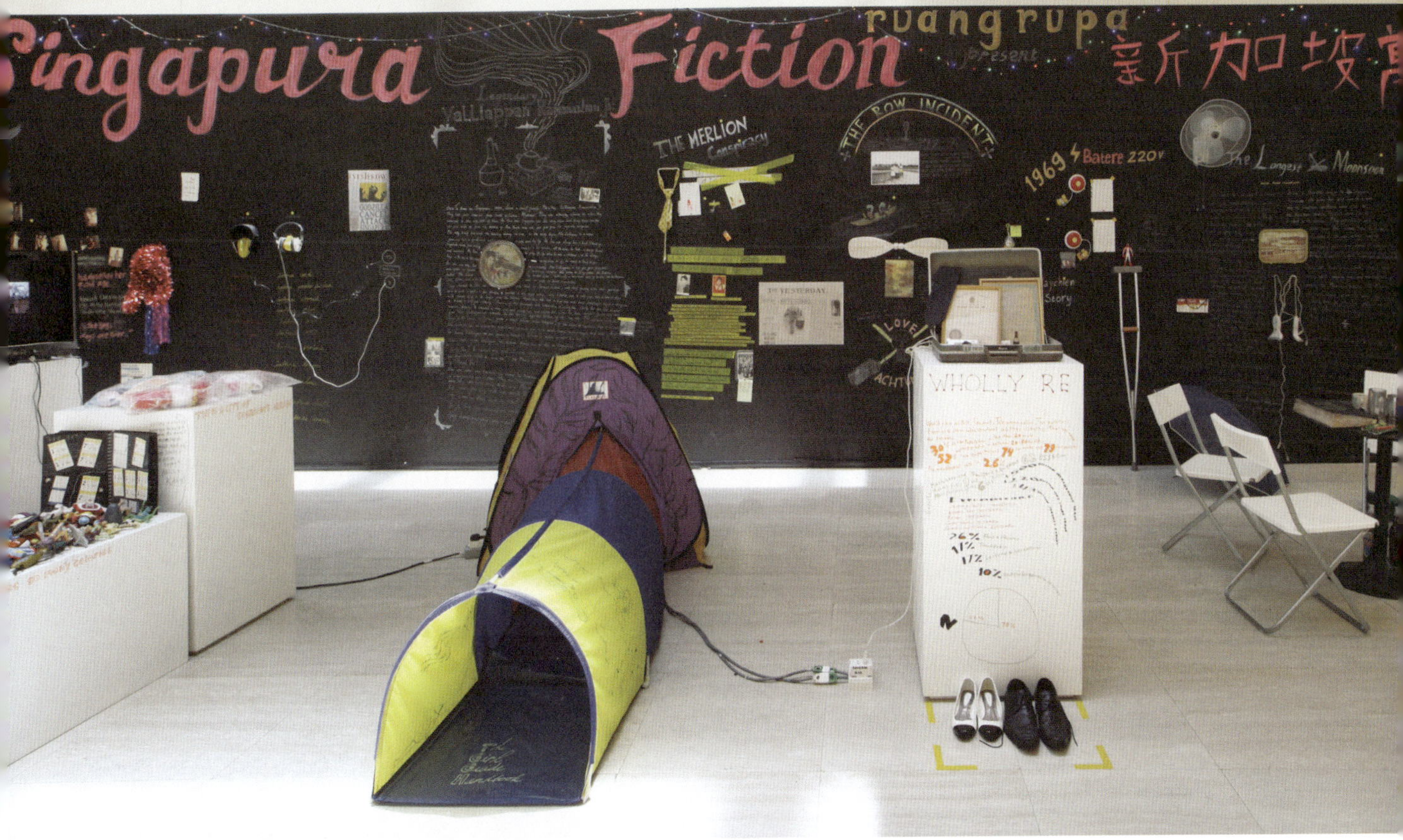

1

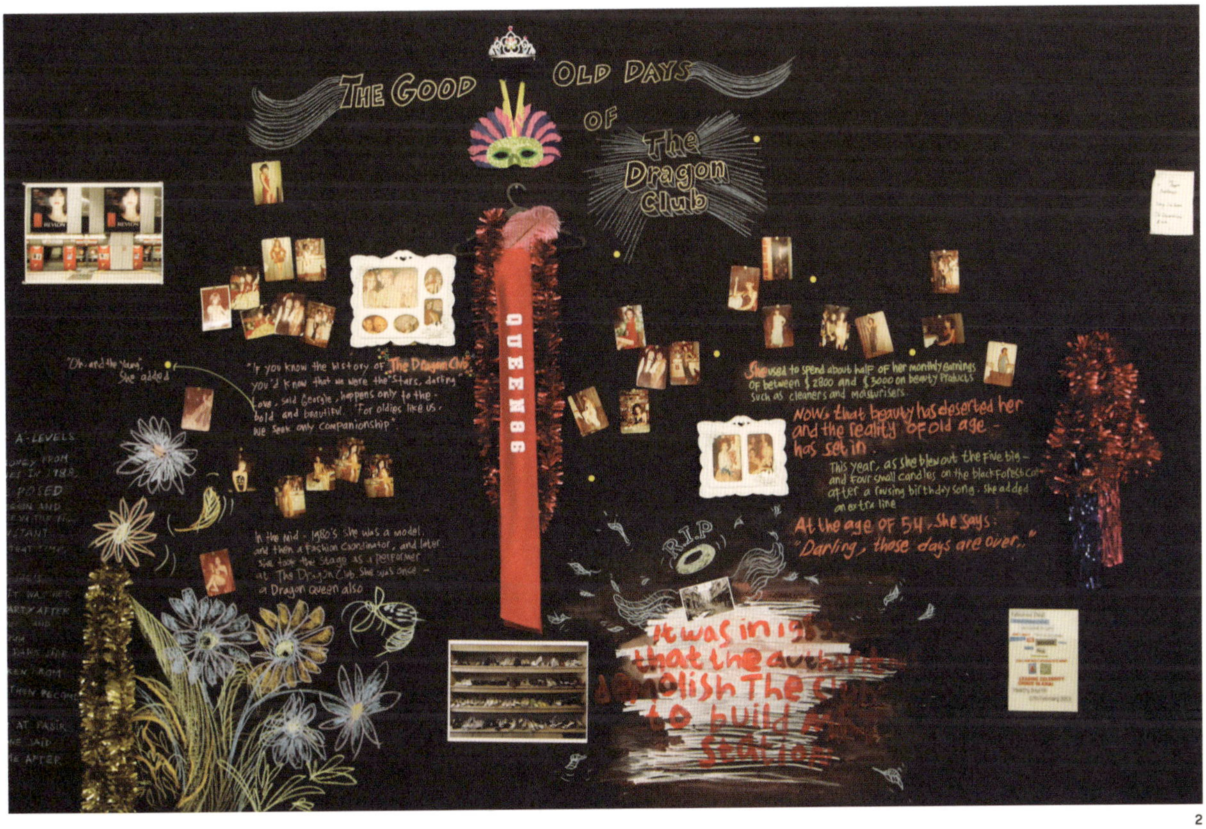

2

previous
1 + 2 – Singapore Fiction, installation, 10th Singapore Biennale, National Museum, Singapore, 2011

3 – Ruangrupa and Norderlicht, Sugar Town Inc, installation, Kunstkring Art Gallery, Jakarta, 2012

4 – Toko Keperluan, installation and performance by Anggun Priambodo, RURU Gallery, Jakarta, 2010

5 – To Give and To Expect Nothing in Return, traveling exhibition, Kedai Kebun Forum, Jakarta, 2010

6 – Ruru.zip, installation, Decompression #10: Ruangrupa 10th Anniversary, National Gallery of Indonesia, Jakarta, 2011

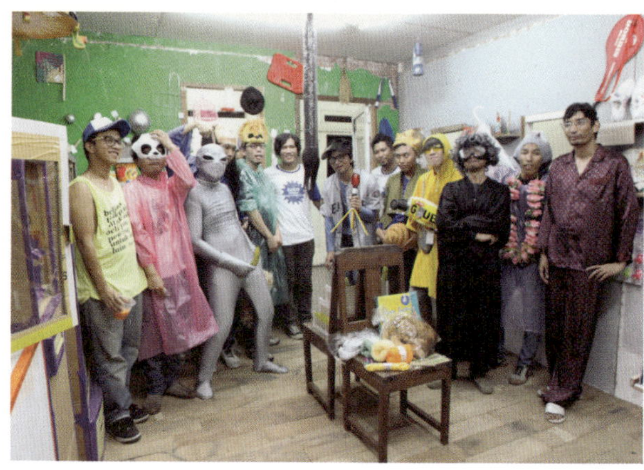

4

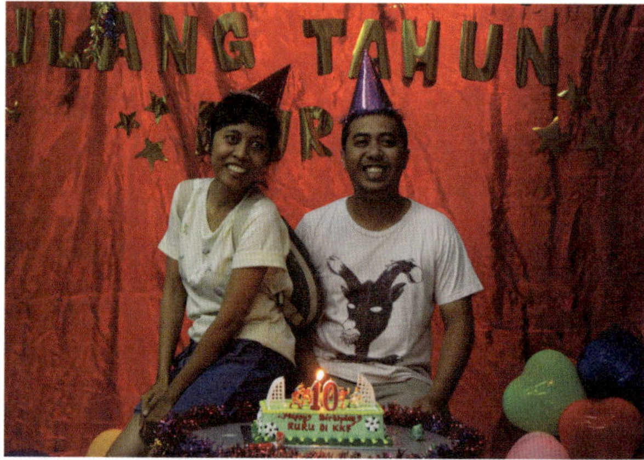

5

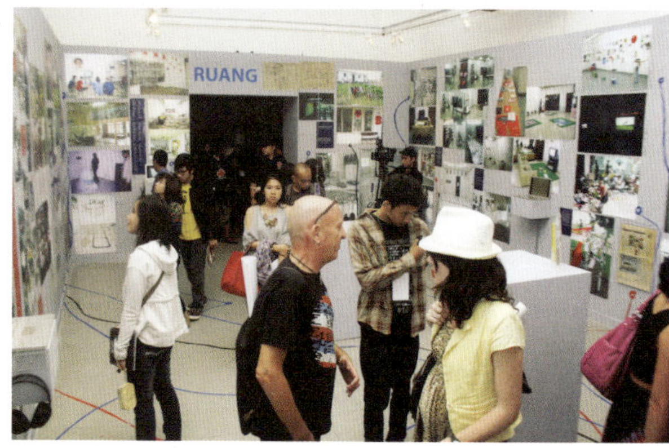

6

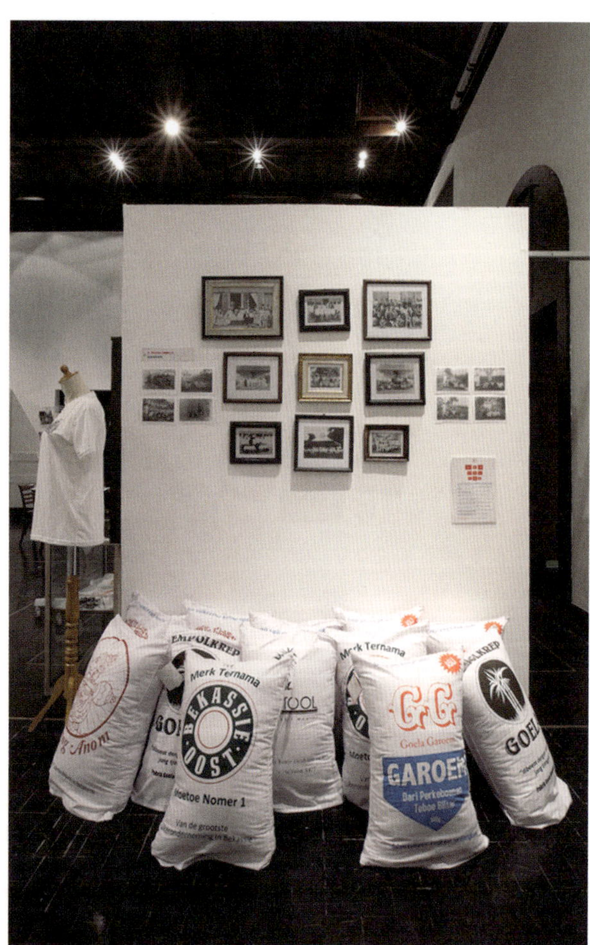

3

7 – To Give and To Expect Nothing in Return, traveling exhibition, Kedai Kebun Forum, Jakarta, 2010

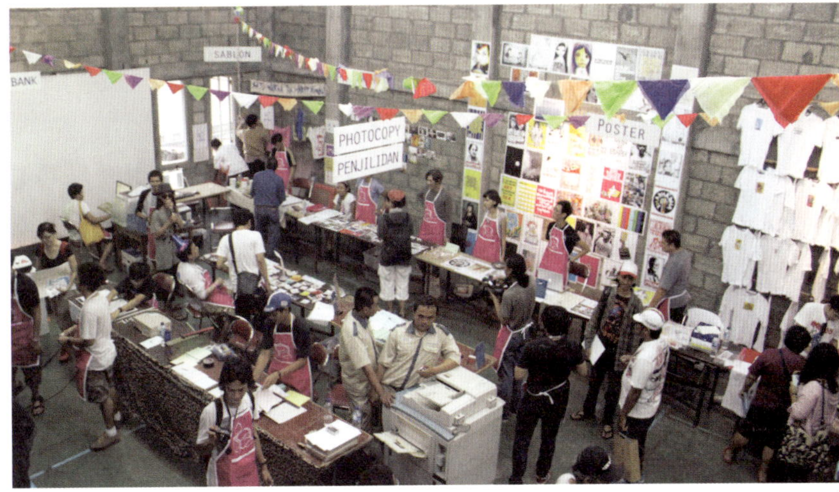

7

How important is each group member's individuality, both in terms of your artistic production and in terms of your relationship with the media? Does anonymity come into play?

Every individual in Ruangrupa is very important and gives meaning to the artistic practice. Since every individual in Ruangrupa comes from a different background of education, culture, and social life, this diversity also strengthens every aspect of our activities as well the artistic production. We have never been anonymous in our work.

What is the relationship between your working methods and your art's "content"? In this sense, does technology tend to play more of a supporting role, or does it lead you in new directions?

Our work is a direct opposition, an antithesis, a resistance, a reaction to the mainstream, but also can be more properly seen as an urgent need that was grown as an implication of an idea development. We play with new media but don't worship it. We try to outsmart it and we try to match its power to a more local context where everyone is using new technology to support their daily communication.

How does your collaboration relate to its cultural, institutional, and commercial contexts? In other words, how would you respond to those who call this a trend?

We make our initiative grow and work as a platform that can continue to hold ideas, passion, excitement, imagination, and dreams—and of course friendship—without having to be too concerned with the group's structure. In order to do that, we should have the ability to understand how people respond to various changes of urban life/forms and space/city and therefore find a working strategy through art.

Who is your audience?

During the last thirteen years there have been significant ongoing shifts in the spaces and the audience for contemporary art. Many artists have become more open to the possibilities of expanding their reach. The individual artist no longer has the monopoly on his or her work of art. And big cities—in this case, Jakarta—can no longer be said to be the only centers of art development. The art world of Jakarta has expanded into a more spacious and free spectrum, which can be used as an assessment and exploration for varieties of styles, models, and art forms. At the beginning, our audience consisted of our friends who had similar interests and passions. Over time, our audience expanded to include junior high school students, artists, intellectuals, NGO activists, and the broader public, especially people in our neighborhood. We're also closely connected to and influenced by the independent music scene. We have invited many bands to perform at Ruangrupa events and starting in 2010, we hold an annual Runagrupa Music Festival (RRREC Fest).

Does your engagement with one another translate into an engagement with the public? How so?

We always work by observing local narrative politics, expanding the concepts of "space" and "public," and inventing new channels for the exploration and definition of communities. We are not attempting to directly oppose the establishment, but at the same time, we are avoiding co-optation. The objective of our activities is the power relations that rule our society, and that's why we provide a place in which various forms of urban activism intersect. Our endeavor is aimed to expand, through discussion, our knowledge and understanding of reality.

8 – <u>T-Shirt Project</u>, 9th Istanbul Biennial, Istanbul, 2009

9 – OK. Video Militia: 3rd Jakarta International Video Festival poster, National Gallery of Indonesia, Jakarta, 2003

10 – <u>T-Shirt Project</u>, exhibition, 9th Istanbul Biennial, Istanbul, 2009

11 – RRREC Fest "The Showcase" poster, Ruangrupa Record Festival, Taman Ismail Marzuki, Jakarta, 2013

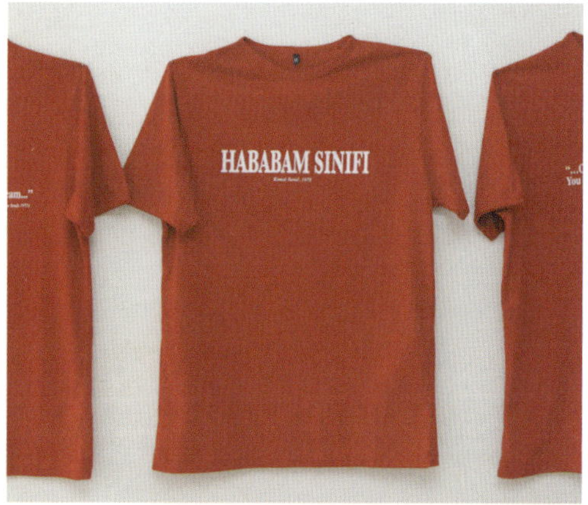

8

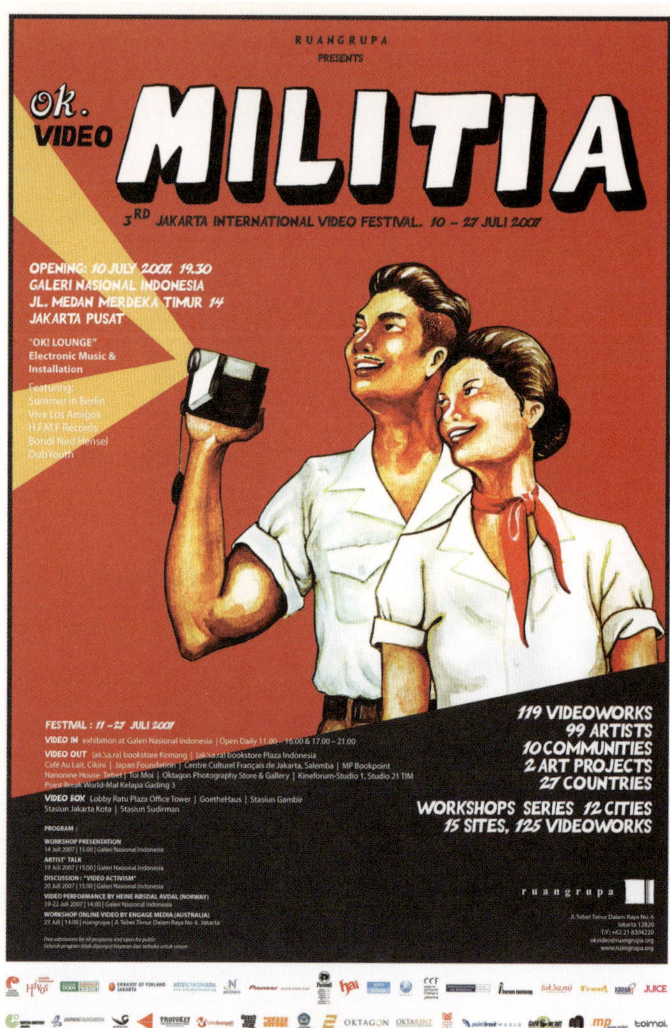

9

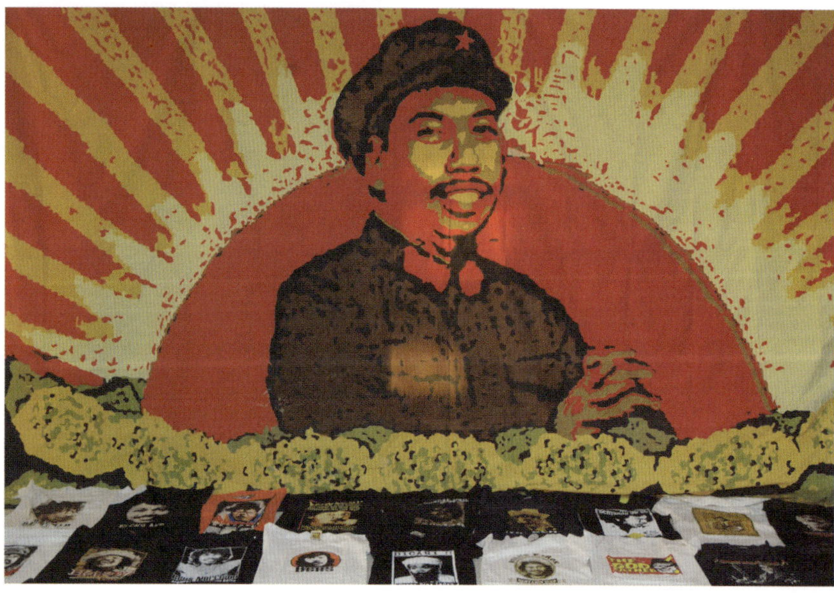

10

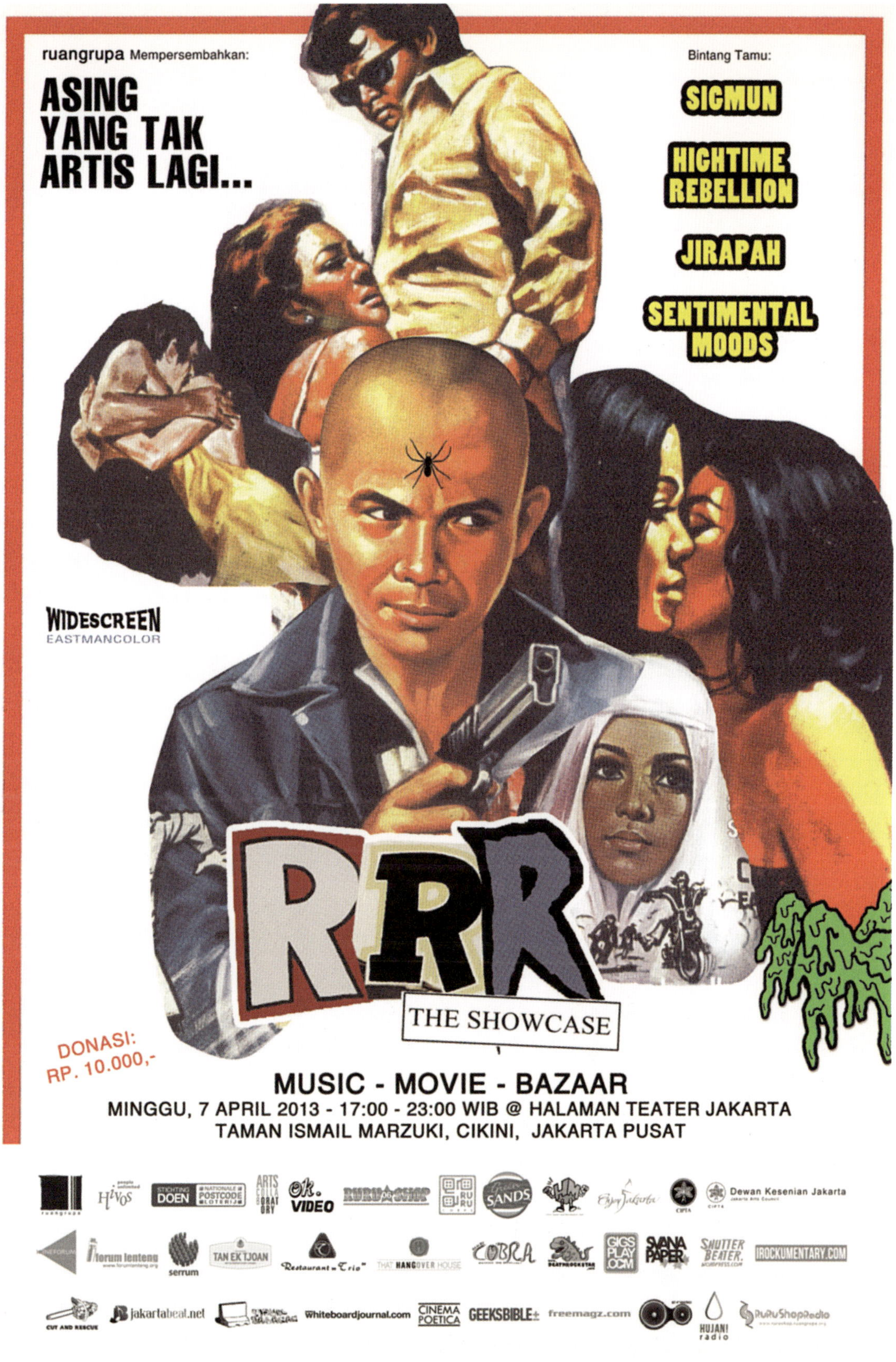

ruangrupa Mempersembahkan:

ASING YANG TAK ARTIS LAGI...

Bintang Tamu:

SIGMUN

HIGHTIME REBELLION

JIRAPAH

SENTIMENTAL MOODS

WIDESCREEN
EASTMANCOLOR

RRR

THE SHOWCASE

DONASI:
RP. 10.000,-

MUSIC - MOVIE - BAZAAR

MINGGU, 7 APRIL 2013 - 17:00 - 23:00 WIB @ HALAMAN TEATER JAKARTA
TAMAN ISMAIL MARZUKI, CIKINI, JAKARTA PUSAT

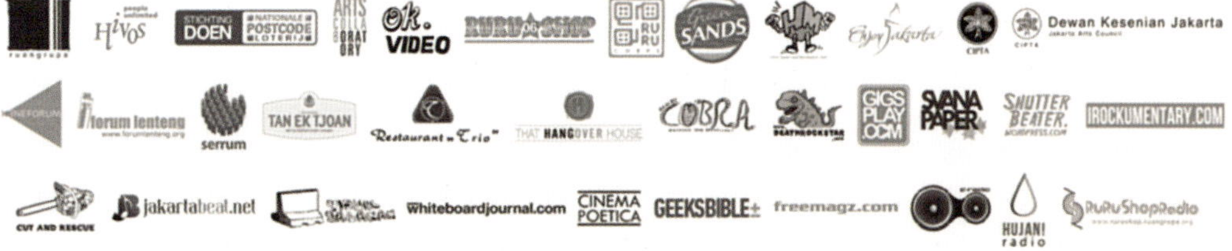

11

ACTIVE SINCE	CITY	WEBSITE
1996	Chicago / Cincinnati, U.S.	simparch.org

SIMPARCH

MEMBERS	ACTIVITIES	RECOMMENDED PUBLICATION
Steven Badgett and Matt Lynch	Painting / Sculpture / Installation	Hydromancy: SIMPARCH with Steve Rowell, Stanlee and Gerald Rubin Center for the Visual Arts, El Paso, 2007

Focusing on site-specificity and the importance of play, SIMPARCH is primarily involved in the creation of recreational wood structures, be they intended for skateboarding, meditation, or fun. Its concern for nature has often brought its work to the countryside, where it has constructed fanciful structures that recall trailer park homes or Airstream trailers.

Why work collaboratively?

We can do ambitious projects much faster. Collective conscience, common goal, spirited, convivial, intensive production.

How do you determine membership? Does physical location matter in this regard?

We began because of a chance meeting in Las Cruces, New Mexico; then one project led to another with no great reason to stop. Besides us, we often ask other people who appreciate the style we work in to join us on bigger projects.

Consistent good people is the way to meet short deadlines.

If considered separately, how do your individual artistic practices contribute to or detract from your work as a group?

One member has a graduate degree and teaches university-level art; the other has a BA and has been a builder-type person since 1987. Our meeting and location/situation inspired a collaboration where experience of both collaborators could be exercised freely.

How are decisions made?

By a kind of erratic dialogue, throwing out half-baked ideas and building upon these fragments in the hope that something will crystallize well enough to put energy into. We find it helpful to remain in an uncommitted zone as long as possible, a real test for curators sometimes. With a residency in Bellevue, Washington, we bought bikes from Craigslist with our transportation budget and rode around a lot trying to think of what to do. We were completely cold, and then Godzilla came up, and that quickly became a viable idea, something to grab onto. We realized we could create our own fiction specific to the location based on this nuclear-era myth/monster. We found a Godzilla-theory essay that was particularly inspiring and watched about ten of the thirty-two Godzilla films.

It became this big puffy lizard lying in a terrarium-like gallery. Godzilla came to destroy Bellevue (home of Microsoft and others) but realized it was futile; he/she gave up in a depressive haze. Kevin Drumm was asked to provide sound for a 5.1 stereo surround system the gallery bought for us. Kevin provided us with something like a malfunctioning coffeemaker—a drone with gurgling, wheezing sounds. It was dumb, but it worked on some levels.

Does each of you have a clearly defined role? If so, what are some of each member's distinct responsibilities?

Evenly shared, save for one of us does more fieldwork, the other more archiving.

How important is each group member's individuality, both in terms of your artistic production and in terms of your relationship with the media? Does anonymity come into play?

Individual interests and satisfactions have to be negotiated and merged within a given project. We prefer to be the entity of SIMPARCH and not identified as individuals, no easy thing usually. Giving lectures as a team can be tricky: the cadence can be off. We've talked about doing lectures as

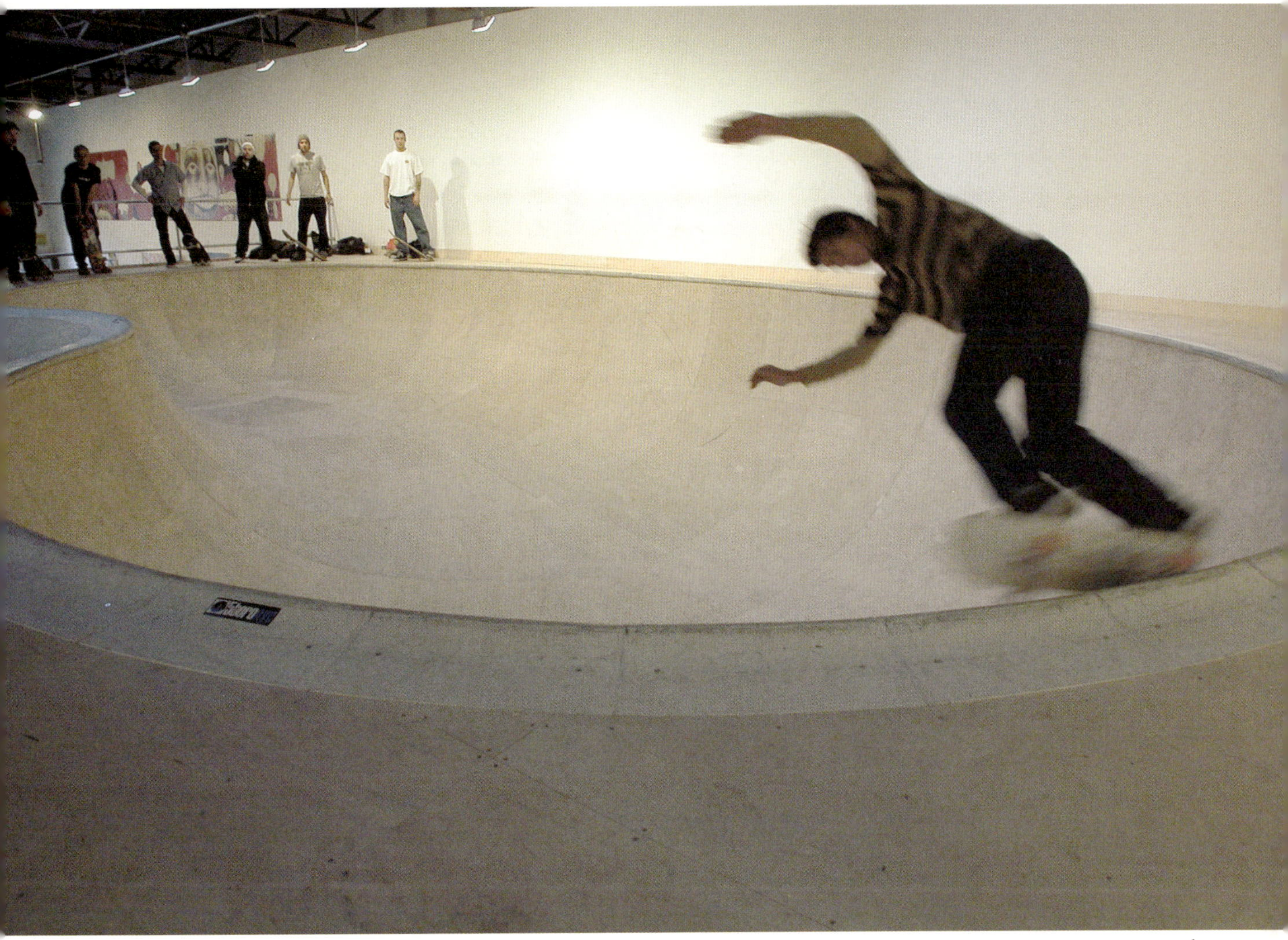

1

1 – Free Basin, wood construction, Deitch Projects, New York, 2003

2 – Free Basin, wood construction, Chicago, 2000

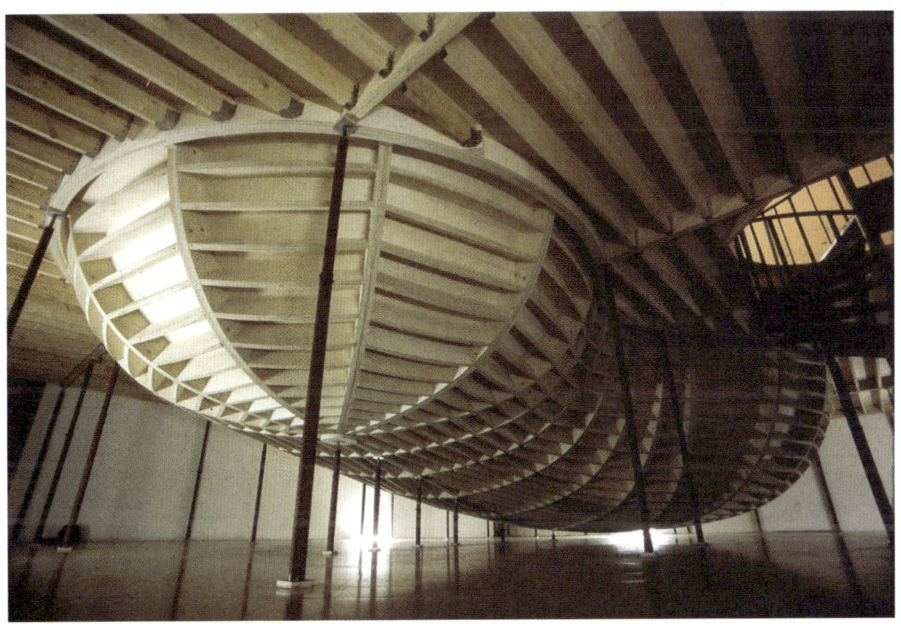

2

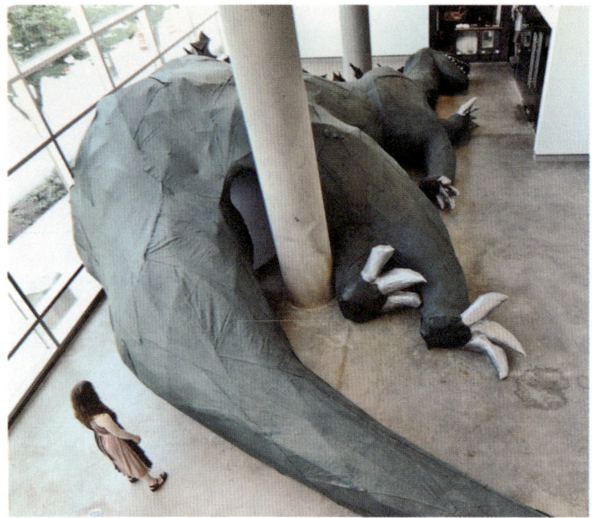

3

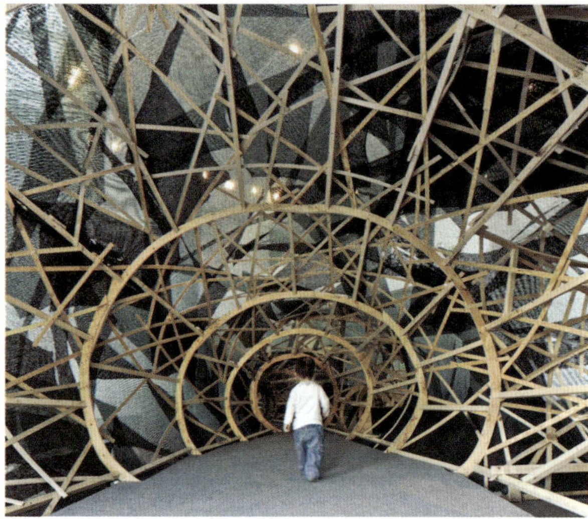

4

dual (not dueling) MCs, passing the mic, etc., à la the Beastie Boys, but we never find time to practice.

What is the relationship between your working methods and your art's "content"? In this sense, does technology tend to play more of a supporting role, or does it lead you in new directions?

We are both purveyors of simp, simposophy, etc., but do not reject new technologies as long as they serve the vision/goal and do not overwhelm it. Our working methods include usually building (hacking) with common materials and can often feel like the content. We have to try to be sure that concept is as strong as the production. It seems every project is a reinvention of our practice. Each one introduces us to a new technique, material, and challenging situation. There is a mutual interest in using a material that can be used in a way it was not intended. Shade fabric as the skin of Godzilla, artificial vines as the stealth garden arbor, truck mirrors to make a glistening mirage/cloud-like sculpture, for example. We can become very focused on specific material use and often a material is intrinsic to a project's aesthetic or gestalt.

A new technology for us would be the electrified livestock fencing that we used in England at the Mary Ward House for an art fair. This mildly shocking wire was fashioned into a garden arbor in the form of a B-2 bomber and was covered with artificial English ivy we brought over in duffel bags.

Steve Rowell provided a sonic overlay of the Shepards Tone, a continuously descending, foreboding drone. Hard to say how we came to that besides thinking about London and the war, the English interest in gardening, a stealthy arbor, garden as refuge and site of disaster. A few people got it—the shock, not necessarily the concept.

How does your collaboration relate to its cultural, institutional, and commercial contexts? In other words, how would you respond to those who call this a trend?

We are very noncommercial. At a lecture a couple years ago we were asked if this was a strategy. Our reply was essentially no, it's a pathology. Relying on the kindness of institutions is how we get by, and the odd grant prize. Collaborative/collective practice seems to be beyond trend status with a consistency of inventiveness and engagement that is years and sometimes decades old, as with Temporary Services, for example.

Who is your audience?

We've always wanted the audience to be broad, beyond the art-world initiated. With Free Basin, the skate bowl, vertical skaters found it to be a perfect armature for their craft; kids love to run around in it; even dogs enjoyed it on occasion. But, ultimately, the mediators of contemporary art appreciated it formally and as social sculpture, so it was funded/installed six times in major venues.

For the work we've done in Wendover, Utah, with the Center for Land Use Interpretation, the audience/users are artists. It's just a few people each year but it is consistent. I guess we are architects in those cases, providing a useful, permanent facility.

Does your engagement with one another translate into an engagement with the public? How so?

That's the goal, to engage people, so, yes—in the sense that we hope our projects offer accessibility and complexity to viewers. That is the perk and justification of our not-so-easy process. And it is appropriate that the process is not so easy. Projects with no rigor will not offer much for maker or viewer. We are lazy in general but understand when we need to work hard to solve a certain problem.

opposite
3 – Exhausted, installation, Open Satellite, Seattle, 2009

opposite
4 – Exhausted (interior), installation, Open Satellite, Seattle, 2009

5 – Will Build to Suit, project for a wood construction, Venice, 2008

6 – Silvas Capitalis (Forest Head), wood construction, Kielder, UK, 2009

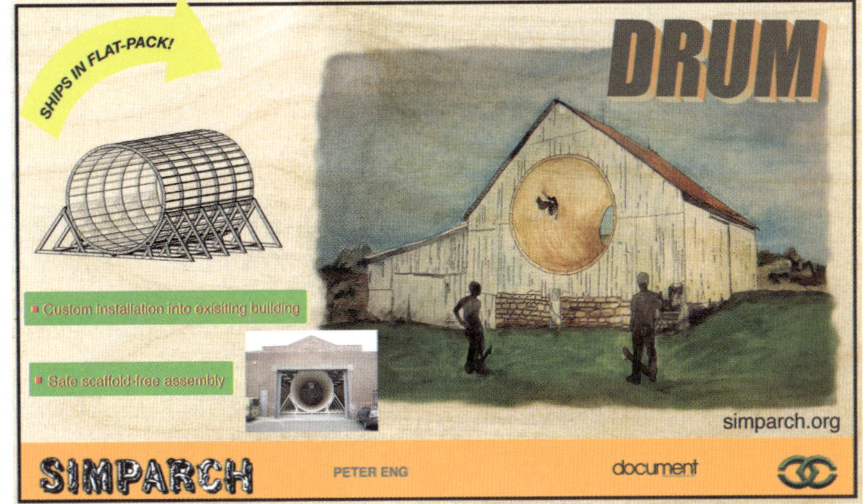

5

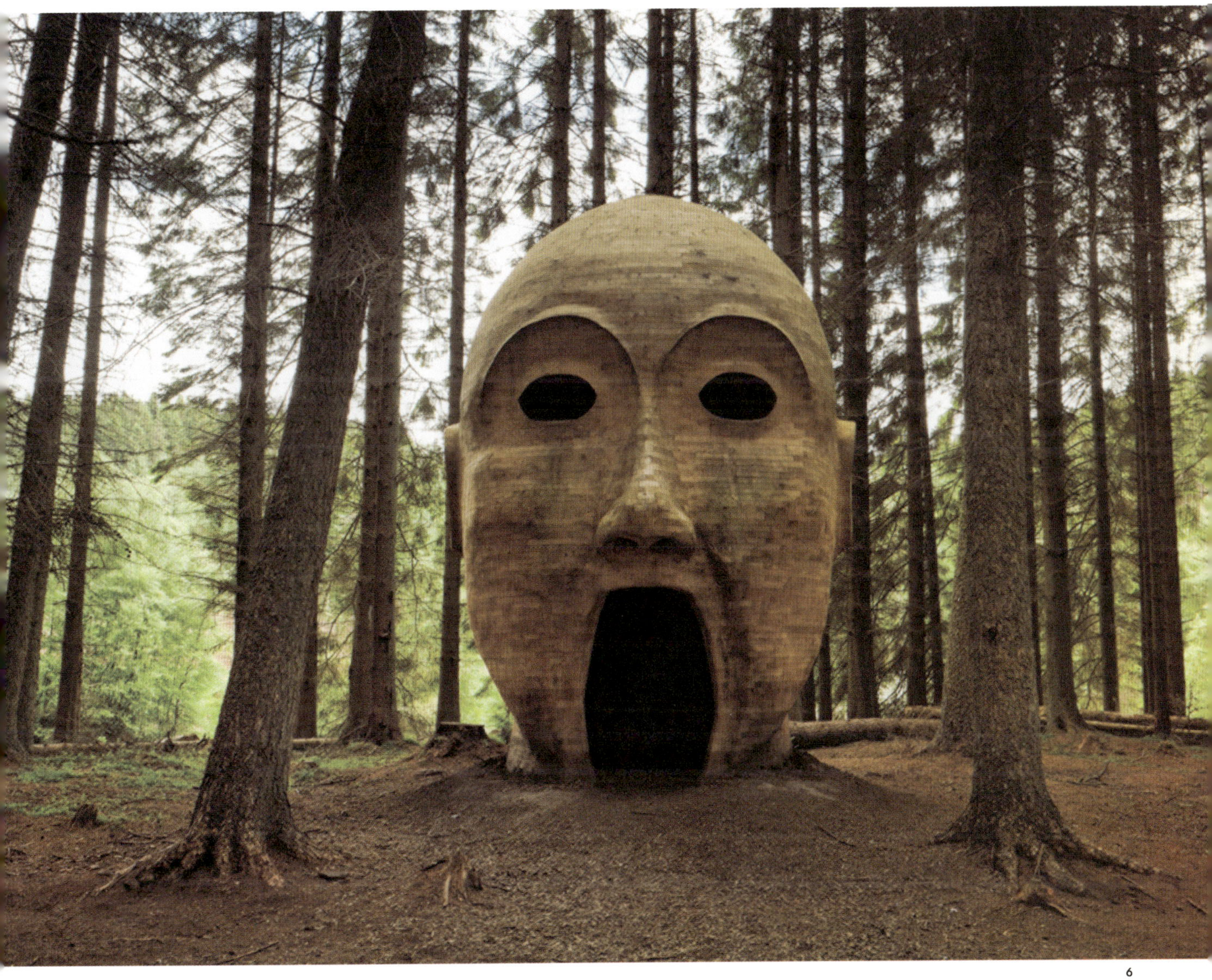

6

ACTIVE SINCE	CITY	WEBSITE
2001	Wilmington, California, U.S.	slanguagestudio.com

Slanguage

MEMBERS	ACTIVITIES	RECOMMENDED PUBLICATION
Full-time: Mario Ybarra Jr., Karla Diaz, Antonio De Jesus Lopez, Emilio Venegas Jr., and Eric Marquez. Part-time: Raul Vasquez, Oralia Rubio, and Betty Marin.	Artist Residency Program, Community Projects, Curating, Merchandising, Music, Painting / Sculpture / Installation, Photography, Public Performance, Urban Interventions, Video, Writing, Youth and Adult Workshops	Elizabeth Hamilton (ed.), Engagement Party: Social Practice at MOCA 2008–2012, MOCA, Los Angeles, 2012

Through community-based projects, seminars, interactive installations, murals, and events halfway between art happenings and block parties, Slanguage explores the modes of production and communication of culture. Particularly interesting for the group is the social value of culture and how this changes depending on the context within which it is presented.

Why work collaboratively?

Working as individual artists is much harder than working as a group. We get things done much faster and easier. Also, creatively, as a group, we get different critical perspectives that make the work stronger.

How do you determine membership? Does physical location matter in this regard?

Membership is based on talent but also ideas, leadership, and critical thinking skills. Members have to be self-starters, contribute with their ideas and innovative methods of production and art making. And although a lot of our members initially were local, we have now expanded our membership globally, depending on where we have worked. Slanguage was initially intended to be our studio, so we have never been institutionalized enough like a museum to ask for a fee. Essentially, the question we ask members is whether they see themselves as a ninja or a samurai.
I (Karla Diaz) lead the team of ninjas based on a ninja-like skill of accuracy, attention to detail, quiet but powerful visual perception, and ability to masterfully attack challenging tasks or projects. The samurai team led by Mario are artists with skills more samurai-driven, that is, abstract, powerful, and direct in their art making, raw at times, with skills that deal with doing big installations, murals, or projects, but also with a strong tactic to leadership and finishing big projects.

If considered separately, how do your individual artistic practices contribute to or detract from your work as a group?

Our individual practices are highlighted and accepted more because of the work we have done at Slanguage. Some of us who have strong art careers are able to use that to help the rest of the group to bring more attention to the Slanguage projects. For example, when some of us get to do individual projects in Boston, in Italy, in Colombia, etc., we talk about the work we do at Slanguage. We then get to come back or do a project with the group. This has opened up numerous collective opportunities.

How are decisions made?

Mario and I are the ones who make the final decisions. We are also the ones who support Slanguage financially. However, we always like to get the group's input before a final decision.

Does each of you have a clearly defined role? If so, what are some of each member's distinct responsibilities?

Yes, well, somewhat. I mean, we know what each one of us will be in charge of doing. This has only been recently (the last three or four years). Before that, Mario and I acted as administrators and we led the groups. It was based on the punk-music concept of DIY (do-it-yourself). And even

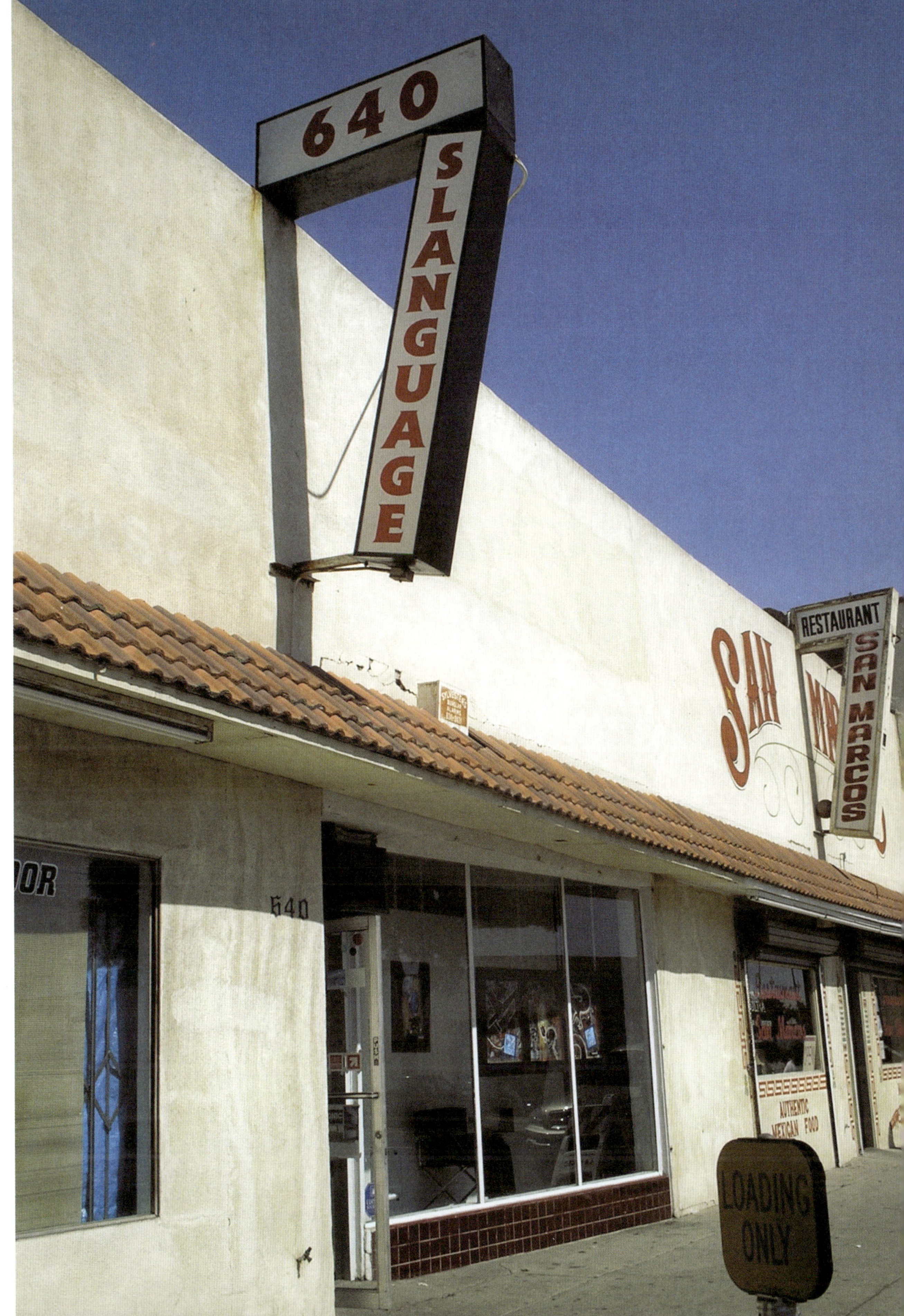
640
SLANGUAGE
RESTAURANT
SAN MARCOS
SAN
640
AUTHENTIC
MEXICAN FOOD
LOADING
ONLY

1

previous
1 – **Outside Slanguage Studio, Wilmington, CA, 2004**

2 – **Slanguage's 10-Year Anniversary, mural, Slanguage Studio, Wilmington, CA, 2012. Design: Mario Lopez**

3 – **Peace in Wilmas, mural, Made in L.A., LAXART, Los Angeles, 2012. Design: Mario Cuen, Mario Lopez, and Raul Vasquez**

4 – **Psychic Cinema Multiplex, installation view, Engagement Party, MOCA, Los Angeles, 2009**

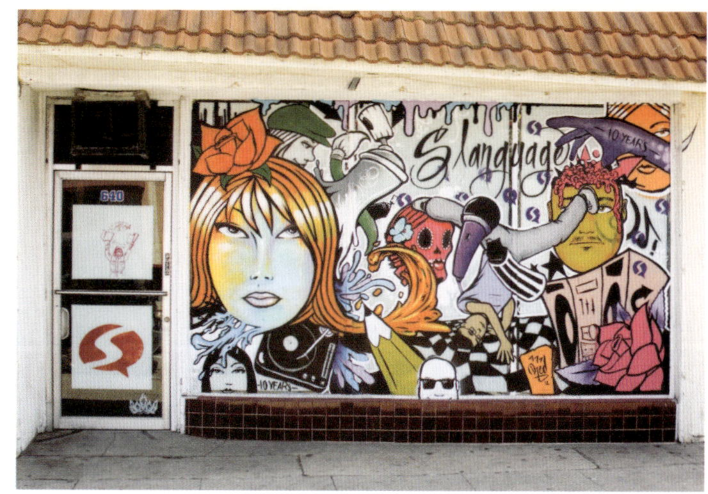

2

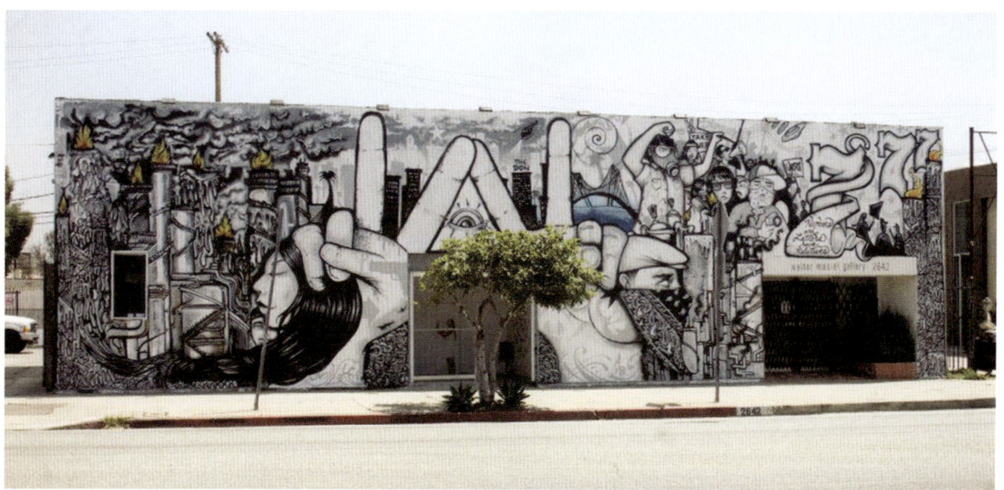

3

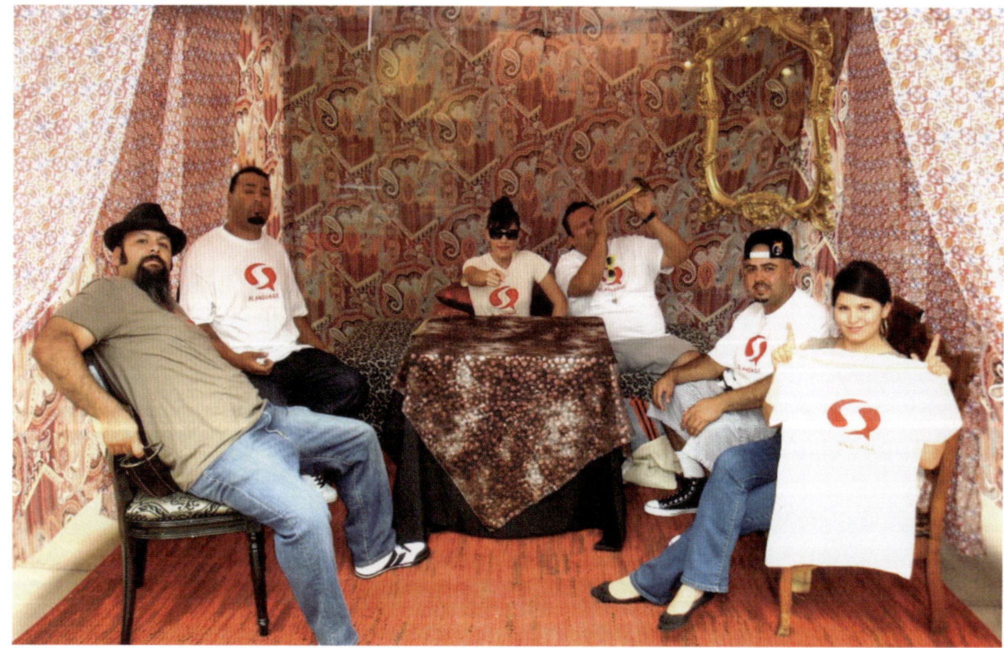

4

though some of it still functions like that, it was really a lead-yourself-and-then-show-me-what-ideas-you-have-to-offer setup. But pedagogically, this concept has always been intentional. We wanted Slanguage to empower artists through their individual artistic strengths. So for now, there are our roles: Mario Ybarra Jr. and I function as directors. I am also in charge of programming and exhibitions, Antonio De Jesus Lopez is installation/exhibition and production manager, Emilio Venegas Jr. is manager of media/design, and Eric Marquez is our master painter.

How important is each group member's individuality, both in terms of your artistic production and in terms of your relationship with the media? Does anonymity come into play?

As a group the member's individuality is very important, especially in terms of production. Since we all have such unique, diverse talents and are at different levels of experience, we all bring something different to the final production. For example, the last project we worked on for MOCA for its Engagement Party series, we did three different events. So we really had to pool all our ideas and resources to get things done. We had contributions by members who were young high school art students, but we also had help from artists who contributed to the performance aspect of the piece, and we had members who were sociologists but were also painters, a theater director to help direct our performances, a dance instructor, and so many other members and community friends who helped us. In terms of the relationship to the media, we'd like to say we are all Slanguage.

What is the relationship between your working methods and your art's "content"? In this sense, does technology tend to play more of a supporting role, or does it lead you in new directions?

How we work and the "content" of our work are always related to one another. Slanguage is a production, a lab, and a process-based, multidisciplinary space. Everything we make—whether it's a song or a painting—we always use it in our artwork. We don't censor ourselves, because Slanguage is the space for questions to be posed, not necessarily answered; it's a space where we can make mistakes, fail, and at the same time we can use our imaginations, dream of possibilities and impossibilities to keep creating. For us, technology has played a supporting role (more advanced social media sites specifically), because it has given us access to a bigger audience in an easy, free, and international visual forum.

How does your collaboration relate to its cultural, institutional, and commercial contexts? In other words, how would you respond to those who call this a trend?

It's a lie that artists don't collaborate; they have been collaborating for centuries. More so, there are many examples of artists around the world who have been doing this work for many years. Museums and institutions have always been supportive of us. However, we don't want to be an institution or completely an anarchist group,;we are in the middle; we occupy a "third space" of sorts where we function as an alternative and move between the official and unofficial. We understand that it always takes a few years for museums or galleries to catch up to what's happening in independent artist-run projects like Slanguage. What excites me about the work we do is that we will always find the new trend. That's what our work and intent is. We have always wanted to make work that speaks about subcultural groups or narratives, of marginalized histories, of ideas and issues that were of cultural, social importance and prominent to visual contemporary art. To us, this "trend," as you say, will pass; we know that. We never meant to be "trendy" but to figure out how we can make art we want to see happen. We have empowered ourselves as artists and instead of waiting, we started to do this ourselves.

Who is your audience?

Our audience is everybody.

Does your engagement with one another translate into an engagement with the public? How so?

We have to know each other to work. Our engagement with each other does translate into an engagement with the public. For instance, when we are doing a project, teaching a workshop, setting up an installation, or doing a performance, I know whom I can rely on for what to help us make the final show happen; knowing them, I understand my audience.

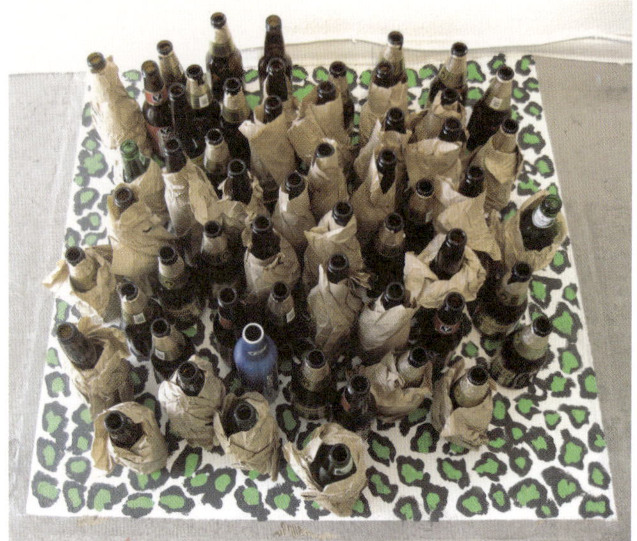

5

5 – Radames "Juni" Figueroa, War Spectacle: The Last Paradise, installation, Slanguage Studio, Wilmington, CA, 2009

6 – Brutalism: A Dance Performance poster, Engagement Party, MOCA, Los Angeles, 2009. Design: Christopher Reynolds

7 – Slanguage Teen Arts Council Summit flyer, Made in L.A., LAXART, Los Angeles, 2012. Design: Emilio Venegas Jr.

8 – Slanguage Studio, installation, ICA, Boston, 2009

opposite
9 – Dislexicon: A Word Performance, performance, Engagement Party, MOCA, Los Angeles, 2009

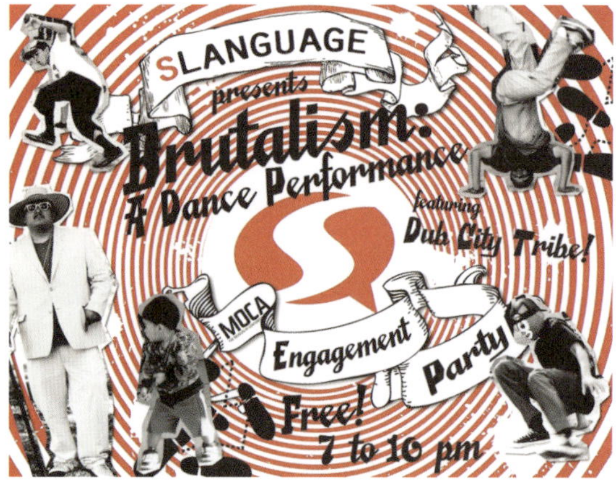

6

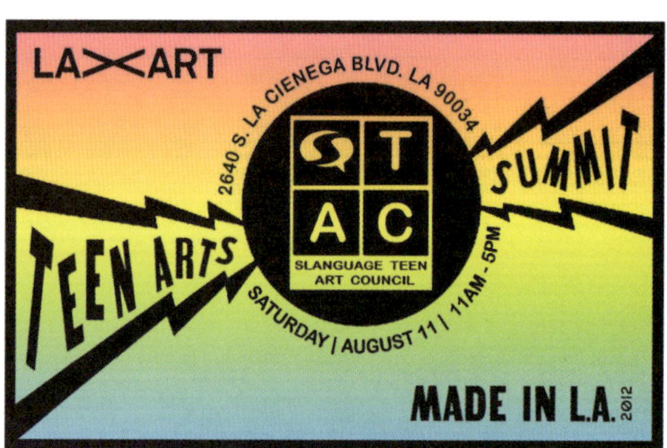

7

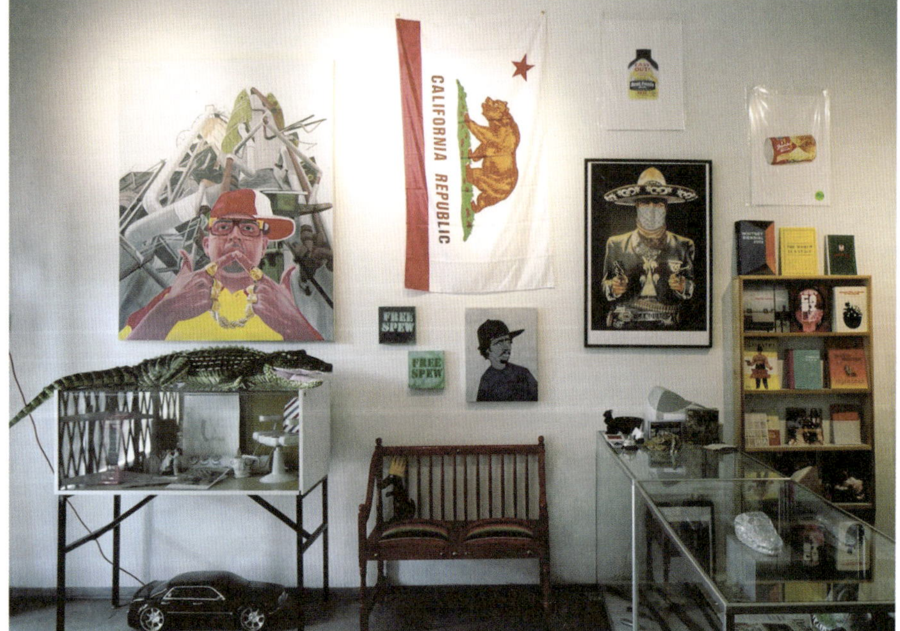

8

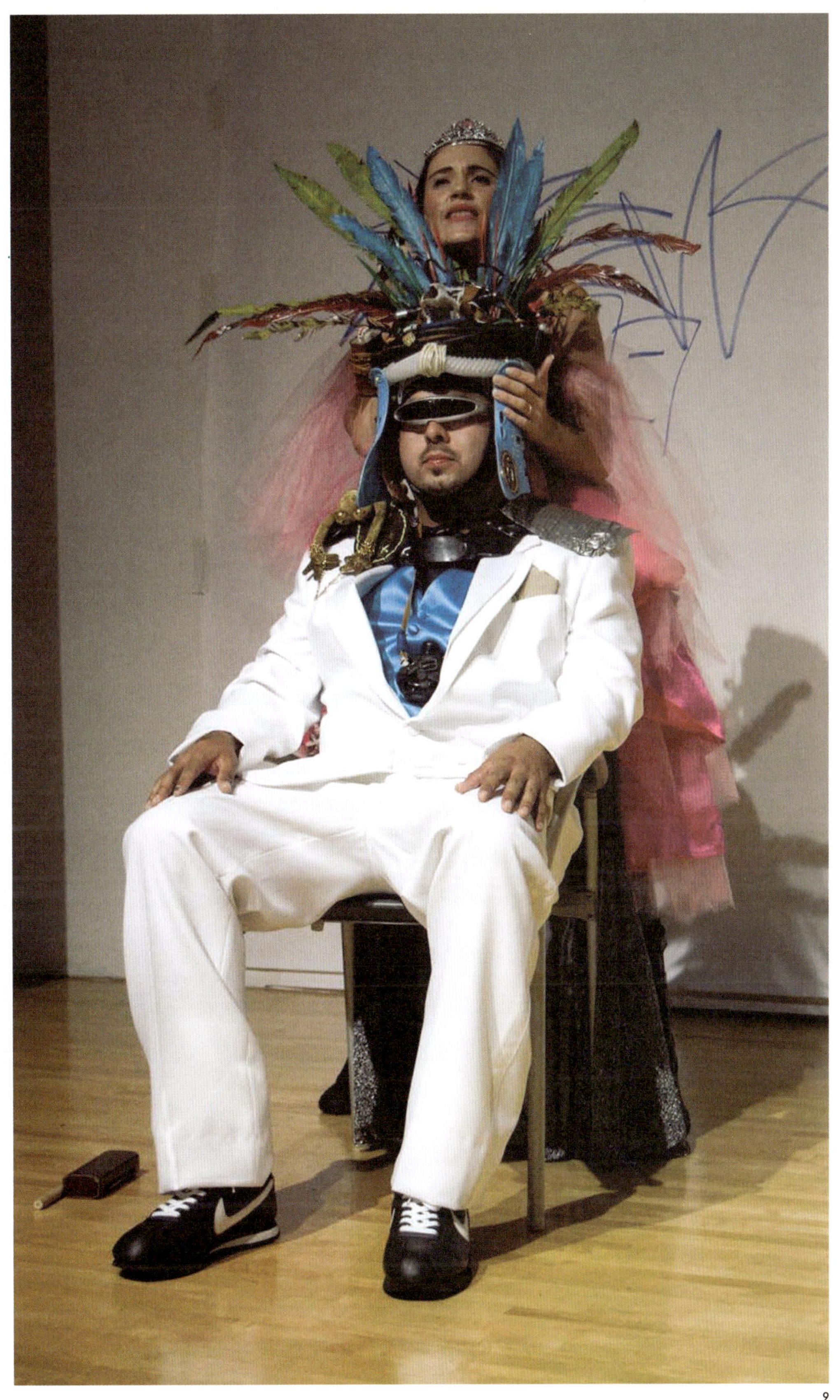

9

ACTIVE SINCE	CITY	WEBSITE
2006	Eurasia	slavsandtatars.com

Slavs and Tatars

MEMBERS	ACTIVITIES	RECOMMENDED PUBLICATION
Anonymous	Community Projects, Merchandising, Painting / Sculpture / Installation, Public Performance, Publishing, Urban Interventions	SLAVS AND TATARS, Not Moscow Not Mecca, Wien Secession / Revolver, Berlin, 2012

Signs and symbols of the loosely identified geographic area of Eurasia constitute the content of Slavs and Tatars' research, which spans from installations to talks and publications. Its work offers the chance to reflect on the regionality of language,and its relation to territorial identity.

Why work collaboratively?

The very term "collaborative," like too many others, has become promiscuous to the point of losing its inherent value. Given the collective nature and propos of our practice, we look to curators, academics, gallerists, and installation crews, among others, each as an integral partner in an often alchemic process that allows for a series of thoughts to resonate spatially, formally, intellectually, and hopefully effectively.

How do you determine membership? Does physical location matter in this regard?

We do not determine membership: it has determined us. Physical location doesn't matter.

If considered separately, how do your individual artistic practices contribute to or detract from your work as a group?

We do not have individual practices as artists.

How are decisions made?

The longer one lives, the more one understands what one likes, what kinds of ideas one is drawn to, which food one prefers, which people, which places, etc. It's important to resist this "raffinement," this narrowing of one's field of activity, and to embrace one's antithesis, to read things we don't agree with, to become friends with people to whom we might not normally be drawn. Collaboration addresses this need urgently: we share interests but our respective understanding of these interests, these phenomena, these people could not be more distinct and different at times.

Does each of you have a clearly defined role? If so, what are some of each member's distinct responsibilities?

Yes, we bring very different skill sets to the table. One of us is more intuitive, more visually articulate, while the other is more analytical and linguistically inclined. We embrace this dynamic entirely and in no way try to change it. Interestingly enough, though, it inevitably leads to an osmotic bleeding of capabilities, from one to another.

How important is each group member's individuality, both in terms of your artistic production and in terms of your relationship with the media? Does anonymity come into play?

This is a very good, if tough, question that continues to haunt us if only because there is no term to define our desire to deflect any attention to us to the work. We do not communicate our personal names, biographies, places we live, etc. Not because we seek anonymity, which strikes us as a very self-conscious, almost dramatic, or at least performative gesture. Rather, it's a disciplinary practice: we are not interested in personalities as much as we are in the work. While we acknowledge the attraction—when we like a work, inevitably one of the first instincts is to find out who is behind it, where s/he is from, etc.—we do not necessarily believe it is a healthy line of questioning; it is one better not indulged.

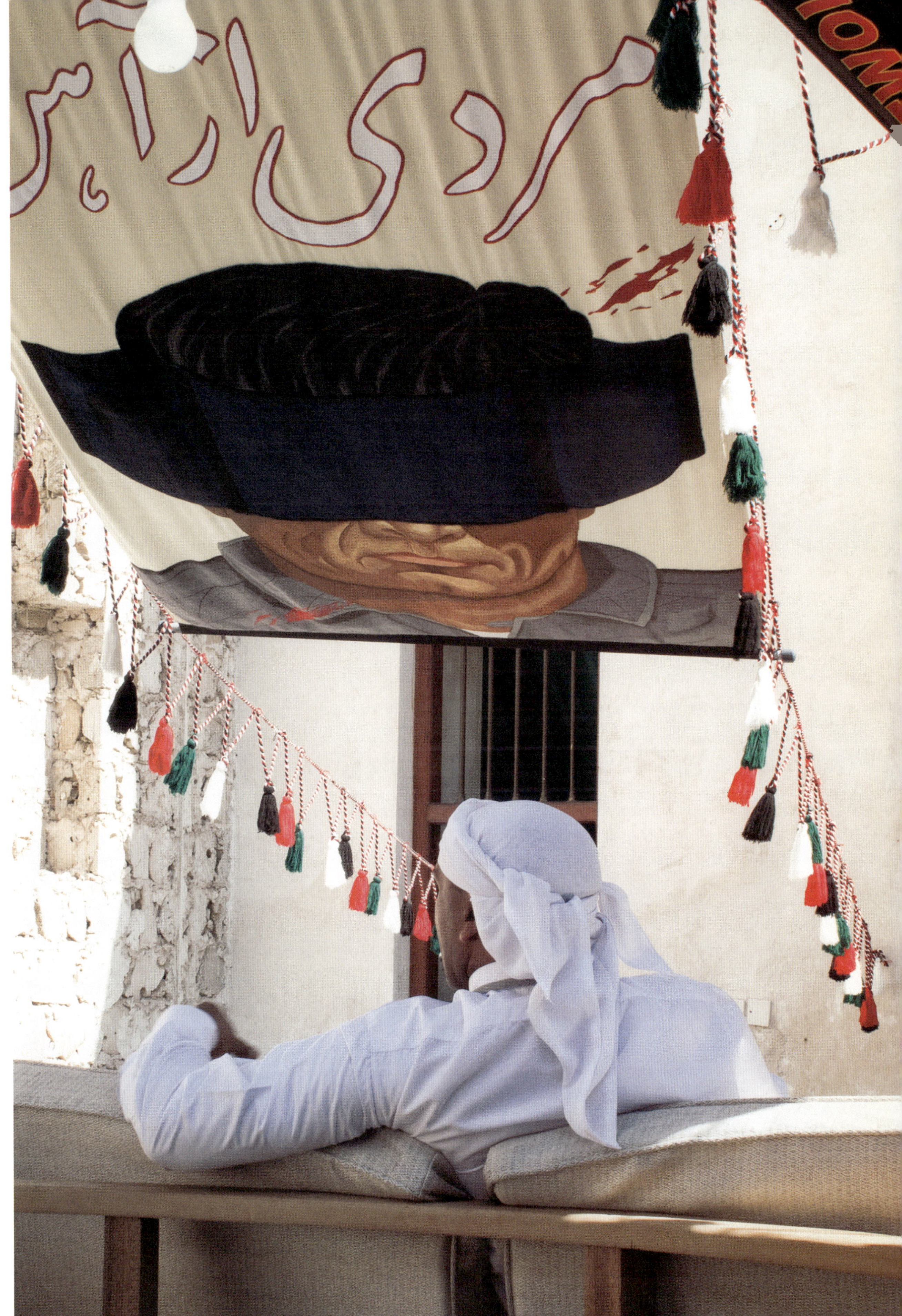

1

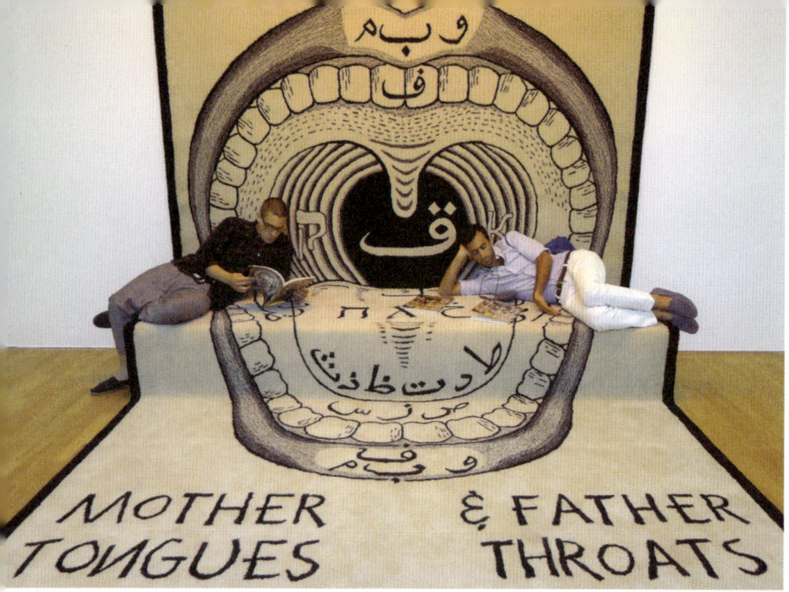

2

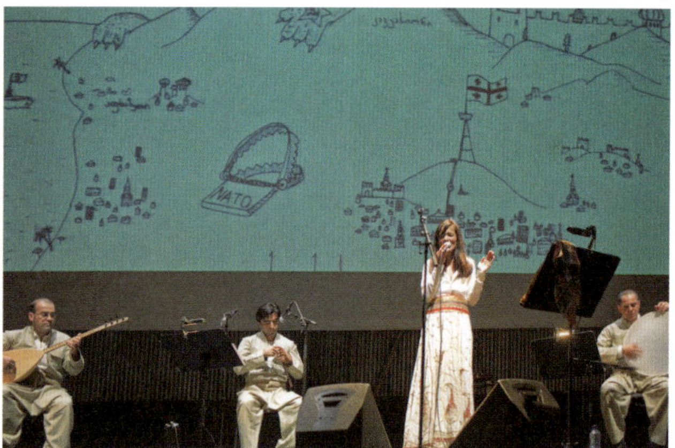

3

KEEP YOUR MAJORITIES CLOSE BUT YOUR MINORITIES CLOSER

Forever & Today
Grand Opening: 13 September 2008, 6-8 pm
141 Division Street, New York, NY 10002
info@foreverandtoday.org | www.foreverandtoday.org
Poster: Slavs and Tatars, 2008

4

What is the relationship between your working methods and your art's "content"? In this sense, does technology tend to play more of a supporting role, or does it lead you in new directions?

Only insofar as technology makes presence all the more crucial. We've never lived in the same city since commencing Slavs and Tatars. We depend a lot on Skype. Otherwise, we meet roughly once a month in person for various exhibition openings as well as research assignments or speaking engagements and then extend these stays to work with each other. In some sense, we are extending the word "opening" to include not just the audience, but also us. As opposed to the traditional dynamic, in which an exhibition opening is a crowning moment of commemoration, of relaxing and reflecting, we use it as a platform to address an existing cycle of work or as a point of departure toward something else.

How does your collaboration relate to its cultural, institutional, and commercial contexts? In other words, how would you respond to those who call this a trend?

To compare practices simply because of their collaborative nature goes to the very heart of the "who/where" line of questioning we are not particularly interested in. We find affinities with other artists but that is because of the line of questioning, be it from an individual or collective, living or dead, artist or theologian. To borrow from the spurious vocabulary of the financial world, though, perhaps we could propose that our practice, like others, is a correction. For example, via a need to tell stories differently, to deliver critique without the insular, impenetrable language or positioning, or to produce political work that is joyful and festive without the emphasis on the destructive and dark.

Who is your audience?

The approach to our work is akin to a bazaar or souk: there's a fanning out of media. Our Friendship of Nations: Polish Shi'ite Showbiz, for example, tells the story of twenty-first century Iran through that of 1980s Poland and Solidarnošç. To do so, we turned to a magazine contribution, a public balloon, an archive, textile works, public billboards, lectures, publications, and craft-specific sculptures. Stemming perhaps from our regional focus, this maximalism allows

previous
1 – **Friendship of Nations: Polish Shi'ite Showbiz, installation, 10th Sharjah Biennial, Sharjah, United Arab Emirates, 2011**

opposite
2 – **Mother Tongues and Father Throats, installation, Moravian Gallery, Brno, Czech Republic, 2012**

opposite
3 – **Hymns of No Resistance, performance, Kaai Theater, Brussels, 2009**

opposite
4 – **Never Give Up the Fruit poster, Forever & Today, New York, 2012**

5 – **Beyonsense, graphics for installation, MoMA, New York, 2012**

6 – **Not Moscow, Not Mecca, cover of the catalog, Revolver Verlag/ Secession, Wien, 2012**

7 – **Beyonsense, installation, MoMA, New York, 2012**

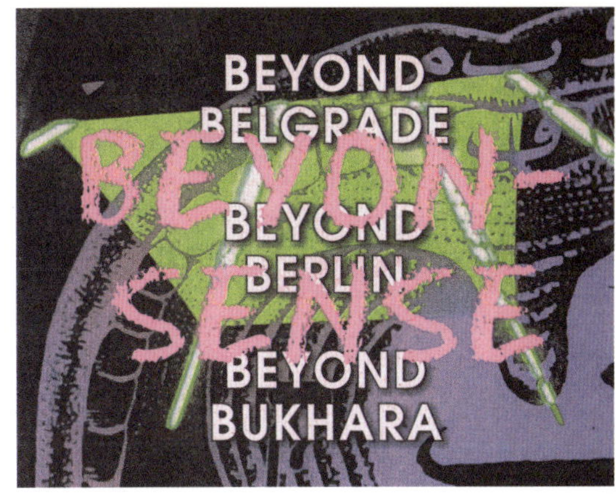

5

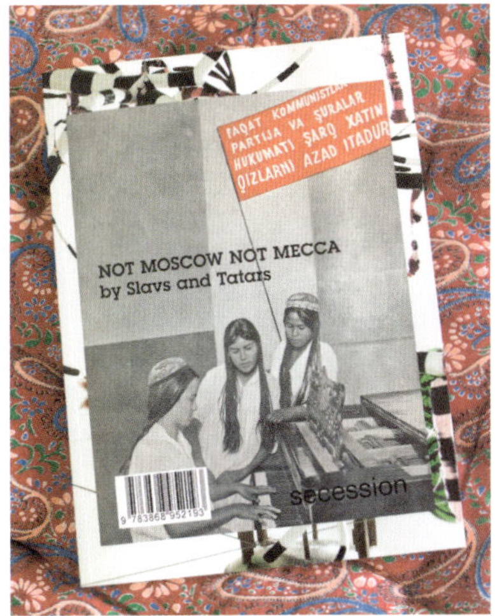

6

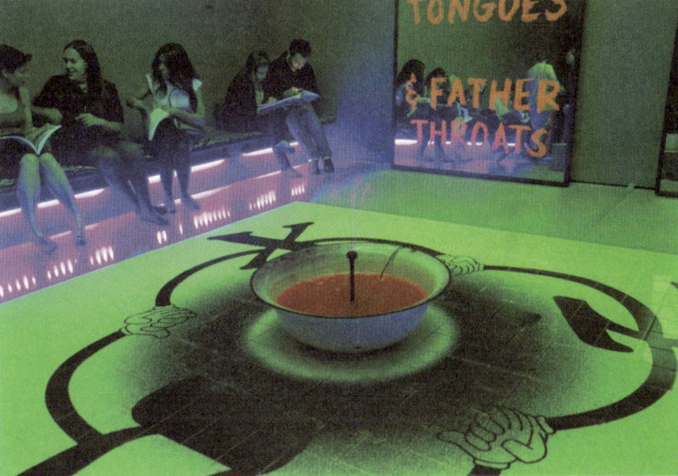

7

the audience different levels of entry into the project. This "not only but also" requires us to engage the audience with generosity, to face our audience, as opposed to making work that could remain insular or only relevant to art professionals. It acknowledges different interests, needs, people—to put it simply, the more literary minded perhaps turn to the book, while the more formal look to the sculptures or vice versa.

Does your engagement with one another translate into an engagement with the public? How so?

Absolutely. Our current cycle of work, The Faculty of Substitution, tries to come to terms with the notion of self-knowledge through engagement with the other, with that which is resolutely not one's self. Today, we not only need intellectual acrobatics but metaphysical ones: substitution requires us to cultivate the agility, coordination, and balance necessary to tell one tale through another, to adopt the innermost thoughts, experiences, beliefs, and sensations of others as our own, in an effort to challenge the very notion of distance as the shortest length between two points. To grasp the nature of political agency in the twenty-first century, we study Muharram and the 1,300-year-old Shiite ritual of perpetual protest (Reverse Joy); to demystify Islam, we turned to communism for our Not Moscow Not Mecca at Vienna's Secession; and it was through mysticism that we proposed an different understanding of modernity with Beyonsense at MoMA.

The Faculty of Substitution attempts to redress this imbalance by playfully, intimately, and formally suggesting a recalibration: of registers, speeds, and form. We look at substitution—from "al-badaliya" to the antimodern, from "la reversibilité" to mystical protest across such disparate figures as al-Hallaj, Joris-Karl Huysmans, and Louis Massignon. How can indirection—looking at something else as a prism onto the chosen subject of study, going somewhere else that initially might not seem relevant, instead of directly heading toward one's destination challenge—the very notion of distance as the shortest length between two points? There is some sass in this circuit: why go straight for the kill when you can circle it, tease it, taunt it out of its strict semantics?

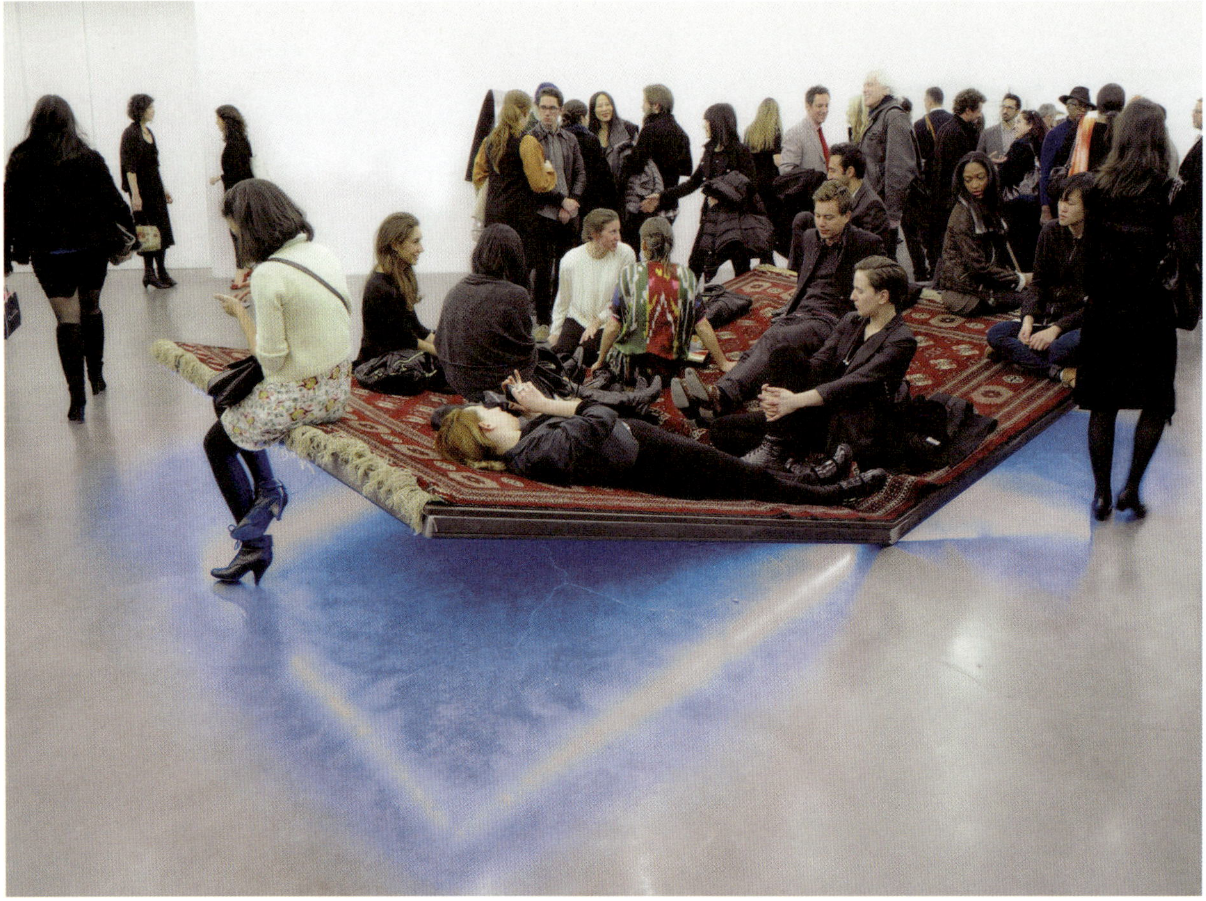

8

8 – PrayWay, installation, part of The Ungovernables, The New Museum, New York, 2012

9 – A Monobrow Manifesto, installation, Frieze Sculpture Park, London, 2010

opposite
10 – The Fragrant Concubine, installation view of Not Moscow Not Mecca, Secession, Wien, 2012

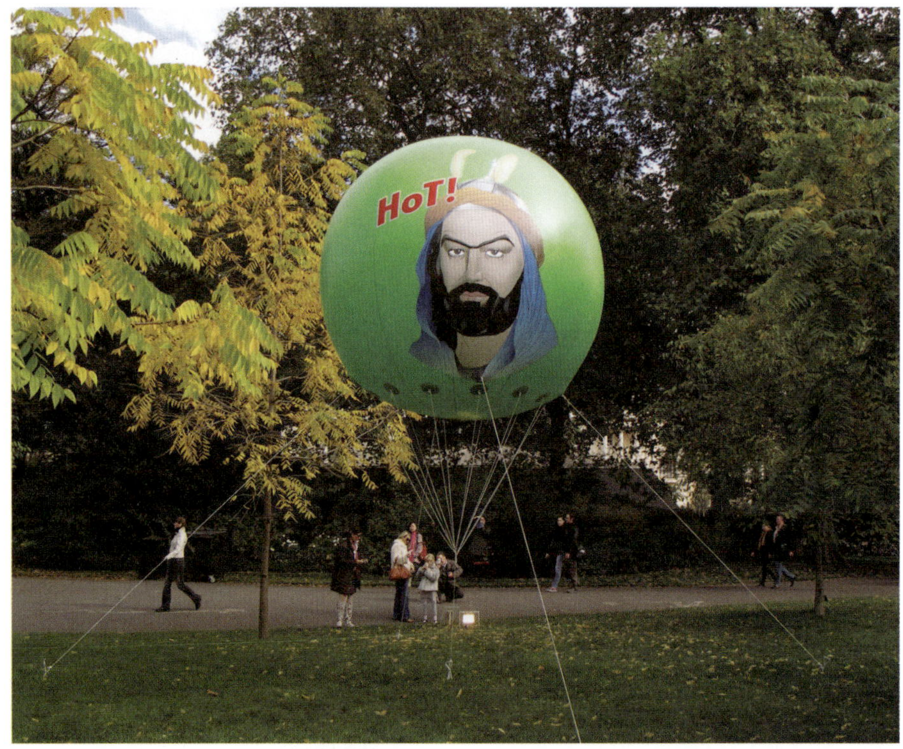

9

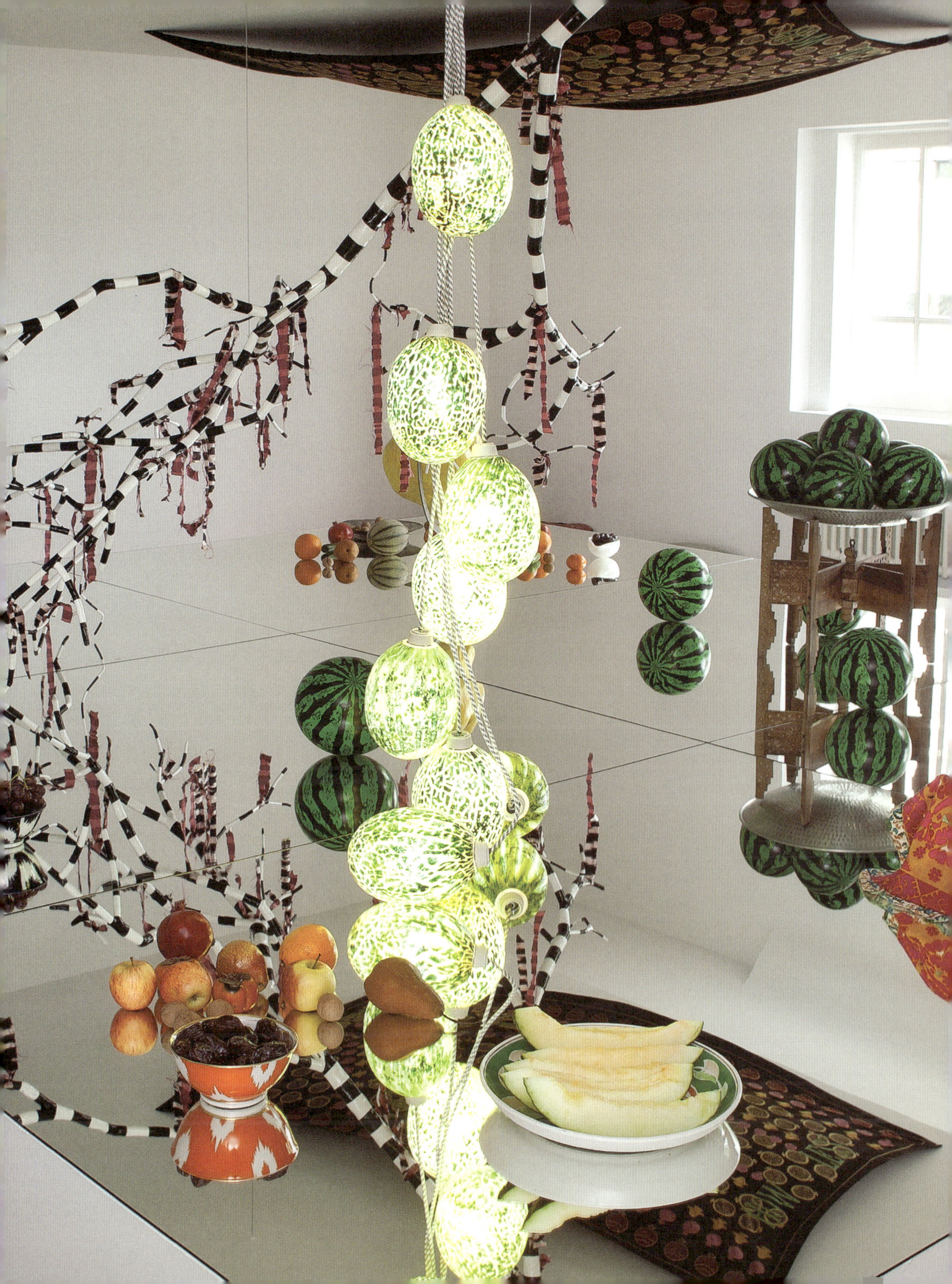

ACTIVE SINCE	CITY	WEBSITE
2004	Paris, France	societerealiste.net

Société Réaliste

MEMBERS	ACTIVITIES	RECOMMENDED PUBLICATION
Ferenc Gróf and Jean-Baptiste Naudy	Installation, Internet Art, Publishing, Urban Interventions	SOCIÉTÉ RÉALISTE, EMPIRE, STATE, BUILDING, CATALOGUE, Editions Amsterdam / Jeu de Paume / Ludwig Múzeum, Paris / Budapest, 2011

Paris-based cooperative Société Réaliste produces graphics, installations, publications, and services to propose a reinterpretation of Western symbols of economics and politics. In its hands, design assumes a dysfunctional dimension, putting into question the value of money, identity, and language, acting as a metaphor for the current process of geopolitical reorganization.

Why work collaboratively?

When we met for the first time, the two of us had already been a part of collaborative projects. We had a lot of common interests, especially artistic references, and we began a continuous conversation about contemporary art practice. The very first project we decided to work on was curatorial research: we were very much interested in "socialist realism," both in how this aesthetic credo became the dominant form of art production in the communist bloc and how fast it disappeared from the official corpus of contemporary art after 1989. The main focus of our research was to try to understand the basic relationship this aesthetics had to cultural politics and public taste in a way that didn't place it in opposition to "Western" contemporary art but in comparison to it. The inversion of the French term for socialist realism, "réalisme socialiste," into "Société Réaliste" became the name of our research, "société" meaning in French both "company" and "society." After some months, we were invited to make an exhibition in a gallery and instead of curating a show, we decided to produce artworks. Therefore "Société Réaliste" became the name of our collaboration. It also came to embody our connection as individuals, as well as our thematic scope and work methodology. it became a kind of third entity between the two of us.

How do you determine membership? Does physical location matter in this regard?

Membership as such is not relevant in the case of Société Réaliste, since it is primarily about our collaboration. To that extent, we are a duo named by a very generic term. It happens very often that people think we are a lot of persons. Which is for the best, considering that we never meant to be perceived as a duo; we never signed works with our civil names; we prefer to be perceived under this potentially multitudinous term. But as a matter of fact, we could not add a member to Société Réaliste; if we did, it would simply become something else. Regarding physical location, we met in Paris and have always worked in Paris. Our collaboration being continuous and regular, we need to meet almost every day. Living in the same city is crucial.

If considered separately, how do your individual artistic practices contribute to or detract from your work as a group?

The fact is that since 2004, we have systematically worked together on all our projects, putting aside our individual practices. Even though we had different backgrounds, one coming from the field of visual and applied arts, the other coming from textual and theoretical practice, we have progressively merged our specificities into one corpus of work in which those practices are equivalent. We consider the variety of our productions, from sculptures to lectures, from Internet-based work to publishing, as synonymous.

How are decisions made?

Out of discussion or obviousness. Most of the time, one of us has an idea that launches a conversation out of which

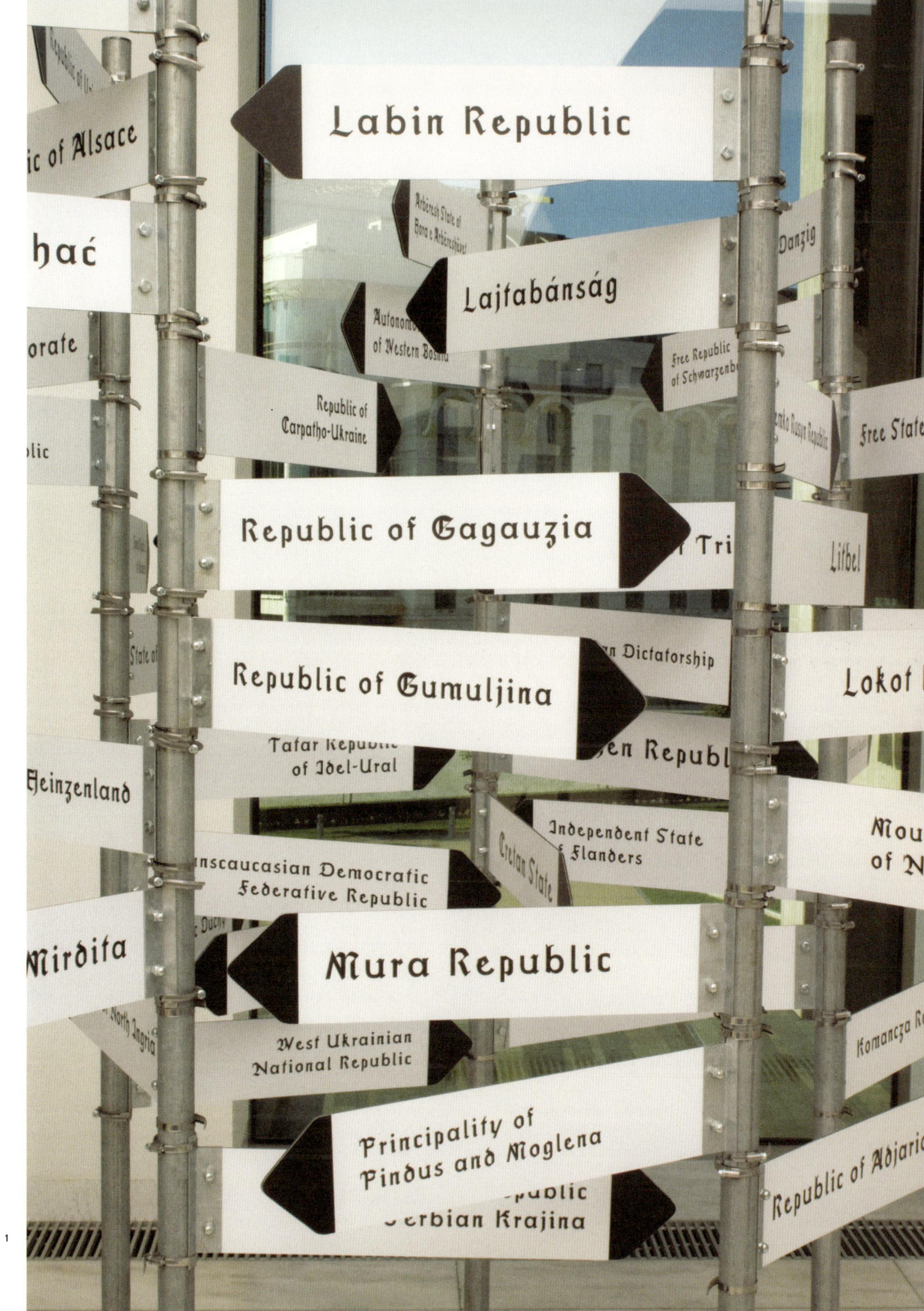

Labin Republic
Lajtabánság
Republic of Carpatho-Ukraine
Free Republic
Danzig
Free State
Republic of Gagauzia
Litbel
Republic of Gumuljina
Tatar Republic of Idel-Ural
Independent State of Flanders
Cretan State
Federative Republic
Mura Republic
West Ukrainian National Republic
Principality of Pindus and Moglena
Republic of Adjaria

1

previous
1 – Windroad, installation, Ludwig Museum, Budapest, 2012

2 – Spectral Aerosion, engraved necurite, 2011

3 – Portrait of Société Réaliste (Ferenc Gróf & Jean-Baptiste Naudy)

4 – L'Avenir Dure Longtemps, Appendix, installation, Les Ateliers Biennale d'Art Contemporain de Rennes, Couvent des Jacobins, Rennes, 2010

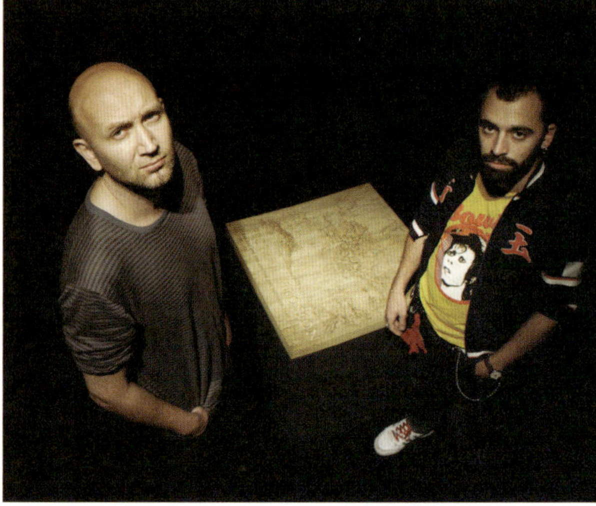

3

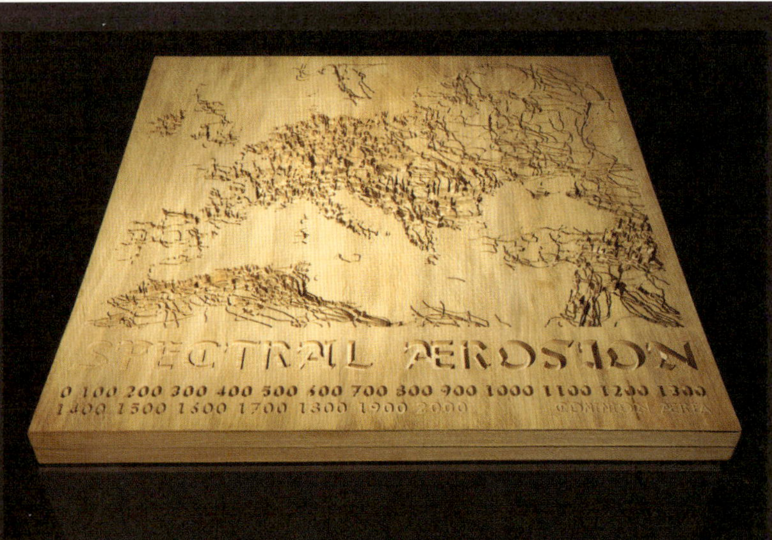

2

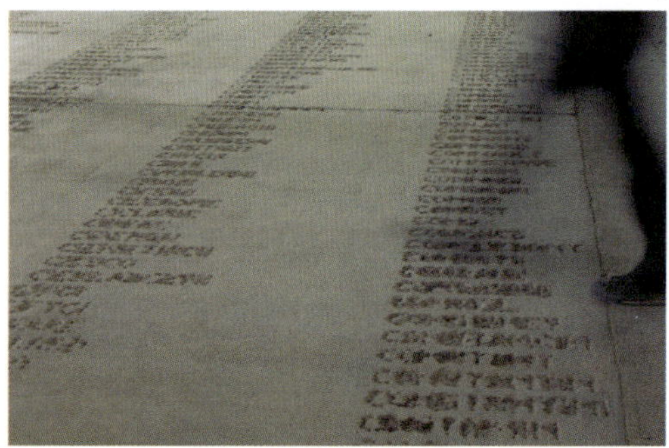

4

we elaborate, up to the moment when it is obvious for the both of us that we have found what we were looking for. The more it is obvious for the both of us, the more it can be named a Société Réaliste's work. If the outcome is incontestable for us, we do it. If one of us doubts, we leave it aside.

Does each of you have a clearly defined role? If so, what are some of each member's distinct responsibilities?

One of the reasons why we call ourselves a cooperative is the necessity of polyvalence. The same way that we make decisions out of discussion, we do construct our works together, without having technical specificities. In a cooperative, everything is shared, responsibility, resources, outcomes, authorship, influence.

How important is each group member's individuality, both in terms of your artistic production and in terms of your relationship with the media? Does anonymity come into play?

If you consider collaborative work as being a vector between a multiplicity of points, Société Réaliste is what lies between the two of us, whatever our individualities happen to be. The excesses of one are always held back by the other, the obsessions of one are opened up by the obsessions of the other, etc. The necessity to find a common language refrains us from egocentric crises and cryptic mumbling. Anonymity is not at stake, because Société Réaliste is a specific name covering a distinct entity made of two precise individuals, but it's better to think of it as depersonalization, or even repersonalization, dissolving into a third entity that we create every day out of the continuous process of working together. Maybe will we know what it is precisely only after its end.

What is the relationship between your working methods and your art's "content"? In this sense, does technology tend to play more of a supporting role, or does it lead you in new directions?

Being inheritors of the conceptual art history and the technological devices we use, the medium is the outcome. We always start from the discourse, from imagination, from ideas, and we progressively go toward its physical realization. Of course, the adequacy between the original idea and the material result that is the artwork is decisive, but we never start from a technique or a technological possibility. This is also a reason why we can make a work vary, change its form throughout time, remake it differently,

5 – EU Green Card Lottery Registration Office, installation, Article Biennale, Stavanger, Norway, 2006

6 – Invisible Hand, graffiti, Galerija Škuc, Ljubljana, 2008

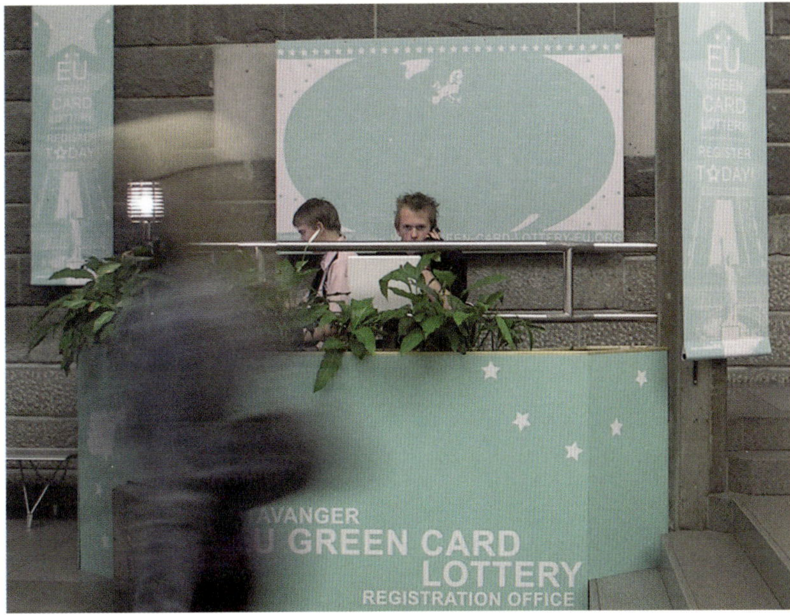

5

6

while keeping its original idea. Sometimes, such as in the case of our EU Green Card Lottery project, the physical objects are only the appearance of the work itself, which is online. But the artwork is not just the website, or the documentation, or the registration offices that we install: it is the whole of it.

How does your collaboration relate to its cultural, institutional, and commercial contexts? In other words, how would you respond to those who call this a trend?

We have never asked ourselves if we are collaborating together because it is a trend. A trend would mean that the collaborative process has never happened before and suddenly appears as a generalized form of working. It is clearly not the case. Since the emergence of modern art, collaboration between artists, art collectives, or duos has been frequent. It seems pretty difficult to consider this as a trend, unless a trend can last for more than a century: from the collaboration between Mayakovsky and Rodchenko to Art & Language, General Idea, or IRWIN, it covers such a long period and such a variety of contexts that it is not representative of something other than modern and contemporary art in general.

Who is your audience?

It depends very much on the project. Most of the time, because of the museum or gallery context, it is the art audience. Sometimes, when we do a public art project or an online project, it is the passersby. In terms of the content and form of our work, potentially, it is everybody.

Does your engagement with one another translate into an engagement with the public? How so?

We do not make participative projects as such, involving the audience as a medium of the work. Our engagement toward the audience is more conceptual and speculative: we do consider people as being able to forge their own key to access and take advantage of our proposals. If our collaboration implies something for the audience, it is the productiveness of working cooperatively, and that if it is viable in the sphere of art, it is as well in any other field.

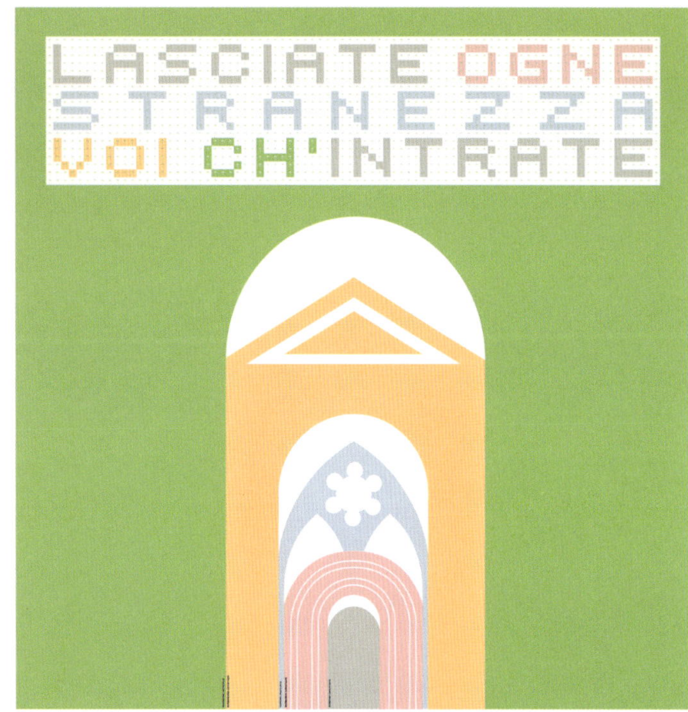

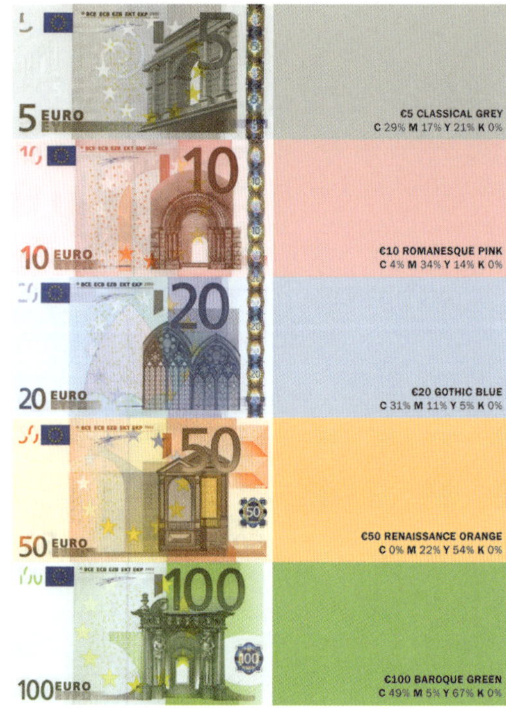

7

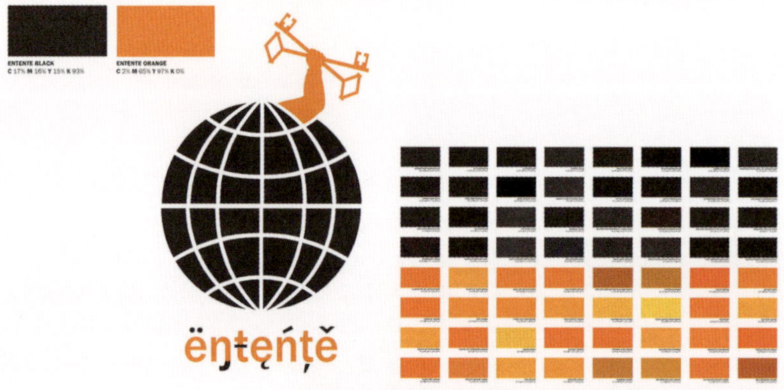

8

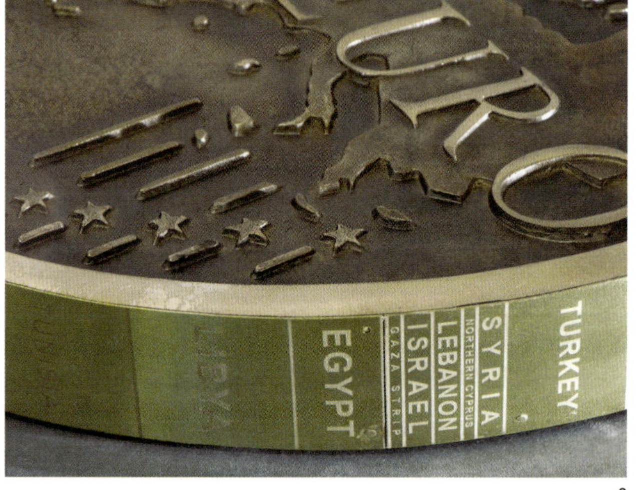

9

7 – Archivolt of Straits, digital print, 2009

8 – Transitioners: Entente, digital print, 2006

9 – Marka: 1 Euro Coin, engraved bronze and copper, 2008

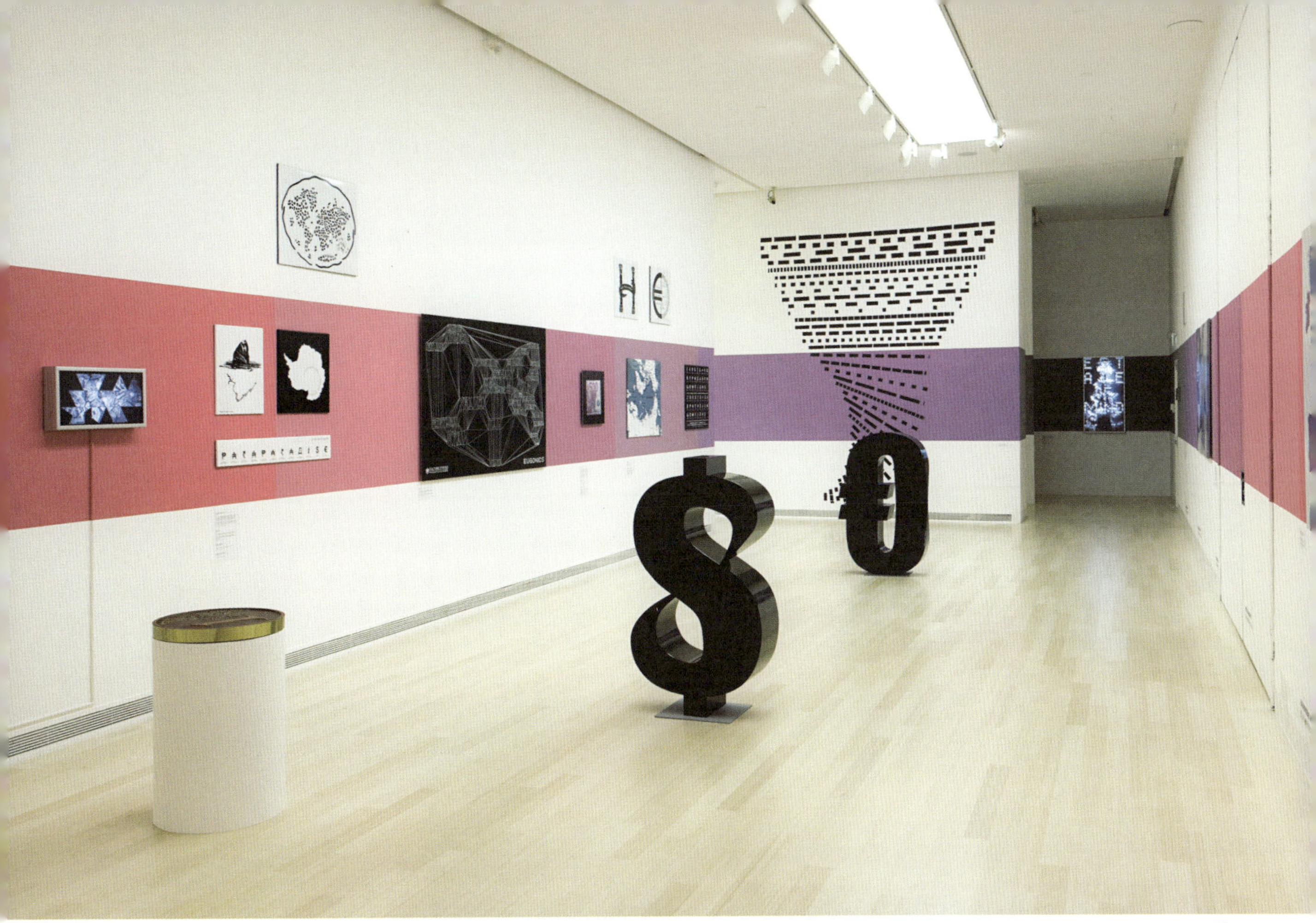

10

10 – Empire, State, Building, installation, Ludwig Museum, Budapest, 2012

11 – New Alphabetical Order, enamel plate, 2009

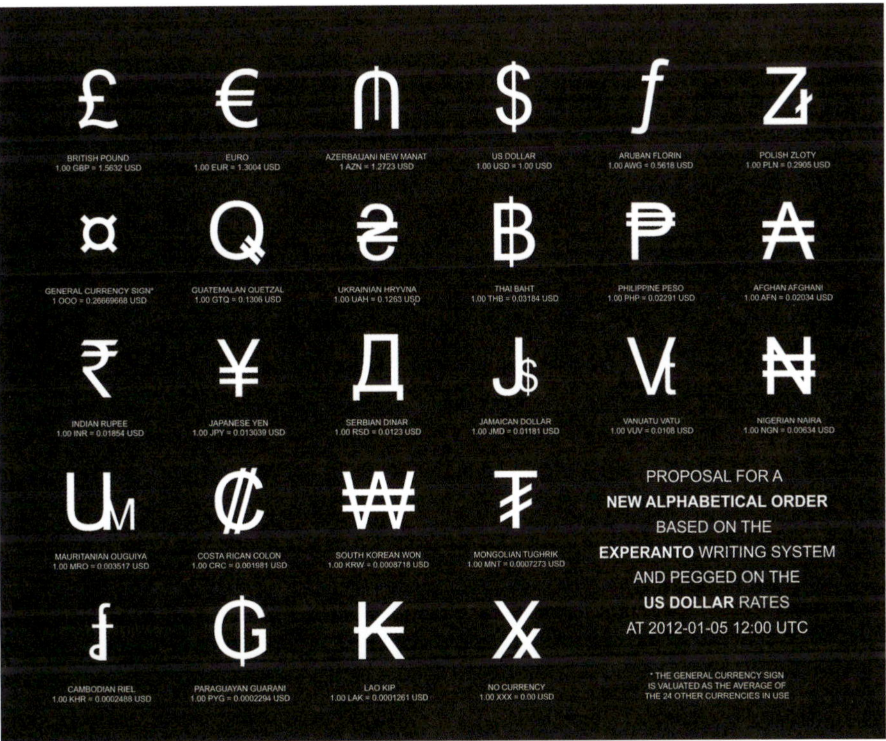

11

ACTIVE SINCE	CITY	WEBSITE
1999	London, UK	spacehijackers.org

Space Hijackers

MEMBERS	ACTIVITIES	RECOMMENDED PUBLICATION
Secret Agents with Agent Names	Brandalism, Community Projects, Culture Jamming, Impersonation, Internet Art, Merchandising, Painting / Sculpture / Installation, Public Performance, Publishing, Situationism, Urban Interventions, Video / Television / Film	Jamie Kelsey-Fry and Anita Dhillon, The Rax Active Citizenship Toolkit: GCSE Citizenship Studies Skills and Processes, New Internationalist, Oxford, 2010

Anarchitecture group Space Hijackers works halfway between art and activism, bringing imagination to the streets of Great Britain. Initially getting attention for its Circle Line Party series, improvised parties on subway trains, the group has expanded its activities to midnight cricket games, carnivalesque military parades, and protests against corporations, the police, and the Olympic Games.

Why work collaboratively?

Collaboration is the only way we can turn our ideas into action. Although many of us have our own solo projects and careers, we still rely on the core network of the group to help with those. Because our ideas are quite complex, they also benefit from many extra pairs of eyes and sets of minds to manifest them.

How do you determine membership? Does physical location matter in this regard?

Our meetings are open. They happen on the third Thursday of every month—usually at our HQ, which also serves as artist studios for many in our collective. Everyone is welcome to come but they have to wear red underwear to prove they are not police. Of course.

Geographic location doesn't really matter—we used to have a Singapore branch and many of our number travel internationally. Quite a few have relocated outside of London. They do the odd hijackery action where they are, but we suppose we can be considered London-based.

If considered separately, how do your individual artistic practices contribute to or detract from your work as a group?

Individuals often have ideas they would like the group to be a part of—and the ones we come up with at meetings are taken as "Hijacker ideas." Individual solo stuff can and does involve a number of Hijackers in its production. Our diversity is our strength. For instance, someone who is more of a performance artist or gamer in his or her solo practice will bring that to certain actions. Graphic designers will come in and take care of the graphic and logo *détournements*. Writers handle the copy; street artists take care of the criminal damage; hackers take care of our Internet presence. Those who can build things, build things. Those who can drink, drink. And dance awkwardly.

How are decisions made?

Whoever shouts the loudest sometimes wins. But usually it's the idea that gets everyone excited or laughing. Sometimes we put it to a vote but we usually come to a decision before it gets that drastic.

Does each of you have a clearly defined role? If so, what are some of each member's distinct responsibilities?

No. We have strengths and skills but those don't predetermine who does what. Some people do tend to come up with more actions than others—but that's balanced out by others being better at editing those ideas into something more coherent or politically clear. It's all very ad hoc. You could say we're

1 – Official Protesters of the London 2012 Olympic Games T-shirt graphics, 2012

2 – Love is…Not War, poster, 2003

3 – Olympic Words, public billboard, London, 2012

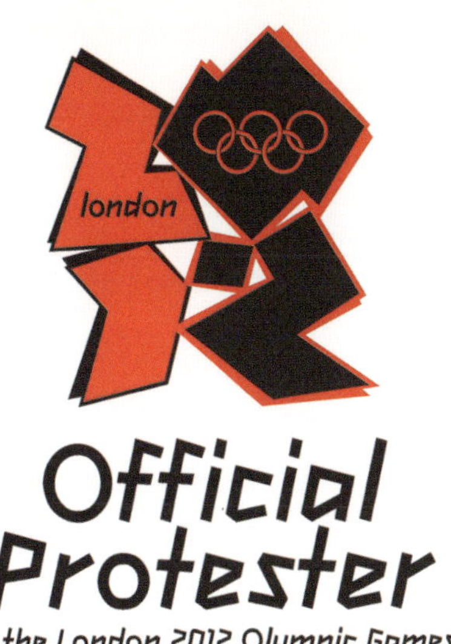

1

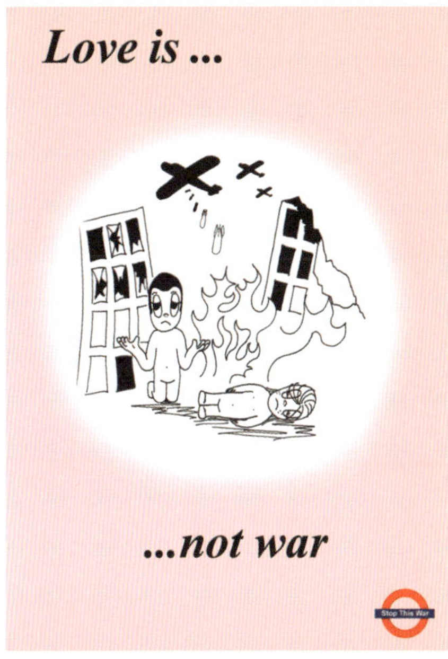

2

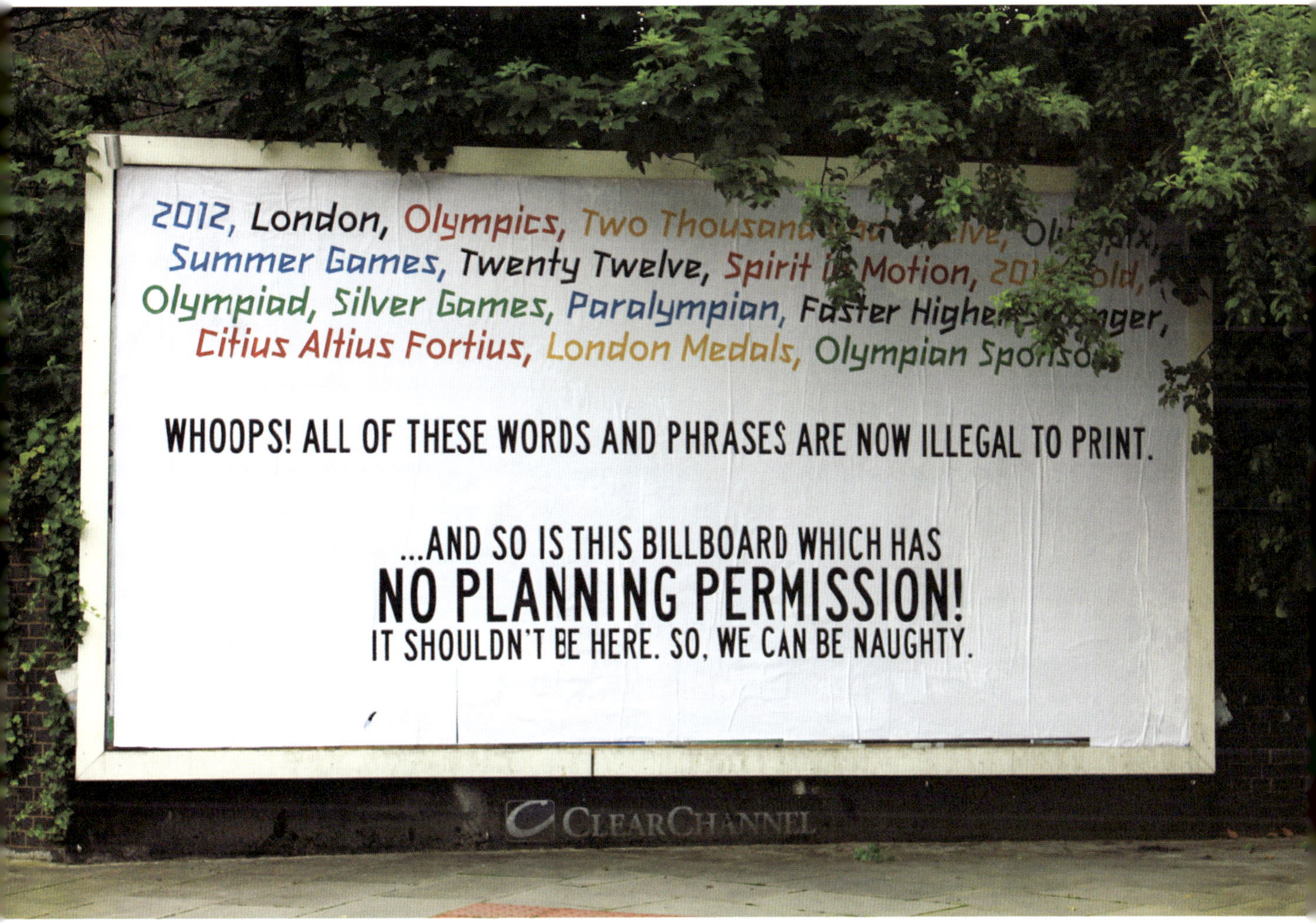

3

more of a disorganization. We're serious about keeping the collective alive but it isn't the be all and end all of our existences.

How important is each group member's individuality, both in terms of your artistic production and in terms of your relationship with the media? Does anonymity come into play?

We all have agent names—you come up with your name at the first meeting you attend. Otherwise you get landed with names like Agent Felchdrinker (who later changed his to CSM). They're not terribly hard to work out, either. We have an Agent Hardcastle, an Agent Jewksy, an Agent Patelaneeta (it's an anagram). We use these in semijokey ways, more like nicknames. We're not too strict about using them unless we're dealing with non-Hijackers. For those dealings we like to keep a certain degree of anonymity, because some of us have rather surprising day jobs. And they do come in handy at demonstrations when you don't want to yell "George!" across a line of police.

Those who feel they can't afford to appear on television don't. Those who are better suited to write things or to do radio take care of that. But not every Hijacker does media. Some of us don't agree with it. For each action, we tend to come up with a party line and stick with that. But we all agree that there's no point in doing things unless people hear about it. It's not hard to figure out who our more prominent media whore agents are but we do try to balance that out a bit.

What is the relationship between your working methods and your art's "content"? In this sense, does technology tend to play more of a supporting role, or does it lead you in new directions?

This depends entirely on the action. For instance, when we declared ourselves the Official Protesters of the London 2012 Olympic Games, we blitzed social media and our extensive media contacts with a story about corporate censorship that spread all over the world. Technology and the global Internet space was the platform. Some of this led to media interest from television and radio—thus bringing things into the "real world." On the whole, we consider that a successful action that shamed LOCOG and Twitter and brought out the point we were trying to make—that the Olympics helped no one but corporations and the government agencies allied to them. Real people and their stories were silenced. By causing enough of a stink we hope that we helped some of those narratives to come out, because the real Olympic legacy is who gets left behind.

Technology is important. As is social media and having working media contacts. It kinda helps that some of us are already part of that world in our daily lives—so we have a deep understanding of how PR and press works.

How does your collaboration relate to its cultural, institutional, and commercial contexts? In other words, how would you respond to those who call this a trend?

We've been around since 1999. We've seen actions that we came up with over ten years ago reappropriated and retranslated by the likes of UKUncut and other more outwardly activist, single-issue groups. That's exactly what we want. We have no particular sense of ownership over ideas—we're usually over the moon when someone decides to hold a Circle Line party of his or her own... or buys a tank or decides to pretend to be a corporation on national TV. We've succeeded by passing that possibility of naughtiness on to someone else.

We're not single issue, either. We tackle power structures in general, and then each action narrows things down to specifics. Space can be physical or virtual so our remit transcends trends and fashions. While the press is busy jumping on bandwagons, we're usually up ahead building the next one.

Who is your audience?

What kind of a question is that? Of course everyone will answer with something mundane like "everybody" or "anyone who'll listen." Seriously...? Dunno...depends on the action. Sometimes it's the world and a government or corporation. Other times it's just us.

Does your engagement with one another translate into an engagement with the public? How so?

Well, if sometimes our audience is the world and other times our audience is us, then...erm...how can we not engage? The point is not to always engage and be engaging but to make sure some change comes out of that effort. Everything else is academic.

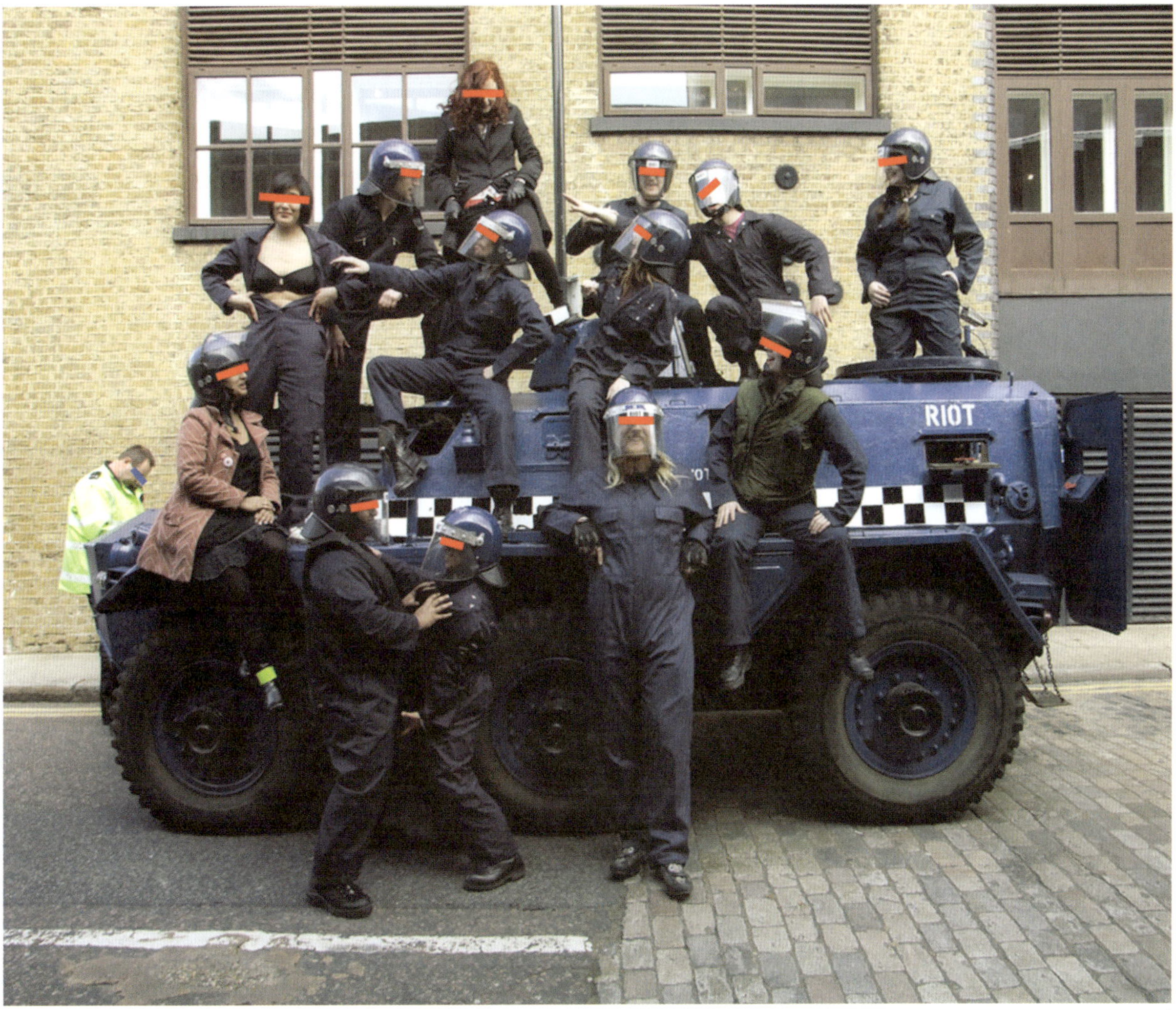

4

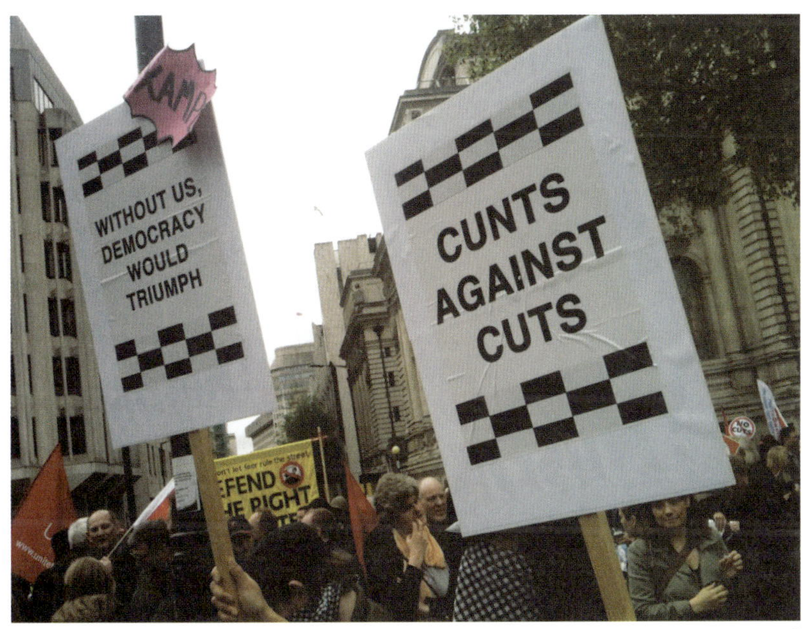

5

4 – G20 Tank, public performance, London, 2009

5 – Police Protest Stall, public protest, London, 2008

ACTIVE SINCE	CITY	WEBSITE
1993	Copenhagen, Denmark	superflex.net

SUPERFLEX

MEMBERS	ACTIVITIES	RECOMMENDED PUBLICATION
Jakob Fenger, Bjørnstjerne Christiansen, and Rasmus Nielsen	Community Projects, Curating, Internet Art, Merchandising, Music, Painting / Sculpture / Installation, Public Performance, Publishing, Tools—the Creation of Tools, Urban Interventions	Barbara Steiner and SUPERFLEX (eds.), SUPERFLEX: Tools, Verlag Der Büchhandlung Walther König, Cologne, 2003

Known for suggesting alternative forms of production, SUPERFLEX has served as model of self-organization for both younger art groups and liberal commercial enterprises. Its open-source beers, biogas units for remote human settlements, and free shops could realistically enter the market but they are also commentaries on the condition of developing countries in a global economy.

Why work collaboratively?

That's a good question. But perhaps we need to understand its opposite to be able to answer it. Why work individually? Or even ask the question: Is there such a thing as individual work? In the creation of things, we are all building on someone else's work and we approach the world as part-time schizophrenics consisting of multiple personalities. So where is the individual actually performing the work? Perhaps it only exists as a social construct applied sometime after the work has been executed. Surely the market seems to like this construct. But that might not be the whole reason. The ego acts in mysterious ways. But to answer the question about working collaboratively, we would simply have to state that individual work does notexist as such and therefore all work is collaborative.

How do you determine membership? Does physical location matter in this regard?

The kernel of SUPERFLEX has always been the three partners. In periods we have worked closely with others, mainly people coming from different professions and disciplines. These people have been close partners, some for years, on individual projects. Often we have shared our office with them as well. Physical location matters but is not always possible. Over the years we have had partners in Amazonas and in Liverpool.

If considered separately, how do your individual artistic practices contribute to or detract from your work as a group?

We don't have an individual artistic practice besides SUPERFLEX. This is not an agreement written in blood but there has simply never been the interest nor the energy. However, if one member suddenly would turn up saying he has written a poetry collection, I believe the others would be surprised but endorse the idea nevertheless.

How are decisions made?

Collectively on conceptual matters and individually on practical matters. Usually persistence is a key factor in decision-making processes. Which side of the argument lasted longest when being challenged. The answer is in the air but needs to be caught. We usually all know when we have it. It's like the invisible hand of SUPERFLEX operating.

Does each of you have a clearly defined role? If so, what are some of each member's distinct responsibilities?

We try to avoid this since specialization is to collectives what gentrification is to cities. It simply makes them boring.

How important is each group member's individuality, both in terms of your artistic production and in terms of your relationship with the media? Does anonymity come into play?

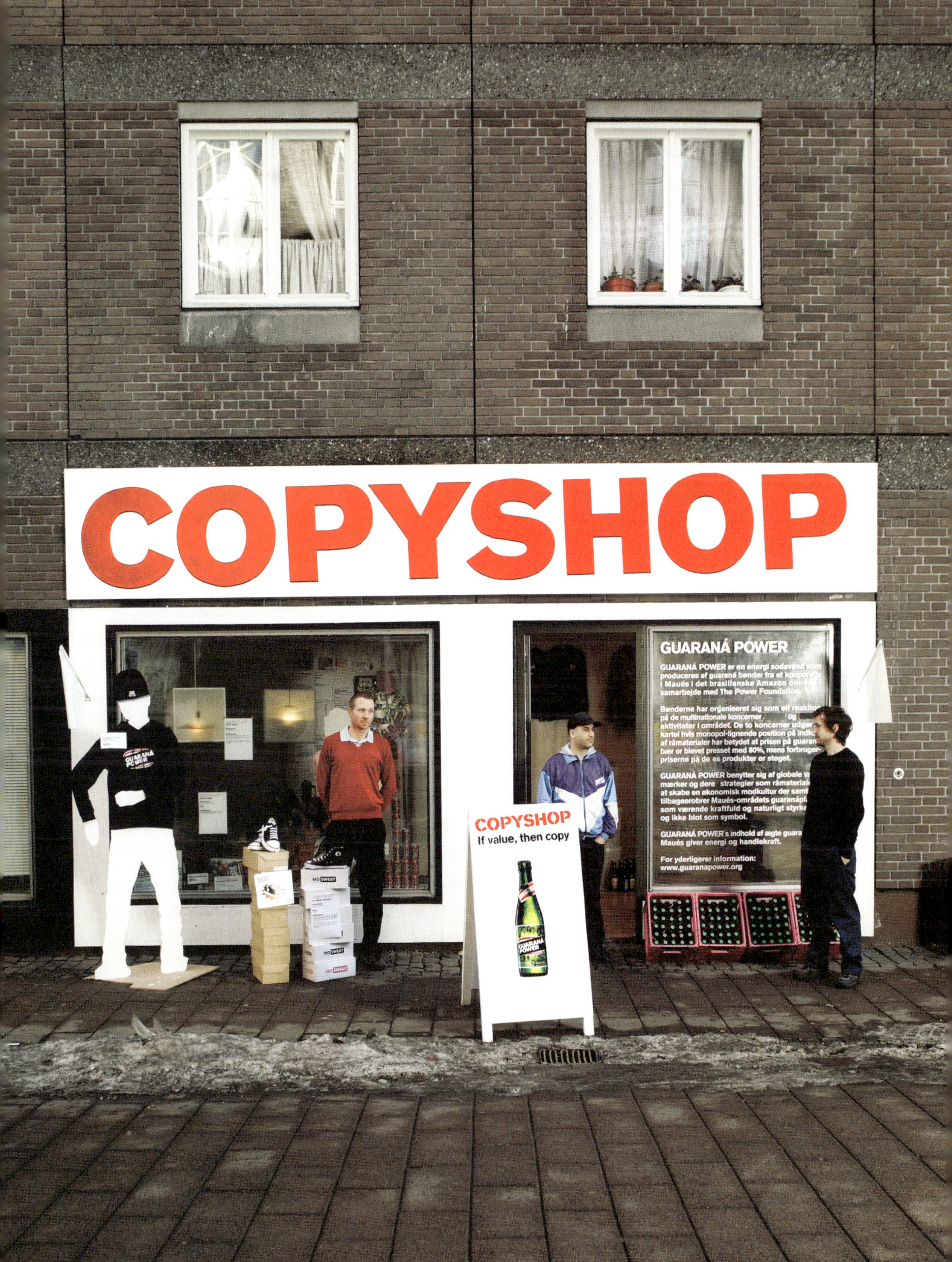
COPYSHOP
GUARANÁ POWER
GUARANÁ POWER er en energi sodavand som
produceres af guaraná bønder fra et kooperativ
i Maués i det brasilianske Amazon område i
samarbejde med The Power Foundation.
Bønderne har organiseret sig som en reaktion
på de multinationale koncerner og
aktiviteter i området. De to koncerner udgør
kartel hvis monopol-lignende position på indk
af råmaterialer har betydet at prisen på guaran
bær er blevet presset med 80%, mens forbruger-
priserne på de es produkter er steget.
GUARANÁ POWER benytter sig af globale
mærker og dere strategier som råmateriale
at skabe en økonomisk modkultur der samt
tilbageerobrer Maués-områdets guaranápl
som værende kraftfuld og naturligt styrke
og ikke blot som symbol.
GUARANÁ POWER's indhold af ægte guara
Maués giver energi og handlekraft.
For yderligerer information:
www.guaranapower.org
COPYSHOP
If value, then copy
NO SWEAT

previous
1 – Superflex in collaboration with Copenhagen Brains, COPYSHOP, store, Copenhagen, 2005–2007

2 – Euro, billboard for the exhibition Show Off, presented at Malmö Konsthall, Sweden, and Point Centre for Contemporay Art, Cyprus, 2012

3 – Guaraná Power bottle packaging, for a soft drink produced in collaboration with a guaraná farmers' cooperative from Maués in the Brazilian Amazon, 2003

4 – Guaraná Power Production/Bar, bottling of Guaraná Power and sales, Venice Biennale, Venice, 2003

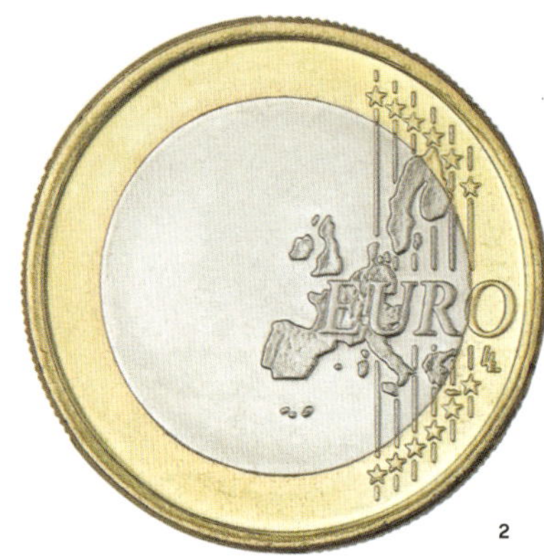

2

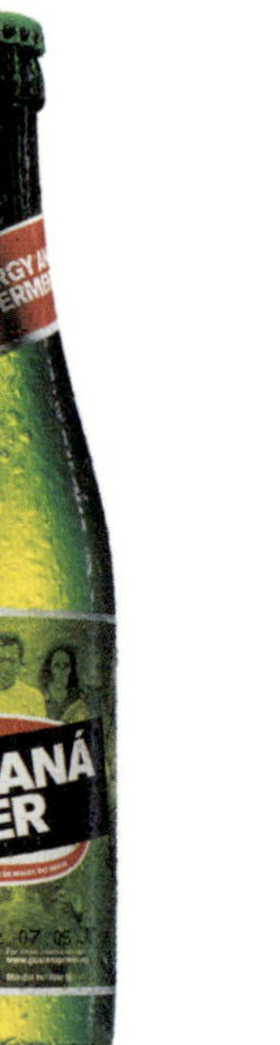

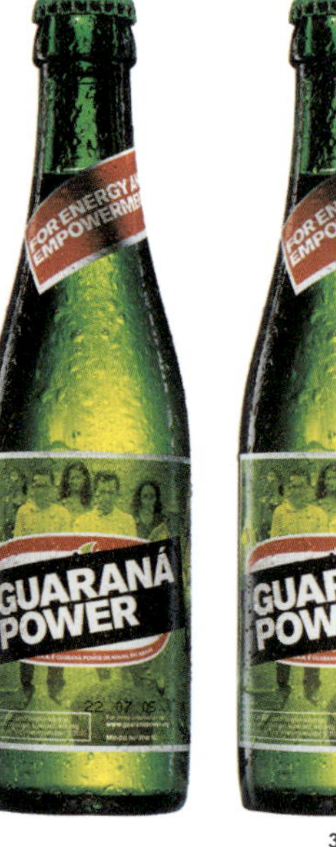

3

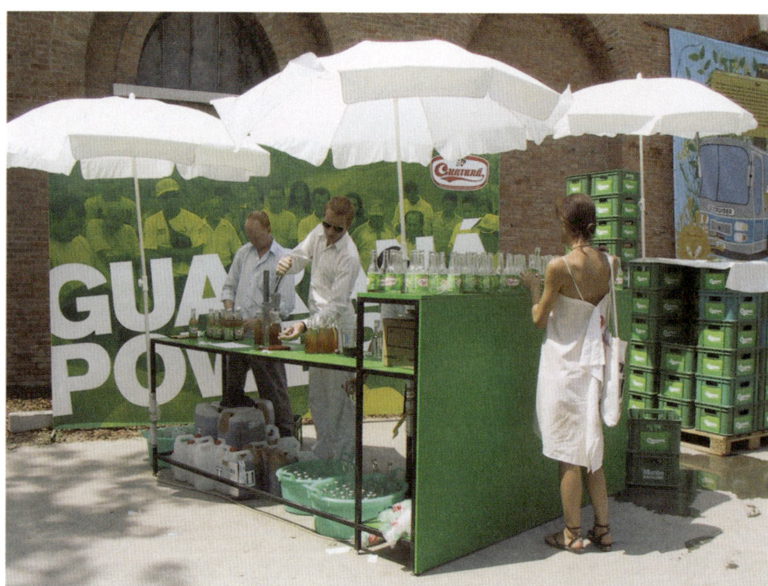

4

We never wanted to boost our individuality, neither in relation to the work nor the media. You will find very few obvious biographical elements in the work and very rarely personal elements being used externally toward the media. On the other hand, the group consists of the collective capital of the individuals. Who they are and what the equation of these personalities brings about. So in that sense individuality means everything and nothing.

What is the relationship between your working methods and your art's "content"? In this sense, does technology tend to play more of a supporting role, or does it lead you in new directions?

A large part of our work has actively produced what you refer to as technology. In 1996 we started conceptualizing and building small scale biogas systems. In 1999 we made an internet broadcasting system, what today is referred to as a content management system, that enabled users not familiar with media production to become media producers. These processes are extremely demanding in terms of time. Perhaps one can argue that the development of these tools was an extension of the power of collective organizing. That the social strength is turned into a technological strength that operates against the idea of making us all into passive consumers.

How does your collaboration relate to its cultural, institutional, and commercial contexts? In other words, how would you respond to those who call this a trend?

Not sure exactly how to grasp that question. But we consider ourselves to be citizens of capitalism. This is the mainframe in which we are operating. To claim anything else would be unwise and to relate to this can hardly be called a trend. Rather, what we deal with is identity politics on a megascale. There are individuals and groups trying to grasp the context they are operating within and what this context makes them into. But really, not much of SUPERFLEX work goes in this direction. Specifically, we are neither turned on nor turned off by the politics of the institutions of art. They

5 – FREE BEER/Brewing Kit, installation at Centre d'Art Contemporain, Geneva, 2007

6 – Rirkrit Tiravanija and SUPERFLEX, Social Pudding, packaging for pudding produced through a workshop, GfZK, Leipzig, 2003, and 1301PE, Los Angeles, 2004. Design: SUPERFLEX and Rasmus Koch

7 – Supergas, Biogas unit, Cambodia, 2001

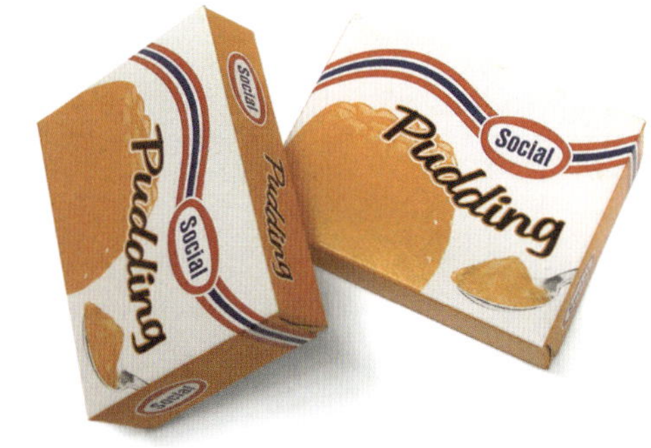

6

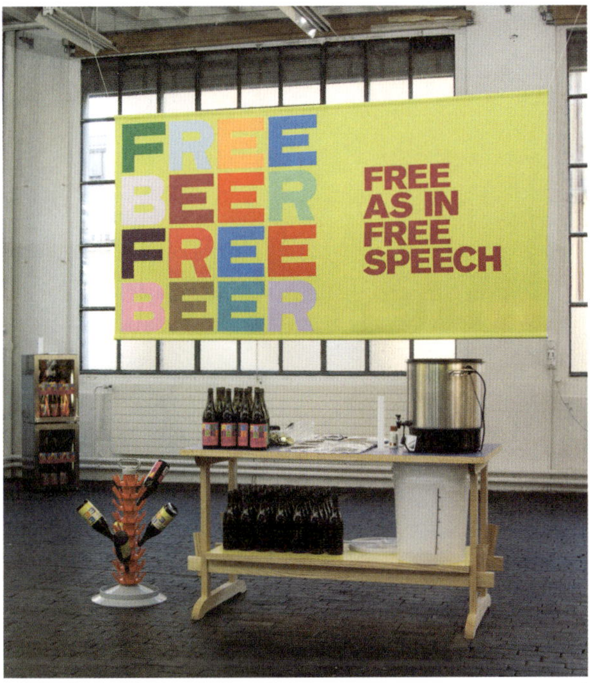

5

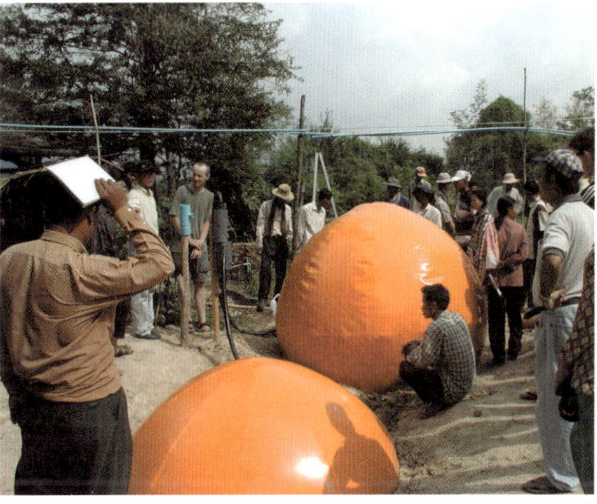

7

exist in the world, as does Starbucks, where we occasionally will buy coffee. But the fact that Starbuck is actually a character in the novel Moby Dick simply does not interest us. We just go there for the coffee. At this moment in time the art world behaves like the imperial British Empire in its heyday, thriving from constant expansion. We are guilty of extensively pirating on this for various purposes. Most probably we have also been pirated upon but we like to believe that the balance is in our favor.

Who is your audience?

At an early point, meaning the last millennium, we started relating to our work as tools. Tools that would acquire their meaning through some sort of use. Basically that the tools would never be regarded as the end product, but rather the cue to something, in a participatory manner. In that sense the audience does not exist. There are users of the tools and the use of tools. In Internet terms this could be referred to as the power of the protocols.

But then again one should be weary with words and what time does to words. Was it not the former president of the World Trade Organization who recently described his organization as one built upon participation? The users are the producers and so forth. So the participatory buzz has reached the higher echelons of capitalism. Another example of the blurring of the audience factor is off course Facebook, which we could regard as a perversion of relational aesthetics. A giant empire whose real audience might just be the CIA.

Does your engagement with one another translate into an engagement with the public? How so?

Not really.

8 – FREE SHOP, Family Mart, Tokyo, 2003

9 – Superkilen, urban park project, urban furniture gathered from more than fifty different countries, Nørrebro, Copenhagen, 2011

opposite
10 – Today we do not use the word "Recession," Lord Councillor Dara Murphy, mayor of Cork, Ireland, signs a decree advocating that for one day, on June 17, 2010, the citizens of Cork should refrain from using the word "recession."

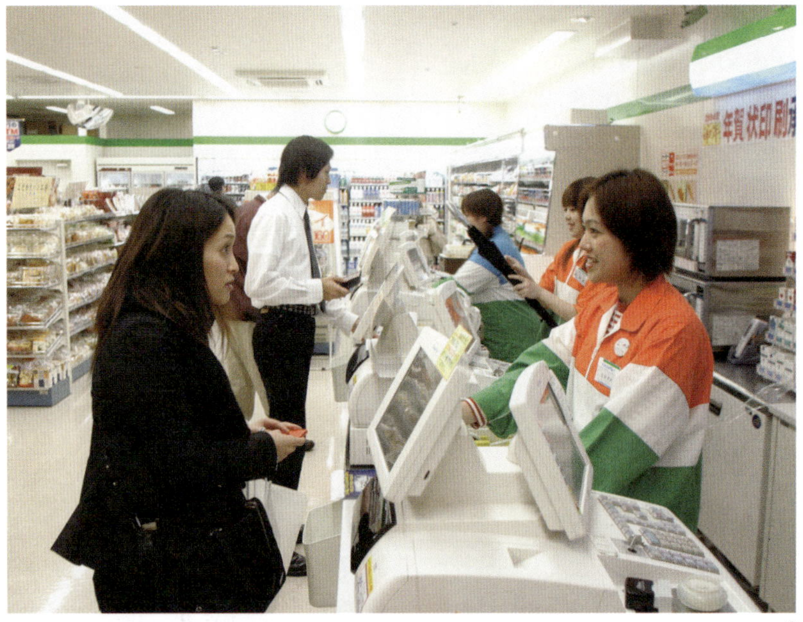

8

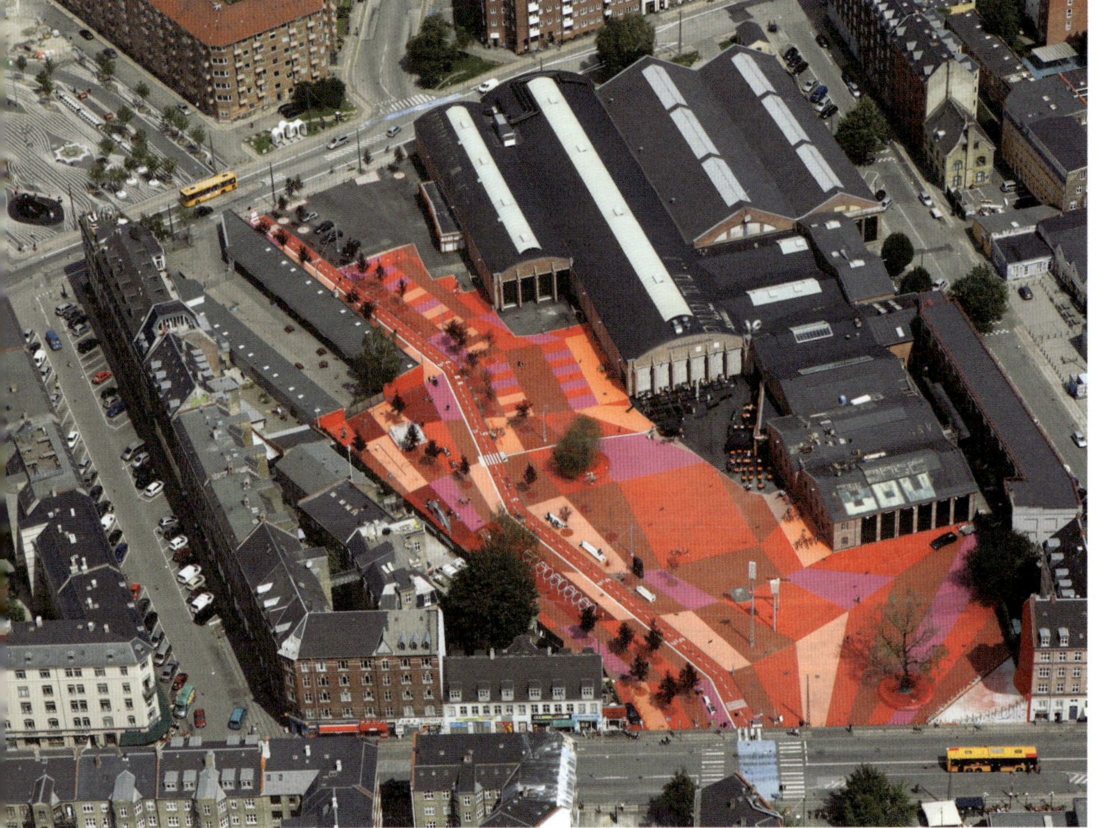

9

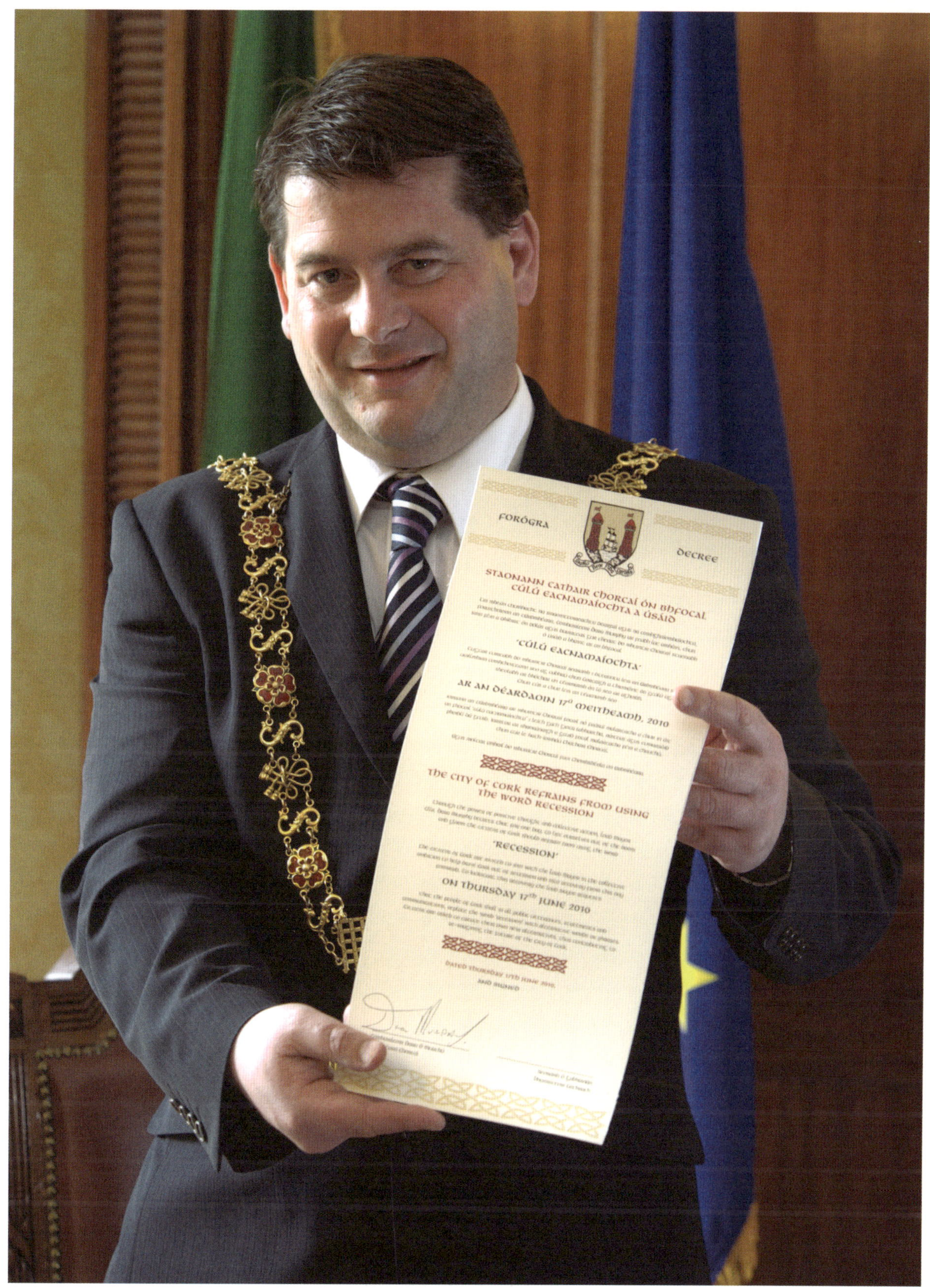
FORÓGRA
DECREE
STAONANN CATHAIR CHORCAÍ ÓN BHFOCAL CÚLÚ EACNAMAÍOCHTA A ÚSÁID
'CÚLÚ EACNAMAÍOCHTA'
AR AN DÉARDAOIN 17ú MEITHEAMH, 2010
THE CITY OF CORK REFRAINS FROM USING THE WORD RECESSION
'RECESSION'
ON THURSDAY 17th JUNE 2010

10

ACTIVE SINCE	CITY	WEBSITE
1998	Chicago, U.S. / Copenhagen, Denmark / Philadelphia, U.S.	temporaryservices.org

Temporary Services

MEMBERS	ACTIVITIES	RECOMMENDED PUBLICATION
Marc Fischer, Brett Bloom, and Salem Collo-Julin	Community Projects, Curating, Music, Publishing, Urban Interventions	TEMPORARY SERVICES (eds.), Group Work, Printed Matter, New York, 2007

Started as an artists' space in Chicago, Temporary Services has become a publisher, curatorial collective, and organizer of community workshops and projects. Its "self-reliance" libraries, nonprofit markets, and publications on anonymous public creative phenomena propose a reconsideration of the role, meaning, and value of culture in the public sphere.

Why work collaboratively?

There is no such thing as work that isn't collaborative. Everyone must rely on other people for their work to get out into the world. Language itself has been shaped by millions of people over the course of centuries. It is through this shared, collaborative work that we have words to signify meaning. Every aspect of bringing art to the world involves the work of others.

We put emphasis on the collaborative nature of human existence. We are interested in collapsing the limiting idea that art is an individual, solipsistic pursuit.

How do you determine membership? Does physical location matter in this regard?

We all started collaborating on work that predated the group. We enjoyed working together and this led us to formalize our relationships as Temporary Services. People joined Temporary Services in a rather organic way, sometimes from being invited or absorbed into meetings or after contributing to early projects.

We started in Chicago but currently live in three different cities. We have worked together for nearly fifteen years, which helps make this current arrangement possible. Our group membership has remained the same since 2002. We often collaborate with others outside of the group on a project basis, but have not tried to expand our membership in recent years.

If considered separately, how do your individual artistic practices contribute to or detract from your work as a group?

We don't proceed with our work from the place of our individual concerns and past or present individual artistic practices, but from the ideas or concerns we share as a group, and the challenges, questions, or invitations that our group takes on. We often talk about how we've maintained our group's work over many years and how life changes impact that. From that point, we could possibly discuss our individual realities, but this is not where we start that discussion.

How are decisions made?

We arrive at a consensus and only work on projects and include participants that all three group members agree on.

Does each of you have a clearly defined role? If so, what are some of each member's distinct responsibilities?

A group is a culture of people that is a complete thing. The production of that culture exceeds the individuals and even the things that they produce. When we work in a group we meet, have discussions, work on ideas, have more discussions, travel together, publish things, make websites, share documents on and offline, go to concerts, and share life in a way that also contributes to the group and becomes a part of the group work and identity. Each of us takes on different things, sometimes doing the same things when the others get tired of doing a boring task.

In a group you have to pay attention to everyone's needs and abilities and proceed from there. If you can't do this, people will drift away and your group will fall apart.

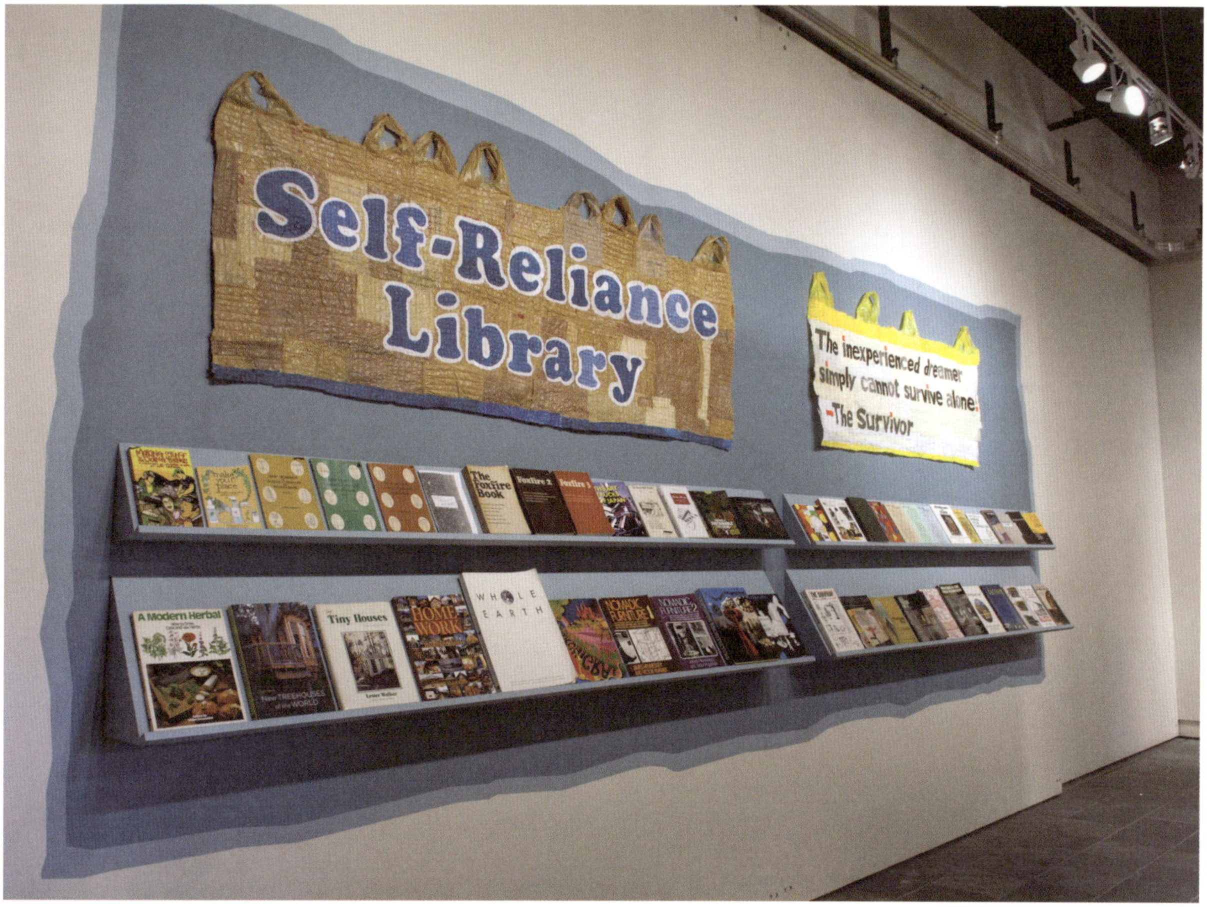

1

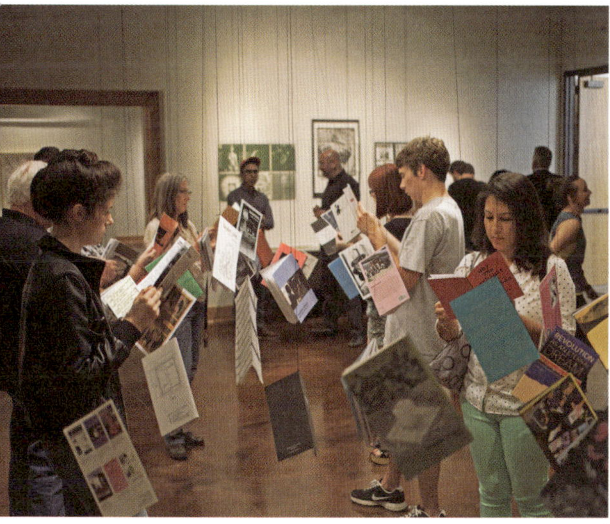

2

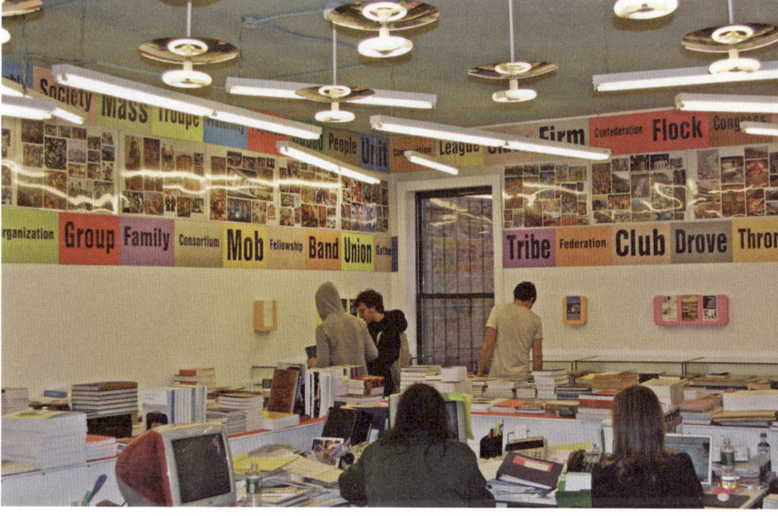

3

1 – Self-Reliance Library and Personal Plastic Banners, installation, Carnegie Mellon University, Pittsburgh, PA, 2011

2 – Booklet Cloud, installation, Texas State University, San Marcos, TX, 2013

3 – Aesthetic Analysis of Human Groupings, installation, Printed Matter, New York, 2007

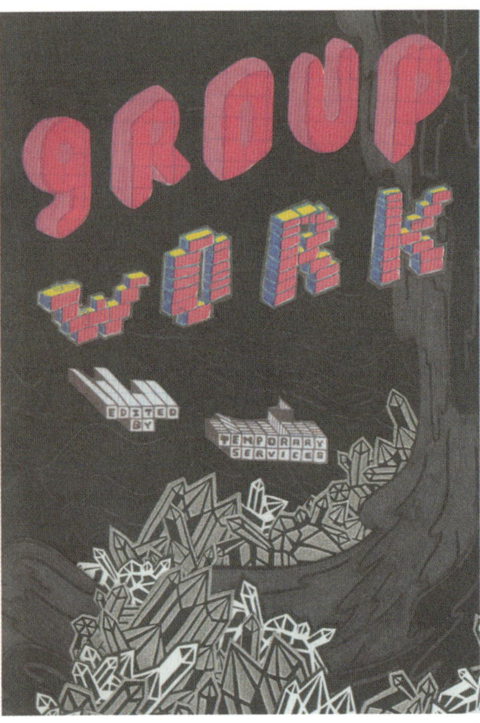

4

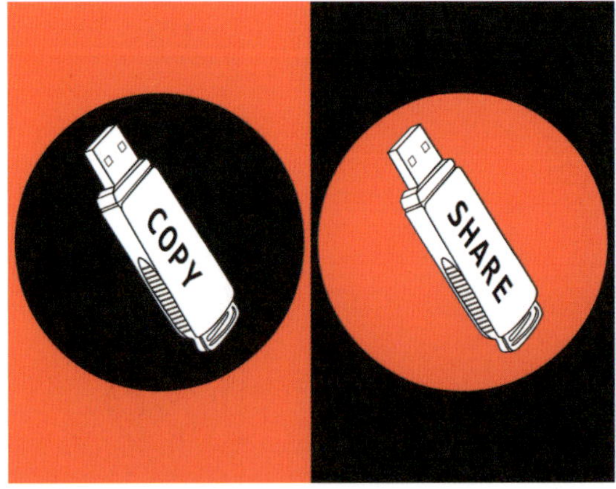

5

4 – Group Work, cover of the book, edited by Temporary Services and published by Printed Matter, New York, 2007. Cover art: Esteban Garcia and Nick Martin

5 – Designated Drivers booklet, inside front and back cover, 2011

opposite
6 – Music Mountain poster, 2012

opposite
7 – Why The Exhibit Was Canceled, cover of the book published by Temporary Services's Half Letter Press, 2001

How important is each group member's individuality, both in terms of your artistic production and in terms of your relationship with the media? Does anonymity come into play?

We author projects under a group name but don't conceal the names of members of the group. Unfortunately, we have had to assert to some people that our work and thoughts equally come from each member of the group. For example, in the past we have answered interview questions collectively as a group (through email, etc.) and then our responses were attributed to only one of us in print. This is a continual problem for many groups. People who are not in the group will assume that the group has some sort of internal hierarchy without asking. They will assume that a member of the group is "more important" based on vague ideas, such as one group member having a more visible presence in a cultural scene than the others. There seems to be a constant need for people to assign leadership to a person in groups in which a leader does not exist.

What is the relationship between your working methods and your art's "content"? In this sense, does technology tend to play more of a supporting role, or does it lead you in new directions?

We take on projects and direct the form our work takes based on our shared interests in the content, what we can manage and maintain, parameters such as where the work will be presented and the budget we have on hand, our skills and the skills of others we are working with outside of the group, and the fact that the three of us no longer live in the same city. Our approach is flexible and responsive to shifting conditions and sites. We have embraced changes in technology as needed and desired but also actively work to avoid extravagance and wasteful approaches to production. A recent project, Designated Drivers, sprung from an invitation to engage newer technologies and we decided to invite artists to work with USB flash drives. These cheap devices, which we used to create a shareable exhibition of many thousands of files selected by twenty artists and groups, are easy to replace when they break and cost very little to maintain. This is something we need to consider with all technology-driven projects, given the economic and environmental instability of the world.

How does your collaboration relate to its cultural, institutional, and commercial contexts? In other words, how would you respond to those who call this a trend?

As we stated in response to the first question, all art is collaborative in nature. Humans depend upon each other for our survival. We are also all part of many groups: our families, those who share our interests, workers, etc. Therefore, people working together in groups is not a trend at all. There is a lot of discussion in the sometimes myopic art criticism world that would lead one to believe that the idea of people working together toward a common goal was created as a postmodernist art project, but most people are savvy enough to understand that the world is much bigger than that and that artists don't live in a bubble.

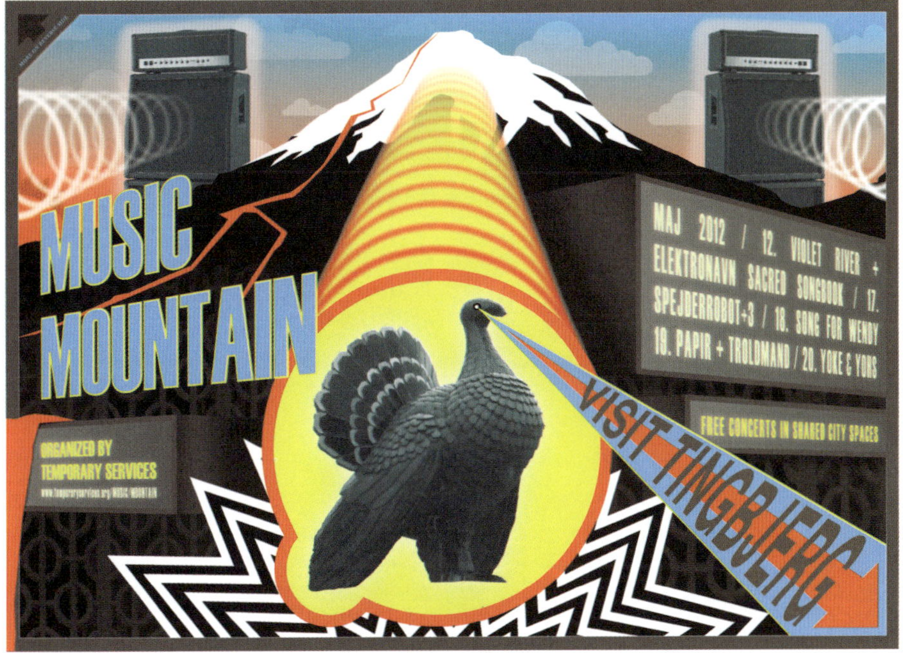

6

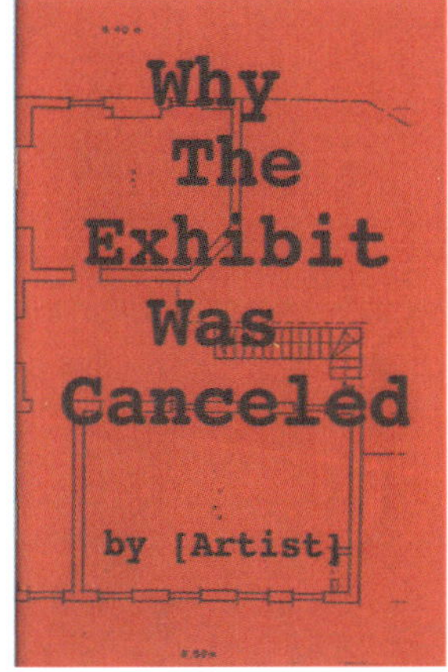

7

It also seems appropriate here to point out that the terms collective and "group" are not interchangeable. The word "collective" has a rich history of political and social connotations and connections that not every group chooses to reference or be connected to. Temporary Services consciously chooses the word "group" when referring to ourselves.

Who is your audience?

This can change dramatically from project to project. It is also hard to define the limits of audience, because we produce so many publications and web-based materials that are seen by many thousands of people who do not always get to see our exhibitions in person. We also give lectures and participate in public discussions: that's an audience as well.

Prisoners' Inventions, our collaboration with an artist named Angelo, has been seen by many tens of thousands of people in exhibitions presented in multiple cities and countries. The exhibition version of the project includes a full-size copy of Angelo's prison cell; the book Prisoners' Inventions features his drawings and writings about the myriad things he has seen cellmates and fellow prisoners invent. While the exhibition is a fully immersive experience, the project has found a large audience through media coverage as well.

Music Mountain, our series of free outdoor concerts in the Tingbjerg area of Copenhagen in Denmark, was only attended by a couple hundred people at most. The project will be viewed more through documentation, the poster that was displayed in public in Copenhagen and Tingbjerg, and stories told by the bands that played and the people who saw and heard their performances.

Ideas circulate widely and uncontrollably. Some projects resonate many years after the fact. Our booklet Why The Exhibit Was Canceled was only seen by a few hundred people when we first published it over twelve years ago. It has since been reprinted and downloaded many thousands of times.

Does your engagement with one another translate into an engagement with the public? How so?

No. Our group's membership has always been clearly defined and does not change from project to project. When we collaborate with others outside of the group, we credit them as equal participants but we do not consider them as members of the group. It wouldn't be appropriate to suggest that they are also responsible and accountable for all of the other day-to-day things that our group is involved with. Likewise, the audience is frequently invited to participate in our projects, and out of this many long, rewarding, and mutually supportive relationships have emerged, but participation does not result in a change in group membership or structure.

8 – Prisoners' Inventions, drawing by Angelo from the book by Angelo and Temporary Services, published by WhiteWalls, 2003

9 – Temporary Services and IC-98, It Is Always Like This, Turku, Finland, 2008

10 – Designated Drivers by Temporary Services and participants, from an exhibition at Texas State University, San Marcos, TX, 2013

11 – Song For Wendy, public performance as part of Music Mountain in Tingbjerg, Denmark, 2012

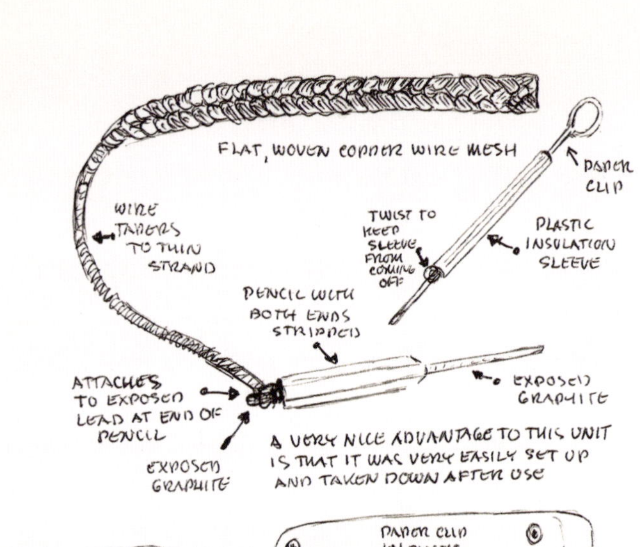

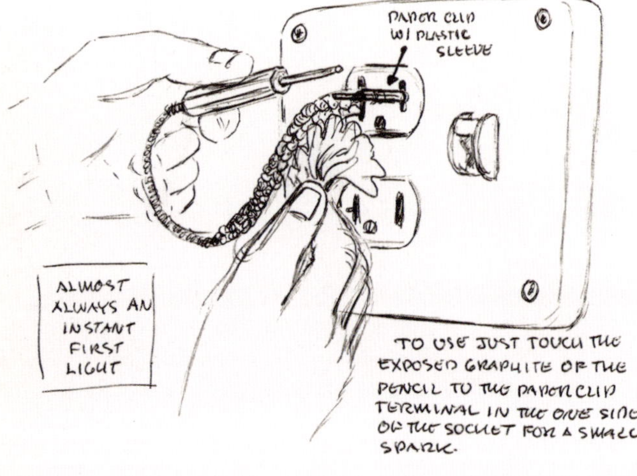

8

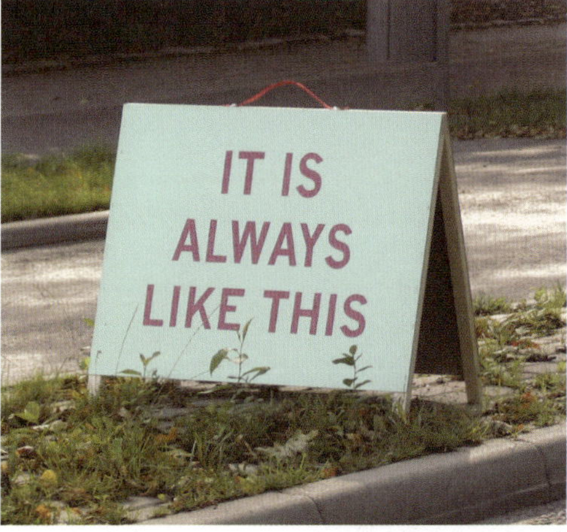

9

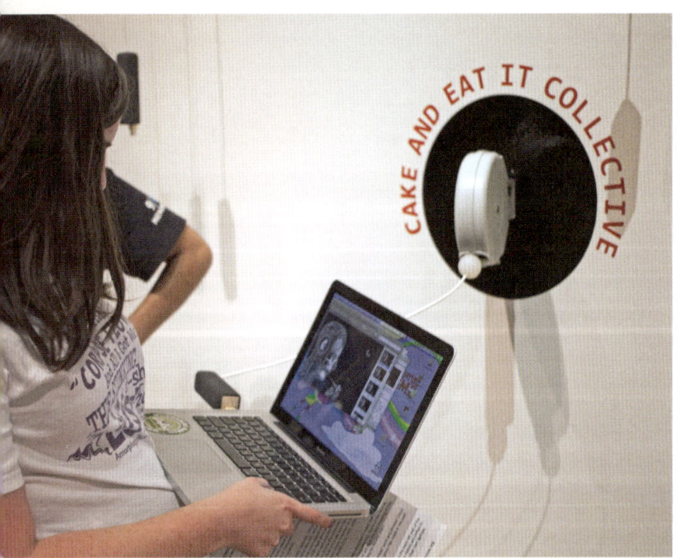

10

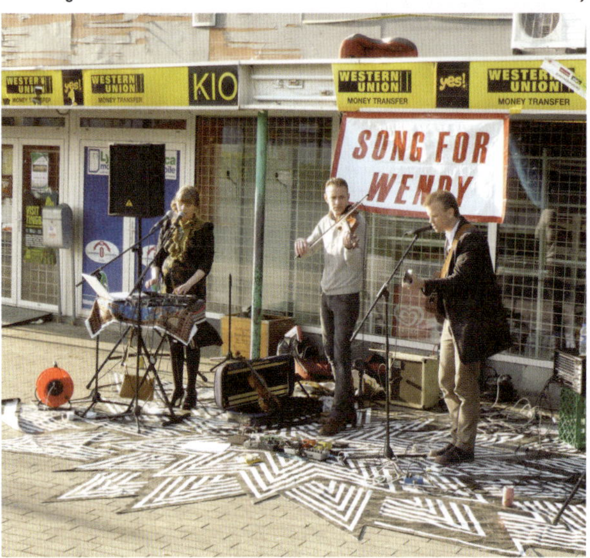

11

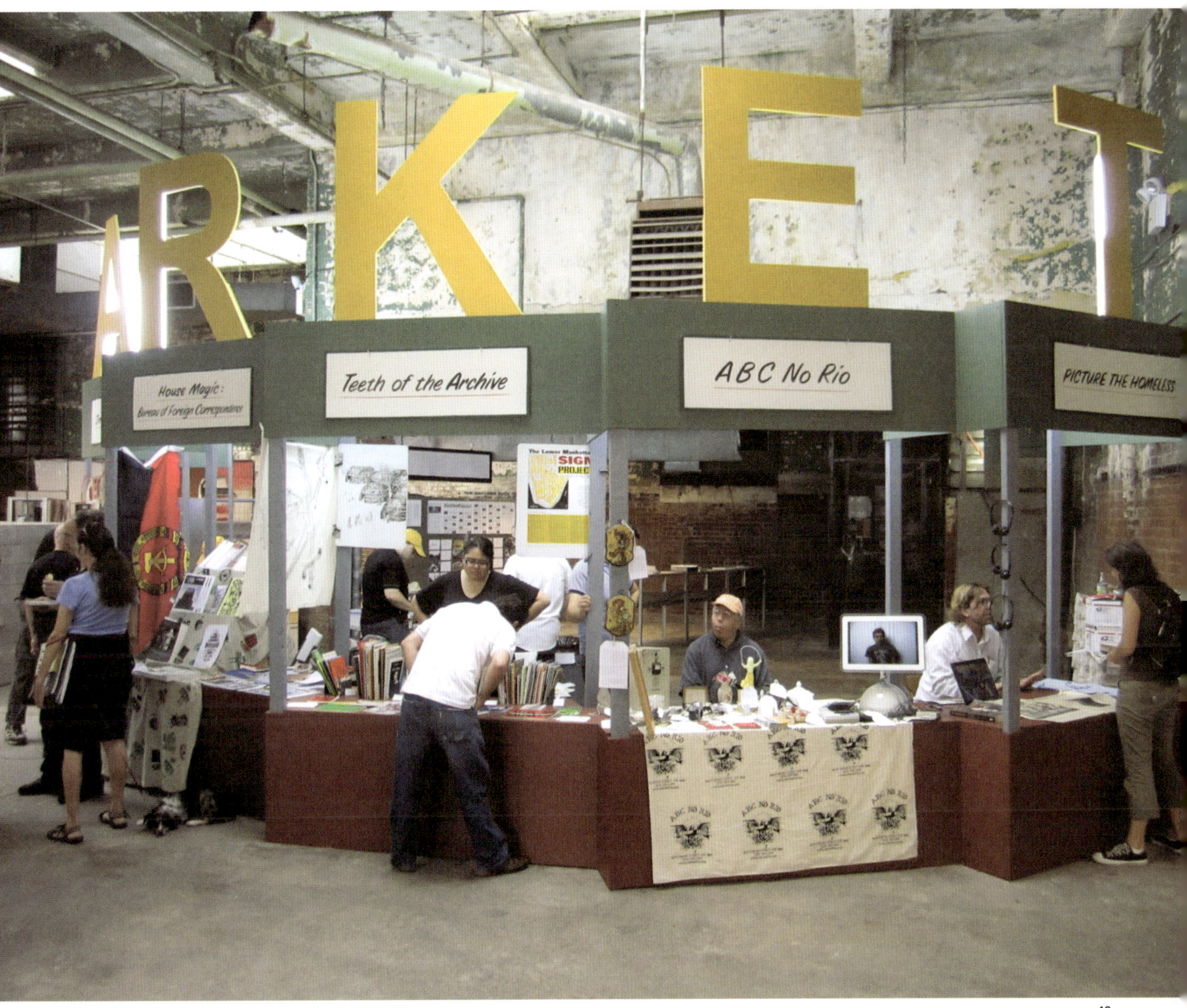

12

12 – MARKET by Temporary Services and participants, from the exhibition Living As Form, curated by Nato Thompson for Creative Time, Lower East Side, New York, 2011

ACTIVE SINCE	CITY	WEBSITE
2002	Milan, Italy / Perth, Australia / Internet	thisisamagazine.com and thisisnotamagazine.com

This is a magazine

MEMBERS	ACTIVITIES	RECOMMENDED PUBLICATION
Andy Simionato and Karen Ann Donnachie	Community Projects, Curating, Internet Art, Merchandising, Music, Painting / Sculpture / Installation, Public Performance, Publishing, Urban Interventions	THIS IS A MAGAZINE, Compendium 6: Pink Laser Beam, self-published, Milan, 2009

This is a magazine, also known as This is (Not) a Magazine, is a multidimensional editorial project that extends its practice from publication to digital art, from performance to curating. So far, more than three hundred artists have taken part in its activities. It doesn't matter where these contributors are located: the Internet is the key.

Why work collaboratively?

Every activity or action is collaborative. I remember reading something about Plato being worried about whether he really had an idea unless it was shared. I think it was Plato. Anyway, in a collaborative activity, with each new artist increases the variables of any situation, and this affords more happy accidents, unexpected results, and postpones predictable resolutions of problems. Collaborative activity also departs from a kind of psychic zero. A psychic zero is a neutral point of departure consisting of every possible new direction simultaneously.

How do you determine membership? Does physical location matter in this regard?

As we are, or not, a magazine, membership is determined at the moment of publication, at the moment of making whatever it was we are making public. Perhaps "membership" is too strong a word for our specific activity, as some "members" may not be aware of their status, for example, in one publication we published a list of Pamela Anderson's favorite books; the list was available on her website at the time, and so we thought she should be part of that publication, leaving her name as a contributor. For the second part of your question, as a primarily Internet-specific publication, we consider geographic location as ineffectual; even when we are aware of the location of the artist, we understand this to be a fluid variable among many.

If considered separately, how do your individual artistic practices contribute to or detract from your work as a group?

TIAM remains an occasional and randomly published articulation of visual experiments in "deviations," the outcomes often resulting from some initial email exchanges or Facebook messaging. Somehow we occasionally manage to publish something, to form a sufficient binding membrane to call what we have done as sufficiently separate from other practices, but once we do manage this small feat, we soon move on. The publication, whether it be a physical book or online movie or whatever, either manages to survive by finding its public or not; either way, we do not interfere with this process, for example, we do not do hold complicated launches or entertain other marketing considerations. Actually, the publication itself is an exhaustive practice.

The publication can also be a space for my own works, so quite occasionally I have contributed, but this has happened less in recent editions, which I have considered more as ongoing performances than as magazines or books, with the various elements appearing to me more as actors; the publication as a stage.

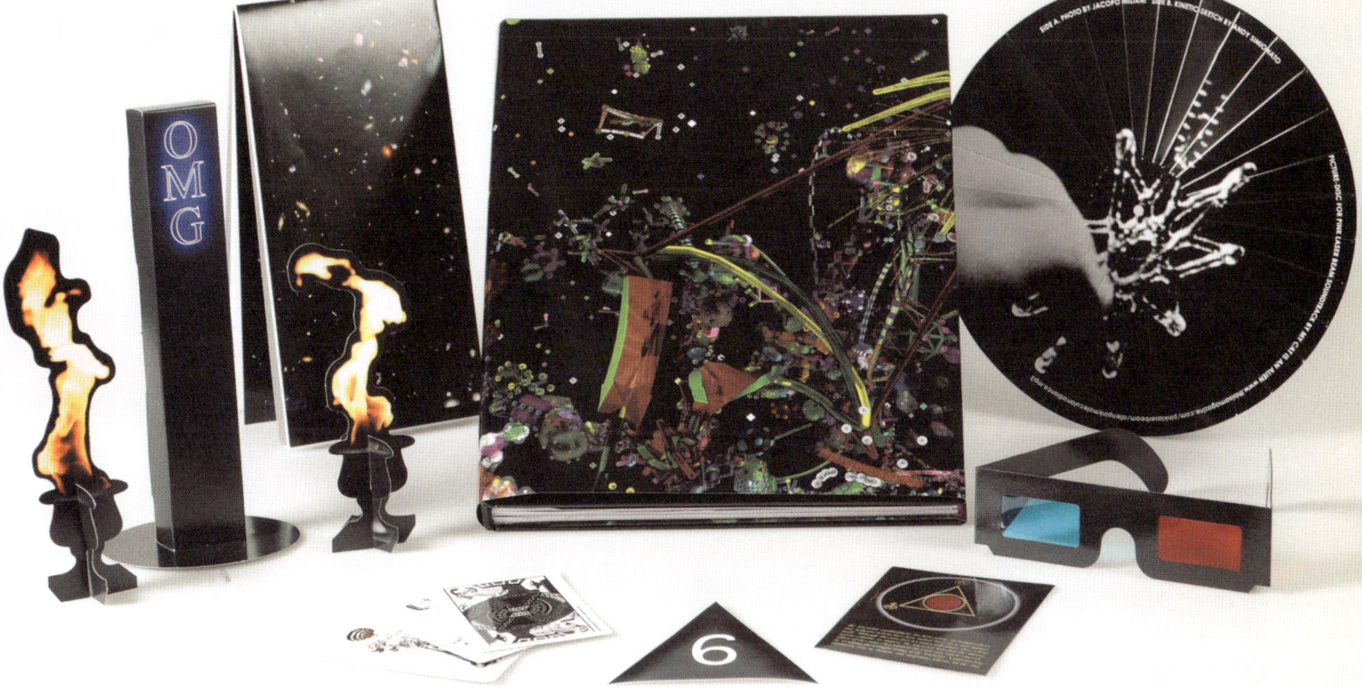

1

1 – Pink Laser Beam, Compendium no. 6 of This is a magazine, 2010. Artworks: AIDS-3D, Center for Tactical Magic, Grant Willing and Donnachie, Simionato and Son

2 – Who I Think I Am, book spread of Compendium no. 5 of This is a magazine, 2007

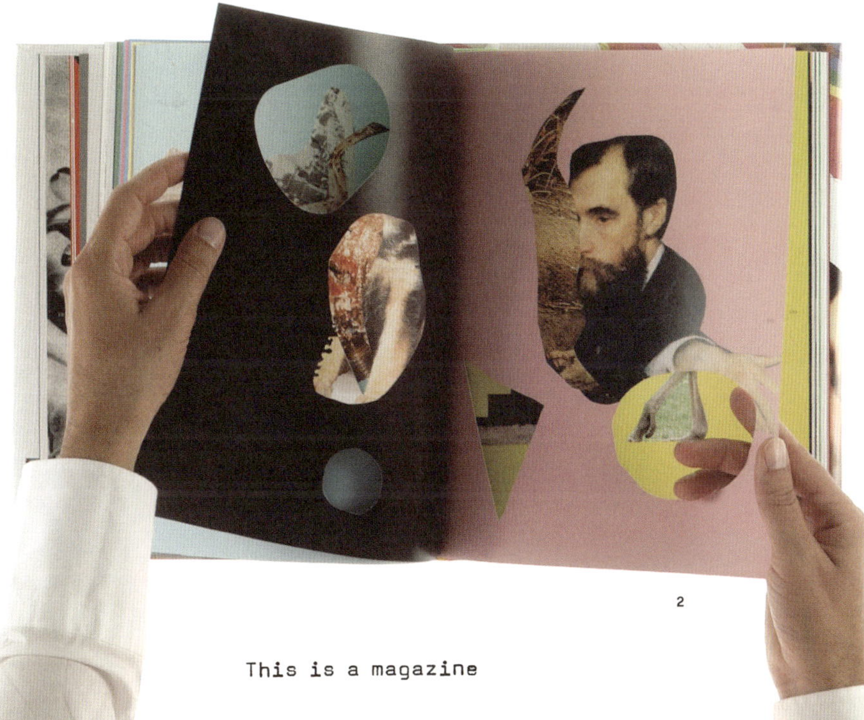

2

How are decisions made?

I could draw the process on a graph with the X axis representing the level of dictatorship and Y axis representing time; the graph would show each decision with an initial and sudden upward spike of autocracy followed by a long, falling tail of diplomacy.

Does each of you have a clearly defined role? If so, what are some of each member's distinct responsibilities?

The focus is on getting the work published, and as we are very few doing the work that would in a traditional editorial organization be executed by many, it is the role that chooses us. When the phone rings, whoever picks it up is the office secretary, when the printer has a problem, whoever can jump in a taxi and drive out [to the printing house] is the graphic artist, and so on.

How important is each group member's individuality, both in terms of your artistic production and in terms of your relationship with the media? Does anonymity come into play?

The artist's individuality is not normally influential in the publication. Indeed, some artists have used pseudonyms, and on other occasions we have intentionally obfuscated identities, such as in the most recent Pink Laser Beam. At the moment this may be the direction we maintain, deferring the association of an individual artist's identity to a specific work or works, not because of any overt aversion to individuality but to experiment with a collective activity that results in a kind of "total work." On the website and within the publication, we announce all the artists and groups involved, and index all the names and websites and whatever, but leave the body of the work, its totality, to refer only to itself.

What is the relationship between your working methods and your art's "content"? In this sense, does technology tend to play more of a supporting role, or does it lead you in new directions?

To consider content in our work is problematic; we deliberately manifest an aversion to the subject, for example, already in the complete name of the project, "This is a magazine about nothing," there is this departure or untethering from the content. In the early stages of the project, in the early 2000s, the technology was influential. For example, we made many decisions about materials that would help reduce the strain on download times for the magazine. This led us to become interested in internet ephemera, flashing GIFs and so on, that were made for an efficient delivery; indeed, they already contain their own delivery system. Again we added algorithmic interactivity and similar components influenced by the user's actions, rather than, say, traditional time-based animations in order to maintain small file sizes. As Internet usage spread and bandwidths and speeds increased, we felt we could allow ourselves greater file sizes, and so we began making the Peep-shows, which were QuickTime movies, but even here we kept their dimensions relatively diminutive. Eventually we moved toward rather conceptually driven works, for example, the Microsoft Powerpoint edition and some other Java-coded works to continue experimenting with available tools. At each occasion there were some works that fit better than others, but most of the time we would announce to the artists what we had in mind and they would react to that with appropriate works or adaptation of works.

How does your collaboration relate to its cultural, institutional, and commercial contexts? In other words, how would you respond to those who call this a trend?

We have no idea of trends; we would probably not notice if our activities were considered to correspond to a trend.

Who is your audience?

There is always the need to imagine an audience (in our case, a reader, I suppose), the need to picture someone who will receive the work in some future, but this future-audience (or future-reader), whomever he or she may be, is destined to remain an illusion. The nature of the book is defined by this absence, and I apologize for appearing evasive in my answer, but this absence is always there. The author writes because he cannot be present when the reader reads, and the reader reads precisely because the author is not there. The audience, as you call it, along with the author, is illusory.

Does your engagement with one another translate into an engagement with the audience? How so?

Continuing from my previous response I would answer that there is a translation of author-author to author-reader engagement. That translation can be identified through the work, which represents the same entropic dimension as any conversation, with an additional complication being that in each instance that conversation is made possible through the illusion of the other.

3 – Swap, Drop and Roll, stamp, Perth Institute of Contemporary Arts, Perth 2012

4 – This is a magazine's Office Desk, Milan, 2010

5 – Pink Laser Beam, book spread of Compendium no. 6 of This is a magazine, 2010

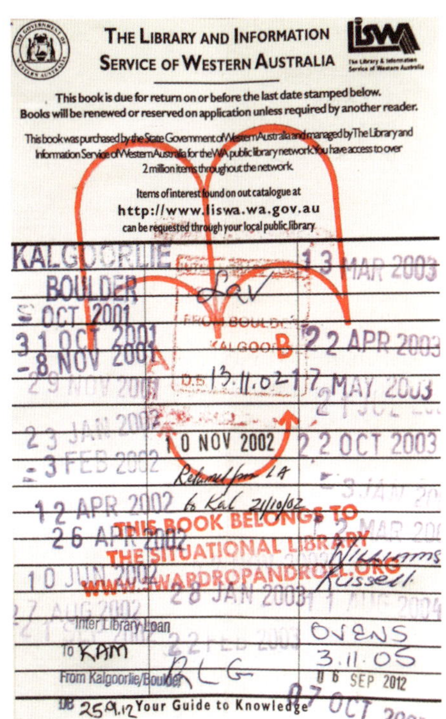
THE LIBRARY AND INFORMATION SERVICE OF WESTERN AUSTRALIA

LISWA

This book is due for return on or before the last date stamped below.
Books will be renewed or reserved on application unless required by another reader.

This book was purchased by the State Government of Western Australia and managed by The Library and Information Service of Western Australia for the WA public library network. You have access to over 2 million items throughout the network.

Items of interest found on out catalogue at
http://www.liswa.wa.gov.au
can be requested through your local public library.

KALGOORLIE BOULDER

THIS BOOK BELONGS TO
THE SITUATIONAL LIBRARY
WWW.SWAPDROPANDROLL.ORG

Inter Library Loan
To
From Kalgoorlie/Boulder

Your Guide to Knowledge

3

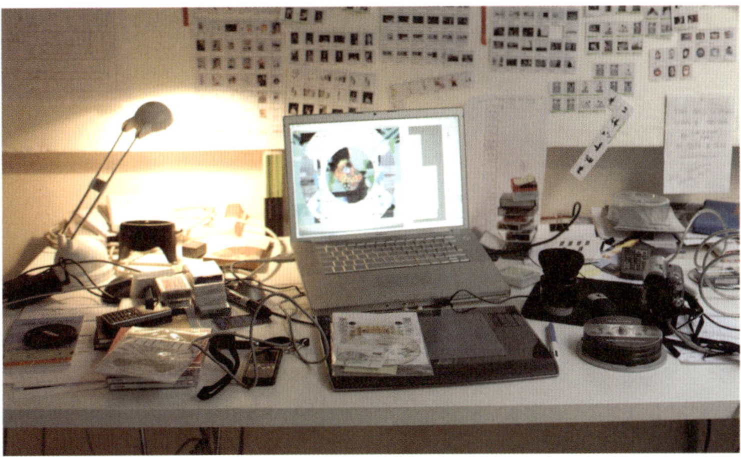

4

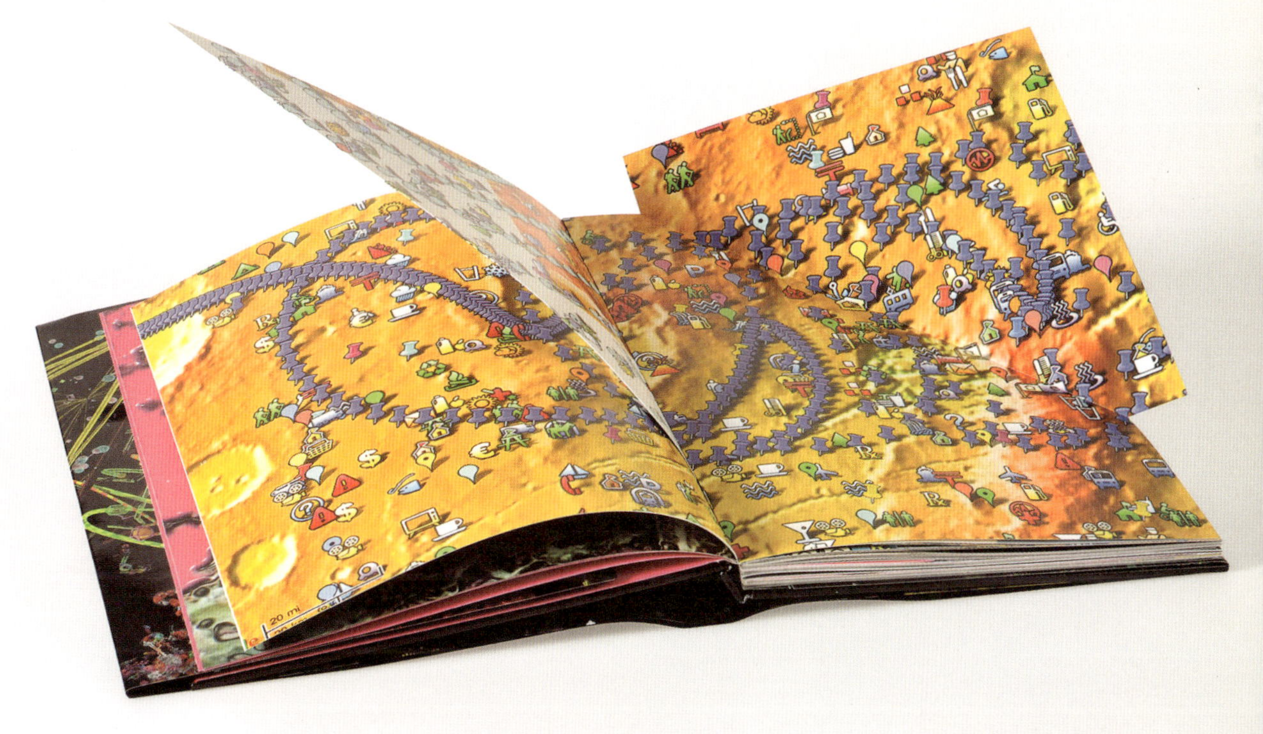

5

6 – Everything Will Be Ok, book cover of Compendium no. 4 of This is a magazine, 2006

7 – Fashion=Fiction, book cover of Compendium no. 2 of This is a magazine, 2003

8 – This is a magazine and Antonio Riello, Only the Good, installation, Kunstverein, Neuhausen, 2011

9 – Swap, Drop and Roll, installation, PICA, Perth, 2012

10 – Who I Think I Am, digital image from Compendium no. 5 of This is a magazine, 2007. Artwork: René Schmidt

opposite
11 – Everything Will Be Ok, book spread of Compendium no. 4 of This is a magazine, 2006

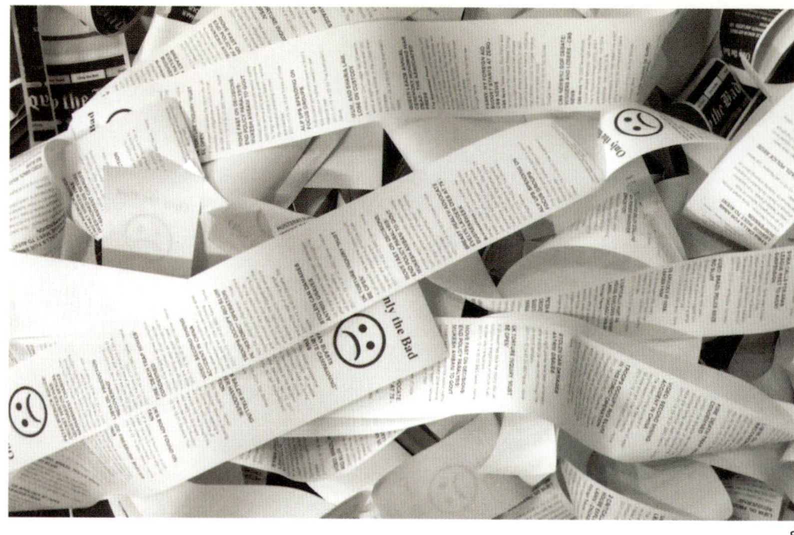

8

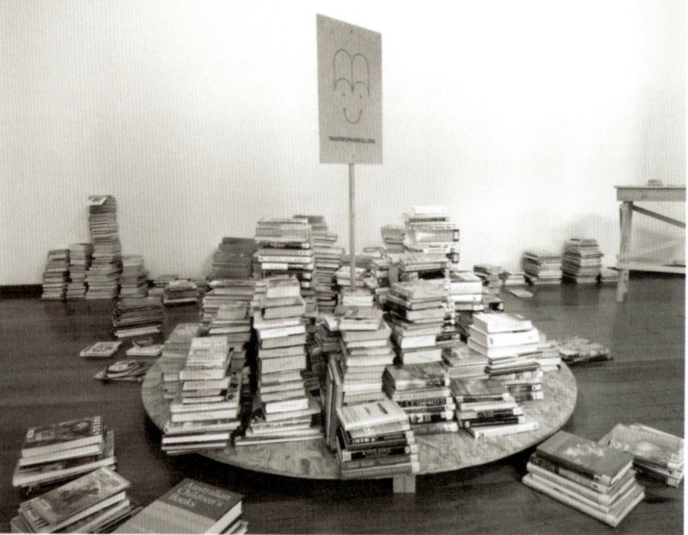

9

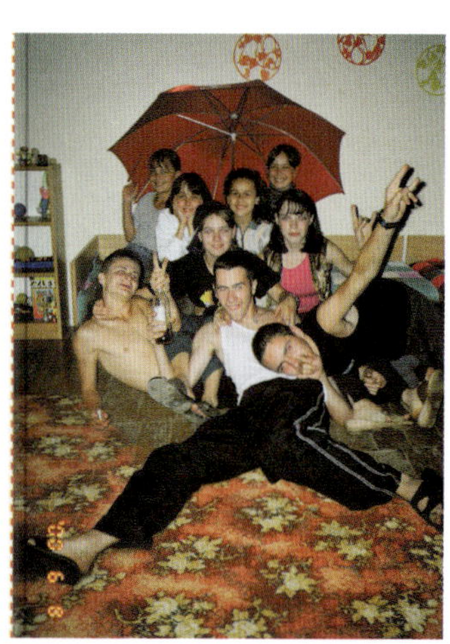

6

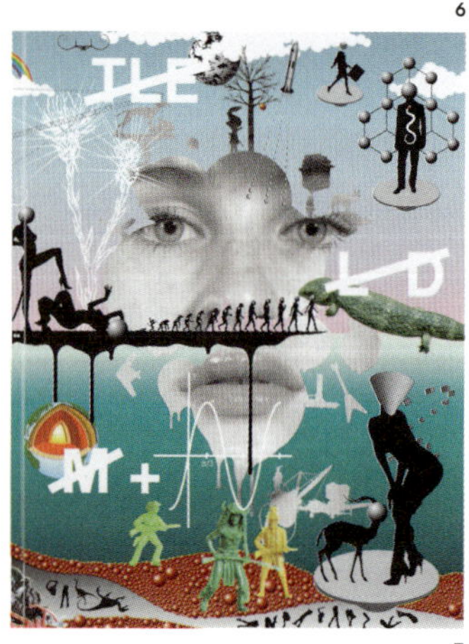

7

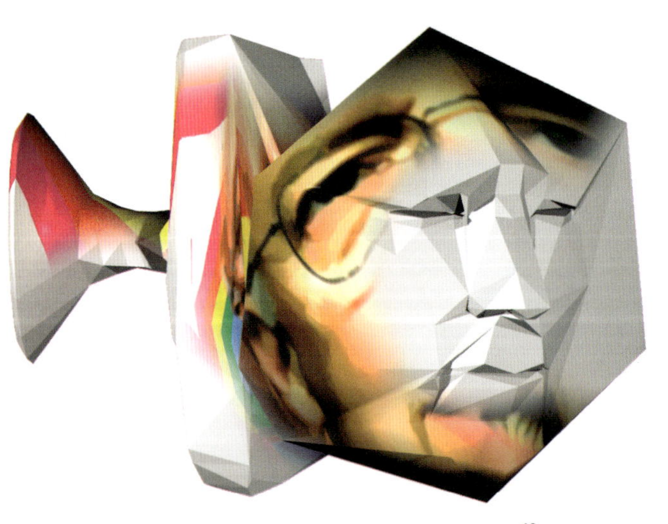

10

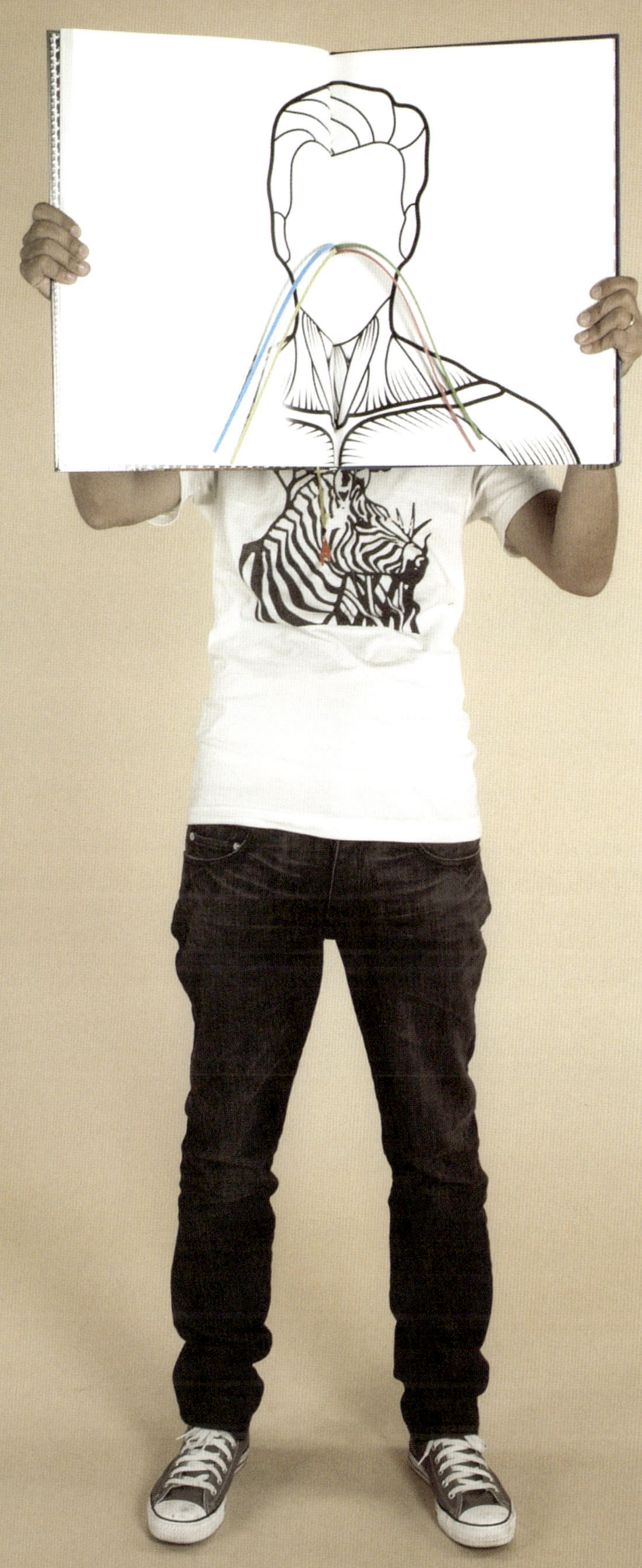

ACTIVE SINCE	CITY	WEBSITE
2002	Tokyo, Japan	picnicclub.org

Tokyo Picnic Club

MEMBERS	ACTIVITIES	RECOMMENDED PUBLICATION
Hiroshi Ota, Kaori Ito, Nami Fukutome, Wataru Noritake, Yutaka Suzuki, Hajime Ishikawa, Kenji Kitamura, Hiroyuki Moriwaki, Toru Kashihara, Yasumi Taketomi, and Noriko Shimuta	Community Projects, Food / Recipe Development, Public Performance, Urban Interventions	Marieluise Jonas and Rosalea Monacella (eds.), Exposure: Design Research in Landscape Architecture, Melbourne Books, Melbourne, 2013

With backgrounds in architecture, urban planning, illustration, and design, Tokyo Picnic Club organizes participatory picnics through the installation of mobile structures in Tokyo as well as other cities in Japan and abroad. Carrying on the legacy of radical architecture groups of the sixties, the collective proposes a physical as well as symbolic interruption of the stressful rhythms of metropolitan life.

Why work collaboratively?

Tokyo Picnic Club was founded in 2002 to celebrate the bicentennial anniversary of picnic, which became popular thanks to the activities of "Pic-Nic-Club," founded in London in 1802. For more than ten years we've been using picnic as our act of expression, covering a wide range of issues and activities, including gastronomy, design, fashion, lifestyles, landscape design, and urbanism. The aim of TPC is to thoroughly redefine the concept and practice of picnic in the contemporary urban context of Tokyo. In order to accomplish that, we always develop cross-genre and synergetic discussions between multiple collaborators.

For example, to produce Picnic Tea (2004), an architect, an urban designer, and a food coordinator had tested dozens of tealeaf blend samples, which would match the atmosphere of "greenfield" (parks, rural landscapes) and "brownfield" (abandoned industrial sites, port areas, contaminated lands). Two tastes were created from this collaboration: Greenfield Tea and Brownfield Tea. A graphic designer conceived the packaging for the tea box, and an illustrator added weird cartoons on it.

How do you determine membership? Does physical location matter in this regard?

Each project requires a wide approach to picnic, so we invite new specialists accordingly. Basically, members are from Tokyo, as the club has been focusing on the public spaces in Tokyo. There is no rule for membership. The club was founded by Hiroshi Ota, Kaori Ito, and Tomoharu Matsuda. Currently the core group consists of about a dozen people but members of the club are closer to one hundred.

If considered separately, how do your individual artistic practices contribute to or detract from your work as a group?

All members have their own career and practices, and normally work individually. But when there is a project about picnic, each member proposes new forms of collaboration and new approaches to TPC activities. One of the reasons we work collaboratively is that the collaboration itself provides the fun of gathering and mutual contribution, like the real act of picnicking.

How are decisions made?

Hiroshi Ota and Kaori Ito, who are the cofounders of TPC, arrange the project, involve collaborators, manage the budget, and plan the schedule. Wataru Noritake, the graphic designer, is responsible for art direction. The three together define the framework for each project. Most of the time, the discussion for the project happens during picnics, with easygoing moods, on holiday afternoons.

Does each of you have a clearly defined role? If so, what are some of each member's distinct responsibilities?

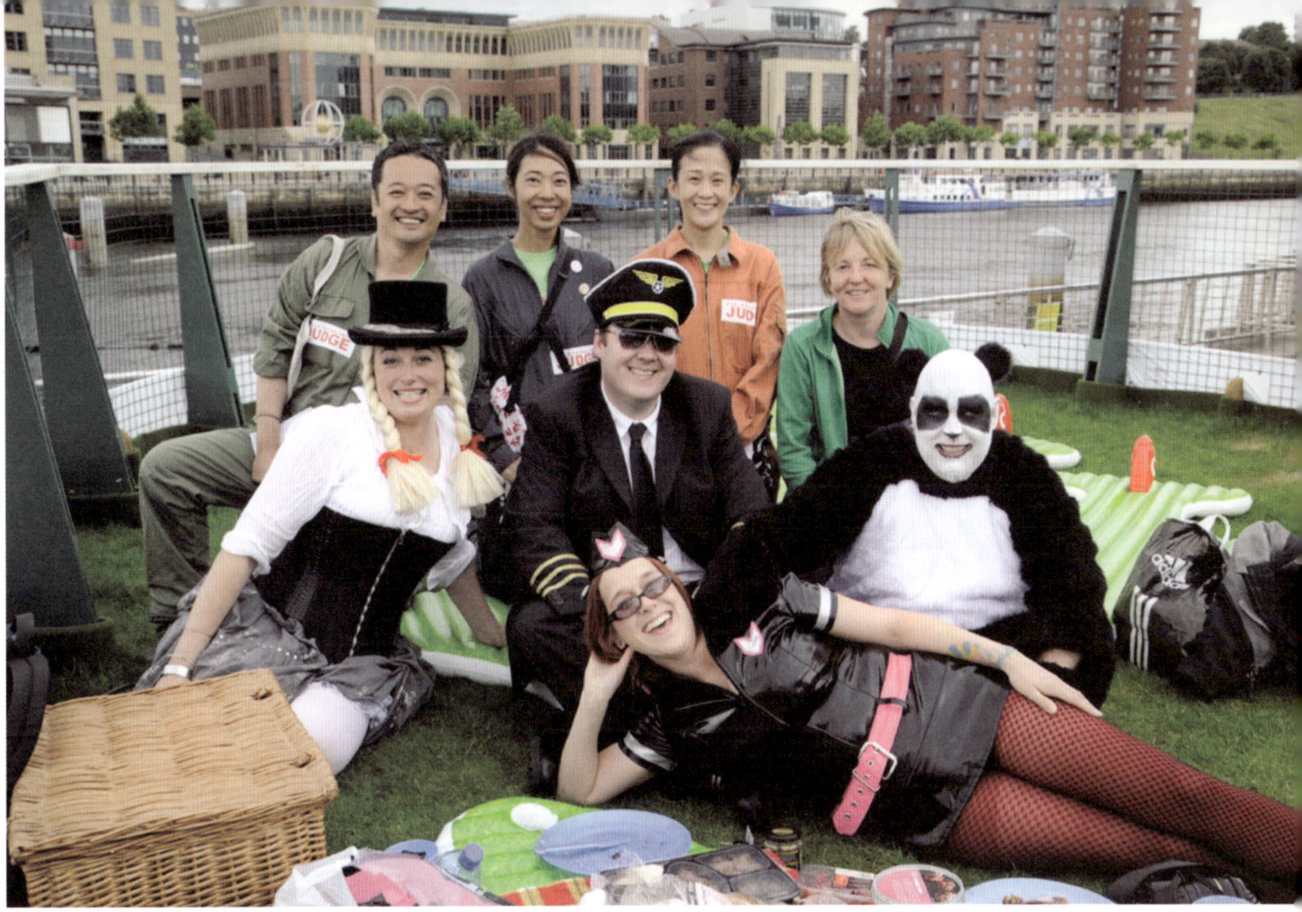

1

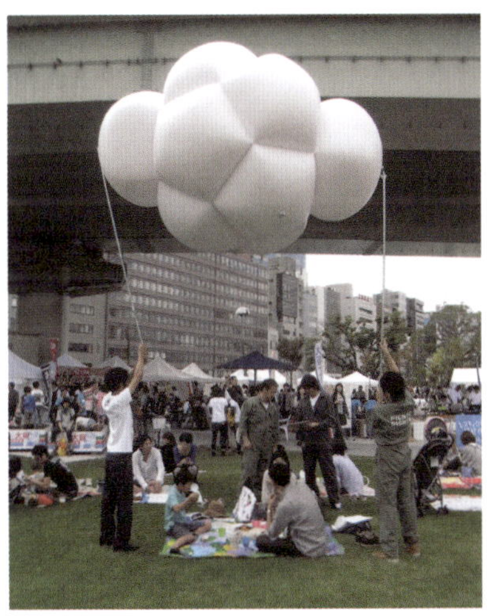

2

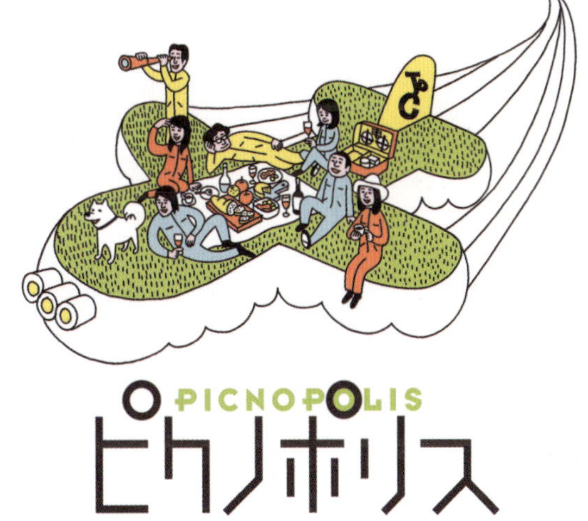

3

1 – Picnopolis Newcastle Gatehead, ten-day and ten-site picnic festival in the UK, 2008. Design: Hiroshi Ota, Kaori Ito, Tomoharu Matsuda, Wataru Noritake, Nami Fukutome, Yutaka Suzuki, and Hiroyuki Moriwaki

2 – CLOUD Camera photo shoot for Picnopolis Osaka, 2011. Design: Hiroshi Ota, Kaori Ito, Wataru Noritake, and Yasumi Taketomi

3 – Picnopolis Newcastle Gatehead illlustration for Picnopolis project, 2008. Design: Kenji Kitamura

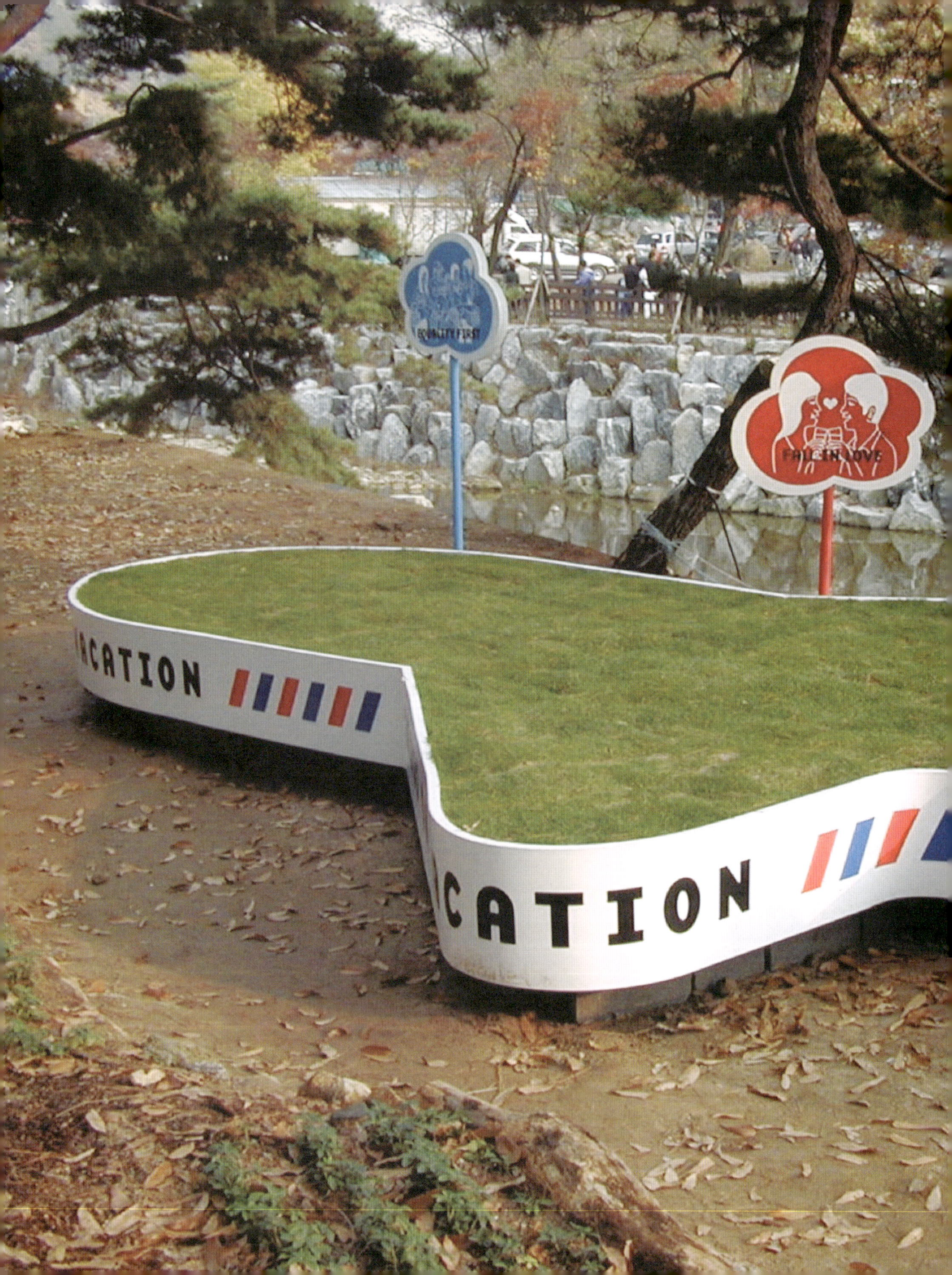

FALL IN LOVE
CATION
CATION

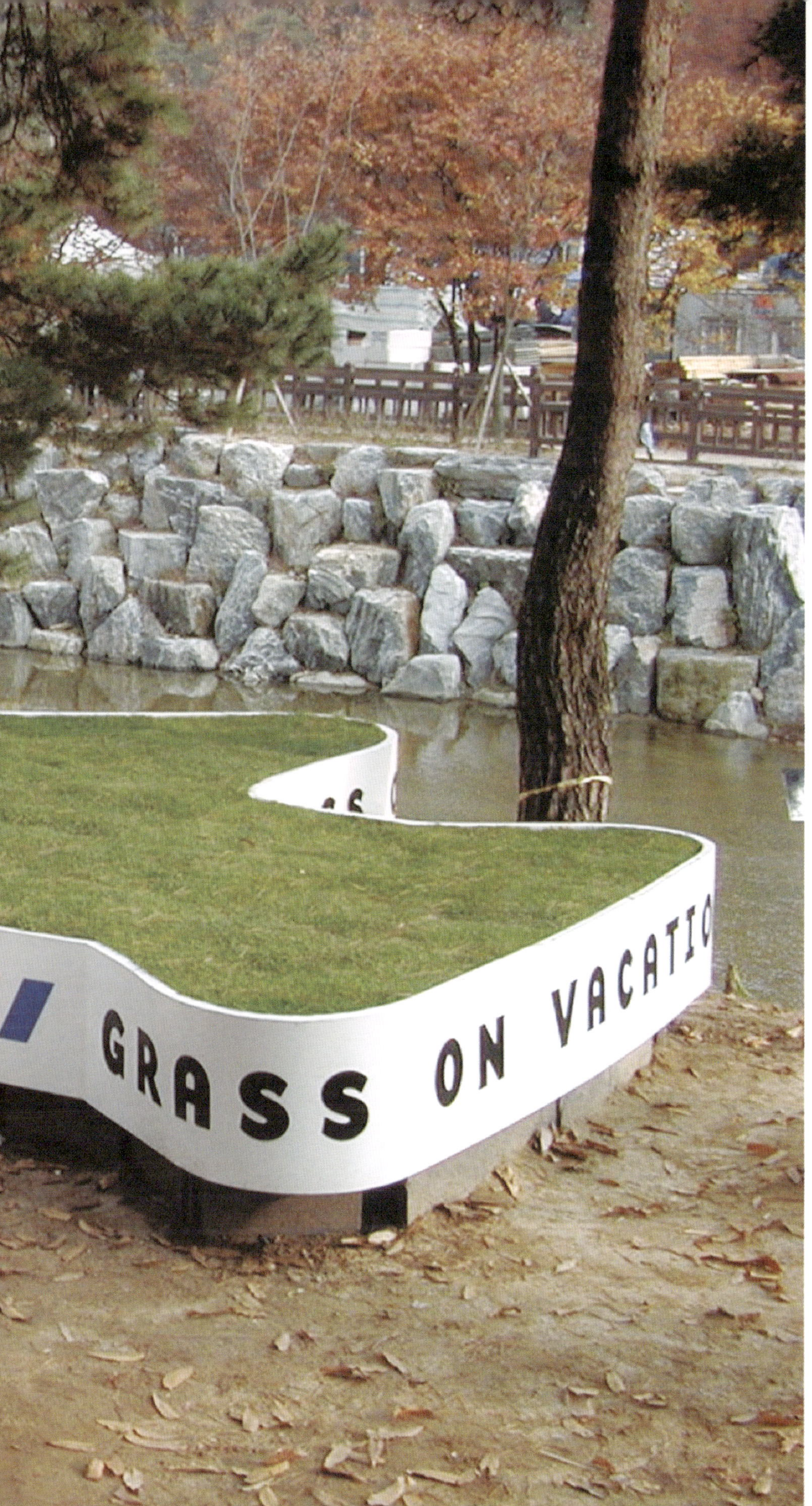

4 – Grass on Vacation, installation for Anyang Public Art Project, Korea, 2006. Design: Hiroshi Ota, Kaori Ito, Toru Kashihara, and Wataru Noritake

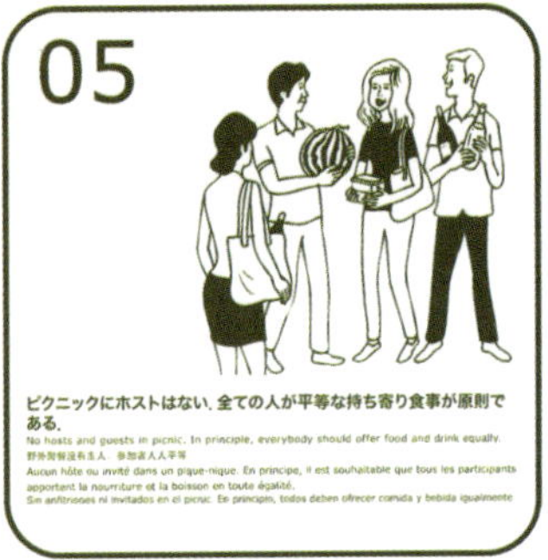

5

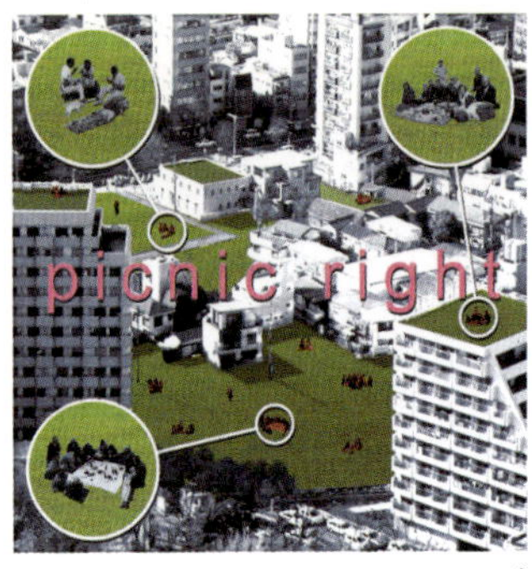

6

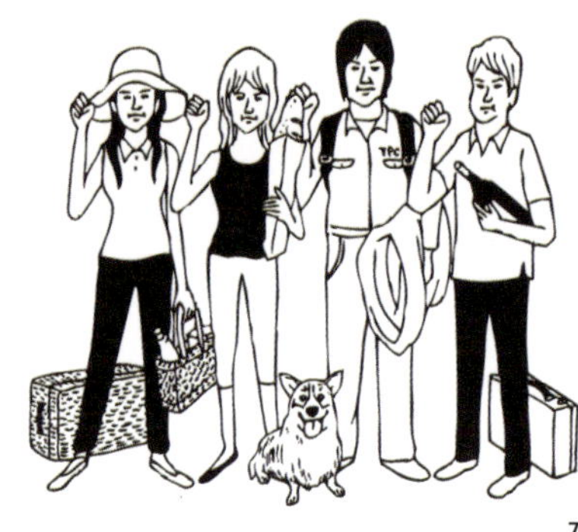

7

As TPC consists of creators from various fields, each member has a clear role and idea to redefine contemporary picnic: Hiroshi is an architect, Kaori is a urban designer, Nami is a food coordinator, Wataru a is graphic designer, Yutaka is a photographer, Hajime is a landscape designer, Kenji is an illustrator, Hiroyuki is an illumination artist, Toru is an architect, Yasumi is an architect, and Noriko is an editor.

How important is each group member's individuality, both in terms of your artistic production and in terms of your relationship with the media? Does anonymity come into play?

Projects are normally credited according to who has primarily developed them, like "Hiroshi Ota/Tokyo Picnic Club," "Yutaka Suzuki/Tokyo Picnic Club." For the public relations, Hiroshi Ota and Kaori Ito mostly talk with media under the title of the club cofounders. But when a journalist wants to discuss our food ideas, Nami Fukutome, our food coordinator, becomes in charge of public relations. As our activities are all "club activity," the presence of members is very clear and anonymity is not so strong.

What is the relationship between your working methods and your art's "content"? In this sense, does technology tend to play more of a supporting role, or does it lead you in new directions?

Ota, Kashihara, and Taketomi are architects and so coordinate the project technically. For example, the production of the project PicnicKIOSK (2005) and the installations of Motherplane (2008) required an engineering approach, but architects worked sufficiently to realize their constructions. Three architects enjoyed temporal art installations that gave totally new experience to their daily practices as architects.

How does your collaboration relate to its cultural, institutional, and commercial contexts? In other words, how would you respond to those who call this a trend?

Ota and Ito are also university professors, so the academic relationship to architecture and urbanism are quite important. As the interests in contemporary public spaces becomes bigger in Japan, the experiences of TPC gets public attention as a unique approach to urban invention in academics.

On the other hand, picnic is naturally associated with commercial contexts, like the promotion program of certain foods/beveragse, the spring campaign in a certain shopping store, or the events for the customers of outdoor fashion brands. If there are any chances to propose new styles of picnic with these commercial clients, we are very free to try projects in the commercial context.

Who is your audience?

It would be ordinary people who are conscious about lifestyles. More than ten picnic clubs have been founded after TPC in Japan, exploring their own methodology of picnicking. We are very happy with this result. After Picnopolis NewcastleGateshead (2008), theorists and activists in urbanism became interested in our assertion of "Picnic Rights," which declares basic human rights to do picnic in the dense and crowded urban circumstance of Tokyo. The understanding of TPC activities has altered from a superficial one to more sympathetic one.

Does your engagement with one another translate into an engagement with the public? How so?

The audience has always had positive reactions and enjoyed being in gorgeous settings with food in a hamper. At the first stage of our activity, they simply wanted to join TPC as members, but after the club had made a slogan of "Think Your Own Picnic" in 2004, they started their own interventions according to their own urban context. TPC is partly responsible for launching a movement and picnic clubs are now in Osaka, Urawa, Shimokitazawa, Kashiwa, Toyama, and other Japanese cities, and each of them is developing its own recipes and styles of picnic.

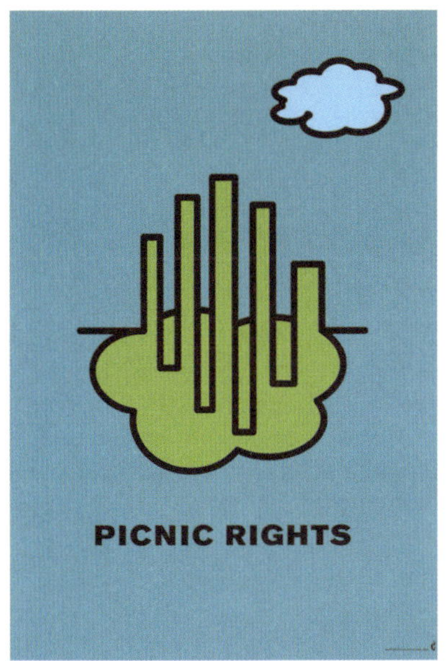

8

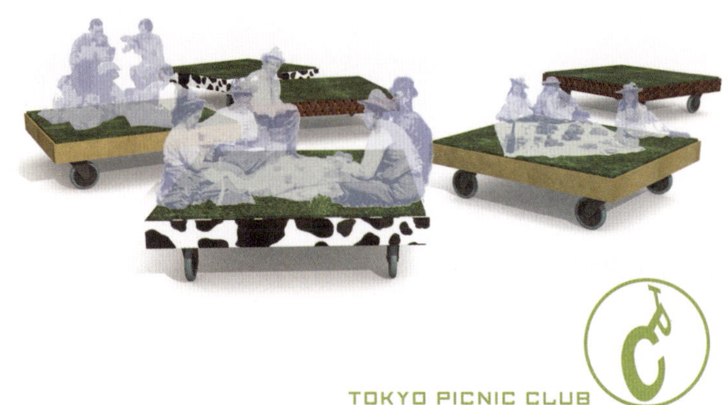

9

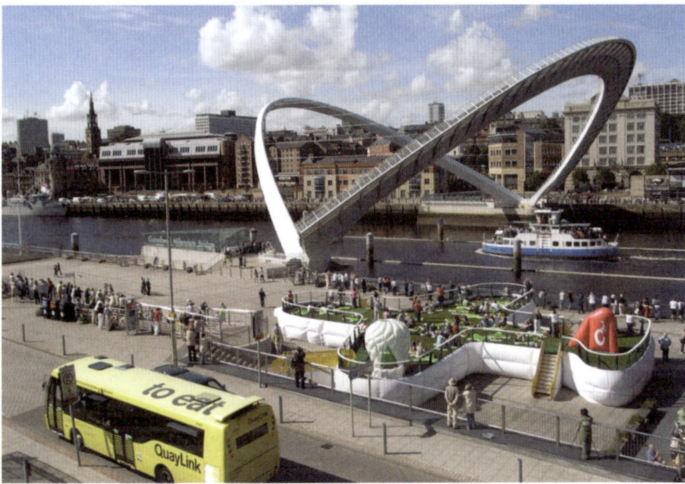

10

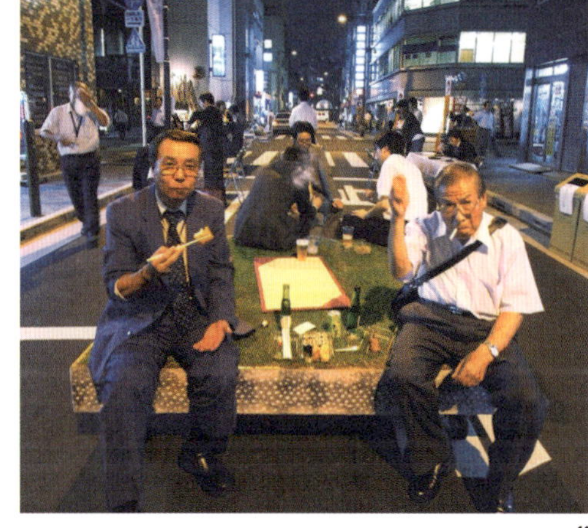

11

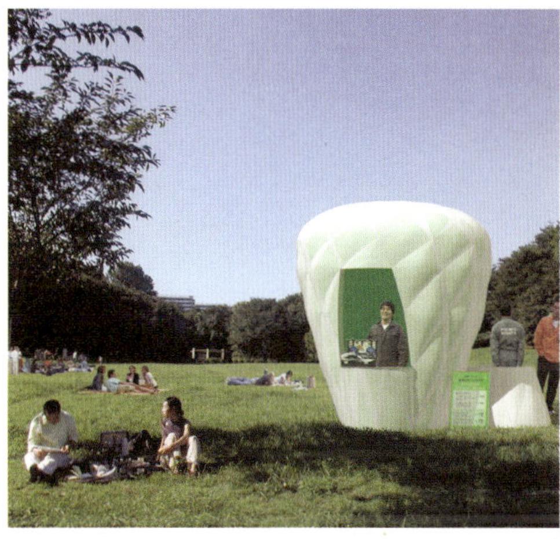

12

5 – "15 Picnic Rules" text and illustrations for Club Manifesto, 2004. Design: Kaori Ito and Kenji Kitamura

6 – "Picnic Rights" illustration for Club Manifesto, 2003. Design: Hiroshi Ota

7 – "Fight For The Picnic" illustration for Club Manifesto, 2005. Design: Kenji Kitamura

8 – "Picnic Rights" poster for Club Manifesto, 2004. Design: Wataru Noritake

9 – Portable Lawn, installation project, Mori Art Museum, Tokyo, 2004. Design: Hiroshi Ota, Kaori Ito, and Hajime Ishikawa

10 – Motherplane, installation for Picnopolis Newcastle Gateshead, 2008. Design: Hiroshi Ota, Kaori Ito, and design neuob

11 – Excursion of Portable Lawn, community project, Kanda, Tokyo, 2005. Design: Hiroshi Ota and Kaori Ito

12 – PicnicKIOSK, installation, Showa Kinen Park, Tokyo, 2005. Design: Kaori Ito and design neuob

ACTIVE SINCE	CITY	WEBSITE
1999	Zagreb, Croatia / Berlin, Germany	whw.hr

What, How and for Whom / WHW

MEMBERS	ACTIVITIES	RECOMMENDED PUBLICATION
Ivet Curlin, Ana Devic, Natasa Ilic, Sabina Sabolovic, and Dejan Krsic	Curating, Publishing	What, How and for Whom/WHW, 11th Istanbul Biennial: What Keeps Mankind Alive?, IKSV, Istanbul, 2009

As a curatorial collective, What, How and for Whom / WHW has developed a metainvestigation on the role of cultural institutions in the articulation of discourses about history and identity. In particular, the Croatian group has focused its attention on the representation of politics and life under socialism, playing an important role in the understanding of collectivism as both a cultural and social practice.

Why work collaboratively?

We came together around the exhibition What, How & for Whom, on the occasion of the 152nd anniversary of The Communist Manifesto, shown in Zagreb in 2000, at a time when rightwing and heavily nationalistic politics, characteristic of the Croatian nineties, were slowly starting to disintegrate. This exhibition focused on complex relations between art and economy, and it put the emphasis on problematic attitudes toward the legacy of the socialist decades and the economic transition the region was then undergoing. These ideas stayed with us over the years. The impact this project had on the public in Croatia prompted us to continue working together and we took the questions from its title as the name of our collective. From the beginning we were aware that our aims of articulating discontent with the governing ideas on art and politics, creating and influencing new ways of producing and interpreting art, and challenging the environment of ossified and closed art institutions carry different resonance when proposed collectively.

How do you determine membership? Does physical location matter in this regard?

Addressing the postsocialist context of Croatia and the legacy of the Yugoslav socialist revolution was always an essential element to our work. We try to relate and translate that to other contexts, regardless of where we work. In that sense, having the physical location does matter, rooting us in a specific starting point, on various levels. We are a tight collective of people and have been in intensive collaboration and communication for years. Yet in the future we would like to think about the ways in which WHW could be more open for new forms of membership and collaborations, and what the advantages and challenges of that new process would be.

If considered separately, how do your individual artistic practices contribute to or detract from your work as a group?

We are not artists but curators. We all studied art history and comparative literature, so when we started to work together we were absolute beginners in a terms of curating. We grew together professionally, influencing each other in relation to not only our content but also organizational issues; influencing each other, learning from each other, finding solutions together. Working together for so long, we've established not only a platform for rethinking the cultural production and political content of art, but also an infrastructure that we share as a common resource and starting point. In recent years we rarely work on individual projects.

How are decisions made?

We try as much as possible to reach our decisions horizontally through discussion and dialogue. Making decisions together involves lots of arguing, but also

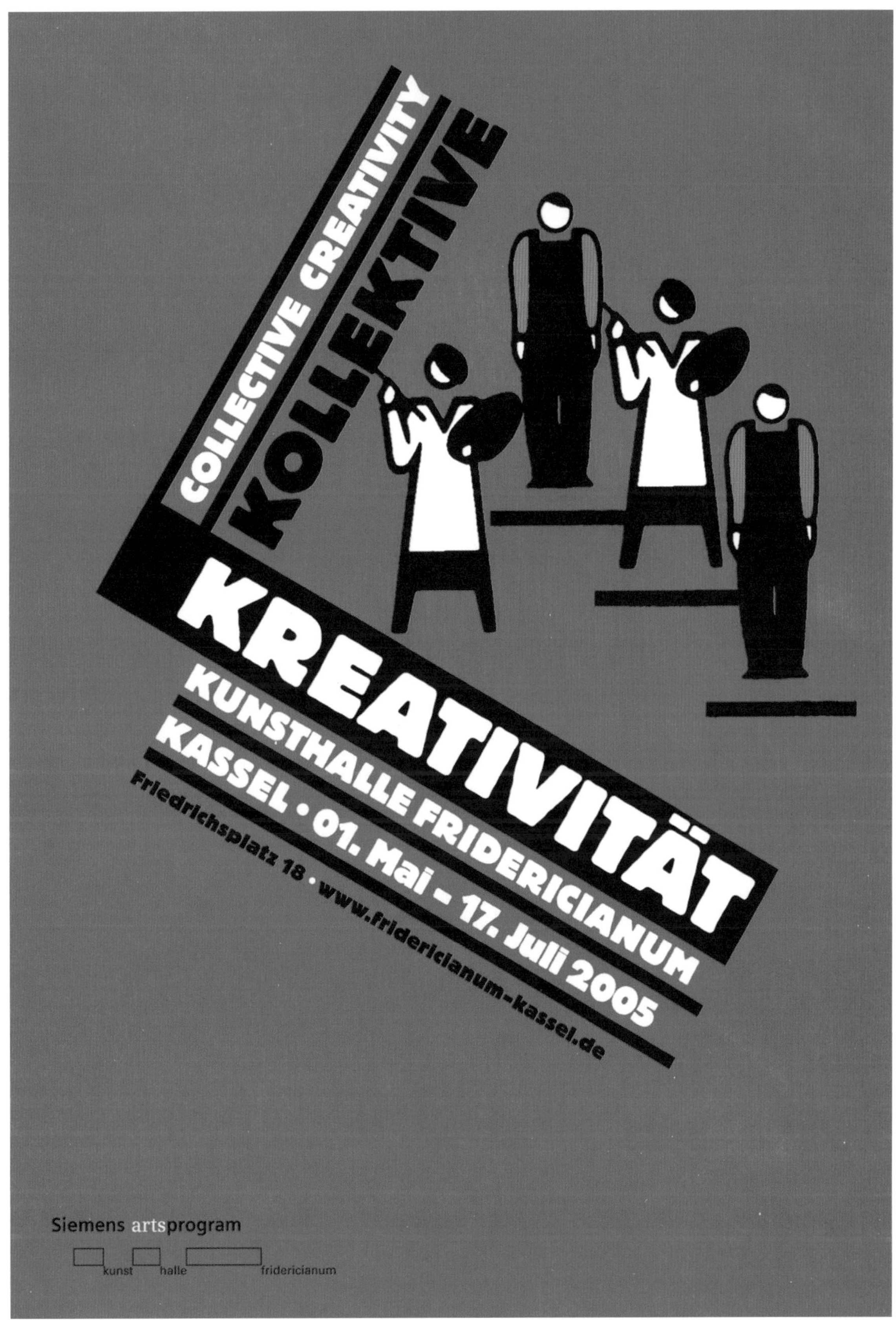
COLLECTIVE CREATIVITY
KOLLEKTIVE
KREATIVITÄT
KUNSTHALLE FRIDERICIANUM
KASSEL • 01. Mai – 17. Juli 2005
Friedrichsplatz 18 • www.fridericianum-kassel.de
Siemens artsprogram
kunst halle fridericianum

1

previous

1 – Collective Creativity, cover of the exhibition reader, edited by WHW, Christoph Keller/Revolver Publishing, Berlin, 2005. Design: Dejan Kršić

2 – Christoph Schlingensief: Fear |at the Core of Things, installation part of the exhibition curated by Kathrin Rhomberg, Gallery Nova, a nonprofit space directed by WHW, Zagreb, 2012

3 – What, How & for Whom, on the occasion of the 152nd anniversary of the Communist Manifesto card, Zagreb, 2000

4 – Sanja Iveković, SOS NADA DIMIĆ, intervention on the facade of the factory Nada Dimić, Zagreb, 2000

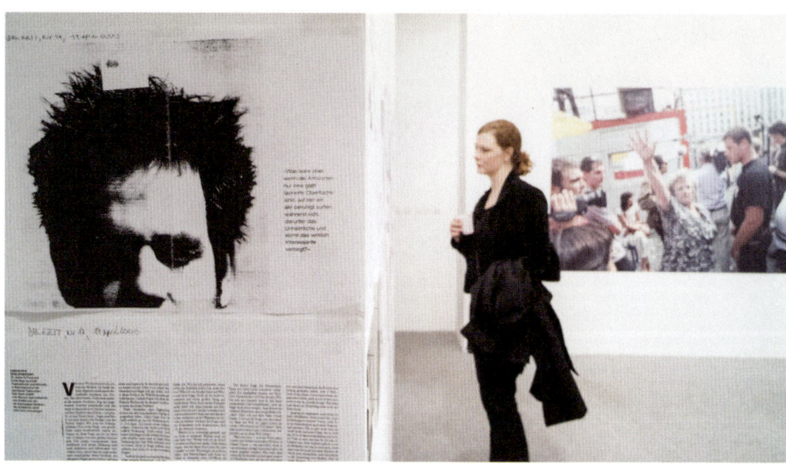

2

Constant revolutionizing of productions, uninterrupted disturbance of all social conditions, everlasting uncertainty and agitation distinguish the bourgeois epoch from all earlier ones. All fixed, fast-frozen relations, with their train of ancient and venerable prejudices and opinions, are swept away, all new-formed ones become antiquated before they can ossify. All that is solid melts into air, all that is holy is profaned, and man is at last compelled to face with sober senses, his real conditions of life, and his relations with his kind.

what, how & for whom

on the occasion of 153rd anniversary of the Communist *Manifesto*

Cristian Alexa | Damir Babić | Maja Licul & Jože Barši | Eldina Begić | Emese Benczúr | Marijan Crtalić | Attila Csörgo | Boris Cvjetanović | Sandro Đukić | Darko Fritz | Jean-Baptiste Ganne | Tomislav Gotovac | Igor Grubić | Aleksandar Battista Ilić | Irwin | Sanja Iveković | Kurt&Plasto | Krištof Kintera | Žiga Kariž | Ivana Keser | Ivan Marušić Klif | Rassim Krastev | Igor Kuduz | Andreja Kulunčić | Matthieu Laurette | Yuri Leiderman | Kristina Leko | Zbigniew Libera | Vlado Martek | Kobe Matthys | Ivo Moudov | Edi Muka | Ola Pehrson | Tadej Pogačar | Marko Peljhan | Renata Poljak | p.RT | Oliver Ressler & David Thorne | Tomo Savić-Gecan | Mladen Stilinović | Anela Šabić | Nebojša Šerić-Šoba | Slaven Tolj | Milica Tomić | Igor Toševski | Goran Trbuljak | Vasily Tsagolov

3

4

the possibility that we influence each other's thinking during this process. That is not to say that there are no conflicts and disagreements, but we tend to consider them as an inevitable and sometimes vital part of working together.

Does each of you have a clearly defined role? If so, what are some of each member's distinct responsibilities?

We don't have clearly defined roles, although we do divide up tasks for organizational reasons. We all feel responsible for the conceptual and practical decisions related to an exhibition, and we reach them through discussions; this approach effectively cancels traditional divisions of roles. At the same time, it continually begs us to practice tolerance, understanding, and commitment with and to one another. This ensures that our working practices are not static but rather always tested and held as provisional.

How important is each group member's individuality, both in terms of your artistic production and in terms of your relationship with the media? Does anonymity come into play?

The questions of individuality and anonymity are closely related to collective work. There are of course good and bad aspects of this dynamic, and the shelter a group provides can become both the source of strength and shield of conformity. This complex and often contradictory dynamic was brilliantly captured by Jon Hendricks, cofounder of Guerrilla Art Action Group, who said that the group is more than a sum of its parts, that the group acts as an united front and therein lies its strength but its self-destruction as well.

What is the relationship between your working methods and your art's "content"? In this sense, does technology tend to play more of a supporting role, or does it lead you in new directions?

For us, producing exhibitions is a way to address questions that we can't pose in other mediums. From the beginning, we were interested in transforming the traditional (and in our view, negative) aspects of the act of exhibition. We make attempts to turn an exhibition into a space that can be used for different articulations of social interaction, outside of the normally absolute domination of private property and representational logic. Nowadays when—as with most other public spheres—the very core of artistic production, as well as institutional practices that we took for granted, is endangered by austerity measures and the pressures of

5 – Gernot Faber, On fire, installation as part of the exhibition I love You, You Pay my Rent, Gallery Nova, a nonprofit space directed by WHW, Zagreb, 2011

6 – On the occasion of 152nd anniversary of Communist Manifesto, cover of the reader, edited by WHW, Zagreb, 2002. Design: Dejan Kršić

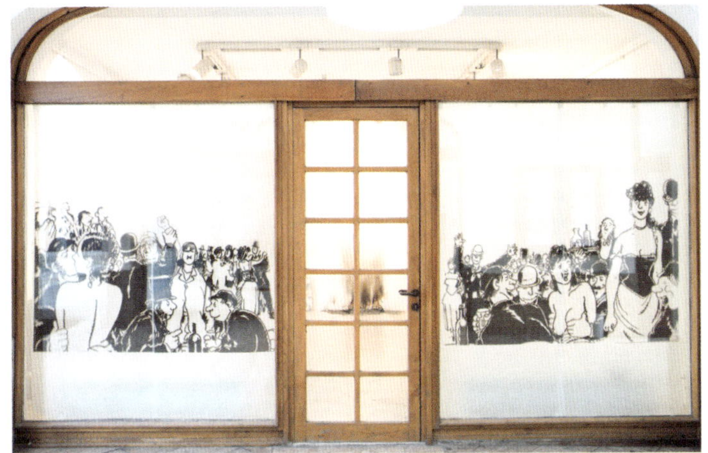

5

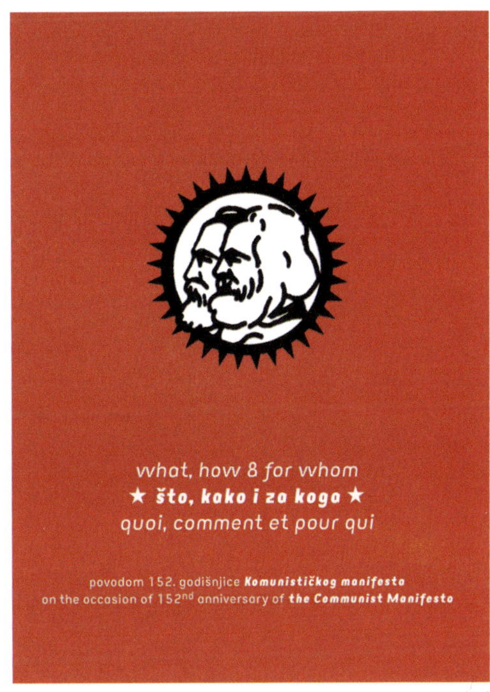

6

infotainment, new technology is offering us ways toward solidarity and the sharing of resources beyond and against the market logic. But the benefits of new technologies should not be taken for granted, and as a collective, we have yet to figure out the best ways of approaching it and dealing with it through our practice.

How does your collaboration relate to its cultural, institutional, and commercial contexts? In other words, how would you respond to those who call this a trend?

Considering that we have been working together for almost fifteen years now, it's quite a long trend, we'd say. In fact, we have seen the interest in collectives increase and then decrease during the past decade. And although as a collective we firmly believe that group work can create a surplus of desires, perspectives, and ideas that infuse each other in a very special way, we have always been quite reserved about glorifying the group's process.

Who is your audience?

Audience is an issue connected to class differences and the question of who has access to culture. In Zagreb at Gallery Nova our program is potentially open to everyone, as all our programs are offered for free. Of course, that does not solve the everlasting last question of our group's title: for whom? Our average audience is mostly coming from cultural circles and this is quite hard to change. But we also believe in a "delayed audience"—the resonance of certain projects that over time will create or reach a new, different audience.

Does your engagement with one another translate into an engagement with the public? How so?

Yes it does, but the process is not linear or literally translatable. Once the exhibition is open, and even before, it is already outside of the curators' hands; it starts a life on its own. As curators, we can try to direct it and catalyze its processes, but we can't predict the interactions it will create. What remains constant from our perspective is the desire to rethink the exhibition as an open and collective resource equally capable of intervening in existing social surroundings as it is in creating new ones. Exhibitions are a form of communication that is in a constant rehearsal.

ACTIVE SINCE	CITY	WEBSITE
1999	New York, U.S.	theyesmen.org

The Yes Men

MEMBERS	ACTIVITIES	RECOMMENDED PUBLICATION
Andy Bichlbaum and Mike Bonanno	Activism, Internet Art, Internet Performance, Media Interventions, Public Performance, Urban Interventions	THE YES MEN, THE YES MEN: The True Story of the End of the World Trade Organization, The Disinformation Company, New York, 2004

This activist duo is known for projects of sabotage and disturbance often associated with the antiglobalization movement. Most of its actions start with the conceit of its members impersonating representatives of real-life corporations or government institutions. In this guise, the Yes Men have appeared on TV newscasts and at academic conventions. Other works include creating a fake copy of the New York Times and building a dystopian living unit to meet the challenges of climate change.

Why work collaboratively?

We partner with progressive organizations that are working on campaigns and are looking to implement our media tactics to garner attention to their causes. Stand-alone hoaxes and media actions can be encouraging, fun, stimulating, etc.—but they really work to their fullest when tied to ongoing efforts toward systemic change. We mainly rely on partner organizations for that (although we'll be more active as we develop our "Action Switchboard," a social network that will have a system of "goals" built in, requiring all projects to serve one). We are also always looking for innovative ways of creating a media spectacle—we only have so many ideas—and our collaborators often bring their own tastes and resources to bear.

How do you determine membership? Does physical location matter in this regard?

We don't have members. We try to inspire as many people as possible to act, and thanks to the Internet we are able to provide a certain level of mentorship remotely if folks aren't based in NYC like us; this is going to increase dramatically when our Action Switchboard is launched. It's always pleasant to work in the same place as collaborators, but that isn't always possible, and we have to figure out new ways of collaborating at a distance, or at least mentoring at a distance, if our tools are to spread.

If considered separately, how do your individual artistic practices contribute to or detract from your work as a group?

We have filmmakers, theater makers, actors, writers, programmers, and graphic designers at the core of our team and a host of other collaborators with other skills. I can't see how any of this could detract from our work, but the fact that we are story and performance oriented is the reason we use the tactics we use and all art forms can contribute to that.

How are decisions made?

On a case-by-case basis with whoever is available.

Does each of you have a clearly defined role? If so, what are some of each member's distinct responsibilities?

Sometimes. Check back with us after we're an official nonprofit.

How important is each group member's individuality, both in terms of your artistic production and in terms of your relationship with the media? Does anonymity come into play?

I'm not sure what you mean by individuality. Of course, everyone brings their own strengths and skills and when interacting with the media, we bring those to bear, whether through writing, acting, or fielding questions. We rely on anonymity in order to pull off most of our projects. We try to give journalists funny excuses to report on the issues we and

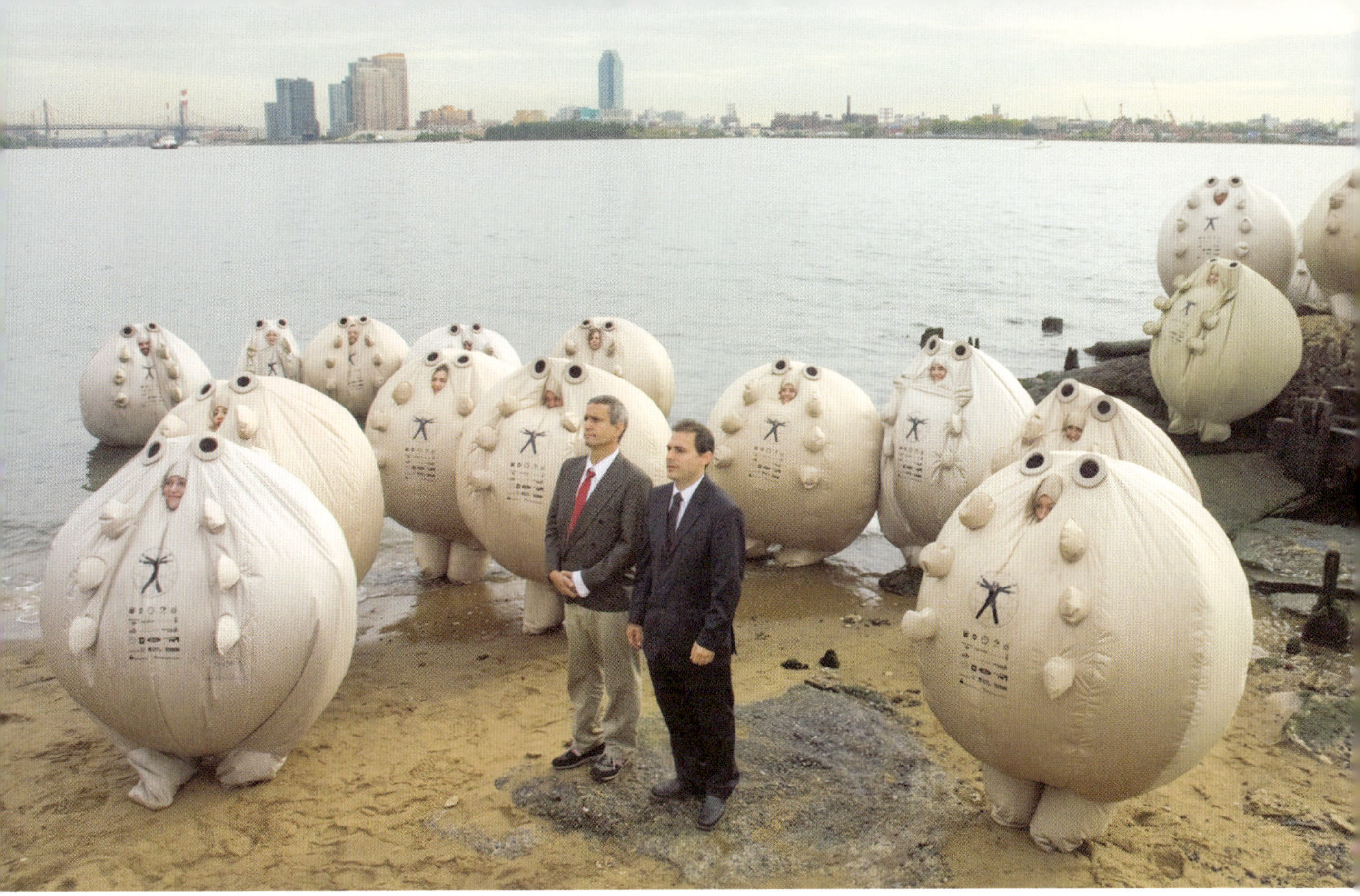

1

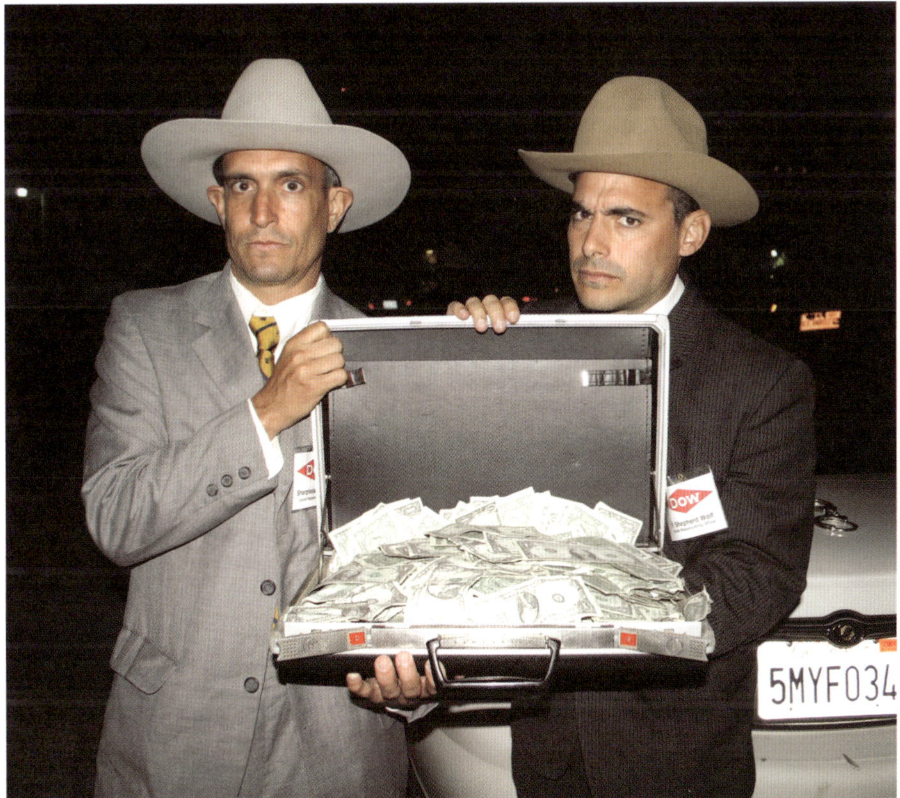

2

1 – Balls Across America, action, 2009

2 – Bush Bus, action, 2004

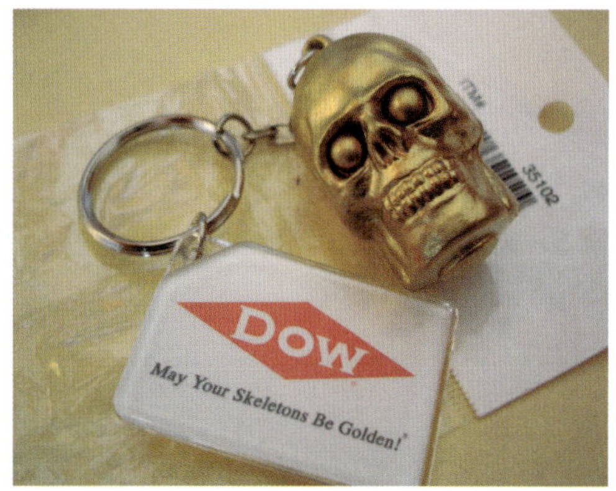

3

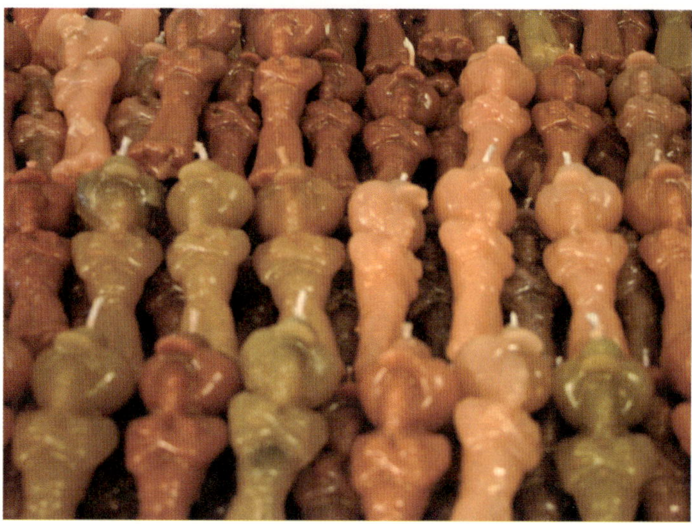

4

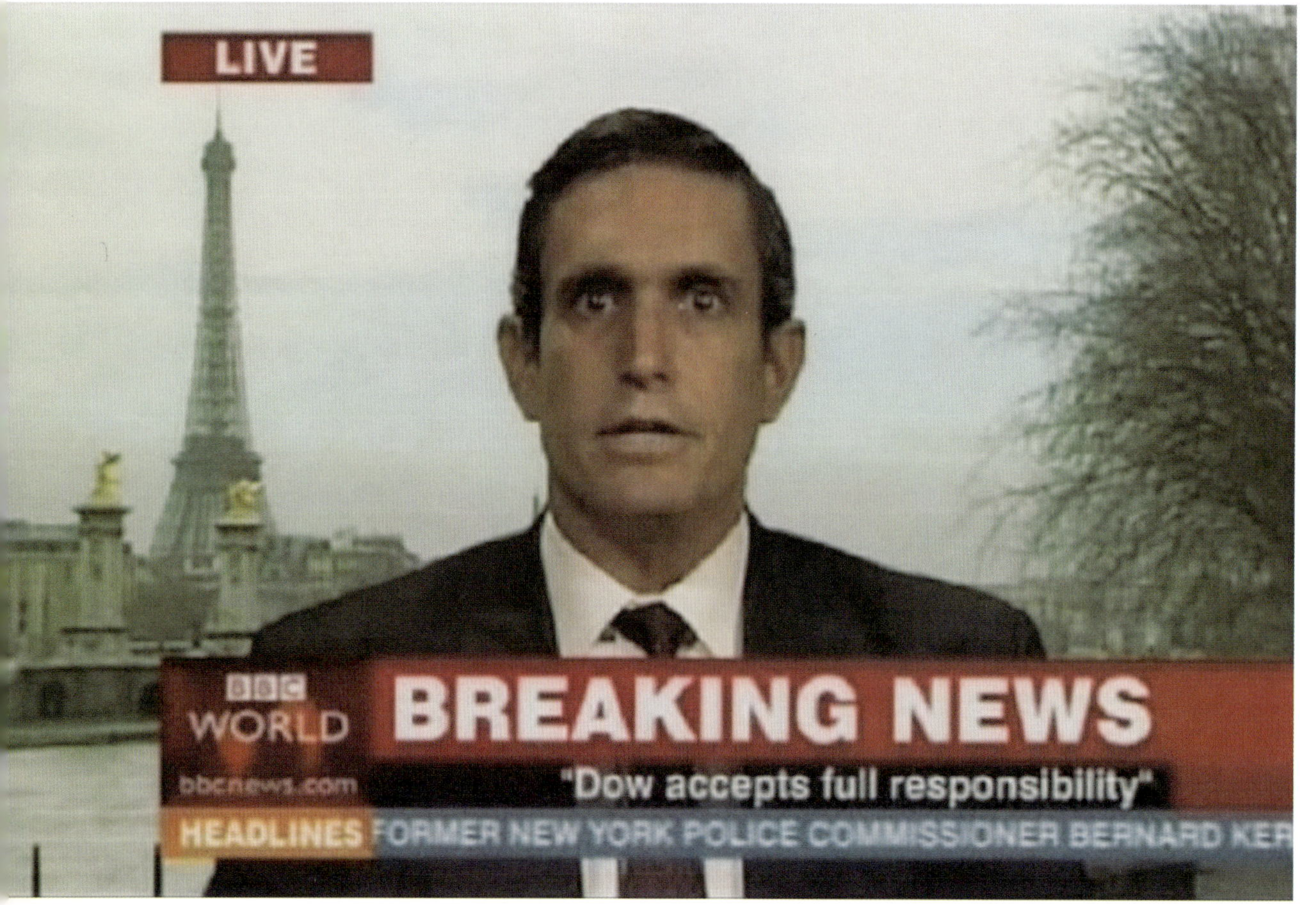

5

3 – Dow's Golden Skeleton, keychain, 2005

4 – Vivoleum candles, used in action, Calgary, Alberta, 2007

5 – The Bhopal Project, action live on BBC, 2004

6 – Chevron Gets Flushed, poster, Yes Lab project, 2010

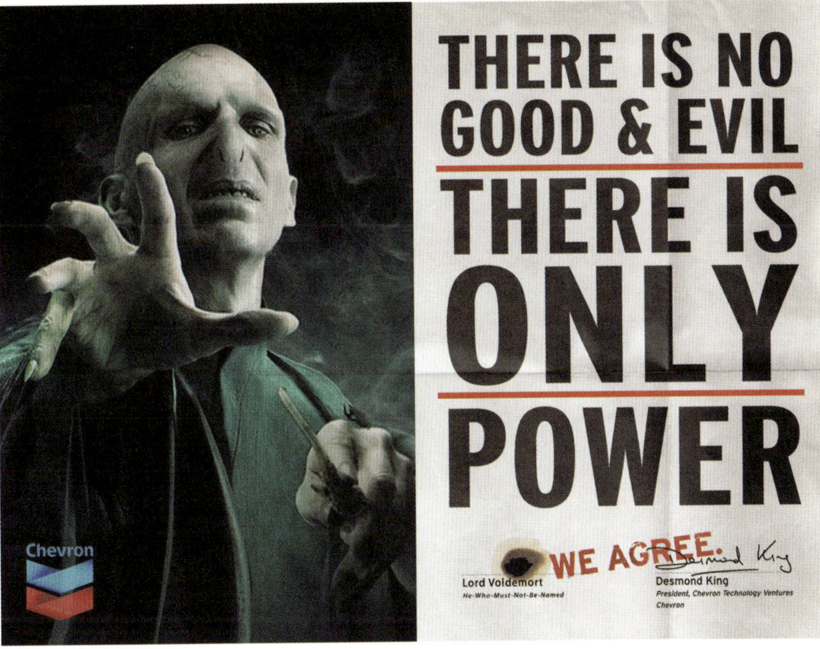

6

our partners think they should be reporting on—often by momentarily pretending to be an existing corporation or other such powerful entity, doing something either insanely good or just plain insane. In the end, we have no intention of remaining anonymous or passing these things off as real beyond a few hours—which is what distinguishes us from those who use these techniques to sell products or promote candidates, etc. (mainly the corporate PR industry). We always reveal who we really are and why we've resorted to subterfuge, but that first part definitely requires some anonymity.

What is the relationship between your working methods and your art's "content"? In this sense, does technology tend to play more of a supporting role, or does it lead you in new directions?

Art? What art? We rely on technology, as everyone always has. Currently, the Internet is perhaps our main medium. Our content is entirely reliant on its qualities. We wouldn't write the same thing in a press release as we would for a shooting script, obviously. The ability to create fake identities online allows us to perform our spectacles by inhabiting virtual roles. The blandness and obsession with appearances that go along with a conference allow us to enter and participate undetected in a world that we are not only not a part of but making fun of. We use the methods of those that we are working against to create the content that works against them.

How does your collaboration relate to its cultural, institutional, and commercial contexts? In other words, how would you respond to those who call this a trend?

We would respond: "GREAT!" If more people caught onto our "trend"—namely, that working to make the world better is fun and rewarding—we really think the world would be a better place. We point out what is already ridiculous in our "cultural, institutional, and commercial contexts" in the hopes of changing them.

Who is your audience?

People who want to make a difference but don't know how, who need an on-ramp to activism, who need to be engaged and perhaps enraged. It also depends on the project we're working on. Sometimes it's the general public and sometimes it's more specifically a company or policy maker whose mind we think needs changing—of course, that usually (or maybe always) involves mobilizing the general public. Right now, we mostly target people who are already disposed to be on the side of progressive movements for environmental, social, and political justice. In the future, we'd like to be able to win over people with aversions to those buzzwords.

Does your engagement with one another translate into an engagement with the public? How so?

I'd like to think we challenge each other to think outside our own experience. Hopefully, that translates into work that is more broadly accessible. We think if it makes us laugh, it will make other people laugh.

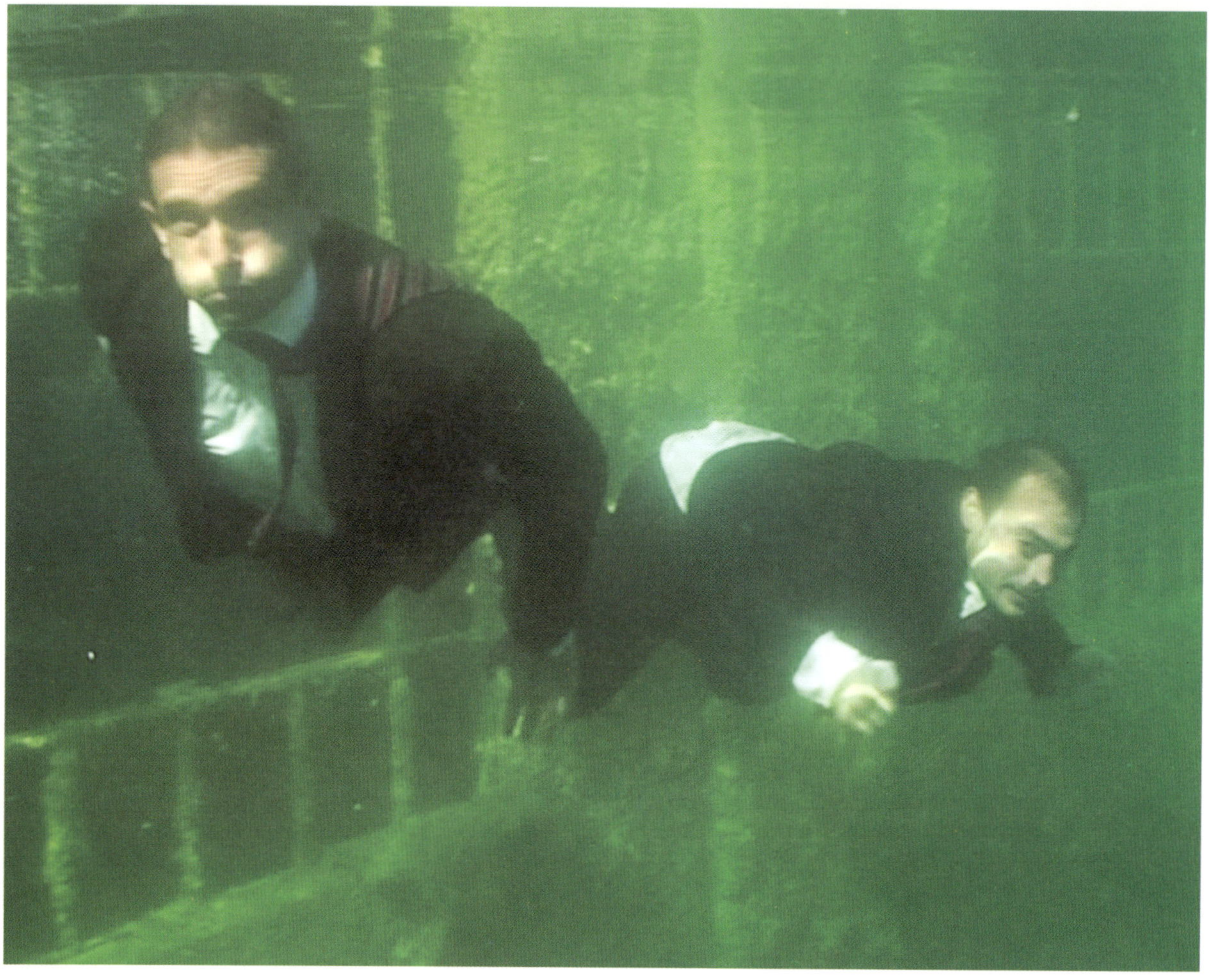

7

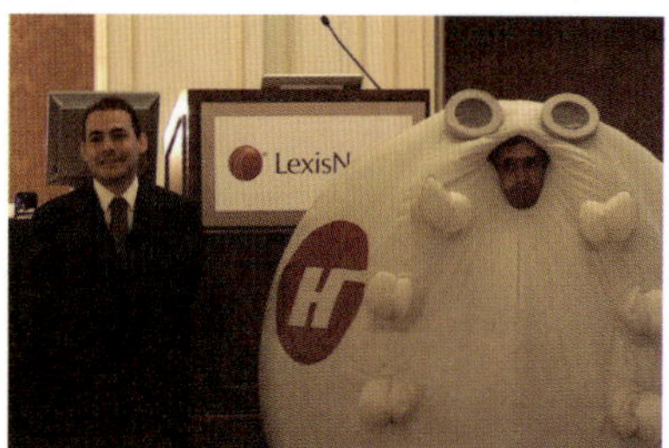
LexisN

8

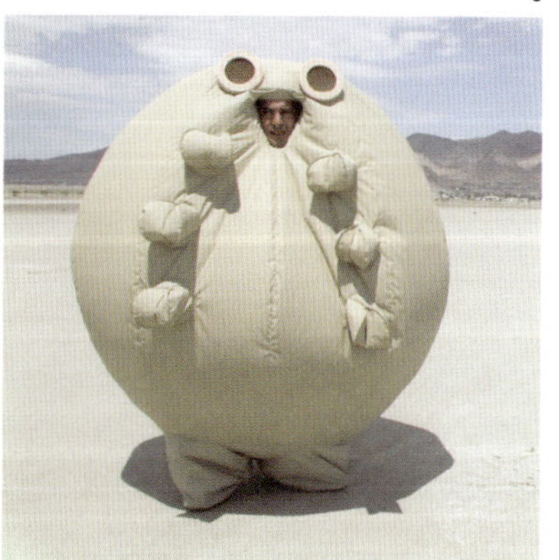

9

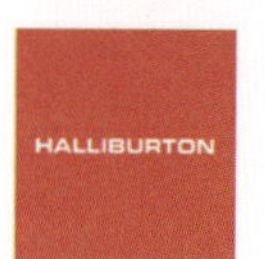
HALLIBURTON

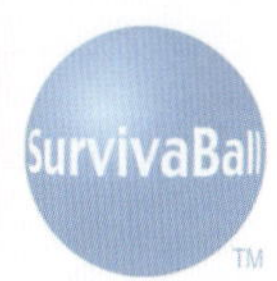
SurvivaBall
TM

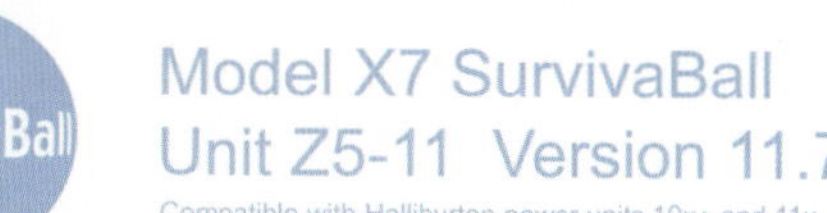
Model X7 SurvivaBall
Unit Z5-11 Version 11.7
Compatible with Halliburton power units 10x+ and 11x
with PP45 adapter and TICC conversion software

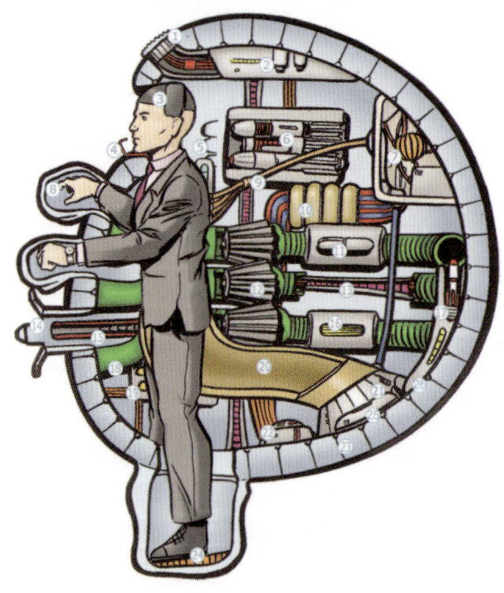

1.SHF antenna with supplementary LF antennae
2.Receiver and data processor
3.Protective headgear with visor
4.Drinking straw
5.External pores (defensive)
6.Defence Enhancement Unit (1 of 3; primary)
7.Food Reprocessor (receives nutrients from Nutrition Refunction Centre, 21)
8.Maniple Pods (for interaction with people, technology and the environment)
9.Nutrition Utility Transfer (conveys nutrients from Food Reprocessor, 6)
10. Electrical Gafting (secures against power loss)
11. Dynamo
12. Motors (powered by dynamo and Maniple Pod plug interfaces)
13. Electromagnetic strips (generate electricity for dynamo and allow external linkage)
14. Maniple Pod deployed as rotor (applicable to all MPs)
15. Defence Enhancement Unit (2 of 3; non-lethal)
16. Power converter
17. Defence Enhancement Unit (3 of 3; rear)
18. Power conduits with inline power converters and dynamo
19. Medical Analysis Unit (runs constant scans on health and energy)
20. Personal Trapment Unit (conveys cast-off to Nutrition Refunction Centre, 21)
21. Nutrition Refunction Centre (extracts nutrients from cast-off)
22. Persistent Nutrition Unit (delivers small amounts on an ongoing basis)
23. Suspension Grid (elasticated cable system)
24. Hyperfine Elasticity Units (impart added momentum)
25. Medical Stability & Emergency Unit
26. Communications and Infrastructure Monitoring Assemblage

10

opposite

7 – Climate Change Dip, still from the documentary The Yes Men Fix the World, 2009

opposite

8 – SurvivaBall Pitch, still from The Yes Men Fix the World, 2009

opposite

9 – SurvivaBall publicity photo, 2006

opposite

10 – SurvivaBall schematics, instruction graphics, 2006

11 – New York Times Special Edition, fake copy of the New York Times, November 12, 2008

"All the News We Hope to Print"

The New York Times

Special Edition

Today, clouds part, more sunshine, recent gloom passes. **Tonight,** strong leftward winds. **Tomorrow,** a new day. Weather map throughout.

VOL. CLVIV . . No. 54,631 — NEW YORK, SATURDAY, JULY 4, 2009 — FREE

IRAQ WAR ENDS

Nation Sets Its Sights on Building Sane Economy

True Cost Tax, Salary Caps, Trust-Busting Top List

By T. VEBLEN

The President has called for swift passage of the Safeguards for a New Economy (S.A.N.E.) bill. The omnibus economic package includes a federal maximum wage, mandatory "True Cost Accounting," a phased withdrawal from complex financial instruments, and other measures intended to improve life for ordinary Americans. (See highlights box on Page A10.) He also repeated earlier calls for passage of the "Ban on Lobbying" bill currently making its way through Congress.

Treasury Secretary Paul Krugman stressed the importance of the bill. "Markets make great servants, terrible leaders, and absurd religions," said Krugman, quoting Paul Hawken, an advocate of corporate responsibility and author of "Blessed Unrest, How the Largest Movement in the World Came into Being and Why No One Saw It Coming."

"At this point, the market is our leader and our religion. No wonder the median standard of living has been declining so much for so long."

Krugman said that the new Treasury bill seeks to ensure the prosperity of all citizens, rather than simply supporting large corporations and the wealthy. "The market is supposed to serve us. Unfortunately, we have ended up serving the market. That's very bad."

Much as Roosevelt, after the Great Depression, put the brakes on C.E.O. wages and irresponsible banking practices, administration officials claim that today we need to rein in the industry that has caused such chaos and misery.

"The building blocks of post-World War II American middle-class prosperity have all been swept away," said House Speaker Nancy Pelosi, who initially op-

Continued on Page A10

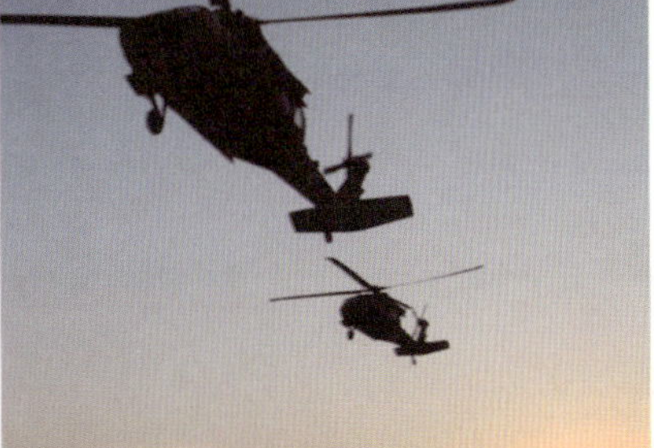

COURTESY ARMY.MIL

U.S. Army helicopters begin moving troops and equipment from Saddam Hussein's former Baghdad palace.

Troops to Return Immediately

By JUDE SHINBIN

WASHINGTON — Operation Iraqi Freedom and Operation Enduring Freedom were brought to an unceremonious close today with a quiet announcement by the Department of Defense that troops would be home within weeks.

"This is the best face we can put on the most unfortunate adventure in modern American history," Defense spokesman Kevin Sites said at a special joint session of Congress. "Today, we can finally enjoy peace — not the peace of the brave, perhaps, but at least peace."

As U.S. and coalition troops withdraw from Iraq and Afghanistan, the United Nations will move in to perform peacekeeping duties and aid in rebuilding. The U.N. will be responsible for keeping the two countries stable; coordinating the rebuilding of hospitals, schools, highways, and other infrastructure; and overseeing upcoming elections.

The Department of the Treasury confirmed that all U.N. dues owed by the U.S. were paid as of this morning, and that moneys previously earmarked for the war would be sent directly to the U.N.'s Iraq Oversight Body.

The president noted that the Iraq War had resulted in the burning of many bridges. "Yet our history with our allies runs deep," he said, "and we all know that friends forgive friends for anything. Or nearly." A spokesperson for the French Ministry of Defense confirmed that France would assist the U.S. withdrawal. "The U.S. helped the Soviet Union defeat Hitler. We do recognize that."

In conflict zones worldwide, leaders and rebels pledged peace. (See "In Conflict Zones Worldwide, Peace Moves," on Page A4.)

On Wall Street, reactions were mixed, with the Dow Jones Industrial Average up 84 points, to close at 4,212. While KBR stock was quickly downgraded to a "junk" rating of BBB-, defense contractors such as Lockheed Martin and Northrop Grumman started up.

Continued on Page A5

Maximum Wage Law Succeeds

Salary Caps Will Help Stabilize Economy

By J.K. MALONE

WASHINGTON — After long and often bitter debate, Congress has passed legislation, fiercely fought for by labor and progressive groups, that will limit top salaries to fifteen times the minimum wage. Tying the bill to a plan of overall reform of the U.S. economy, the bill echoes a similar effort enacted by President Franklin Roosevelt in 1942, which was followed by the longest period of growth for the middle class in U.S. history.

"When C.E.O. salaries remain stable thanks to high taxation of high salaries, there's little incentive to take big risks with shareholders' money, and the economy remains in a steady growth mode," said Senator Barney Frank, one of the bill's co-sponsors. "But when C.E.O. salaries can fly through the roof, there's a very strong incentive for C.E.O.s

Continued on Page A10

TREASURY ANNOUNCES "TRUE COST" TAX PLAN

By MARCUS S. DRIGGS

The long-awaited "True Cost" plan, which requires product prices to reflect their cost to society, has been signed into law.

Beginning next month, throw-away items like plastic water bottles and other items which are wasteful or damaging to the environment will be heavily taxed, as in many developed countries. Steep taxes will also apply to large cars and gasoline.

The new plan calls for a 200 percent tax on gasoline, comparable to the one long in effect in most European countries. Companies and consumers are already switching in droves from inefficient gas vehicles to new electric cars. "We suddenly have a waiting list 200 names long for the EV1," said Jake Cluber, the owner of Cluber Chevrolet in

Continued on Page A10

Recruiters Train for New Life

As a ban is imposed on recruiting minors, ex-recruiters nationwide look for new work. The Times follows one on his job-hunt odyssey through Manhattan and surrounding areas.

BY BARRY GLOAD, PAGE A12

Last to Die

Two proportional monuments — one to the Iraqi dead, 300 feet high, and one to the American dead, 15 feet high — are unveiled in Baghdad, and a five-year-old boy whose lifespan coincided with that of the Iraq War is remembered.

BY J. FINSTERRA, PAGE A5

USA Patriot Act Repealed

Eight years later, a shamefaced Congress quietly repeals the much-maligned USA Patriot Act, unanimously... or almost.

BY SYBIL LUDINGTON, PAGE A8

Evangelicals Open Homes to Refugees

Up to a million Iraqi exiles — nearly half of the total — will find sanctuary in Christian homes across the U.S., vows the National Association of Evangelicals. Other denominations are expected to follow.

BY W. WILBERFORCE, PAGE A7

Public Relations Industry Starts to Shut Down

The public relations industry has been criticized for misleading the American people, corrupting politicians, and even helping to start wars. Now, it's beginning the process of shutting down for good.

BY LOUIS BECK, PAGE A10

Ex-Secretary Apologizes for W.M.D. Scare

300,000 Troops Never Faced Risk of Instant Obliteration

By FRANK LARIMORE

Ex-Secretary of State Condoleezza Rice reassured soldiers that the Bush Administration had known well before the invasion that Saddam Hussein lacked weapons of mass destruction.

"Now that all of you brave servicemen and women are returning, it's important to us to reassure you, and the American people, that we were certain Hussein had no W.M.D.s and that he would never launch a first strike against the U.S.," Ms. Rice told a group of wounded soldiers at a Veterans' Administration hospital yesterday.

"I want you to know that if we had had the slightest suspicion that Saddam could use W.M.D.s against you, we never would have sent hundreds of thousands of you to be sitting ducks on the Iraqi border for several months."

Mr. Rice was referring to the fact that by August 2002, eight months before the ground invasion, the US had over 100,000 troops stationed in countries throughout the Gulf, a number that grew to over 300,000 shortly before the 2003 attack on Baghdad. Most of these were within range of the Scud missiles used by Mr. Hussein in the 1991 Gulf War, that could easily have been fitted with chemical or biological weapons if they had existed.

Rice noted that in the 1991 Gulf War, Hussein had used missiles to launch attacks on Israel, which made him popular with Arab citizens throughout the Middle East.

"Do you really think we would have given Saddam a major public relations coup by allowing him to annihilate tens of thousands of you right there on holy territory?" asked Ms. Rice.

Former Secretary of State Henry A. Kissinger responded to Ms. Rice's revelation without surprise. "Of course this was the case. When Israel believed Iraq had nuclear weapons in 1981, they didn't attack on the ground — they bombed from the air. That's a pre-emptive attack. If you believe deterrence will not prevent an attack and that your enemy has W.M.D.s, then the last thing you do is station your troops right next door."

ABC's George Stephanopoulos

Continued on Page A5

Popular Pressure Ushers Recent Progressive Tilt

Study Cites Movements for Massive Shift in DC

By SAMUEL FIELDEN

The spate of reform initiatives undertaken by the Administration and both houses of Congress can be attributed directly to grass-roots advocacy, according to a comprehensive study due out this month.

"In education and health care, most notably, but also in housing, banking, and the environment, we have documented unprecedented responsiveness on the part of political leaders," said Dr. Joyce Wellmon, director of the Plains Institute for Policy Analysis, a New York-based think tank. "Our data show a direct correlation between the level of activity of particular coalitions, on the one hand, and specific legislative action, on the other. It's popular pressure that is responsible for the swiftness and scope of legislation emerging from the White House and Congress."

The institute's report shows a three-fold increase in the incidence of letters, phone calls, faxes, and email received by congressional offices, 88 percent of which were from people who identified themselves as new members of particular activist organizations.

See nytimes-se.com for more

The report includes extensive interviews with House and Senate staff, who speak of "unimaginable change," a "dramatic policy shift," and "a new era of accountability" since the elections.

"Not since the Great Depression has the interaction between popular movements and public leaders been so robust," said Jorge Lazaro, head of the U.S. Government Accountability Office. Lazaro cited, in particular, the Wagner Act, also known as the National Labor Relations Act of 1935, which recognized the right of workers to organize and bargain collectively with their employers.

"Roosevelt showed no interest in the Wagner Act until it became clear the unions were going to force it through regardless," Mr. Lazaro noted. "At that point he jumped on it and helped push it into law."

Mr. Lazaro also pointed to the Depression-era organizing of the Farmers' Holiday Association, when farmers refused to sell or bid on crops, blockaded roads, and even once used a torpedo to halt a train carrying livestock into Iowa. Such direct actions helped push courts and legislatures to adopt measures that granted relief from debt caused by low crop prices.

"The similarities between the two periods are remarkable, and the lesson that emerges is simple: if you want change, keep our feet to the fire."

Dr. Wellmon agrees. "The only reason the current President and Congress have been able to implement all these changes, was because of pressure from popular movements that made them have to."

The Plains report, due out next month, cites the work of groups associated with United for Peace and Justice, an umbrella for anti-war groups, for galvanizing public support for ending the war, and for pushing the Administration to resist the oil lobby and other interest groups. It also cites the work

Continued on Page A6

KC IVEY/THE NEW YORK TIMES

Protests organized by Witness Against Torture helped pave the way for the close of the Guantánamo facility.

Nationalized Oil To Fund Climate Change Efforts

By MARION K. HUBBERT

Congress has voted to place ExxonMobil, ChevronTexaco, and other major oil companies under public stewardship, with the bulk of the companies' profits put in a public trust administered by the United Nations, and used for alternative energy research and development in order to solve the global climate crisis.

While unusual, this is not the first time the government has chosen to take control of large corporations. From 1942 to 1944, U.S. car factories were retooled in order to produce tanks for the war effort. And Fannie Mae and Freddie Mac were both created as "government sponsored enterprises" with a significant amount of government oversight.

"We can do what needs to be done," said Senator Charles Schumer, Democrat of New York. "Our planet's survival is at stake. Plus, public pressure hasn't given us much of a choice."

Not everyone felt the move was a good idea. "The climate crisis may or may not be real," declared Senator Kay Bailey Hutchison, Republican of Texas. "I'm an agnostic and I'm staying that way. But sea

Continued on Page A5

INTERNATIONAL A4-5

Gitmo, Other Centers Closed

The notorious Guantánamo Bay, Cuba detention camp will be closed, along with a network of secret C.I.A.-run facilities in Eastern Europe, Afghanistan and elsewhere. PAGE A24

Iraqi Refugees Worldwide Celebrate Withdrawal

Two million Iraqi exiles, and three million internal refugees, celebrated the end of hostilities and began making plans to return to their homes. PAGE A4

NATIONAL A6-9

Conflict of Interest Law Will Stop Revolving Door

The "Revolving Door" bill will prohibit high-ranking corporate officers from holding public office for ten years upon leaving their companies, and public officials from accepting management positions at large corporations for the same period. Coupled with the Ban on Lobbying bill, the bill will reduce the influence of large corporations on public policy. PAGE B1

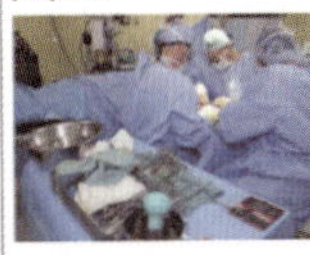

Health Insurance Act Clears House

While almost all are celebrating the passage of the National Health Insurance Act, which finally brings the U.S. up to par with other developed nations, representatives of Kaiser, Cigna and other health insurance companies are vowing to "fight tooth and nail" to protect their interests. PAGE A7

Bush to Face Charges

Most observers weren't surprised by the high treason indictment itself, but rather by the party that brought it. The case could also provide an unexpected boost to the International Criminal Court, paving the way for more indictments. PAGE A5

BUSINESS A10-11

Corporate Personhood Gets Real

An initiative to abolish limited liability will make shareholders pay for the crimes their corporations commit — even if they only own one or two shares in a mutual fund. PAGE A11

NEW YORK A12

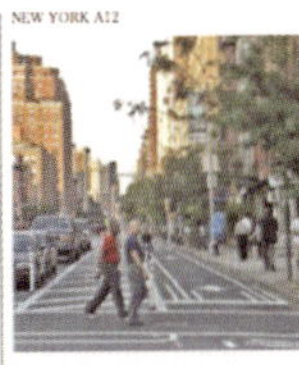

Bicycle Lanes Inaugurated

With the completion of the 9th Avenue bike lane and groundbreaking on other avenues, New York is on the (bike) path to becoming as livable as other world cities. PAGE A12

EDITORIAL A13

A Lobbyist Defends Lobbying

The Ban on Lobbying bill is not without victims. PAGE A13

Thomas L. Friedman

The columnist resigns, and will put down his pen to take up a screwdriver. PAGE A13

A Baboon Troop's Experience

A particularly peaceful baboon troop may have lessons to teach us. PAGE A13

More Inside The Times.
PAGE A2 ▸

8 92015 12023 9

92015

11

BIBLIOGRAPHY

Bavo, ed. Cultural Activism Today: The Art of Over-Identification. Rotterdam: Episode Publishers, 2007.

Billing, Johanna, Maria Lind, and Lars Nilsson, eds. Taking the Matter Into Common Hands: On Contemporary Art and Collaborative Practices. London: Black Dog, 2007.

Bishop, Claire. Artificial Hells: Participatory Art and the Politics of Spectatorship. London/New York: Verso, 2012.

Blauvelt, Andrew, and Ellen Lupton, eds. Graphic Design: Now in Production. New York: Walker Art Center/Cooper-Hewitt National Design Museum, 2011.

Bourriaud, Nicolas. Relational Aesthetics. Paris: Les Presses du Réel, 2002.

Deitch, Jeffrey, and Kathy Grayson, eds. Live Through This: New York 2005. New York: Deitch Projects, 2005.

Greenwald, Dara, and Josh MacPhee, eds. Signs of Change: Social Movement Cultures, 1960s to Now. Oakland: AK Press, 2010.

Hapkemeyer, Andreas, and Letizia Ragaglia, eds. Group Therapy. Bolzano, Italy: Museion, 2006.

Haydn, Florian, and Robert Temel, eds. Temporary Urban Spaces: Concepts for the Use of City Spaces. Basel/Boston/Berlin: Birkhauser, 2006.

The Invisible Committee. The Coming Insurrection. Los Angeles: Semiotext(e), 2009.

Jansen, Gregory, and Robert Klanten. Art & Agenda: Political Art and Activism. Berlin: Gestalten Verlag, 2011.

Joo, Eungie, ed. The Ungovernables: The 2012 New Museum Triennial. New York: Skira/Rizzoli, 2012.

Kester, Grant H. Conversation Pieces: Community and Communication in Modern Art. Berkeley: University of California Press, 2004.

——The One and the Many: Contemporary Collaborative Art in a Global Context. Durham, NC: Duke University Press, 2011.

Klein, Naomi. No Logo. New York: Picador, 2000.

Lamunière, Simon, ed. Utopics: Systems and Landmarks. Zurich: JRP Ringier, 2009.

Lee, Pamela. Forgetting the Art World. Cambridge, MA: MIT Press, 2012.

Lomme, Freek, ed. Who Told You So?! The Collective Story vs. the Individual Narrative. Eindhoven, The Netherlands: Onomatopee, 2013.

Metahaven and Marina Vishmidt, Uncorporate Identity. Baden, Switzerland: Lars Müller Publishers, 2010.

Miessen, Marcus. The Nightmare of Participation (Crossbench Praxis as a Mode of Criticality). Berlin: Sternberg Press, 2011.

Miessen, Marcus, and Shumon Basar, eds. Did Someone Say Participate?: An Atlas of Spatial Practice. Cambridge, MA: MIT Press, 2006.

Möntmann, Nina, ed. New Communities. Toronto: The Power Plant/ Public Access, Toronto, 2009.

Pasternak, Anne, ed. Creative Time: The Book. New York: Princeton Architectural Press, 2007.

Rancière, Jacques. The Politics of Aesthetics. London: Continuum, 2004.

Shirky, Clay. Here Comes Everybody: How Change Happens When People Come Together. London: Penguin Books, 2009.

Sholette, Gregory. Dark Matter: Art and Politics in the Age of Enterprise Culture. London: Pluto Press, 2011.

Stimson, Blake, and Gregory Sholette, eds. Collectivism After Modernism. Minneapolis: University of Minnesota Press, 2007.

Temporary Services, eds. Group Work. New York: Printed Matter Inc., 2007.

Thompson, Nato, and Gregory Sholette, eds. The Interventionists: Users' Manual for the Creative Disruption of Everyday Life. Cambridge, MA: MIT Press, 2004.

Thompson, Nato, ed. Living as Form: Socially Engaged Art From 1991–2011. Cambridge, MA: MIT Press, 2012.

What, How and For Whom, eds. Collective Creativity. Frankfurt: Revolver Publishing, 2005.

ACKNOWLEDGMENTS

I'd like to offer deep gratitude to Princeton Architectural Press for believing in and embracing this book and its subject—it's an honor to have my first book published by such a prestigious publishing house.

I'm particularly thankful to Paul Wagner for giving the perfect corresponding visual form to all the material I've collected, and to my editors Nicola Bednarek Brower and Jay Sacher—and Jacob Moore, who helped along the way—for their patience and commitment. Thanks for sharing my vision from the first moment.

This book would not be here without the tremendous generosity of all the numerous artists involved. Thank you all for being so excited to be part of it and working so hard on your contributions and satisfying my pressing requests for information and images.

Special thanks go to those who believed in the project in the early stages of the process: Assume Vivid Astro Focus, Fallen Fruit, and This is a magazine. I'd also be remiss in not mentioning all the galleries and museums that have sent me images or granted me the rights to publish them. Thank you for helping these artists develop alternative forms of cultural productions.

Even if they were not directly involved, I'd like to thank all the students I've had since I started my academic career five years ago. I've talked about many of the artists featured in this book in the courses I've taught at NABA, Milan, and Parsons, New York, and particularly at Rhode Island School of Design, Providence.

This book is dedicated to my grandfather, Francesco, who has supported and encouraged me my entire life. I am appreciative of my parents Anna and Santi, and my siblings Chiara and Paolo, for their unconditional love. Thank you for believing in me. Finally, a special thanks to my beloved wife, Giulia, who stands by me every single moment and tolerates my growing piles of books in our apartments.

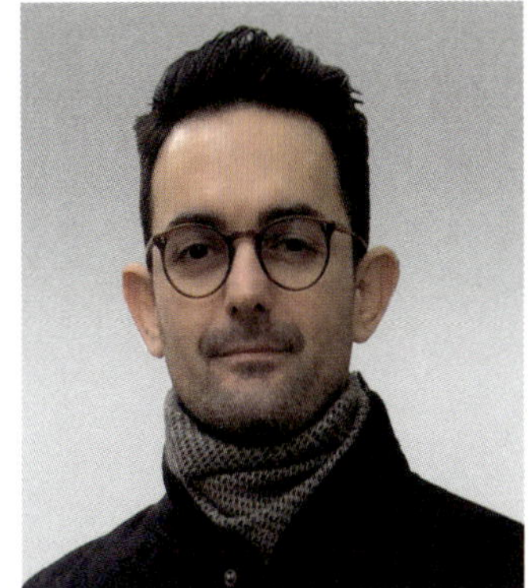

Francesco Spampinato is a contemporary art and visual culture historian, writer, and artist. He teaches at Rhode Island School of Design, Providence, and has taught at Parsons School of Design, The New School, New York, and NABA, Milan. His writing has appeared in Apartamento, DAMno, Flash Art, Kaleidoscope, L'Uomo Vogue, and Waxpoetics among others. He lives and works in New York.

Published by
Princeton Architectural Press
37 East 7th Street
New York, New York 10003
www.papress.com

978-1-61689-268-5

Printed and bound in China by C&C Offset Printing, Ltd.
17 16 15 18 4 3 2 1 First edition

Editors: Nicola Bednarek Brower, Jay Sacher, Barbara Darko
Design: Paul Wagner
Design Assistance: Benjamin English, Amrita Marino

Special thanks to: Meredith Baber, Sara Bader, Janet Behning, Megan Carey, Carina Cha, Andrea Chlad, Barbara Darko, Ali Dawes, Russell Fernandez, Will Foster, Jan Hartman, Jan Haux, Mia Johnson, Diane Levinson, Jennifer Lippert, Katharine Myers, Rob Shaeffer, Sara Stemen, Kaymar Thomas, Joseph Weston, and Janet Wong of Princeton Architectural Press —Kevin C. Lippert, publisher

Library of Congress Cataloging-in-Publication Data
Spampinato, Francesco, 1978–
Come together : the rise of cooperative art and design / Francesco Spampinato. — First edition.
pages cm
ISBN 978-1-61689-268-5 (paperback)
1. Artists—Interviews. 2. Group work in art. 3. Arts, 21st century.
I. Title.
NX160.S635 2014
700.6—dc23

2014006393

CREDITS

All images courtesy the artist unless otherwise noted.p. 2: Image courtesy Åbäke / **p. 9: 3.** Photo by Vincent Diamante Licensed under Creative Commons / **p. 11: 5.** © 2013 George Maciunas Foundation Inc. All rights reserved / **p. 13: 6.** Photo by Ryan Lackey Licensed under Creative Commons / **p. 14–15:** Image courtesy Improv Everywhere and Chad Nicholson / **p. 26: 1.** Photo by Melanie Bonaj; **2.** Photo by Dan el Hadad / **p. 28–29:** Photo by Chantapitch Wiwatchaikamol / **p. 30:** Photo by Marouissa Rebecq / **p. 31: 5.** Photo by Marouissa Rebecq; **6.** Photo by Chantapitch Wiwatchaikamol; **7.** Photo by Romain B. James / **p. 32: 8.** Photo by Marouissa Rebecq; **9+10.** Photos by Chantapitch Wiwatchaikamol / **p. 33:** Photo by Marouissa Rebecq / **p. 35: 1.** Photo by Tom Powell. Courtesy the artist and the Suzanne Geiss Company, New York; **2.** Photo by Alfred Piola. Courtesy the artist and the Suzanne Geiss Company, New York; **3.** Photo by Edourard Fraipont. Courtesy the artist and the Suzanne Geiss Company, New York / **p. 36: 4.** Photo by Anne Hansteen Jarre. Courtesy the artist and the Suzanne Geiss Company, New York / **p. 37: 5.** Photo by Matthu Placek. Courtesy the artist and the Suzanne Geiss Company, New York; **6.** Photo by Hans-George Gaul and Assume Vivid Astro Focus. Courtesy the artist and the Suzanne Geiss Company, New York / **pp. 38–39: 7.** Photo by Atushi Yoshimimine and Assume Vivid Astro Focus. Courtesy the artist and the Suzanne Geiss Company, New York / **p. 40: 8.** Photo by Mauro Restiffe and Assume Vivid Astro Focus. Courtesy the artist and the Suzanne Geiss Company, New York; **9.** Photo courtesy the artist and the Suzanne Geiss Company, New York; **10.** Photo by Li Inc. Courtesy the artist and the Suzanne Geiss Company, New York / **p. 49: 1.** Photo courtesy the artist and ICA London / **p. 51: 6.** Photo courtesy the artist and SMART Project Space, Amsterdam; **7.** Photo courtesy the artist and ICA London; **8+9.** Photos courtesy the artist and Van Abbemuseum, Eindhoven / **p. 52: 11.** Courtesy the artist and Moderna Galerja, Ljubliana / **p. 55: 1.** Photo by Melanie Humann; **3.** Photo by Georg Reinhardt / **p. 57: 5.** Photo by Melanie Humann; **6.** Photo by Britt Dunse; **7.** Photo by Heidi Lusser; **8.** Photo by David Baltzer / **p. 58: 9+10.** Photo by Thomas Hauck; **11.** Photo by Georg Reinhardt; **12.** Photo by Timo Wulff / **p. 59: 13.** Photo by Heidi Lusser / **p. 63: 3.** Courtesy the artist and Gio Marconi Gallery, Milan / **pp. 64–65: 5+6.** Photo courtesy Albert Fuchs / **p. 66: 7+8.** Courtesy the artist and Balice Hertling Gallery, Paris; **9.** Courtesy the artist and Quartier des Bains, Geneva / **p. 67: 10.** Courtesy the artist and Deste Foundation, Athens / **p. 69: 2.** Photo by Tom Powell Imaging / **p. 70: 3.** Courtesy the artist and V1 Gallery, Copenhagen / **p. 71: 4+5.** Photo by Tom Powell Imaging; **6.** Courtesy the artist and Perugi Arte Contemporanea, Padova / **p. 72: 7.** Courtesy the artist and Loyal Gallery, Stockholm / **p. 83: 1.** Photo by Ines Schaber. Courtesy the artist and Freymond-Guth Fine Arts, Zurich; **2.** Courtesy the artist and Freymond-Guth Fine Arts, Zurich. Photo by Johannes Raether / **p. 84: 3.** Courtesy the artist and Freymond-Guth Fine Arts, Zurich / **p. 85: 4–6.** Courtesy the artist and Freymond-Guth Fine Arts, Zurich / **p. 86: 7–8.** Courtesy the artist and Freymond-Guth Fine Arts, Zurich; **9–10.** Courtesy the artist and Freymond-Guth Fine Arts, Zurich. Photo by Rafael Suarez / **p. 95: 1.** Photo by Tod Seelie / **p. 96: 3.** Photo by Public Netbase / **p. 97: 4+7.** Photo by Julian Abrams / **p. 98: 10.** Photo by Carlo Mari and Bozidar Zrinski / **p. 102: 4.** Courtesy the artist and LACMA, Los Angeles / **p. 105: 9.** Courtesy the artist and LACMA, Los Angeles / **p. 119: 3.** Photo by Pall Stefanson / **p. 125: 1.** Photo by Chad Nicholson. Courtesy the artist and Chad Nicholson; **2.** Photo by Katie Sokoler / **pp. 126–127: 3.** Photo by Chad Nicholson. Courtesy the artist and Chad Nicholson / **p. 128: 4–8.** Photo by Chad Nicholson. Courtesy the artist and Chad Nicholson / **p. 129: 9.** Photo by Dave Bledsoe, FreeVerse Photography. Courtesy the artist and FreeVerse Photography / **p. 135: 1.** Photo by Oskar Proctor. Styling by Hannah R. Hopkins. Make-upby Lucy Pearson; **2.** Photo by Tom Saunderson / **p. 137: 3.** Photo by Tom Saunderson; **4.** Photo by Yuri Pattison; **5.** Photo by Anna Kari / **p. 138: 6.** Photo by Polly Braden; **7+8.** Photo by Bradley Zero Phillip; **9.** Photo by Florence Early / **p. 139: 10.** Photo by Linda Nylind; **11.** Photo by Polly Braden / **p. 141: 1.** Photo by Meinke Klein / **p. 143: 5.** Photo by Killian Lodo; **6.** Photo by Meinke Klein / **pp. 144–145: 8.** Photo by Matthew Septimus / **p. 153: 3.** Photo by Naho Kubota / **p. 171: 1.** Photo by Tomasz Pasternak; **2.** Photo by David Schmidt / **p. 173: 4.** Design by Yotam Hadar; **5.** Photo by Kfir Bolotin / **p. 196: 3+4.** Courtesy the artist and Open Satellite, Seattle / **p. 197: 5.** Courtesy the artist and Country Club Gallery, Cincinnati; **6.** Photo by Steve Rowell / **p. 198: 1.** Photo by Karla Diaz / **p. 203: 9.** Photo by Patrick Miller / **p. 205: 1.** Photo by Elizabeth Rappaport / **p. 206: 3.** Photo by Esther Eggermont / **p. 207: 6.** Photo by Christine Wurning; **7.** Photo by Donald Rasmussen / **p. 208: 8.** Photo by Patrick McMullan / **p. 209: 10.** Photo by Oliver Ottenschläger / **p. 211: 1.** Photo by Tamás Bujnovszky / **p. 212: 2.** Photo by Dejan Habicht; **3.** Photo by Uros Hocevar / **p. 213: 5.** Photo by Uros Hocevar; **6.** Photo by Dejan Habicht / **p. 215: 10.** Photo by Tamás Bujnovszky / **p. 221: 1.** Photo by Brian Buchard / **p. 222: 3.** Photo by Jeppe Gudmundsen-Holmgreen / **p. 223: 5.** Photo by Francis Ware / **p. 227: 1.** Photo by the Miller Gallery / **p. 246: 2.** Photo by Ivan Kuharić; **4.** Courtesy WHW and Sanja Iveković / **p. 247: 5.** Photo by Ivan Kuhari. Courtesy WHW and Gernot Faber / **p. 249: 1.** Photo by Anna Huix